THE CHRISTIANS

PETER McKENZIE

THE CHRISTIANS
Their Practices and Beliefs

An Adaptation of
FRIEDRICH HEILER'S
Phenomenology of Religion

ABINGDON PRESS
Nashville

The Christians

First published in Great Britain 1988
SPCK
Holy Trinity Church
Marylebone Road
London NW1 4DU

U.S. edition published by Abingdon Press,
201 Eighth Avenue, South, Nashville, Tennessee.

Library of Congress Cataloging-in-Publication Data

McKenzie, P. R. (Peter Rutherford)
  The Christians: their practices and beliefs: an adaptation of
Friedrich Heiler's Phenomenology of religion/Peter McKenzie.
  p.   cm.
  Adaptation of: Erscheinungsformen und Wesen du Religion.
  Bibliography: p.
  Includes index.

  ISBN 0-687-07661-7 (pbk.)

  1. Christianity. 2. Phenomenology. I. Heiler, Friedrich,
1892-1967. Erscheinungsformen und Wesen der Religion. II. Title.
BR121.2.M39 1988
200—dc19

Printed in Great Britain by
Latimer Trend & Company Ltd, Plymouth

CONTENTS

Acknowledgements

The author and publishers are grateful to W. Kohlhammer Verlag, Stuttgart, and to Frau Anna Elisabeth Heutling, for their permission to use Friedrich Heiler's *Erscheinungsformen und Wesen der Religion* as the basis for the present work, and to Professor Dr Hans-Jürgen Greschat and Dr Martin Kraatz for their advice and support.

In addition, the author would like to thank all those who assisted in the preparation of the various drafts of the manuscript during the ten years in which he has been working on this adaptation: especially his colleagues, including Douglas Brear who has read and made comments on the whole manuscript; his students who have discussed so many of its themes with him; and above all his wife Renate for her help at every stage.

The extract from 'Lord of the Dance' by Sydney Carter is reproduced by permission of Stainer & Bell Ltd, London, and Galaxy Music Corporation, New York.

Unless otherwise stated, biblical quotations are from the Revised Standard Version of the Bible, copyright 1946, 1952, © 1957, 1971, 1973 by the Division of Christian Education of the National Council of the Churches of Christ in the USA, and are used by permission.

Thanks are due to the following for permission to use the illustrations reprouced in this book:

Axel-Ivar Berglund: 13b
E J Brill, Leiden: 2 (S Amberg-Herzog), 17b (Roger David)
British Library: 7c, 10
British Museum: 6
Camera Press: 5a (Phillippa Berlyn), 13a (William Hamilton), 15 (Roger Wood)
Ernesto Cardenal: 17a
Gabinetto Fotografico Nazionale, Rome: 20
Giraudon, Paris: 12
Librairie Albert Guillot, Lyon: 7a, 7b (Jean Doresse)
Sonia Halliday Photographs: 5b
Peter Hammer Verlag, Wuppertal: 17a
Heckel, *Glaube und Form* (Berlin-Steglitz): 1

John Hillelson Agency: 9 (Elliott Erwitt)
Hirmer Verlag, Munich: 3b, 4
Alfred Lammer: 16
Moscow Patriarchate: 11
Musée de L'Homme, Paris: 14
Parrinder, *Religion in an African City* (OUP): 3a
Popperfoto: 13c
John Rylands University Library, Manchester: 8
Edwin Smith: 18
Frank Spooner Pictures: 19 (Adams)

Abbreviations

BCP   The Book of Common Prayer.
CENERM   Centre for New Religious Movements, Selly Oak Colleges, Birmingham.
CH   *Scottish Psalter and Church Hymnary*, rev. edn. London, Oxford University Press, 1929.
CMS   Church Missionary Society Archives, Birmingham University Library.
DACL   *Dictionnaire d'archéologie Chrétienne et de Liturgie*, ed. F. Cabrol and H. Leclercq. Paris, Letouzcy et Ane, 1924–53, 30 vols.
EKG   *Evangelisches Kirchen-Gesangbuch*. Karlsruhe, Verlag Evangelischer Presseverband für Baden, 1965.
EJ   *Encyclopaedia Judaica*, Jerusalem, Keter, 1972, 16 vols.
ER   *The Encyclopedia of Religion*, ed. Mircea Eliade. New York, Macmillan, 1987, 16 vols.
ERE   *Encyclopaedia of Religion and Ethics*, ed. James Hastings. Edinburgh, T. & T. Clark, 1908, 13 vols.
HWDA   *Handwörterbuch des deutschen Aberglaubens*, ed. H. Bächtold-Stäubli. Berlin, Walter de Gruyter, 1927–42, 10 vols.
KiiG   *Die Kirche in ihrer Geschichte: Ein Handbuch*, ed. K. D. Schmidt *et al.* Göttingen, Vandenhoeck & Rupprecht, 1961–.
LThK   *Lexikon für Theologie und Kirche*, ed. Josef Höfer and Karl Rahner. Freiburg, Herder, 1957–67.
MMM   *Man, Myth and Magic: An illustrated Encyclopedia of the Supernatural*. London, Purnell for BPC Publishing, 1970–72, 112 parts.
NCE   *New Catholic Encyclopedia*. New York, London, McGraw-Hill, 1967–79, 17 vols.
NDLW   *A New Dictionary of Liturgy and Worship*, ed. J. G. Davies, London, SCM, 1986.
ODCC   *The Oxford Dictionary of the Christian Church*, ed. F. L. Cross and E. A. Livingstone, London, New York, Toronto, Oxford University Press, 1974.
RAC   *Reallexikon für Antike und Christentum; Sachwörterbuch zur Auseinandersetzung des Christentums mit der antiken Welt*, ed. Theodor Klauser. Stuttgart, Hiersemann, 1950–, 12 vols. to 1983.
RB   *The Roman Breviary*. New York, Benziger, 1964.
RE   *Realencyklopädie für protestantische Theologie und Kirche*, ed. A. Hauck. Leipzig, J. C. Hinricks'sche Buchhandlung, 1896–1909.
RGG   *Die Religion in Geschichte und Gegenwart: Handwörterbuch für*

       Theologie und Religionswissenschaft, ed. Kurt Galling. Tübingen, J. C. B. Mohr (Paul Siebeck), 1957–63.

ThWNT   *Theologisches Wörterbuch zum Neuen Testament*, ed. Gerhard Kittel and Gerhard Friedrich. Stuttgart, W. Kohlhammer, 1949–79, vols. I-X/2. The references given may easily be found in the corresponding volume of the English translation.

UJE   *Universal Jewish Encyclopaedia: An authoritative and popular presentation of Jews and Judaism since the earliest times*, ed. Isaac Landman. New York, Ktav, 1969, 10 vols.

Introduction

In this work, Christianity will be presented, I believe for the first time, in detailed phenomenological form. It will not be the approach of theology, though use will be made of theology in the form of religious concepts, e.g. creation or revelation (see below, Part Two). It is also not a history of Christianity though extensive historical material will be found in its pages. It is to be distinguished, again, from sociology or psychology of religion but these will also not be altogether neglected (especially in Chapter 13, and Part Three). We shall have occasion to come back to these other approaches later in the introduction.

What, then, is phenomenology of religion? Very briefly, phenomenology of religion (*ER* 11, 272ff.) makes use of the materials provided by the history of religions, theology, sociology and psychology of religion, as well as its own direct observations. Out of these materials significant religious phenomena disclose or manifest themselves to the interpreter. This is the primary stage and is often known as hermeneutical phenomenology (Brennemann, 1982). These phenomena may then be grouped under categories and sub-categories which have the widest possible application across religious traditions. Such groupings facilitate comparisons between phenomena which in turn help to bring out their meaning. We may call this stage morphological phenomenology. Finally, the categories themselves are further grouped into a unified field. This process is the culmination of the systematic phenomenology, argued for by Joachim Wach (Wach, 1924) and carried through in 1961 by Friedrich Heiler (Heiler, 1961).

The value of the study of religion proceeding along such lines has been long recognized, particularly in the area of religious education. In today's Britain, for instance, the religions of the ethnic minorities – Islam, Hinduism, Sikhism, Buddhism, Zoroastrianism, Afro-Caribbean religions – not to mention the many varieties of the Judeo-Christian traditions, may come together almost in the same classroom. Understandably, a massive government report, *Education for All* (1985), declared in favour of the phenomenological approach to religious education 'as the best and indeed the only means of enhancing the understanding of all pupils, from whatever background, of the plurality of faiths in contemporary Britain ...' (p. 474). Phenomenology of religion was long represented in Britain by E. O. James who made outstanding contributions to the subject (James, 1933, 1950, 1958, 1959, 1961, 1962, 1965, 1966). Lancaster, Leeds and Leicester are among university centres which have concerned themselves with the theory and application of the phenomenological method in the study of religion. But the way forward has, in my experience, been held up by the lack of two things: wider access to Continental phenomenology, including that of Heiler, and the provision of a phenomenology of the dominant religious tradition in the Anglo-Saxon world – Christianity. The present work attempts to make further progress in the field of religion by providing a Heilerian phenomenology of Christianity.

Since the early 1970s I have been making frequent use of Heiler's phenomenology of religion. It has been found helpful again and again for the phenomenology courses at Leicester where categories are worked with such as sacred action, images and symbols, myth, sacred space and time, sacred word and silence, sacred community, sacred person and deities. I have long seen the need for students and the wider English-reading public to have greater access to Heiler's work. The latter is at present known only in the shortened form of an early work on prayer, *Das Gebet* (Heiler, 1923a). Twenty-six years after the appearance of Heiler's phenomenology, no translation is yet in sight.

What the English reader and student of religion is deprived of in particular is (a) the very much more complete set of morphological categories that is to be found in the *Erscheinungsformen*, (b) their arrangement into concentric circles to provide Joachim Wach's *Systematik* for the field of religion, and (c) his inclusion of a great deal of Christian material as well as material from other religions, the result of his major studies of Catholicism and Orthodoxy as well as his lifelong interest in popular religion and ecumenism. (We shall come back to these points later.)

When, about ten years ago, a colleague in the field of religion raised the question of a work on the Christians, their beliefs and practices, it became clear to me that this had already been done by Heiler – if the large phenomenology of religion could be adapted for the purpose. There were other phenomenologies of religion available in English, but there was an urgent need for a phenomenology of Christianity to enable this part of the field to be presented in the same terms as those of the other religious traditions. It should not be the case of having a phenomenological approach to the other religions, but theology or history when it came to Christianity. Failing a translation of the complete phenomenology of Heiler, which would of course be welcome, it seemed the best solution would be to aim for an adaptation in the form of a phenomenology of Christianity but setting that religious tradition in the context of others and interpreting it according to the categories of morphological phenomenology.

The interpretative categories as well as most of the material for the phenomenology of Christianity set out in this work are thus the result of an adaptation of an already existing phenomenology of religion: that of the distinguished Marburg historian of religion, Friedrich Heiler (1892–1967; *ER* 6, 249f.). Heiler's work, published in 1961 (revised edition 1979), is entitled *Erscheinungsformen und Wesen der Religion* (Manifestations and Nature of Religion). Still available in German, it leads the history of religions series of more than forty volumes called *Die Religionen der Menschheit* (The Religions of Mankind) issued by the publishing firm of Kohlhammer of Stuttgart, Germany.

Why this work on religion should lend itself as an exploration of one religious tradition, namely, Christianity, calls for further discussion, the first part of which concerns Heiler's phenomenological method, the second part having to do with the kind of material which Heiler uses to illustrate his categories.

The Methodology. Heiler's interpretative categories stand solidly in the morphological tradition extending back over almost a hundred years. They are by no means chosen without regard for early phenomenologists. He makes use of themes that have been developed since the 1880s by scholars such as Chantepie de la Saussaye, Bertholet and Lehmann in their *Lehrbuch der Religionsgeschichte* (Chantepie, 1925), Van der Leeuw (Leeuw, 1963), Eliade (1963; *ER* 5, 85ff.) and Kristensen (1960). Over the years these categories have been adjusted to take account of the increasing body of knowledge made available by historians of religion and also by anthropologists, sociologists, psychologists, archaeologists and others. It is true that some of the earlier positions taken up by scholars in the field of religion have become outdated: for example, their often obsessive concern for the origins and evolution of religion. Nevertheless, the categories themselves have stood up remarkably well under the continuous expansion of knowledge of the world's religions. This was due in no small measure to the fact that from the outset the categories took into account not only the religions of Asia but also the traditional or ethnic religions.

The categories employed by Heiler are readily seen in the table of contents of this work. They may be grouped and arranged within three concentric circles: the outer circle represents the world of religious *manifestations*. Its categories include the sacred object (both natural, and made by hand), sacred space, sacred time, sacred number, sacred action (purification, sacrifice, unification), the sacred word (from and to the Deity), sacred silence, sacred writing, sacred person and sacred community. An inner circle of religious *concepts* follows: the concept of Deity (or lack of it), creation, revelation, salvation and eternal life. Inside that circle is another, that of religious *experience* (both in its normal and supranormal forms). Within the three circles is found the object of religion: ultimate reality (revealed and hidden). Each of these categories is capable of further subdivision enabling detailed comparisons across religious traditions. Such categories may be seen in different ways. They may be viewed as enduring structures, ideal Platonic forms or essences. Eliade and some of his followers seem at times to view them in this kind of way (Brennemann, 1982). They may also, however, be regarded as a loose grid, facilitating the grouping of various religious expressions. What both these views have in common is an acceptance of the importance of retaining such morphological categories. Underlying this retention of the categories is the assumption that religion, including its truth claims and its forms of personal experience, is to be taken seriously. Some would object to such a postulate as being too 'theological' (Rudolph, 1985). On the other hand African and Asian scholars in particular seem disinclined to abandon such a postulate in favour of some form of massive Western or Marxist 'objectivity' (Ursula King in Whaling, 1984).

Objection has also been taken to some of Heiler's categories, particularly those in the inner circles. Those making up the first, outer circle can hardly be objected to, since they appear in virtually all the preceding phenomenologies. Moreover, sacred community must be regarded as of particular value since it takes in the province of sociology of religion with its concern for the study of social groups and their leading religious figures. The first of the inner circles, with its series of major religious concepts, has elicited the objection of too much influence of Christianity and theology. Yet both Chantepie and Lehmann-Bertholet have included sections on doctrines among their categories. Moreover each of the concepts named lends itself just as easily to interpretations from the side of the traditional or ethnic religions, even as it does for Christianity. The third circle, that of religious experience, has been called into question as laying too much emphasis on the psychological and the para-psychological. But here too there are precedents in early phenomenologies. Moreover, it would lead to a definite impoverishment if one were to exclude *a limine* the whole area of psychology and para-psychology of religion. Lastly, if the category of Deity is objected to in the name of Theravāda Buddhism, a non-theistic tradition, it should be said that Heiler is aware throughout of what he calls mystical religion, with its reluctance or refusal to entertain concepts of Deity.

For others fewer categories would suffice. Ninian Smart has popularized six 'dimensions' (Smart, 1968) while Eric Sharpe has opted for four 'modes' (Sharpe, 1983). Such a reduction may appear at first sight an advance over against the more numerous categories of traditional morphological phenomenology. Yet there is a danger that the doctrinal, mythical, ethical, ritual, experiential, social *dimensions* or the existential, intellectual, institutional and ethical *modes* will be too general to facilitate the kind of detailed comparisons possible with the broader range of categories. The effect of the categories *is* precisely a broadening one. The category of sacred object, for example, is not made explicit in the six dimensions or four modes, yet brings in a whole world of natural symbolism and religious iconography, with a range of sources other than the written or spoken word.

Even if it be conceded that in respect to the choice and deployment of categories, Heiler 'kept to the phenomenological rules' (Sharpe, cited in Whaling, 1984), it has now to be asked whether it can be legitimate to apply such broad themes to one specific religious tradition, namely Christianity. If the categories of interpretation are drawn from the widest possible range of religious traditions, should they be used to try and make a profile of one particular religious tradition, namely Christianity? On the one hand it may narrow down the range of material grouped under the categories, on the other hand, Christianity's own special character may come too short. The boundaries that mark it off from what is not 'Christian' (whatever that may be held to be) may become blurred and obscured (Sykes, 1984).

These are important considerations. There are risks involved, but I am convinced these risks must be taken to formulate a phenomenological profile of Christianity in a comparative religious setting. It must still retain much of the character of a phenomenology of religion, but the emphasis will be on Christianity. If it is feared for the distinctiveness of that faith, we may remind ourselves that this is being documented at every point in the very material itself. Augustine of Hippo and Gregory the Illuminator occur only in Christianity, as do the rites of Baptist Christians in the Niger delta. The self-identity of Christianity is preserved in the historical particularity in which certain people, understanding themselves to be Christians, practise this rite, hold to that belief and share in the associated experiences. Again, it can be argued that the time has now come for such a 'Copernican' step. Christianity has become a world-wide, multi-cultural faith, whose followers, numbering almost a third of mankind, come out of countless different religious backgrounds. Why should Christianity not be interpreted in categories of the widest possible application? Finally, even in terms of Christianity's own inner intentionality, its self-identity has always been seen by some at least as an eschatological universalist faith, a community with in principle unlimited commensality, and, by implication at least, with no permanent boundaries standing to separate it from other religious traditions.

The practical gains from a phenomenology of Christianity are clear. First and foremost there is the freedom to explore religious meaning. We may read whole histories of Christianity without forming much of an idea as to how ordinary Christians practised and conceived of their faith. We are hurried from one *event* to the next. In a phenomenology of Christianity the place of the event is taken by the successive unfolding of the meaning. The historical flux is captured and put to work to explore the nature of Christian *phenomena* in a comparative context. Change and development, origins and influences are still there down to present-day secularized forms of erstwhile religious expressions – but meaning is dominant. Above all, with phenomenology's categories there is an enforced shift away from official, normative religion towards popular religion (*ER* 11, 440ff.) with its customary and folkloric practices.

Again, while there are available to English readers several phenomenologies of religion (including Kristensen, 1960; Van der Leeuw, 1963; and Eliade, 1963), there is as yet no careful and detailed application of phenomenological categories to Christianity in English. Moreover, none of the standard phenomenologies of religion in English devotes much attention to Christianity. A more recent work, Ninian Smart's *The Phenomenon of Christianity* (1979) does, it is true, consider various forms of Christianity, including major denominations, in their historical context and also to a lesser extent in relation to other religious traditions. But *The Phenomenon of Christianity* is not yet a *phenomenology* of Christianity. The emphasis is different in three respects: first, the six dimensions referred to above are employed instead of the more numerous categories and sub-categories. Then, the object appears to be a profile of major denominations and confessions, instead of more individual, popular and folkloric forms. Finally, there is a concern to emphasize distinctiveness rather than to document the similarity of forms across a wide range of traditions. All this is not intended to detract from the book's wealth of interest and insight; but rather to suggest that there is still an important place for the kind of detailed phenomenology of Christianity which is offered here.

It would only be proper, however, to acknowledge what this kind of phenomenology of Christianity does not provide. What emerges will be seen to be very much in the nature of a series of brush strokes, or to amount to at best not more than 'approximation' (Kristensen, 1960). Little attempt is made, for instance, to give a connected account of specific Churches, denominations, orders and religious movements within Christianity (*NDLW* 315ff.; Molland, 1959; Smart, 1979). There will of course be references to these, sometimes at length, under the different categories. But the principal focus is on the Christians themselves rather than on their collective life as Churches and denominations.

Others may miss a greater attention to the social context of the religious phenomena being compared. It has been argued that the classical phenomenological categories, such as are presented here, can no longer be applied in a global way because the social and religious context of such manifestations is not provided in detail. The resultant 'limitative' approach (Platvoet, 1982) goes, however, to the opposite extreme. It narrows the focus to a few religious phenomena and eschews any overall perspectives. Paradoxically, however, the limitative approach has demonstrated that even single phenomena imply a whole world in themselves. And so universality, excluded from the front, arrives through the back door. The approach of a broadly phenomenological study of Christianity does take context seriously, but this context takes an inter-religious rather than a socio-religious form.

The Material. Besides the provision of detailed phenomenological categories, this work also offers a wealth of materials brought together under the various categories and sub-categories. Even Heiler's sharpest critics have had to acknowledge this fact. It has been Heiler's achievement to have provided in his phenomenology of religion a detailed study of Christian practices and beliefs set in the context of those of other religions. In the present writer's experience of teaching Christianity for more than twenty years, and phenomenology and history of religion for much of that time, there is no one else who so far has managed to bring together (1) a clearly phenomenological stance in the tradition of Chantepie, Joachim Wach and Van der Leeuw; (2) an insistence upon a broad history of religions approach with materials drawn from traditional or ethnic religions as well as Hinduism and Buddhism, Sikhism and Zoroastrianism, Islam and the religions of China and Japan, as well as many others; (3) a strong interest in the psychology, sociology and iconography of religions; and all this with (4) a profound scholarly understanding of Christianity (Heiler, 1941). The last mentioned is marked by an unusual ecumenical breadth. Friedrich Heiler grew up in Catholic Bavaria and never lost his affection for and intimate knowledge of Western Catholicism (Heiler, 1970). He became an ecumenical Lutheran under the influence of Nathan Söderblom

(Misner, 1981), was a warm admirer of Eastern Orthodoxy (Heiler, 1971), and displayed a far-sighted appreciation of the piety of other non-Western forms of Christianity (Heiler, 1924).

All these interests, and more, colour the rich tapestry of materials that go to make up this phenomenology. In addition one should draw attention to the strong biblical base and interest in the history of salvation, the many references to the church Fathers, popes and reformers, the constant recourse to the inner world of the mystics, and the many examples of popular piety especially those from southern Germany. For those more accustomed to the normative or theological articulations of Christianity (see under Part Two, below), this diversity of religious forms may appear bewildering. Even so it represents only a fraction of the still largely unknown and unrecorded religious expressions of world Christianity (Andrew Walls, in Hinnells, 1984). Despite all the attention given to the Latin tradition, Eastern Orthodoxy and the non-Western world, the present work will still be seen by some as too Western, too European and too Protestant. However, the breadth of the categories does provide the basis for the building up of a more balanced picture as our knowledge of ecumenical Christianity increases. The reader may well be able to add to the material given here from his or her own experience of religious phenomena drawn from the Christian or, indeed, the other religious traditions of mankind.

It should be stressed that the work that follows is an *adaptation*. What does adaptation mean? The adaptation from a phenomenology of religion to a phenomenology of Christianity is intended to be an extension not a distortion of Heiler's work. For it interprets Christianity in terms of Heiler's categories and retains sufficient comparative material to provide a context firmly set in the world of religions. That the adaptation does represent an extension and not a distortion is evidenced by the fact that there is built up cumulatively an astonishingly full and rounded picture of a universal faith. The fulness of materials on Christianity in Heiler's phenomenology is actually the bringing together of the results of many other separate works on the subject.

The adaptation has been carried out by a combination of translation, paraphrase, condensing and selecting. The material drawn from other religious traditions has had to be somewhat reduced, yet sufficient has been retained, for example on the mystery cults of antiquity, to remind the reader of the comparative dimension, i.e. that Christianity is part of the inter-religious context, both historically and phenomenologically. The very full German references to sources and further reading have also been reduced; basic references, however, and important and characteristic Heilerian sources have been widely retained. To these, English references have been added; with all references given both in brief form in the body of the text, and again in full at the end of the book. Reference has also been made where appropriate to hymns and other material current in the Anglo-Saxon world; and at some points, e.g. in Chapters 1, 2 and 5, the text has been slightly amplified.

In some other respects also account has been taken of the fact that twenty-five years have elapsed since Heiler's work first appeared. Less emphasis has been placed on the idea of evolution from simple beginnings up to the emergence of the so-called 'higher religions', an idea which influenced Rudolph Otto and to a lesser extent Friedrich Heiler. However, the basic notion of development in the history of religion remains in evidence. Again, the rather pejorative term, 'primitive religion', has been rendered throughout by the more adequate and respectful 'traditional religion'. The term 'higher religion' has been avoided where it might suggest in any way that 'traditional religions' are to be regarded as in some sense 'lower'. Some material has also been added from the non-Western (and non-Eastern) world, including the continents of Africa and Latin America, so important for contemporary world Christianity. Reference has been made for example to African religions and liberation theology. Other developments such as the Second Vatican Council and the women's movement have also been recognized. Similarly, the references to further reading have been updated, an instance being the inclusion of the phenomenologically-important *Encyclopedia of Religion* edited by Mircea Eliade, which has just appeared in fifteen volumes with an index volume still to be delivered at the time of writing. Finally, to the reader who finds that 'so much' non-Christian material has been retained, one must emphasize again that world Christianity can only be understood in the light of the 'tacit dimension' provided by the other religions of mankind.

All these features, I believe, make for a reasonably up-to-date phenomenology of Christianity, a useful adjunct to the *Erscheinungsformen* for the English-speaking world. Those who may be led through this work to wish to have the full Heilerian range of material, with all original details of sources should by all means consult the German original, *Erscheinungsformen und Wesen der Religion* (Stuttgart, Kohlhammer Verlag).

We turn now to ask, in a preliminary way, the Christians – who are they? The work that follows seeks to explore their religious world. The question of their identity within this world of theirs may be approached on two levels. First, we might take account of Christianity in its various official, public, intellectual, collective forms, at the 'macrocosmic' level. This may be said to be the usual approach that is taken. The other way – just as often neglected – is to take seriously the individual, popular, private, inward emotional forms, those on the microcosmic level. An instance of the latter: if a person climbs slowly towards a sacred place, in tears all the while, and this 'pilgrim', let us say, calls himself/herself a Christian, do we not have to take this 'sacred action' to be an important expression of Christianity? It or a similar action should therefore find a place in any treatment of the subject. In the work that follows both macrocosm and also microcosm are able to find a place, both official and popular religion, through the use of the phenomenological method. First, though, a word should be said about Christianity in the usual sense of the term, that is, on the level of the macrocosm, by way of a short historical synopsis.

The world has been seen by Christians as deriving its meaning from the 'sacred history' (*Heilsgeschichte*) outlined in the Jewish Scriptures, the Christian Old Testament. This history goes back to Adam and ultimately to God. Such a wide-ranging perspective is supported by the two genealogies given in the New Testament for the founder of Christianity. In the Gospels the ancestry of Jesus is traced either to Abraham (Matt. 1.1–17) or to Adam the 'son of God' (Luke 3.23–38.). Even when viewed more externally as one religious movement in history among others, the world of the Christians is extensive indeed. From a small sect within Palestinian Judaism it has grown to where it is found in most countries of the world (Barrett, 1982). Its progress through the centuries may be checked by reference to the year of the present era: 1987 as I write. The Christian era according to the Western calendar begins on 1st January in the year one, the notional date of the birth of Christianity's founder. The actual date, however, is unknown, although 6th January or 25th December have been adopted as a day on which to celebrate his birth (see below, Chapter 4). Also a matter of uncertainty is when Christianity may be said to have begun – whether at the beginning of sacred history itself or at some point during the life of Jesus, e.g. at his baptism, or else sometime after his death, for instance at the day of Pentecost, the 'birthday' of the Church. Certain it is however that Christianity now embraces a time span of at least nineteen and a half centuries.

During this long period of time Christianity, like other religious traditions, has developed a multiplicity of forms and tendencies rather like a growing tree putting out its branches, some of which flourish, while others remain small, and still others wither away. The extent to which in the course of time the tree and its branches may have slowly changed into something different or else have remained basically one and the same religious movement, is also a matter of debate. Perhaps this much could be offered by way of a preliminary sketch of Christianity's progress through the centuries:

After an initial period in the Greco-Roman world of some three centuries, marked by steady growth and the emergence of a variety of religious forms, Christianity obtained the sometimes doubtful advantages of political recognition and support. It also spread well beyond the confines of the late Roman empire, separating gradually over centuries into broadly Latin and Western, and Eastern, Greek-speaking areas. There followed a 'medieval' period of roughly a millennium during which time Germanic and Slavic peoples came under the influence of the Christian faith and helped to create some of Christianity's most spectacular achievements in terms of civilization, culture, learning and spirituality. In the East, Nestorian Christianity spread as far as India and even to China (where it was known as 'the luminous way').

The transition to the last, 'modern', period is difficult to pin down precisely either in the West or the East. Indeed, with the new, world-wide expansion of Christianity beginning in the fifteenth century, the very terms East and West become inadequate markers. But the long upheaval in Western Christianity during the sixteenth and seventeenth centuries brought about by the Reformation and its aftermath, does indicate a watershed in one respect: the unity of medieval Christendom effectively breaks up. In eastern Europe and Asia, successive invasions of Arab and central Asian Muslims represent a more external threat for Christianity comparable to the internal disruptions and national reconstructions experienced in the West. The invasions in the East extended also over a millennium from the seventh to the seventeenth centuries.

In more recent times, both in the West and to a lesser extent in the East, Christianity has been confronted increasingly by what has been termed 'secularization', the increasing autonomy from the religious domain claimed by one area of life after another: the political, economic, social, legal, the sciences, the arts, and many other fields. Even the sphere of religion itself has been seen more as confined to individual piety than as embracing public life and its institutions as well. In their way, too, other movements, such as Rationalism, Romanticism and Socialism have also had a profound effect upon Christianity. To take up only the last of these, Marxist influence has been potent not only in the West and in Eastern countries including Russia and China, but also more recently in Latin America and Africa. Christianity has been compelled *nolens volens* to come to terms with such challenges. To what extent it should rethink its message and structure in the light of these new movements and ideologies is a matter of intense debate.

Understanding Christianity in terms of its many and complex historical developments is clearly a task of some magnitude. It is the task that historians of Christianity set themselves. Fortunately there is a variety of histories already, designed to meet the student's needs, from one-volume surveys to multi-volume compendia (Reynolds, 1977; Bainton, 1966; Latourette, 1975; Rogier, 1964ff. and *ER* 2, 348ff.). The historical approach is undoubtedly of help in tracing changes and developments, in trying to determine what happened at a given place and time, and why it happened. To elucidate such questions the historian has developed appropriate categories for historical interpretation and is well able to discuss events and movements in these terms. In the work that follows recourse will have to be made to such works.

Yet, as the earlier remarks on phenomenology have indicated, this book is not primarily about Christianity in terms of its history. The reader should not expect to find a straightforward, detailed, chronologically-ordered series of developments; though there is as it happens much historical material in it. It is rather about Christianity in the context of the religious life and the religious experience of Christians.

The advantage of the phenomenological approach compared to the historical one is seen in the case of the study of Christianity in Africa. Even under the guidance of an Africa-centred historiography, Christianity tends to emerge as something very different and separate from both Islam and African traditional religions. For African Christians this sense of separateness has needless to say posed a long-standing problem, one that is reflected in the massive literature that has grown up concerning the 'indigenous' Church (*NDLW* 268ff.).

To make further progress, historical concerns with change and development, origins and influences, have to give way before another series of interpretive categories, those of phenomenology, which as we have seen, have not just been derived from the Western historical tradition, and from that of Christianity itself, but rather from the widest possible range of the religious traditions of mankind. Such categories, as we shall see, will, if applied to the study of Christianity, soon have the effect of having it viewed as a 'world religion'. It will be a world religion not just in terms of its numbers and geographical extent but in terms of *structure*. When it is worked out in this way, Christianity can no longer be maintained to be in principle or in practice separate from, say, African traditional religions or Islam or Indian religions, or even from Europe's own Celtic or Germanic religions, or even from Australia's aboriginal religious systems. No matter from what cultural and religious area of the globe Christianity is being experienced, it will be seen to be truly 'indigenous' in the sense of being structurally an integral part of the religious experience of mankind. From such a point of view, denying the indigeneity of the Church in Africa or anywhere else must be seen as the result of applying inappropriate interpretative categories.

It should perhaps also be added that Christianity can not be studied as a 'world religion' with the categories and approach of theology, unless these, as with those of history, are subordinated to the categories and approach of phenomenology. Traditional Christian theology is concerned (properly) with the uniqueness of the Christian faith. Its structure lies within this presupposition. The structure of phenomenology on the other hand is the proper systematic for the whole field of religion and therefore there is a sense in which it alone can provide the proper structure for Christianity *as a world religion*.

A final word on that part of the phenomenological approach which was earlier called *hermeneutical* phenomenology. What follows may best be viewed not as a kind of static array of classified material, but as a dynamic process for experiencing what a religious tradition such as Christianity is all about. The loose grid of categories drawn from a wide range of religious traditions may appear at first sight rather abstract and static. Yet they should be regarded not as important in themselves, but as intended to function simply as markers and facilitators for the symbolic descriptions of religious phenomena, as significant expressions of living religion. They are what stream up out of people's encounter with and apprehension of ultimate reality. These expressions are in turn then grouped loosely into religious manifestations (Chapters 1 to 13), religious concepts (14 to 18) and religious experience (19 and 20). Although separate for the sake of analysis, these three concentric circles do of course belong together in every instance. Such significant instances are intended to strike a chord, to effect a resonance in the reader's own experience: for religion is not only a tale that is told, it is all about a life that is being lived.

PART ONE

The World of
Christian Phenomena

1

Objects Sacred to Christians
1: Natural Objects

(1) The stone, mountain, earth, water, fire and storm

One place to begin a study of the beliefs and practices of Christians is where some objects of significance to them are found. Christians are concerned with the invisible One beyond all sense perception, and yet, paradoxically, they communicate with the Deity, normally, in and through sensory forms. Their religious life is expressed through the world of the body, its glance, its word and its gesture. Even their spiritual concepts are derived from the impressions received through the senses. The central biblical notion of spirit (Greek *pneuma*) comes from the movement of the wind as perceived by the senses. The simplest sensory stimuli may evoke the highest forms of religious inspiration. Thus the inaugural vision of a West African prophet began after he saw three leaves on the wheel of his steam-roller (Omoyajowo, 1966). Although some Christians have tended to react against the excessive reliance upon the sensory element in their cultic religious life, it is thoroughly interwoven into the earliest traditions of the Christian religion. Jesus healed by the laying on of hands and by the use of his spittle. His followers anointed the sick with healing oil. Jesus washed the feet of his disciples as an exemplary action symbolizing purification, forgiveness and humility. Christians find the presence of God even in a child in a manger, in water, that of baptism, and in bread and wine of the Lord's Supper. Anything can become a 'hierophany', a disclosure of the sacred.

In the remainder of the chapter, consideration will be given to some of the objects taken from the natural world which many, including Christians, see as disclosures of the sacred. One further point should be cleared up at the outset. Christianity is usually regarded as a religion of history, not as a religion of nature. Such classifications may have a point, but cannot be pressed too far. Just as African traditional religions are as concerned with the life of people in society as with nature and the cosmos, so too Christianity is as much concerned with nature as with history and the course of events. This becomes clearer in the consideration of some natural objects which may not be thought of at first as being closely connected with the Christian religion.

The first sacred natural object to be considered is the *stone* (*ER* 14, 49ff.). Signs of the cult of stones in the shape of stone cairns, standing stones and stone circles (*ER* 9, 336ff.) are still with us today and bear eloquent witness to the Deity as everlasting. Although some might not think of Christians being related to such cults, it is all too true that Christianity and other religions have incorporated basic insights learnt from the stone hierophanies of early days. Through its early Judaic heritage and its early western Semitic environment, the Christian religion has been firmly rooted in, as well as continually influenced by, the cult of stones. An example is Gilgal (Heb. for stone circle), an early Semitic shrine near Jericho. *Bethel*-stones, popular among the early western Semites, enter the Christian tradition through the Hebrew patriarch Jacob, who slept on such a stone, had a vision of Deity and recognized the stone as *Bethel* or a sacred shrine (Gen. 28.17). He then poured a libation of oil. Following this he set up a memorial stone pillar (*massēbāh*) where the Deity (YHWH) spoke to him and he responded by anointing it with oil and pouring a libation (Gen. 35.14). He and his uncle Laban made a covenant (*berīth*) upon a *massēbāh* (Gen. 31.44ff.). After a victory over the Philistines, Samuel the judge set up a boundary stone which has also become for many Christians a symbol of the power of the Deity; its name, *Ebenezer*, finding its way into numerous hymns (1 Sam. 7.12).

The veneration of sacred stones was forbidden in early Judaism (Deut. 16.22) and in early Christianity by missionaries among the Germanic peoples. But it lived on in linguistic images of great vividness (Wenschkewitz, 1932). The invisible Deity is praised as a 'rock' (Ps. 18.2; 31.3f; 40.2, etc.) in the awareness that the latter is a traditional hierophany of invisible being and power. Christ is seen as the 'corner stone' of the arch. It is rejected by the builders because, with its peculiar shape, it did not fit in the wall (Ps. 118 [LXX 117].22; Mark 12.10; *ThWNT* 1, 792f). The stone which was rolled back before the tomb of Jesus is thus also a symbol of his resurrection (Morison, 1930). The disciple and apostle Peter is associated with a 'rock', used both as a symbol and as a play on words. 'Thou art Peter (Aram. *Kepha*, Greek *Petros*), and upon a *kepha* (Greek *petra*, 'rock') I will build my *ecclesia*' (church; Matt. 16.18). The apostle is here a symbol of the steadfastness of the *ecclesia* of Christ (*ThWNT* 6, 103–9). Moreover every Christian is called to be a stone in a spirit-filled temple. 'And like living stones . . . built into a spiritual house . . .' (1 Pet. 2.5). This is echoed in the rites for the dedication of a church. Finally, Christian mystics employ the stone as a metaphor for the Deity and as everywhere sacred. God is addressed by Mechthild of Magdeburg (1210–82/94) as 'Thou exalted Stone'; while Francis of Assisi simply loved the stone as part of nature. Because Christ is called the corner stone, he, Francis, walks over every stone with reverence.

Like the stone, the *mountain* (*ER* 10, 130ff.) has also had special significance for Christians. They draw inspiration from references in Scripture to the Deity (YHWH) as a Mountain God (1 Kings 20.23, etc.) with many centres of divine power: Mt Sinai, Mt Peor, Mt Hermon, the mountains of Lebanon, Mt Tabor, Mt Gerizim and Mt Zion. From these help will come (Ps. 121.1). Not only the prophet Elijah, but also Jesus, and later, saints and mystics including Benedict and Francis, preferred the mountain as a place for prayer and contemplation. The mountain is a favourite image of gradual purification in Dante's *Divine Comedy*. In the old Preliminary to the Roman Mass the priest said (Ps. 43.3): 'O send forth thy light and thy truth, that they may lead and bring me to thy holy mountain, thy dwelling place.' Christian mystics compare the different stages of contemplation to climbing a mountain. Saint John of the Cross entitled one of his mystical works *The Ascent of Mount Carmel*. For Mechthild of Magdeburg, God was the 'Mountain'. Henry Suso speaks of 'a wild mountain range of the Whence beyond God'. Angelus Silesius sings: 'God is indeed the ground of all being; and yet he to whom God would show himself must ascend the peak of the eternal mountain.'

Like the mountain, the *earth* (*ER* 4, 534ff.) has been venerated since the earliest times. Often this was as a mother goddess, with a strong emphasis upon fertility and a close connection with the dead. Christians followed Jewish prophets in rejecting Ishtar the mother goddess of the western Semites; but many traces of the cult of the earth are found in the Judeo–Christian tradition. When he hears of the loss of all his children and property, Job prostrates himself upon the earth, the mother from which he has come and who will receive him at death (Job 1.20f.). The Psalmist recalls having been formed 'under the earth' (Ps. 139.15). Jesus Sirach sees the earth as 'the mother of us all' (Ecclus. 40.1). The ancient myth of the marriage of 'heaven and earth' lives on in the Bible as a linguistic image for the cosmos (Gen. 1.1 etc. and Mark 13.31 etc.). The belief in the earth and the belief in salvation may occasionally converge (Isa. 45.8), but on the whole the earth is firmly placed in the relationship of the creation to its Creator (Acts 4.24 etc.). The veneration of the earth emerges again in the mystics. Saint Francis includes Mother Earth in his 'Hymn to the Sun'. In pantheist thought and in the art and poetry of the Romantics, the Christian vision of a renewed earth (Rev. 21.1) lives on. It has recently emerged in a new sensitivity to the earth as the common environment of animals and plants, as well as of mankind. 'Mankind, animals and plants participate in one and the same world and environment. That means that they stand in relationship to one another and have to rely on one another' (Tierhilfswerk, 1981).

The sacredness of *water* (*ER* 15, 350ff.) is also part of universal religious belief, and in this Christians also share. *Sacred springs and rivers* (*ER* 12, 425) bring life, fertility and healing. Catholic pilgrim chapels are often built over springs. Names such as Santa Maria Fontana betray the enduring faith in the sacredness of the spring. At a shrine in Eichstätt, Bavaria, the spring becomes the Virgin's tears, and these are in demand all over the world. The miraculous healings at the pilgrimage centre of Lourdes and elsewhere also increase the sacredness and power of the water.

Sacred rivers have traditionally included those referred to in the Bible. That the Euphrates river is regarded as sacred (it is mentioned in the creation stories, Gen. 2.14 etc.) appears from a vision of the Apocalyptist (Rev. 9.14), where four angels are found beside this great river. Even more is the river Jordan celebrated in Christian hymns, sermons and homilies. It obtained a central place in the Christian geography of salvation through the baptism of Jesus in its waters. The running water of rivers has the power which cleanses a person from sin (see below, Chapter 5).

Sacred water is kept by many Christians in special containers. The Roman Church, thus, has three different forms of consecrated water: that consecrated on the Sunday; baptismal water consecrated on the nights of Easter and Pentecost; and 'Gregorian' water used for consecrating churches. In the Eastern Church, an important place is given to the consecration of water on the feast of Epiphany, which, if possible, is celebrated at rivers, and counts as one of the sacraments. A Roman Catholic prayer of consecration stressed the sacredness of water as 'living, regenerative and purifying'.

Water features also in the primordial mythology and cosmology of Christianity. It is the original matter out of which the world is formed (Gen. 1.2), the primordial ocean, similar to *Apsū* in the Babylonian creation myth. The Deity (YHWH) has established the water upon the seas and the streams of water (Ps. 24.2). The creation myth (Gen. 1.1–2.3) stresses that the spirit of God hovers above the water. The four rivers are named in the myth of Paradise (Gen. 2.10ff.); while the Ode of Solomon (11.6) has it that the 'Spring of the Lord' brings about a state of ecstasy. In prophetic, eschatological visions, the cosmological theme occurs again. In the vision of Ezekiel (chap. 47), water springs up from the threshold of the temple and becomes a 'river of life'. Zechariah (14.8) prophesies that living water will flow out of Jerusalem, one half to the sea eastwards and the other half to the sea westwards. Continuing this theme the New Testament Apocalyptist sees a pure river of water of life, clear as crystal, proceeding from the throne of God (Rev. 22.1).

Water is also a symbolic, linguistic image in Judeo-Christian writings. It stands for the divine life and grace. The Deity is a 'spring of living water' for prophet and psalmist (Jer. 17.13; Ps. 23.2). The image of water is a favourite one for the Johannine writings of the New Testament. In the story of Jesus and the Samaritan woman, the well of Jacob symbolizes the Jewish law, while Christ provides water which quickens into everlasting life (John 4.14). The Latin hymn *Veni Creator* praises the Holy Spirit as the 'living fountain'. The Christian mystics took up the same theme, Mechthild of Magdeburg speaking of the 'Fountain of the eternal Deity' and of the 'flowing Trinity'. For Angelus Silesius, the Deity is a well from which everything comes and a sea to which it all returns. Modern people are aware that in a physio-chemical sense they are largely composed of water. They delight, as of old, in taking the waters, whether as baths, sauna, or river, lake or beach. These have not lost their powers of renewal. It has also not escaped the far-seeing that the sense of sacredness of water has actually played a major role in preserving the limited, pure waters of spring and rain, on which all life depends (Liebmann, 1973).

The cult of another of the elements, that of *fire* (*ER* 5, 340ff.), has also become a part of many religions. Fire has been seen to have a twofold significance: on the one hand it drives away harmful and evil powers (its *apotropaic* function); on the other hand it is the source of welcome warmth, light and life. It also has a doubleness in its divine and human character: it has its origin in heaven; but has been discovered by man, and has to be cared for and preserved by him. In Western Europe, the Spring fire for the Deity (Indo-Germanic Wotan) promoted fertility in crops and people. After the coming of Christianity, Wotan was demonized as 'Winter' and burnt in South German 'Judas fires'. Some part of the Spring fire also remained in the rite of the consecration of fire in the Frankish church which passed from there into Roman Catholicism in general. The prayer of consecration in the Mass includes a strongly apotropaic motif, that of driving away the devil. Further west, in Ireland, the fire of the Celtic goddess of wisdom Brigit was transferred to the Christian abbess Brigit of Kildare, where it was cared for by nuns.

More importantly, the cult of fire continues for Christians in the burning of *candles and lamps*. In Rome, where the Saturnalia fire of the winter solstice was once ignited, Christmas candles are now given out and lit instead. On All Souls' day in Catholic areas, lighted candles are placed on graves to drive away harmful powers. A candle is lit by Catholics and placed before a sacred picture or statue as an offering. Before the emperor of Byzantium a candle was carried as a sign of his sacredness. It was also carried before the Roman pope. Early Christian writers inveighed against the traditional Roman practice of burning lights before icons of the deities; but later the same custom spread among Christians themselves. The Christian Church took over the practice of solemnly lighting candles in the evening. Candles and lamps were lit before altars, and, later, on the altars and before icons of Christ and the saints. As in the Jewish synagogue, the Church in East and West had an eternal light burning as a symbol of the presence of God. The Easter candle symbolizes for many Christians the risen Christ. In the Easter liturgy of both East and West, including some Protestant as well as Anglican and Catholic churches, all other candles or lights are ignited from the one Easter candle. In the Greek Orthodox Church, the cry goes forth: 'Come ye, take light from the light unquenchable.' But it is the natural fire which still remains sacred for Saint Francis. At sunset he sings, 'May you be praised, my Lord, through my brother the fire, through whom you illumine the night.'

In mankind's religious history, fire has often been the manifestation of Deity, for instance, as Agni, Atar or Hestia/Vesta. For the early Israelites, the Deity, according to some scholars, was originally also a fire or volcano deity. The burning bush which Moses encountered (Exod. 3.2) has caught the imagination of Christians and has even, along with the cross of St Andrew, become a crest or monogram for Presbyterians. Yet this hierophany may derive from a volcanic eruption: 'The whole of Mount Sinai smoked because the Lord drove down the mountain with fire' (Exod. 19.18). The Elijah legend has the prophet ascending to Yahweh in a chariot of fire (2 Kings 2.11). Fire also has an important place in Christian eschatology. Notions of a world conflagration, originating in Indo-Germanic, Indo-Iranian and Hellenistic (Stoic) ideas, passed from thence into early Christianity, with its vision of the heavens passing away in fire and the elements melting from its heat (2 Pet. 3.12). There are earlier biblical references (e.g. Deut. 32.22) to the Deity's fire of judgement and wrath which burns down into the deepest underworld and up into the mountain strongholds. Indo-European and prophetic-Judaic concepts merge in the Roman liturgy for the dead, which celebrates him 'who will come to judge the dead through fire'. Hell, in the prophetic and apocalyptic view, has the form of a furnace which burns with fire and sulphur (Rev. 21.8). Purgatory also implies a fire of refinement and punishment (see Chapters 5 and 18, below).

Fire is also taken as a positive symbol of the nature of Deity in the biblical writings. The Deity led the people of Israel out of Egypt by night with 'a pillar of fire' (Exod. 13.21). His throne is fire (Dan. 7.9). He is 'consuming fire' (Heb. 12.29). The eyes of Christ are like a flaming fire (Rev. 1.14). The Spirit is like fire (Matt. 3.11; and Acts 2.3). Jesus' calling is like the throwing of fire (Luke 12.49). Fire is an image beloved of Christian – as well as Islamic – mystics. Mechthild of Magdeburg's revelations were of 'fire'. Angelus Silesius sings: 'Where God is a fire, my heart is the hearth.' Fire is an image for the love radiating from the sacred heart of Jesus. Gertrud of Helftae (1256–1302) speaks of the flame of divine love from the sacred heart which makes the soul glow with warmth. Blaise Pascal's conversion was experienced as 'Fire, fire, fire' (Caillet, 1945, 131ff.).

Atmospheric phenomena, especially the *storm* (*ER* 9, 487ff.; 12, 201ff.) (including lightning, thunder, wind and rain), have had, and still have global significance in the history of religions. Christians too have taken such phenomena with deepest seriousness as sacred symbols of Deity. *Lightning* has been seen as an especially numinous manifestation. The Deity looses his lightning bolts (Ps. 18.14). The future coming of the Messiah will take the form of lightning (Luke 17.24). The Apocalyptist has a vision of lightning, along with thunder and voices, coming from the throne of Christ (Rev. 4.5). Jesus sees Satan fall from heaven like lightning (Luke 10.18). For Angelus Silesius, God is simply a lightning flash. *Thunder* is associated with lightning. The Deity when giving the law was seen and heard by the people in lightning and thunder claps (Exod. 20.18; 1 Sam. 7.10; Ps. 18.14f.). In a *storm* the Deity appears (Nah. 1.3). His words are carried by the *storm wind* (Ps. 148.8). The Reformer, Martin Luther, cried out to the mother of the Virgin Mary in a storm, and made a solemn vow which changed his life and the course of Christian history. The New Testament associates the *wind* with the Spirit. For early Christians the latter is like the wind (Acts 2.2). The Spirit blows where it will (John 3.8). In his 'Hymn to the Sun' Saint Francis of Assisi praises Brother Wind and the weather.

(2) The sun, moon, stars, heaven and light

The *sun* (*ER* 14, 132ff.) is a religious phenomenon of the greatest importance for the cultus and piety of all times. By cultic rites it was caused to rise. Its appearance was greeted with prayer and praise. Sun beliefs and cultus were so deeply rooted in religious life that Christianity as a monotheistic religion in the Judaic tradition, could only attempt to transform without eliminating them. The Roman traditional festival of *Sol Invictus* (the Unconquered Sun, a central imperial deity), was celebrated on 25th December, which became the birthday of the founder of Christianity. The female sun deity of spring, for the Anglo-Saxons, was *Eostra*, with April as *Eosta* ('Easter') month. In addition to this, sun beliefs were transmitted to Christianity through Judaism. Josiah, the reformist king of ancient Judah, sought to repress the sun cult of a predecessor, King Manasseh (2 Kings 21 and 23). Even so, Psalm 19, which begins 'The heavens are telling the glory of God', goes on to include an early praise song to the sun hero who 'like a strong man runs his course with joy'. God is praised by a prophet as the 'sun of righteousness' (Mal. 4.2); and prayer is made in the Book of Enoch to the evening sun (83.11).

The solar cult exerted a strong influence on Christianity during its first three centuries through the rival cults of Mithras and *Sol Invictus*. Even for Christianity's founder, the sun was an image of divine love that embraces good and bad alike (Matt. 5.45). On the mountain of transfiguration, Jesus' face shone like the sun (Matt. 17.2; cf. Rev. 1.16). The day of resurrection is *dies solis, sunùntag*, Sunday. For Cyprian, Christ is 'the true sun and the true day.' In Christian worship also, the cult of the sun finds expression in the sacred action of *orientation*. The sanctuary itself is 'oriented' towards the rising sun (see also below, Chapter 3). Early Christian candidates for baptism stretched out their hands and spat towards the west as a sign of abjuring demonic power. Then they turned towards the east to greet Christ as the rising sun. The sun running its course comes into the hymn of the canonical hours (*NDLW* 140ff.), for instance Lauds, which included the words, 'O thou true Sun, shine thou upon us with the brightness of thine everlasting light.' This is continued in Protestant hymns, for example, that addressed to the Sun of Righteousness (*EKG* No. 218). For Christian mystics the sun is an image of God. Mechthild of Magdeburg prayed to God as 'My Sun, thou chosen Sun'; while Henry Suso spoke of God as the 'supernatural sun'; and Christ as the sun's zenith. Saint Francis' 'Hymn to the Sun' ('We praise you for Brother Sun') continues in its own way the veneration of the sun.

The cult of the *moon* (*HWDA* 6, 477ff.; *RGG* 4, 1094ff.; *ER* 10, 83ff.) is also world-wide. The moon is traditionally related to menstruation and women's illnesses. Its cult was opposed by the Hebrew prophets (Deut. 4.19; 17.3), but was firmly rooted in popular western Semitic religion. During the late Roman empire, early Christianity was also confronted by the widespread veneration of *Luna*, together with *Sol*, as seen in the tauroctony reliefs of the Mithraic cult of the time. Nevertheless, the Easter celebrated by the early Christians was itself linked to the moon, being celebrated on the first Sunday after the first full *moon* after the spring equinox. As an object of veneration Mary the mother of Christ was later given the moon as her symbol along with a mantle of stars. And the medieval mystic Mechthild of Magdeburg conceived of God as the full moon.

The *stars* (*RGG* 1, 662ff.; *HWDA* 1, 632ff.; 9, 396–689; *ER* 14, 42ff.) have traditionally been experienced as living, divine beings, the 'ears' of the God of heaven. Particular stars and constellations have also had their significance. The astrological zodiac (4000–2000 BC, in Babylon) assumed widespread importance in different religions down to the late Roman empire, and even beyond, for example in Western and Asian traditions. In astrological interpretation, types of human character and destiny correspond to houses of the zodiac. Divination in the form of astrology would link the cosmos to man, as 'microcosmos', by means of the notion of 'sympathy' or harmony. The cult of the stars reinforced the sense of fatalism in the Greco-Roman world. Men were captive to the world powers or elements. From these, escape was sought by means of magic, by the gnostic redemption myth, by Mithras' graded initiation, by Neoplatonist mysticism, and especially by worship of the stars and their propitiation by sacrifices (Cumont, 1956). Christianity opposed the astral cult; but down to the present day astrology has maintained a place of some influence even among Christians as a form of divination. Many newspapers and weekly journals provide horoscopes as a regular feature.

In the medieval period, Dante (*Purg.* 30, 109ff.) was prepared to assign a place of relative influence to the stars. The great theologian Thomas Aquinas also gave the stars a degree of power over the cosmos, but not over the reason and free-will of man. In Christian art of the medieval period, many of the symbols are of astrological origin. Certain saints, for instance, are distinguished by a star or stars (Roeder, 1955). The Renaissance witnessed a revival of astrology, especially among the Renaissance Popes Julius II, Pius III and Leo X. Romanticism, Classicism, Theosophy, Occultism, Anthroposophy and even National Socialism – all made use of astrology in some degree. But other tendencies in Christianity resisted the influence of the stars. Christian leaders, including individual popes and Reformers, rejected astrology. The personalism felt by Christians with regard to the Deity, and the persistent indeterminism in Catholic dogmatics and ethics also supported such opposition. But the star cult lives on in other forms than astrology; e.g. there is the celebrated star of Bethlehem in Matthew's birth narrative (2.1–13), featuring in Christmas cards and plays. It could refer to a particular astral constellation. The *magoi* could also be Magian priests of Ahura Mazda or Mithra (*ThWNT* 4, 360ff.). Only later do they become three kings.

Other linguistic star images are found in Christianity. Mary has a gown of stars and is addressed as Morning Star. Hail (Mary) Star of the Sea is found in a hymn. In Protestant belief, Jesus is also praised as 'Star'. Jesus is the great Star of Wonder who has appeared out of Jacob. It is the same form of address as in Babylonian and southern Arabian traditional religions, though now filled with christological content. Compare also the hymn of Philip Nicolai of 1599, 'How beautifully shines the Morning Star', based on the reference in Revelation 22.16 (*EKG* No. 48). But, equally, the natural stars are called upon, in Ps. 148.3, to praise God, and this is also firmly in the spirit of Christianity.

Not only the stars, but *heaven* itself (*ER* 13, 343ff.) has proved a manifestation of Deity. The whole expanse of the sky, the totality of light, the connection of heaven with both sun and night stars, the atmospheric phenomena, often of the most dramatic kind, and the fruitful, essential rains – all these and more have contributed to the impact made by the heavens upon Christians, as indeed upon people of many other religious traditions. Above all, the heavens were seen as the dwelling-place of the Deity. Originally the heavens had been seen as linked with the earth in a primordial divine marriage. The heavens were either male (China) or female (Nut – Egypt). They were Djeus, the shining one, for the early Aryans, Dyaus Pitar in the Vedas, Varuna/Ouranos for the Indo-Europeans, Khshathra for the early Iranians. In early Judaic thought, which passes into Christianity, heaven is the throne, earth is the footstool of Yahweh (Isa. 66.1). In one of the Psalms (104.2), we find the Babylonian concept of the tent of heaven and the mantle of stars. Elsewhere (1 Macc. 4.10; 12.15, etc.) we find heaven (*shāmayim, ouranos*) being used instead of the name of God as this has become too sacred to utter. Similarly in Matthew, the Kingdom of heaven really means the Kingdom of *God*; while the lost son confesses in Luke (15.21) that he has sinned against 'heaven' and before his father (*ThWNT* 5, 496–543). This faith in 'heaven' Christians share with the whole of mankind; everywhere where men lift up their hands to heaven is there this testimony to a universal faith.

Fire, sun, stars and the heavens all combine to make *light* a hierophany of the divine (*ERE* 8, 47ff; *RGG* 4, 357ff.). Light is also a symbol for the divine much developed in Gnosticism and Neoplatonism, and has left its mark clearly upon the New Testament and the writings of the Fathers. In the Jewish Bible light is a symbol for God and his help: those in darkness have seen 'a great light' (Isa. 9.2). Jesus makes use of light symbolism in the Sermon on the Mount (Matt. 5.14ff.). So does Paul (Rom. 13.12; 2 Cor. 4.6; 6.14; Phil. 2.15). Early Jewish and Hellenistic light symbolism join hands in John's Christ-mysticism. For John, Christ is the 'light of the world' (John 1.4f.; 8.12). Those who believe are 'children of light' (12.36). Christ is eternal light, holy light. Athenagoras' hymn, 'Hail, gladdening Light', has become the vesper hymn of the Greek Church and of many congregations in the West; yet it goes back to Aristophanes' praise of Dionysos. In the Greek Orthodox Easter night liturgy is the declaration, 'Now all is filled with light that is in heaven, on earth and under the earth.' On the same night the Western Church consecrates the sole Easter candle with a hymn to light. In the liturgy for the dead, light symbolism is offered to lighten the darkness of death. 'May perpetual light illumine them' is the repeated plea.

In Eastern monasticism, Symeon the New Theologian (949–1022) fathered a whole mystical theology based on light. Contemplation of the divine *doxa* (effulgence) found visible expression in the seeing of a wonderful light. Linked to a yoga-like prayer technique, this light mysticism was carried further in the fourteenth century by Gregorios Sinaita, a monk of the famous monastery at Mt Athos. Another Gregory, Gregory Palamas, provided a foundation for this with a theory concerning the uncreated energy of the light of God which transfigured Christ on Mt Tabor and which perceptibly illuminates a person in a state of inner peace. (In Buddhist literature, followers of a Tibetan lama may attain the Buddha-nature with a salvation body full of light.) The teaching of Gregory Palamas, however, occasioned the Hesychast controversy during which he was accused of belief in a twofold deity (ditheism; see also below, Chapter 7).

Western mysticism sees the soul, rather than the body, as the bearer of God's light through its oneness with the Deity. As Angelus Silesius put it: 'I am eternal light, I burn without ceasing, my taper and oil are God, my spirit is the vessel.' Protestant hymns carry this further, singing of 'Morning rays of eternity, light of inexhaustible light' (*EKG* No. 349).

(3) Trees and plants

Living nature stands alongside inanimate nature as a hierophany of the sacred, revealing the mystery of growth and decay, of living and dying. The cult of the *tree* (*ERE* 12, 448–57; Mannhardt, 1904–5; *RGG* 1, 842f.; *HWDA* 1, 946ff.; E. O. James, 1966; *ER* 15, 26ff., 242ff.) influenced Christianity at many points and even furnished it with its central and characteristic symbol of the wooden cross. Down to the present day trees have been venerated as deities, special trees being regarded as specially sacred. The Slavic Deity Perun manifested himself in the form of an oak, though he was also associated with thunder and the storm. The oak and the ash were revered in Celtic and Germanic religion. The sacred tree of life stood in Old Uppsala before the arrival of Christianity. At the birth of a child, a tree of life was planted: thenceforth the child's life was bound up with that of the tree. In a Ghanaian town a row of trees represented the chiefs of that place.

Even the branches of trees, broken off at particular times, bear the latter's sacredness within themselves, as in the case of the *baresman* branches of Iranian religion. Christianity shares in the veneration of trees and branches at many points. A telling example is in the Catholic Palm Sunday cultus where palm and olive branches are distributed and carried about in solemn procession, the olive branches as a symbol of heavenly anointing, the palm branches, following biblical precedent (Mark 11.8; Matt. 21.8), as signs of the victory of Christ in the resurrection (*HWDA* 6, 1365ff.). In the Niger Delta, early Baptist Christians tied branches to their doors, windows and roofs during the days leading up to New Year's Day. At midnight on New Year's Eve they were taken down to the waterside and cast into the water, bearing away the old year with its sicknesses and evils (George, 1971).

The *wreath* of greenery (*HWDA* 5, 381–428; *RAC* 1. 1010ff.; Baus, 1965) has the power of the branch to put forth leaves and buds. It was worn for sacrificial festival and marriage rites. The *rosary* is a form of wreath which gives practical aid for counting petitionary formulae and short prayers. It also wards off harmful powers. The materials of the rosary (e.g. snake bones) often carry a sacred power. In Poland, during a storm, it was customary to circumambulate the house three times carrying the rosary to ward off harm. The rosary came into Christianity from Indian Hinduism and Buddhism, through Islam (*ERE* 10, 847ff.).

The *tree without leaves*, the pole or pillar, is also sacred in that it bears in itself the power of putting forth spring leaves; and as such has exerted a strong influence upon Christianity. The cultic pole of the western Semites was placed against the altars of the hill shrines, and in the temple at Jerusalem as well (Judg. 6.26; Deut. 16.21f.). The two pillars of Solomon's temple (2 Kings 7.15) were the (Sumerian) tree of life and the tree of truth (*RGG* 1, 637ff.). The tree of life lived on among European Christians as the *maypole* (*HWDA* 5, 1515ff.). The latter is still to be seen in some villages, e.g. in Bavaria. It used to be erected before the dwelling of a newly-married couple and laden with many emblems and objects so that the pole's power of life and growth would enter into them. The freedom tree of the French Revolution represented a secular form of the sacred tree (Mathiez, 1964), while the popular *Christmas tree* is a late form of the Germanic tree cult (Lauffer, 1934). Despite the widespread popularity of the Christmas tree, Christianity would appear to have placed itself at some remove from the veneration of tree deities (e.g. the West African *Ìrokò*, the Celtic goddess of the Ardennes, *Dea Arduinna*, or the Black Forest *Dea Abnoba*). However, there are references to the spirits of trees, the *ēl* or *'elōn*, in the Hebrew Scriptures; while during the Middle Ages many old Germanic tree shrines were absorbed into the cult of the Virgin Mary. A later cult legend explains the connection by the miraculous discovery of an icon of Mary in the tree concerned.

The sacredness of trees can turn a whole forest into a shrine. In West Africa many townships and villages have their sacred groves nearby. In Israelite religion *ashera*-poles were erected 'under every green tree' (2 Kings 16.4). Indo-Germanic peoples loved clearings as cult places. An example is the sacred oak forest for Thor near Dublin. Some of these later become associated with Mary.

The *sacred tree* is also a complex, multi-valent symbol in the Christian tradition (*ERE* 12, 747ff.; *RGG* 3, 251f.; Reno, 1978). Just as the sacred fig-tree under which the Buddha received enlightenment played so large a part in the subsequent spread of Buddhism; so in Christian sacred history the 'tree' of the cross on which Christ was crucified (*arbor crucis*) came to take on the meaning of the *world tree* (*arbor inversa*), itself of immense influence in early Indo-Germanic religion (*HWDA* 5, 487–499); and also the *tree of Paradise* in its twofold form of the *tree of knowledge* and the *tree of life* (*lignum vitae*), prominent in Sumerian religion and the Bible (Widengren, 1951; Eliade, 1963; *RGG* 4, 250f.; *HWDA* 5, 960ff.). The tree of the cross is thus linked with creation and Paradise and with the last things where the tree is beside the river of life and its twelvefold fruits are for healing and salvation (Rev. 22.2). In a derivative sense, the sacred tree also becomes an image of the pious and righteous. The mystic, Hugo of St Victor, refers to the tree of the virtuous, an image taken from the Psalms where the righteous are planted near the tree of life, growing and putting forth greenery and fruit (Ps. 1.3 and 92.13).

During the late Middle Ages, Gothic art represented the tree of the cross with leaves and fruit and roots. Christ hangs on the cross from which a great current of life flows. It is the 'love tree' of the medieval mystics. Henry Suso, for instance, compares the cross to the may-tree, as do German and Dutch hymns. Angelus Silesius sings of the *arbor crucis* as *arbor vitae* whose noble fruit is life itself. From this it is but a short step to seeing the tree in terms of deity and divine grace. Mechthild of Magdeburg speaks of a revelation of God in which he (God) refers to the tree of his Holy Trinity and grace as the most beautiful tree of the holy Deity. For Angelus Silesius greening and flowering are images for the inner life and mystical union.

Along with trees, *plants* have also been seen as sacred throughout the history of religions and not least in Christianity. They are sacred for their value as fruit, for their healing properties, for their powers in warding off various evils, and, finally, as an elixir of immortality. The *lawn*, with its carefully cut grass, so cultivated in England and elsewhere, is a reminder of the sacred space strewn with greenery spread out for the sacrifice in early Indo-European and Iranian times (*barhis-baresman*). The Greeks, Romans, Slavs and Estonians attached great significance to *mistletoe*, widely found hanging in English homes at Christmas time even today (*HWDA* 6, 381-93). It was regarded as sacred by Celtic and Germanic peoples for its healing and apotropaic powers.

Faith in the power of sacred plants lives on in certain Christian rites as well. The blessing of plants (*HWDA* 5, 440ff.) takes place during the Feast of the Assumption of Mary, especially in Southern Germany, having originated in the ninth and tenth centuries. Ears of corn and flowers including especially those with the names of Mary or Our Lady are blessed through the saying of prayers and the sprinkling of holy water. Examples of the latter include Lady's Candle (Mullein, *Verbascum thapsus* L.) and Lady's Slipper (*Cypripedium calceolus* L.; Conolly, 1982). Some flowers are also associated with the Christian year: Candlemas bells (snowdrops), Lent lilies (daffodils) and the Easter rose (primrose). Others are dedicated to a saint: St Peter's herb (cowslips) and St John (the Baptist)'s wort (*Hypericum perforatum*; Greenoak, 1985). The presence of plants and herbs in houses was held to be a safeguard against fire and lightning. Today the increasing presence in homes and offices of tropical plants, such as rubber and cheese plants, is valued largely for aesthetic reasons. Any religious background is largely unconscious. Earlier, plants and herbs were placed in fields and behind the stalls of animals for blessing and fertility, and protection. During storms they were burnt in the hearth. They were also placed in the marriage bed and in the beds of children. Bundles of lavender under Victorian pillows or in chests of drawers for the scent they gave off, are a late reminder of the earlier religious motivation.

Plants were also blessed at Easter, the Festival of the Chains of Peter and the Vigil of John the Baptist which in the Vatican included the blessing of Carnations. (Vigils [*vigiliae*, *RE* 20, 632f.] incidentally are festive preparations for the celebration of the main festival. The German Brethren have vigils before Good Friday and Easter. Methodists and other Protestants have vigils or 'Watch Night' services at Christmas and New Year's Eve.) Of the different plants, *corn and seed corn* were regarded as especially sacred. The new-born would often be put into a basket of seed corn and then have it sprinkled over them. The bridal pair were strewn with seed corn. A vessel of corn is placed in the Greek Orthodox church at the service for the burial of the dead (*Pannychis*). The last sheaf of corn possesses great sacred power. In the festival or wedding today where rice or confetti is sprinkled over the bridal pair the same symbolism is carried on. The fruitfulness of the grain is transferred to men and women and their offspring. The ear of corn must be regarded as a common form of European Christian symbolism for fruitfulness, just as the *lily* signifies the virginity of Mary, the mother of God, and the *rose* is an image of beauty and secrecy. In the language of the Christian (and Sufi) mystics, the last-named flowers are especially important.

(4) Animals and nature

In human history and prehistory, the *animal*, even more, if that were possible, than in the case of plants, has been regarded as sacred. And in this, Christianity has, over the years, participated very extensively. Even the Deity has manifested itself to people in animals: on the one hand in the latter's strangeness, uncanny or evil qualities and, in some cases, overpowering force; on the other hand, in the attractive and lovable character of animals especially some domestic ones (Van der Leeuw, 1964, 66f.; *HWDA* 8, 778-948; *ERE* 1, 483-535; *ER* 1, 290ff.).

In many parts of the world – one thinks, for example, of the American Pacific North-West or of Australia – animals have won a prominent place in people's cultural heritage as ancestors and clan *totems* (*ERE* 12, 393ff.; *HWDA* 8, 1034ff.; *ER* 14, 573). Particular animals, such as the raven or bear, are not hunted or killed (except for communal meals), and form a special relationship with groups or individual humans. They may also be superhuman actors in creation myths, culture heroes and trickster figures (*ER* 15, 45ff.). It is impossible that Christians could avoid becoming entangled, so to speak, in the veneration of animals, either those important for the area where they live, or else those which play a prominent part in Christian sacred history. Such animals include the following: the *bear* was sacred from prehistoric times; and is still regarded as such among the Ainu of Japan. It features in the folklore of the Germanic and Slavic peoples. The *steer* embodies wild force and generative power for Near Eastern and Indian peoples. The wild *boar* is also sacred for the Germanic peoples. More widespread is the power of the *serpent* or snake (*ER* 13, 370ff.). A phallic symbol, the serpent appears in dreams and visions as an image of generation and power. The serpent is firmly anchored in the consciousness of Christians through the references to it in Genesis 3, the story of the fall. The cult of the snake appears among early gnostic Judeo-Christians known as Ophites (*RGG* 4, 730) and also in contemporary snake-handling groups in North America.

Another sacred animal is the *heron* of ancient Heliopolis in Egypt, which later becomes the *phoenix* (*RGG* 5, 357f.; see also below), a powerful symbol in medieval Christianity. The *horse*, although sacred in Indo-Iranian religion, and also among the Germanic and Celtic peoples, as well as in parts of Africa, was, as the object of a sacrificial cult, opposed by Christian missionaries, both in Europe and Africa. The *fish* was regarded as sacred in the ancient Near East. The storm deity Dagon was later represented, or mis-represented, by a fish symbol. Fish have also been held as sacred in parts of South America and West Africa. As early as the third century AD fish appear in Christian symbolism, drawing upon the gospel stories of fishing and the meal of bread and fish (see also below, p. 30, and Chapter 7). The *donkey* or ass, whose braying makes it one of the oracular and prophetic animals (*HWDA* 9, 939ff.), has a place in Christian sacred history not only through its role in the entry of Jesus into Jerusalem (Matt. 21.2–7), but also, more directly, as a sacred oracular animal: Balaam's ass (Num. 22). The *cock*, of widespread significance in African and Asian religions, is associated with Peter's denial (Mark 14.72 and parallels).

Parts of animals, too, have been regarded as sacred. Animal skulls have been placed on or before shrines and ordinary houses to ward off evil powers. During their time in Russia, the radical Reformation sect of the Hutterites had their pastors place a horse's skull before the bridal pair to remind them of the transitory character of earthly life and to ward off harmful influences (*HWDA* 8, 847ff.; Holzach, 1980).

The veneration of animals has passed through various transformations, some of which have left their mark on Christian faith and practice. The first was that found in western Semitic religion (as recorded in Lev. 11 and Deut. 14), where sacred animals became tabued as 'unclean' – the camel, hare, badger, pig, weasel, mouse, bat, certain kinds of bird, the serpent and the lizard. There was to be a clear separation between these unclean animals (called *qādōsh*, sacred) and the clean animals (called profane or *chol*). The swine that were unclean for the Jews were sacred also for Syrians, fellow western Semites. Only later did more ethical ideas of cleanness and uncleanness, i.e. involving 'purity and danger' come in (Douglas, 1966). Traces of sacred animals being used for cultic and sacrificial purposes are also found in the Bible, e.g. where cow ash mixed with water served as a lustration for washing away sins (Num. 19.9).

The transformation that occurred when images of animals replaced real ones also appears in the Judeo-Christian tradition. A golden steer image of Yahweh/Baal was placed by Jeroboam I in the temples of Dan and Bethel (1 Kings 12.28f., 32). Possibly a steer image was in the ark of the covenant, if the latter was of Canaanite origin. A bronze serpent (*nehushtan*) was worshipped down to Hezekiah's time by the Israelites (2 Kings 18.4). Animals were associated with spirit beings which manifested through them. He-goat and ram demons (*se'irim*, Lev. 17.7, and Azazel, Lev. 16.8ff.) were worshipped by the Israelites in the desert.

The cult of animals also found expression in animal legends and myths, some of which have exerted a powerful influence in shaping the Christian world-view. Three groups of these appear in cosmological, anthropological and soteriological myths. First, there are the animals appearing in myths of creation, such as the serpent and dragon. The seraphim of biblical visions are originally rather unangelic desert snakes (Kaupel, 1930). The *dragon* (*ER* 4, 431ff.) comes from a conflation of the most important familiars of the soul, the serpent or lizard, the lion and the bird. The dragon myth of Sumeria and Assyria returns in the Israelite cosmology (Day, 1985), where Yahweh kills or splits apart Rahab or Leviathan (Ps. 89.10; Job 26.12). The same dragon appears in a more shadowy form as *Tehom* in the Priestly codex (Gen. 1.2). Perhaps the cherubim (Assyr. *kuribu*, Greek *gryps*, Engl. griffin) are also monstrous dragons. In Christian legends there emerge a number of saintly victors conquering dragons, especially St Michael and St George. The latter first kills a dragon which had brought disaster to the town near Lasias in Cappadocia. King Selbios sacrificed a child to it daily until the lot fell upon his own daughter Margareta. This twelfth- to thirteenth-century legend goes back to an earlier ninth-century Coptic story by Theodor of Euchaita, and even, perhaps, to the myth of Perseus and the sea monster. Traditional religious shrines and sacred places were often thought the seat of a dragon. Pictures of dragons were later carried in Christian processions. Out of this custom there developed dragon slaying in the form of a mock battle staged during the Corpus Christi festival (Mitterweiser, 1930; Michael, 1947; Browne, 1985).

Animals appearing in anthropological and soteriological myths include those in which there is manifestly a strong feeling of relatedness between man and beast. Werewolf stories and tales of those who go berserk (in bear-skins) are of such half-human, half-animal figures. When people are tired of human life, they may change into the form of animals. Reincarnation adds to the idea that people will be reborn according to their moral deserts, it may be as some form of animal (see also below, Chapter 18).

Already with such a thought, the third, eschatological, group of myths is reached, which is very much more central to Christianity. In the Christian Apocalypse, the cosmogonic dragon myth returns. The dragon pursues the woman (Mary, the *Ecclesia* or Church) who is with child (Rev. 12.1–6). Michael fights against the 'old serpent' (of Gen. 3.4ff.) and throws him to earth. The dragon is bound for a thousand years, then loosed to lead astray the nations and, finally, to be thrown into the lake of fire (Rev. 20.10). This account may well betray the influence of Zoroastrian eschatology where the dragon Azi Dahaka, loosed by Ahriman, consumes one-third of humanity, and destroys the fire and the plants before being destroyed in turn.

The significance of animals continues in the animal symbolism of Christian iconography. This was already codified in the *Physiologus* (Curley, 1979, Treu,

1981), an ancient work which originated in Egypt in the second century AD and portrays forty-one animals interpreted symbolically. It was to become a classic handbook of Christian art during the medieval period. Among those included, the *dove* represents the soul, the Holy Spirit (Mark 1.10), Mary, the Eucharist and the vessel for holding the consecrated host. The *peacock* is the image of immortality (originally, however, the apotheosis of Roman emperors). The *lamb* stands for the Redeemer (John 1.29; Rev. 5.6, etc.) and for believers in the Good Shepherd (John 10). The *pelican* symbolizes Christ who opens his breast and allows his blood to pour out. In *Adoro te*, the communion hymn of St Thomas Aquinas, there is a reference to Christ in the sixth stanza as 'pious pelican' (omitted from the English version). The *fish* (see also above) is an image of Christ present in the water of baptism, and the Eucharist. *Ichthus*, the Greek word for fish, forms an acrostic for the words *Iesous Christos Theou (H)uios Soter* (Jesus Christ God's Son Saviour). The *lion* is a symbol for the power of Christ whom Revelation (5.5; cf. Gen. 49.9) calls the 'lion of the tribe of Judah'. According to medieval zoology, the lion wakes his cub on the third day, so it becomes a symbol of Christ who rose on that day. The lion is treasured as a symbolic guardian of church portals, as it was in ancient Near-eastern temples. The *phoenix* (see also above), the image of temporal renewal in Egypt, becomes in eternal Rome the symbol of the resurrection. The *eagle* was a symbol of resurrection and immortality; while for the mystics it represented the vision of God and mystical union. The *cock* was the herald of light, symbol of watchfulness on church towers and spires. The *nightingale* symbolized the longing for heaven and the praise of God. The *lark* stood for humility. The *bee* was the symbol of virginity because of belief in its parthenogenesis. The *unicorn* which finds sleep only in the lap of a virgin, is a symbol of chastity and therefore an attribute of Mary (*RAC* 4, 839–62; Rüdiger, 1977). The *lion* (*ER* 8, 556ff.), *ox* and *eagle* are also symbols of the evangelists Mark, Luke and John, based on Ezekiel's vision (1.5, 10) and that of Revelation (4.6ff.; *RGG* 2, 703)., Also included was the zodiac which came to be featured in the apse, on the portal or on the floor of churches.

Animals were also used as symbols of demonic powers. The *dragon*, as previously mentioned, is an image of Satan (Rev. 12.13, 20). The *serpent*, whose head Mary crushes, is the Devil (see also above). *Swine* depict lasciviousness, as in representations of St Anthony in the desert. The *wolf* stands for the hypocrite. *Animal heads* in medieval churches stand for demons and sinful persons. Animals may also represent the seven deadly sins: *bears* indicate unchastity; while covetousness also appears in the form of a wolf. The *beast* in the Book of Revelation is an image of the Roman emperor Domitian who had divine honours paid to himself (Rev. 13–20).

This means for Christianity that despite their multivalent symbolism animals tend to be grouped into divine sacred ones on the one hand and the satanic and uncanny ones on the other. In other religious traditions, this same dualism may be found. In Hinduism and Buddhism, however, the dualism is subordinated to the migration of the soul through the animal world as well as the human and divine worlds, which leads in turn to the age-old Indian view of the refusal to harm all living creatures (*ahimsa*). Buddhist friendship embraces all living things. The Buddha drew lions and tigers to himself through such friendship. The *cow* represents for the Hindu, and for many Parsi Zoroastrians, the whole of non-human creation. The old rites of cultic veneration of the cow symbolize the brotherhood of man and beast, an ethical valuation which lives on in Western Christianity in the reverence for life of Albert Schweitzer and others.

Also influencing Christianity is the Israelite tradition with respect to animals. They are regarded in the main as fellow-creatures with man. 'Thou helpest *man and animal*' (Ps. 36.6). Animals are exhorted to praise the Lord (Ps. 148). Hence the command to man to love animals. The righteous man has pity on his cattle (Prov. 12.10). In the eschatological messianic kingdom of peace, wild animals, now transformed, have a part (Isa. 11.6). Jesus lived in the desert among animals (Mark 1.13), and gave his disciples power to tread on serpents (Mark 16.18). Some early Christian martyrs prayed slowly with crossed arms and caused a bear and a panther to retreat. Desert monks of Egypt, Libya and Syria fed, watered and bound up the wounds of animals of the desert, including buffaloes, wild goats, forest asses, hyenas and lions. The shrine of St Thekla in Cilicia (Seleukia) possessed an animal park. Pilgrims to the shrine brought animals as offerings for her (Kötting, 1950). Columba of Iona and the Iro-Scottish monks followed those of the desert and transmitted the love of animals to the Anglo-Saxons and the continent. Anselm of Canterbury was a known friend of animals. St Francis was even more notable in this regard (Armstrong, 1973).

There are two main sources for the Christian love of animals. The first motive is faith in creation. Paul in his letter to the Romans (8.19ff.) proclaims, as did Zarathustra long before him (Gathas, *Y.* 29), the solidarity of men and animals in suffering and the longing for redemption. The other motif is eschatological, the recovery of the paradisal state of purity and innocence which man possessed before the fall. The enmity between man and animals, thus, is post-lapsarian. A new aeon has begun with Christ and continues with his saints. It should be noted that the Judeo-Christian love of animals was also taken up by the Qur'ān and Muslim saints.

For religious faith, including Christianity, *nature* – from the stone to the sun and stars – forms the theatre in which the divine is manifested (*ER* 10, 324ff.). It is true that the Hebrew prophets were concerned to stress its symbolic character and to deny the identity of nature and the divine. Biblical nature poetry, moreover, does not praise nature as God, but rather the glory, wisdom and love of the Creator (Ps. 104.24). It is not a question of the praise of the nature deities, therefore, but of nature's creator (Ps. 148; Song of Thr. 59ff. or Dan. 3.59ff.). Nevertheless, there is still a personal relationship to nature in that the latter is directly addressed and called upon to praise the all highest. This theme is part of the morning prayer of praise in many Christian churches.

Daily, worshippers glorify the greatness and sacredness of nature as the creation of God. This was defended in the second and third centuries AD against Marcion's rejection of nature in favour of grace as the purest act of the alien God. God is not only the God of man's salvation but also the God of nature, creator as well as redeemer: the good creator not the trickster demiurge. The resurrection of Christ means the sanctification of nature, and the anticipation of nature's transfiguration at the eschaton (*ERE* 9, 201–54).

The Eastern Church celebrates the Easter rite in communion with the whole of nature, by proclaiming: 'Now all is filled with light: heaven and earth and beneath the earth. Let the whole creation therefore celebrate the resurrection of Christ in which it is established.' Augustine found in nature not God but a testimony to its having been created by him. A higher power gives all creatures life, power, beauty and joy, as it gives these to the heart of man. Mankind thus stands in a brother–sister relationship with nature. Francis' nature mysticism made this into a personalized inner experience. Creatures were a 'Thou' as they were to the Hebrew psalmist; but Francis calls them brother and sister of the *one family*, including brother wolf as well as sister cicada, nature inanimate as well as animate, brother sun, sister moon, brother wind, brother fire, and sister mother-earth. This was an enormous step forward in Western understanding of nature. Roger Bacon, a pioneer of modern natural science came from the Franciscans. Under the influence of this approach, and including Stoic and Neoplatonist motifs, there arose in the late Middle Ages a modern nature veneration which went further than the Bible, Augustine or Francis. The Stoics taught that Zeus, as the divine world spirit, revealed himself in nature; while Neoplatonism considered nature to be interfused with the world-soul as an image of the spiritual cosmos. It was John Scotus Erigena who brought Neoplatonist nature mysticism into Christian thought; Wolfgang Goethe espoused nature piety; and Schleiermacher saw religion as the contemplation of the all. Romantics, Victorian nature poets: Keats, Shelley, Wordsworth, Coleridge and Tennyson, along with the painters Turner and Constable, all influenced the steady emancipation of the religion of nature from the religion of salvation, even though for Francis they had gone together: the poetry of sunset and evening star was for him inseparable from the assurance of salvation, youthful mysticism was one with the incarnation and the cross, while the one who sang of the beauty of nature had at the same time the stigmata of the crucified (Summers, 1950).

From the love of nature have also grown up and proliferated the various physical and life sciences, world exploration, mountaineering, sports and hobbies of all kinds. In recent days has been added the concern for the ecosphere (Emmel, 1977; *ER* 4, 581ff.): for environmental pollution, the contamination of rivers, lakes and oceans, for the health of urban communities and the preservation of tropical forests, rural and historically important areas. Above all, there is concern over the ultimate form of pollution: a radioactive earth (Bertell, 1985).

2
Objects Sacred to Christians
2: Artefacts

(1) Common forms of cult object made by hand

The Divine accommodates itself to mankind by revealing itself through objects in their natural surroundings. It stoops even further to the human level by seeking to communicate with humans through the images and objects which they themselves have made. In the area of religious iconography (*ER* 7, 2ff., 67ff., 97ff.), Christianity made its own fresh beginning and contributed its own distinctive forms and attitudes. Eventually these became part of the long tradition of religious symbols and icons, but there remained among Christians widely divergent attitudes about whether such divine accommodation through images is really possible; and in what measure such icons may be venerated. In what follows a series of objects made by hand is examined. They have in common the fact that they have been discovered to possess or convey religious significance on a wide scale.

From time immemorial the *weapon*, for example, has been regarded as sacred. In the Roman and Germanic religious traditions, oaths were taken on the shield, lance, javelin and sword, while the double-axe was the symbol of deities over a wide area of Europe, Asia and Africa. In Christian history few incidents were more fateful than the consecration of the *shields* of Constantine's army before the victorious battle of Milvian Bridge. They were inscribed with the cross monogram (☧ or ✝) following upon a vision or visions of the Christian God which came to Constantine. There is also ample evidence for the continuation of oath-taking involving weapons in the crusading tradition in Western Christianity. Even today, many can conjure up in the mind's eye a picture of a knight taking a solemn oath on lance or sword as he kneels facing the altar in full armour. In Germanic religion the *hammer* of Thor played a role in the sanctification of marriage. This lingered on in Christianity in the *anvil* which served as an altar for the marriages of runaway couples in Gretna Green.

The *staff* (*ERE* 11, 811ff.) has greater significance in the Judeo-Christian tradition. With his staff, Moses turns the Nile into blood, calls into being frogs, flies, locusts; and produces storms, thunder and hail (Exod. 7ff.). With his staff (Exod. 14) he divides the water, leads the people through on dry land and destroys the pursuing Egyptian host. Later he strikes the rock with his staff and water gushes forth. Elijah's staff has the further power of making iron swim on water and awakening the dead (2 Kings 6.6; 4.29). The association of the staff with the serpent, found earlier in Babylonia, returns in the Mosaic legend when Moses at God's command throws down his staff before Pharaoh and transforms it into a serpent. The Egyptian sorcerers try to do the same but Moses' staff swallows theirs up (Exod. 7.9). The staff here is the image and instrument of divine power. In early Christian art, Christ is depicted as the thaumaturgos who awakens Lazarus from the dead with his magic staff. The staffs of Christian bishops and abbots reflect those of Moses and Aaron (*LThK* 2, 508f.). On the T-shaped staff of the bishops of the Eastern Church is a snake's head; while snakes are at the foot of the Western staffs. Another form of the staff is the royal sceptre. The sceptre is the means through which the honour and majesty of the Christian ruler is manifested. By extension this becomes the judge's staff or the chancellor's mace. Related to the staff and also originally a sacred artefact is the *flag* (*LThK* 3, 1340f.; Goldammer, 1954/5). Originally the flag was often the sign of the presence of the Deity. In Christianity flags were a feature of Byzantium and also of Western Europe where they appeared in processions from the tenth century. The early form of the flag consisted of the processional cross with a cloth attached. The blessing of the flag stresses the nature of the Church as the militia of Christ.

Another symbol common in the history of religions is the *disk* and *wheel* (*HWDA* 7, 463ff.; see also above, Chapter 1). The sun-disk or chariot wheel represents the sun's passage across the heavens in stone age and bronze age Europe, and in a more spiritualized form the teaching of the Buddha in Asia. With the Christian mystics it is likewise spiritualized. For Hildegard of Bingen the Deity is a wheel; while Henry Suso speaks of 'the eternal Sun-wheel'. The allied symbol of the ring (*HWDA* 7, 702–14; *LThK* 8, 900) also stands for the sun, but in addition symbolizes a bond or fetter, and a sign of authority. The early Roman custom of exchanging rings was continued in the Christian wedding ceremony. Similarly the ring worn by the images of Germanic deities and chiefs was retained in the Western Church, from as early as the seventh century, in the form of the bishop's ring. The ring was worn as a sign of authority and, very possibly, to ward off evil powers. It was also a *signaculum fidei*, an image of the charismata bestowed by the Spirit, and of the sacred bond with the Church. From the twelfth century onwards abbots also wore the ring. But the first to wear it were the Christian nuns. Nuns' rings are mentioned by Ambrose, Bishop of Milan, as early as the fourth century. They stand for the marriage of the holy virgin with Christ and the dedication of her entire life to God. Since the thirteenth century the ring has been conferred at the time of the nun's taking of her monastic vows.

Given its prophetic character and ascetic tendencies, Christianity would seem at first glance to have set itself firmly against all symbolic representations of human sex organs; and yet some influences in this direction are discernible. In the history of religions the phallus (*ERE* 9, 815–31; *ER* 11, 263ff.) was often considered sacred as the bearer of the human power of generation, the vagina represented the power of giving birth and both together symbolized the triumph of life over death. They also stood for the mystery of sexual union and the wonder of procreation. Phallus/vulva symbols were an integral part of the fertility rites. They have been found in stone age cultures, in Africa, among the western Semites, the Greek maenads, in the Roman fertility festivals, and in the lingam in Indian temples and houses or as amulets of the Lingayat sect in India. Against the Roman, Greek and Germanic fertility cults Christianity declared its firm opposition, even as prophetic Judaism had done in the case of the western Semitic ones. It drew strength from the conquest or sublimation of the sexual. Yet the sexual symbols kept coming back. As late as the eighteenth century a phallic fertility rite was observed in Upper Bavaria. An image called St Leonard's Nail was carried through the fields in a procession. There it was embraced and kissed by young girls. Ancient phallic ceremonies survive also in the Roman consecration of baptismal water. The Easter candle is plunged into the water accompanied by prayers which make it clear that the purpose of this act is to impregnate the water and make it fertile. However, on the whole the ascetic tradition in Christianity turned what was positive and sacred into what was negative and to be rejected. The result was at once positive in releasing energies for the cultural and spiritual; and also negative in seeing the sexual as unclean and to be feared. It has taken modern biology, depth psychology and perhaps, most recently, the women's movement amongst other influences, to help to restore something of the naturalness of traditional peoples with regard to their sexual powers.

All the sacred artefacts mentioned so far may be considered less central to Christianity than the *cross* (*ERE* 4, 324ff.; *RGG* 4, 45ff.; *LThK* 6, 242–54; *RE* 11, 92; Bonnet, 1971; *NDLW* 201f.; *ER* 4, 155ff.). In it Christianity has laid hold of a universal symbol which it has succeeded in historicizing and developing in the direction of the greatest spirituality. The cross reaches back to the days when man made the discovery that his world could be expressed in terms of four quadrants. It became an especially widespread symbol among the Sumerians, the Hittites, the Minoans and the Amerindians. It became the stylized form of the tree of life and of fertility; indeed, in the Egyptian symbol of the ankh (☥) it came to stand for life itself (Okafor, 1984). The cult of the cross emerges relatively late in Christianity. According to legend the Empress Helena, wife of Constantine, discovered the cross of Christ in Jerusalem. From there its veneration spread to the whole Church. Various stages may be traced: first, fragments of the true cross were venerated. Then the empty cross was erected either as a processional cross secured to the altar during the service; or, since 1100, as a standing cross on the altar. This happened first in the Eastern Church without the crucifix or figure of Christ, a form of the cross which continues down to the present day in Nestorian churches and is also found in many Protestant and Anglican services. It is in Romanesque art that we find the figure of Christ on the cross, first of all clothed, then as a sign of Deity, almost naked; also with a crown, victorious. As such Christ was represented as the impassive conqueror, corresponding to the Johannine interpretation of Christ's death upon the cross (John 19.30). It is Gothic art which first represented the crucified one as the 'man of sorrows' (Isa. 53.3) with his 'sacred head sore wounded' (J. S. Bach). This led in turn to the cross becoming a symbol for the mystery of the atonement. The special veneration of the cross on Good Friday goes back to ancient Jerusalem practice. In the Roman Church's Good Friday liturgy the cross is unveiled with the call to behold the wood of the cross on which hung the salvation of the world. Many Protestant Christians who have banished the crucifix or even the empty cross from altar or communion table, nevertheless may allow pictorial representations of the cross and crucified in church rooms, if not in the sanctuary itself; and most retain the cross as a linguistic image, as in the hymn of the Unitarian John Bowring: 'In the cross of Christ I glory, towering o'er the wrecks of time.'

One form of the cross, the *swastika* ('four gammas' [Γ], 卐 *svastika*, 卍 *sauvastika*; *HWDA* 3, 1345ff.; *RGG* 3, 31f.; *ERE* 4, 329) is very widespread and has an ambivalent meaning in Christianity. Its meaning has been traced back to the Elamites (4000–3000 BC). Male and female forms (*svastika* and *suvastika*) appear in India. In the Judeo-Christian tradition there may be an early reference to it as the sign on Cain's forehead (Gen. 4.15), the sign of Job (Job 31.35) and the sign of deliverance (*tau*: Π) given to the prophet Ezekiel. Christians used the swastika in the Roman catacombs. It found its way onto coins, coats of arms, bells and vestments during the medieval period. The wide variety of meanings given to the symbol may be summed up in the three words: life, fertility and luck. In recent times Fascist movements have adopted the swastika as a presumed symbol of the Aryan racial heritage, thereby giving it for others a strongly negative value. This has in turn led to its adoption by some radical youth groups as a form of protest against the felt tyranny of the 'establishment'.

(2) The image and its forms

To a greater degree than the cult objects we have just been considering, *images* (Bevan, 1940; Sierksma, 1960; *ERE* 7, 110–60; *RGG* 1, 1268ff.) display human or anthropomorphic traits, though the degree of anthropomorphism may range from the photographic likeness of the 'iconic' image to the abstract, stylized representation of the 'aniconic'. The materials from which the image is made also vary very greatly. It may be of stone, or wood of a sacred tree, it may be of more enduring terracotta or bronze or other metals. It may be decorated, too, with silver or gold, and be clothed like a human person. The image may be sculptured or in the form of a painting. Wooden images can have nails driven into them, symbolizing sicknesses, or the worshippers, or petitions to the deity. Christianity has shared fully in all the profound symbolism of the image. But it has also profoundly distrusted the image as a consequence of its Semitic heritage. Affirming the image were the early-acquired influences from its Hellenistic environment.

The supernatural or wholly-other quality of the image is preserved in many ways: it may be through its unnatural size as in the case of the giant statue of the Christian emperor Constantine. It may be its uncommon colour. In Altötting and Rocamadour the Mother of God figure is black, as was the goddess Artemis of Ephesus two thousand years earlier. It may also have a partly non-human form, that of an animal or bird (theriomorphic). Or it may be accompanied by an animal (a familiar). Christopher, the Christian saint, has the head of a dog in Byzantine art. Prominence may be given to the sexual features of the image to emphasize the powers of procreation and life. Ethiopian images of the Virgin have the devotee, perhaps a bishop, being suckled at her overflowing breasts.

A further 'unnatural' but numinous feature in the image is the manifold form of limbs, especially arms, sense organs, eyes or ears, and especially the head. Such images are found in Christianity in the shape of the three-headed figures of the Trinity or the seven-headed Madonna of Aufkirchen in Austria (*ERE* 12, 457f.). Even more startling are images which are deliberately repulsive in character. The appearance may be distorted or deformed. There are Christian images of martyrs and saints being tortured or put to death in gruesome fashion, or over-realistic portrayals of the crucifixion (Matthias Grünewald). Another form of the sacred image is that which contains the most sacred part in its interior. This may consist of a sacred substance to which access is gained by an opening in the stomach. Or it may be a modified form of this, as in the case of the Christian image of the divine Trinity, with icons of the Father and Son and a theriomorphic Spirit in the interior of a Madonna image to which access is gained through two doors which are hinged sections of the Virgin's own body.

Apart from unusual features that attest its sacredness, the image becomes what it is by *consecration* (*ER* 4, 59ff.). When an image is consecrated the Deity condescends to imbue with life what would otherwise be a lifeless statue made by human hands. As in Hinduism and Buddhism, the icons of the Eastern Church and the images of the saints in the West receive a special consecration. Ultimately, however, the image is regarded as having its origin in heaven. This fact gives it its sacredness, and not any aesthetic qualities which may be present in the image as a work of art. So it must be said that finally the image is *not* made by human hands, but derives its being and life from the beyond (*RAC* 1, 68ff.). But equally it may behave in a very human fashion. It may laugh, speak, perspire, weep tears, shed blood, turn away, move, and if dishonoured or neglected, may utter a solemn curse or bring about sickness or death. Of such a character are the images and icons of Christ, Mary and the holy saints and martyrs in the popular belief of many Christians (Günter, 1910).

Some of the forms in which the image is venerated may also be mentioned. There is firstly the devotional gesture (*NDLW* 247ff., 381f.; see also Chapter 5, below) which may involve an act of genuflection or prostration before the image. The latter may be kissed, or its hand kissed, or it may be stroked. Again, the object of veneration which is mediated by the image or even localized in it, may be invoked and addressed in an act of prayer. Then again, offerings of all kinds may be brought and laid before it. These may include food, flowers, incense and lights. Further, the image may be carried about in procession to bring the Deity's blessing to the town or country. In Eastern Christianity it is icons which are carried in this way; whereas in the West statues of the saints are taken on procession, sometimes even to remote places, in recent days by motor vehicle or aeroplane. In this way the Madonna of Fatima in Portugal makes a veritable pilgrimage. Finally, images are cared for or badly treated. They may be washed, clothed and decorated, played and danced to, taken out on visits and put to bed. Such has been the treatment given to the image in Egypt and elsewhere. What appears in Christianity is their ill-treatment to the verge of desacralization on certain occasions. If prayers were not heard by the Deity, i.e. favourably answered, Christian images were dishonoured, beaten, whipped or even thrown away, in a manner reminiscent of the periodic desacralization of cult objects in Aboriginal religion (Weidkuhn, 1965). Neapolitan fishermen used to bring a statue of their patron Saint Peter to sea, and whip it if it did not bless their catch. Similarly a farmer in the Black Forest is known to have thrown his crucifix out into open ground so that it could feel what the constant rain was like.

Three forms of image and icon have been popular with Christianity as in other religions: the *amulet*, the *devotional statuette or icon*, and the *coin or medallion*. The amulet (*RE* 1, 467ff.; *ERE* 3, 392–472; *DACL* 1, 1784–860; *HWDA* 1, 374ff.; *LThK* 1, 462ff.; *RAC* 1, 397–411; *RGG* 1, 345ff.; M. Howes, 1975; *ER* 1, 243ff.) Latin *amuletum* from *amoliri* to remove, Greek *apotropaion*, *phulaktērion*, may be worn suspended from the neck or wrist or apart from the person. Its primary function is apotropaic, it wards off harmful powers. Through its presence it preserves a person's health and well-being. In Greece, Syria, Egypt, Ethiopia, Persia, Central Asia, India and Japan amulets have long been important. In the Judeo-Christian tradition, there are several early references to amulets worn on people and animals (Judg. 8.21; Isa. 3.16ff.). Early Christianity fought against the practice of wearing amulets; but amulets rapidly gained ground from the fourth century onward. Secret signs, bells, coins, and tokens became popular as amulets. Some of the clergy produced amulets to meet the demand despite continuous opposition from church councils. The cross, eucharistic bread, relics, icons, wax and oil from pilgrim centres, holy water and salt were also used in the medieval period. Post-tridentine catholicism reformed and regularized the wearing of devotional aids (the cross, the rosary, the sacred heart of Jesus or Mary, medallions with saints' pictures, etc.). As in the case of Islam, a common form of amulet or phylactery has consisted of a fragment of sacred writing hung about people and animals or placed on poles to protect the fields (see also below, Chapter 10).

The devotional statuette or icon may be traced all the way back to palaeolithic times where miniature images were sometimes placed on tiny altars (Gimbutas, 1974). In the Eastern Church the icon dates from the Egyptian custom in antiquity of making portraits of the deceased. Christian icons date from the fourth century, the earliest examples preserved in the monastery of St Catherine in Sinai coming from the sixth century. Icons spread from Byzantium to Italy, Armenia, the Balkans and so to Russia. Portable icons are the small pictures painted on wood against a gold background, of Christ, Mary, the saints and biblical scenes. Their painting was always a sacred act, subject to the strictest canons. In the West the small devotional image appeared from the fourteenth century. In it a group of figures was depicted, representing themes from the life of Mary and Christ. The figures of Christ and John were taken out of the scene of the Last Supper; or that of Jesus being scourged from the story of his passion. In the fifteenth century there arose the sacred heart symbol. It became popular as a flaming heart encircled with thorns, not only among Catholics but also among Lutheran pietists. Some devotional images and pictures were sold at places of pilgrimage and are in widespread use today (*LThK* 1, 505; Spamer, 1930).

The coin or medallion (*ERE* 3, 699–710; *RGG* 2, 1310f.; *HWDA* 3, 596–624; Laun, 1924) was originally a convenient form of sacrificial offering for the priesthood and cultus. The metal pieces had a picture of the Deity together with an animal or plant symbol or attribute. Thus the emperor Constantine was depicted on a Roman coin with the image of the Deity *Sol Invictus*, the unconquered Sun, next to the cross monogram (see above). Later the image of the Mother of God appeared on coins called *Frauentäler*. The typical medieval coin was the *Kreutzer*, with the cross as its image. In Byzantium, also, a picture of Christ appeared on coins, while in the West symbols of the saints in the form of the lamb and the fish appeared. In addition coins often bore sacred inscriptions, such as Emmanuel, or Mother of God, help! Later came other inscriptions, including INRI (*Iesus Nazarenus Rex Iudaeorum*), *Pater Noster, Ave Maria*, Hallelujah and Amen.

(3) Iconic and anti-iconic tendencies

The strong tension in Christianity between the love of images and the suspicion of them is certainly not absent from other religions. Indian religions have been friendly to icons and images, as is well known, and yet the reforming movements of the Jains and the Buddhists were originally without images, apart from the *stupa* or house for relics. Later, symbols of the fig-tree, the lotus, the wheel and the empty throne came into the veneration of the Buddha, and finally statues of the Jina, the Buddha and Bodhisattva. The image comes to be regarded positively as an appearance through which Reality reveals itself. It is a symbol for meditation, to be left behind at the higher levels of meditative experience. Other religions were also imageless at the beginning. Early Japanese Shinto had simply the solar disk of the goddess Amaterasu. Only under Buddhist influence were statues made of the gods, and a picture – though not a statue – of Amaterasu. Early Indo-European religion was also imageless. The invisible deity was invoked on strewn sacrificial greenery. Imageless religion lived on in early Vedic and Zoroastrian religion, and among the early Roman and Germanic peoples. Later the cult of the icon entered Italy, India and Iran (under the Achaemenids), but later Zoroastrians from Roman down to Parsi times were imageless apart from icons of the Prophet Zarathustra and the fire, as the 'body' of Ahura Mazda. Similarly, some modern Hindu reformers have also turned to a faith without images.

Christianity found itself in the Greco-Roman world, an environment friendly to images. But its roots were in Judaism, whose prophets had reacted

strongly against western Semitic forms of image veneration. Judaism's position
had varied over the centuries (*RGG* 1, 1271f.; *RE* 3, 217–21). It began as an
aniconic, nomadic cult of sacred stones, some of the latter being carried about
in the ark of the covenant. Then, coming into the western Semitic, Canaanite
environment, it had wooden images of Yahweh covered with sheet metal, also
steer images cast in metal. It was when the Israelites extended their veneration
to the images of other deities that the prophets raised their voices in protest
(Isa. 44.10; Jer. 10.3ff; Hos. 13.2). This led to a tabu being placed upon image
veneration in the cultus of Yahweh (Exod. 20.4; Lev. 26.1; Deut. 27.5). In
Hellenistic times, Jewish anti-iconic tendencies joined forces with those of the
Greek philosophers, such as Heraclitus, Xenophanes, the Stoics and Plutarch.
Porphyry however defends the cult of images in his work on the subject. Only
the ignorant take these for wood and stone. Is a stele only stone?, he asks. Or is a
book only paper? The opposition to images in Judaism was continued in Islam,
which venerated the black stone in the *Ka'aba* at Mecca. Guru Nanak was led
to reject the Hindu cult of images. Imageless Sikhism, however, soon found
itself with the sacred writings, the Holy Granth, venerated as the living Sahib
or Lord.

Against the background of all these other developments, we have to chart the
changes in the Christian view of images (*RGG* 1, 1273ff.; *RAC*2, 318–41; *RE* 3,
221–6; Schöne, 1959). Originally, Christianity was without images, as in
Judaism and other religions. But early on, in an extreme Hellenistic environment, icons of Jesus began to be venerated. Even in the Epistle to the Hebrews
(1.3) Jesus is spoken of as the *eikōn* of the invisible Father; while in the Gospel
of John (14.9) Jesus says, 'He who has seen me, has seen the Father.' The
Synod of Elvira (313 AD) forbade pictures of Jesus and their veneration, but in
the Eastern Church (Heiler, 1971) Basil the Great (d. 379) commended them,
as did many of the monks of the day. Alongside pictures of Christ others
appeared of the Mother of God, saints and angels. By the sixth century the cult
of icons had become widespread. John of Damascus (d. before 754) based his
justification of the cult upon Neoplatonist ideas. These in turn became the basis
for the teaching about the subject at the Seventh Ecumenical Council of Nicaea
(787). According to these ideas, the venerator of the icon ascended from the
sōmatikē to the *pneumatikē theōria*, from the bodily to the spiritual contemplation. There was also a further motif. The icons became matter that was imbued
with divine power (*energeia*) through the name of God 'and his friends'.

The champions of religion without images, on the other hand, saw image
veneration as enmity to God-created matter, and as a denial of the incarnation
of God in Christ. So argued the Nestorians and the Paulicians. In 723 the
Muslim Caliph Yazid intervened in this controversy and ordered the removal of
all icons from Christian places of worship in his territories. Under Islamic
influence too, Bishop Constantine of Phrygia continued to struggle against the
veneration of icons. He won over the Byzantine emperor, Leo the Isaurian
(716–41), who was called *sakēnophrēn* (the one with the mind of a Saracen)
because of his liking for things Islamic. In 726 and 730 Leo ordered the removal

of sacred pictures from the churches. This action brought on the iconoclastic controversy in the Eastern Orthodox Church (*RE* 3, 223–5; Martin, 1930). The monks, motivated by theological and material interests, fought for the icons since the emperor was bent upon a measure of church reform which included the monasteries as well. In the year 757 the Council of Constantinople condemned the veneration of icons as the work of Satan and a form of idolatry. Leo's son, Constantine Kopronymos, sought to crush the monks' opposition but only succeeded in provoking a more widespread reaction to these iconoclastic measures. In 787 an ecumenical council rescinded the acts of the previous 'pseudo-synod' and proclaimed that the veneration of icons aroused a longing for the 'prototype' which the icon represents. The victory over the iconoclasts is celebrated each year in the Eastern Orthodox Church by the festival of Orthodoxy (Heiler, 1971). The cult of the icon in Eastern Christianity (*RGG* 3, 670ff.) has since become of immense importance. The *iconostasis* or icon screen, coming perhaps from the ancient temple (*LThK* 2, 467ff.; *DACL* 7/1, 31–48), separates the holy of holies from the nave of the church where the worshippers are gathered. Icons, many of them of the Mother of God, were venerated as miracle-working, especially in Russia. On the walls of houses icons occupied the place of honour.

Initially the West was more rationalistic and cautious in its approach to icons and images. Gregory the Great and Alcuin gave them a place for pedagogical reasons and for decorating the church interior. This position was endorsed by synods at Frankfurt (794) and Paris (825). It is true that because of the danger of their abuse, Argobard of Lyons (769–840) and Claudius of Turin (d. about 827) demanded their complete removal. However, the veneration of images and pictures won out in the end although they did not obtain as much recognition in official dogmatics and liturgies as they did in the Eastern Church. The images received their sacred character, moreover, through a special act of consecration. The solemn *oratio* or prayer of blessing of the Roman rite was a meditation upon what was represented and also a prayer for the merits and grace of Christ, the Blessed Virgin Mary and the Saints. In popular piety these last named although in heaven, are believed to be present in the icon or image. They are localized, as was held to be the case in the ancient world. Hence the Mother of God figures at Altötting, Andechs, Lourdes and elsewhere. Legends also tell of miracles (see below, Chapter 8) wrought by images of Christ and the saints. Mary comes alive and gives her breast to the worshipper (as depicted, indeed, in many icons of the Ethiopian Church). Images and icons are 'discovered' in forests, springs, rivers and lakes. Those who dishonour the saints' images are miraculously punished (Günter, 1910). In Germany pictures and images are placed in the 'Lord's corner'. Their veneration in the West, though not perhaps as intense as in Eastern Christianity, may nevertheless include actions such as prostration, the kiss, the hand-kiss, offering of flowers, lighting of candles and the hanging of votive pictures. Petitions are also made before the image. The latter may even be clothed with costly garments and hung with jewellery. As in the ancient world, pilgrimages are made to images.

The cult of the eucharistic *host* in Western Christianity rivalled that of the image. Its essence was the veneration (called *latreia*) of the present Christ in the consecrated host, the elements of bread and wine. Whereas in the early Church and in the East the Eucharist was conceived of primarily in terms of a mystery drama and a communion meal, in the West what was dynamic and symbolic in character becomes static and transformational. Christ is regarded as being present body and soul, both divine and human, in the consecrated host. The communion cup for the laity disappears. The host remains an object of veneration. The worship accorded to God and the incarnate Christ is now extended to the eucharistic form of Christ (Heiler, 1923). The eucharistic Christ, approached with prayer and devotion by the believers, was preserved in different ways: either in a *columba* (literally 'dove'; see above, in Chapter 1); or a *turricula* ('tower'), the former hanging from the altar, the latter from a baldachin over the altar in a shrine or coffin like a reliquary either on the altar or in a wall cupboard. From these there developed the Gothic wall shrine for the sacrament or the tabernacle on the altar.

As with images of the deities in the ancient world, icons in the Eastern Church and relics in the early Western Church, so also the host was carried in a God-bearing procession called the *Corpus Christi* procession(*RGG* 2, 1165ff.; *LThK* 4, 405f.). It was taken through the streets of the town or out into the fields, first covered in a chalice, then open in a crystal vessel or golden monstrance. The first recorded Corpus Christi procession took place in Cologne in the second half of the thirteenth century. Others followed in Würzburg, Augsburg and Hildesheim. At first these took place only on the Corpus Christi feast-day itself. Then it was performed on other occasions as well. It quickly won a special place in the hearts of Catholics. At the time of the Reformation (Denzinger, 878), it acquired a dogmatic character in conscious opposition to the position of the Reformers. Even in recent times, in one south German city, the route of the Corpus Christi procession was elaborately laid down in flowers beside the provincial headquarters of the Protestant Church.

In addition to the processions, the host was shown covered in the pyx (*NDLW* 453f.) or uncovered in the monstrance (*NDLW* 377) to be venerated during services in side chapels. Late medieval piety placed great stress upon actually seeing the host (Browe, 1933). The further practice arose in the sixteenth century of the eternal devotion of the monstrance, which was now put on view permanently. Contemplative orders of nuns were founded who took up the contemplation of the host. They divided the day into watches and formed a guard of honour as for the dead. In recent times, such devotional practices have been castigated by the women's movement as the 'necrophilia of patriarchal religion' (Daly, 1979). But the cult of the Eucharist continues to flourish with Corpus Christi chapels in many places. There the host is on display day and night, a practice that goes back to the Roman empire where the image of Isis was being venerated in the same way. The cult of the sacrament in the West was very much the same thing as the cult of the icon in the East. In both cults, the same kind of legendary motifs are operative, including miracles of all kinds (Browe, 1938).

The opposition to images, present from the beginning in the Judaic heritage of Christianity, broke out again at the time of the Reformation in sharp reaction to the widespread cult of the image in the Western Church. Iconoclasm made its appearance in the early days of the Reformation at Wittenberg, and later in the Radical and Calvinist-Zwinglian reformations it spread to Reformed, Anglican and Independent groups. Lutherans abandoned the cult of the Eucharist, the Saints and the Virgin Mary, but refused to part with the crucifix and pictures of Christ and the saints. Among the reformed groups, the Quakers represent the sharpest form of Puritanism. For them, the sacrament and all icons disappear entirely; or put another way, the whole of life becomes sacramental and the whole world an icon of the deity.

(4) Sacred dress and sacred colour

Associated with the image and the cult object is the sacred *vestment* (*ERE* 5, 40–72; *HWDA* 4, 1458–515; 3, 1709ff.; *RGG* 3, 1646ff.; *NDLW* 521ff.; *ER* 3, 537ff.; 14, 410ff.). Clothing may also become sacred and has played a prominent role in Christian rites, with attitudes varying towards it as in the case of images. Dress, including the sash or girdle, the mantle, the shoes, gloves, head covering and also the shrouding of the dead, attains its sacredness in a twofold way: firstly, through its proximity and relationship to the wearer. It becomes the wearer's representative, an extension of the person. By putting on the clothing of another, one assumed his or her sacred power. In West Africa, for instance, the priests of Sango dress as women and plait their hair in the women's style, thereby acquiring their mysterious power. Similarly, a woman of the southern Slavs would place her dress upon a fruit tree then put it on, so that the tree's fertility would be transferred to her and she could bear a child. The son was in turn put into his father's shirt so that he would have the latter's strength. In early Israel, Jonathan and David exchanged clothes and weapons as the seal of their friendship (1 Sam. 18.3f.). Moses put Aaron's clothes on Eleazar as the sign of the transfer of office from the former to the latter.

Allied to the idea of representation by proximity is the second way by which clothing acquires sacredness, namely, through its use in cultic actions, where it comes into close association with the sacred. Everyday clothes are taken off and replaced by others set aside for the purpose, when acts of worship are performed. Afterwards the reverse process occurs. Priests accordingly have their vestments prescribed within narrow limits. 'These are the clothes you shall make', the Priestly codex stresses (Exod. 28). Even the Jewish lay person must wear a prayer shawl (*tallīt*) (*UJE* 10, 159f.). In the Christian tradition (J. Braun, 1907/1964, and 1912; Dix, 1945; Lotz, 1949; Mayer-Thurman, 1975; Mayo, 1984), quite early on clerical vestments begin to make their appearance. In cut and colour they were no different from profane dress. But they were as far as possible cleaner and purer than ordinary dress. By the seventh century profane dress had changed while the early Roman vestments remained the same as before, worn now over everyday clothes. From the ninth century onwards, liturgical vestments became more and more costly and elaborate. They also received a special rite of blessing. They were regarded as sacred objects and could not revert to profane use. They were kept apart in a special place, the sacristy. In terms of medieval symbolism, the individual vestments came to represent the passion and glory of the incarnate Son of God, who was represented on earth by the priest. They also came to signify the priest's inner struggle against the powers of evil and the cardinal sins of flesh and spirit. Vestments veil the human and leave behind the profane. They signify the total yielding to the service of God and Christ. Through them the priest becomes the bearer of the sacred, removed from the profane sphere. He speaks and acts in place of God.

Basic liturgical vestments include the *alb*, the *tunic* and the *chasuble*. The alb is a long, white linen garment with sleeves, over which is worn a three-quarter length garment with short sleeves, the tunic. On the street and on special occasions the chasuble was added as an over-garment. The latter was basically a piece of great round cloth reaching to the knees, with an opening for the head in the middle. Subsequently changes came about in this vestment. The short sleeves of the tunic became longer and wider, and became the *dalmatic* worn by deacons in the West, bishops in the East. The chasuble underwent changes in styling also and attained in the end the well-known 'double-bass' shape. For higher clergy the distinctive insignia was the *pallium*, a circle and pendant of white cloth with black crosses. For the lower clergy it was the *stole* or 'yoke', a long ornate scarf made of silk. In addition, the *maniple*, another ornate scarf, was worn over the left forearm. With the alb, a girdle called the *cingulum* was put on. Worn around the neck was another form of scarf, a square cloth called the *amice*. Later forms of sacred dress included the *cope*, *pluvial* or *cappa*, a mantle of silk or velvet originally designed to protect the wearer from the cold during processions. In colder climates such as those of England and Germany, there developed the well-known surplice or *superpelliceum*. Late developments also were the liturgical dress for head, hands and feet, including the tiara, mitre and biretta. The last-named was the ordinary head-covering for men and women in the late Middle Ages.

The Reformation at first brought little change in these vestments. Luther gave his followers complete freedom to continue with those in general use. But those still widely used for the Eucharist came increasingly under attack from the radical wing. Gradually the choir garment or surplice came to be worn for services over the clerical street dress (the black cassock). For preaching the Roman practice of removing the Mass vestment was continued and after the time of Luther was extended to the celebration of the Eucharist as well. Calvinists also tended to take a less friendly view of the eucharistic vestments. During the Enlightenment voices were raised against these 'old fashioned' costumes. During the next century the Prussian *Talar*, thought to derive from

Luther, began to replace the white surplice and coloured Mass garments in German Protestantism. Further north in Scandinavia, the medieval Roman practice continued especially in the Swedish Lutheran Church. Anglicans too kept the earlier practice despite certain Puritan and Calvinist simplifications. Their vestments included the cassock and surplice, and sometimes the alb and either chasuble or cope. In North America Episcopal Churches followed Anglican practice and other Churches followed their lead. At the other extreme, small Reformed Churches or sects either adopted the Geneva or academic gown or dispensed with any gown at all, returning to early Christian practice by wearing clean and neat street clothes. Lutheran and Reformed Churches found themselves somewhere between these two extremes.

Clothing and vestments have also taken on other meanings as well in the Judeo-Christian tradition. They feature as literary images and symbols. The cosmos has been likened to the vestment of God, a notion common also to Greek and Germanic religious thought. The God of heaven is thought of as wearing a mantle of stars. 'Light is the vestment thou hast put on' (Ps. 104.2). The vestment also served as a symbol of blessedness. The blessed wear glorious garments (1 Enoch 62.4). The great multitude which the Apocalyptist sees is 'clothed in white before the throne and before the Lamb' (Rev. 7.9). Each martyr will receive a white robe (Rev. 6.11). They have washed their clothes and made them dazzling white in the blood of the Lamb (Rev. 7.14; *ThWNT* 4, 247–56). Paul also uses the image of clothing when he speaks of 'the putting on' of the 'incorruptible' and of 'immortality' (1 Cor. 15.54). Again, clothing is the symbol of the sanctity of the redeemed. Paul speaks of 'putting on Christ' (Rom. 13.14). The Epistle to the Ephesians speaks similarly of 'putting on' the new man who is created according to the divine original, God, in true righteousness and holiness (Eph. 4.24).

Sacred objects, especially vestments, have certain *colours* (*RGG* 2, 874f.; *RE* 5, 755–62; *HWDA* 3, 1189–215; *NDLW* 178ff.; Haupt, 1941; *ER* 3, 562ff.). Just as a person selects colours for dress or home so also do the religions of the world have their special colours, deliberately chosen to provide for their followers an immediate aura of the numinous. These sacred colours include white, red, blue, green, yellow, gold and black. The extent to which Christians share in this colour symbolism will be looked at in two ways: first, in terms of individual colours; and then in terms of an overall colour combination or colour canon.

In many respects *white* (*HWDA* 9, 337–58) may be regarded as the basic colour of the sacred. It is the colour of light, of eternity, of purity, holiness and joy. It is the colour of the basic vestments of Christian priests of the Eastern, Western and African Churches (but see also below, under black), just as it is for those of Obatala, Isis and Ahura Mazda. On the mount of transfiguration, Christ's clothing was white, as were the clothes of the blessed in the Apocalyptists's vision (Mark 9.3; Rev. 7.13). The baptismal robe of the early Christian was also white. Neophytes kept them on for eight days after the baptism. The Sunday on which they took them off is called Whit(e) Sunday.

White is also the principal colour of the bridal gown in Christian weddings. It was also the colour of the burial shroud for Roman Catholic infants dying in the age of innocence.

A second sacred colour which enjoys almost equal status is *red*. It is the colour of energy and activity, the symbol of blood, the bearer of life. As such it has been the colour associated with sacrificial rites by which the life of man is renewed. Red is the original colour of Easter eggs, the symbol of young life, which in Southern Germany are often hidden away in fields and bushes. Red is also the colour of the bridal veil in Italian weddings, following age-old Roman practice (the *flammeum nuptiale*). Consecrated Christian virgins in the Western Church also wore the *flammeum*. Red is also used as a colour for vestments and adornment of Christian priests, particularly the highest church officials. As the colour of the sun and fire, it is also used as the colour for the angels in the icons of the Greek church. The colour depicts their fiery nature. As the colour of life, red is widespread as the sacred colour in the cult of the dead. It is probably the oldest sacred colour known, going back to the earliest use of red ochre for burials in Africa, up to 100,000 years ago. Red vivifies the dead – and keeps them away from the living. Red wards off evil powers, yet along with black is itself the colour of the demonic.

Blue is sometimes regarded as a colour of lesser significance despite its connection with the sky. Blue-purple was the colour prescribed for priestly robes in ancient Israel (Exod. 28). Blue is the apotropaic colour against the 'evil eye'. In the Christian tradition deep blue-violet became the colour for penance in the West. It was the colour of the bruises made by repeated self-flagellation. In Eastern churches the ouranic symbolism of this colour has been taken up. Many churches are painted sky blue both outside and in.

Green (*HWDA* 3, 1180) is the colour of vegetation and fertility. It is the liturgical colour in the Christian year between white and black, occurring between Epiphany and Lent, and again between Trinity and Advent (see below, Chapter 4).

Yellow (*HWDA* 3, 570–89) in the Christian tradition seems to have been scarcely regarded as an important symbol except in a spiritualized form as the colour of reason for mystics such as Tauler. It is different however with the colour *gold*. Gold is the colour of the sacred in Eastern Christianity, especially for icons; while in the West, cult objects and paintings are often of gold, or gold in colour.

The colour of the magical, of Satan and the Devil, and even more, of the dead and of mourning, is *black* (*HWDA* 7, 1431–60). For the medieval mystic black was the colour of sensuality. The Lutheran *Talar*, the Geneva gown, and the Catholic outdoor dress, the cassock, are all black (except perhaps in tropical countries). Although the movement for liturgical renewal has led to the return of light and colour to the vestments worn in Christian services of worship (Lotz, 1949), the black Protestant vestment has stubbornly held its ground. From smaller Reformation communities such as the Hutterites, who wear black for everyday dress, we learn that they do so not only as a sign of mourning for their martyrs and confessors during five centuries of persecution; but also as the symbolic affirmation of their rejection of the 'fallen' world to which they no longer belong.

In addition to the individual colours, groups of colours have also become important for the various religious traditions. And so we may speak of the colour canon which is unique to a particular religious movement or tradition. The ancient Jewish colour canon, for instance, appears to have been made up of the following colours: purple-red, for the majesty of God in the exalted aspect; purple-blue, the divine majesty in the aspect of condescension; scarlet-red, the divine zeal and wrath; and white for the divine love and mercy (*RE* 5, 762). In West Africa, to take another instance, Yoruba traditional cult-groups have distinctive sets of colours which symbolize a particular deity or *òrìsà*: blue and yellow for the deity Òrunmìlà, representing divine wisdom; red and white for Sàngó, divine force; red and black for Èṣù, who represents divine unpredictability. Obàtálá's cult group has, as noted above, the colour of the eternal creator, white. In the same way the colours of the Christian Church (J. Braun, 1912; Eisenhöfer, 1932) formed into a set pattern slowly over the centuries. In the Eastern Church white was taken as the colour for festivals, purple or violet for penance, and black was the colour of mourning, especially on Good Friday. The Western Church developed a colour canon in the twelfth century for the different festivals of the Christian year (see below, Chapter 4). These colours were: red, white, green, violet, and black. In the sixteenth century Pius V prescribed this colour canon for the whole Latin Church. More and more, the Churches of the Reformation and the Anglican have tended to adopt it as well, although with many variations and alternatives. *White* is the colour for the festivals of Christ, of Mary, and of those of non-martyred saints and confessors, holy virgins and widows. It symbolizes divine light, the holiness and virginity of the soul and the Transfiguration. *Red* is the colour for the Passion, Pentecost, and the Apostles' and Martyrs' days. It symbolizes the suffering of Christ, the Holy Spirit's tongues of fire, and the blood-witnesses to the faith. *Green*, as noted earlier, is the church colour representing the days after Epiphany and after Trinity Sunday. *Black* is the colour of Good Friday. Earlier it stood for times of penance, and for Masses said for the dead. *Violet*, the colour for penance and self-mortification (see above), is the colour also for Advent and the Lenten period. It used to stand also for the Ember days at the beginning of the four seasons of the year observed in Catholic and Anglican churches as a time of penance, likewise over a long period in German Protestantism. It was also the colour for the Rogation Days on which processions were held to intercede for bodily and spiritual well-being (*RE* 3, 248f., 593). Finally, it symbolized the festival of the Innocents which is celebrated by the Church in East and West in memory of the massacre of the children at Bethlehem by Herod (Matt. 2.16–18; *RE* 20, 282; Bottermann, 1982, 108–11, during which children played the parts of bishop and abbot: Young, 1951). Thus, among Christians, as among members of other religious traditions, the power of colours lives on as it did long ago for prehistoric man.

3

Sacred Space
in the Christian Tradition

(1) The open space

Sacred objects with their colours are closely associated with sacred *space* (*NDLW* 26ff.; H. W. Turner, 1979; Eliade, 1957; 1963; Mirsky, 1976; J. G. Davies, 1982; Marvell, 1985; *ER* 1, 382ff.; 2, 71ff.; 12, 526ff.). Sacred space is a primary apprehension of religious man. It has to do with his perception of the world, of how it is founded, constituted and ordered. This awareness was universal long before the rise of Christianity. Sacred space is a creation of divine action. It is revealed by divination, or constituted as such by rites of consecration. Sacred space becomes a significant centre and point of orientation for human life and activities. It is 'a little piece of heaven on earth' (Turner, 27). A feature of sacred space, long ago noted by Chantepie de la Saussaye, is its persistence through time and across religious traditions. Where once was a Celtic shrine or Roman temple may now be a Christian church. A Christian church building may in turn find itself a Hindu or Jain temple or mosque. In what follows, some basic forms of sacred space will be identified which have been important for Christians over the centuries.

The open space is one of the oldest forms of sacred space. It serves as a shrine, bounded by sacred stones or a stone circle. It is also defined by a mountain or hill, by a spring, trees, a sacred grove or an open clearing in a forest area. The open space was an important shrine for Celtic and Germanic peoples. In the *ciric garth* ('circle guard', 'churchyard') a cross would be placed to indicate its conversion to Christian use.

In antiquity, the *temenos* (Greek) or *templum* (Lat.) (*ERE* 7, 789ff.) was originally a precinct or cult-place. The cultus in antiquity was often performed in the open air. Offerings would be placed on the altar which was out in the open in the form of a stone, stone heap, stone wall or wooden table (*ERE* 7, 333–58; *RGG* 1, 251ff.; *HWDA* 1, 825ff.; *RAC* 1, 310–54). The image of deity was housed in a small shrine or covering. The enclosure was 'delimited' (*sancire*) and therefore 'sacred' (*sanctus*). Entry was forbidden to armed and unauthorized persons. Even those permitted to enter the enclosure had to purify themselves and to make the appropriate rites of expiation. Such enclosures are found today in places as far apart as India, Indonesia and Africa.

Often within sacred enclosures were the *graves* (*ER* 14, 551ff.). Christians, following the example of the Jews, began to make the first catacombs in Rome about the beginning of the third century under Pope Callistus. They were a subterranean cemetery (*RGG* 3, 1171ff.). The graves of the martyrs were specially sacred. Since the fifth century the catacombs were replaced by cemeteries and since the eighth century these have been specially consecrated (*LThK* 4, 373ff.) after the manner of the consecration of churches.

Among open spaces of significance to Christianity may be mentioned the Mass rock at Cahirkeem in south west Ireland, now marked by a cross, where priests celebrated the Eucharist in secret during the eighteenth century when this was banned under penal laws. Another large rock beside a deserted mountain road in Westmorland is known as Fox's pulpit, where in 1652 he preached to a thousand Seekers. John Wesley and George Whitefield continued Fox's use of open spaces a century later with their open-air preaching (*NDLW* 399f.). Wesley widened the open space to include the whole surface of the globe when he declared that the world was his parish.

One last feature of the open space is the *sacred way* (Fohrer, 1939; *HWDA* 9, 214ff.). The pathway to the *temenos* is sacred. Even the ordinary way, where two ways cross or three ways meet, is sacred (*HWDA* 5, 516–29; *ERE* 12, 330ff.).

(2) The covered space

(a) The cave

Covered space early on joined open space as sacred. Natural caves and grottos (*HWDA* 4, 175ff.; *ER* 3, 127ff.) served in prehistoric times for religious and cultic purposes. Sacred objects were preserved by Australian peoples in caves, and the uninitiated were denied entrance to them. Oracular shrines were also in the form of caves in Greece, as were cult centres for the Celts and early Cretans. These cave shrines may have been survivals from earlier days of the cave dweller. The grotto of Zeus on Mount Ida was famous, so too was the grotto on Mount Parnassus. Christianity (Gervers, 1979; E. O. James, 1965) early on took part in the tradition of the cave. The *Protevangelium* of James, dated somewhere between the second and third centuries, asserts that Christ was born in a cave or grotto. This claim is echoed by the Alexandrian Father, Origen, and in the art of Byzantium. Origen refers to the cave site or grotto at Bethlehem which was associated with the nativity as early as about 135 AD. There is a striking parallelism here between Mithraic and Christian beginnings. Mithras was born from the generative rock amid a blaze of light. Christ, according to the *Protevangelium*, was born in a cave if not out of rock; also, like Mithras, in a blaze of light. The Mithraeum was an image of the world-cave for the initiates. The Churches of San Clemente and Sta Prisca in Rome were themselves built over Mithraea. There was a 'thematic and symbolic continuity' (Gervers). Grottos also served as dwellings for Christian saints. Benedict stayed in a sacred cave in Subiaco, Francis of Assisi in a grotto (*Fonte Colombo*). The grotto at Lourdes has become famous as a Christian place of pilgrimage (see also below, section three). Less so, and originally more inaccessible, is the cave chapel of Our Lady of Rocamadour half-way up a cliff in the Dordogne.

(b) The house and home

The house (*ER* 6, 438ff.) is also a shrine. In the foundations of houses in antiquity sacrifices and sacred objects were often walled up or buried. The building sacrifice expelled the dangerous powers residing in the soil. Early West African Christian missionaries took over traditional practice and buried a bottle with messages under the foundations (in Ibadan and Işeyin [CMS CA2]; also at Igbore, Abeokuta, on 23/11/1868 [CA2 070, 54]). The house often had a sacred enclosure, hedge or fence. The threshold acquired sacred significance. A survival of this is seen in the wedding custom of the bride being carried over it into the matrimonial house. The threshold was also a place of sacrifice (*HWDA* 8, 1509–43). The door likewise was sacred, being guarded by protective deities. Apotropaic amulets were also placed over doors (*ERE* 4, 846ff.; *HWDA* 8, 1185ff.). The *mezuzah* (*UJE* 7, 526f.) for example was placed on door posts in Jewish homes. The *pantry* (*penus*) was likewise a sacred area of the Roman house, being protected by its deities, the Penates. The Roman *domestic hearth* (*ERE* 6, 559ff.; *RGG* 3, 234ff.; *HWDA* 3, 1758ff.) had particular significance, being connected with the sacred fire. It was also the centre for the cult of the dead, who were buried in a separate shrine or beneath the floor not far from the hearth. The Christian domestic house has still, in recent times, continued to retain some sacred corner or shrine as the focus of worship and sacred centre of family life in the home. There may also be a sacred symbol or cult object: in many Russian Orthodox homes in the form of an icon. In one domestic house in southern Ireland (Castletownbere, West Cork, 23/3/83) the sacred niche is at the top of the stairs. It consists of a small statue of Christ with Sacred Heart. Before it is a tiny fluorescent cross. There is also a flask of holy water from the pilgrimage centre of Knock. Where a house has no special niche or spatial focus of worship, the persons in the family have the Scriptures as the focal point. Prayers may be said sitting or kneeling. Even here, however, there appears to be a customary space for worship, be it the living room or dining room.

(c) The house of God

Of greater importance than the domestic house is the house of God (*domus Dei*; *ERE* 12, 236ff.; Clements, 1965; Kraus, 1966; H. W. Turner, 1979). The dwelling place of the Deity stands often, as it did at Old Uppsala, close to a natural shrine, a meadow, tree or spring. Simpler forms include the huts of Siberian shamans or of the rice mother of Malay people, or the traditional shrines of the Yoruba *òrìsà*, or the *Mbari* shrine of Ala among the Ibo; or, in the Hebrew Scriptures the tent of meeting or covenant (Exod. 26 and 27). As a miniature Solomonic temple, it may reflect the memory of the tabernacle of the nomadic period. Out of the tabernacle the house of God (*Beth 'Elohīm*) emerged. The temple (*ER* 14, 368ff.) developed out of the palace of the gods, which was to be as magnificent in its way as earthly palaces. Early on it is given a cosmic significance. The Accadian *ziggurat* is made in the image of the world-mountain. At the top was a table and a resting place for the Deity. Some

English war memorials also have a small room at the top of the arch accessible only to the Deity and the spirits of the dead.

The temple is also a cult-place, but sacrifice, hymns and prayers may be carried on in an anteroom or even in the open. It is also important as a centre of oracles and of healing, hence the widespread practice in antiquity of 'incubation', sleeping in the temples (Hamilton, 1906; *RGG* 3, 755f.). As a result of the incubation the worshipper expects to have a dream or vision of the Deity which either has a healing effect, or else gives the worshipper a message to his advantage. The custom of incubation lives on in Greek pilgrimage churches and also in some independent healing Churches in Africa. Also a feature of the traditional temple was its role as refuge or asylum. Those seeking protection were safe if they touched the altar or an image of the deity, since these were regarded as being filled with divine power. Medieval churches preserved this right of asylum even if it was subject to violation in practice, as for instance when Thomas Becket was killed before the altar at Canterbury (Hilgen, 1981; *RGG* 1, 668). More than an asylum for individuals, the temple also conferred protection on the whole community. The Yoruba town of Oshiele was once saved from destruction, its ruler asserted, because Olórun would not allow his 'sacred house', a great iron-roofed church, to be polluted by the enemy (CMS, CA2 070, Jnl. W. Moore, 14/8/1878).

The building of temples became widespread in the religions of the ancient world; but for Christians it is the early temple of the Israelites in Jerusalem that has possessed an enduring fascination (*ER* 2, 202ff.). It was built by Solomon according to the ancient pattern with a holy of holies as a darkened shrine in which were the ark of the covenant and the cherubim. At the doorway were the two pillars also found in Sumerian temples. Similar temples were built for Yahweh at Bethel and Dan in the northern kingdom. Later the Jerusalem temple was renewed: in the seventh century Assyrian cult forms were introduced but after Josiah's reform, such foreign cult objects were removed. Still later, after the victory of Nebuchadnezzar (605 BC) new cult forms were again introduced. Shortly after this, in 586, the temple itself was destroyed. A second temple was later built under Zerubbabel.

Israel firmly believed that Yahweh was present in his sacred shrines, especially those of Zion and Gerizim. This is made clear in Solomon's prayer of consecration for the new temple: 'I have built thee an exalted house, a place for thee to dwell in forever' (1 Kings 8.13). The prophets, too, are imbued with this belief in the presence of Yahweh in his temple. Hence Isaiah's famous vision (Isa. 6.1): 'I saw the Lord upon a throne, high and lifted up, and his train filled the temple.' Ezekiel received this oracle of Yahweh from the temple: 'Son of man, this is the place of my throne and the place of the soles of my feet, where I will dwell in the midst of the people of Israel forever' (Ezek. 43.7). And the Psalmist sings: 'This is my resting place forever; here will I dwell, for I have desired it' (Ps. 132.14). The yearning for Yahweh's dwelling place echoes from the temple hymns and pilgrim songs: 'How lovely is thy dwelling place, O Lord of hosts! My soul longs, yea faints for the courts of the Lord. One thing I have asked of the Lord, that will I seek after; that I may dwell in the house of the Lord all the days of my life' (Ps. 84.1f.; 27.4). With such utterances and many more, from prophets and Psalter, Christians have identified, with heart and soul throughout the ages.

Through the Deuteronomic reform the priests first made known their demands for one exclusive cult centre and hence the abolition of the cultus and ancient Yahweh shrines in the land. In harmony with this requirement the whole of the existing sacred writings, including historical and prophetic books, were edited anew by the so-called Deuteronomists. But the changes in priestly theory were only slowly translated into practice. The traditional Hebrew sacrificial cultus lived on in Samaria and in Egypt.

The love for the temple was mingled with a passionate criticism of it on the part of the prophets. Jeremiah was sharply opposed to any reliance on the idea that because the temple was Yahweh's, no evil could befall the people. The cultic presence of Yahweh he held to be of no use without its being accompanied by moral living on the part of the worshippers (Jer. 7.4–7). Israelite prophetism criticized the cultic presence of Yahweh in the temple from the standpoint of a purer concept of God as well as from ethical considerations. A prophet of salvation called Trito-Isaiah received this word of Yahweh: 'Heaven is my throne and the earth is my footstool; what is the house which you would build for me, and what is the place of my rest?' (Isa. 66.1).

With Jesus the same love for the temple and criticism of it are apparent. The twelve-year-old Jesus says to his parents: 'Did you not know that I must be in my Father's house?' (Luke 2.49). He is also full of zeal for the preservation of the temple's holiness. He drives the money changers out of the temple, on the authority of God's word (Isa. 56.7). At the same time the outpouring of God's powers as revealed by Jesus' healing miracles went beyond God's presence in the cultic shrine: 'Something greater than the temple is here' (Matt. 12.6). Further, there issues from the mouth of Jesus the prophecy that sounds fearful to Jewish ears: 'There will not be left one stone upon another' (Matt. 24.2). 'I will destroy this temple that is made with hands and in three days I will build another' (Mark 14.58).

An echo of this word of Jesus is found in the sermon of Stephen (Acts 6.14). This eschatological faith in the disappearance of the temple is also alive in the New Testament Apocalyptist (Rev. 21.22). The love of the temple and the criticism of it are also found in Paul: on the one hand he undertakes a pilgrimage to Jerusalem, prays in the temple and even takes on himself the Nazarite vow of the shaving of the head in the temple and the offering of the prescribed sacrifice (Acts 21.26). On the other hand he proclaims on the Areopagus in Athens: 'The Lord of heaven and earth does not live in shrines made by . . . human hands' (Acts 17.24). The Fourth Gospel proclaims the end of all confinement of God's presence to a particular cult-place. In conversation with a Samaritan woman, Jesus says: 'The hour is coming when neither on this mountain (Gerizim) nor in Jerusalem will you worship the Father . . . The hour is coming and now is, when the true worshippers will worship the Father in spirit and truth' (John 4.21ff.).

The Judaic belief in the temple gradually changed in early Christianity. The temple became for Paul an image of the dwelling place of God in the individual's soul and body and in the whole congregation. 'Do you not know that you are God's temple and that God's spirit dwells in you?' 'Do you not know that your body is a temple of the Holy Spirit?' (1 Cor. 3.16; 6.19). In the deutero-Pauline letters this image is employed particularly for the *ecclesia* of Christ. 'Christ is the cornerstone in whom the whole structure is joined together and grows into a holy temple in the Lord; in whom you also are built into it for a dwelling place of God in the Spirit' (Eph. 2.20ff.; cf.1 Pet. 2.5). The 'household of God' is 'the church of the living God', 'the pillar and bulwark of the truth' (1 Tim. 3.15). Hippolytus also says: 'The Church is not called a place, nor a house built out of stone and mortar; nor can a person by himself or herself be called a church. For a house tumbles down, and a person dies. What then is the Church? The holy gathering of those living in righteousness' (*Div. Inst.* iv, 13.26).

This spiritualization of the temple concept had of course begun with the Hebrew prophets. From the same period also there grew up a new appreciation of the value of the gathering together of the believers for worship. The Jewish synagogue (*ER* 14, 209ff.) took its rise most probably during the Babylonian exile after the temple had been destroyed. It was a place of prayer, which acquired its sacredness not from any external building or cult object, but rather from the gathered congregation. The first synagogues were probably the houses of prophets. In the Greco-Roman world the interior took the rectangular form of the *basilica*, with a raised part for reading. But even this place of prayer had its own cultic centre: the holy tabernacle with the scripture rolls, also called the ark, shrine or temple. The tabernacle, originally moveable, was placed during the service in the direction of Jerusalem. Later it became stationary and stood in an apse or niche. Made of wood or marble, it might be covered by a baldachin and an embroidered curtain.

In the earliest Christian cult-place (*LThK* 5, 991ff.; *RGG* 3, 1348–411) the Babylonian house-gathering of the prophet lived again. Christian worship services were celebrated in the houses (in addition to the temple and synagogue services). In the larger towns these might be the well-appointed houses of more affluent members. The *atrium* served as the room for the cult-gathering. The third-century house-church in Dura Europos, meeting in a private house built in the first century, may be a fairly representative example.

The house-church was in time replaced by the *basilica* which was built after the style of the courtroom, public hall or market hall, not that of the temple. It was seen as the house of the congregation, created by it in the image of the heavenly Jerusalem (*RAC* 1, 1225–9; Stange, 1950; Krautheimer, 1965). As in the house-church, the altar was still a moveable, wooden table on which the sacred meal was celebrated. Behind it were the *cathedra* of the bishop and the seats of the presbyters. This house of God still possessed no other sacredness than that of the congregation and that of the eucharistic mystery celebrated by them at the holy table.

Early on the sacrament or *mysterium* was interpreted as a priestly sacrifice. This was Cyprian's view in the third century. As a result, the communion table became more of a cultic centre. With the table was associated the *concessio*, the tomb of the martyrs. In the basilicas the altar (*NDLW* 6ff.; J. Braun, 1924; *ER* 1, 222ff.) came to be built over the tomb of martyrs and saints, thus continuing the practice of worshipping at the tombs of confessors on the anniversaries of their passion and death. The Eastern Church, however, stayed mainly with the moveable wooden table. But there arose there also a close connection between the altar and the relics of the martyrs. In the East the mysteries could be celebrated only on an *antiminsion*, an embroidered silk cloth into which the relics of the saints were sewn. In the West they took place over a stone slab below which were the relics. In this way the altar attained a localized holiness in a double sense: through the sacramental Christ and through the remains of the saints. The sacredness of the altar found its strongest expression in the Latin rites for the consecration of churches (Muncey, 1930). Their high point was the consecration of the altar and the grave of relics nearby. So even in early church times when the church *basilica* was still purely a room for public gatherings, the transition to the sacred building was complete. The church with the altar symbolizing Christ and the grave of relics is no longer exclusively a place for gathering together in worship; it has already become a temple.

It was otherwise with the mosque (*masjidu*) of Islam (*ER* 10, 121ff.) whose relation to the synagogue, and its stronger emphasis on devotion and obligatory prayer, led to a type of mosque based on the house of the prophet. Despite the centrality of the sacred cult object, the *Ka'aba* (*ER* 8, 225f.) in the mosque at Mecca, the *masjid-al-jumaa* (Friday mosque) became analogous to the synagogue of the word. Since the worship service consisted of prayers and the sermon the mosque like the synagogue was the place of gathering together for common prayer. (It also served as a school and even as a university.) Like the Christian basilica with its relics of saints and martyrs, the mosque has been combined with a tomb of the founder or a saint. In addition, the prayer niche (*mihrāb*), facing towards Mecca, corresponded to the niche with the tabernacle of the law facing Jerusalem and in form resembled the apse of the Christian basilica. What is distinctive about the mosque in terms of sacred space is the way it is marked off from the profane world. The numinous character of sacred space in Islam has been well described by Rudolf Otto (R. Otto, 1932a).

In contrast to the Islamic developments the localized, physical sacredness of the Christian building was more and more strongly emphasized in East and West. The *presbyterium* or apse, the holy of holies, became separated off by barriers (*cancelli*) from the worshippers in the nave (*NDLW* 264f., 481). A further step was thus taken in the direction of the ancient temple where the holy of holies was closed off to such an extent that only the priest had access to it. The rails were raised into a screen (Nestorians and Copts) a curtain (Nestorians and Armenians) a stone wall (Ethiopians) or, in the Greek Orthodox Church, into a screen with pictures (*iconostasis*; see Chapter 2 above). By these varied means the holy of holies was cut off completely, especially by the iconostasis which enabled access to the altar only by three doors. The middle one was partly opened in the service and enabled a view of the altar, but during the most sacred part of the liturgy, namely during the consecration of the elements, it was closed and the curtain was drawn.

In the Western Church the altar was brought into greater prominence in another way. It was placed at the midpoint of the intersection between the apse and the nave. The plan of the church becomes now the *crux capitata* (†) instead of the *crux commissa* (T). The altar was covered with a baldachin and became an independent little temple, concealed from the view of the worshippers by a curtain during the most sacred part of the sacrifice of the Mass. The hollowed-out place for the martyrs under the altar was widened and became a crypt with an arched roof and its own independent altar. From the baldachin there often hung the *turricula* or *columba* (see above, Chapter 2) which contained the eucharistic Christ. Upon the latter, worshippers began to fix their gaze even apart from the times of the Mass. As a concomitant of the growing belief in transubstantiation, there emerged thus a third, physical shrine in addition to altar and martyr's tomb, namely that of the reserved Eucharist. Altars and shrines for relics multiplied. The external tower, originally missing altogether or else built beside the church, was now built into a church building above the intersection of transept and nave or above the front facade. The church achieved thus the character of 'a safe stronghold'.

In the Gothic churches the altar was given more prominence partly by being placed higher up – and more importantly by the towering retable, a panelled frame with pictures, often great works of art, and statues. At the same time there emerged more prominently the place for preserving the Eucharist, in the form of the tabernacle for the sacrament. It grew out of the simple cupboard in the wall and rose up to the ceiling as a tower of great artistry. Under the influence of mysticism perhaps, Gothic architecture (Goldammer, 1969; Simson, 1956; *RGG* 3, 836) was seized by a boundless urge towards infinity. The Romanesque walls lost their massive burden and were dissolved into soaring pillars over which floated the delicate roof tracery.

In the renaissance and baroque churches the high altar became the dwelling place of *Deus praesens* through the transfer to it of the tabernacle for the sacrament and through the building up of the altar to include giant paintings or statues. The side altars also emerged into greater prominence. On them, shrines for relics or reliquaries are found. Christ is present with his saints in the church; and the church is again a temple in the age-old, traditional sense. The Renaissance also brought about the architectural return to the ancient temple with its classical harmony and restfulness of style. The baroque sought in its turn to achieve, out of the newly awakened life of the Catholic reformation, an overwhelming effect through movement, the heaping up and exaggeration of forms.

The Reformation turned against this whole line of development as a prophetic counter-movement. The church, it was felt, must become again a house of assembly, *domus ecclesiae* (H. W. Turner, 1979). The living, worshipping, celebrating congregation gathered round God's word is the true church, not the eternal building. There is no 'sensorily-perceived' presence of God depending on some external 'steeple-house': as George Fox, the Quaker founder, put it (Nickalls, 1952). The Calvinist wing of the Reformation was radically puritan in its approach, Lutheranism was more conservative. The former removed most, if not all, cult objects: the altars, the icons or images and the tabernacle for the host; only the pulpit and the communion table remained. Lutheranism emptied the tabernacle, removed the side altars, but retained the main altar as a cultic centre, as a sign of *Deus praesens*, no longer as a place of sacrifice. Hence, the liturgy, which requires the minister to turn away from the people towards the altar, a feature also of Lutheran-Reformed (United) Churches as well. The double centre of Lutheran churches – altar and pulpit – is apparent in Protestant baroque churches in which the pulpit is above and behind the altar. Anglican churches and also, though not always so prominently, Methodist churches, have also retained this double centre; Baptist and Congregational tend more towards the Calvinist forms.

Modern Catholic church building is also inspired by Reformation motifs. Its style is christocentric and it seeks in association with the *liturgical movement* (Hammond, 1960; Jungman, 1965, Koenker, 1954; *NDLW* 307ff.) to leave aside everything peripheral and to reflect upon what is central. It returns thus to the Eastern church: the high altar is prominent but the superstructure now disappears. The table becomes a spiritual place of sacrifice with believers crowding round the altar. Modern Protestant church building is contrariwise influenced by the value placed on the liturgical dimension and is closely associated with modern Catholic church architecture. The altar emerges into prominence in simplicity and stylish elegance. Even before Catholic and Protestant theology found the way to one another, modern church architecture of both confessions prepared the way to unity through their convergent movement. An early movement of convergence is seen in the Gothic revival. Led by A. W. N. Pugin, the Cambridge journal *Ecclesiologist*, the Oxford Tractarians and Ruskin, it strongly influenced churches in the Anglo-Saxon world (H. W. Turner, 1979, 241ff.).

Christianity thus shows a tension between the ancient belief in the sanctity of the cult-place and the prophetic-evangelical faith in God's infinity and spiritual presence. This tension comes to expression in Psalm 24 which may have been sung at an Israelite festival held to consecrate the temple; and which even today is sung at Christian services held to dedicate churches: 'Lift up your heads, O gates!/and be lifted up, O ancient doors!/that the king of glory may come in' (Ps. 24.7). Both movements, in tension with each other, come together in the belief in the incarnation. The eternal one enters space and time and becomes finite, in Christ. Christ is present not only in history but also in the *mysterium* of the cultus. The cultic place is sacred in the sense of Genesis 28.17, the word of

Jacob in the Bethel story: 'How awesome is this place! This is none other than the house of God (Beth-El) and the very gate of heaven.' These words begin the liturgy of the Roman festival for the dedication of a church; and take on visible expression in the numinous church building, with its varied and numerous types of church architecture. An example would be evening worship in the Orthodox cathedral in Athens or the Anglican at Gloucester, where all combines to give an overwhelming experience of the numinous. At the same time, however, the eschatological character of the Christian hope permits only an imperfect realization of that perfect divine presence which will come only at the end (Rev. 21.3).

(3) The place of pilgrimage

Sacred space may also be found 'out there' beyond the local shrine and temple and meeting house in the sacred city or goal of pilgrimage (*ERE* 10, 10–28; Raphael, 1973; V. Turner, 1973; Sumption, 1975; *ER* 11, 327ff.). These places of pilgrimage are found in Hinduism, Buddhism and Islam, also in Judaism and Christianity. Jerusalem is for Israel not only the central point of Palestine where all the tribes gather (Ps. 122.3f.). It is also the *centre* (*ER* 3, 166ff.) for the whole world. Even the Gentiles will come to Mount Zion in the last days (Isa. 2.2ff.). It was to Jerusalem that Gentiles did come, since for Christians the notable place of pilgrimage is the place of the suffering and death of Christ. Pilgrims have been visiting the holy places in Jerusalem and Palestine at least since the pilgrimage of the fourth-century Spanish nun Etheria. Alongside Jerusalem must be placed other important places of pilgrimage in Eastern and Western Christianity: Rome, with the alleged graves of the Apostles Peter and Paul and those of the martyrs; then Trèves, with the sacred mantle of Christ; Aix-la-Chapelle, with the relics of Christ and the saints; Cologne, with the relics of the three kings and the brothers Maccabaeus; Santiago de Compostela (H. Davies, 1982), with the grave of James, and Marburg, with the church of Saint Elizabeth; as well as Loreto, with the sacred house from Nazareth and the numerous places of pilgrimage devoted to Mary: Altötting, Maria-Zell, Maria Einsiedeln, Andechs, Kevelaer, Tschenstckau (Poland), La Salette and Lourdes (France), Fatima (Portugal). The last two became famous through appearances of Mary (*RGG* 4, 761f.). Finally, there are the Franciscan places of commemoration: Assisi and Padua.

Jerusalem was spiritualized in early Christianity as the place of eternal blessedness. 'You have come to Mount Zion and to the city of the living God, the heavenly Jerusalem' (Heb. 12.22). 'And I (John) saw the holy city, new Jerusalem, coming down out of heaven from God, prepared as a bride adorned for her husband' (Rev. 21.2). Subsequently Jerusalem became an image of the Church. The Latin hymn for the consecration of churches (*Caelestis urbs Jerusalem*) includes this image. In English-speaking countries a hymn by William Blake, sung to the tune 'Jerusalem', includes the lines, 'And did the countenance divine/Shine forth upon our clouded hills?/And was Jerusalem builded here/Among these dark satanic mills?'

Finally, pilgrimage itself becomes the symbol of a spiritual journey rather than a physical one. As in Hinduism, Islam and Sikhism, so also in Christianity: 'Now we could make truly Christian pilgrimage, namely, if we diligently read the prophets, psalms and evangelists, then we would journey to God not through holy cities, but through our thoughts and heart: that is the true blessed land and paradise of eternal life' (Luther).

(4) Heaven as sacred space

Beside the temple or the place of pilgrimage, *heaven* or *the heavens*, may be regarded as sacred space. Early venerated as a deity of light, as the abode of the primordial creator or originator of the world and the social order (Söderblom, 1926, 93–116), heaven was associated in Jewish faith with Yahweh. 'To thee I lift up my eyes, O thou who art enthroned in the heavens' (Ps. 123.1). Christianity followed Judaism in this association. Jesus prays, 'Our Father who art in heaven' (Matt. 6.9). The spiritualization of the age-old faith in heaven took place early on in Hellenistic Christianity. Heaven became a synonym for salvation in the here and now '(God) raised us up with him and made us sit with him in heavenly places in Christ Jesus' (Eph. 2.6). And again, 'Our commonwealth is in heaven' (Phil. 3.20). Augustine calls the souls of the just and the saints heaven since God has his dwelling place there. Luther suggests that the Christian does not have to perform good works in order to get to heaven, but he must have heaven in his heart.

(5) Orientation in sacred space

Faith in God's presence in space finds visible expression in prayerful *orientation* (*ERE* 10, 73–88; *RGG* 4, 1690f.; *LThK* 7, 826ff.; *ER* 11, 105ff.). For many people such as Max Müller's Samoyede woman, the rising sun sets the direction: 'Every morning I step out of my tent and bow before the sun and say: "When thou risest I too rise from my bed." And every evening I say: "When thou sinkest down I too sink down to rest"' (Müller, 1889, 569). In the case of the early Romans and Jews (Dan. 6.10), the direction of prayer was towards the central shrine, the temple, a practice eventually followed by Islam as well, in turning towards the *Ka'aba* in Mecca (*sura* 2, 136ff.). In early Christianity also the practice of orientation came to be adopted. In Christian catacombs the dead were placed facing the east. It was natural that the direction for prayer should also be towards the east. Yet it was not simply towards the rising sun, but rather towards the place from which Christ had ascended to heaven and to which he would return again. For Christ is in the east. Jerusalem, or to be more precise, the Mount of Olives, is the centre of the world, the *axis mundi*. Christ becomes the sun of salvation. The orientation of the altar is found in the Church of the Nativity in Bethlehem and in the Hagia Sophia in Istanbul. There is orientation of the entrance to the Church of the Holy Sepulchre in Jerusalem. The orientation of the church and altar leads to that of the priest at the altar during the celebration of the liturgy.

(6) Sacred space and sacred way

The world and man (*homo viator*) are in movement and subject to constant change. The Deity, in one aspect, remains eternally at rest. *Sacred space* gives religious people a sence of identity in terms of unchanging structures and forms (Mol, 1975). The *sacred way* on the other hand enables them to cope with change and movement through a dynamic movement or progression of their own. This tension between the concepts of the place and the way was investigated by the Swedish scholar Edvard Lehmann (Lehmann, 1917). Over against the eternally resting Deity is the way of cosmic events and the religious striving of many. In China, the way (*Tao*) was the cosmic order, the order and rhythm of the seasons, growth and decay. The *Tao* of the universe is the way of heaven (*Tien Tao*) and the way of earth (*Ti Tao*). The human *Tao* should correspond to the cosmic *Tao*. Man in his individual and social life has to be in harmony with the eternal law of the world. In India the way of salvation (*mārga*) took the way of good works (*kārma-mārga*), magic rites (*tantra-mārga*), insight through meditation (*jñāna-mārga*), liberation through psycho-somatic exercise (*yoga-mārga*) and devotion or the love of God (*bhakti-mārga*). The Buddha taught the eightfold path of right views, right resolve, right speech, right conduct, right livelihood, right effort, right mindfulness, right concentration. In the Hellenistic mysteries and in mysticism, including medieval Christian mysticism, there is commonly a threefold way, the way of purgation, the way of illumination, and the way of union. Islamic sufism also has its way of salvation, with various stations leading the soul to divine reality.

In early Israel, the way had a twofold significance. On the one hand it is God's way with, or plan for, the world. This is seen as personal, unfathomable decision of the will, rather than in terms of an impersonal law. 'My thoughts are not your thoughts, neither are your ways my ways ... For as the heavens are higher than the earth, so are my ways higher than your ways' (Isa. 55.8f.). On man's side, the way is to proceed according to God's moral law. In the early historical books Yahweh says: 'I have chosen Abraham that he may charge his children and his household after him to keep the way of the Lord by doing righteousness and justice' (Gen. 18.19). Isaiah has this oracle (Isa. 2.3): 'Come, let us (the peoples) go up to the mountain of the Lord,/to the house of the God of Jacob; that he may teach us his ways/and that we may walk in his paths.' *Derekh* (way) became a favourite expression of Jewish piety as it is reflected in the Psalms, for instance the 'Song of Songs' concerning the law of Yahweh, the 119th: 'I have chosen the way of faithfulness, ... Teach me the way of thy statutes' (119.30,33). The image of the two ways was also an important one in Judaism: 'Behold, I set before you the way of life and the way of death' (Jer. 21.8). It recurs in the Sermon on the Mount where 'the easy way to destruction' and the 'hard way to life' confront one another (Matt. 7.13f.). Likewise in the second-century work *Didache* (1) where the way of life and that of death are explained in greater detail in terms of the New Testament ethical teaching. The image of the way is reinterpreted in the Fourth Gospel with Jesus himself being described as 'the way' (14.6). Later it appears as an important element in the Qur'ān (e.g. *sura* 2, 5–9).

The notion of the way includes the *journey into heaven* (Eliade, 1970; Cohen, 1974). The basic form of the journey into heaven is shamanic. In a state of trance, supported by his congregation, the shaman journeys on their behalf to the underworld or to heaven to meet the Deity. This shamanic pattern is prevalent in the history of religions (Cohen, 1974, chaps. 2 and 3). On Iranian soil the idea of the journey into heaven also flourished – an example being Zarathustra's journey to meet the Wise Lord, Ahura Mazda. From there it penetrated into Judaism and Christianity; and also influenced Hermetic mysticism, Gnosticism and later Islam. The view persisted among Fathers of the Eastern Church that the soul had to go after death through a series of stations in which it is subjected to judgement. In Western piety the journey into heaven was viewed in a more exclusively ethical light and interpreted in terms of the earthly pilgrimage through life. In this sense it was portrayed in the famous work of the Baptist, John Bunyan, in his oft-reprinted work *The Pilgrim's Progress from this world to that which is to come* (1678). The image of the journey into heaven appears in a more spiritualized form in the mystics. Angelus Silesius sings, 'Christian, do not think of the journey into heaven as a long one. The entire way thence is not even a single step away.' So in the sacred way and sacred space, the images of place and way come together in a final *coincidentia oppositorum*.

4

Sacred Time and Number
in Christianity

(1) The substratum of nature festivals

Just as sacred space is separate from the profane, so also with *sacred time* (Van der Leeuw, 1964; Eliade, 1957 and 1963; *HWDA* 9, 889–97; *RGG* 3, 162f.; *NDLW* 133ff., 259f., 477f.; *ER* 2, 547ff.; 3, 323ff.; 6, 360ff.; 7, 454ff.; 8, 41ff.; 12, 535ff.; 13, 148ff.). Why must one day be more sacred than another when the sun makes every day in the year equal to every other day? Jesus Sirach (Ecclus. 33.7ff.) answers for all religions, including Christianity:

> By the Lord's decision they were distinguished,
> and he appointed the different seasons and feasts;
> some of them he exalted and hallowed,
> and some of them he made ordinary days.

The concept of time is itself basically religious. The Latin '*tempus*' comes from the same root as *templum* and *temenos* (from *temnein* 'to cut'). Sacred time is the place where the caesura, the cut, occurs. This moment rises up out of the evenness of everyday life. Sacred time is thus the time of transition, like the *twelve nights* (*HWDA* 9, 979–92) between Christmas and Epiphany and the New Year festival (*HWDA* 6, 1020–45; *RGG* 4, 1419f.; *ER* 10, 415ff.). These turning-points between the old and the new require rites through which people can ward off dangers and secure blessings. These are the *rites of passage* (van Gennep, 1960; *HWDA* 8, 1217–51; *ER* 12, 380ff.).

In many religious traditions, including Christianity, sacred time is bound up with the life of nature. The festivals of traditional peoples often celebrate the lambing season through offering of the first-born in the form of the shearing of sheep, and the clipping of the ears of domestic animals. For the Israelite nomads the offering of the first-born took place at the *pesach* festival, which lives on also in the Christian rite of the Last Supper and the christological symbol of the lamb. Fisher-folk celebrate the appearance of shoals of fish. There are reminiscences of this in New Testament stories involving the catching of large numbers of fish (Luke 5.6; John 21.6). The sowing and harvest festivals of agricultural peoples are also represented in the Judeo-Christian tradition. In ancient Israel there was the festival of the first barley harvest (*massōth*). The *massōth* were the old form of unleavened food. The festival of Weeks took place in the wheat harvest. It was so named because it occurred seven weeks after the Massōth festival. There followed the festival of Tabernacles during the harvesting of fruit and grapes. All these festivals were taken over from an agricultural people, the Canaanites, by the Israelites, an ethnic group of semi-nomads, who transferred these rites from the Canaanite deities, the Baalim, to their own Deity Yahweh. These festivals live on in Christianity, being constantly brought to mind through the liturgical and devotional reading of the Old Testament. But other nature festivals have also persisted in the Christian tradition.

The early Roman *ambarvalia*, a procession round the field, was continued by the Latin Church in the festival of the evangelist Mark on 25th April, as well as in the three Rogation Days before Ascension Day. The harvest thanksgiving festival was also retained in the Christian Church as a whole (*RGG* 2, 602). The Germanic spring festival (*HWDA* 3, 161ff.), concerned with the driving away of winter, also persisted in the Christian tradition. It paralleled the Hindu *holī* festival of the full moon in March when a straw doll is burnt in the course of the rites. For many people in the southern hemisphere, the originally northern fire rite, historicized as Guy Fawkes' day, has become an apotropaic rite of spring concerned with driving away winter. The spring rite continues today in northern Christianity through the Easter fire in which the image of winter, Judas, is burnt. Festivals of the sun occurred at the winter and summer solstice and the equinoxes. The winter solstice was the time of the Sumerian New Year festival while it was also celebrated by the Germanic peoples, and by Mithraists as *Mithrakāna* or *Mihrāgan*. It is preserved in the Jewish *Chanukkah* festival of lights and above all in the Christmas festival. The festival of the summer solstice lives on in popular custom as Midsummer eve, the time of transformation (Shakespeare's *Midsummer Night's Dream*; J. M. Barrie's *Dear Brutus*). In place of the old summer solstice festival, many Christians have, as part of their liturgy, the festival of John the Baptist.

Other festivals are at the time of the new moon and the full moon. In ancient Israel the festival of the New Moon was a day of rest like the Sabbath. The Israelite Sabbath was perhaps derived from the Babylonian day of the full moon *Ṣabbattu* (*ERE* 10, 885–93). It should be noted in passing that the term Sabbath has a firm place in Christianity either as the Lord's Day (Sunday), or in the Hebrew form of the Seventh Day. Moreover, Easter retains a lunar element in that it follows the first *full moon* after the vernal equinox.

There were also festivals which included times of fasting and penance. As in Judaism and Islam, Christianity has its special days of penance and prayer: the Ember days, the Vigils, Rogation Days and other times of fasting (see also Chapter 5 below). The festival for the dead, common in other religions, is found among Roman Catholics and Anglicans as All Souls' Day, observed on 2nd November. The Reformation did its best to abolish it but during the Enlightenment it returned with the Sunday for the Dead, on the last Sunday of the church year; or in more recent times, with Remembrance Day observed on the Sunday nearest to Armistice Day of World War One (11 November 1918) or, in Australasia, to Anzac Day (25 April 1915). There were also days of misfortune (*HWDA* 8, 1427–40; 3, 899ff.). The Greeks and Romans had these days of impurity and tabu, which passed over into popular piety. An example of these is Friday, a day sacred to the Germanic deity Freya and, before her, to the

Roman goddess Venus. For Christians, Friday can be both unlucky and lucky at the same time.

(2) Celebrating the saving events

The change from nature festivals to those based on saving events took place in the ancient mystery religions. In the latter, the dying and rising of the saviour deity was presented in the form of a drama. The Phrygian mysteries of Attis and Cybele were celebrated from 15th to 27th March each year. They culminated in the day of burial, the *sanguis*, and the festival of joyous resurrection (*hilaria*). For other religions also a change occurred in the concept of sacred time. Although the link with the nature festivals still remains, a distinction is introduced by the re-presentation and commemoration of a saving event. The birth and other events of the life of the religious founder and saviour figure are now celebrated. Thus, for example, the Jains and Buddhists celebrate saving events in the life of Mahavira and the Buddha, the Hindus those of Krishna, the Muslims those of Muhammad, whose birth and death are celebrated on the same day, and Sikhs the birth of the Gurus.

The linking of sacred history with sacred time in this way is especially strong in both Judaism and Christianity. The Judeo-Christian calendar is concerned throughout with the events of holy history. What was past becomes present. There occurred what has been called one of the great revolutions in the history of religions (Eliade, 1957, 110f.; Wyatt, 1979). Through the Deuteronomic reform the nature festivals of the Israelites acquired their character as events in the history of salvation without losing their original character as nature festivals. The Sabbath serves to call to mind the creation. The Passover, the festival of the first-born of the flocks and beginning of the harvest, recalls the exodus from Egypt. Pentecost, originally the harvest festival, comes to commemorate the giving of the law on Mount Sinai. The feast of Tabernacles for the grape harvest was a reminder of the people's sojourn in huts during the traversing of the desert. The Purim festival which arose in the Jewish diaspora or dispersion during the Persian period, commemorates the downfall of the enemies of Judaism. The Chanukkah festival at the winter solstice is devoted to the dedication of the temple under Judas Maccabaeus. The lament for Tammuz, the dying god of the nature-cycle, is transformed into the lament for the destruction of the temple.

The *Christian year* (McArthur, 1953; E. O. James, 1961, 199–271; *RGG* 3, 1440ff.; *ER* 3, 439ff.) is built in turn upon the Israelite one, and centres upon Easter and Pentecost, the first Christian festivals to be commonly celebrated. In place of the history of Israel, or superimposed upon it, comes the saving history of mankind with its centre the incarnation, passion and resurrection of Christ. The change of view is reflected in the move away from the Jewish date of Easter. Originally, the Christian Church celebrated Easter on the same date as the Jews, namely 14th Nisan, regardless of when the date occurred in the week. This custom was retained among Christians in Asia Minor. The rest of the

Church however began to celebrate Easter as the *day* of resurrection on the first Sunday after the spring full moon. After a long controversy, the latter view prevailed at the Council of Nicaea (325). Even so, differences arose in the calculation of Easter as between the Roman and the Celtic Churches (Heiler, 1941, 148f.). Today, the calendar of the Russian Orthodox Church still differs from that of the Western Church.

At the same time Christianity began to link up with other traditional nature festivals. The festival on 25th December of the unconquered Sun (*Sol invictus*) became that of the birth of Christ (*HWDA* 9, App. 864–968). The festival of Dionysos and the birthday celebration of Aion on 6th January became the festival of Epiphany. The early Roman festival of purification on 2nd February became the festival of Mary's purification. The Passover festival was given the name of the goddess of spring, Ostara, in the Germanic world. The Ember fast days derive from nature festivals and are rivals to the traditional Roman festivals of seed-time and harvest. The liturgical year of the Church got its present form generally speaking in the seventh-century Gregorian Sacramentary. Since the eleventh-century liturgical books (*NDLW* 96ff.) have been set out according to the church year. In the thirteenth century religious reflections and symbolic meanings began to be added. The name 'Church Year' was first used in the collection of sermons by Pomarius of Wittenberg published in 1589.

In the church year the dramatic cycle of the history of salvation is renewed, from the expectation of the Messiah by the people of Israel until the final coming of the Lord. Because the time of preparation for the coming of Christ in the Old Testament already records the hidden activity of Christ, the whole of the church year represents the life of Christ in both the historical sense and also the trans-historical. The church year could be said to be an immense structuring of time in terms of the sacred.

Advent is the time of yearning for reconciliation with God and the hope of the Messiah's coming. The object of the Christmas festival is the birth of Christ in a threefold sense: in Bethlehem, in the human soul and in the eternal bosom of the Father. On the feast of Epiphany, Christians celebrate the adoration of the wise men in Bethlehem, the baptism of Christ in the river Jordan, the marriage of Cana in Galilee. On Palm Sunday the entry of the Messiah into Jerusalem is celebrated, on Maundy Thursday the institution of the Lord's Supper, the washing of the disciples' feet and the betrayal and arrest of Jesus; on Good Friday is the crucifixion; on Easter Eve, the resting in the grave; on Easter Eve comes the high point in the Eastern Orthodox liturgy and now also for the Western Church again – the resurrection of Christ; in the Easter period comes the gospel of the Forty Days closing with the ascension into heaven; and at Pentecost are the sending of the Spirit and the birth of the Christian Church. After the completion of the historical drama of salvation the Western Church immerses itself in the mystery of the inner life of the Godhead on Trinity Sunday. The Sundays of the ensuing period are without special festivals; but are there for reflecting upon the expansion of the Kingdom of God and the problems of Christian living.

Two other groups of festivals are traditionally embedded in this cycle of festivals of Christ, namely those devoted to Mary and the saints. The former includes Mary's conception, birth, Presentation in the temple, Annunciation, Visitation, the Seven Sorrows of Mary, especially under the cross, and Mary's Assumption into heaven; with the saints' days it is not their birth that is celebrated, except in the case of John the Baptist, but rather their death, the saint's true 'birthday', often also the date on which their relics have been transferred. A special day also is the commemoration of a church's consecration. In Germany this is celebrated on the third Sunday in October, in the Church of England on the first Sunday. Thus, for believers the whole revelation in terms of sacred history is spread out like the sun's rays passing through a prism.

The saving mystery of Christian feasts and festivals is not concerned merely with the recalling of what is past. Rather, it is a present event. Hence, in the liturgy the call comes again and again of 'today'. 'Today Christ is born of a virgin in Bethlehem' – just as in the temple of Kore in Alexandria the call rang out each year in the night from the 5th to the 6th January: 'Today in this hour Kore the Virgin has given birth to Aion.' 'Today Christ is nailed to the cross'; 'Today Christ is risen from the dead.' The reading of the gospel, too, does not assume the form of a narration of a bygone event; but rather of a divine activity in the present, taking place before the eyes of the worshipping congregation.

The *Christian week* is the church year in miniature, beginning with the celebration of *Sunday* (*ERE* 12, 103ff.; *LThK* 9, 687ff.; *HWDA* 8, 87–99). In early Jewish Christianity the Sabbath was observed in the same way as among Jews generally. In Hellenistic Christianity, even in Paul's time, Sunday emerged instead of the Sabbath as 'the day of the Lord' (Rev. 1.10). Sunday was even taken over by the Jewish-Christian Ebionites as the Christian Sabbath. The celebration of the Sunday was based on Christ's resurrection 'on the third day' after Friday, the day of the crucifixion. But it is not improbable that the reverse is the case, namely that the resurrection as the rising of the 'sun' of the Spirit was first of all placed on the *dies solis*, the day of the sun. On Sunday also the creation of light was recalled and the sending of the Spirit was celebrated.

On weekdays (*HWDA* 9, 687ff.) early Christian practice partly followed and partly diverged from the Jewish. Two fast days were taken over; but instead of Monday and Thursday, Wednesday and Friday – the days of the betrayal and crucifixion – were observed with a gathering for worship, *statio*; hence the name 'station-days'. In the West Saturday was added as a third fast day. According to a later and more elaborate interpretation of the weekdays, on Monday the angels are praised, Tuesday the apostles, Wednesday the Holy Spirit, Thursday the instituting of the Lord's Supper, Friday Christ's death, and Saturday the Mother of God.

The months are significant in the devotional life of Western Catholic Christians. March is dedicated to Joseph, May to the Mother of God, June to the Sacred Heart of Jesus, September to the Guardian Angels, October to the Rosary and November to All Souls.

The times of the day were also associated with this history of salvation, especially the third hour, called *Terce*, with the Holy Spirit, the sixth (*Sext*) with the crucifixion; and the ninth (*None*) with the death of Christ. In the Eastern Church and also in that church which was so much influenced by it, namely the Celtic Church, every prayer hour had a twofold relation to the creation and fall on the one hand, and to the life of Christ on the other. This is especially characteristic of the Coptic Church. At midnight Adam and Eve come into this world of sorrows – Jesus is born, institutes the Lord's Supper, rises from the dead. At dawn Adam and Eve bestir themselves and look for work – Jesus appears to the women after the resurrection. At the third hour Adam is created and led into paradise – Jesus appears before Pilate. At the sixth hour Adam stretches out his hand towards the forbidden fruit – Jesus reaches out his hands towards the cross. At the ninth hour Adam is cursed by God – the earth trembles at the crucifixion of Christ. In the evening hour of vespers Adam is driven out of paradise – Jesus dies and the curtain of the temple is torn in two.

(3) The sacred year

Beside sacred days and months is the *sacred year* (*RGG* 3, 799f.; *LThK* 5, 979f.). Every seventh year was a Sabbath year in Israel. It served as a time for the land to lie fallow, for the wild growth to be given to the poor, and for the remission of debts. Every fiftieth year was a year of jubilee in which houses leased to others were returned to their original owners, and slaves and serfs went free. Under the Romans, also, jubilee years were introduced in 249 BC, on the basis of a person's maximum life-span of a hundred years. It was repeated in 146 BC, and again, by Augustus, in 17 BC. Domitian repeated it in 88 AD and it was again celebrated in 204 AD by Septimius Severus. Pope Boniface VIII transferred this custom to the Church and instituted a Christian year of jubilee (*LThK* 5, 125f.; *RGG* 3, 961f.). During that year all pilgrims to Rome would be given a plenary indulgence, a 'jubilee indulgence'. Originally it was intended to be every hundred years, following the example of ancient Rome. Then in 1343 its frequency was reduced to every fifty years; later, in 1389, to every 33 years; and finally, in 1470, to every 25 years. Recent holy years have taken place in 1950 and 1983. Special holy years were also decreed. 1926 was the 700th anniversary of the death of St Francis. 1933 was nineteen centuries after the death of Christ.

At the commencement of such a year the door of jubilee is opened at St Peter's and at the end of it is walled up again. From this ecclesiastical year of jubilee, other secular and religious jubilees and centenaries have sprung. The Roman Church, for instance, celebrates the centenaries of the death of great saints, e.g. Augustine, Albertus Magnus or Elizabeth. Protestant Christians have corresponding centenaries. 1963 was four hundred years after the

Heidelberg Catechism; 1983 five hundred years after the birth of Martin Luther; 1985 three hundred years after that of Johann Sebastian Bach. All individual churches, of whatever communion, tend also to observe anniversaries of their founding. Thus, Brixworth church in Northamptonshire celebrated its 1300th anniversary in 1980, while the church of St John in Leicester celebrated its first centenary only in 1985.

(4) The world aeon

World periods (*ERE* 1, 192–205; Eliade, 1959; *ER* 1, 128ff.; 2, 461ff.) appear with the Sumerians and Babylonians and are connected with the signs of the zodiac. Speculation about cosmic periods spread to Greece, Persia and India, and Shiite Islam. There tend to be cycles and periods where evils increase until a redeemer or saviour appears. Four cosmic periods appear in Iranian religion and four world kingdoms in Daniel (2.32; 7.3ff.). The teaching about world periods became also a part of the Christian theology of history. Following the much earlier figure of Montanus (Strobel, 1980), Joachim of Fiore (*RGG* 3, 799; Reeves, 1976; Benz, 1934) distinguished not four but three world ages (1) the Kingdom of the Father (the Old Testament), the time of servitude, of the law, of the 'letter' and of married people and the laity; (2) the Kingdom of the Son (the New Testament), taking an intermediate position between the flesh and the spirit, the age of the clergy and of church institutions; and (3) the Kingdom of the Spirit (prophesied for 1260 AD), the fulness of time, the period of freedom, the time of the monks, of the eternal gospel, of a new 'order of the righteous', of the 'spiritual church'.

Not only are segments of time seen as bearers of the sacred, but also time itself. Time (*Kāla*) in the Vedic texts is a primordial deity, creator of heaven and earth. Zoroastrian Mazdaism knew of *Zurvan akarana*, primordial deity of uncreated time. Zurvanites held Zurvan to have originated both Ormazd and Ahriman. Manichaeism and Uigurean Buddhism also held time to be a primordial deity. Chronos was for the Greeks the father of Zeus. In Hellenistic Egypt Aion is the image of the deity, the soul of the cosmos. And in Germanic religion even the Gods are subject to the end of time (*Ragnarök*). Given this impressive evidence of the connection between religion and time it is understandable to find it extended into Christianity also (*ThWNT* 1, 197ff.; Cullmann, 1951; *RGG* 1, 193ff.; *LThK* 1, 680ff.). The theory of aeons appears in the New Testament where Christ is described (in 1 Tim. 1.17) as the king of the aeons; while speculation about the aeons has an important place in Christian gnostic theosophies. The concept of the aeon lives on in the Church's liturgy in which the ceaseless cry is heard, 'As it was in the beginning, is now and ever shall be, world without end (*eis tous aiōnas tōn aiōnōn; in saecula saeculorum*)'.

The concern with days and years and aeons led to the practical ordering of time by means of *sacred calendars* (*ERE* 3, 61–141, *RE* 21, 914ff.; *ER* 3, 7ff.). In ancient cultures days of sacred and cultic significance were fixed in calendar form by priests, scholars and officials who were expert in astronomy, astrology and oracular divination. The publishing and observing of the calendar was of extreme importance since profane as well as cultic life turned upon the character of the individual days. For the Aztecs, the Egyptians, Babylonians, Indians, Greeks, Romans and Iranians, this was especially true. In China the yearly publishing of the imperial calendar was carried out with great solemnity and ceremony. Early Christianity found itself with the existing Roman calendar which featured the Julian year. With some reforms this has remained down to the present day. The *months* of the calendar are also the same. The Jewish *week* of seven days (also favoured by oriental cults), however, was preferred to the classical Roman reckoning by Calends, Nones and Ides, but the *years* were at the same time not numbered in terms of a general era. The years were counted after a certain consul, or after the founding of Rome or Antioch. In Egypt years were counted from the accession of Diocletian (284 AD), which was linked in turn with the great persecution which soon followed. Easter was based on a sun cycle of months, first an 84-year cycle, then in the fifth century, a 532-year cycle based on the work of Anianos, an Egyptian monk, about 400 AD. This 532-year period represents a 19-year moon cycle multiplied by a 28-year sun cycle. Anianos began his cycles with the creation of the world which was reckoned, using the Bible as the basis of calculation, at 5492 BC. In 525–6 a Scythian monk, Abbot Dionysius Exiguus, added a calculation to these Alexandrian cycles, 'from the incarnation of Christ'. He thus became the founder of the Christian calculation of time. The incarnation of Christ was put at 25 March, year one. It was still centuries before the 'Christian era' came into general use. The Anglo-Saxons adopted the 532-year cycle, Celtic Christians adhered to their 84-year cycle. The Venerable Bede (d. 735 AD) published the larger scheme and won acceptance for it in France, where it was later adopted by Charlemagne. But there were other competing world eras: Julius Africanus Sextus (d. after 240) put Jesus' birth at 5500. Anianus himself had it at 5501. The Byzantine Empire's era (seventh century) began at 5509 BC. The Jewish era began 3761 BC. Bossuet, following Archbishop Ussher, also began to count the years before Christ (4004 to the creation). Meanwhile Pope Gregory XIII had reformed the calendar with a Bull dated 24/2/1581. This was for us 24/2/1582 because the Pope dated year one from 25/3/1 whereas we reckon from 1/1/1. For us the Pope's year one began 25/3/1 BC. Dating from 1/1/1 became common in Europe after the sixteenth century.

The calendar as developed is now in general use, though the notion of the incarnation as the centre of time and history has been dwarfed by the expansion of geological and astronomical time back as far as fifteen thousand million years. It should also be noted, moreover, that there are other important calendars still in use, including the Islamic, the Jewish, the Zoroastrian, the Hindu, and the Buddhist. The Christian calendar is nevertheless practical in that it unites sun and moon cycles. Even if the actual date of Jesus' birth should ever be ascertained with certainty, it is unlikely that this new fact would change the dating of the 'Christian era'.

(5) The sacred number

Space and time are brought together in the *number*, which participates in the sacredness of both. The number lends supernatural power to the objects with which it is in contact (*ERE* 9, 406–17; *LThK* 12, 1025ff.; Hopper, 1930; Heller, 1936; *ER* 11, 12ff.). Number speculation is from time immemorial but is first found in Sumeria and Babylon. Numbers are part of those things handed down from mythical and primordial time. This is the case in early Israelite religion and in Christianity whose number speculation was based on the Old and New Testaments. *The Key to Holy Scripture*, attributed to Melito of Sardis (d. 195) but based on Augustine's numerology, illustrated this approach. Mechthild of Magdeburg, a Beguine mystic, took this further. In her revelations number symbolism occupies a prominent place, parelleling that of Jewish Kabbalah and Islamic number speculation. These tendencies,reflected in the *Zohar*, a popular Kabbalistic work of the thirteenth century, were later to influence Western occultism. The popular song, 'Green grow the rushes O', contains some interesting number symbolism based on early religious and folkloric sources. The following are some numbers with varying degrees of significance for Christians:

One: stands at the head of all numbers. It is really not a number but the symbol of primordial unity, non-polarity and divinity. Christianity takes over the central confession of Judaism that Yahweh is one (Deut. 6.4). It is also influenced by Neoplatonist mysticism based on 'the one'.

Two: is the number of opposition, of polarity. The year is divided into two by the two equinoxes. Right and left are two, as are sun and moon, day and night. The Cosmic-All Deity first separated into two: heaven and earth. Male and female are two. There are two tables of the Mosaic law; two covenants, Old and New; two *aeons*, present and future; two natures of Christ, divine and human; two forms of the Christian mystic's life: contemplative and active – symbolized by two pairs of sisters: Leah and Rachel, Mary and Martha. There is also the gnostic and Hellenistic *dualism* reflected in the writings of Paul and John, and the apocryphal writings. More recent is a whole micro-technology based on binary numbers, not to mention in anthropology the concern with binary opposites, the resolution of which forms a basic theme in many myths.

Three: is the most sacred number, the divine number, the pre-eminent number; a number which signifies totality and completion: it has beginning, middle and end. The whole of the history of religions is replete with triads. Several categories of these may be distinguished: (a) *The divine triad*: Yahweh appears before Abaham in a triad of angels (Gen. 18). Jesus-Mary-Joseph is a familiar triad in popular Catholic piety. (b) *Metaphysical triads*: these include the gnostic triad of Father, Mother and Son; God, Counsel and Reason; or in Neoplatonism: the One, the Spirit and the World Soul. The Christian doctrine of the Trinity represents a primordial phenomenon inasmuch as it goes back to an effectual impulse in the ancient Near East towards a triadic ordering of divine powers. The Christian Trinity developed into a metaphysical triad under the influence of gnostic and Neoplatonic mysticism: the Father equals Being; the Son – Thought; the Spirit – Love. It also developed from a position whereby the Spirit is under the Son who is under the Father (Subordination-ism) towards a position of equality of natures of the divine persons (*homoousia*, equality in substance). Finally it developed from the 'economy' of the *sacred history*, in which the Deity takes part, where the Father is Creator, the Son Redeemer, and the Spirit the Sanctifier, to a position where the Trinity expresses the inner relationship of the eternal Godhead (Gerlitz, 1960). (c) *Anthropological and psychological triads*: Augustine contributes to these with his three faculties of the Soul: Being, Knowing, Willing; or Memory, Understand-ing, Love. (d) *The Cosmological triad*: the ancient cosmology divided the cosmos into heaven, earth and underworld, a view still held by Paul (Phil. 2.10). (e) *The chronological triad*: an example is the three successive kingdoms of Joachim of Fiore – those of the Father, the Son and the Spirit (see above). (f) *The ethical triad* is found in Christianity in the triadic theological virtues of faith, hope and love (1 Cor. 13.13), themselves based on other ancient divine triads; or the medieval mystical way of purification, illumination and union. (g) *The liturgical triads*: the Hebrew temple had three parts (1 Kings 7); the Christian year has three periods – Christmas, Easter, Pentecost. Three is the number of consecrat-ing bishops. Aaron's blessing is threefold (Num. 6.24) and has passed into Protestant as well as Jewish liturgies. The threefold call of 'holy' in Isaiah's temple vision has become a part of Jewish and Christian liturgies world-wide. There is also the Greek Orthodox Church's threefold circumambulation (see further, under the number seven) around the altar during the marriage rite. (h) *Legendary triads*: these include the three vine branches in the dream of the Pharaoh's cup bearer (Gen. 40.10); the three months the child Moses was hidden (Exod. 2.2); the three days of darkness in Egypt (Exod. 10.22f.); the three times Elijah stretched himself over the widow's dead boy to revive him (1 Kings 17.21); the three young men in the fiery furnace (Dan. 3); the three days and three nights in which Jonah was in the belly of the fish (Jonah 1.17); and the three days in which Paul could not see (Acts 9.9). In recent times the triad has continued to hold its own as a mythic framework. According to Hegel's philosophy the movement of the human spirit in history follows the triadic rhythm of thesis, antithesis and synthesis. For Marx this became a dialectical progression through traditional, capitalist and classless societies.

Four: a cosmic number: four is the number of the winds, the number of the quadrants, the cardinal points of the compass, the seasons, the forms of the sun's appearance, the phases of the moon. Ancient Iran knew four world periods, Daniel four world kingdoms. Revelation sees four beasts standing around the throne of God. Its author sees four differently coloured horses upon which sit the four deadly 'Riders of the Apocalypse' (Rev. 6.1ff.). Most obvious for Christians is four as the number of the 'gospel makers'.

Five: the traditional number of the planets and of Venus whose temple had five sides. The pentagram was often found on early pictures of the Virgin Mary. On church walls the pentagram became the basis of magical rites. It was a symbol of the cosmos, a microcosm. Five is the marriage number, the number of the wise and of the foolish virgins in the parable (Matt. 25.1ff.). Jesus feeds 5000 people with five loaves (Mark 6.35ff.). Christ has five wounds, the object of popular Christian devotion. And five crosses were made at the Roman rite for the consecration of the altar.

Six: a number of the macrocosm, symbolized in the figure of the six-pointed hexagram, important in the Chinese I-Ching divination and for the number of the Holy Immortals in Iranian religion. Six is the number of the days of creation (Gen. 1). The seraphim have six wings (Isa. 6.2). Six jars served for the miracle of turning water into wine at the marriage of Cana in Galilee (John 2.6).

Seven: a cosmic number, in the ancient world the number of planets with the sun and moon. Augustine followed a tradition which went back to the Babylonians when he regarded the number seven as the universal one, whole and perfect. Mary wears seven veils as did Isis, Ishtar and Venus before her. There are seven days in the week. The seven eyes of Yahweh signify his omniscience (Zech. 4.10). Wisdom builds her house on seven pillars (Prov. 9.1). As the cultic number, seven are the altars which Balaam builds and to which he brings as offering seven steers and seven he-goats (Num. 23.1ff.). The *massōth* (unleavened bread) is eaten for seven days after the Passover festival (Lev. 23.6). The feast of Tabernacles lasts seven days (Lev. 23.8), also the consecration of the altar (Exod. 29.37). On the seventh day of the seventh month the sevenfold lustration with blood takes place at the sacrifice of the atonement (Lev. 4.6). The year of jubilee (see also above), was celebrated after seven times seven years (Lev. 25.8). The daily prayer of praise is said seven times (Ps. 119.164). Seven steps lead to the temple of Solomon corresponding to the seven stories of the Babylonian temple, and in the temple stands the candelabrum with seven branches (Exod. 25.31ff.). The dedication of the temple lasts twice-seven days (1 Kings 8.65). The Hebrew word for swearing an oath (*shaba*) comes from the seven sacred objects before which the oath was taken.

Seven is also the legendary number for the miraculous: Noah sent forth the dove after seven days (Gen. 8.11). In his dream the Pharaoh saw seven fat and seven thin cattle, seven fat and seven lean ears (Gen. 41). Seven priests carry seven trumpets before the ark; on the seventh day they circumambulate the city of Jericho seven times (Josh. 6.4; on the *turnus sacralis*, see also above under 'three'. From the Judeo-Christian tradition, the number seven passed into Islam, where on pilgrimage at Mecca seven circumambulations are made of the *Ka'aba*). Elijah sent his servants to look for rain seven times (1 Kings, 18.43f.). Seven thousand refuse to bow the knee to Baal (1 Kings 19.18). Naaman dipped himself seven times in the Jordan following Elijah's instructions (2 Kings 5.10). The boy raised by Elisha sneezes seven times (2 Kings 4.35). Seven is also the eschatological number: the light of the sun is sevenfold in the messianic age (Isa. 30.26). The importance attached to the number seven in Israelite religion carries over into early Christianity as well. In the doublet of the feeding of the multitude the latter are satisfied with seven loaves (Mark 8.5f.). Jesus drives seven demons out of Mary Magdalene (Luke 8.2). The unclean spirit that has gone out takes seven worse spirits with him (Matt. 12.45). The son of the captain at Capernaum is healed of fever at the seventh hour (John 4.52). The Lord's Prayer contains seven petitions. Seven deacons were installed by the apostles in the earliest Christian congregation (Acts 6.3). The apocalypse names seven congregations, seven angels, seven lampstands, seven seals, seven horns of the victorious lamb, seven eyes, seven trumpets, seven spirits, seven suns, seven heads of the beast, seven plagues, seven golden scales. The Christian tradition knows seven gifts of the Holy Spirit, seven refuges (*LThK* 10, 1099), seven sorrows and joys of Mary, seven works of mercy, seven Catholic sacraments, seven virtues (four cardinal and three theological), seven mortal sins (as there were seven lists of sins in Babylon). The seventh is the day of the second burial service. The Christian legend of the seven sleepers, also found in the Qur'ān (*sura* 18.20ff.), concerns seven brothers who in the persecution of Decius (251) took refuge in a cave and fell asleep. The cave was walled up and they awoke only when the cave was opened, then they died. If it rains on their day (27 June) it is thought it will rain for the following seven weeks.

Eight: eight persons were saved in Noah's ark (Gen. 6.18). Christian Gnosis knows of eight heavens. The star of Mary in the catacomb of Priscilla has eight points, as has that of Venus and Ishtar. According to Augustine eight represents the resurrection, hence the early Christian baptistery has the form of an octagon.

Nine: the number of perfection (3 × 3), was a special number for many peoples. For Christians the sacred time of Jesus' death was the ninth hour. Christian theology counts nine choirs of angels (*NCE* 1,516). The nine-day period of devotions, called *novena*, is a popular feature of Roman Catholic piety (*LThK* 7, 1064; *NCE* 10, 543f.).

Ten: the number ten signifies wisdom, and like nine also perfection. Ten is the number of the commandments, the code of apodictic law fundamental to the Judeo-Christian tradition (Exod. 20). Abraham gives Melchizedek the tenth, or tithe (Gen. 14.20). The tithe in the land, both of fruits and of animals, is sacred to Yahweh (Lev. 27.30ff.) and is reserved for the Levites. The tithe as a detailed set of regulations was criticized by Jesus (Matt. 23.23) and replaced by free-will offerings by the early Church. It was reintroduced between the fifth and ninth centuries in Western Europe for the maintenance of the clergy, charitable purposes (see below under fasting) and to finance the building of churches. The administration of the tithe was subject to abuses which church reformers strove to correct. The tithe was eventually abolished (in France in 1789, in Italy in 1887) being replaced by state taxes and free-will offerings. It lives on in Protestant church groups. Ten is also the number of the plagues of Egypt (Exod. 7ff.). It is the number of the measurements of Solomon's temple

(1 Kings 7.2ff.; *LThK* 9, 1037f.). Ten lepers were cleansed by Jesus (Luke 17.11ff.).

Twelve: like ten, is of far greater significance; a cosmic number, the number of the houses of the zodiac, the number of hours, the number of months, the number of aeons (for Christian Gnostics), the number of tribes in Israel and the sons of Jacob, the number also of the minor prophets. Jesus came into the temple about twelve years old (Luke 2.42). Twelve is the number of the apostles. After the feeding of the five thousand twelve basketsful were left over (Mark 6.43). Twelve is also the apocalyptic number: the woman clothed with the sun has twelve stars (i.e. the zodiac) in her crown (Rev. 12.1). The heavenly city has twelve gates (Rev. 21.21). The foundations of its walls are adorned with twelve kinds of precious stones. Twelve thousand are sealed out of each of twelve tribes, so one hundred and forty-four thousand worship the Lamb (Rev. 7.4ff; 14.1). The tree of life bears fruit twelve times each year (Rev. 22.2). The Apostles' Creed has twelve articles. There are twelve Sibyls. And the Rule of St Benedict (Chapter 7) counts twelve grades of humility.

Thirteen (Böklen, 1913): the number of Nergal, the god of the dead and in Babylon an unlucky number. But it can also be the number of a new beginning. In the Old Testament Solomon built his palace in thirteen years (1 Kings 7.1), and the temple gate was thirteen cubits wide (Ezek. 40.11). Although in Western Europe, thirteen is an unlucky number, in popular Catholic piety the number thirteen is sacred. The Madonna appeared in Fatima (Portugal) on the thirteenth day of the month (De Marchi, 1956).

Fourteen: the genealogy of Christ is divided into three groups of fourteen generations (Matt. 1), fourteen being a number which brought luck in Babylonia and Egypt. There are fourteen helpers in time of need, according to medieval popular Catholic piety. The fourteen fearful demons are the 'opposite numbers' of the fourteen heavenly helpers.

Fifteen: the number (3×5) of Ishtar. There are fifteen 'gradual' Psalms in the Old Testament. The hymn in First Corinthians (13) counts fifteen forms of love. The Christian rosary includes fifteen mysteries, five joyful, five sorrowful and five glorious.

Seventeen: ten signifies the law and seven the gifts of the Holy Spirit. Seventeen therefore is the sacred number of all those who attain the blessedness through the fulfilment of the law by the power of the divine spirit (Augustine).

Twenty-two: is the number of the letters in the Hebrew alphabet which are symbolically interpreted in the Jewish Kabbalah. It is also the number of the medieval Tarot cards.

Twenty-four: is the number of elders around the heavenly throne of God (Rev. 4.4).

Thirty: is a number for the dead. There were thirty days of mourning for

Moses and Aaron (Deut. 34.8). The Catholic Mass for the Dead (*LThK* 3, 569f.), which is held thirty days after a person dies, is called 'the thirtieth'. Josiah offered thirty thousand lambs and goats at the Passover (2 Chron. 35.7). Judas betrayed Jesus for thirty pieces of silver (Matt. 26.15).

Forty: forty (4×10, 5×8) is a number of totality. The flood lasted for forty days and forty nights (Gen. 7.4,17). Forty years the Israelites wandered in the desert (Exod. 16.35). Forty days Moses, Elijah and Jesus were in solitude (Exod. 24.18; 1 Kings 19.8; Mark 1.13). Jonah announced that Nineveh would be destroyed in forty days (Jonah 3.4). David, Solomon and Joash reigned for forty years. There were forty days between the resurrection and ascension of Jesus (Acts 1.3). There were forty martyrs of Sebaste, in North Africa. In Catholic piety there is a devotion of forty hours with special prayers and processions before the sacrifice of the altar.

Fifty: the fiftieth year is the year of the jubilee in Israel. The fiftieth day after the resurrection of Christ is the Day of Pentecost (Greek 'fiftieth'). Fifty is the number of Ave Marias in a Rosary (*ERE* 10, 849ff.).

Seventy: the spirit of Moses came upon seventy elders (Num. 11.24). The Babylonian exile will last for seventy weeks of years (Dan. 9.24). According to legend there are seventy translators of the Greek Bible (called the Septuagint–LXX). Jesus' disciples should forgive others seventy times seven times (Matt. 18.22).

One hundred and fifty-three ($1 + 2 + 3 + \ldots 17$): is the number of fishes which the apostles caught in the sea of Tiberias (John 21.11). It corresponds to the number of types of fish in ancient zoology.

Six hundred and sixty-six: is the number of the beast in the Apocalypse (Rev. 13.18).

Whatever the attraction of number, and today is witnessing an unprecedented expansion of numeracy through information technology, the ultimate, the Deity, eludes final numerical analysis. Nor should we forget the implicit critique of all sacred times and numbers that appears in Christianity at the outset, namely that while some hold to sacred times others consider all times and, by implication, all numbers, to be equal and alike (Mark 2. 18–28; Rom. 14.5). This resistance to special times and numbers like the interest in number symbolism, runs through the Christian Church from the earliest days.

5
Christian Sacred Action
1: Purification

(1) Elements of cultic action

Some of the practices of Christians have already entered into the discussion of objects of significance, Christian perceptions of sacred space and, even more perhaps, those of sacred time. But these practices have now to be looked at more directly in terms of the theme of *sacred action*. In the sacred object, the Divine manifests itself in perceptible form. In sacred space the Infinite condescends to what is bounded and limited. In sacred time and number, the Eternal becomes present, the Immeasurable accommodates to measurement and number. All are forms of God's contact with man. Yet man does not want simply to take from God. He wants to give to him at the same time. He tries not only to make images or symbols of him, but also to respond actively to what he receives from God. An outward form of this reciprocal action between God and man is the cultus, a 'mystery drama', which presents and celebrates the acts of God through human actors (*ERE* 12, 752–812: *ER* 12, 405ff.; 15, 445ff.).

The practices of Christians are not to be taken simply as an interesting collection of customs. Basically they (and also those of other religious traditions) are concerned with the appropriation of the sacred, of the salvation offered to men, as an event in space and time (Goldammer, 1960, 328ff.). The cultus is concerned with this reciprocal appropriation by God and man in a particular place and at a particular time. It is circular in character: it repeats itself again and again; and yet this mystery-drama is always an event, an action. In early Roman Missals, the canon of the Mass, the central part of the service, is described as *actio*, action. The succession of elements in the cultic action are like different scenes in a drama. The preparatory stages lead slowly up to more unitive ones. This is especially the case in the long liturgies of the Eastern Church; but even in many Protestant services the same progression of 'scenes' has been maintained. The cultus, despite all its loss of meaning to many today, remains still, for Christians across the world, as for those of other faiths, nothing short of *ultimate reality*. It is the ever-new miracle which orients them towards the future, provides them with an interpretation of the past, and gives power to face up to the problems of the present.

The essence of cultic action may be uncovered by distinguishing it from other religious categories, such as religious objects, forms of sacred space and time, and also, still to be considered, sacred sound and word. Stripped down to a bare consideration of gesture and movement, sacred action may be distinguished from other forms of body movement (Brennemann, 1982, 107ff.). The latter range from instinctual movements (reactions to danger and need) and rhythmic motion or repetitive 'body-chant', on the one hand, to gestures in a play or speech, and objectively planned, assembly-line movements on the other. Sacred action, by contrast, is that form of action which symbolically points beyond itself and thus 'thematises the world' (Brennemann), even recreates the world for the participants.

Movement in sacred action takes on certain analogies. One of these is God's action in creation; another is man's search for union with him by pilgrimage. Similarly the cessation of movement, stillness, has also many meanings, such as, for instance, the Sabbath, when God rests, or the stillness of contemplation of the Eternal. Gesture (*NDLW* 247ff., 381f.; *ER* 6, 188ff.; 11, 461ff.) and positioning or body posture (*NDLW* 437ff.) are both important. In the Roman Mass, for instance, the priest must exactly position the finger with which he touches the Body of Christ between the consecration of the elements and the purification of the chalice, so that the eucharistic sacrifice is not made impure. Similarly, acts of prayer and blessing involve the movement and positioning, not only of the body (by standing, kneeling, sitting or lying), but also of arm, hand and fingers. Some Protestants in south Germany clasp the hands together with interlaced fingers, while praying. Catholics, on the other hand, press the hands together with straightened fingers, in the manner of Albrecht Dürer's 'praying hands'. Some Pentecostalists pray with both arms raised and hands open and apart. Christian icons and images illustrate such symbolic positioning. Another gesture is the bow, from the waist, or the head lowered and raised, or even the eyes lowered and raised. In Anglican services a bow is often made by the clergy towards the altar. The same bow is made by a Reformed elder on Remembrance Sunday after placing a wreath under the window commemorating the fallen. A rubric for the Roman Mass directs the officiant to raise and lower the eyes as he utters a part of the formula of consecration. Bending the knee (genuflection) is often associated with Catholic veneration of the Blessed Sacrament, but it is equally made by many European Protestants before receiving the Lord's Supper. Partial or full prostration of the body is associated with Hinduism, Chinese religion, sacred kingship in European history and, more recently in Africa, where Christians also participate in African kingship ceremonies. Such gestures convey a wide spectrum of feelings: of approach, of oneness, of turning away from, of reverence and veneration, and of absorption in the Deity as overmastering reality. Even the most 'ordinary' service of worship is, as Otto has shown (R. Otto, 1932b) a mild form of mystical 'concentration', in which the reality of the Deity is felt and expressed in facial expression, eye movements and the movements of the lips.

Mimesis or imitation is also a powerful element in cultic action. The once-and-for-all saving event is imitated through the cultus, which becomes an analogous happening. The transcendent becomes immanent, sacred history is re-enacted. Thus in Bavarian mountain valleys during Christmas, families will sleep on straw in imitation of the Christ child. In handing round the elements at the Lord's Supper, Reformed Christians imitate the original supper as recorded in the biblical words of institution. In the Eastern Church, the Mass is a recapitulation of the whole of sacred history, just as some African sermons which start from Genesis and end at Revelation.

In approaching the wide field of Christian sacred action a systematic approach is taken in terms of three stages: Purification, Sacrifice and Unification. These correspond broadly to the pattern of traditional religious rites, including the basic steps of the mystery cults and of Christian sacramental rites and mysticism. The remainder of the chapter will be devoted to different forms of rites of purification.

(2) Driving away dangerous powers

It might seem as if the driving away of dangerous powers is an inappropriate place to begin the discussion of Christian rites of purification. Yet many features of Christian worship, many rites of purification, have an 'apotropaic' character: they ward off dangerous powers (*HWDA* 1, 129–49: 3, 435ff.; 7 1386ff.). This was the case in Europe more clearly in past days; it is still the case in many parts of global Christendom.

Traditionally these powers or spirits are driven away through making sounds or noise, especially during times of transition where people are prone to dangerous influences, e.g. on New Year's night, or on their wedding night. Survivals of this are found in New Year's fireworks, or the 'stag' party before the marriage. Drums have also apotropaic significance (*HWDA* 8, 1166ff.; Wieschhoff, 1933; Weman, 1960; *ER* 4, 494ff.). In Central Africa, Baptist Christians use talking drums, in place of bells, to summon people to church. The public character of the drums testifies to the truth of what they are saying and dispels the darkness of falsehood (BBC Radio Four, 13/5/78). In origin, bells (*ERE* 6, 313–18; *HWDA* 3, 868ff.) also had the function of driving away dangerous powers at the beginning of cultic action. The apotropaic significance of ringing church bells during a thunderstorm is clear: they drive away the storm demons.

Another, at first sight, unlikely form of warding off dangerous powers is by spitting (*HWDA* 1, 149ff.; 8, 325–44; *ERE* 11, 100ff.; *ER* 14, 37f.); for instance, spitting before demons. Saliva was traditionally regarded as a soul-substance which has the power to drive away evil. In antiquity, it was customary to spit before epileptics: epilepsy was counted as a 'sacred sickness'. Hence, the Apostle Paul could write to the Galatians that they did not treat his temptation in the flesh as trivial, nor did they spit in front of him (Gal. 4.14. Interpreting the temptation in the flesh as epilepsy goes back to J. B. Lightfoot. Others have found no evidence for the diagnosis of epilepsy). Spitting was also part of early Christian baptism. In the Roman rite the priest touched the baptizand with saliva. Another apotropaic rite concerns the use of fire to drive away bad spirits. This practice, common among the Indo-European peoples, has been retained in the Catholic consecration of fire on the night of Easter Eve. Its apotropaic character is made clear in the prayer of blessing which refers to the driving away of the Devil (see above, Chapter 1).

The heating and burning of woods and resins to produce *incense* (*HWDA* 7, 521ff.; 526ff.; *ER* 7, 161ff.) also has apotropaic character; and has to be seen as part of the Christian tradition. The burning of incense from the heart and liver of the fish drives all bad spirits away, according to the angel's words to Tobias (Tob. 6.7). Ancient Rome knew of this practice. It lingers on in southern Germany where Catholic houses are 'smoked out' on the Feast of the Three Kings (6th January) with a frankincense specially consecrated for the occasion. Complementary to this is the burning of incense to attract the Deity and good spirits through incense. In the story of the flood it is told that after he had smelt the pleasing odour, Yahweh promised he would never again put his curse upon men (Gen. 8.21). In the incense used in religious traditions including the Christian (Atchley, 1909; *ERE* 7, 201ff.; *LThK* 10, 783f.; *NDLW* 265f.), both meanings may be discerned. The apotropaic character is, however, especially apparent in the censing of the altar in the Eastern and Western church, where a full circle is made around it. In the Western church the funeral coffin is censed in the course of circumambulation (see further in Chapter 6, below).

Describing a circle has also to do with driving away or protection from dangerous powers. The *sacred circle* or circumambulation (*HWDA* 8, 1302–78; 5, 462–78; *ERE* 8, 321ff.; 3, 657ff.; Oesterley, 1923; Korvin-Krasinsky, 120f.; Backman, 1977; *ER* 2, 509ff.), refers to the making of a circle around sacred objects such as the altar, the image of Deity or the dead, so that the devotees may be protected from hostile powers, or protect their own sacred power and increase it. This rite is connected with the sacred dance (see below, Chapter 7). A more intensive form of banning evil powers is the *binding* or chaining through bonds (*ER* 2, 217ff.). The term 'to bind' is used in connection with the banning of demons. On the other hand, the breaking of the bond imposed by hostile powers is described as 'loosing'.

The sacred gesture has an apotropaic effect. The raised hand (*ERE* 6, 492ff.; *HWDA* 3, 1379ff.) in a gesture of commanding, keeping away, preventing and banning, is one form often used by Christians.

Another is the raised three fingers (including the thumb), the gesture of swearing an oath, or the form of the Latin benediction. Another form of the gesture is the V-sign made with two fingers, the gesture of compelling and banning hostile powers; more recently the sign of victory. In contrast to the elaborate *mudra* (hand signs) in the tradition of the Buddha (A. C. Moore, 1977, 150ff.; *ER* 10, 134ff.), Christians have developed the *sign of the cross* (*LThK* 6, 265ff.; *HWDA* 5, 535–62). In this sign a powerful apotropaic gesture entered into early Christianity. Tertullian mentions it in the early third century, while Cyril of Jerusalem later stressed its effectiveness in driving away demons. Antony, the father of Christian monks, adds that demons rapidly disappear when one protects oneself by means of faith and the sign of the cross. The sign of the cross is made when something frightening or disturbing supervenes, at the mention of hated persons, when lightning is seen, a funeral cortège passes, or after an anxiety dream in the night. It is also made in other contexts than the apotropaic: as a sacred gesture accompanying prayers and personal devotions, during the liturgy of the Mass or the Eucharist, before the crucifix, or with grace at mealtimes. It is made in two forms: outwardly towards another, or inwardly towards oneself. The Eastern form has the hand touching forehead, breast, right shoulder and left shoulder; the Western form is forehead, breast, left shoulder, then right. Not all Christians make this sign. It is held to be an unnecessary outward ceremony by some churches of the Reformation.

A further apotropaic action is that of the sacred or magic eye to counter the evil eye (*ERE* 5, 608ff.). It lives on in many religions including Christianity, for instance in north-east Africa, and also in European folklore. The basis is the suggestive power of the look. The power of the eye is held in check by means of an eye-shaped amulet, often of silver and blue (the colour of Osiris' eye of heaven), of metal or stones. The evil eye is distracted or overcome by the equal and opposite power of this sacred eye; or other amulets.

(3) Rites of elimination

Alongside apotropaic rites in effecting the removal of evil or dangerous powers are the rites of *elimination*. These are concerned with the transfer of the tabued material or sin to another object, human or animal. The Greek *Thargelion* festival was a good example of this. A prisoner was loaded with the sins of the people; then he was stoned and burnt, and his ashes were scattered over the sea. The rite more familiar to Christians is that of the 'scapegoat' held by Israelites on the Day of Atonement in post-exilic times. The high priest would place both hands on a goat and confess all the transgressions of the people so that these were transferred on to its head. The goat was then sent out into the desert where the demon Azazel lived (Lev. 16.20ff.; *RGG* 5, 902f.). The concept of the scapegoat influenced Paul's conception of the vicarious atoning death of Christ as the elimination of sin. It also stands for those eliminatory practices or 'distancing devices' by which even today the community tends to shift its guilt for its violence on to a minority. 'The prime example of this technique is anti-Semitism, by which the modern world perpetuates modes of feeling that originated in . . . the ancient world' (Maccoby, 1982, 34ff., 186). Cultic rites of elimination may also, however, be based on other cultures than those of the ancient Near East. Early Baptist Christians of the Niger Delta took over the traditional *amagba* rite of the Kalibari people. A week before New Year, branches were tied to the doors, windows and roof of the house. At midnight, after the New Year's Eve watchnight service, the branches were carried down to the waterside; then they were whirled around the head and thrown into the water to the accompaniment of the chant: 'Old year go away/Sickness go away/ All evil things go away/Let good things come/Let children come/Riches come/ And peace come' (George, 1971).

Another form of elimination is the removal of inhibiting or binding articles of clothing, leading to partial or total *nakedness* (*ER* 11, 7ff.). In Greek religious cults, girdles had to be removed. Often, too, women had to unbraid their hair and allow it to fall free. It is still laid down in the Eastern Church that the person to be baptized and confirmed appear without a girdle. Similarly, it is often required that the devotee should be barefoot when taking part in prayer or cultic acts. In the story of the burning bush Yahweh says to Moses: 'Take off your shoes' (Exod. 3.5), a command that is observed by Japanese Shintoists, Hindus, Sikhs, Buddhists and Muslims when in the temple or at prayer. Removal of shoes is also customary among some West African Christians, for example in the Celestial Church of Christ; while in Europe some Catholics also remove their shoes during the veneration of the cross on Good Friday.

Complete nakedness is an older rite than partial uncovering. A person had to appear naked before the Deity whose image was also naked and of great beauty. Nakedness was the rule in antiquity for prayers, sacrifice, the cult of the dead, the sacred dance, incubation or sleeping at the temple, and when prophesying. After disappearing from cultic practice, religious nakedness lived on in popular love and fertility customs (*HWDA* 6, 823–915). In early Christianity, the baptismal liturgy assumed that the person to be baptized was fully naked. Cyril of Jerusalem praised the neophytes who were naked before the eyes of all but were not ashamed: they bore the image of Adam, who was himself naked in paradise and unashamed.

To a greater extent than in baptism, sacred and total nudity lived on in some Christian sects or movements: first of all among some gnostic Christians, then in the Adamites (*RE* 1, 64f.; *MMM*, 2017–19; Büttner, 1959) and other groups during the medieval and modern periods. The Adamites took their name from the first man who lived in a condition of total nakedness. The basic idea was that the Church is paradise and the state of paradisal innocence is re-presented in the cultus. The Adamites found support in one of the *Agrapha* of Jesus. In a gospel fragment found in Egypt the disciples ask: 'When will you appear to us and when will we see you?' Jesus answers: 'When you are naked and unashamed.'

The followers of Priscillius, whose teaching derived from Egypt, also appear to have practised ritual nakedness. The accusation of praying in the nude was made against Priscillius (*RE* 1, 64; H. Chadwick, 1976). Sacred nudity was encountered in the Beguine convents of the Middle Ages, and in the Brethren and Sisters of the Free Spirit. Individual cases were known among the Taborites and Dutch Anabaptists. The accusation of sacred nudity was a typical charge levelled against medieval dissidents such as the Waldensians. Yet no less a person than Francis of Assisi had his brother Rufino preach in the church naked. He did the same himself. He climbed up into the pulpit naked and preached about the nakedness of the crucified one. In the early days of the Quakers, prophets and prophetesses appeared naked. Adamites reappeared in Germany during the modern period, went naked at services and in their houses; some survived in Russia into the twentieth century. In 1925, an Adamite group was reported in California under Anna Rhodes and her husband, whose farm became the Garden of Eden. The English legend of Lady Godiva, first recounted by Roger of Windover in the thirteenth century, also gives an instance of an ordeal involving total nudity. The original purpose of her ride across Coventry may have been forgotten, but in its later form it is still a rite of elimination to ward off the heavy tolls the people had been subjected to by her husband Leofric, Earl of Mercia. The medieval mystics followed the Neoplatonists of antiquity in regarding total nakedness as an image for inner detachment and mystical purification, rather than as a cultic action. Dionysius, following Philo and Plotinus, saw in ritual nakedness an allegory for the soul. It represents the divine simplicity. Mechthild of Magdeburg is not afraid of giving the image an erotic colouring, when she speaks of 'love uncovering itself'.

Paradoxically, the same purpose of effecting the removal of dangerous powers is served by the opposite rite of covering (*HWDA* 7, 1207ff.; 8, 1591–609). Here the profane had to be shielded from the holy. While the one takes off the profane, the other covers it up. In many religious traditions priests and officiants wear some form of head covering. The pious among the early Israelites veiled their heads during the theophanies, as did Elijah in the wilderness (1 Kings 19.13). In the post-exilic period, there arose the custom of putting on the prayer shawl called *tallīt* ('the protecting'). Paul wanted women to cover their heads for similar, religious reasons (1 Cor. 11.5). The use of vestments in cultic actions (see above, Chapter 2) is also an eliminatory rite in covering up the profane when approaching the holy.

Sweeping away the profane or what is tabued also belongs to the rites of elimination. Just as African peoples made use of a 'spirit broom' which could remove the evil powers, so, also, the act of sweeping out the sacred place, sweeping the path leading to it, trimming lawns, and preventing signs of dirt or disorder, are all related to the rite of elimination. This can be extended to the keeping clean of the domestic home (Douglas, 1966).

(4) Rites of purification

Rites of purification are outward acts which enable a state of pollution or impurity to be overcome or removed by means of powerful, symbolic substances (*ERE* 10, 455–505; *HWDA* 4, 1084–99; Van der Leeuw, 1964; Kristensen, 1960; *ER* 12, 91ff.). Among these substances are some of the most powerful natural symbols in the history of religions. *Fire* is one (see also above, Chapter 1). According to Numbers 31, Moses commanded the Israelite warriors, after a retaliatory raid on the Midianites, to purify all metal objects with fire. According to Paul, in the New Testament, the testing and purification of man will take place at the last judgement 'as through fire' (1 Cor. 3.13ff.; and compare the Zoroastrian *Yasna* 34, 4 and *Bundahishn* 30, 17ff.). John the Baptist speaks of the messianic baptism through fire (Matt. 3.11). Origen, the Alexandrian Father, built on Stoic teaching when he conceives of the fire of the coming of the world conflagration as 'purifying fire'. At the final judgement, all men without exception will have to cross the river of fire. The one with serious sins will have to spend longer in this refining fire. The latter, however, must be regarded as temporal and transitory, not as everlasting hell-fire. It is not even an actual, physical fire, but exists in the mind. Every person sets alight the flame of his own fire and will not be thrown into some fire that is already burning, outside of himself. This teaching of Origen (and Clement) was extended further in Western Christianity. But it assumed a more material character in the shape of the early medieval doctrine of purgatory (see also Chapter 18), as represented in the works of Gregory the Great. The mystics in turn refined and spiritualized the doctrine. Especially was this so in the case of Catherine of Genoa (von Hügel, 1923, 1, 283ff.; 2, 230ff.).

Of still greater importance for purification is *water* (see above, Chapter 1). Water is a substance which purifies from sin and pollution in the same way as it washes away material dirt. Modern ideas of hygiene provide a further extension of the analogy in their concern to provide a germ-free, aseptic environment. The most comprehensive form of purification with water is through total immersion, whether in a bath or in running water, a rite which forms part of the Judeo-Christian heritage. On the Day of Atonement the high priest and the one leading the sacrificial goat had to undergo a ritual bath. Synagogues were built with baths alongside. Ritual baths for purification were especially important to the Essenes and baptist sects east of the Jordan at the time of the rise of Christianity. For Greco-Roman religious cults as well as for Islam later, it was no different. In early Christianity, as we shall see shortly, it was part of the initiatory rite of baptism.

As a substitute for total immersion, rites of washing (*ER* 1, 9ff.) appeared. Wash basins have been found at the entrances of ancient temples and in traditional shrines. For Israelite priests the washing of feet was prescribed before they carried out their offices (Exod. 30.18ff.). In the Christian cultus of East and West the most prominent rite of washing became that of foot washing. It took place on Maundy Thursday; and in early times was often regarded as a sacrament (*ERE* 5, 874ff.; T. Schäfer, 1956). A hand-washing rite is also customary for the priest before and during the Catholic Mass. Ritual washing, a substitute for total immersion, is itself represented by the rite of sprinkling. The Israelites were sprinkled in the temple with a special water of purification, made by mixing water with the ashes of a heifer (Num. 19.9). The holy water used for rites of sprinkling by the Roman Church is mixed with consecrated salt, another substance with sacred powʿer. It is consecrated, with exorcisms, on the Sunday. The Roman high office begins with the solemn sprinkling of the faithful. Often the latter are also sprinkled at the end of the Mass. The Roman Church uses holy water for consecrations and rites of blessing called Sacramentals (from their similarity to the sacraments), an example being the funeral rite. Catholics also sprinkle themselves with holy water as they enter and leave the church. Many even do so when they leave their home or return to it, morning and evening. They also sprinkle graves with it, and in many places farming people sprinkle their cattle. Besides simple washing and sprinkling there are more comprehensive rites of lustration (*ER* 5, 56f.). In the Greek Orthodox Church on the feast of Epiphany, the faithful are sprinkled with water that has been solemnly consecrated in a river, a spring, or, if need be, in a simple basin;

while in the Syrian Orthodox Church repeated sprinklings of holy water occur during the Whitsunday service with the congregation kneeling for prayer.

Alongside the rites of washing and purification which are repeated again and again, there is the once-for-all, initiatory rite of *baptism* (*ERE* 2, 367–411; *LThK* 9, 1311–23; *RGG* 6, 626–60; *ER* 7, 224ff.). Baptism, especially that of infants, has even less claim to be exclusively Christian than have other Christian rites. Germanic peoples, for instance, baptized their newly-born children in ice-cold rivers. Boniface required that those so baptized should be baptized again in the name of the triune God. Proselyte baptism has been customary among Jews from the earliest times down to the present day. As a rite, it comes before circumcision. For the baptist sects east and south-east of the Jordan, baptism was also an initiation rite. Amongst these sects was that of John the Baptist. The baptism of John possessed eschatological significance. Baptism as the seal of repentance effected the rescue of the one baptized from the wrath of God at the last judgement.

Christians, in company with Jews and Buddhists, have adopted a dialectical position with regard to washing and baptismal rites. They are conscious of the prophet's protest against relying upon the outward performance of lustration rites. Jeremiah declares: 'Though you wash yourself with lye and use much soap, the stain of your guilt is still before me, says the Lord . . .' (Jer. 2.22). Yet, despite this, so great was the significance of cultic purification that washing became a favourite image in religious language. To the *same* prophet comes this oracle (Jer. 4.14): 'O Jerusalem, wash your heart from wickedness, that you may be saved.' The Psalmist declares in a similar vein (51. 2.7): 'Wash me thoroughly from my iniquity, and cleanse me from my sin. Purge me with hyssop and I shall be clean. Wash me and I shall be whiter than snow.' The image of baptism is used eschatologically in the sermon of John the Baptist: the Messiah 'will baptize you with the Holy Spirit and with fire' (Matt. 3.11). Christ, too, describes his sacrificial death as a 'baptism' (Mark 10.38; Luke 12.50).

The rite of purification is taken over, but at the same time simplified, made more concentrated, and spiritualized. Baptism has become the foundation sacrament of Christianity, not primarily by reason of the sanctifying power of water and of washing, but because of its connection with the redeeming work of Christ. As Thomas Aquinas declared: 'All the virtue of the sacraments derives from the suffering of Christ.' The Johannine allegory of the water and blood which flowed from the wound in the side of the Crucified (John 19.34), is concerned with the fact that the sacraments arise out of the saving death of Christ. The baptism of John became the 'eschatological sacrament' of the early Christian Church (Cullmann, 1948; Manson, 1952) although Jesus, according to John's Gospel, did not baptize but allowed his disciples to do so (John 4.1f.). In the early Church, baptism was already seen in relation to the crucified and risen Jesus. It was performed in the name of Jesus. The name of Jesus was pronounced over the one being baptized (Acts 2.38). In Pauline Christianity baptism acquired further significance: baptism is the image of dying, being buried and rising again with Christ (Rom. 6.3ff.). Even vicarious baptism of those already dead was the rule in the early Church (1 Cor. 15.29), a practice which is continued in the Church of Jesus Christ of Latter Day Saints. Together with the interpretation given in terms of one's insertion into the history of salvation, there was added also the age-old, initiatory theme of regeneration, death and rebirth (Van der Leeuw, 1964). It became the bath of rebirth (Tit. 3.5). Mother Church gives birth to its children in the maternal womb of water. So runs the prayer for the Roman rite for the consecration of baptismal water on Easter Eve. Then, with the growth of the doctrine of original sin, baptism became a rite of purification not only from personal sin, but also from original sin.

The rite of baptism (*LThK* 9, 1007; Heiler, 1971) consisted originally of total immersion three times in water. Soon pouring or sprinkling (*RAC* 2, 185–94) came in as a substitute for immersion, particularly in the case of baptism of the sick. The Eastern Church, however, has retained the practice of baptism by immersion down to the present day. In the West, baptism by infusion (wetting or moistening) became more and more widespread in the medieval period. Yet early Lutheranism allowed a choice between immersion and pouring, as the Anglican Book of Common Prayer and the Roman Church also allow at the present day. Protestantism and Anglicanism were content for the most part to practise baptism by sprinkling, or even by wetting with fingers dipped in water. Baptists and Disciples of Christ (Churches of Christ), following the radical Reformers, have largely persisted with total immersion associated with believers' baptism. Their view of baptism has found support among the independent churches of Africa.

Water for baptism is specially consecrated in Eastern and Roman churches. In the latter, this takes place on Easter Eve and in the Vigil of Pentecost. The rites include the admixture of the oil used for the catechumens' confirmation and the immersion in the water of the Easter candle. In the old rite of Braga, in Portugal, a wooden cross was put into the water (see also above, Chapter 2). The substance of the water itself had to be specially prepared by this 'mystery' rite.

(5) Purification by blood

Blood is more powerful and effective than water (*HWDA* 1, 1434–63; *LThK* 2, 537–42; *RAC* 2, 459–73; *ERE* 2, 714–19; *ER* 2, 254ff.). Blood is the bearer of the soul or life, and is one of the most powerful means of driving away evil. The Israelites gained protection against the angel of death by smearing their doorposts with the blood of the passover lamb (Exod. 12.7). The leper was sprinkled with blood as part of healing and cleansing rites (Lev. 14.2ff.). The greatest rites which involved sprinkling with blood took place on the Day of Atonement. The blood of the sacrificial animals was sprinkled before the curtain of the holy of holies, on the horns of the altar for the offerings and over the ark of the covenant (Lev. 16.11ff.). The Israelites were not alone in the use of blood as a means of purification. It was also widespread in the West among the Germanic peoples as well as in the Mediterranean world, for instance in the mystery cult of Attis and Cybele. In the *taurobolium* and *criobolium* rites of the latter, the initiate was purified and reborn by the blood of a steer or a ram.

Purification by blood was already subject to criticism in antiquity and doubt was cast on its effectiveness. In Christianity, the New Testament revelation of salvation in Christ was held to have done away with the blood rites of the old covenant. But the *blood of Christ* (*RGG* 1, 1329f.; *ThWNT* 1, 171ff.) becomes one of the most important images in the New Testament doctrine of redemption. According to the Gospels, Jesus himself represented his sacrificial death, through the emptying of the cup, as the blood of the new covenant poured out for many (Mark. 14.24). These words said over the cup, however, present us with a difficult problem. Perhaps it is death by stoning that is meant, such as Stephen the first martyr had to endure. Perhaps the scene of the Last Supper has been reconstructed to fit in with the Pauline view of salvation. In any case, redemptive and saving power are once again being attributed to blood, the blood of Christ, as the Pauline and deutero-Pauline writings make clear.

The blood of Christ is an expiation (Rom. 3.25). Through this blood mankind has been made righteous and is protected from the wrath of God (Rom. 5.9). Reconciliation through Christ's blood is particularly emphasized in the deutero-Pauline letters, especially Ephesians and Colossians. The last mentioned refers to the 'peace through the blood of his cross' (Col. 1.20). Also in the First Epistle of Peter, which reflects the spirit of Pauline thought, in the First Epistle of John and in the Apocalypse, redemption is seen as the result of the blood of Christ: 'The blood of Jesus Christ makes us free from all sin' (1 John 1.7). The redeemed in heaven have 'their clothes made white in the blood of the Lamb' (Rev. 7.14). The most comprehensive theology of blood, however, is that contained in the Epistle to the Hebrews, which also at the same time gives the greatest degree of spiritualization to the image of the blood of redemption:

> He entered once for all into the Holy Place, taking not the blood of goats and calves but his own blood, thus securing an eternal redemption. For if the sprinkling of defiled persons with the blood of goats and bulls and with the ashes of a heifer sanctifies for the purification of the flesh, how much more shall the blood of Christ, who through the eternal Spirit offered himself without blemish to God, purify your conscience from dead works ... (9. 12–14).

The theology of blood made itself at home in Christianity, encouraged by the increasing 'realism' in which the eucharistic wine was identified with the blood of Christ. Through the mysticism of Bernard of Clairvaux which was centred on the suffering and death of Jesus, a meditation arose on the blood of Christ, represented in the hymn attributed to him, 'Hail, O head covered with blood'. Blood is often seen to trickle down medieval crucifixes. Angels catch in chalices the blood which gushes out of Christ's body. Theological speculation attributed to the blood of Christ – even to the smallest drop – the power to blot out sins.

The hymn of the cross by Venantius Fortunatus and the communion hymn *Adoro te* attributed to Thomas Aquinas have entered into the common heritage of Western Christianity. Fortunatus' hymn contains these lines:

> From His patient body pierced
> Blood and water streaming fall:
> Earth and sea and stars and mankind
> By that stream are cleansed all.
>
> (*CH* 108, v. 3)

In the hymn 'Thee we adore' (*CH* 319, v. 3), we find these lines: 'Fountain of goodness [originally: pious pelican, see above, Chapter 2] Jesus, Lord and God,/Cleanse us, unclean with thy most cleansing blood.' There arose even a special festival of the 'Precious Blood of Christ'. It was extended to the whole Latin Church in 1849 by Pius IX. Brotherhoods and companies were founded by the Order of the Most Precious Blood. Bernard's mysticism of the passion was revived in pietism. William Cowper's eighteenth-century English equivalent was: 'There is a fountain filled with blood/Drawn from Immanuel's veins' (*CH* 692). From Moody and Sankey in the nineteenth century we have: 'What can wash away my stain?/Nothing but the blood of Jesus!' (Sankey, 183). There is a link between the mystical-pietist-evangelical stress on the blood of Christ or his wounds, including theological speculation concerning his blood's atoning power, and the age-old, traditional, view of blood as apotropaic, purifying and strengthening. It is true that blood has become the symbol of the self-sacrifice, obedience and self-giving of the Redeemer on the cross. But the image of blood would never have been applied to all this, nor would it have acquired such fascination and power if the whole of antiquity had not been permeated by faith in the mysterious, numinous power of real blood. The Salvation Army hymn, with its stirring march tune, gives tangible proof of the connection between the idea of faith in the blood and that of blood as a symbol of life: 'There is power, victorious power/In the blood of our Lord Jesus Christ.'

The reaction of liberal theology against the blood theology of pietistic orthodoxy is understandable, but there are three considerations to be borne in mind: what is involved is a symbol or image. It is a matter of debate whether Christ did in fact shed blood on the cross since the loss of blood during crucifixion is slight and death usually supervenes from other causes than through blood loss. Again, it should be recalled that the image of blood was used relatively sparingly in the early Church; in the message of the Synoptic and Johannine Jesus it appears nowhere at all; and though it is a feature of Pauline and deutero-Pauline writings, and the Epistle to the Hebrews, the latter makes quite clear the allegorical or symbolic character of the image. Finally, other images are employed to interpret the sacrificial death of Christ, including that of buying free from servitude to Satan (manumission).

(6) Mortification of the flesh

Asceticism (*ERE* 2, 63–111 and 225–35; *RAC* 1, 749–95; *LThK* 1, 928ff.; O.

Chadwick, 1958; *ER* 10, 112ff.) is also a rite of purification, with many forms, including vigils (refraining from sleep), fasting, flagellation and even sacred suicide (i.e. refraining from further living). Sleep and the night can be a source of pollution and danger. In the Roman Breviary, the Matins hymn for Monday had these words: 'So each transgression of the night/Be purged by thee, celestial light.' Refraining from sleep has long been considered necessary for those preparing for cultic activity. The Jewish high priest had to keep watch before the Day of Atonement. Jesus was accustomed to spending the night awake (Luke 6.12). Paul and Silas prayed to God and sang praises at midnight (Acts 16.25). Nocturnal services and vigils (*LThK* 10, 606f.) were customary in the early Church. Nocturnal services took place in the catacombs on the anniversary of the martyr's death; and nocturnal convocations were held on fast days or Station days, especially Wednesday and Friday. Monks and ascetics of the fourth century held daily vigils. Before major festivals nocturnal services were held. Easter night was even called the 'Mother of vigils' by Augustine, while the service for the dead was a 'vigil-though-the-night'. Later the vigil was moved to the evening before the festival (except for Easter) and the day before became known as Vigil. In Western monasticism the vigil was called *Matutin* (later *matins*) already in Benedict's day. The purely cultic-ascetic waking was spiritualized through Jesus' warning to 'watch', 'keep awake and pray' (Mark 13. 35,37; 14.38) and the warning of Paul: 'Let us not sleep, as others do, but let us keep awake and be sober' (1 Thess. 5.6; 1 Pet. 5.8). Clement of Alexandria considered that one should often get up from one's bed during the night and give praise to God. For they are blessed who watch for the Lord and make themselves like the angels who are called the watchers.

Refraining from eating (*ERE* 5, 759–65; 12, 618ff.; *RGG* 2, 881ff.; *HWDA* 2, 1234–43; *LThK* 4, 31ff.; Gandhi, 1944; *ER* 5, 286ff.) like the vigil, is a powerful form of purification. With fasting we have to distinguish between complete fasting and abstaining from particular foods and drinks, especially meat, fish and wine. Fasting has apotropaic power: its purpose is to drive away harmful powers of the dead penetrating into one's person: the spirits of the dead hover around the house and may poison the food. Fasting by the pregnant woman or both parents serves to protect the child from demonic powers. Abstaining from flesh was influenced by the fear of the harm the soul of the animal could do to those who ate the meat. Fasting, however, also served as a means of acquiring power, a powerful will, for example, as in the case of warriors, hunters and fishermen. The relatives remaining behind would also support them through fasting. Fasting is in addition a means of obtaining visions, ecstatic experiences and the gift of prophecy. It is a means of overcoming sterility and barrenness. It is, above all, necessary in preparing for cultic activities, circumcision and initiation rites, sacred dances, sacrifices and especially rites of communion.

These features are characteristic of a wide range of religions. Apart from traditional or ethnic religions, including those of the Greco-Roman world, fasting is found very widely practised in Jainism, Buddhism and the religion of Gandhi, Hinduism. Gandhi repeatedly practised the Hindu penitential fast over the acts of violence of his followers or his opponents. Both Islam and

Christianity were influenced by Jewish practices of fasting (Strack and Billerbeck, 1928). The festival of Purim includes a fast day and a day of free celebration and rejoicing. Special fasts were ordered in times of public crisis. Thus the prophet Jonah made the following demand in Nineveh: 'Let neither man nor beast, herd nor flock, taste anything; let them not feed, or drink water' (Jonah 3.7). In addition to such public fasts, it was open to individuals to fast privately, usually twice a week. Jesus fasted forty days and nights (Matt. 4.2ff.) following the example of Moses and Elijah (Exod. 34.28; 1 Kings 19.8). The motif of apotropaic fasting emerges clearly in the words of Jesus (according to some manuscripts): 'This kind (of unclean spirit) cannot be driven out by anything but prayer *and fasting*' (Mark 9.29).

In early Christianity, common fasting accompanies secret fasting. The *Didache* (8.1) prescribes fasting on Wednesday and Friday, clearly distinct from the Jewish Mondays and Thursdays. In the West, Saturday was added and the Wednesday disappeared. The Latin Christians called the fast 'station' because the Christian, like the Roman soldier, was at his post against the enemy (Satan). In the Eastern Church, and in the West, fasting is recommended before one receives the sacrament: before baptism, communion and ordination. In the last mentioned, both the ordained and the officiant are to fast. In the Eastern Church four periods of fasting emerged: the forty-day fast before Easter, first instituted by the Council of Nicaea (in 325); another after Easter, the 'apostles' fast', lasting from the first Sunday after Pentecost until the feast of Peter and Paul (on 29th June); before Christmas (14 November to 25 December). To these three times, also found in the Celtic Church, a fourth was added: the Marian fast from 1 to 15 August: before the feast of Mary's Assumption into heaven. Originally, complete abstinence until sundown was required during this period. During the forty-day fast only one meal a day was taken, and that meal was of dry food. No drinks were allowed. In the Eastern Church these rules are still for the most part strictly observed. The eating of butter was allowed in the week before the forty-day fast, thus easing the transition from normal eating to fasting. The West observes only the major fast. The Advent fast fell into neglect. Instead of the long Advent fast, four seasonal fasts were observed called Ember, including the Marian fast, referred to above, which also had spread to the West. These fasts took place in the week of Pentecost, in the third week of September, and in the third week of Advent. There were in addition vigil fasts on the days before major feasts. The ordinances for fasting have in recent days been greatly relaxed in the Western Church.

Fasting was employed above all as a means of doing penance. Year-long fasting, or abstinence, was imposed upon penitents for especially grave sins. Such penitential fasting was considered to be a form of penitential punishment. It was given for medical and pedagogical reasons in the Eastern Church; and in the Western Church served to make up for what had been done wrong (*satisfaction*). Alongside the prescribed fasts were the voluntary fasts which constituted a means of sanctification. The legends of the saints are full of extended fasts. The pattern of saintliness depicted in the saints in the Roman

Breviary includes the ideal of fasting to the point of emaciation. The Reformation led to the widespread abolition of fast days. Yet Luther himself commended fasting before the major festivals (vigil fasts), also the Friday fast and the pre-communion fast.

There has been criticism of fasting especially in Zoroastrianism and Judaism. Jeremiah received the oracle of Yahweh: 'Though they fast, I will not hear their cry' (Jer. 14.12). Jesus opposes fasting as a form of self-display (Matt. 6.16ff.). In the presence of their master, his disciples, who are compared by Jesus to wedding guests, should not be fasting (Mark 2.19ff.). Luther fought against the concept of fasting for the sake of merit. Fasting, he held, cannot help a person towards the forgiveness of his sins. Yet there are important psychological effects from fasting in the form of control of one's mental faculties, the calming of the passions, the gaining of freedom for prayer and for sacrificial surrender to the Deity, the capacity for spiritual vision and illumination. Fasting before major festivals continues to be of importance for the believer himself to appropriate and experience the secrets of salvation.

Fasting has also had social significance in Christianity as in other religions, including Islam (*ER* 13, 90ff.): it has made it possible for man to bring God a tithe of his time, the tenth of the year (see also above, Chapter 3). That which has been saved up through fasting may be placed at the service of one's neighbour, as Leo I long ago recognized. Nathan Söderblom recommended just after the First World War that only bread and tea be taken on a Friday and that the savings be used to support the starving in the Russian civil war. In more recent years many similar acts of fasting and abstinence have been undertaken, especially by young people, both in order to achieve simplification of life-style and in order to place the results of 'sponsored' activities at the service of their neighbours in need.

The most severe form of the fast is that 'unto death'. It is known in Hinduism chiefly in the form practised by Gandhi. Less well known is that of the dissident Cathars of medieval Europe whose rite of *endura* involved a happy fasting to death (Lambert, 1977).

Parallel to fasting as an ascetic rite goes flagellation, or the subduing of the body and its passions by beating or devices which cause discomfort and pain. Voluntary flagellation, in a state of exalted devotion, is a common phenomenon in the history of religions, in the traditional cults such as those of West Africa, in the Greco-Roman world and in Shi'ite Islam at the festival of Muharram.

Involuntary corrective flagellation was practised in the early Church and later on in the mission field. Voluntary flagellation, which was known in early Christian monasticism, became widespread among clerical and lay people in medieval Europe. Taking their authority from Paul's words: 'I pommel my body and subdue it' (1 Cor. 9.27), they would sing hymns and flagellate themselves. Flagellation was regarded as a substitute for the recitation of the 'penitential psalms' (Pss. 6, 31, 37, 50, 101, 129 and 142) in expressing sorrow and the desire for pardon. A ceremony of collective flagellation took place in monastic houses every Friday after confession. In the wandering flagellant communities was an eschatological motif of expecting God's punishment at an imminent judgement day. The Black Death in the fourteenth century led to their revival. Eventually, extreme forms were condemned by several Popes and the Council of Constance (1417), and they were suppressed by the Inquisition. But flagellation has nevertheless continued to the present day, in Latin countries particularly, and among brotherhoods and orders, such as *Opus Dei*.

The most extreme form of flagellation is sacred suicide (*ER* 14, 125ff.) such as that practised by the Donatist Christians of North Africa in the fourth and fifth centuries (Frend, 1952; Büttner, 1959). In a state of exaltation, a group of *circumcellions* ('those who live around the shrine') would hurl themselves over a cliff. The place where they fell to their death would be commemorated by specially inscribed stones. The mass suicide of 383 members of the James Jones cult (R. Howes, 1982; Kilduff, 1978) in Guyana in 1978 had the eschatological motif of some of the medieval flagellants. It offered also a parallel to the fast-unto-death.

(7) Chastity and celibacy

Abstaining from sexual intercourse, or chastity (*ERE* 3, 474–503; *HWDA* 4, 1291–303; *RGG* 3, 753ff.; 1259ff.; *ER* 6, 144ff.), is a final form of purification to be considered. Sexuality has been especially associated with forms of purification in the world's religions (Parrinder, 1980). In the Latin *castus* from which the word 'chastity' is derived, there is the negative connotation of doing without or refraining from. It is an age-old idea that sexuality 'pollutes', not perhaps in the modern hygienic sense, but in that of being filled with dangerous powers and demonic forces. Conjointly with the fear of the demonic in sexual life, goes the sense of awe at the mysterious power of generation and life which finds expression in phallic rites and those of sexual union with the Deity (see below, Chapter 7). But this sacred power of the sexual comes up against that of the cultus.

Chastity is prescribed for priests and other participants in the cultus before all ritual action. Of particular importance is refraining from sex before initiation rites. The requirement of celibacy for the priesthood is especially strict. During their period of service in the temple at Jerusalem, priests on duty had to live apart from their wives, an example being Zacharias (Luke 1.23). This requirement of the ancient temple cult was taken over by the Christian Church. Up to the present day, the Eastern Church requires its married priests to remain chaste on the night before the celebration of the liturgy. In individual churches there is also a set period after the service during which chastity is enjoined. In the Middle Ages there was a period of chastity extending for some days before and after a communion which the laity had to observe in the same way. (This prescription has now been relaxed in the Roman Church.) Chastity was required of the faithful during 'sacred times', especially during a time of fasting. Paul already commended temporary abstention from sex to married people for the purpose of fasting and prayer (1 Cor. 7.5).

Permanent celibacy (*ERE* 3, 271ff.) was already required of certain priests and priestesses in antiquity. Vestal virgins served under this rule for thirty years, after which they were free to marry. Their chastity ensured the well-being of the state whose sacred fire they watched over, much as the woman watches over the domestic hearth. The breaching of the rule of chastity was seen as a fearful sacrilege.

Against this background it is not surprising that from the earliest times Christians have held celibacy in high regard. Jesus himself appears to have regarded it as a rare phenomenon. 'Not all men can receive this precept. There are eunuchs who have made themselves eunuchs for the sake of the kingdom of heaven' (Matt. 19.11–12). But, despite this, celibacy was soon exalted above marriage. It is true that the requirement of celibacy for all those baptized did not prevail among the main body of Christians, even though all held in high regard the unmarried, celibates, ascetics and widows. Throughout, the traditional motif was operative, according to which the sexual pollutes or makes impure. 'It is these who have not defiled themselves with women, for they are chaste; it is these who follow the Lamb wherever he goes' (Rev. 14.4). Besides ideas of pollution and power, there is a second motif: that celibacy makes possible the undivided surrender to God (1 Cor. 7.32). Here Christ himself figures as the archetype of virginity. Under the influence of this view, Mary was changed from being the Galilean mother of a large family into the eternal virgin whom her parents, acting on a vow, had consecrated to service as a temple virgin (*Protevangelium* of James). The early Christian ascetics, men and women, were the forerunners of the monks and nuns. They still lived together, very frequently, but in spiritual wedlock (*ERE* 1, 177ff.). Throughout early Christian literature there resounds a paean of praise to virginity. Chrysostom, for instance, wrote that virginity is the better way to the degree that the steersman is better than the ordinary seaman, the commander is better than the soldiers, heaven is better than the earth and angels are better than men.

Despite the high value attached to celibacy, deacons, priests and bishops in the Eastern Church, and initially also in the Western Church, were not compelled to stay permanently unmarried (Lea, 1907). Up to the seventh century there were married bishops in the East while priests are still today allowed to marry. Gregory of Nazianzus was the son of a bishop and a saintly mother, Nonna. At the Council of Nicaea a celibate bishop, Paphnutius, energetically opposed the introduction of compulsory celibacy for priests. Only the second marriage was forbidden there. It was not until Trullanum (692) that this was extended to priestly marriage in general.

The Latin Church, which extolled a greater degree of asceticism, compelled its clergy early on to become celibate. The Synod of Elvira (300) called for lifelong celibacy in all deacons, priests and bishops after ordination, under pain of deposition. The cause of this remarkable difference between East and West lies in the fact that the Western Church early on introduced the *daily* celebration of the Eucharist. This made it necessary for complete celibacy throughout the week, and not just a temporary one before the Sunday observance. The demand for celibacy in the West was also reinforced by Augustine's theory that original sin was transmitted by the act of procreation. Sexual union was thus disfigured with the blemish of impurity from which he who celebrates the holy mysteries must keep himself free. Pope Siricius (384–99) referring to Leviticus: 'Consecrate yourselves . . . and be holy' (20.7), declared that Christ, the bridegroom of his Church, wanted to find it pure and spotless at his return. All priests and Levites were bound to preserve the continence and chastity under an eternal divine law. Leo I (440–46) even forbade 'carnal cohabitation' to subdeacons. Such laws, however, were repeatedly broken in the West. Resistance to the law of celibacy was especially strong in Germanic lands. The Goths who had received the faith from the Eastern Church, and the other Germanic peoples who had received it from them, knew nothing of priestly or episcopal celibacy. Numerous conciliar and papal decrees sought vainly to impose it. Even prohibiting married priests' attendance at services proved fruitless. Finally Gregory VII (1037–85) decided to act ruthlessly. He ordered the separation of all married priests from their wives. Even then celibacy prevailed with difficulty and never completely. In Iceland and northern Sweden, priestly marriage maintained itself up to the Reformation when it received fresh sanction to continue. In other countries secret marriage often took the place of the public one. Only after the Council of Trent – which felt compelled to make priestly celibacy the norm against Protestant married priests – was the requirement of celibacy more widely observed, without, however, its succeeding in eliminating concubinage altogether. Rome now began to urge celibacy upon the uniate Eastern Churches, beginning with the Church of the Mar Thoma Christians in South India. One motive of the Curia had to do with ecclesiastical politics: a celibate clergy appeared to be more independent of local princes and thus a more effective instrument of papal policies.

Celibacy is rooted in large measure in a traditional religious conceptual world in which the sexual is seen as pollution and he who has to do with the sacred must remain *pure*. Modern biology has undermined this conception and sees sexuality as a natural function, a part, a piece of the cosmic harmony, as something willed by God, as it was already manifest in the Chinese *Weltanschauung* where *Yang* and *Yin*, the male and the female are the two basic cosmic principles. In the modern world the demand for celibacy is no longer motivated by the idea of the pollution of sexual life and its association with the transmission of original sin. Instead, Catholics base their concern for celibacy upon the undivided *self-giving* of man to God and his fellows. Thomas Aquinas pioneered this view when he characterized the 'evangelical counsels' (poverty, chastity, and obedience) as the instrument of perfection. The celibate was able to give himself to God and his fellow-men without other human bonding. The energies which are required for raising a family are freed for religious and moral purposes. There is truth in this justification. There have been creative spirits in every age who have refrained from marriage on account of their calling. Examples include Mahavira and Gautama Buddha in India, John the Baptist,

Jesus and Paul, Origen, Basil of Caesarea, Augustine, and countless church teachers and saints, men and women; also Protestant mystics such as William Law and Gerhard Tersteegen; philosophers including Descartes, Kant and Kierkegaard; artists, such as Michelangelo and Raphael, and musicians such as Beethoven and Brahms. In this connection there ought not to be forgotten the innumerable *castrati*, the ethereal beauty of whose voices filled the churches and cathedrals of Western Europe over many centuries, and at least down to the time of Haydn, to whom it was suggested that he might retain his place in the cathedral choir in Vienna if he were to undergo this operation: he refused, and went (Geiringer, 1947, 34f.). One should also not forget the 'ordinary' unmarried men and women, whose lives have been a source of enrichment to others such that these rise up and call them blessed.

A second motive, in addition to undivided self-giving, is the polarity of church life, made up of a 'domestic' pole and an 'heroic' pole which support and complement each other (T. S. Eliot, 1974). The requirement for sexual abstinence within marriage can only be fulfilled if the celibate and sacrificial life of the priest provides married people with a living example. The history of Protestantism shows that without celibacy and monasticism there is a danger that Christianity can become too bourgeois and respectable. The third motive for the retention of celibacy is the age-old one of church politics: the freedom of the Church over against the state, the independence of the clergy as a militia of Christ. Against this must be set the need to provide sufficient priests in areas such as Africa where not enough celibate candidates are forthcoming.

6

Christian Sacred Action
2: Sacrifice

(1) The gift sacrifice

Celibacy and monasticism are forms of self-surrender and abstinence. Offered
to the Deity they are forms of *sacrifice* (Hubert, 1964; E. O. James, 1933;
*ERE*11, 1ff.; *RGG* 4, 1637ff.; Kristensen, 458ff.; Van der Leeuw, 1964;
Burkert, 1972; *ER* 12, 544ff.). Sacrifice is a sacred action. One 'makes' a
sacrifice. The object sacrificed, the person or persons offering sacrifice, the
transactional or communicational character of the action are all of significance.
The traditional *gift sacrifice* (*ERE* 6, 197ff.; Mauss, 1954; *ER* 5, 552ff.) places
the emphasis in addition on the one to whom the sacrifice is made. Gifts are
made to the Deity partly as a recognition of the latter's originating power e.g. to
make things grow; partly to make glad, win over, or ensure continued favours,
and partly to turn away displeasure by expiation. The sacrifice of the *first-fruits*
(*ERE* 6, 41ff.; *LThK* 3, 1054f.) is important in this context. In the early
Israelite narrative of the sacrifice made by Cain and Abel (Gen. 4.3f.), Abel as a
shepherd brings the first-born of his herds; Cain as a farmer, the first-fruits of
this crops. The offering is accompanied by a prayer–commentary ('I bring this
to you . . .'). It signifies dependence and recognition that the powers of growth
and fertility are sacred and beyond man's reach. Man possesses nothing
inherently, but gives back a small part as a token that all belongs to the Deity
and comes from his hand. Thanks and praise are also important motifs. But
there is the further thought of ensuring continued giving by the sacrifice of a
part of what has been received. The thought of the blessing being continued is
reflected in the practice of leaving the *last sheaf* (*HWDA* 2, 950ff.) to stand in
the field to ensure subsequent harvests.

The first-fruits sacrifice is found particularly in Israelite religion (*HWDA* 2,
1976ff.; *RGG* 2, 608ff.) whence it passes into Christianity. 'The firstfruits of
your ground you shall bring unto the house of the Lord your God' (Exod.
23.19). 'All the firstling males that are born of your herd and flock you shall
consecrate to the Lord your God' (Deut. 15.19). In Semitic religion the first-
born son was regarded as belonging to the Deity. This idea lay behind the
sacrifice of children in Canaan and elsewhere. It was however replaced by the
sacrifice of animals. In Israelite religion a lamb or (for the poor) two turtle
doves served as a substitute (Lev. 12.6ff.). The sacrifice of the first-born is
retained in the New Testament as a central image. Christ has become 'the
firstfruits of those who have fallen asleep' (1 Cor. 15.20). Christians have the
'firstfruits of the Spirit' (Rom. 8.23), are the 'firstfruits of his creatures' (James
1.18); chaste souls are the 'firstfruits for God and the Lamb' (Rev. 14.4). The

liturgy of the Catholic Apostolic Church, which is based on those of the Eastern, Roman and Anglican Churches, describes the bread and wine of the Eucharist as 'the firstfruits of our possessions'.

The gift and food sacrifice differs from the sacrifice of praise and thanksgiving. Yahweh orders the Israelites not to 'appear before me empty handed' (Exod. 23.15). Everything valuable to man is brought to the Deity: animals, fruit, cakes, drinks, flowers, ornaments, and weapons (*ER* 8, 537ff.). Underlying the gift sacrifice is: I give in order that thou mayest be able to give. The gift binds and places the recipient under an obligation. It binds giver and recipient together. Gift sacrifice sets up a state of friendship between giver and receiver; both have a share in the power that is given.

The problem of how the sacrifice gets to be possessed and enjoyed by the Deity is only secondary. The fruits left standing rot away; springs, rivers, lakes, swallow up their sacrifices; the sacrifices of the earth deity rot in the ground. In the case of the 'sacrifice of the whole' (*holocautōma*) the sacrifices are burnt; the fire serves as the means by which the sacrifice is brought to the deity.

The relationship set up between man and the Deity by gift-giving is very different from that between men themselves. The Deity is infinitely more sacred, more unknowable and more powerful than man. The Deity may decide not to give the people offering the sacrifice what they are asking. So there is no simple exchange of goods and services. The gift is rather equivalent to the offering of oneself. The offering of a gift is to offer a part of oneself. To accept a gift is to accept the giver, the person that accompanies the gift. Early Christian converts in West Africa used to rub their offering over their bodies before handing it over, as a sign that they were giving themselves in the same act, a practice which was discouraged as 'unchristian' by the mission authorities.

Closely related to sacrifice as a form of gift-giving is the notion of communication between man and the Deity and this world and the spirit world. The French sociologists Hubert and Mauss, in their important study of sacrifice (Hubert, 1964), concluded that what was common to all sacrifice was the attempt to establish communication between man and the Deity through an intermediary. Through the act of consecration the victim becomes an intermediary between the sacrificer and the Deity. Through being sacrificed, the victim opens up a channel of communication between the profane world of men and the world of the spirit. Through this channel of communication, sacred power is able to flow from the Deity to the sacrificer.

(2) The offering of incense

Of the many forms of sacrifice, one which gained entry into Christianity is the offering of incense (Atchley, 1909; *NDLW* 265f.; Nielson, 1986; *ER* 7, 161ff.; see also Chapter 5, above). The incense sacrifice had a cosmic significance in the tobacco smoking of the Ojibwa Indians, for whom it served not only as an entry into states of trance; for the smoke, sent in all directions to the divine beings, was a sacred action which repeated the myth of the creation of the world through the tobacco smoking of the Creator (W. Schmidt, 1926). In the religions of antiquity the pleasant smell of the sacrifice was offered to the Deity. The Greeks and Romans had a special incense altar near the image of the Deity. As among the Canaanites, incense was offered in the temple of Yahweh at Jerusalem. It was offered every day, morning and evening, on the altar of the smoke offerings. Every food sacrifice was accompanied by incense and laid on the show-bread. The priestly codex gives precise details for the preparation of the incense (Exod. 30.7f. and 34ff.).

Incense became spiritualized as an image. The Psalmist prays: 'Let my prayer be counted as incense before thee' (Ps. 141.2). This tendency is continued in the New Testament (*ThWNT* 2, 808ff.) where the Apocalyptist interprets as the prayer of the saints the golden bowls full of incense in the hands of the twenty-four elders and the incense in the angel's golden censer (Rev. 5.8; 8.3f.). Paul says: 'We are the aroma of Christ to God' (Eph. 5.2). At the same time, early Christianity nursed an antipathy towards the use of incense itself. The strewing of incense before Roman traditional deities was regarded as evidence of falling away from Christ. Christians who performed this rite, often at the request of Roman officials, were known as *thurificati* (those who have burned incense). Yet, even so, it was not possible to prevent some Christians using incense for funeral rites; and after the triumph of Christianity over the traditional cults, incense even gained entry into Christian services of worship. From the fourth century onwards, vessels of incense were placed before altars and the tombs of martyrs, first of all in the Church of the Holy Sepulchre at Jerusalem, then in the great basilicas of the West, and later even before images and icons of the saints.

The censing of the altar and of the church at the beginning of the service is already mentioned by Dionysius the Areopagite in the fifth century. In the West, incense was employed for the rite of the Mass later than it was in the East. In an early Roman liturgy it served for the veneration of the book of the Gospels. Thereafter it enjoyed ever wider use. In the solemn Roman Mass a comprehensive censing of the altar takes place at the beginning of the offertory. Incense accompanies acts of consecration of churches and cultic worship of the sacrament (before the sacramental blessing and during processions). In Catholic liturgies, the early threefold significance of incense lives on: it is apotropaic; it brings a sacrificial offering; and it offers a symbolic image for prayer, inward sacrificial self-giving and the good works which flow from love. In the Church of England the use of incense was common during the seventeenth century and especially in the later nineteenth century and onwards under the influence of the Tractarian movement. It appears in Reformed traditions as a literary image.

(3) Blood sacrifice and human sacrifice

Blood sacrifice (*ERE* 4, 649–671) is found in most religions and even today in Africa, Latin America and parts of Asia, including India. In the sin offering of the Old Testament temple cult, the sprinkling of blood was the decisive act.

'The priest shall dip his finger in the blood and sprinkle part of the blood seven times before the Lord in front of the veil of the sanctuary, and the priest shall put some of the blood on the horns of the altar of fragrant incense before the Lord which is in the tent of meeting, and the rest of the blood of the bull he shall pour out at the base of the altar of burnt offering' (Lev. 4.6f.). A special sprinkling of blood took place on the Day of Atonement. The high priest brought the blood of the he-goat behind the curtain and besprinkled the sacred tabernacle; 'Thus he shall make atonement for the holy place, because of the uncleannesses of the people of Israel, and because of their transgressions, all their sins' (Lev. 16.15f.). In these passages, the close connection between the blood sacrifice and rites of purification is easily discernible. The blood sacrifice serves to still divine wrath and to bring about divine reconciliation; and at the same time to drive away the dangerous powers that have accumulated in the holy of holies. But the idea of substitution of the human by the sacrificial animal is also apparent. Apart from the special potency of the blood, the death of the victim was important because death is the entry into another, more sacred realm. When the consecrated victim is killed, it undergoes a transition from the ordinary, profane world to the sacred realm to which it belongs in essence. Such considerations do not belong to remote antiquity for some Christians. Megas (cited by Burkert, 1972, 16) describes a Greek Orthodox rite in Cappadocia by no means untypical of parts of the Eastern Church: a stone altar for the sacrifice stands in the chapel of the most holy. On it incense is burnt and when the candles have been lit, prayers are said and the stone is covered with a wreath. Then the officiant takes the animal, a sheep or goat, and brings it into the chapel. He leads it three times round the altar. Children throw grass and flowers on it. Then the owner of the animal makes the sign of the cross with the knife three times and kills the animal to the accompaniment of words of prayer, during which time the priest (*popē*) stands at the main altar. The blood has to be sprinkled over the stone. Then follows the dividing up of the animal for the communal meal, the *popē* receiving those parts of the animal assigned to priests of antiquity. It must be recognized, however, that, although the forms of the ancient blood sacrifice have been preserved, an inner transformation has taken place in the meaning of the rite, such as we find also in the ritual slaughter of the sheep or goats at the Islamic *Id-al-Adhan*. The purpose of the rite has become the communal meal shared with the poor and needy.

Human sacrifice (*ERE* 6, 840–67; *HWDA* 6, 156–74; *RGG* 4, 867f.; Kristensen, 1960; *ER* 6, 515ff.) has been widespread in the history of religions. Sometimes *anthropophagy* (Arens, 1979) has been seen as human sacrifice, whereas it concerns rather the appropriation of the sacred substance of those (such as prisoners of war) who are, in principle, already part of a sacred world. Human sacrifice was rather seen as a communication to the nature deities, the sun, vegetation, in the case of the traditional religions of Mexico and Peru, by which these deities were filled with new power. Similarly in Germanic religion, humans were offered at the spring and autumn equinoxes to strengthen the natural processes of growth. *Foundation sacrifices* (*ERE* 6, 109ff.; *HWDA* 1,

962ff.; *RGG* 1, 935; *ER* 5, 395ff.; see also above, in Chapter 3) also involved human offerings. Living persons as well as those immolated in a special rite were buried under, or in, the foundations of walls of buildings, fortresses or bridges in Japan, in Canaan, and among the Celts and Germans. Even in the Middle Ages, children are known to have been walled up at the laying of the foundation stone of fortresses, city walls and bridges.

Human sacrifices have a strongly propitiatory function. Particularly in times of disaster and national need, the wrath of the deity or deities must be assuaged. There is a sense that this wrath is increased by repeated transgressions until only a human sacrifice can bring about the required satisfaction. Children and young women possessed a concentration of sacred power which made them especially preferred as offerings. Child sacrifices were early on practised in western Semitic religions. Even in Israel this cult of Moloch (*RGG* 4, 1089f.) was carried on. At Topheth the cult place in the valley Ben Hinnom, near Jerusalem, children were sacrificed to the Deity: first they were killed, then laid in the arms of the divine image, whence they slid down into a pit of fire (Jer. 2.23; 19.5ff.; Ezek. 23.37).

Prisoners of war have already been mentioned in connection with anthropophagy. Taken prisoner in the sacred rite of warfare, their physical death simply actualized their sacred status. In early Israel the spoils of war belonged to Yahweh. Articles of value had to be destroyed or placed in the temple. They were *herem*, under the ban by virtue of their sacredness (*harem*). Samuel punished King Saul for disregarding this command of Yahweh. Saul had spared the Amalekite king, Agag. So Samuel himself undertook the dispatching of the king (1 Sam. 15). The Germanic peoples held similar views regarding the sacrifice of prisoners of war. In Mexico, mock wars were staged so that the participants could obtain prisoners for sacrifices. In West Africa, expeditions were made to obtain slaves for the European export trade (Inikori, 1982); and it is difficult to exclude the possibility of a sacrificial motive.

Amongst various types of sacred person who were offered, or offered themselves in sacrifice, we may mention briefly the sacrifice of the king (Frazer, 1922, 157ff.; *Sacral Kingship*, 1959), where in times of national misfortune or a threatened decline of his natural powers, it was necessary to renew the life-force of the nation by this means. Similarly, many associated with him (*HWDA* 3, 1082–103) were sent to accompany him to the spirit world, either by voluntary suicide, or being placed in the grave with the deceased. The burial of royal slaves with their deceased masters was practised in West Africa; while in India, the voluntary immolation of widows (*satī*) was a similar form of sacrifice for the dead. In Japan, *junshi* (the voluntary death of the vassal at the death of his lord) was similarly observed. Perhaps the most dramatic form of human self-sacrifice was the sacred action of *devotio* (Versnel, 1980; Eliade, 1979, 224ff., citing Livy) performed by a Roman commander when his army was in danger of being defeated. Having solemnly devoted the army to Di Manes and Earth (*Tellus*), Decius (*c.* 340 BC) plunged into the thick of the enemy and fell beneath a hail of missiles. His troops, set free from 'religious fears', pressed on to victory. Through Decius' expiatory sacrifice, the wrath of the deities was stilled.

(4) Substitute sacrifice

The loss of such valuable men and also animals led, in the various religious traditions at varying times, to reforms in human and blood sacrifices in the direction of *substitute sacrifices* (*HWDA* 2, 964–74). West African archives contain many instances where the traditional authorities in the nineteenth century agree to substitute sacrifices. At first, human sacrifice was replaced by the offering of an animal. The sacrifice of Isaac by Abraham represents a mythological reflex of this transition; a ram takes the place of the first-born son (Gen. 22). Greek, Roman, German and Chinese accounts report similar substitutions of humans by a ram, a hind, a human figure of metal, clay or straw. Dolls serve as substitutes for children. At bottom is the thought that with sacrifices the appearance counts as much as the real thing.

A prominent form of the substitute sacrifice is *votive offerings* containing figures or figurines of humans and animals. By hanging up pictures of sick limbs or people or animals in the shrine, healing, it was believed, could be achieved. A characteristic example of objects with the power of sympathetic magic is found in the account of the capture of the ark of the covenant by the Philistines (1 Sam. 6), which led to an epidemic of tumours and a plague of mice. The Philistines sent back the ark together with five golden tumours and five golden mice, which are described as *'āshām*, guilt sacrifices.

Pilgrimage chapels of the Greek Orthodox and Catholic Churches have continued this tradition. Every possible human organ, even the heart of the loved one, and all kinds of animals, including horses, cattle, sheep and goats are represented. The image and the original are bound together by a magical or mystical bond. Through hanging up the icon of picture in the shrine, supernatural healing power pours into the sick body or limb. In the immediate vicinity of the Deity or its image sickness, disease and pestilence vanish.

Instead of costly animals as sacrificial offerings, animal-shaped sacrificial cakes (*HWDA* 3, 173–405; 9, 945ff.) were sometimes made. In the cult of Astarte and Artemis these took the form of a stag. The small animals, e.g. horses and pigs, found on Christmas trees go back to Germanic sacrificial cakes. The tasty bread rolls in Germany called *Brezeln* (*bracellum, braciolum,* 'bracelet') are a substitute for the bracelets which were given to the dead to take with them to the spirit world. The snail-shaped cakes go back to the swastikas which were likewise given to the dead to ward off harmful powers and as a sign of life and luck. Another and far more important substitute for valuable and complicated sacrifices is the coin, medallion, or sacrificial money (see above, Chapter 2). The value of the metal was secondary. Another form of substitute sacrifice is that by symbolic action rather than by symbolic object. The death of a person may be suggested and not actually carried out. In German popular fertility customs, the place of human sacrifices by drowning has been taken by naked girls being thrown into the water or sprinkled with it. In these customs the blood sacrifice of a human being is rendered completely harmless.

One further substitute sacrifice widely practised by Christians, is that of *hair sacrifice* (*ERE* 6, 474ff.; *HWDA* 3, 1239–88; *RGG* 3, 1f.; *LThK* 4, 1293f.; *ER* 6, 154ff.). Hair has long been sacrificed to the Deity. Sometimes this ensures a person's spiritual and even physical power, as in the Samson saga (Judges 16). Hair sacrifice was bound up with the Nazirite vow which Paul took upon himself (Acts 21.24). The *tonsure* (*ERE* 12, 385ff.; *RE* 19, 836ff.; *LThK* 10, 207f.) of Christian monks, nuns and priests also goes back to the hair sacrifice. Tonsure has become a common practice amongst Christians since the fourth and fifth centuries. It has taken different forms: there is the tonsure of Peter in which a crown of hair is left and the centre of the crown is shaved. Then there is the tonsure of Paul, according to which the head is completely shaved (Acts 21.24). The tonsure of John or James, on the other hand, involves the shaving of the front of the head from ear to ear. This follows the style of the Druids and the Celtic Church. It is important to note that the tonsure of Buddhist monks and nuns, who shave off all their hair, has a different origin. It is a seal of the completely equal place taken in the monastic community through the rejection of the castes, the external characteristic of which is a particular hair style. In West Africa, prisoners of war are shaved to indicate loss of rank. New recruits to the army are likewise shaved to indicate the sacrifice of civilian status.

(5) Sacrifice of sexuality

Circumcision (*ERE* 3, 659–80; *RAC* 2, 159ff.; *RGG* 1, 1090f.) is a widespread substitute sacrifice practised by numerous peoples (not the Indo-Germanic, Mongolian or Finno-Ugric ones). Some extend the rite to both sexes. It is performed at infancy (Gen. 17.9ff.), at puberty, also before marriage. When Yahweh met Moses and sought to kill him, Zipporah circumcised the foreskin of her son as a substitution for the life of Moses and described him as a 'bridegroom of blood' (Exod. 4.24ff.). In addition circumcision is an age-old fertility rite analogous to the first-fruits sacrifice. It serves to secure the procreative power of the male and the power to give birth of the female. In the Israelite Priestly codex it becomes 'a sign of the covenant' (Gen. 17, 10ff.). The Deuteronomist carries its significance further in speaking of a 'circumcision of the heart' (Deut. 10.16). Paul too speaks of circumcision as 'a matter of the heart, spiritual and not literal' (Rom. 2.29). The author of the Epistle to the Colossians sees in baptism 'the circumcision of Christ made without hands' (Col. 2.11). Despite this reinterpretation by the New Testament, the festival of Jesus' Circumcision is still observed in East and West on 1st January and the Jewish circumcision rite has been retained by Ethiopian and Syrian-Nestorian Christians. In East Africa in the nineteenth century, Christian missionaries campaigned against female circumcision (Murray, 1976). Supported by the women's movement, African women in the twentieth century are continuing the fight against genital mutilation (Assaad, 1980; Koso-Thomas, 1987).

Castration (*ERE* 5, 579ff.; *ER* 2, 109ff.) goes even further. In the cult of Attis and Cybele in antiquity, the priest eunuchs offered up their power of procreation to the great Mother, the goddess of fertility (Vermaseren, 1977). Castration is used by Jesus as an image for the voluntary abstention from marriage (Matt. 19.12). He draws attention thereby to the painful 'surgical intervention' it makes in one's natural life. A millennium later, the uncle of Héloise took it upon himself to have her lover and secret husband, the brilliant scholastic theologian, Abelard, castrated by force. Out of this sacrifice came greater spiritual inwardness and an even deeper bonding of them both.

The giving up of chastity or virginity is another form of the sacrifice of sexuality. Sometimes termed *sacred prostitution* (*ERE* 10, 404–9; 6, 671–6) it consists in the surrender of one's chastity to the male or female deity who is represented by the temple priest or visiting stranger. It originally represented an imitative fertility rite. According to Herodotus, every Babylonian maiden had to offer her virginity as sacrifice in the temple of Ishtar. Besides this practice for the generality, there was the professional group of temple prostitutes. In Babylonia, the latter were called *kadishtu* 'the sacred ones', or *harimtu*, 'those excluded from profane life'. Temple maidens of Aphrodite received the name of 'hierodules'. The hierodule (*ER* 6, 309ff.) was also found in the western Semitic culture of Yahweh (Deut. 23.18) and even in the temple of Yahweh at Jerusalem under the same (Babylonian) designation of *Kᵉdeshā*. But sacred prostitution met with the sharpest opposition from the prophets. Amongst the reforms of Josiah the king was the closing down of the sacred brothel in the temple of Jerusalem (2 Kings 23.7). The prophet Micah continued to attack the institution of the *Kedᵉshōth* (1.7). Since then sacred prostitution has come under the condemnation of Christian ethics. There was little attempt to understand it in terms of the characteristic, traditional way of religious thinking. Sacred prostitution and phallic worship celebrated the mysterious reproductive power of humanity and were a form of sacrificial self-giving to the deity of fertility. In due course sacred prostitution gave place to symbolic substitutionary practices, e.g. through symbolic sacred marriage in the temple. In Christianity it lived on in the New Testament image of the 'bride' of Jesus. Christian ascetics also speak of 'brides of Jesus' who give up to Christ not only their soul but also their body.

(6) The spiritualization of sacrifice

The critique of physical, material sacrifice began before, and apart from, Christianity as a step in the internal reform of individual traditions, including that of early Israel. The Psalmist has the following declaration of Yahweh:

> I will accept no bull from your house,
> no he-goat from your folds.

> For every beast of the forest is mine,
>   the cattle on a thousand hills . . .
> If I were hungry, I would not tell you;
>   for the world is mine and all that is in it is mine.
> Do I eat the flesh of bulls,
>   or drink the blood of goats?
>
>   (Ps. 50.9f., 12f.)

Ethical considerations are added to this altered concept of Deity by the prophets. Samuel asks: 'Has the Lord as great a delight in burnt offerings and sacrifices,/as in obeying the voice of the Lord?' (1 Sam. 15.22). Amos proclaims that Yahweh requires not sacrifice, but justice and righteousness (Amos 5.21ff.). Through Hosea, Yahweh declares:

> For I desire steadfast love and not sacrifice,
>   the knowledge of God, rather than burnt offerings.
>   (Hos. 6.6)

Jesus repeats this demand (Matt. 9.13). Amos, Micah, Isaiah and Jeremiah all announce in effect that Yahweh hates external sacrifices and cultic acts as sacrilege and abomination, and requires instead of the sacrifice a moral attitude and action. In the Ebionite Gospel, Jesus declares: 'I have come to bring an end to sacrifices, and if you do not give up sacrificing there will be no end to the wrath of God.' The destruction of the temple, prophesied by Jesus (Mark 13.2), brought its cultic sacrifices to an end. The overturning of the tables of the traders in the temple forecourt (Mark 11.15) points in the same direction.

Sacrifice, under the influence of this prophetic critique, is not completely rejected, but transposed into the moral and spiritual key (Wenschkewitz, 1932; *RGG* 4, 1647ff.). The Epistle to the Romans speaks of a 'reasonable' sacrificial service. For 1 Peter (2.5) it is 'spiritual sacrifice'. So the prayer of praise and thanksgiving is considered as a sacrifice. The prophet Hosea can speak in grotesque images such as 'the bulls of our lips' (Hos. 14.3). The Psalmist exhorts: 'Offer to God a sacrifice of thanksgiving and pay your vows to the Most High' (50.14); and again: 'He who brings thanksgiving to me as his sacrifice honours me' (50.23). The Talmud and Philo continue the same theme as does the Epistle to the Hebrews (13.15): 'Through him let us continually offer up a sacrifice of praise to God, that is, the fruit of lips that acknowledge his name.' The same thought is echoed by the Fathers, and comes to clear expression in hymns, such as that of Paul Gerhardt. Should God desire a sacrifice, instead of incense a hymn will be offered and instead of a slain lamb, a prayer (*EKG* 348, 5).

The study of the sacred Scripture has also counted as sacrifice in Talmudic Judaism, more explicitly, perhaps, than in Christianity. In both Judaism and Christianity, the attitude of penitence becomes a sacrifice. 'The sacrifice acceptable to God is a broken spirit' (Ps. 51.17). In the end, every ethical virtue and achievement counts as sacrifice. Just as the *Bhagavadgītā* (4.24ff.) describes self-control, yoga and insight as sacrifice; and the Buddha commended ceaseless giving as sacrifice rich in blessing; so, too, in the Judeo-Christian tradition, Jesus, the son of Sirach (Ecclus. 35.1) declares that: 'He who keeps the law makes many offerings; he who heeds the commandments sacrifices a peace offering.' According to Tobit (4.11), to give alms is a good sacrificial gift: 'For all who practise it charity is an excellent offering in the presence of the Most High.' In Christianity, moral sacrifice is seen partly as the control of bodily drives, and partly as the activity of sacrificial love: 'To present your bodies as a living sacrifice, holy and acceptable to God' (Rom. 12.1). 'Do not neglect to do good and to share what you have', writes the author of Hebrews, 'for such sacrifices are pleasing to God' (Heb. 13.16). True sacrifices, for Augustine, are to fight for the truth even to the shedding of our blood, true incense is to burn with fervent love and to practise humility and the works of mercy.

Mystical self-surrender to God is also to be counted as sacrifice. It is achieved through prayer, the refraining from all concupiscence, desire and wanting, from all that is contrary to the will of God. Augustine emphasizes again and again that we ourselves must become the sacrifice; and that no sacrifice is more pleasing to God than the sacrifice of self. In the *Imitation of Christ* (4, 8), Christ says to the soul, 'I seek not your gift, but yourself . . . Offer yourself to me, and give yourself wholly to God; so shall your offering be acceptable.' And the soul answers: 'Lord, in simplicity of heart I offer myself to you this day . . . as an act of homage to you, and as an act of perpetual praise' (4, 9, 1). In the mysticism of Islam, notably that of Jelāl-ud-dīn Rūmī, the same interpretation of sacrifice is to be found. The fusion of inward prayer and sacrifice in this way represents the culmination both of prayer and sacrifice. And yet prior to, and above all human sacrifice, is the divine sacrifice. Man is not in a position to present a sacrifice to God. God himself is in the final analysis the power of sacrifice and even the sacrifice itself. This was seen long ago in ancient India where Prajapati is both creator and also sacrificial victim; and it is, as we shall now see, no different in the Christian tradition.

(7) The one blood sacrifice

The Christian faith knows only *one* blood sacrifice, that of the Son of God on the cross: 'Christ having been offered *once*' (Heb. 9.28). 'For Christ our paschal lamb has been sacrificed' (1 Cor. 5.7). 'Christ . . . gave himself up for us, a fragrant offering and sacrifice to God' (Eph. 5.2). This sacrifice is a 'mystery hidden for ages and generations but now made manifest' (Col. 1.26). A whole theology of sacrifice is developed in the Epistle to the Hebrews. The rich sacrificial cult of the old Covenant appears here as a foreshadowing of the once-and-for-all sacrifice on the cross. 'Christ, through the eternal spirit offered himself to God' (Heb. 9.14). 'He has appeared once for all at the end of the age to put away sin by the sacrifice of himself' (9.26); he has 'offered for all time a single sacrifice for sins' (10.12); 'by a single offering he has perfected for all time those who are sanctified' (10.1). How this was translated into a traditional religious context is seen in a West African foundation rite, where the 'sacrifice' was planted in an earthern pot and buried under the foundations of a new church building. It consisted of a scrap of paper on which was written in Yoruba: '*On si li etutu fun ese wa*' (He is the propitiation for our sins) (CMS CA2 070, 54: W. Moore, Jnl 23/11/1868, 1 John 2.2).

This sacrifice made once and for all is the object of dramatic presentation in the eucharistic sacrifice of the Lord's Supper: 'We have an altar (for sacrifice) from which those who serve the tent have no right to eat' (Heb. 13.10). Tent means here the temple of the Old Testament. On the basis of the Epistle to the Hebrews, the Fathers of the Church built up the theological theory of the eucharistic sacrifice (*RGG* 4, 1051ff.; Schulte, 1959). The once-and-for-all character of the sacrifice of Christ is carefully preserved. The Eucharist is a memorial, a recapitulation of the one sacrifice of Christ on the cross, and thereby a true sacrifice; it is not seen as a repetition but as a re-presentation of the one sacrifice in the context of a cult drama.

Christians who celebrate the Eucharist are imitators of the great sacrifice. The Eucharist is a mystery drama analogous to the mysteries of Osiris and Attis, in which the fate of the Deity is set forth. The eucharistic sacrifice in this respect is perfectly bloodless and spiritual. According to Gregory of Nazianzus, the priest offers this sacrifice when with a 'bloodless' stroke he parts the Body and Blood of the Lord, whereby the voice serves as his sword. This separation is shown liturgically in the form of the 'slaying of the Lamb' in the preparatory act of the Byzantine liturgy in which the priest uses a 'lance' to separate the pieces of bread which are to be consecrated in the eucharistic rite which follows.

This early Christian conception of sacrifice became more unrestrained both in the West and in the East during the Middle Ages as a result of popular piety and the theology which accompanied it. The sacrifice of the Mass was described as a bloodless renewal of the sacrifice of Golgotha having expiatory power itself. In reaction to the crudity of some medieval views of sacrifice, Luther and Calvin raised their sharp polemic against the alleged idolatry and blasphemy in the idea of the sacrifice of the Mass itself.

The Eucharist, however, remains in the central place of the cultus and this inevitably moves the sacrifice of Christ into the mid-point of Christian faith and life. The sacrifice of Christ is no mere play acting. It is not a feather bed, but an appeal to continuous self-sacrifice. It is the source of the Christian's 'living sacrifice' which has to be practised daily. The Pauline 'Christ mysticism', as it is called, includes 'suffering with Christ' (Rom. 8.17) 'sharing his sufferings' (Phil. 3.10), with 'Christ being formed' in his followers (Gal. 4.19). The mystical union between Christ and Christians constitutes the unifying principle linking the daily sacrificial life of the individual with the Christ who sacrificed himself on the cross.

The highest form of self-sacrifice with Christ, however, is the martyrdom which was considered by the early Church as being one with the sacrificial death of Christ (Campenhausen, 1936). The unity of the Christian's 'living sacrifice' with Christ was worked out most fully by the medieval mystics. In the

Imitation of Christ (4, 8, 1), Christ says: 'I freely surrendered myself to God the Father for your sins, with my hands spread out on the cross and my body stripped. I kept nothing back, but let all be transformed into a sacrifice to appease the divine anger ... You, too, should of your own free will offer yourself ... as a pure and holy offering ...'

The sacrificial idea in the Christian faith finds its culmination in the sacrifice on Golgotha and in the mystical participation of the individual Christian in this sacrifice. Here the sacrifice is no human achievement but divine grace. God comes first to man, he sacrifices himself first and indeed he does this from all eternity. The human sacrifice is simply the elaboration, the realization and the imitation of the divine sacrifice and of communion with him. It is mystical union, not just purification.

The history of sacrifice may often appear to us as full of senseless cruelty and waste. Yet, through the cult of sacrifice, mankind has learnt the secret of fulfilling social obligations, giving oneself in love to others, and abstinence. Sacrifice has been the school of social ethics and mystical communion with God.

7
Christian Sacred Action
3: Unification

(1) Dramatic presentation and imitation

Early Christianity grew up in the context of the *mystery drama* (*ERE* 4, 867–907; 9, 70–83; *RGG* 2, 262ff.; *ER* 10, 230ff.). The mystery drama is a presentation through symbolic forms of the acts of the Deity which are full of blessing for the human participants. This drama is no play-acting but supreme reality, expounded and elaborated in the accompanying recitation of myths and prayers. The object of the mystery drama is to appropriate the divine blessing by presentation and imitative repetition. This is true whether for the dramas of early Mexico, the North American Indians, e.g. the Algonquin, the Greek-Italian *Mimus*, Attic comedy, or the Germanic ritual drama whose theme was the dying and rising of nature. Throughout, the aim was to encourage new, burgeoning life. European medieval drama and Indian drama have also grown up out of those earlier religious dramas, as have the Japanese pantomimes which enacted religious myths with the aid of masks and dance, e.g. the enticing of the sun goddess out of her rock cave.

Of great importance are the mystery dramas of the Near Eastern and Mediterranean religions. Mystery dramas were presented in Babylonia and Assyria especially at the New Year festival. At such festivals the passion and rising again of the deity-of-the-Year was presented. Bel was arrested at the entrance to the underworld, beaten and wounded; his clothes were stripped off; he was led into a cave in the mountains. The city was in an uproar. Bel's spouse petitioned the sun and moon to spare the life of the imprisoned one. She went to the gate of the tomb in search of him. In the end Bel was brought back to life from the dark mountain; and the song of the world's creation was sung in his honour. In another New Year drama, the battle of Marduk with Kingu and Tiamat was presented in symbolic rites. The New Year festival in Sumerian, as in earlier and later Babylonian, times had as its purpose the reviving of the world after the conquest of the forces of chaos.

In Egypt (Bonnet, 1971, 568ff.; Clark, 1978), it was the Osiris saga that was presented in dramatic form, especially in Abydos. It concerned the most terrible event in Egyptian religion. Osiris falls under the sword of Seth; his limbs are cut up and scattered. Isis seeks them weeping. Seth is conquered by Horus; the body of Osiris is found, put together and reanimated. There follows a reordering of the world, with Horus ruling over the living and Osiris over the dead. The fate of Osiris is relived by the participant in the cult who may say: 'As Osiris truly lives, so do I; as Osiris is not destroyed, so will I also not be destroyed.' In Rome, the drama was presented every year from 28th October to

1st November, in almost the same way as in Egypt. Heart-rending lamentations of priests and devotees could be heard. Then, when the corpse was found again, put together and revivified, endless jubilation echoed through the temple and along the streets.

The Hellenistic mysteries (*RGG* 4, 1232ff.; Reitzenstein, 1927; Godwin, 1981; *The Mysteries*, 1955) were influenced by Eleusis, a pilgrimage centre of international repute. Here, too, a fertility myth was presented in dramatic form. Kore, the daughter of the earth goddess Demeter, plucks flowers in the meadow. Hades comes and abducts her in his chariot. In despair, the mother seeks her daughter, until Hermes brings her back and makes peace between the parties in dispute. A sacred marriage between Demeter and Zeus is staged by hierophants and the priestess of Demeter. As the fruit of this marriage a child or an ear of corn in a basket is taken about in open procession.

In the cult of Attis (*RGG* 1, 687; *RAC* 1, 889–99; Vermaseren, 1977) a mystery involving birth, death and resurrection is also celebrated. On 15th March, the entry of the reed bearers took place. As a child, Attis had been left abandoned on the banks of the Sangarius river in Phrygia, only to be discovered by Cybele. On the day of the spring equinox a pine tree was felled and brought by the tree bearers into the temple on the Palatine hill in Rome. The tree, which was wrapped in woollen bandages like a corpse and wreathed with violets, represented the dead Attis. On the following day the devotees fasted and lamented for Attis. The priest-eunuchs flagellated and wounded themselves. Frenzied neophytes castrated themselves. Secret vigils took place in which the initiates had, as a new Attis, to unite themselves with the mother-bride. On 25th March the festival of joy was celebrated amidst tumultuous scenes of rejoicing: Attis had awakened from the sleep of death. On 27th March a silver statue of Cybele was led under a shower of flowers down to the stream Almo where it was bathed.

In the atmosphere of these salvationist mystery cults, early Christianity was transformed from an eschatological and messianic movement, expecting the return of the crucified and risen Christ, into a salvationist mystery cult (S. Angus, 1925; H. Rahner, 1963). In the central service of worship, the celebration of the Eucharist, the saving mysteries of birth, death and resurrection were presented; but, in contrast to the traditional mystery cults, they were not at first shown in a colourful external display, but rather in a condensed, symbolic action that proclaimed 'the death of Christ' (1 Cor. 11.26). The Last Supper of Jesus constituted the beginning of this development. The parabolic action in which he symbolized his death, was embedded in the supper and served as the anticipation of the glorious meal to come.

The dramatic character of the eucharistic celebration achieved greater prominence later, especially in the Eastern Church. The iconostasis, or screen, lends to the inner shrine the character of a stage, similar to the theatre in antiquity. The traditional procession takes place twice in the Eastern Church: the first, called the 'little entry', with the book of the Gospels, the second, the 'great entry', with the prepared offerings of bread and wine. During the consecration of the bread in Eastern churches, the doors are closed. Syrian Christians close off the apse with a curtain, whereas in the West, earlier, a curtain was drawn across the baldachin, or canopy over the altar.

The other form in which salvation history is dramatized in Christianity is represented by the church year, the focal point of which is the Easter festival (see also above, Chapter 3). The days of penance and fasting were followed by the rejoicing of Easter night when the baptism of neophytes took place. This celebration of the passion and resurrection took dramatic form in Jerusalem where the holy places were visited in procession, and during the reading of the sacred texts the different acts of the passion were solemnly presented, from the entry of Christ into Jerusalem on Palm Sunday to the resurrection on Easter night. From Jerusalem, the passion week liturgy spread to the whole Church, East and West. Its main stages are: (a) the entry into Jerusalem, portrayed as a drama with the entry of a bishop riding on a donkey, and the welcoming of Christ with palm and olive branches; in the West, earlier, a Christ figure was led along on a 'palm-donkey'; (b) the celebration of the Lord's Supper and the washing of the disciple's feet on Maundy Thursday; (c) the adoration of the cross of Christ and the burial, on Good Friday; (d) the observance of the resting in the grave on Easter Eve; in south Germany a sacred grave was constructed in which the figure of the body of Jesus rested; (e) the celebration of the resurrection on Easter night; the risen one was symbolized in East and West by the lighting of the Easter candle; the mysterious event of the resurrection was symbolized in the Eastern Church by pushing open the church door with the cross.

Despite the connection between the Easter week liturgy and the ancient mystery cults, one difference is claimed by Christians, that their sacred action is related to historical events, the last act only, that of the resurrection, being conceded as a supra-historical mystery. Around the Easter week are then grouped the remaining festivals of the Christian year: Christ's birth, epiphany, teaching in the temple, ascension, and the sending of the Spirit. The measure of dramatization in terms of liturgical symbols still did not fully meet the needs of the people; so in the tenth century there arose *mystery plays* (*ERE* 8, 690ff.; *RGG* 4, 1238f.; Young, 1933; Craig, 1955). The biblical narratives were presented by players in masks. The house of God at first provided space for these plays, then the churchyard before the church (cemetery). There were passion plays, plays about the Antichrist, the last judgement, the twelve virgins, the lives of the saints, miracle plays, plays about Mary Magdalene and St George and the dragon. In post-Reformation times the great spiritual processions with masks took place in the context of the *Corpus Christi* festival (see above, Chapter 3). They were especially encouraged by the Jesuits. Down to the present day mystery plays are still the custom in some places, e.g. the passion plays in Erl, Thiersee and Oberammergau. The last mentioned has achieved world fame. The mystery play, it should be noted, carries over into Islam also. Shi'ite Islam knows of a passion play: the martyrdom of Hussain.

(2) The touch and the kiss

The blessing of the sacred, which is experienced so intensely by participants in the mystery drama, constitutes the latter into a single complex rite of unification. Within such rites and festivals are particular actions which also give expression to the sense of union or communion with the divine. The *touching* (*ER* 14, 578ff.) of a divine manifestation is one immediate form of union. It may be a sacred natural object, or a sacred image of the deity; it may be the altar of a shrine, a sacred relic, or a person. The worshippers stroke the sacred object, especially the hand or knee of the statue, and embrace it. The touching of sacred objects is common today in India, where it is practised by Hindus, Christians, Sikhs and Muslims. The aim is both the expression of veneration and also the reception of the divine into body and soul. So strong is the impulse to touch that it became spiritualized as a literary image. The Hebrew 'to stroke the face' (Exod. 32.11 etc.) became an expression for prayer. 'To embrace' is a favourite image with Mechthild of Magdeburg and other medieval mystics. The mutual touching of two persons can have the same significance as the touching and embracing of the sacred object. Such a unification rite may be seen in the modern encounter group (W. C. Schutz, 1972).

Especially widespread is the act of *kissing* the holy object (*ERE* 7, 739ff.; *HWDA* 5, 841–63; *RGG* 4, 189f.). In the religions of antiquity the kiss is the exchange of soul-substance. The worshipper kisses sacred stones and amulets, a sacred tree, the earth, the threshold of the temple, the altar, the image of deity. Steer images in Canaanite and Israelite religion were kissed by the worshippers. In the language of the Israelite religion, the kissing of Ba'al had the same significance as genuflection (1 Kings 19.18).

Kissing the foot of the divine ruler was a widespread custom, as in Egypt. Many images and pictures of deities and saints have been worn out by much kissing. In Eastern Christianity icons and the priest's cross are kissed, in Western Christianity the book of the Gospels, the chalice and paten and also relics. At the solemn adoration of the cross on Good Friday, the wounds of the Crucified are kissed. The foot-kiss is also practised with saints' statues, e.g. the statue of St Peter in Rome. At the consecration of the holy oil on Maundy Thursday, the vessels of oil are kissed. The faithful kiss the hand of the priest, the ring of the bishop and the cross on the shoe of the pope. The pope, in turn, has often been seen to prostrate and kiss the 'soil' on arrival at the country of his visit.

The mutual kissing of two persons has also the same significance as the kissing of sacred objects. Samuel kissed Saul when he anointed him as king (1 Sam. 10.1), thereby transferring to him his spirit-substance. In the kiss of peace (*ODCC* 784f., 1055; *NDLW* 250f.), the kiss entered into early Christianity and assumed an important place in the liturgy of both baptism and Eucharist.

Early on, Paul advises the young Christian congregations to 'greet one another with a holy kiss' (Rom. 16.16; 1 Cor. 16.20; 2 Cor. 13.12; 1 Thess. 5.26; cf. 1 Pet. 5.14). The same injunction is found in a series of early Christian liturgies. The kiss is also the symbol of reconciliation which precedes the offering of gifts in the African and Roman communion rites. Originally both sexes kissed each other freely. In the third century, however, the demand arose for the separation of the sexes. Eventually, the liturgical kiss became a priestly ceremony in the West: until recently, only the clergy gave one another the kiss of peace in the form of a 'continental' embrace, while the laity were only allowed to kiss the kissing plate (*osculatorium, pax*). In the Byzantine liturgy, the priest kissed only the altar and the plate on which the eucharistic bread was offered. The general kiss remained only for the liturgy of Easter night. In the Church of England the pax disappeared from the Prayer Book of 1552. In recent times the liturgical movement has attempted to restore the kiss of peace (or a 'sign' of peace) in the form of a handclasp. In 1971 the pax, as a handclasp, was introduced into the Anglican communion liturgy at the beginning of the communion, before the reception of the bread and wine.

The Greek Orthodox Church rite for the dead also included the touching and kissing of the hands and the forehead of the deceased. In one of the hymns for the dead the call goes forth: 'Come, brother, let us give the deceased a last kiss as a thanksgiving unto God.' The following words are also put into the mouth of the deceased: 'Come, then, all ye who have loved me and bestow on me the last kiss.' This beautiful rite of unification goes back to the liturgy for the dead in remote antiquity.

The significance of the kiss is also seen in its persistence as a linguistic symbol for the mystics. Its use was especially encouraged by the verse of the Song of Solomon (1.2): 'O that you would kiss me with the kisses of your mouth.' Bernard of Clairvaux says: 'We should not only gaze at him (the heavenly bridegroom) but kiss him.' 'In the kiss we are united with him' (*Sermon on Canticles*). Bernard built up a whole ladder of steps to the mystical kiss. The kiss of the feet is penitence, the kiss of the hands contemplation, the kiss of the mouth the inpouring of the Holy Spirit. Here the kiss lives on as the mediating of spirit-substance. In his theology of the Trinity, Bernard also employs the image of the kiss. The Spirit proceeds from the Father and the Son even as the true kiss is communing between the one kissing and the one being kissed. Among other examples, the Dominican Margareta Ebner prays: 'Give us the kiss of thine eternal peace through the heart into the soul.' In a sermon attributed to Meister Eckhart, these words are found: 'If it should happen to a soul to receive a kiss from the Deity, then it will be totally fulfilled.' And Zinzendorf prays: 'My Jesus, greetings and a thousand kisses.'

(3) Anointing with oil

Another form of unification rite is that of blessing and consecration. Like the touch and the kiss, there occurs the transmission of sacredness and power. Blessing (*NDLW* 93ff.; *ER* 2, 247ff.) is a communication of power to persons and to objects, and even to the Deity. The Hebrew *barakh* has a double significance: to bless and to praise. The hymn of praise is in origin a communication of power to the Deity (see below, Chapter 8). Similarly consecration (*NDLW* 192ff.; *ER* 4, 59ff.) also involves a transmission of sacredness: it is a blessing laden with power. In distinction to the blessing, consecration has as its main object the mediation of lasting sacredness, of being placed permanently in the possession of the Deity.

Blessing and consecration take place through contact with substances laden with sacredness and power: through washing with sacred or consecrated water, through smearing with blood, through smearing with spittle, and through *anointing* with oil or fat. All of these forms of blessing or consecration are apotropaic, in driving away dangerous powers; they also communicate sacredness. The anointing of sacred stones was widely practised in ancient Canaan. In the Bethel story Jacob anointed the stone which had served as a pillow because of the dream he had of the ladder reaching up to heaven (Gen. 28.18). The book of the law orders the anointing of the tabernacle, the altar of burnt offering and all its utensils (Exod. 40.9ff.). Anointing is, above all, a rite of consecration: it communicates lasting power and sacredness to an object or person. It is chiefly kings, priests, and prophets who receive, through anointing with oil, the power to carry out their office. Samuel poured a flask of oil over Saul and said: 'Has not Yahweh anointed you to be prince over his people Israel?' (1 Sam. 10.1). 'The men of Judah came and . . . anointed David king over the house of Judah' (2 Sam. 2.4). The anointing of the king became a normal practice in Christianity also. From the end of the tenth century the Byzantine emperors were anointed; while Western rulers were anointed on the head with chrism from the seventh century onwards. Later, these were anointed only with catechumen oil and that on the right arm and between the shoulders.

The anointing of priests accompanied that of kings. In post-exilic times in Israel – perhaps under Babylonian influence – the high priest was anointed on the head; later all the priests were so anointed. The aetiological legend on the subject (Exod. 40. 12ff.) tells of the anointing of Aaron and his sons: 'You shall . . . anoint them, as you anointed their father, that they may serve me as priests: and their anointing shall admit them to a perpetual priesthood throughout their generations.' For Israel, the anointing of prophets is the communication of spirit substance as in the royal consecration. Samuel received the commission to anoint David and 'the spirit of Yahweh came mightily upon David' (1 Sam. 16.13); similarly with Elijah: 'and Elisha you shall anoint to be a prophet in your place' (1 Kings 19.16).

It was therefore only natural that anointing with oil, called *unction* (*ERE* 12, 509ff.; *LThK* 7, 702ff.; *NDLW* 511ff.) should become for Christians one of the most essential forms of communicating sacramental power. The earliest form known in the Christian tradition is unction for the sick (*LThK* 7, 714ff.). During the time of Jesus' public ministry the apostles 'anointed with oil many that were sick and healed them' (Mark 6.13). In the early Church, unction of the sick was carried out by the elders with laying on of hands and prayer (James 5.14). Out of this arose the sacrament in the Eastern Church called *euchelaion*, in the Latin Church *oleum infirmōrum* or extreme unction. In the Eastern

Church the forehead, nose, cheeks, mouth, breast and hands were anointed; in the Latin Church the eyes, ears, nose, lips, hands and feet, and earlier, also the loins. In the Eastern Church the oil was consecrated by the priest before anointing the sick; in the Latin Church the consecration of the oil for the sick is carried out by the bishop and takes place on Maundy Thursday. The prayer of consecration of the oil by the Roman Church includes the petition that it may be, to all, 'celestial medicine for mind and body'. In 1936, the Church of England provisionally approved the reintroduction of the rite of unction, together with the imposition of hands, for the sick.

Catechumen unction, or the oil of exorcism (L. L. Mitchell, 1978), was originally little different from the anointing oil for the sick. In the early Church, catechumens were anointed all over, even as is now the case with baptizands in the Eastern Church. In the Roman Church, only the breast and shoulders were anointed. The apotropaic character of this anointing is apparent in Cyril of Jerusalem's *Mystagogic Catechesis* (2, 3): the oil of exorcism 'drives away all invisible powers of evil'. But this anointing is not only a negative warding off, but also a positive communication of power. So Chrysostom writes: 'Baptizands are anointed with oil like athletes who enter the stadium.'

The most sacred form of all is the 'oil of thanksgiving' or 'oil of gladness' (after Psalm 45.8), called *muron* (oil of myrrh or chrism). In the West this oil is mixed with balsam and consecrated on Maundy Thursday. In the Greek Orthodox Church, instead of myrrh the finest olive oil, similar to the anointing oil of Israel, is used and mixed with numerous (13–57) aromatic substances. It is only consecrated every seven years on Maundy Thursday, even less often in the Coptic Church. The consecration of oil is called 'a mystery' by Dionysius the Areopagite. At the consecration of the myrrh the bishop prays: 'Send down thy Holy Spirit upon this myrrh and make it a royal, spiritual oil of anointing, that it may protect life and sanctify soul and body unto an oil of gladness . . . Through the descent of thy Spirit, longed for and holy, make it into a vestment of immortality and a seal which makes perfect.'

Here the idea of the powerful substance comes together with the symbolism of sacred dress (see above, Chapter 2). In the East, the forehead, eyes, ears, mouth, breast, hands and feet are anointed with myrrh; in the Western Church only the forehead is anointed (together with the laying on of hands). In the East, the anointing with chrism is called seal (*sphragis*) a term which originates from the mysteries and Gnosticism. The prayer for the consecration of the oil in the *Euchologion* of Serapion runs: 'Mayest thou, through the divine and invisible power of our Lord Jesus Christ, send down into this chrism divine heavenly power, that those who are baptized and anointed in the saving sign of the Only Begotten . . . may participate in the gift of the Holy Spirit. Protected by this seal may they remain strong and steadfast, unharmed and invulnerable.' According to the Roman prayer of consecration on Maundy Thursday, the anointing with chrism signifies the solemn conferral of the threefold office of all Christians: royal, priestly, and prophetic. Thereby it continues the whole anointing ritual of antiquity.

In the Roman Church, the anointing of hands with catechumen oil takes place at the ordination to the priesthood. At the episcopal consecration, the head is anointed with chrism, also the hands. Both rites are accompanied by the singing of the canticle, 'Come creator Spirit'. At the consecration of churches, church walls, the resting place of relics, altar and bells are anointed with chrism.

The anointing with oil soon passed over into a more spiritualized form as symbolic language: *Mashīah* is the 'anointed one'. Jesus declares at the beginning of his public ministry (Luke 4.18): 'The Spirit of the Lord . . . has anointed me', thereby taking in a personal way, and as messianic, a passage in the book of Isaiah (61.1f.). Acts (10.38) continues: 'God anointed Jesus of Nazareth with the Holy Spirit and with power.' This anointing is transferred by Christ to those who believe in him: 'God . . . has anointed us (*chrisas*, RSV: commissioned); he has put his seal upon us and given us his Spirit in our hearts as a guarantee' (2 Cor. 1.21f.). 'You have been anointed by the Holy One' (1 John 2.20). The ninth-century hymn for Pentecost, *Veni Creator*, speaks of 'the anointing Spirit' and 'thy blessed unction from above' (*CH* 182). It is often sung at services of induction and installation of ministers and clergy.

(4) The laying on of hands

A special form of the unification rite by touch is the *laying on of hands* (*RGG* 3, 53f.; *LThK* 4, 1343ff.; *HWDA* 3, 1398ff.; *NDLW* 400ff.; *ER* 11, 97ff.). A principal purpose of the rite is the conveying of divine power through sensory contact. The imposition of hands was widespread in the ancient Near East to bring about new life and healing. In Israelite religion, the laying on of hands is frequently mentioned: as blessing (Jacob blesses Ephraim and Manasseh, Gen. 48.14); at the transferral of office (Moses transfers his office to Joshua as his successor, Num. 27.18); and at the consecration of the sacrificial animal (Lev. 3.13). In rabbinic Judaism it is practised more often, above all at the ordination of rabbis. Here is found the notion of a chain of the laying on of hands which stretches from the rabbis back to Moses.

By the laying on of hands, Jesus and the apostles practise healing (Mark 5.23; 6.2; 8.23ff.; Luke 13.13; Acts 28.8). In Samaria Peter and John communicate the Holy Spirit by the laying on of hands to those who have been baptized (Acts 8.17). Through the imposition of hands the grace of the Spirit and the authority of the bearer of the Spirit are transferred to the office-bearer at ordination. 'I remind you to rekindle the gift of God that is in you through the laying on of my hands' (2 Tim. 1.6). According to an apocryphal gospel, Jesus commissions the disciples by the laying on of hands.

The imposition of hands is also a part of the rite of baptism and, more especially, at the reception into the catechumenate: it belongs in the Western Church to *confirmation* (Lampe, 1951). The latter is often called 'the laying on of hands'; and takes place equally in Protestant forms of confirmation ('Receive the Holy Spirit'). In earlier times, it was the custom also at absolution in the

Roman Church. The latter Church also prescribes it, as does now the Church of England, at unction for the sick, blessing of the sick and exorcism. At the consecration of baptismal water the hand is held over the water, and at the Eucharist during the prayer 'Now, therefore' it is held over the gifts of oblation.

Above all, however the imposition of hands constitutes the essential action at the ordination of deacons, deaconesses and priests, bishops' consecration, in part also the consecration of monks, and, in the East, the consecration of the abbot. In the ordination of Protestant ministers, the consecration of Protestant bishops and at the blessing of Protestant deacons and deaconesses, the laying on of hands has been retained. The chain of the laying on of hands ensures the apostolic succession of the Church's office-bearers. In early succession-lists the formula runs: 'He received the hand of priesthood through NN ...' Through the laying on of hands a stream of power goes from hand to hand, from Jesus and the original apostles down to the present day. There are those, however, for whom such 'linear' succession is less important than the 'vertical' power from on high, conferred by the direct descent of the Spirit. Even among such 'charismatics', the laying on of hands frequently forms part of the informal liturgy of the prayer meeting.

(5) The sacred dance

The experience of divine power is also the starting point and the goal of the *sacred dance* (*ERE* 10, 358ff.; Oesterley, 1923; Van der Leeuw, 1930, 1963; Backman, 1977; *ER* 4, 203ff.). For some traditional peoples, the sacred dance may be even more important than sacrifice. Traditional dancers respond to the whole range of the rhythms of the world about them: nature, economic activities, social relations with spirit-beings, men and animals. Their dancing also expresses a whole range of inner emotional responses. The dance thus has many purposes, many 'intentionalities'. It wards off sickness and death by concentrating and releasing sacred power. It may also ward off, by the same means, hunger, storms, floods, volcanic eruptions, dangers from eclipses of the sun and moon. Even the wedding dance has as one of its purposes the warding off of harmful powers that may threaten the bridal couple. The same is also true of dances of death. More positively, dances may be performed to ensure good hunting, to make the crops grow, to bring rain, and to create favourable conditions for success in time of war.

The sacred dance is frequently one of imitation. Or, to put it another way, it operates by analogy. The desired object (harvest, game, victory, rain, etc.) is presented in dance movements. This leads to the acquisition and concentration of sacred power, including the power over animals (Lonsdale, 1981). Similarly by imitation, the dancers become deities or spirits, especially in masked dances, also in possession dances, and thereby acquire divine powers. In sacred dances of this kind very often a circle is described. Such circumambulation can lead to the mystic-ecstatic dance where man incorporates into his own realm and person the life of the Deity or of the cosmic process as a whole.

The religious dance was very much a part of the Judaic and Greco-Roman background of early Christianity. In ancient western Semitic religion, the rhythm of the cosmos and the rhythm of the dance came together in the dancing deity: *Baʿal markōd*, Lord of the Dance. In the biblical narratives, the dance takes place in honour of the Deity or as an expression of thanksgiving and joy, especially at victory in war, but also as harvest thanksgiving. After the victory over the Egyptians during the exodus, Miriam and the women performed a victory dance (Exod. 15.20). Similarly, when the Israelites returned victorious from a campaign against the Philistines, 'the women came out ... singing and dancing ... with timbrels, with songs of joy, and with instruments of music' (1 Sam. 18.6). After bringing back the ark of the covenant, King David 'danced before Yahweh with all his might' (2 Sam. 6.14; 1 Chron. 15.28). The biblical word for festival (*hāj*) means a cultic dance, a term similar to the Arabic term for pilgrimage (*hajj*), which involves the cultic circumambulation of the holy shrine (*Kaʿaba*). The dance was included in the early Jewish liturgy. The Psalmist exhorts the worshipper to 'praise his name in the dance' and 'sing praises unto him with timbrel and harp' (Ps. 149.3). In exilic times, the prophet receives the words: 'Smite with thine hand and stamp with thy foot' (Ezek. 6.11) suggesting that worship included a stamping and clapping dance.

The presence of the dance in Judaism influenced its entry into early Christianity, but this influence was greatly reinforced by Greco-Roman religious dance forms, especially those of the mystery cults. The latter had highly developed dance rituals. To disapprove of the dance was considered by the Greeks to be even a form of blasphemy. Among the gods who danced were Apollo and Dionysus. These became divine models for two opposite forms of religious response. The Apollonian is an ordered contemplative dance which leads to an inner calm and quietness in the dancer. The Dionysiac form in contrast to this is ecstatic and intoxicating. The dancer is swept away by the power of the dance and loses control of the self. This emptying of the self (called *fana* by the Sufis) is often described in terms of death and release. Both these types – the Apollonian and the Dionysiac – found expression in Christian dance forms; and yet the religious dance in Christianity was not simply a survival from other traditions. It was part of Christian worship in its own right. The Gospels contain the reproach: 'We piped to you, and you did not dance' (Matt. 11.17; Luke 7.32). In the early Church, the dance was an accompaniment to prayer as an expression of the believer's desire to move upwards from earth towards heaven. Clement of Alexandria wrote: 'We raise our heads and our hands to heaven ... and move our feet just at the end of the prayer ... In this way we reach blessedness and deliverance from the chains of the flesh which our soul despises' (cited by Backman, 1977, 22).

Dance in early Christianity was also seen as an imitation of the dance of the angels. The latter were believed to dance in heaven, and to provide a pattern for dance on earth. Basil of Caesarea went further and described the Christian life on earth as the counterpart of the heavenly dance. In a letter, he wrote: 'Could there be anything more blessed than to imitate on earth the ring-dance of the angels?' (cited in Backman, 25). His contemporary, Chrysostom, was passionately opposed to earthly dancing, but nevertheless shared with Basil his praises of the heavenly dance: 'God did not give us feet to serve him in pedestrian ways, but rather so that we might dance with the angels.' After death, the soul was believed to join in the dance of the angels. Yet this heavenly dance was anticipated eschatologically in a ring dance around the altar and the sacrament called the *chorea*. It was held at the time of formal initiation by baptism and reception of the Eucharist. The *chorea* was modelled on the angels' dance and celebrated the mystery of the resurrection. Such was the intensity of this unitive rite that the angels were believed to come down and join in the dance around the altar, thus bringing the earthly participants into immediate contact with divine beings. Dances were also performed around the graves of martyrs to honour the martyr and to return the love of God which he manifested while on earth. Later these dances were performed for Mary and the saints. Down to the present day, a dance of priests is customary in the Ethiopian Church; while a dance-like circling around the altar and the lectern with the icon, by the priest with bride and bridegroom, is a feature of the marriage rite in the Byzantine Church. In the West, the dance is continued in the churchyard dance and the dance for the dead. The models for the dance were not only provided by the angels, martyrs, saints and Mary. Christ also was the divine model. The idea was often expressed of the dancing Christ, an image which has been preserved down to the present. A song for Shrove Tuesday from the fifteenth century embodies this theme: 'Jesus, he must dance the lead,/and the virgin Mary. All must pay his rhythm heed/To reach God's sanctuary' (cited in Backman, 1977). The twentieth-century folk-song by Sidney Carter, entitled 'Lord of the Dance' contains these words:

> I danced on a Friday when the sky turned black;
> Its hard to dance with the devil on your back.
> They buried my body and thought I'd gone:
> But I am the dance and I still go on.

Ecstatic dance was never far from the Christian dance, especially among the gnostic Christians where it was linked with the mystical vision and the dissolving away of the barrier between this world and the next. Dionysius the Areopagite speaks of the soul which is taken into the immediate circle of the Deity and in a simple and ineffable way circles round his eternal *gnosis*. The ecstatic dance lived on in the West in the medieval *chorizantes* and *dansatores*, groups who seemed to exhibit a 'dancing sickness' or 'choreomania'. In the East there were similar groups, including the Russian *Chlysty* and *Skopsty*. Forms of sacred dance have been preserved in the Corpus Christi dances of Mexico and Spain. In Mexico, the persistence of the traditional Indian religious dance form is discernible. In the Syrian Orthodox Church of South India, ring-dances enacting biblical themes and performed by men were popular down to the 1950s at least. In Africa, many Churches, including especially the independent

Churches, have allowed free expression to the people's irrepressible urge to express their joy and thanksgiving in dance. Often, however, the style changes there from the earth-oriented traditional form to the characteristic Christian upwards-moving dance.

The dance has been used as a compelling image in medieval mysticism especially by Mechthild of Magdeburg. The soul dances after Christ who dances on ahead or plays to the soul. The heavenly dance makes manifest the blessedness of the souls made perfect and the angels. It is linked with the cosmic dance of the stars which in Dante's great vision, is moved by love, 'the love that moves the sun and other stars' (*Paradiso* 33, 145). The visions of the mystical dance found concrete form in pictures of the heavenly ring-dance by Fra Angelico. Out of the heavenly dance has also emerged the dance of death (*la danse macabre*) which assumed countless forms of expression in late medieval art and drama (J. M. Clark, 1950; *LThK* 10, 228).

Alongside the popular tradition of the sacred dance in Christianity has gone an almost puritan distrust of the earthly, profane dance forms. As a total form of expression, which abolishes all distinctions between the heavenly and the earthly, the sacred and the profane, it could quickly assume the more orgiastic, Dionysiac forms. These were believed to introduce idolatrous elements into the Christian dance. As early as the fourth century, what were described as frivolous and indecent dance movements and improper songs accompanying them, were strongly condemned. Warning after warning concerning the excesses the dance was prone to showed the strength of its hold on the people. The Germanic and Slavic peoples, amongst whom Christianity spread, had their own religious dances which they naturally wished to employ as a way of expressing their new-found faith. More often than not, however, and this applies to Christian missions virtually world-wide, the church authorities regarded the dance form as 'heathen' or 'idolatrous'. Van der Leeuw also points out that the sheer bodily nature of the dance often posed a problem. In much Christian thought the spirit was stressed to such an extent that, contrary to the implications of its own incarnational teaching, the body was regarded as sinful: the flesh was to be mortified, not allowed free expression. Moreover, the dance, while liberating the dancer from bondage to the physical and earthly, also could arouse earthly desires from its very movements. It was not until the Reformation, however, that opposition to the dance became effective. The dances around the maypole disappeared, as did those in churchyards. But beyond Western Europe, fortunately perhaps, 'the dance goes on' as an essential form of sacred action, an unitive rite which thematizes the world, recreates divine order, releases divine power, and provides bodily expression of pure spirit.

(6) Sexual union

As a rite of unification with the Deity, *sexual union* or sacred marriage (Eliade, 1963; *ER* 6, 317ff.) has, even more than with the sacred dance, been accorded a negative as well as a positive status in the Christian tradition. Sexual unification with the Deity is based on the nature of the sexual act and its connection with fertility. The ecstatic emotional side of sexual union provided analogous concepts of divine and heavenly bliss; it also possessed important powers which made nature fruitful. Over thousands of years agricultural rites enacting a symbolic sexual union with the Deity show the importance of these motifs in the history of religions. Examples include the horse sacrifice of the Vedic cultus, in which the queen places herself beside the sacred victim. This rite persisted also in the Celtic sacrifice where the king copulated with a dead mare. Such sexual rites continued down to recent times in the form of popular customs: fields were thought to be fertilized when naked girls danced on them or gave the ploughman a kiss. Carnival times were also a reflection of earlier agricultural fertility festivals; as is the throwing of confetti at weddings. Confetti and rose petals have replaced spring blossom.

The symbolic representative of the Deity could be a sacred person as well as a sacred animal or object, as in the case of rites of sacred marriage performed with the priest or priestess, temple maiden or sacred teacher, or the stranger. In the course of time such rites tended not to be acted out, but to be performed symbolically (as in the case of human sacrifice). Thus, symbolic nuptials were celebrated with ithyphallic images of deities. In many mystery cults a bridal bed would be prepared on which the initiate would be united with the deity through visions. Even in recent days, in Benedictine convents, a bridal bed would be prepared, following the nun's taking of the veil, and decorated with flowers. The rite of *dedication to virginity* (*LThK* 4, 1213; Münster, 1955) is the marriage to Christ as bridegroom. A crucifix is placed on the pillow, in the company of which the newly-wedded virgin celebrates her wedding night. The Dominican mystic Margareta Ebner took a very large crucifix to bed with her. The sexual motif is here intertwined with social and religious factors in a profoundly symbolic rite.

The primordial motif of sexual union with God lives on also in linguistic symbolism, as with the prophet Hosea. In his marriage to a prostitute, the prophet appears as the representative of Yahweh, his wife represents the unfaithful adulterous people of Israel (Hos. 1.2). Even the Song of Solomon, originally a collection of secular love songs, came to be interpreted as an allegory, with Solomon as Yahweh and the beloved as Israel. In the Pauline writings this Jewish motif combines with the Hellenistic sacred marriage. This relationship of the Church to Christ is that of bride to bridegroom: 'The two shall become one'; 'This is a great mystery . . . I take it to mean Christ and his Church' (Eph. 5.31f). Hippolytus and Origen took over the allegorical interpretation of the Song of Solomon; and from there it was passed on into the common medieval hermeneutical tradition.

The way in which the marriage between the Church and Christ was understood was given an individual form in early Christian asceticism. The holy virgins consecrated to God became brides of Christ united with him (*Christo copulatae*). They consecrate their bodies to Christ and dedicate to him their chastity. A further degree of individualization followed in Christian

Gnosis and mysticism. Following Indian and Neoplatonist mystics who made use of sexual union as an image for mystical union, Origen, father of Christian bridal mysticism, declared that the soul was the bride of the Logos, united with it in a spiritual marriage. He interpreted the Song of Solomon in terms of this individual relationship. The writings of Makarios the Egyptian took this individualist bridal mysticism still further. The mysticism of Bernard of Clairvaux exploits the Song of Solomon in exhaustive fashion and depicts in its images the bliss of the soul united with Christ and the misery of times of separation. The graphic character of the imagery is again intensified in the case of Mechthild of Magdeburg where the full realism of a sexual union with God appears once more. God marries the soul with all his might in the bed of love. A parallel to Western bridal mysticism is afforded by that of the Indian Krishna cult, where Radha, the beloved of Krishna, symbolizing the soul, experiences the torments of separation as she does the joys of the nearness of the loved one.

The image of loving intimacy and sexual union passes over into that of pregnancy and birth. Plotinus speaks of 'the soul filled with God becoming pregnant', Origen of 'being pregnant by the Holy Spirit'. There is an underlying conception here of the supernatural conceiving which was widespread in the traditional and ancient world (see also Chapter 16 below). For the way it is referred to in Christianity, the pattern was set by Luke's narrative which speaks of supernatural conception (Luke 1.35). The birth of Christ out of the human heart in a spiritual sense is referred to by Thomas Aquinas. Angelus Silesius sings: 'Mary it is who bears the Son of God physically, while I do so inwardly, through the Spirit, the eternal father.' Sometimes there was a return to physical realism, as when nuns so far identified with Mary as to believe that they were actually pregnant. Margareta Ebner, in similar vein, suckled an image of the child Jesus.

The idea of sexual union with the Deity is a natural human symbol. Psychoanalysis has underlined the fundamental character of human sexuality, which so permeates our unconscious and also our conscious activities and thoughts. 'No one', wrote Van der Leeuw, 'is able to remove the sexual completely from any relationship, even from that to Deity' (Van der Leeuw, 1964, 232). A close relationship persists, positively or negatively, acknowledged or unacknowledged, between the erotic experience and all those, including the religious, cultural and artistic ones, which are concerned with the ultimate in life. In Christianity, as in varying degrees in other religions as well, religious attitudes vary widely in regard to sexuality, but all alike draw religious power from the same source. The traditional primordial view that sexuality is at least an analogue of heavenly bliss is never too far beneath the surface.

(7) Incorporation of a sacred substance

Related to union with the Deity through love and sexuality is 'substantial' union, where a divine substance is incorporated into the human person. The soul becomes 'deified' through the enjoyment of sacred food and drink. The traditional forms of substantial union are the sacrificial meal and the elixir of immortality. The cultic or sacrificial meal (Bammel, 1950; *HWDA* 2, 1022–59; 5, 1490–507; 8, 156–234) is one of communion with the Deity, and is found in many forms, including that of the totemic mysteries where the totem animal, considered by clan members to be sacred and protected, is taken and consumed in a communion meal. There man takes the divine being into himself in order to be one with him. In traditional and ancient cults the sacrificial animals were considered to be not only offerings to the Deity, but also themselves divine and filled with divine power. They had therefore to be consecrated with special rites. In the sacrificial animal the Deity itself was consumed. Nothing of what was offered therefore was to be brought back into profane life, all had to be consumed or burnt on the spot. In other forms of the sacrificial meal the Deity was invisibly present and participated in the meal. Called upon through a special prayer (*epiclesis*), the Deity would eat together with those sharing in the sacrifice. The sacrifice was a communion meal partaken of by God and man. It was common among the Germanic peoples, where the sacrificial animal lived on in certain kinds of cakes. Although these bread rolls, pancakes or cakes were only a substitute for the more valuable sacrifice of animals, it was nevertheless believed that through the blessing of the priest divine powers would enter into them which would pass into those enjoying them, such that they would experience rich blessings and the forgiveness of their sins. Crescent-shaped rolls or buns are one such sacrificial offering, in this case a substitute for the ram's or cow's horns.

Along with the sacrificial food is found the sacred elixir of immortality (*HWDA* 8, 1150–65; Kircher, 1970; *ER*, 5, 96ff.). Like the dance, or the consuming of narcotics, the sacred liquor brings about a state of ecstasy and makes a person divine and immortal. Fermented mare's milk was a sacred intoxicant for the Tartars and Kalmuks. Strong tea was used by the Seminole Indians to induce a state of trance. In the Indo-Germanic world a favoured form of sacred elixir was made from honey. Honey possessed the power to ward off sickness and danger. In the more solid form it was called nectar, in the liquid form ambrosia. Milk (*HWDA* 4, 243–93) and honey (*HWDA* 4, 289–310) are the food of the gods. In the paradise of the primordial past and of the age to come, milk and honey are flowing. The initiates of Attis drank milk and honey after the *taurobolium* rite. The custom of drinking milk and honey also lived on in the early Christian rite of baptism (*LThK* 7, 201; *HWDA* 6, 375–80). Among the Germanic peoples mead made from honey was the sacrificial elixir. It was consecrated through a special formula and was then capable of transforming a person. The old sacred drinking rite of the Germanic people (*NCE* 873f.) is found in Swedish *skål* drinking, and in the German expression: 'Beer sayings are true' and will be fulfilled. Something of this is found in the custom of '*minne* drinking', drinking in the name of the saints, which has been a feature of the cultus of the Church. Such saints have included Stephen, George, John, Martin, Gertrude, Emmeram, Olaf, Benedict, Leonard, Bernard, apart from Mary and Christ (*HWDA* 4, 745–60). This custom has continued down to the continued down to the present in 'drinking to St John'. On the festival of John the Evangelist (27 December), the wine of St John is blessed and handed to the faithful with the words: 'Drink the love of St John.' The legend of origin has it that the apostle took away the poison from a poisoned chalice handed to him, by making the sign of the cross over it. In the Catholic church of south Germany consecrated wine is handed to the bridal couple and the wedding guests after the nuptial Mass.

Intoxication and drunkenness serve as symbols for being filled and united with God especially in the language of the mystics. Sufi mysticism developed a whole genre of 'drinking' poetry; one of the praise names of the Sufi is the one who is 'drunk with God'. The image of drunkenness is already present in Philo's work: he speaks of sweet and sober intoxication. This paradoxical juxtaposition of words probably well describes what was seen as drunkenness in the Pentecostal experience (Acts 2.12f.). In the morning hymn of Ambrose, 'O splendour of God's glory bright', which was sung on a Monday at Lauds, the English, 'The Spirit's wine, that maketh whole,/and mocking not, exalts the soul', conceals the notion of sober intoxication in the Latin *sobriam ebrietatem*. Augustine and Bernard of Clairvaux write in similar vein. The medieval German mystics often speak of thirst for *Minne* and drunkenness from *Minne*. Teresa of Jesus, the Spanish mystic, also speaks of intoxication with heavenly wine.

(8) The sacramental meal

The *sacramental meal* occupies a special place in the Greco-Roman mystery religions, whose proximity to early Christianity we have already had occasion to refer to. In the mysteries of Dionysus, the initiate confesses: 'I lead a pure life since I, as shepherd . . . completed the meal with raw flesh after passing the night in a state of ecstasy.' It was similar in the Eleusinian mysteries, and in those of Atargatis where the sacred fish served as food (see also above, Chapter 3). The fish were kept in dams near the temples and were not to be touched. They were consumed in the sacred meal in the belief that in them the flesh of the Deity itself was being consumed (Cumont, 1956). The fish (*ichthus*) became a favourite symbol of the eucharistic body of Christ, whereby the Greek word was interpreted as a christological acrostic. In the cult of Attis, the initiates practised periods of fasting, then ate and drank out of musical instruments, in this case different types of drum. The sacramental meal consisted probably of fish, bread and wine. In the Mithras cult, a communion celebration took place with bread and water which were consecrated and mixed with honey and wine (instead of the Iranian *haoma*). It was a memorial celebration of the meal which Mithras shared with Helios (the Sun deity) before the former's ascension to heaven. The cult of Serapis also had a communion meal. A communion *ostrakon* (tablet) invites the communicant to the table of the Lord Serapis at 9 a.m. in the Serapeion. From such practices one may understand the warning of the Apostle Paul: 'I do not want you to be partners with demons. You cannot drink the cup of the Lord and the cup of the demons. You cannot partake of the table of the Lord and the table of demons' (1 Cor. 10.20f.). Also, in the cult of Sabazios, a vegetation deity similar to Dionysus, who was conflated with Yahweh Sabaoth, sacred meals were celebrated similar to those of the cult of Attis. These meals were interpreted as the anticipation of the eschatological meal of heavenly blessedness.

Although the early Christian Lord's Supper (Lietzmann, 1979) has to be understood against the background of the communion meals of the mystery cults in the ancient world, its point of departure is to be sought rather in the Jewish *kiddush* which was said on the evening before the Sabbath and the Passover at the beginning of the family meal, also at a meal of friends (*habura*; R. Otto, 1938; Jeremias, 1955). At the blessing of the wine the family head prayed: 'Blessed art thou, O Lord our God, King of the universe, who hast created the fruit of the vine'; and at the blessing of the bread: 'Blessed art thou, O Lord our God, King of the universe, who bringest forth bread from the earth.' Jesus performed this *kiddush* with his disciples as friends (*haberim*). The stories of the miraculous feeding of the five thousand and four thousand in the desert (Mark 6.32ff.; 8.1ff.) are based on the memory of such common meals. Jesus 'gave thanks' means 'he spoke the *berakha* (blessing)'. This meal is at the same time the anticipation of the glorious eschatological meal, as with the Sabazios mysteries. It signifies further a declaration of loyalty inasmuch as the common meal binds together the participants in a supernatural bonding.

Jesus' farewell meal had its special character: 'I shall not drink again of this fruit of the vine until that day when I drink it new with you in my Father's kingdom' (Matt. 26.29). A short but fearful interim lay between this meal and the meal in glory. In view of his imminent sacrificial death, Jesus carried out a parabolic action after the manner of the Hebrew prophets (Fohrer, 1953; Lindblom, 1967). As Jeremiah broke a jug in pieces and put on a yoke (Jer. 19.10ff.; 27.2ff.), and Ezekiel cut off his hair and burnt and scattered it (Ezek. 5.1ff.), so Jesus represented his death by means of the breaking of bread. He accompanied this action with some words of interpretation: 'This my body'; according to most of the New Testament texts he spoke also words of interpretation over the cup: 'This is my covenantal blood'.

These words of institution, as they are called, have been handed down to us in very different forms. Besides those of Paul (1 Cor. 11.23ff.), Mark (14.22ff.), Luke (22.15ff.) and Matthew (26.26ff.), there are the numerous early Christian liturgies. The Lucan passage presents a serious problem. In early manuscripts, including Codex D and early translations, the words about blood are missing. In the remaining manuscripts and translations they are supplied from the Pauline text. In Luke are also other words about the covenant: 'As my Father appointed a kingdom for me, so do I appoint for you that you may eat and drink at my table in my kingdom, and sit on thrones judging the twelve tribes of Israel' (Luke 22.29f.). The exact words spoken at the farewell meal cannot be ascertained with certainty: above all, the question whether Jesus himself gave the commission to repeat it: 'Do this in remembrance of me' (1 Cor. 11.24f.);

and whether he linked the cup with his blood. With reference to the second question, there are two possibilities: (a) the cup at the Last Supper simply possessed eschatological significance but had no connection with blood, the latter stemming from Pauline theology; (b) the blood formula was left out of the Gospel of Luke – which originated on Roman soil – out of consideration for the secret rites of the early Church and their slandering as Thyestean (i.e. cannibalistic) feasts.

The early Church celebrated meals in common and experienced in these the presence of the Risen One. Individual resurrection narratives are a clear reflection of these common meals. Jesus had shared his meals with the disciples. Hence, those at Emmaus 'recognized' him in the 'breaking of bread' (Luke 24.31.35). The presence of the risen Jesus gave the meal its joyful character: 'They partook of food with . . . glad hearts, praising God' (Acts 2.46f.). It is not impossible that the memorial of the death on the cross was also held in 'the breaking of bread'. It is remarkable, however, that there is no reference to the death on the cross and sacrificial redemption in the earliest eucharistic prayers of the *Didache* (9f.). These prayers represent the transforming of the Jewish *kiddush* prayers by an eschatological outlook coloured by Johannine emphases. The Lord's Supper, the Eucharist, becomes the anticipation of the Kingdom of God coming at the end of history. The bread is the symbol of the future oneness of the Church of Christ. No recitation of the words of institution occurs, the latter is still missing in the Syrian-Nestorian *anaphora* (eucharistic prayer; *NDLW* 10–17) and in the other early liturgies.

The Eucharist soon took on wholly new characteristics on Hellenistic-Christian soil. Paul had grown up in an atmosphere of mystery cults which were familiar with the sacred drama in the form of sacred communion. He did not consciously take over traditional cultic forms from, say, the Mithras or Attis cults; but unconsciously interpreted along their lines the sacred meal of the earliest Christians and their tradition of the Last Supper (1 Cor. 11.23ff.). He had received the words of institution 'from the Lord', that is, in a vision, probably, from the mouth of the risen *Kurios*, not from the tradition of the earliest Church. To receive the Eucharist has for Paul an immediate connection with the redeeming death of Christ which lies at the centre of Pauline theology. The Eucharist here is a dramatic presentation ('proclamation') of the death of Christ. It is thus a sacrifice, and at the same time a sacrifical meal. The bread and wine mediate in a real way the *koinōnia* (communion) with the Body and Blood of Christ (1 Cor. 10.16), *are*, in fact, the Body and Blood of Christ. Paul expressly draws a parallel between the Lord's Supper and the meals of the mystery deities. Unworthy eating and drinking has the effect of a curse which produces sickness and death as its consequence (1 Cor. 11.27ff.). The elements are placed in immediate relationship to Christ's presence, something that does not appear to have been the case in the earliest Christian community. This conception of Paul's is continued by Justin, who speaks of the food over which the thanksgiving is spoken as the flesh and blood of the incarnate Christ. The Lord's Supper is also for Paul the sacrament of the Church's unity: 'Because there is one loaf, we who are many are one body, for we all partake of the one loaf' (1 Cor. 10.17). The Pauline account of the Lord's Supper emphasizes the formal institution of the sacrament though according to Mark's Gospel, it was not so much a case of deliberately setting up an institution as, with everything else, of its being spontaneous and born out of particular circumstances. If it was an 'institution' then it was so only as the transforming of the old custom of the *kiddush* in the light of the expected *parousia*.

The Pauline interpretation of the Lord's Supper was of immense significance as far as the course of future developments was concerned. The Pauline words of institution, or vision of institution, influenced the Synoptic Gospels of Mark and Matthew and entered into the independent tradition of the third Gospel. It formed the basis for the Johannine interpretation of the Eucharist. What is new in the latter is the linking of the sacrificial eating and drinking with the receiving of eternal life. Here, too, may be seen the influence of that interpretation of the sacrificial meal which is characteristic of the Hellenistic-oriental mystery rites. Two strata may be distinguished: (a) in the basic writing, what is said about the bread of life is strongly spiritualized: 'I am the living bread which came down from heaven; if anyone eats of this bread he will live for ever' (John 6.51). (b) The edited text is strongly realistic: 'Unless you eat the flesh of the Son of man and drink his blood you have no life in you; he who eats my flesh and drinks my blood has eternal life, and I will raise him up at the last day' (John 6.53f.). Here, too, as with Paul, we have the identification of bread and flesh, and of wine and blood. This paradoxical identification is an external cause for offence (*skandalon*); notwithstanding the fact that what follows is no magical communication of eternal blessedness through eating and drinking, but rather a spiritual one: 'The words which I have spoken unto you are spirit and life' (John 6.63).

The deutero-Johannine thought was taken further in the Greek concept of the food and elixir of immortality. Very early Greek, and even Indian, ideas of ambrosia and nectar (*amrtam*) became popular once more. Ignatius (*Eph.* 20.2) described the Eucharist as the 'medicine of immortality'. Irenaeus provides a detailed theory about this: the Body and Blood of Christ are the seed of the resurrection body; the human body is nourished from the flesh and Blood of Christ and attains in this way the capacity for resurrection: it is immune against corruption or decomposition. Firmicus Maternus held a similar view; and it returns again and again in the Greek and Latin Fathers. Epiphanius describes the Eucharist as the 'power of reanimation'; Gregory of Nyssa says: in the Eucharist 'the Lord is bonded with the bodies of the faithful so that through the unification with the immortal one, man may also participate in immortality.' The belief in its power for resurrection explains the custom of handing the Eucharist to the dying as food for the journey (*ephodion, viaticum*). Chrysostom says: 'Those who have received the sacrament with a pure conscience shall depart hence . . . under the protection of guardian angels.' The early Christian custom, still observed by St Benedict, of placing the consecrated bread in the mouth or on the breast of the deceased, was later forbidden by the Church.

With the idea of the food of immortality was linked that of Hellenistic deification. 'God's Son has become man in order to make men divine' (Athanasius). The Eucharist is a permanent incarnation for the purpose of divinization. The communicants, according to Cyril of Jerusalem (*Myst. Cat.* 4, 1), become 'one body and blood with Christ'. According to John of Damascus, the goal of receiving the Eucharist is divinization and immortality. All the motifs of the Church's interpretation of the Eucharist have clear parallels in the mystery cults of antiquity. Out of the *berakha* of the Last Supper emerges a liturgy of mysteries. The condition for participating in these is initiation through baptism. No catechumen, still less a member of another religious cult, was allowed to participate in these mysteries. Hence the warning call of the deacon before the beginning of the mystery actions: 'Let no uninitiated person be present' (Brightman, 1896, 41).

Theological speculation occupied itself with the way in which Christ was present in the elements (Dunkerly, 1937). In the East as in the West, two directions were taken: a pneumatic-spiritualistic one and a metabolic-realistic one. Clement and Origen are the fathers of spiritualism in the East, Tertullian and Augustine in the West. Bread and wine are figures and signs of the body of Christ and only 'in a certain fashion' can the sacrament of the Body and Blood of Christ be his real body and his real blood. Soon this spiritualism began to come up against the realism of the doctrine of transformation, transubstantiation or change. The latter found in the Eucharist not only a sanctification of the elements but a transformation. In the East, Cyril of Jerusalem and John of Damascus represent these conceptions, as do in the West the early Gallican liturgy and the Spanish Mozarabic rite. Isidore of Seville makes an attempt to bring both positions together. In the Carolingian renaissance, John Scotus Erigena and Ratramnus represent Augustinian spiritualism, Paschasius Radbertus (in the ninth century) the view of metabolism. The controversy was repeated in the eleventh century between Berengar of Tours and Lanfranc. Metabolism emerged as the victor. At the Roman synod of 1059, Berengar was compelled to acknowledge that after consecration bread and wine are not merely *sacramentum* (i.e. sanctified signs) but also the true Body and Blood of Christ and in a sensory way, not merely in the sacrament but in reality, are taken hold of by the priest, broken and chewed up by the teeth of the faithful (Mirbt, 1924, 144f.; *RE* 2, 606–12).

The transformation of the communion elements is not interpreted in East and West in quite the same way. In the East it is seen as an organic transformation analogous to the process of digestion in the human organism, or as 'assumption', analogous to the taking of a human body by the Logos; in the West it is viewed as transubstantiation, the transforming of the substance of the bread and wine into the substance of the Body and Blood of Christ. With the reception of Aristotelian metaphysics, the doctrine of the relation of substance to accidents was applied to the Eucharist. After consecration, there remain only the accidents of the bread (form, colour, smell and taste). These accidents pertain no longer to the substance of bread and wine, but to that of the Body and Blood of Christ. The scholastic theories were made into dogmas at the Council of Trent. Alongside these another theory maintained its place for much of the Middle Ages, that of consubstantiation, according to which the earthly and the divine substance are present at the same time in the communion elements (see also below, Chapter 8).

Connected with this development there occurred also others: (a) There was in both East and West a change in the form of distribution; the Eucharist was given in the East with a spoon, in the West it was put into the mouth. In the West, moreover, it was received kneeling. (More recent practice includes reception into the hands, standing.) (b) Again, the customary leavened ordinary bread was replaced in the West by unleavened bread, which was given a special form, the host, impressed with pictures, about the end of the first millennium. (c) The chalice was withheld from the laity and only the bread was given. This arose from fear of dishonouring the sacrament through spilling, besides the difficulty in procuring the wine. It was first described at the Synod of Lambeth (1281). Whereas Leo the Great had threatened those who despised the cup with excommunication, and Gelasius I had called this sacrilege, the Council of Constance (1415) condemned the demanding of the cup for the laity as heretical and threatened its advocates with dire punishment.

The consequence of this realistic attitude towards the sacrament was the turning of the *mysterium* away from the dynamic towards the static and the emergence of a veneration of the elements, at first during the Mass and then apart from the Mass (see above, Chapter 2). In connection with the increasing realism with which the sacrament was viewed, countless legends of eucharistic miracles came into being in the Middle Ages, mainly stories of bleeding hosts (Browe, 1938). Thus the history of the Christian Communion shows the ceaseless influence of primordial religious motifs and concepts. Over against this realistic symbolization there stands the spiritualizing tendency of the mystics. In place of the materialist view of the Eucharist there entered a more personal one. The 'sacred things' become signs of the personal presence of Christ as Lord and Bridegroom, with whom the individual soul is united in a mystical union. From a psychological standpoint this union is the same as the sacred marriage. Hence, the Byzantine liturgy of the Presanctified: 'Give, that we all, who share in these sacred things, may be one with Christ himself' (Brightman, 1896, 349). The high point of this mystical view was reached by Symeon the New Theologian through whom eucharistic mysticism is joined to a mysticism of light (see above, Chapter 1). Even more personal is the eucharistic view of the medieval mystics. The Eucharist becomes a 'sacrament of *minne*', a spiritual wedding. For Meister Eckhart, the soul was united to God much more closely than are soul and body which together make up a person. Here the host has nothing of the impersonal character of the early Christian mysteries and food of immortality. Everything materialistic and magical is stripped away from it: it is now merely a sensory sign for the presence of the Redeemer, Friend and Bridegroom of the individual soul. This applies also to the eucharistic hymn, *Adoro te devote*, attributed to Thomas Aquinas:

Thee we adore, O hidden Saviour, thee,
Who in thy sacrament dost deign to be:
Both flesh and spirit at thy presence fail,
Yet here thy presence we devoutly hail . . .
O Christ, whom now beneath a veil we see,
May what we thirst for soon our portion be,
There in the glory of thy dwelling place
To gaze on thee unveiled, and see thy face.

For this personalistic mysticism, the receiving of the sacrament may, in the final analysis, be dispensed with. The mystic can receive communion 'spiritually' at any time if he entertains a longing for union with Christ, and prepares himself for it inwardly. This spiritual communion he can receive 'a thousand times a day and oftener, wherever he may be and whether he is sick or well' (Meister Eckhart). Such personalistic mysticism which closely impinges on bridal mysticism, has been a dominant form of Catholic piety. The pious one seeks the personal Christ in the sacrament. During the time that her home town was placed under interdict, Catherine of Genoa journeyed secretly outside its walls in order to be able to communicate. 'It seems to me', she said, 'that if I were dead I should return to life to receive thee' (Hügel, 1923, I, 115). Daily communion is practised by many of the faithful in the Roman Church, for many decades also in the Anglican Church. It was especially propagated by Pope Pius X, who recommended children's communion from the moment when they can distinguish between the earthly and the heavenly bread. Children in the Eastern Church receive communion from the time of their baptism.

Profound changes took place in Protestantism. For Luther the Lord's Supper was first and foremost the visible Word (Augustine). It made more plain and certain the comforting word of forgiveness; it was a seal of saving grace; and an associated form of the proclamation of the word ('given for you' and 'poured out for you'). The relationship of word and sacrament is like the letter and its seal; the latter is not absolutely necessary. With this revolutionary interpretation, but also as a conservative spirit Luther connects faith in Christ's true presence in, with and under the bread with faith in a real eating of the Body and Blood of Christ. Against Zwingli he emphasizes in the Marburg colloquy the pronounced realism of the 'is' of the words of institution. He holds fast thereby to the old doctrine of consubstantiation. He knows of consecration but not of transubstantiation of the elements. The real presence of the Body of Christ he brings into relationship with Christ's ubiquity. In connection with the realistic sacramental faith, Luther holds firmly to the early Greek view that the reception of the Body and Blood of Christ implants the seed of the resurrection. The Formula of Concord (Chap. 7) teaches that by the power of the words of institution, all communicants united sacramentally with bread and wine, receive orally the true Body and Blood of Christ – the believers unto the forgiveness of sins, the unbelievers to their judgement. Lutheranism has also preserved the Roman liturgical custom by which the host is placed in the mouth and is received kneeling.

Calvin described the sacrament also as the seal of the word (Wallace, 1953). In the Calvanist view of the sacrament, however, the emphasis is placed on the spiritual nourishment of the soul rather than on the comforting words of forgiveness. Luther's favourite text was the words of institution, Calvin's was the Johannine narrative of the bread of life which, despite Luther's protest, he related to the Eucharist. Citing Augustine, Calvin championed psycho-physical parallelism: with bodily eating and drinking there goes the parallel spiritual enjoyment of the Body and Blood of Christ, which are not on earth but in heaven. The unifying bond between the two is the Holy Spirit. Christ is present only according to his divine power; Luther's doctrine of ubiquity Calvin found 'monstrous'. Only believers receive and are bodily nourished by the Body and Blood of Christ. Unbelievers receive only the visible elements. With respect to the liturgical rite, Calvinism restored the forms of the early Church: sitting or standing, ordinary bread, and the bread and the cup (common or individual ones) given into the hand.

Zwingli interpreted eating and drinking as a memorial celebration and an act of commitment rather than a mystical reception of grace. Man acts, he does not simply receive. The community of Christ's disciples is openly apparent in the Lord's Supper. The 'is' in the words of institution has the sense of 'signifies'. The Zwinglian rite succeeds in returning to the form of the Jewish *berakha*. Bullinger reached a more profound view: the Lord's Supper is the spiritual appropriation of the redeeming death of Christ and spiritual union with him. This interpretation was to prevail among Swiss church people. A clear example of this is the communion hymnody of the Swiss Reformed Church which differs little from that of the Lutheran. The Reformed view of the Lord's Supper is also to be found in the smaller, Free Churches of Protestantism. In these the fellowship idea of the early Christian communal meal is especially valued. The Lord's Supper of the Moravian Brethren is characterized by joy as was that of the early Church.

Protestant modernism called for the continued decatholicizing of the sacrament. Liberal theology referred to magical notions which adhered to early Christian sacraments from their links with the Hellenistic mysteries, and demanded the elimination of every magical element so as to leave a purely spiritual understanding of the sacraments. The consequence of this spiritualism, however, was the decline of the Eucharist to the point of disappearance. A great number of Protestants went to the Lord's table at their confirmation for the first and last time.

An opposing movement in Protestantism was the sacramental one which strove for the renewal of the early Christian faith in the sacrament. It began in the Oxford Movement of Newman and Pusey which restored the Anglican Church to a sacramental one (P. Schaefer, 1933). A parallel movement arose in German Lutheranism in the mid-nineteenth century. After the First World War another sacramental movement arose in the Lutheran and Reformed churches in Germany and in Scandinavian Lutheranism, and also in the Reformed churches of Switzerland, France, the Anglo-Saxon countries, among the Waldensians, and even among the Remonstrants (Arminians) and Unitarians. In African churches the same concerns were accompanied by a strong movement to link up with the traditional religious heritage of African Christians (Idowu, 1965). Everywhere may be seen a higher valuation of the sacrament, often also a return to realism, if not that of Rome and the Middle Ages, then to the forms and approach of the early Church and of the East.

The Christian communion meal is an especially clear example of Christianity's connection with the history of religions (Bammel, 1950). The sacred meal is not only the sacrament of Christians; it is also that of mankind as a whole. No one knew so well the connection between the Lord's Supper and the mystery cults as did the Fathers of the Church. In their evident perplexity over this, they came, from Justin onwards, to accept the idea that the true sacrament was being imitated by 'demons'. This was historically an absurdity, yet it bore witness to the structural similarity of the sacred communal meal, as a unitive rite, in its many forms; and also the underlying reality of commensality, sharing a common table at mealtime (Okafor, 1981), whose ultimate form cannot stop short of universality. 'Men will come from east and west, and from north and south, and sit at table in the kingdom of God' (Luke 13.29). The Eucharist is the 'sacrament of ecclesiastical unity' (Aquinas). The mystical body of Christ, the great congregation of all who are seeking the Deity, whose number and names are known to God alone, is here visible. Christianity becomes a mystery religion through Paul and John. Yet, despite this development, the link is never given up with that which originally constituted it, namely an eschatological expectation. In this sense the sacred meal points beyond itself to the appearing of the Lord and the setting up of the Kingdom of God, the community of the blessed. This double character of the Lord's Supper is expressed in the early Christian communion cry: *Marana tha* (1 Cor. 16.22; *Did.* 10.6) which has a double meaning: 'Our Lord comes', and 'Our Lord, come!'. This is the last prayer of the New Testament (Rev. 22.20).

(9) The covenant

The final form of union to be considered is the voluntary concluding of a *covenant* between man and God. Typical of traditional religions in its concern for the covenant is that of the Yoruba (Idowu, 1966). In the East, Mithra the Lord of the wide pastures is a covenantal deity. In Roman religion, the peace of the gods is a peaceful relationship between the state and the deity. Dangerous disturbances of the peace must be avoided through regular lustrations. The Israelite *berīth* (*ThWNT* 2, 106–27; *LThK* 2, 770ff.; *RGG* 1, 1513ff.), literally 'eating' or 'meal' (sacrificial meal) is, according to Robertson Smith, the making of a blood brotherhood, and the concluding of a covenant as a mutual exchange of power. *Kārat berīth*, to cut the covenant, is to pass through between the backs of sacrificial animals which have been divided into two with the aim of a mutual cursing: in the event of a breach of contract, both of the contractual partners wish for themselves the fate of the animals thus divided in two. Such a *berīth* was concluded between Yahweh and Abraham as an exchange of obligations (Gen. 15). A further covenant takes place between Yahweh and Moses (Exod. 24). God promises the people of Israel leadership, protection, victory and conquest; the people promise obedience to the law of Yahweh and the worship of him alone. The covenantal obligation is sealed by the sprinkling of blood and communion (Exod. 24.8). Priesthood and kingship likewise rest upon the covenant of faithfulness. This covenant becomes spiritualized with the prophets into a covenant of the last days. This is especially the case with Jeremiah:

> Behold, the days are coming, says the Lord, when I will make a new covenant with the house of Israel and the house of Judah, not like the covenant which I made with their fathers, when I took them by the hand to bring them out of the land of Egypt, my covenant which they broke . . . But this is the covenant which I will make with the house of Israel after those days: I will put my law within them, and I will write it upon their hearts; and I will be their God, and they shall be my people. (Jer. 31.31ff.)

The 'eternal covenant', the permanent state of the covenant in relation to *shālōm* is proclaimed by the prophets (Ezek. 16; Isa. 55) and by the law books influenced by the prophets: the Book of the Covenant, the Decalogue, Deuteronomy, and the Priestly codex. In the Priestly history, the covenant is extended backwards in time: here the covenant of God with Noah appears under a sign, the rainbow. The Priestly history (Gen. 17) considers circumcision to be a sign of the covenant although earlier it had been a fertility rite in the cult of Yahweh.

In the Greek Bible, the translation of *berīth*, *diathēkē*, becomes a term which refers to sacred history. It tells of the gracious guidance throughout the history of salvation in which the whole initiative devolves upon God regardless of the communal relationship grounded upon this (*ThWNT* 2, 127ff.). *Diathēkē* also serves to express the difference in the New Testament (*ThWNT* 2, 132ff.; *RGG* 1, 1516ff.) between the preparatory saving events of the Old Testament and their fulfilment in Christ. Especially sharp does this difference appear in the Pauline words of institution: 'This is the new covenant in my blood' (1 Cor. 11.25); also in the Epistle to the Galatians, where the difference between the covenant of the law, made on Sinai, and the covenant of promise, made with Abraham, is made clear. Both in Galatians (4.22ff.) and also in the Epistle to the Hebrews (chap. 9), the Greek significance of the *diathēkē* is equal to testament, i.e. the last determination and disposition. Irenaeus speaks of three diathēkai (*foedera*; Seeberg, 1920): (a) the natural law in the heart of man, (b) the decalogue as the law reformed (*lex reformata*), and (c) the recapitulation of the moral law in Christ, the eternal law with spiritual sacrifice.

The covenantal or 'federal' theology revived during the Reformation (Seeberg, 1920). The Anabaptists called themselves 'comrades of the covenant', Zwingli considered paedobaptism a 'covenant' which corresponded to the

Pauline interpretation of the Abrahamic covenant. Bullinger pursued this thought further, as did Calvin. Under humanist influence, distinctions were drawn between the 'covenant of nature' ('work covenant', Polanus), the 'covenant with Adam' and the 'covenant of grace'. Cocceius based on this his work on federal theology (1648) in which the covenant of work is replaced by the twofold 'economy' of the covenant of grace. At the beginning, however, there stands the primordial 'treaty' between Father and Son. Federal theology was to exercise a strong influence upon Reformed theology and Pietism. Characteristic in this regard is the use of formulae drawn from Roman law. Two partners stand facing each other, not with equal rights, it is true, since one of them, God, is sovereign. Here the connection between the Roman *pax* and the Israelite *berīth* comes to light. For the Christian Church, the place of the covenant of circumcision is taken by the covenant of baptism; it is a widespread Christian custom to renew the covenant of baptism at the first communion, and in Catholic churches annually thereafter at the Easter vigil, following the consecration of the baptismal water. An oft-sung hymn in German is 'My baptismal covenant lasts for ever'. The baptismal covenant is also celebrated in Protestant hymns, and in the inscribing of the names of baptized on a cradle roll, where they and their parents are periodically reminded, during special rites in church or Sunday school, of their covenantal obligations.

8

The Sacred Word
1: From the Deity

(1) Forms of the sacred word

(a) Singing, murmuring and the cadence

Sacred action and *sacred word* (Mensching, 1937) are closely associated. The latter underlines the sacredness of the former. The word becomes sacred through association with sacred action, sacred space and sacred time. But even apart from these, the word may bear the sacred in itself just as sacred action also thematizes the world without a word being spoken. Even the way the word is uttered also thematizes the world apart from its contents. The word is part of the wider category of sacred sound which has already been mentioned in connection with apotropaic rites and unification rites, especially the sacred dance reflecting the music of the spheres (see above, Chapters 5 and 7). It is true, however, that Christianity has been strongly associated with the word, and even where non-verbal sound is present (organ music, woodwind and brass, drums, bells, rattles), the word is rarely far away.

The *sung word* (*ERE* 9, 5–61; *RGG* 4, 1197ff.; 1201ff.; *HWDA* 4, 677–84; 9. App. 424–85; 6, 633–90; Goldammer, 1960, 272ff.; *ER* 3, 204ff.) is sacred in origin. The modulation of the voice has something wonderful in itself as have the sounds of nature and other beings. The sacred origins of singing are apparent in the words *epōdē* (Greek) or *incantatio* (Latin) from which comes *enchanter* (Fr.) or *carmen* (Latin) from which is derived (French) *charme*. The Norse word *galdr*, magic saying, comes from the verb *galan*, to sing, especially used for birds' voices. Traditional magical singing lives on in religious speech-song or chanting, the monotoned recitations of sacred texts, with relatively little rising and falling of the voice. Read in this manner are the canonical texts of the Vedas, the *Tripitaka* throughout the Buddhist world, the Sikh *Granth*, the Qur'ān (Nelson, 1980), the Avesta, the liturgical texts of Jewish synagogues and those of Christian Churches in East and West.

In Eastern Churches as in the Roman Church, there occurs the juxtaposition of 'real' singing and chanting. Also in the Catholic Church, prayers in the vernacular may be said in a sacral monotone, not as in the average Protestant Church, where the words are stressed according to meaning. The chanting of the priest at the altar was also retained in Lutheran Churches where, in contrast to the Roman Church, the words of institution of the Lord's Supper are often sung. Rationalism voiced its disapproval of the singing of the liturgy by the priest. However, the liturgical movements in the Anglican and Protestant Churches, including the Oxford Movement in Britain and the Berneuchner and

Alpirsbacher in Germany, have been concerned to reintroduce sacral singing and chanting.

In the course of time cultic singing became separate from profane singing. As with cultic vestments and sacred language, cultic singing represents an early form of singing that has died out. Living language and singing are subject to constant change and development, but cultic singing, along with all things cultic, remains the same for long periods. Christian cultic singing goes back to the Syrian, Greek and Roman cult singing of antiquity. The individual Christian Churches formed their cultic singing independently, each following its own tradition, whether Syrian, Egyptian, Armenian, Greek, Slavic, Roman, Celtic, Gallic, Spanish or, more recently, African. In the West the Roman form superseded the other forms. It had itself emerged out of the Italian folksong; and after the reforms of Gregory the Great it became known as Gregorian (*RGG* 2, 1848f.). The Gregorian chant is in unison in accordance with the closing words of the Preface (Rom. 15.6) 'that together you may glorify with one voice . . .'. Only gradually during succeeding centuries did polyphonic music spread to other parts of the liturgy, at first in the Latin Church, then in the Byzantine (Russian and Greek; *RGG* 2, 1207–17). Lutheranism also followed Gregorian plainsong in both the singing at the altar, and also its congregational singing (*RGG* 2, 1474ff.). In individual churches (in Switzerland and Britain) polyphonic congregational singing was cultivated; in others, however, part-singing was only for the choir. In the Roman Church and also in part of the non-Roman Churches of the West, there arose a move to return to the old Gregorian forms and also to purely vocal song (without organ accompaniment); a similar move in the Greek Church was for returning to the old Byzantine melodies. In such movements there lives the awareness of numinous or 'mystical' singing.

The *repetition* of the sacred recitation and cultic song constitutes a special form of these. It may be in part literal repetition and there may be in part some variation to the meaning. (1) The continual repetition of a *refrain* or response is widespread among the praise songs and chants of traditional peoples. In the liturgy of the Greek Church the call comes after each petition of the intercessions: Lord have mercy, *Kyrie eleison*, Slavic *Gospodi pomilui*; in the Roman litanies, the short petitions are repeated: 'Pray for us', 'Redeem us, O Lord'. The earliest Western litany is that of All Saints. It was especially beloved in the Irish Church (Plummer, 1925). Roman Catholic litanies arose on the pattern of these Irish litanies. The most popular is the Marian litany. They have now found their way into the books of common worship of many denominations. (2) Repetition of the same thought often leads to a new linguistic formulation, and so arises the *parallelismus membrōrum*. We find this linguistic parallelism in Germanic traditional religious songs, and in the canticles, psalms and prophecies. A greater part of the New Testament writings is also largely cultic texts, 'liturgical catechetics'. Their rhythmic-liturgical character is especially plain in the hymn to love (1 Cor. 13) and in the high priestly prayer (John 17). The first completely colometric translation of the

New Testament, for reading aloud, appeared in 1922 (A. Loisy); and since then many biblical translations have followed this example.

The external divisions in cultic songs or recitations are marked in two different ways: (a) through the exchanges between a cantor or prayer leader and the congregation, a practice widespread in the cultus of traditional religious groups and in antiquity; it has also been customary in Christian psalm and hymn singing; (b) through the antiphonal song, with two choirs of a different or the same type of voice (boys' and men's choirs, or two women's choirs). Antiphonal choirs were also featured in the cultus of antiquity, both in the Roman traditional cultus and in that of the Jewish temple. From Syria it spread to the remaining areas of the Christian Church. The antiphonal form is the more distinguished one in the Church's services of worship.

The *murmur* or *whisper* is another form of the word that is found not only among traditional peoples and in antiquity, but also in the Christian cultus. The compulsive prayers in Babylonian religion were spoken in 'a soft voice'. Prayers were whispered softly into the ear of particular deities of antiquity, such as Aphrodite who thus received the praise name of *Psythiros*, 'the whispering one'. Murmuring and muttering constitute forms of prayer alongside the loud prayers and the completely silent ones. In Eastern church liturgies many prayers are spoken softly by the *mustikos* or priest while the choir is singing. In the Roman Mass the canon or main part was still being sung during the seventh century along with the Preface or preliminary part, yet in such a way as to be just audible to those standing nearby. In the ninth century the soft recitation of the canonical prayers became the rule.

Normal speech tones occupy a prominent place in the cultus, above all in the sermon as a free proclamation of the word. From there it also spread to the free prayers of Protestant Churches and religious movements. But even here the need arises for making some difference from the purely profane. Since the 'catholic' or 'sacral' character of the cultus has to be avoided, the difference can only be created by colouring the human word by means of religious pathos, the so-called 'pulpit pathos' or religious cadence. This created an intermediate stage between sacral speech or song on the one hand and profane speech (or song) on the other. The religious cadence does, however, tend to have a repelling effect. Professors of speech in seminaries wage a constant battle to keep down its hydra-like forms.

(b) Extemporizing and lallation

Against fixed and stereotyped formulae for worship, there arose again and again a counter-movement. All great epochs in the history of religion are creative with regard to language, and have a tendency to transform it. These include: early Christianity, the Franciscan movement which encouraged preaching in the vernacular of the people, the mysticism of the Middle Ages and, above all, the Reformation. Luther is the greatest creator of German Christian language, besides Mechthild of Magdeburg and Meister Eckhart. In Britain, John Wycliffe, William Tyndale and the composers of the Authorised Version of 1611 likewise had a profound effect on English language development. Parallels lie also to hand in Hinduism and Buddhism, Islamic sufism and the Sikh *Granth*.

Free speaking and praying secured a place in the worship of the Jewish synagogue and in the early Christian Church. Paul gives a clear picture of this: 'When you come together, each one has a hymn, a lesson, a revelation, a tongue or an interpretation.' So let each speak 'in turn'. All things should be done 'decently and in order' (1 Cor. 14. 26ff.). Tertullian can boast of Christian prayer in worship services because it comes from the heart. Apart from hymns and prayers sung together, all prayers in early Christian times were improvised, an inspiration of the moment, spoken by prophets and later by ordained office-bearers, but always free. Still later, prayers were written down before the service and then recited or read out. Thus arose the collections of prayers (Sacramentaries), notably the *Leonianum* and *Gregorianum*.

A special form of charismatic speech is speaking in tongues, *glossolalia* (*ThWNT* 1, 719ff.; *LThK* 4, 972ff.; *RE* 21, 749ff.; Samarin, 1972; Hines, 1962; Williams, 1981; *ER* 5, 563ff.). It is a compulsive and automatic speaking in a state of religious enthusiasm and dissociation, without any control by the rational mind. Very different forms of it are found: forms of language, whether it be that of the mother tongue or a foreign dialect or even a foreign language; forms *like* language whether a distortion of ordinary speech or an imaginary language or else a simple stammer and lallation that form words and syllables. Glossolalia flourished in early Christianity, following on from the miracle of Pentecost (Acts 2) as a continuing phenomenon in individual Hellenistic Christian congregations such as Corinth (1 Cor. 14.26). The fact that glossolalia was unintelligible made necessary its interpretation through special charismatics (*hermēneutae*, interpreters). Glossolalia burst out again in post-apostolic times in Montanism, then in Protestantism, in the prophetic Camisard movement at the end of the seventeenth century and beginning of the eighteenth, in the nineteenth-century Catholic Apostolic Irvingite movement, likewise in the evangelical revival movements, and finally in the Pentecostal movement of the twentieth century (Hollenweger, 1969; Massey, 1976; Laurentin, 1977). The danger in religion of turning too much towards forms of dissociation is very real, above all by the repeated forcing of oneself into ecstatic psychological states. There is evidence to suggest that it may take more and more effort to break out in tongues (Goodman, 1974). The problems of those unable to speak in tongues have also been noted (N. G. Holm, 1980). They may easily be led to conclude that they are permanently unworthy to receive the spirit baptism poured out on those near at hand. Yet this form of speech is still of value. In glossolalia is revealed the inadequacy of human speech to convey the religious, in the same way as does the mystic through silence (*HWDA* 3, 962ff.).

(c) The sacred language

The tendency towards the separation of the sacred and the profane led towards the rise of whole *sacred languages* (*ER* 8, 439ff.), not just to different ways of uttering words. Although the living, spoken language is caught up in constant change, the liturgical language remains one and the same throughout the centuries, even millennia, a symbol for the eternal beyond time, the 'wholly other'. The unintelligibility of the sacred texts puts a veil over their contents. This incomprehensibility is further enhanced as the cultic language belongs to a quite different language group from that of the country concerned. Early Roman traditional prayers were still in use in the imperial period despite their unintelligibility. Amongst some traditional peoples, individual Bantu peoples for instance, another language, a Hamitic one, may be used in worship. The cultic language of the Sumerians became the sacred language of their Semitic conquerors. The Babylonian texts are similar to the much later Christian missals in Latin and the vernacular; they are designed to facilitate understanding of the foreign cultic language. The language in which the different sacred writings found expression also became sacred languages, for example, those of the Vedas, the Avesta and the *Tripitaka* of Theravāda Buddhism. The Sanskrit of Mahāyāna Buddhism spread to China, Tibet and Japan where today individual texts and formularies are recited, such as *Om mani padme hum* (O jewel in the lotus flower), though the cultic language has remained that of the vernacular.

In the context of the wider religious concern for sacred languages, it is possible to discern similar phenomena in Judaism and Christianity. The Hebrew language was, and remained, the language of the Jewish Bible: even in Aramaic times it continued as the language of Scripture and the cultus. Hence the need arose for Targums (paraphrases of the biblical texts). Hebrew was the cultic language even of diaspora Judaism. Only for a time was it supplanted by the Greek language. In the orthodox synagogue service, only the sermon was delivered in the vernacular. However, Reformed and Liberal synagogues have introduced the vernacular into other parts of the liturgy, only the most solemn ones, the *Shema* and the Aaronic blessing, are spoken or sung in Hebrew. The Hebrew-Aramaic language was likewise retained in a number of formulae in Greek Christianity and in other Christian languages as 'tokens of origin': *Hallelujah, Hosanna* and *Amen* have maintained their place as exclamations from the days of the temple cultus. In the Aramaic *Marāna tha* (Our Lord comes! O Lord, come! – 1 Cor. 16.22; *Did.* 10, 6) the most important early Christian invocation has been preserved. The form of prayer address, Abba, likewise Aramaic, comes from the mouth of Jesus himself (Mark 14.36). The *Eloi, Eloi* (My God, my God, why have you forsaken me? Mark 15.34) resounds in the passion story, the *Ephphatha* (Be opened, Mark 7.34) in the Roman baptismal rite. Still more Hebrew words have been preserved in the Gospels, such as *Rabbuni* (Master, Mark 10.51; John 20.16) and *Talitha kumi* (Little girl, I say to you, arise, Mark 5.41), or *Corban* (given to God, Mark 7.11).

Elements of Greek are to be found in the different Latin liturgies. The early cultic vernacular language (*NDLW* 519ff.) was Greek; popular Latin became the liturgical language first in Africa, then in Spain and finally in Rome and Gaul (*LThK* 5, 1028ff.). The Greek *Kyrie eleison* has kept its place in the Latin Mass. The *Trisagion* (*Hagios ho theos, hagios ischuros, hagios athanatos* – Holy is God! Holy and strong! Holy immortal One!) is intoned in the Roman Good Friday liturgy. In the Gallican liturgy whole hymns were sung in Greek. As in the case of the Latin liturgy, so also have numerous Greek elements been preserved in the Syriac, Armenian and, most of all, in the Coptic liturgies. The Latin language became the church language for the whole of the West after the defeat of Homoian Christianity. The Germanic peoples, who initially used the Gothic language or their own vernacular in Homoian Christian services of worship, were slowly subdued and won over to the Roman faith. In the East, the vernacular took the place of the Greek everywhere, including Coptic (Egyptian), Syriac, Armenian, Georgian, Slavic (Stökl, 1961; Spinka, 1968) and later still Romanian. All these languages have become just as much church languages as did the Byzantine Greek. In the course of time it became necessary to replace the church language which had become unintelligible by the vernacular tongue, at least for parts of the liturgy. So Arabic replaced Coptic and Syriac; Malayalam took the place of Syriac in South India. The Reformation returned to the early Christian practice of using the vernacular in services of worship. These languages of the people, above all the language of the Luther Bible and that of the Book of Common Prayer have, it is true, themselves long since become sacred languages. Vatican II took a momentous step in replacing the Latin language of the Mass by the vernacular, while many Anglican churches have replaced the Book of Common Prayer by the Alternative Service Book; in both cases with arguments similar to those used a millennium before by the Bishop of Rome, to allow church Slavic in Moravia when the bishops of Bavaria wished to enforce the use of church Latin (Hellmann, 1964).

The rise of the sacred language discloses an inner necessity. Religious language tries to express the stability and unchanging character of the divine; and at the same time the sense of mystery and the ineffable. The language of worship is just as statuesque as liturgy and sacred Scripture, and this not only in Christianity but in other religions equally. The hymns of the Vedas have been unchanged for at least three thousand years; the sacred texts of the Avesta, in the earliest sections, for at least two thousand five hundred, as with those of the Buddhist *Tripitaka*, the Jewish psalms and *Torah* (the narrative parts of the Hexateuch being nearer three thousand years old). The Jewish *Shemone Esre*, or Eighteen prayer, and the prayers surrounding the *Shema* are the same today as at the time of Christ. The Christian Greek and Latin liturgical texts go back in part to the second century, mostly to the fourth and sixth centuries, as a whole to the sixth to eighth centuries. The Anglican Book of Common Prayer is four hundred years old as are Lutheran liturgies and individual Reformers' prayers and liturgies. Their main structure arises out of the earlier Catholic heritage. The Qur'ān and the worship of the Islamic community world-wide have had one language for 1350 years: Arabic. According to ancient rule the

Qur'ān should not be recited in any other tongue. This rule was first broken by the Ahmadiyyah, a movement founded in India in 1880. The sacred language has immense significance for the cultus. Behind what appears to be a blind clinging on to sacred language is a concern about distorting, falsifying, desacralizing, disturbing and weakening the sacred word from God and to God.

(2) The oracle and the prophetic word

The *content* of the sacred word, as distinct from its forms, may be structured phenomenologically by considering first the word from God, then the word to God. This corresponds to religious experience of the prevenient grace of the Deity. 'It was you who first moved me and made me look for you', prays the author of *The Imitation of Christ* (III, 21). Prayer is in the profoundest sense, grace: not man seeking God but God seeking man. God's word therefore has precedence before man's word.

A form of the sacred word of the greatest significance in the life of traditional peoples and those of antiquity is the *oracle* (*ERE* 4, 775ff.; *RGG* 4, 727ff.; 4, 1628ff.; 4, 1664ff.; Guillaume, 1938; *HWDA* 6, 1255ff. *et passim*; *MMM passim*; *ER* 4, 375ff.; 5, 513ff.; 9, 345ff.; 11, 81ff., 454ff.). The Deity (who is not always thought of in personal terms) makes his/her/its will known and reveals what is to be. In many forms of oracles and divination one may distinguish between the giving of oracles in the context of cultic divination which is mostly in the hands of divines and priests; and the personal and charismatic giving of oracles by the seer or seeress. The instruments of cultic divination are many: sticks, arrows, lots, dice, nuts, peas; the flight of birds and the voices of birds; the neighing of horses harnessed to a cultic waggon driven by priests; animal entrails, especially the liver; the blood of victims; the drinking vessel; in addition there is the observation of stars (see above, Chapter 1), the interpretation of dreams (*ERE* 5, 28–40; *RGG* 6, 1001ff.; *LThK* 10, 326ff.; Freud, 1978; *ER* 4, 483), especially dreams at graves and shrines. The infinite variety of these divinatory objects is due to the basic assumption of a correspondence between this world and the spirit world. Because the spirit world initiates real change in the sensory world any object or part of the world about us may be used as an agent through which the deities and spirit powers may communicate with men. The instruction to men is contained in the *oraculum* or saying. The Israelites had a special place for these oracles, the tent of oracles (of Yahweh) at the shrine of Kadesh where *urim* and *thummim*, the sticks or arrows of their system of divination, were kept (Exod. 28.30; Lev. 8.8). Using lots analogously to the Arab stick oracle, there proceeded the pronouncement of Yahweh called *Torah*, literally the casting of the lot to obtain the judgement of Yahweh. Greek centres of oracular divination in antiquity were Dodona, where priests prophesied from the rustling leaves of the sacred grove of Zeus, and Delphi, where the Pythia chewed laurel leaves, breathed in the vapours coming from a cleft in the ground and in a state of trance spoke mysterious words which were interpreted by priests. These interpreted by priests. These translated her words into ordinary speech and issued them as oracles of Apollo.

Besides the system of cultic oracles stands the direct revelation of oracles from the Deity or Numen through seers and seeresses who are endowed with charisma and are not related to an oracular institution. Such were the Germanic and Celtic seeresses. The doyenne of the Greek individual seeresses is Cassandra, the prophetess of doom. Equal fame was attained by the Sibyls. A series of them was named in the literature of the ancient world according to their country of origin. Their sombre verses, uttered in Homeric language and containing prophecies of doom, were collected together and so arose the literature known as the Sibylline oracle. From Greece Sibylline prophecy came to Italy. Cumae, in Campania, became their home. The oracles of the Sibyls of Cumae were written down in the Sibylline books and kept in the Capitoline shrine. In AD 81 they were burnt, but soon after Sibylline sayings were gathered from all over the known world by the Roman state and replaced in the newly-built Capitol. These however exhibited a different character from that of the Greek Sibyls: they resembled rather those of the Delphic oracles. As often as fearful omens arose to pose a danger for the state, the Senate caused these books of oracles to be consulted in order to determine the necessary expiatory measures. The books continued to be consulted down to the emperor Julian; only under Stilicho (365–408) were they destroyed as dangerous survivals of 'paganism' in the early fifth century.

The Sibylline oracle was also taken up by diaspora Judaism in Alexandria and made the pattern for new, admittedly fictitious, oracles which, as 'heathen' parallels to the prophets' prophecies of doom, were designed to promote the religious message of Judaism in the Greco-Roman world (Charlesworth, 1983). Christian Sibyls now built upon these Jewish ones. They imitated the Greek Sibylline oracles in form and language and interwove fabricated prophecies with the genuine traditional oracles. In this manner there arose a whole corpus of Christian Sibylline oracles which Christian writers, above all Lactantius, made use of for apologetic purposes. The prophecy of the Saviour in the fourth Eclogue of Virgil, which was given a messianic interpretation, was taken to be a prophecy of the Cumaean Sibyls (see also below, Chapter 12).

With the Sibylline oracles, contact was also made with the apocalyptic, prophetic books of 'late' Judaism (the Book of Enoch, the Ascension of Moses, the Fourth Book of Ezra, and the Apocalypse of Baruch; *RGG* 1, 464ff.). These prophecies are reflected in part in the New Testament Apocalypse (*RGG* 1, 407ff.; 4, 822ff.; *LThK* 1, 696ff.) which represents a compendium of apocalyptic expectation. In the Middle Ages it provided the impulse for a new literature of Christian prophecy (Nigg, 1954; Cohn, 1971). This culminates in the commentary on the Apocalypse by Joachim of Fiore (Reeves, 1976). In the fourteenth century other tractates of prophecies followed and finally, in the sixteenth century appeared Nostradamus' book of prophecy which is still widely cited at the present day (Cheetham, 1979). Along with the concern in the West for its classical literary oracles and prophecies should be added the continuing importance, especially among Christians of independent churches in Africa and elsewhere, of the interpretation of dreams and visions, and of divination by means of the Bible or biblical passages.

Oracles and divination live on among Christians whose faith retains a strongly traditional cosmological orientation (*The Church in a Changing Society*, 1978, 372f.; see also below, Chapter 9). And yet, more comprehensive in the shaping of the Christian faith and life has been the *prophetic word* (Hübscher, 1952). The latter has given its name to the 'prophetic' religions of Zoroastrianism, Judaism, Christianity and Islam, apart from numerous prophetic movements within and without these. Prophets, as a category of sacred person, tend, as we shall see later (in Chapter 12) to arise in any religious tradition at critical times, as religious formulators of a new form of the faith. The prophetic word appears very plainly in the Israelite religion (*ERE* 10, 384ff.; Lindblom, 1967). 'Whatever I command you you shall speak' (Jer. 1.7; cf. 23.28). The prophet experiences a compulsion to proclaim the word; all resistance is useless; he must carry out God's commission: 'If I say, "I will not mention him,/or speak any more in his name", there is in my heart as it were a burning fire/shut up in my bones/and I am weary with holding it in,/and I cannot' (Jer. 20.9). Or, from a Christian apostle, 'Woe to me if I do not preach the gospel' (1 Cor. 9.16).

The content of the prophetic word is, first, the absoluteness of God. *Yahweh 'ehād*, Yahweh alone is God, Lord and King. Second, there is the call for the spiritual worship of God and the observance of basic ethical norms. Third, the prophet proclaims the wrath of God upon the disobedient people, the destruction of his own people: 'Behold, I am bringing upon this city and upon all its towns all the evil that I have pronounced against it, because they have stiffened their neck, refusing to hear my words' (Jer. 19.15). A fourth element is the preaching of salvation. Israelite prophecy included from the beginning the promise of mercy for the remnant of the people. Gradually, this changed into the promise of a golden age for the whole of Israel. Finally, the prophecy widened out to a universal gospel. The peoples and nations participate in the glory of God's people. Thus, prophecy includes God's revelation of himself, his moral demands, and his revelation of judgement and grace. This word of revelation possesses divine power, magical power. 'Is not my word like fire, says the Lord, and like a hammer which breaks the rock in pieces?' (Jer. 23.29). The word which is uttered through the mouth of the prophet bears – like a magical incantation – the power of self-realization: 'My word . . . that goes forth from my mouth . . . shall not return empty, but . . . shall accomplish that which I purpose, and prosper in the thing for which I sent it' (Isa. 55.11).

Prophecy from a state of possession revived afresh in early Christianity (*ThWNT* 6, 781ff.; *ERE* 10, 382ff.). The preaching of John constitutes a summary of Israelite prophecy, the main feature of which is: 'Repent, for the kingdom of heaven is at hand' (Matt. 3.2). Jesus took over the same form of words employed by John (Matt. 4.17). His gospel is the fulfilment of the

Israelite prophecy of salvation. It is prophetic in form; its crucial content however is the nearness of the Kingdom of glory and the forgiveness of sins. The prophecy of the earliest Church is linked with pentecostal, spiritual enthusiasm. Its content, couched in messianic and eschatological terms, is the testimony to the resurrection of Christ and the proclamation of the *parousia*, the coming of the Lord. The Christian service of worship was a place of prophecy. A vivid picture of this is given in the first Epistle to the Corinthians (14). The prophets had the right to preach and pray as they wished: 'Allow the prophets to utter thanks as often as they desire', exhorts the *Teaching of the Twelve Apostles* (*Did.* 10,71).

As the Israelite prophets do in the name of Yahweh, so also do the early church prophets in the name of Jesus Christ: through their mouth Christ himself speaks. Examples of this occur in the circular letter of the Apocalyptist: 'I am the Alpha and the Omega' (Rev. 1.8). 'The words of the first and the last, who died and came to life' (Rev. 2.8). Many words of Jesus handed down in the Gospels came in all likelihood not from the mouth of Jesus, but rather from the mouth of the risen Christ who speaks through the mouth of the prophets. For instance: 'Where two or three are gathered in my name, there am I in the midst of them' (Matt. 18.20). The high-priestly prayer of Jesus (John 17) may have been spoken first of all by a Christian prophet at the Passover festival of the congregation in Ephesus (Loisy). Gradually, charismatic prophecy was replaced in Christian services of worship by the preaching and prayers of the recognized office-bearers. It burst out again in the Montanist movement (Kraft, 1955; *RGG* 4, 1117f.), but was unable to hold up the consolidation and crystallization of the liturgy. Only in the second millennium did it revive in the Joachimite movement, in the various enthusiastic movements of Protestantism (Quakers, Camisards and revivalist movements of the eighteenth and nineteenth centuries) and, recently, in the Christian prophet movements of Africa and elsewhere (see also above, section one).

(3) The mythic word

A quite different form from the oracle or prophetic word is the *mythic word* (*ERE* 1, 117ff.; *RGG* 4, 1263–74; Van der Leeuw, 1964; Eliade, 1963; Lyttleton, 1983; *ER* 10, 261ff,); yet myth must also be regarded as a word from God. There is a close connection, in this case, with sacred action or ritual (Hooke, 1934; E. O. James, 1958; Watts, 1968). Myth interprets ritual and accompanies it. Both are concerned with the primordial encounter with the sacred and the Deity. They are declarations in word and action of mighty events. Myth deals with the life and work of Deity. It is concerned with what transcends time and history, yet, paradoxically, sets these transcendent events on a level with history. There are many levels of myth. Popular myths are to be distinguished from literary and theological forms of myth. But whether popular or spiritualized in form, the mythic word is an inescapable form of the word from God and constitutes a fundamental dimension of religious expression.

Various kinds of myths may be distinguished. *Theogonic* myths tell of the origin of deities. Deities may be 'born' or 'proceed' out of an earlier deity (e.g. the earth). Brahma proceeds out of the navel of Vishnu, the goddess Athene out of the head of Zeus, Yahweh is associated with a volcano (Exod. 19). Theogonic myths are associated with *cosmogonic* or creation myths (*ERE* 4, 125–79; Long, 1963; Sproul, 1979; Maclagan, 1977; *ER* 4, 94ff.). These range widely from those of traditional peoples in their rich variety, to those of the ancient world which have expanded into cosmologies in epic form, such as the Babylonian creation myth *Enuma Elish* which was recited at the New Year festival. The creation of the world from chaos, through the creator deity's conflict with the cosmic monster lay behind the Israelite creation narrative and that of an even older version of it which is only partly included in Exodus and Leviticus. The beginning of the older version has been replaced by the creation narrative of the Priestly source. Even so, the Babylonian monster Tiamat is still discernible at different places in the Hebrew Bible (see Chapter 1, above). The cosmogonic myth which has survived all subsequent transformations in Christianity is that of the creation of the world through the oracular word of God (Gen. 1).

To be distinguished from the cosmogonic myths are the *cosmological* or nature myths (*ER* 4, 100ff.). These portray the mystery of daily and annual growth and decay as a once for all, unique sequence of events. Individual forms include sun, moon and astral myths; and, above all, myths which represent the seasons of the year: the most striking forms of the latter are the Egyptian myth of Osiris and the descent into hell associated with Ishtar. Traces of ancient sun myths are found in the Samson saga (Judg. 13–16) and the Psalms (19.5ff.).

Anthropological myths of the creation of man, of paradise and the fall (*RGG* 5, 95ff.; Budde, 1952), are associated with myths of creation. Through these the origin of sin and death is explained. There is a vast range of myths of the origin of death (Abrahamsson, 1951). Also linked with myths of primordial times are the myths of the flood, which again are world-wide in distribution and exhibit characteristic features (*ERE* 4, 545–57; *LThK* 9, 590ff.; Heidel, 1949; *ER* 5, 353ff.). These include the annihilation of the former race of men and the survival of a couple or family who form the beginning of a new humanity under a new dispensation. In Christianity the myth of the flood (Gen. 6–9) has maintained its place down to the present. It has even lent its power in disguised form to views concerning the nuclear threat (Chernus, 1982). Nevertheless, the myth of the creation of man, and of woman taken from man's side, of paradise and the fall, with the garden of Eden, the tree of life, the serpent, and the eating of the fruit – these have been even more important for Christians in providing images for understanding and structuring existence as created and fallen.

Also linked with myths of creation are the *patriarchal* myths which go back to primordial times and the origins of a people through the actions of a deity or deities, or mythical beings, who live as a people's primordial ancestors. The Hebrew Scriptures contain such myths of patriarchal hero figures, whereby a people or ethnic group traces its origins to a family and ethnic patriarch (Gunkel, 1922; Thompson, 1974, Seters, 1975). *Cult* myths, often found with patriarchal myths, offer on the other hand an aetiological explanation for a shrine or ritual. The shrine is held to be founded by a deity, the ceremonies introduced or instituted by a divine being also. Such cultic myths are found in archaic and traditional societies. Especially characteristic is the Jacob myth which explains the divine origin of the shrine at Bethel as a stone cult (Gen. 28.19ff.), and the Isaac myth in which the replacement of human sacrifice by animal sacrifice is made clear (Gen. 22). The deepest meaning of the cult myth may be sought in the motif of the Deity (and not man) as establishing communication between them.

Soteriological myths of the revealer and saviour tell of the descent of the divine redeemer to rescue mankind from evil and sin. One form of the saviour myth brings it close to the patriarchal myth, namely, the traditional myth of the bringer of culture and salvation (Ehrenreich, 1906; Lanczkowski, 1974). Human or animal *numina* bring men tools and weapons to help them in the struggle for existence. They also give them medicines and magic formulae. Out of the bringer of salvation has arisen the great saviour and redeemer figure central to the religions of antiquity. In the cult of Osiris is found an intermingling of the saviour myth with the nature myth. In the mysteriosophic cult of Mithras, the main stages of the myth of the saviour figure are clearly depicted in many of the tauroctony reliefs, e.g. those from Neuenheim and Osterburken. In Buddhism and Hinduism saviour myths are also present. The Buddha-to-be steps down from heaven to earth to bring release from the cycle of births full of suffering. He also in a supernatural manner enters the womb of a virgin. A Vishnu avatar in the form of a fish rescues the first man, Manu, in an Indian flood myth. In Christianity, the myth of the revealer and saviour has also a position of prominence. The myth may be outlined as follows: God speaks to the patriarchs, to Moses, to the judges, to the kings and to the prophets. At the end the long-awaited Son of God (Hick, 1977) descends to the earth, born of a virgin (*RGG* 3, 1068f.) clothed in human form, unrecognized by the demons (*kenōsis*, incarnation). The redemption of mankind was mythically depicted by their ransom from bondage to Satan or through the latter's conquest (by deceiving him), or by eliminating the power of sin, after the analogy of the scape-goat or else through appeasing the divine wrath by means of a vicarious sacrifice after the model of the Passover lamb (see above, Chapter 6). There follows the descent into the underworld (*ERE* 4. 648ff.; *RGG* 3, 408ff.; *LThK* 5, 358ff., 450ff.) and the setting free of the righteous forefathers from the grave, the ascent into heaven (*RGG* 3, 333ff.; *LThK* 5, 352ff.), and the return from heaven to judge the world after the final cosmic catastrophe. A few critics also count the narratives of Christ's baptism in Jordan and the Last Supper, including the command to institute it, as cult myths which are designed to explain the institution of both sacraments through Christ; they are then brought into the closest possible connection with the redemptive blood of Christ through the flowing of the water and blood from the wound in the side of the dying saviour (John 19.34). The resurrection narratives are also included among the myths of institution inasmuch as they

explain the moving of the Christian Easter festival to the Sunday and the origin
of the Christian Sunday celebration in place of the Sabbath. Through a process
of parallelism, there grew up a Marian myth around the Christian saviour myth
in the course of the centuries. The main stages of the Marian myth are: the
immaculate conception (and preservation from original sin), the virginal
conception through the Holy Spirit, the supernatural birth, the co-redemption
of mankind by Mary under the cross, and the bodily assumption into heaven.

Also to be distinguished as types of myth are myths of the *beyond* and myths
of the *last days* (eschatological myths). Examples of the former include the
Adapa myth, the Gilgamesh epic, which shows man's search for eternal life, the
underworld myth of Odysseus' descent into Hades and ascension myths such as
Elijah's ascent into heaven (2 Kings 2.11) or that of the ascension of Mithras.
Christ's descent into Hades and ascent into heaven can also be seen as a myth of
the beyond. Eschatological myths furnish a dramatic representation of the end
of the world (*RGG* 2, 650ff.). The primordial events are repeated in the last
days, including the struggle with the monster of chaos (see above, under
cosmogonic myths). Zoroastrian eschatology influenced Jewish apocalyptic and
through the latter early Christian eschatology. German myths of the end of the
world as represented in the *Völuspa* formed a parallel but with a stronger
element of fate and pessimism.

It is possible to discern certain developments in the history of religious
myths. Archaic myths of the traditional world are widened and elaborated in a
poetic and theological way. The early Indo-European peoples present in
various ways the dualism between the forces of light and darkness, and this
theme lives on in later religious developments, for example, in Manichaeism
(*RGG* 4, 714ff.). In Buddhism, sun myths, saviour myths and eschatological
myths live on in a new form in the legend of the Buddha. In Israelite religion,
old mythic motifs live on into later times under an ethical and prophetic
monotheism (*RGG* 4, 1274ff.). They are still present in the medieval mysticism
of the Kabbalah (Sholem, 1949). It was natural for myth to find a place in the
Christian religion. The whole Christian doctrine of salvation, as laid down in
the New Testament, appears permeated with mythical motifs (*RGG* 4, 1278ff.).
They are nevertheless restrained, transformed and transfigured, and become
part of Christian doctrinal development. Particularly is this so in the case of the
creation myth, the myth of paradise and the fall, the myth of the revealer and
saviour, and the Marian myth. Christian theology carried out a task of immense
proportions in spiritualizing and transforming these mythical motifs. The
Gnostics, the Alexandrines, the Cappadocians, Augustine, the Scholastics
and mystics, the Reformers, the Pietists and Rationalists and modern
theologians – all have wrestled in their own way with the spiritualization of
the *mythos*. Resisting them were popular religion and popular theology
(Vrijhof, 1979). The latter are a reminder that we can only think and speak of
the Deity mythically, i.e. symbolically. Even the leading exponent of demy-
thologizing, Rudolf Bultmann, understood by this programme not the elimina-

tion of myth, but its interpretation for the present day (Bultmann, 1960; *LThK* 3, 898ff.).

(4) The sacred legend

A special place alongside myth is taken up by the *legend*. (*RE* 11, 345ff.; Günter, 1910; Delehaye, 1962; *LThK* 6, 450ff.; *RGG* 3, 26ff.). The word itself comes from *vita legenda*, the life (of saints) to be read (in the daily office of prayer). The book in question is called *Legendarium*, or in the case of martyrs, *Martyrologium*. The legend may often have incorporated material drawn from myths. But there is an important difference between legends and myths. Legends centre around an historical person and their object is to present the saint in his relationship with the Deity, men and all living creatures. The 'legendary' saint stands in a continuous relationship with the supernatural, lives with and out of the Deity, operates with the power of God. Traditional religions and the 'world' religions (including Hinduism, Jainism, Buddhism, Taoism and Islam) have all engendered numerous legends; as have Israelite religion (*RGG* 5^2, 49ff.) and later Judaism (Buber, 1972), earliest Christianity (*RGG* 5, 1308ff.), the early Church (legends of martyrs and monks; Delehaye, 1962), Byzantine Christianity (Benz, 1953), medieval Christianity (legends of Mary and the sacrament; Guerber, 1909), and recently the independent African Churches (Orimolade, n.d.). The characteristic form of legend in Christianity takes its pattern from the *Life of Anthony*, the father of the Christian monastic movement. The fixed pattern for legends is especially clear in the readings for the second nocturn of the Roman breviary.

The core of all legends is the miracle story. The miracle legend has a complex structure. It rests on historical foundations, not merely because the person of the saint or prophet is historical, but also insofar as the events narrated have an historical nucleus, a residuum of fact. The person living uninterruptedly with the Ground of his being releases psychic and physical powers. These hidden powers, of which most people are scarcely aware, are released by prayer and meditation. They include: (1) the overcoming of gravity and bodily sensitivity (levitation and anaesthesia), the increased capacity to endure suffering (the martyr can bear incredible agony and torture because he can 'switch off' his body), and increased bodily powers (bursting of fetters); (2) the power of healing: saints, through contact (e.g. laying on of hands), an imperative word and concentration of the will, undertake healing face-to-face or at a distance; (3) *cardiognosia* (the discerning of the psycho-physical state of a stranger, knowing the thoughts of others) and telepathy (the apprehending of events taking place at a distance); in connection with (4) prophetic seeing into the future (proclaiming one's own and others' destiny beforehand); (5) influencing the destiny of others (rescuing them from danger, but also bringing effectual curses upon their head); (6) calming the wildness of animals; (7) influencing the natural elements (especially wind and weather and natural catastrophes). All these phenomena are to be found in the lives of particular saints of all times and in all religions including Christianity. In any one given case, however, it is not usually possible to determine what is historical and what is unhistorical.

Such historical and psychological facts as there are have been greatly exaggerated, decked out and elaborated, and transferred to other persons. Moreover, the elaboration and decking out with further details increase with the telling and retelling of the legend. This process may be studied even during the person's life-time, e.g. in the case of Sadhu Sundar Singh, an evangelist converted from the Sikh religion to Christianity (Appasamy, 1958). The concept of miracle working is also bound up with the traditional view of the way the spirit powers operate in the sacred cosmos. When all these different factors come together we have the formation of the saints' legends in the different religions including Christianity, where they become bound up with that religion's dogmatic and ethical teaching.

Legends travel not only within a particular land and religious area, but also in foreign lands and amongst other religions. The legends surrounding Elijah and Elisha set the pattern for the New Testament miracle stories (as also for the prophet legends of Islam). Buddha legends travelled, in the form of the story of Balaam and Joasaph (bowdlerizing of Bodhisattva; *ERE* 7, 567ff.; *RAC* 1, 1193ff.), through Persia and Syria to Byzantium and into the Western world. As St Joasaph, the Buddha obtained a memorial day in the Greek saints calendar and the Roman list of martyrs. The legend of the miracle of the rose was transferred from Elizabeth, queen of Portugal, to Elizabeth of Thüringen and moved on to the Wartburg. The influence of biblical motifs, the feeding miracles of Elijah and Elisha (1 Kings 17.14ff.; 2 Kings 4.1ff.) and of Jesus, is also discernible in the legend of St Clare of Assisi (Baker, 1978).

The legend takes the saintliness and miraculous power of the mature sacred person back into his or her early childhood, as the infancy narratives of John, Jesus and the Buddha show. The visit of the twelve year old Jesus in the temple at Jerusalem (Luke 2.41ff.) has a parallel in the Buddha's visit to the temple and the school. The legend depicts in this way the psychological fact that the religious power of the sacred person is already embodied in the immature child. Again, the close connection of the saints with the whole of creation is intensified to the point where the entire cosmos participates in the events of their lives. Just as the birth, enlightenment, the first sermon and the death of the Buddha were accompanied by miraculous events in nature, so also was the death of Jesus on the cross (Matt. 27.51ff.).

Of importance in all religions, including Christianity, are the 'dogmatic' miracles. By means of these, proof of the truth of one's own religion and the falsity of the foreign religion or sect is offered before the whole world. The Egyptian diviners could not measure up to the miraculous power of Moses (Exod. 7 and 8), as Simon the magician could not equal that of the apostles (Acts 8.4–24). The exaltation of the saints by the Deity is confirmed by the miracles of healing which occur at their graves and in answer to the prayers offered to them or through them. The 'all-powerful intercession' of the Mother of God is shown in the countless healing miracles which she performs for the faithful. The prayer offered to her is able to lead to victory over enemy hosts; and, indeed, to rescue from the hand of the devil of him who has signed a pact with him, as in the Theophilus legend, the oldest legend of Mary and the prototype of the Faust saga. The truth of the faith is also shown by the power of martyrs who defy the torments and murderous assaults of their persecutors – both Christian martyrs and others, such as the Japanese prophet–martyr Nichiren, over whose head the drawn sword splinters in the hand of the executioner who has suddenly been blinded. The other face of these miracles of the martyrs is the frightful punishment which overtakes their persecutors.

The truth of one's own religion is also especially confirmed by the miracles wrought by objects sacred to it. The healing miracles produced by sick people touching the cross of Christ, which the Empress Helena had rediscovered, attest both the authenticity of the cross and also the divinity of Christ. Terrible plagues come upon the Philistines who have stolen the ark of the covenant (1 Sam. 5.6ff.); similar punishments come upon those who have dishonoured images of Christ and the saints or the consecrated host. Indeed, even the involuntary touching or seeing of a sacred object draws upon itself fearful consequences. Thus blindness fell upon the monk who wanted to see the sacred mantle in Trèves. Just as in the Eastern Church numerous miracles are associated with icons, so also are those in the Western Church linked with the consecrated host (see above, Chapter 2). All these miracle stories take for granted a long dogmatic development. The icon miracles could only occur after pictures had been recognized as earthly representations of heavenly truths (see above, Chapter 2); the miracles of the host only after theological speculation had developed belief in the transubstantiation of the bread into the Body of Christ (see above, Chapter 7). The increasing belief in the devil, which set in with the growth of monasticism and led to ever more grotesque forms during the Middle Ages, produced countless legends concerning the devil's powers of seduction and the saints' ability to ward them off. Thus the legend conforms on the one hand to generally uniform historical and psychological principles, while on the other hand it takes on everywhere a contemporary colouring.

The critical approach to legends began in Rennaissance humanism and continued in the Reformation. Luther was aware of the 'sub-Christian and pagan' character of the motifs of many of the legends, derided them as *Lügende*, lies, but allowed individual legends to stand as examples of faith. The men of the Enlightenment saw nothing but priestly invention in the legend, but others, including Herder, showed more understanding for its value. Romanticism was enthusiastic over the legend, as for medieval life and thought in general. Modern *Religionswissenschaft* has recognized the historical and religious significance of the legend if seen in a critical light. Catholicism identified the legends too closely with the history of the saints, Protestantism rejected them out of hand as 'catholic'. But the legend is older than Catholicism and testifies to the similarity of all popular religious speculations and to their continuity over thousands of years. The same thing holds *mutatis mutandis* for the New Testament legends, especially the infancy and passion legends. In the latter also, poetic and historical motifs intermingle so that it is difficult to separate one from the other. The New Testament Gospels, however, are much more soberly written than the apocryphal gospels. Despite being entwined with legends, Christianity's heart is revealed better in the narratives of the evangelists than the dogmatic formulations of the Councils, be they those of Nicaea or Trent. According to Harnack, the words and external history of Jesus would not suffice without the legends (in the widest sense) which reflect the impression he made upon his disciples.

(5) Didaskalia, parable and allegory

The taught word of the master, *didaskalia* (Mensching, 1937; Wach, 1925) is the creation of a single personality, born from the fulness of religious experience and insight, not as with the prophetic word, out of ecstasy and auditions. Characteristic of *didaskalia* is one-to-one teaching, group instruction and the public sermon. In the first, divine wisdom is revealed by the master to the disciple. Related to the *guru* and disciple relationship in Hinduism is the mystagogic instruction in Hellenism. Examples of the latter are found in the Fourth Gospel: Jesus and Nicodemus, Jesus and the Samaritan woman, Jesus and the man born blind and the disciple on the breast of the Lord (John 3; 4; 9; 13.25). Individual instruction is also the rule in early monasticism.

Besides this group instruction is also found. Examples are the conversations of K'ung-fu-Tzu and Socrates in the circle of their disciples. The latter described his pedagogical work as that of a midwife. The Buddha preaches first to five disciples in Benares. They make up the nucleus of the *sangha* or community. We find group instruction also with the Jewish rabbis. Their example was followed by Jesus. His sayings may be divided into conversations or apophthegms, be they controversies or instructional conversations, and *logia*: wisdom sayings, prophetic and apocalyptic sayings, and sayings about the law (Bultmann, 1972; Riesner, 1984). The group instructions of Jesus involving his disciples and apostles are to be clearly distinguished from his public sermons which betray a prophetic character. But characteristic of group instruction is the added explanation given to parables used in the public sermon (Mark 4.10ff.). The word of the master bears the hallmark of absoluteness, even more than does the prophetic oracle,because it has universal validity. The Buddha declares in his first sermon: 'The liberation from death has been found' (*Mahāvagga* 1, 6). Jesus speaks 'with authority' (Mark 1.22). Esoteric group instruction is also found in the Hellenistic mystery cults and in the Christian mystery rite. The classic example of the latter is the *Mystagogic Catechesis* of Cyril of Jerusalem (see above, Chapter 7). Esoteric group instruction is also characteristic of Christian monasticism and Islamic sufism. The master of novices introduces them to the rules of the order (Caesarius of Heisterbach, 1929). In the prologue to the *Rule* of Benedict are the words of the Psalmist:

'Come, O sons, listen to me, I will teach you the fear of the Lord' (Ps. 34.11).

The third form of *didaskalia* is the public sermon. It is given regularly, not occasionally as with prophetic proclamation. The Buddha's sermon is public: he expressly emphasizes that he has made no distinction in his teaching between what is esoteric and what is exoteric (Digha-Nikaya 2, 100). The same applies to Jesus' sermon at the sea of Galilee, the sermon on the mount, and in the synagogue and temple – 'I have spoken openly to the world' (John 18.20). Likewise, 'Paul and Barnabas spoke out boldly' (Acts 13.46). Paul used to preach in the synagogues; he spoke also, however, before the Gentiles in public places as at the Areopagus in Athens (Acts 17.16ff.). The content of the word of the master is the doctrine of salvation in the form of teaching the *way* of salvation. The seer of the *Upanishads* discloses the secret of the unity between the ground of the soul and Deity. The Buddha preaches the four Aryan truths of suffering, its cause, the elimination of that cause and the way leading to this. The content of the gospel of Jesus (*ThWNT* 2, 705ff.) is the coming Kingdom of God. The background of Jesus' gospel is the prophetic sermon of judgement, the message of the nearness of the last judgement. Over and above this rises the message of blessedness in the coming Kingdom. The gospel is the continuation of the prophetic message of salvation. Similarly the preaching of forgiveness of sins is the continuation of the prophetic message of comfort. It is directed towards the 'poor in spirit', the 'hungry and thirsty' (Matt. 5.3ff.), the 'little ones' (Matt. 18.10). This sermon, however, calls for both decision and confession since it is not human preaching but God's proclamation (Matt. 10.20; Mark 8.38). In the first Christian community, Jesus' gospel of the Kingdom of God becomes the gospel of Jesus Christ and that of the crucified, risen and exalted Lord. Adolf von Harnack speaks of a 'double' gospel in the New Testament. With Paul, the earliest congregation's preaching of the gospel becomes linked with the myth of the redeemer who comes down from heaven, suffers, dies and rises again. Through this connection with the prophetic proclamation of the gospel, the *muthos* of the ancient world already undergoes a transformation. Its content is no longer a natural phenomenon but a sequence of recent historical events. As the word of the crucified one, this proclamation of saving history is paradoxical, 'a stumbling-block to Jews and folly to Gentiles' (1 Cor. 1.23).

The main means of the master's instruction is the *parable*. The greatest religious teachers were masters of the language of parables: the seers of the *Upanishads*, Gautama Buddha, Ramakrishna, Plato, Plotinus, the Hebrew prophets, Jesus (*ERE* 9, 628ff.; *RGG* 2, 1614ff.; Jeremias, 1962; 1966; Dodd, 1978; Linnemann, 1966; Te Selle, 1975), mystics such as Meister Eckhart, and philosophers such as Kierkegaard (Oden, 1978). In this century two great Indian speakers-in-parables have appeared: Rabindranath Tagore and Sadhu Sundar Singh. The deepest religious truth cannot be uttered in abstract philosophical or theological formulations, but in simple parables taken out of the life of nature and of everyday human life. Examples are the parable in the *Upanishad* about salt that dissolves in water: it makes plain the absorption of the individual soul in the divine infinity (*Chandogya Upan.* 6, 12f.); the Buddha's parable of the man who is hit by a poisoned arrow but will not allow it to be drawn out until he knows everything about arrow, poison and archer – he is like the man who got to the bottom of all the world's problems philosophically before he accepts the message of salvation (*Majj. Nik.* I, 426–32); Plato's parable of the cave dwellers who are chained with their backs to the mouth of the cave and see only the shadowy images on the wall, but when free, can gaze at the real world illuminated by the sun – thus man rises up from the imperfect representations to the perfect heavenly forms (*Rep.* 7, 514ff.); Plotinus' parables of the beggar waiting at the gate of the rich man and of the man who waits for the sun to rise (*Enn.* 5, 5, 8) – show that the miracle of ecstatic union with God can only be passively awaited; the parable of Meister Eckhart of the man whose love for his wife is so great that he puts out an eye of his own so as to be quite equal with her, symbolizes the renunciation of divine majesty by the Son of God at the incarnation; the parable of Sadhu Sundar Singh of the man who gave a blood transfusion to save his gravely injured son, shows how Christ on the cross poured out his blood for fallen man.

The parables of Jesus, which are to be distinguished from the many comparisons, images and metaphorical sayings in his teaching, are concerned to tell a story about an interesting individual happening or case. They contain both proclamation of God's Kingdom and also instruction in how to respond to the experience of it (*paraenēsis*), and are known by their titles: the asking friend (Luke 11.5–8), the unjust judge (Luke 18.1–8), the sower (Mark 4.3–9) and par.), the barren fig tree (Luke 13.6–9), the banquet (Luke 14.16–24 and par.), the lost son (Luke 15.11–32), the dishonest steward (Luke 16.1–8), the entrusted pounds (Matt. 25.14–30 and par.), the ten virgins (Matt. 25.1–13), the weeds among the wheat (Matt. 13.24–30), the unforgiving servant (Matt. 18.23–35), the same wages (Matt. 20.1–16), the wicked vine-dressers (Mark 12.1–9 and par.), the two debtors (Luke 7.41–3) and the two sons (Matt. 21.28–31). Related to these are the example stories: the good Samaritan (Luke 10.30–7), the rich farmer (Luke 12.16–21), the rich man and Lazarus (Luke 16.19–31), the Pharisee and the tax collector (Luke 18.10–14), also the order of precedence at the feast (Luke 14.7–11) and the true guests (Luke 14.12–14; Bultmann, 1972).

The *allegory* (Bultmann, 1972), as a poetic, theological composition, is distinct from the parable. Whereas the parable is related to a single theme, the point of the story, which however opens up a wholly new world view, the allegory is a parabolic narrative wherein every single detail has its significance in spelling out the features of the religious cosmology. It is therefore a story which is essentially more artificial than the parable. The two genres come together in the story of the vine-dressers who beat the messengers of their master and finally killed even his son (Mark 12.1ff.). The allegory is a story in narrative form which has a mystical sense or received such through subsequent interpretation. Many stories in the Synoptic Gospels became allegories in the Hellenistic environment. The centurion at Capernaum (Matt. 8.5ff.), the Syro-Phoenician woman (Mark 7.24ff.) and the centurion under the cross (Mark 15.39) are interpreted as representatives of the gentile world which is accepting the gospel of Christ. Here at least historical recollections are present in some measure, but in the case of the Fourth Gospel the allegorical narratives appear to be freely composed, e.g. Jesus' dialogue with Nicodemus (John 3) and the Samaritan woman (John 4), the raising of Lazarus (John 11), Jesus' words to his mother and to his favourite disciple under the cross (John 19.26f.) and the race of the disciples to the grave (John 20.1ff.). These serve to illustrate the mystical-gnostic saving truths of the Fourth Gospel.

The Song of Solomon is only in a secondary sense an allegory. Already in Judaism it was interpreted as the relationship between Israel and Yahweh (see above, Chapter 7). In Christianity it was interpreted in terms of the relationship between Christ and the Church, Mary and Christ, above all Christ and the individual soul (Origen, Bernard of Clairvaux). *The Pilgrim's Progress* by John Bunyan (see above, Chapter 4) is an allegorical work in the grand style. Similar allegorical stories are popular in the Hindu tradition and in Islamic mysticism ('Attār and Rūmī).

(6) Dogma and creed, law and sermon

All religions have their credal formularies (*ER* 4, 138; Rodd, 1987), either put together in a separate rational, easily assimilated form, or implicitly in liturgical songs and chants, as in the traditional and ethnic religions. *Dogma* appears in early Buddhism in the formula of the threefold refuge (in the Buddha, the *Dharma* (*ER* 4, 329ff.) – the teaching of salvation, and the *Sangha* – the community) and the four Aryan truths (suffering, the cause of suffering, the end of suffering and the way to end suffering). The dogma of one God in Judaism has found lapidary form in the *Shema*: 'Hear O Israel: Yahweh is our God, Yahweh alone' (Deut. 6.4 alt. rdg.); that of Islam in the call: '*Lā ilāha illā 'llāhu*. . . There is no God but God and Muhammad is the messenger of God.' The expanded form of the Islamic confession of faith is as follows: I believe in Allah and the prophets and the books and his angels and the resurrection after death. Mazdaism too has its confession and creed in the *Yasna*. In West Africa, followers of Shango celebrate their 'hero', 'sorcerer king', 'lightning flash' (McKenzie, 1976). Christianity too has its creeds, much elaborated from early beginnings.

Christian dogma arose out of the formulae, *Kurios Iēsous Christos* Christ is Lord (Phil. 2.11) and 'Father . . . Son . . . and . . . Spirit' (Matt. 28.19). The trinitarian dogma was developed in the encounter with Gnosis. It progressed from the history of salvation into metaphysics. As Adolf von Harnack put it in a classic way: Christian dogma 'in its conception and development is a work of the Greek spirit on the soil of the Gospel' (Harnack, 1961). The oldest confession in dogmatic form is the baptismal creed, erroneously named 'Apostles', which stemmed from the second half of the second century and was expanded on Roman soil. The Council of Nicaea expanded the second article through a series of christological expressions (*RGG* 4, 1454f.). The confession of faith which had been enlarged with Nicene terminology was called the Nicene-Constantinopolitan Creed, acknowledged by the whole of Christendom. Ecumenical councils added further definitions to the Nicene dogma. Christological terminology attained its greatest precision in the Chalcedonian definition; in Latin garb this appeared in the Athanasian Creed which originated in southern France or Spain.

The positive formulations of the councils were usually accompanied by the cursing of those who taught differently; 'The Catholic Church anathematizes . . .' (Council of Nicaea). 'If someone does not confess that God is truly Immanuel and therefore the Holy Virgin is the Mother of God (*theotokos*), let him be *anathema* (placed under the ban).' This anathematizing is an ancient cursing formula which was imported into Christianity by Paul (1 Cor. 16.22; Gal. 1.8; *ThWNT* 1, 356f.; *LThK* 1, 1494f.). The Western Church, as distinct from the Eastern Orthodox Church, continued to produce dogmatic formulae and those who rejected them were cursed under the words *anathema sit* 'May he be under the ban'. Whole series of such canons are contained in the definitions of the Tridentine and First Vatican Councils. The most rigorous observance of the formula counts as the indispensable condition for attaining eternal blessedness. The Athanasian Creed begins with the words: 'Whoever wishes to be saved it is necessary that before all things he should hold fast to the Catholic faith.' This Catholic faith is contained in the trinitarian and christological formulae which follow. The numerous dogmatic definitions and anathemas fill a large handbook called the *Enchiridion Symbolorum* (Denzinger, 1979, ET 1957). The Protestant Churches have also created their confessions and creeds which have a binding character (*RGG* 3, 1012ff.; *LThK* 2, 149ff.; Schaff, 1905; Bettenson, 1975). But in recent years the ecumenical movement has led to a new stress on the doctrines and creeds which the Churches have in common. The points in history where divergences arose are also being reconsidered (Schlink, 1983).

What corresponds to dogma in the field of ethics is the *moral law* (Mensching, 1941; *ERE* 7, 805–89; *RGG* 2, 1511ff.; *LThK* 3, 815ff.; Westermarck, 1926). It is older than the law of faith and grew out of regulations covering tabus and sacrifices, also from oracles. The Babylonian king received his laws from the Sun god (Codex Hammurabi; *RGG* 3, 51f.). The Greek king was known as *themistopolos*, i.e. guardian of the *themistes*, the regulations which he had received from Zeus. These are sayings filled with religious power which have binding force like sacred formulae (*mantra, manthra*). Of the Jewish collections of law (Kornfeld, 1952; *RGG* 3, 175ff.; Stamm and Andrew, 1967), the oldest, including the decalogue, are of pre-exilic origin. A large part, however, are only post-exilic. The Israelite law was held to be the revelation of the divine will. In Deuteronomy under prophetic influence, the love of God took its place as the first of the commandments (Deut. 6.5). The law and faithfulness to the law were celebrated by Jewish piety to an overwhelming extent (Ps. 119). Early Christianity made a tremendous effort to gain freedom from the law. Its pioneer and herald is Paul. Colossians emphasized that Christ 'nailed to the cross' had 'cancelled' the 'bond' which contained the 'legal demands' (*dogmata*; Col. 2.14; cf. Eph. 2.14f.). Christianity itself, indeed, soon became again a legalistic religion. Jesus' moral guidance was interpreted as law, as in the case of Matthew's sermon on the mount. Even the Pauline letters contain formal 'tables' of the law (Rom. 12.9ff.). Councils and popes issued ethical and cultic laws with binding legal authority. Fulfilling the will of God and obeying the law become the same thing.

The *sermon* (*ER* 11, 494ff.) is found in the religions of the world: the prophetic religions, the mystical religions; the religions of the book and the religions of oral tradition. The sermon brings together the different forms of the word from God; it is at the same time doctrinal teaching and moral law, prophecy, gospel and testimony. The Buddha sent out his disciples with the command: 'Preach the doctrine' (*Mahāvagga* 1.11). The risen Christ commissioned the apostles to 'teach all peoples' (Matt. 28.20). Theravāda and Mahāyāna Buddhism employ the sermon to instruct the laity through monks and priests respectively. The priest of Shango in West Africa preaches a long sermon in the market place of a traditional city (McKenzie, 1976, 35). The Jewish sermon (*ERE* 10, 220ff.) is a creation of the synagogue, a fruit of the exilic period. The Christian sermon (*ERE* 10, 215ff.; Dargan, 1905 and 1912) is linked to that of the synagogue, but also has its roots in the popular sermon of wandering preachers (Stoics, Cynics and Pythagoreans (Bultmann, 1910). The early Christian missionary sermon (Harnack, 1962) was given not only in synagogues but also in streets and public squares. It was replaced by instruction and exposition of Scripture in worship services. The Christian sermon was long regarded as inspired; the bishop only gave the text to the preacher during the service itself. Origen was a master of the biblical homily. In the case of the Cappadocian Fathers we can observe the transition from the simple homily to the rhetorical sermon as a work of art. The Western sermon derived from the Eastern Church. The greatest preachers in the West were Ambrose and Augustine. After a period of decline, during which, however, a revival of the missionary sermon took place among the Celtic and Anglo-Saxon *peregrīnī*, there followed a renaissance of the sermon in the Carolingian period. Then the creative powers of the sermon dried up again; the early medieval sermon bears the impress of imitation. There followed a period of revivalist preaching in the form of the crusade sermon, the sermon of Franciscans calling for repentance, and of Dominicans directed against heresy and calling for faith (d'Avray, 1985). Over against these were the Cathari sermons, full of ancient Eastern dualism and calling for the acceptance of martyrdom (Wakefield and Evans, 1969).

The sermons of the later Dominicans bear a mystical character (Meister Eckhart, Tauler). Alongside the ecclesiastical and monastic sermon there arose a free lay sermon among the Waldensian *barbas* (Tourn, 1980) and the Lollards of Wycliffe. A new epoch for the sermon began with the Reformation: the biblical sermon arrived. In the centre stood the gospel, admittedly very differently interpreted: by Luther, as the newly-discovered consolation of the grace of God which forgives sins; by Calvin, as the sermon on the sovereign rule of God; and by the Baptists, as the call for the holy community. The sermon of testimony to the gospel, a feature of the sixteenth-century Reformation, gave place to orthodoxy's sermon of instruction, which was in turn replaced by the revival sermon which pressed for the conversion of the individual (Spener, Jonathan Edwards). This was superseded by the rationalistic and moralistic sermon of the Enlightenment. Neo-Lutheranism renewed the sermon of testimony in the form of teaching; the revival sermon found its home in Methodism (the Wesley brothers and George Whitefield) and in the Salvation Army (William Booth). In post-Tridentine Catholicism, a renewal of the sermon took place in the appeal for renewal of faith over against the heretics (Canisius). It gave way to the classical, rhetorical sermon represented by Bossuet, and the popular moral homily of an Abraham a Sancta Clara (Ulrich Megerle; *RE* 1, 110–112).

The fathers of the modern Protestant sermon are Herder and Schleiermacher (Schleiermacher, 1876–7). The nineteenth century witnessed the danger of a modernizing and aestheticizing of the biblical message. Examples are Harry Emerson Fosdick, F. W. Robertson and Charles Spurgeon (Blackwood, 1947). The evangelical revival sermon (*ER* 14, 38f.) continues with the legendary Billy Graham; while the early Christian improvised sermon has been revived in African Churches. The Christian sermon has also influenced other religions. Not only reformist religious movements such as the Indian Brāhmo-Samāj (Hinnells and Sharpe, 1972), but also Buddhism and Islam (Denffer, 1980; 1981) have received some stimulus through the Christian sermon, which in recent days has become audible to many through radio and television. But despite this influence the sermon has its own parallel history in other religious traditions. The sermon calling for faith is especially common in Japanese Buddhism of the *Shin* sect and the Jōdo sect which believe in justification *sola fide*. In Islam the sermon (*hutba*; *ERE* 10, 222ff.) is given by the *hātib* or spokesman for the group which conducts the Friday service from the *minbar*, pulpit or lectern, or a raised place. Thus, in myriad sermons and other forms mentioned in this chapter, the word from God, the word concerning ultimate reality, is constantly brought home to religious people, among them the Christians.

9

The Sacred Word
2: To the Deity

(1) Primordial sounds, blessing and cursing

The word from God finds its echoing response in the word to God (Heiler, 1923; *LThK* 4, 537–51; *RGG* 2, 1209–34; *ER* 11, 489ff.; 13, 20ff.). No religion is without revelation; and equally, none is without prayer – in the widest sense of the word. Prayer is rooted in the being of man, in his responding nature. Such responses to revelation in the form of meditation, contemplation and prayer may not involve the turning towards a personal Deity. There are also words which may carry a sacred power in themselves without being recognizable as a clearly defined word to God. These include the numinous, *primordial sounds* (Otto, 1943a, 203ff.; 1972, App. 3). Primordial religious sounds are the immediate response to the impress of the sacred. In India, and in those countries influenced by Indian religions, the greatest currency has been given to the sacred syllable *Om*. *Om* is the most sacred of all syllables in Brahmanism. It is the shortest linguistic summary of the secret of Brahman, and is probably identical with the Semitic *aun*. This is a sound of numinous shuddering, a characterization of the negative-numinous (in Otto's terms) that finally takes the form of evil magic and the demonic. Perhaps also *Yahu*, an old Dervish cry, is such a primordial sound which then became the name of God; or it was a name or praise name whose context was lost. Similar mystical primordial sounds are contained in the invocatory formula *io, io*, with which the prayers of Aeschylus began. At the mass for the dead of the Buddhist Tendai sect in Japan, the priests sing endlessly the vowels 'a-e-o'; while in West Africa Ogboni cult members praise the Deity with the call: '*Hééepà, Hééepà!*'. While little in the way of primordial sounds still continue in Christianity, there appear to be increasingly in the Western world those who practise forms of meditation with little sense of their prayer-responses being directed to a divine being.

Not only such primordial sounds, but every serious and solemnly-spoken word uttered with deliberate concentration is sacred for traditional persons. The word is here a powerful and magical entity like the song (see Chapter 7, above). It carries in itself the power of realization, like the sympathetic magical act of miming. This magical idea of the 'wish-word' lives on in the fairy tale. Grimm's 'Table, be covered!' illustrates perfectly the power of the magical formula (*HWDA* 1, 1157–72). Often the wish-word is the commentary that goes with the wish-action.

The formula bringing luck or good fortune is called the *blessing* or blessing-wish; misfortune is caused by the *curse* or harmful wish (*ERE* 4, 367–74; Brun, 1932; *HWDA* 7, 1582–620; 2, 1636–52; *ER* 2, 247ff.; 4, 182ff.). Both blessing and cursing are one in their magical and powerful effect. The Hebrew *bārakh* signifies to 'fill with power'; it is therefore used in the double sense of to bless; in the one instance power is communicated to man, in the other to God. Still today *baraka* means in Arabic the magical power or blessing communicated in all possible ways. The power-laden wish-word is made more powerful, first, through repetition (three times or seven times). Still more power is attained by blessing or cursing through the uttering of a deity's name. In everyday life, the word of blessing retains a significant place through greetings and salutations formulae (*ERE* 11, 104ff.; *ER* 13, 24ff.).

The most frequent form of blessing and cursing is to assign the wish-fulfilment to a deity which gives or condemns. In place of 'Be blessed' or 'Be cursed' comes 'May God bless/curse/punish you'. Here blessing and cursing are subordinated to the will of God who directs the way they are applied, retaining in his hand how they are put into effect. The magical word of blessing or cursing approaches a prayer and yet it is not a complete prayer. For the position of the one blessing or cursing is oblique and indirect in relation to the deity. One form of this consists of the handing over of a person to the chthonic or demonic powers (*paradidonai tois chthoniois* or *tō satanā*, 1 Cor. 5.5; Deissmann, 1911, 303ff.). The blessing and curse are irrevocable, as in the blessing by Isaac (Gen. 27). After this blessing for the first-born has been pronounced upon the deceitful Jacob, he (Isaac) cannot take it back nor can he pronounce a blessing of equal value upon Esau. Blessing and cursing are especially effective when uttered by 'power-laden' persons: the family head, the chief, the king, the divine-healer, the priest, the stranger, the beggar, and the one imploring help. Blessing and cursing are thought of in terms of a powerful substance which enters into the body of the one blessed or cursed or at least hovers about a person. The blessing turns back to the one blessing if spoken over someone who is unworthy, as is said in the words of commission uttered by Jesus (Matt. 10.13). According to the view of antiquity, the curse had a contagious power. Therefore the one cursed or ostracized was tabu. Everyone who eats or drinks with him is infested with his curse-power, his 'social death' (Hasenfratz, 1982). This primordial idea lives on in the excommunication of the Roman Church; whosoever has social intercourse with an excommunicated person, falls himself under the ban. Indeed, because of this the curse is no less dangerous for the one pronouncing it. One protects oneself against these dangers by causing a curse uttered against a contemporary to be followed by a blessing for oneself.

Blessing and cursing live on in the prophetic religions including Christianity. The Aaronic blessing (Num. 6.24) was part of Israelite temple liturgy and is also used to this day in Christian liturgies. In the Roman Church special power is ascribed to the blessing given by the new priest, bishop and pope. There is a German proverb to the effect that to obtain the blessing of a new priest one should wear out a pair of shoes; to get his first blessing, one should ride one's horse to death. From the loggia of the Vatican the pope gives his blessing 'to the city and the world' (*urbi et orbi*), radio and television rendering powerful assistance. The curse also lives on. It is given powerful expression in the piety of the Hebrew psalms (Mowinckel, 1924). The enemies of Israel, its oppressors and tormentors, are cursed with these cruel words amongst others: 'O daughter of Babylon, you devastator! Happy shall he be who requites you with what you have done to us! Happy shall he be who takes your little ones and dashes them against the rock!' (Ps. 137. 8f.). Taking over these cursing psalms presented difficulty for the Christian conscience. One sought therefore to subject them to a spiritual interpretation by applying them to the enemies of God and the Church, to Satanic powers and evil thoughts. Benedict gave the last-mentioned interpretation to the 'child' cited in the psalm verse, in the prologue to his Rule.

Enlightened traditional piety came out against the person from whose mouth a curse issues. The New Testament also rejects the curse. Jesus says: 'Bless those who curse you' (Luke 6.27); Paul: 'Bless and do not curse' (Rom. 12, 14). Yet it was not long before the curse found its way into the ecclesiastical documents of councils and popes. Heretics and church-political opponents were cursed. An especially horrific example is the curse Clement VIII placed upon the emperor Louis the Bavarian: 'May he be cursed in his going out and coming in. May the Lord strike him with madness, blindness and frenzy of spirit. May Heaven send down its lightning upon him. The wrath of almighty God and the blessed Peter and Paul come upon him in this world and the next. May the whole world fight against him, may the earth open and swallow him up. May his name be blotted out from his generation, and may the memory of him perish from the earth. May the elements rise up against him. May his dwelling-place become a desert, and all the merits of the blessed dead and the saints put him to shame and make known to him their wrath. May his sons be driven out of their dwellings and be delivered up into the hand of those who shall destroy them before his eyes' (Mirbt, 1924, 225). In the West such curses become increasingly ineffectual. By the eighteenth century, in the hands of a Lawrence Sterne, the curse is elaborated to the point where the immense edifice collapses in a gust of laughter (Sterne, 1967).

(2) The oath and compulsive prayer

A variant form of the curse is the *oath* (*ERE* 9, 430ff.: *RGG* 2, 347ff.: *HWDA* 2, 659ff.: *LThK* 3, 727ff.). In origin the oath is a conditional curse placed on oneself and often linked with an ordeal or with sympathetic magic. The latter shows the fate of the one who breaks the oath. Especially favoured in traditional religions was the dismembering of a sacred animal, between both parts of which the oath-taker proceeds, or the breaking to pieces of a symbolic object such as a calabash. The words of an oath supply a description of this fate. The assertive oath sometimes forms the introduction to the divine judgement or ordeal (by fire or water; *ERE* 9, 507ff.; *HWDA* 3, 994—1064: *RGG* 2, 1807ff.; Leitmann, 1953). For those unable to take the oath the ordeal is substituted. Directed towards the future is the promissory oath. Another form of conditional self-cursing is the pledging of a valued object. One swears by that which is dearest:

the father, by the head of his children; the woman fond of jewels, by her most valued piece. The words of the conditional curse have the power in themselves to bring about the stated consequences in the event of the oath being broken. In order that the words of the oath-swearer should attain this magical potency, there follows the touching of the valued objects with other objects of great power: stones, oath rings (Germanic peoples), a part of the body, the sacrificial animal and weapons.

In the course of time Christian shrines come to take the place of these and so the altar, the crucifix, relics, the container for the sacred host, the Bible or Gospels became the new objects of power – just as *Olorisha* in West Africa swear by the matchet of Ogun, Muslims swear by the Qur'ān, Sikhs by the Granth, Zoroastrians by the Avesta. In the original formula for the oath the name of the Deity did not necessarily form a part. But later the Deity was acknowledged to be the determining power, for example: 'If I do not say the truth or do not hold to my promise, may God punish me thus and so.' Or else God was called upon as witness and helper. Thus the curse contained in the oath becomes the judgement of God. Yet despite the Deity's association with the oath, there remains an element of compulsion. The one swearing the oath retains in his hand whatever it is that may become his fate; the power of the curse hovers about his head and sooner or later is discharged when he becomes an oath-breaker. The faith in magical power has the consequence that one tries to secure oneself against the effects of the curse by all kinds of manipulation. The Franks stole relics out of reliquaries so that with their aid the loading of the oath words with cursing power would not take place. In southern Germany the 'cold' oath was preferred. Here the effect of the oath gesture (three raised fingers) was nullified by the opposite gesture made by the fingers of the left hand held downwards!

Compelling oneself and compelling God is the theme of the much debated words of Jesus: 'Do not swear at all' (Matt. 5, 34ff.). Man has no power with his oath. By giving a pledge or putting a curse upon himself he 'cannot make one hair white or black'. Jesus rejects the oath because of this belief in its magical power. Although in the first instance he has in mind not the oath taken in court but everyday oath-taking, some smaller groups in Christendom have interpreted the saying in the sense of a radical rejection of every confession of faith and political oath of allegiance.

Christian theologians gave the oath quite a new interpretation: taking the oath means calling upon God as witness to the truth. At the same time they restricted the promissory oath to guard against possible misuse. The oath becomes a recognition of God's sovereignty as highest law-giver and judge who obliges a person to do nothing that contradicts his will and the dictates of conscience. Both the Roman Church and the Reformer Martin Luther are at one in this view. Yet despite such a moral and spiritual interpretation, the Roman Church gives a wide scope to the oath through the Tridentine profession of faith and the anti-modernism oath (Denzinger, 1979). In different forms of this oath the old idea of self-cursing persists. An apostate, heretic or schismatic promises upon his return to the Church to remain in fellowship with it. He emphasizes this promise by adding the following self-curse: 'If for whatever cause or reason I should separate myself from this unity, which Heaven forbid, may I as oath-taker be found guilty of everlasting punishment and have my place in the world to come with the original cause of disunity' (Mirbt, 1924, 589).

Related to the curse is the *compulsive prayer* or conjuration (*HWDA* 1, 1109ff.; 2, 32ff.; 8, 1546ff.; *RGG* 1, 1091f.; 2, 832f.; *RAC* 2, 169ff.; *MMM* 3, 857ff.; Richards, 1944; *ER* 5, 225ff.). It differs from the curse in that it is directed towards spirit beings who are thought to be dangerous and hostile. Hence the 'you'-form in contrast to most of the cursing formulae. The compulsive prayer has a double significance: removal, keeping away and banning of the spirits; or else attracting, compelling, rewarding and appeasing them. The first part is often accompanied by some drastic action or by loud noises with instruments (see above, Chapter 5). The conjuration is mostly accompanied by the command to go away, to leave a place, an object or a person. Often numerous compelling imperatives are strung together. The conjuration may also be linked with a magical action which makes the former quite plain. In an early Saxon compulsive prayer against worms, the latter are banned into an arrow which is placed on the affected part, at the same time the following conjuration is pronounced: 'Go out, Worm, with your nine little ones, / Out of the marrow into the arteries, / From the arteries into the flesh, / From the flesh into the skin, / From the skin into this arrow' (*HWDA* 9, 1546). When the worm has crawled into the arrow it is shot into the forest where the sickness demons dwell.

Not everyone has the power to compel demons. Banning them is an art which either has to be learnt or comes as a special gift. There are both professional and charismatic practitioners. Especially suited for compulsive prayers are chiefs, healer-diviners, shamans, priests and prophets. An ordinary person can also conjure spirit beings if the correct formula is known. The conjuring of demons is not only a part of traditional religions; it is also an important feature of the religions of antiquity, especially of Egypt, Babylonia, Iran and India. Belief in spirits and the art of compelling them became widespread in Hellenistic Judaism. Jesus' time was a heyday for the banning of demons. Many Greeks and Jewish rabbis conjure demons just as Jesus and the apostles do (*ThWNT* 2, 1–21). Jesus' activity in driving out demons belongs to those historical traits which are best attested. It seems to have differed from professional banning of demons in antiquity through the absence of all external, secretive practices. The driving out of evil spirits occurs through the power of imperative speech only: 'I command you, come out!' (Mark 9.25; cf. 1, 25; 5.8). In the apostles' driving out of demons, the naming of Jesus' name becomes the most important means of banning. The name causes the named one to be present and lends unfailing power to the conjuration.

In place of the free, charismatic banning of demons a permanent rite gradually comes into being. There also arose a special office in the Church, that of exorcist (*ODCC* 493f.), which has continued as a form of ordination in the Roman Church down to the present day. The conjuration of demons is a part of church ritual, both of the Eastern Orthodox (Rudloff, 1938) and of the Roman. An essential feature of many traditional religions and those of antiquity is thereby preserved into modern times. At the beginning of the Roman rite of baptism there occurs the command to the spirit to 'go out from him'. The conjuration was followed by a lengthier exorcism at the baptism of infants. At the adult baptism there was a whole series of these. Recently, however, the exorcism in the order for infant baptism became optional, while those for adult baptism disappeared, though they are provided for at various stages of the catechumenate (1972 Order for Adult Initiation).

A conjuration belongs to the consecration of water on the Sunday and to that of the holy oil on Maundy Thursday. The 'great exorcism' in the *Rituale Romanum* is carried out with great solemnity on those possessed with evil spirits: 'I adjure thee, serpent of old . . . God commands thee . . . go out, go out, go out, give place.' A special form of demon-conjuration is the renouncing of the devil (*ERE* 1, 49ff.; *RAC* 1, 558–64; Kelly, 1985). In the Eastern liturgy of baptism, the one being baptized is asked three times after he has been turned to face the West: 'Do you abjure the Devil? And all his works? And all his angels? And all serving of him? And all his glory?' The one being baptized answers each time: 'I abjure'. 'Hast thou abjured Satan?' 'I have abjured, I have abjured.' 'Then blow and spit upon him' (see also above, Chapter 5).

An ancient tradition of mankind is here preserved. There lives on in the compulsive prayer the consciousness of the reality of evil as a terrible power. Independent African Churches have many rites for driving away evil spirits and countering the activity of witchcraft; though problems may arise where spiritual means are grasped at to deal with what is best handled in other ways, e.g. with the techniques of modern medicine. In the history of conjuration in Christianity what comes through ever more clearly is the commanding power of the word, not in itself as a word of man, but as the word of God: 'The majesty of God commands thee.'

(3) Invocation and confession

Calling upon a higher being, *invocation* (*epiclesis, advocatio*: *RAC* 5, 577ff.) may occur through the primordial, non-verbal sounds of piping and clacking, frequently also through the sounding of a bell (see also above, Chapter 5), as is heard today in Shinto and Hindu temples. Ancient verbal invocations are the Greek *elthe* (come), Latin *veni*. The epiclesis often takes the form of a compulsive prayer. Important is not so much the form of address but the attitude. As long as a person believes in trying to compel the higher being, compulsive prayer is present. As soon, however, as a person bows before the higher being, makes himself dependent on that being, knows himself to be in need of help from this being, we are dealing with invocatory prayer in the real sense. But even this is still permeated with the belief in the mysterious power of the word.

The epiclesis in prayer form takes on a twofold character: first, there is the liturgical epiclesis. The Deity is invoked for the sacrifice and cultus. In early Indo-Germanic religion the gods were invited to seat themselves on sacrificial greenery spread out for the purpose. In the temple cultus, the deity is called into the divine image. The latter only becomes a sacred object and symbol of the divine presence when inhabited by deity. In the epiclesis of the early Christian community, the risen Christ is called to come near to the worshipping congregation (*LThK* 3, 935ff.; *RAC* 5, 585ff.; Goldammer, 1941). This call in turn has both a present and an eschatological reference: it also implores the return of Christ in glory ('*Mārana thā*, Our Lord, come!'). The epiclesis of the Acts of Thomas (50): 'Come and have fellowship with us', is a eucharistic one; it asks for Christ's presence at the Supper. In place of this personal epiclesis there emerges later a more impersonal form: the calling down of the Spirit or the Logos on the elements of bread and wine (see Chapter 7, above).

The epiclesis as prayer in the narrow sense, is different from the liturgical epiclesis. God is being called upon to help. This cry for help has become the introductory invocation of the canonical office of the Western Church including the Church of England: 'O God, make speed to save us. O Lord, make haste to help us' (BCP). For the mystics the epiclesis as prayer has the aim of unification rather than seeking help. 'Come' is the formula of those who hunger and thirst after God. *Elthe* is the ever-recurring cry in the invocatory prayer of Symeon the New Theologian: 'Come, true Light, come eternal Light . . . Come for my poor soul has longed for you and still longs for you; come, the Alone to the alone . . . Come, my joy, my glory, my constant bliss.' *Veni, Creator Spiritus* ('Creator Spirit! . . . Come') and *Veni Sancte Spiritus* ('Come, Thou holy Paraclete') are the call of two medieval, pentecostal hymns still widely sung today. 'O come, O come, for no day or hour will know happiness without you', cries the author of *The Imitation of Christ* (3, 21).

The cry of the person far from the Deity is the primordial sound of real prayer. The cry for closeness bespeaks the awareness of one's inability to come to the Deity. Therefore one implores the opposite: God's coming to man. Yet the coming of the Deity to man is somehow felt to be a judgement upon him. The Holy One comes to the unholy, the Pure to the impure, the Strong to the weak. All rites of purification do not suffice. Therefore one confesses before the Deity one's profanity, impurity, sinfulness and guilt. The prayer of penitence is part of the religion of humanity, including as well the Israelite-Christian religion of revelation. The *confession* of sin (Heiler, 1923) is found in traditional religions and in antiquity, notably Babylonia, Egypt and ancient India. The preaching of the Israelite prophets also had the effect of sensitizing the conscience: 'Against thee, thee only, have I sinned' (Ps. 51.4). The Psalter (*LThK* 2, 822f.) includes some of the profoundest confessional prayers (the seven penitential psalms), above all the psalm *Miserere* which has become a prayer of confession in Christian liturgies. Jewish piety was later enriched by further prayers of confession (Neh. 9.33ff.; Dan. 9.4ff.). The confessional prayer was given a central place in the Day of Atonement liturgy. It also received a place in the early Christian liturgy. Even greater was the place created for the confession of sin called *apologia* (*DACL* 1, 2591–601) in Western worship, in the Mass, Prime and Compline in the canonical office, and at unction for the sick. In the *Confiteor* ('I confess . . .'), the praying congregation calls God and the heavenly world as witness to its sinfulness. Its confession of sin comes to a climax in the threefold cry: 'My fault, my fault, my own most grievous fault'. The prayer of penitence was renewed in the liturgy of the Reformation. Olaus Petri, the Swedish reformer, and Calvin composed prayers of confession in which recognition of man's total corruption and powerlessness is linked with complete trust in God's mercy and Christ's act of redemption.

Confession (*ERE* 3, 825ff.; *RGG*1, 1541ff.; *ER* 4, 1ff.) however, is not only 'before God' but also before the representative of God, be that priest or congregation. As such, confession is not some invention of the Roman Church: it is an institution of mankind. Traditional peoples and those of antiquity are familiar with confession before the community, the family or the priest. In Babylonia whole lists of sins were read out to the penitent. Similar confessional lists of sins obtained in early India. These tables of sins have made their way through the millennia from culture to culture. Their form is still reflected in the arrangement of Western and medieval tables of sins.

Early Christianity recognized a mutual confession of sins before the brethren (Jas. 5.16). Public penance (*RGG* 1, 1544ff.; *LThK* 2, 802ff.) which was imposed for serious transgressions (murder, adultery, apostasy), was later replaced by secret confession before the bishop or confessional priest (Groupe de la Boussière, 1983). In the Eastern Church the laity adopted the monastic custom of confessing before a 'spiritual father' who did not have to be a priest. Private confession of a non-sacramental kind before the 'soul friend' was a custom in the Irish Church. It was popularized by Irish monks on the continent and after public confession had been repressed took on sacramental character. In the Western Church it became the means of educating the traditional peoples, Germanic and Slavic, who were flooding into Christendom.

Confession is carried out before the priest: 'I confess before the Almighty . . . and you, reverend priest in the place of God . . . .' Up till the sixteenth century, however, lay confession (*LThK* 6, 340f.) still counted as a valid substitute. Beside 'secret confession', public confession was also practised in monasteries. The place in the chapter room on which it was made is called the *culpa* ('fault') stone. On the wall was often a large fresco of the Crucified between the two thieves; and after the confession beatings were frequently administered. Private confession was zealously promoted in the early days of the Reformation. Luther praised it as a 'delightful thing'. Confession was seen in close association with the certainty of salvation which was reinforced by the absolution which followed. After its decline in the age of Enlightenment, private confession was revived in the nineteenth century by the Anglican Oxford Movement and Neo-Lutheranism (*LThK* 2, 838ff.).

(4) Adoration, praise and thanksgiving

Confession of sins and the seeking of forgiveness are a prerequisite for fellowship with the Deity. What is profane may not associate with what is holy. But even the one to whom forgiveness has been granted remains of no worth over against the divine. He or she falls down in *adoration* (*RGG* 1, 355f.) before God's power and holiness. Prayer is linked here with the gesture of devotion: prostration, kneeling, standing, bowing; raising, crossing or folding the hands (Heiler, 1923, 98ff.; Ohm, 1948). Indeed, the gesture is more important than speaking. Awe and dread cannot be expressed in words. But often this attitude does seek expression in words, and then, with marked preference for a form of address in the third person rather than for the more intimate second person. In ancient hymns such as the Hebrew Psalms there occurs an alternation between he and thou/you (found also in the opening *sura* of the Qur'ān), for instance, 'The Lord reigns; he is robed in majesty . . . ; thou art from everlasting' (Ps. 93, 1f.). The threefold 'holy' which Isaiah heard from the mouth of the angel (Isa. 6.3), was probably the devotional formula in the Jerusalem temple service: *Kādōsh, kādōsh, kādōsh.* It recurs in expanded form in the Christian liturgy: *Hagios ho theos, hagios ischuros, hagios athanatos* (Holy is God! Holy and strong! Holy immortal One!) (see above, Chapter 8). Then it passes over into the 'thou' of the petition, 'Have (thou) mercy upon us'. Sometimes, too, adoration is expressed in the second person, then remains reticently circling around the thought of holiness: 'I adore and worship thee'. A devotional meditation in the thou-form is the priestly silent prayer in the Chrysostom liturgy which accompanies the *Trisagion* of the choir: 'Holy God, thou who dwellest among the saints, thou who art glorified with the threefold holy voice of the Seraphim and art worshipped by all the heavenly host . . . thou who hast raised up thy humble and unworthy servants to stand before the glory of thy holy altar and present unto thee the worship due unto thee; accept thou O Lord from the mouth of us sinners the threefold holy song of praise' (Brightman, 1896, 369).

Adoration is closely related to *praise and thanksgiving*. While adoration is directed towards God's holiness and unapproachableness, praise and thanksgiving are offered to his glory, power and mercy. The hymn or song of praise contains in its early and traditional forms a recounting of the divine praise names, honorific titles and epithets, followed by exclamations: *Hééepà* (Praise!), *Svāhā* (Salvation!), *Triumphe* (Victory!), or *Axie* (Worthy!). The praising has as its purpose the enhancing of the power of the Deity so praised, as is seen in the double significance of the Hebrew *bārakh* (bless, praise). There developed also the poetic glorification of the Deity's works in nature and in human life. Often the praise passes into narrative myth which depicts the mighty works of the Deity in the past (see Chapter 8, above).

A corpus of praise songs or *poetic hymnody* (*ERE* 7, 1–58; Heiler, 1923, 161ff.) is found in many religious traditions, in virtually all, if oral praise songs and chants are included. The Deity called upon is the only one, the highest one, ruler of heaven and earth. Sometimes poetic hymnody develops into a fine flowering, as for instance in the hymn to the deity Aten of the Egyptian king Akhenaten: 'Thou dost appear beautiful on the horizon of heaven, / O living Aten, thou who wast the first to live. / When thou hast risen on the eastern horizon, / Thou hast filled every land with thy beauty. / Thou art fair, great, dazzling, high above every land; / Thy rays encompass the lands to the very limit of all thou hast made' (Thomas, 1958, 145). The Hebrew hymnody or Psalter is closely related to the hymnody of the ancient Near East. God is praised as creator and also as saviour and redeemer. Faith in Yahweh implies exclusive worship of this one God, creator of heaven and earth. Besides his activity as creator are placed his deeds in holy history, in the exodus from Egypt, in the victory over the Canaanites, in the help given against the peoples who were fighting the Israelites. The depicting of Yahweh as active in holy history is developed further in the late Israelite prayer: 'Thou art the Lord, thou alone; thou hast made the heavens, . . . the earth and all that is on it, the seas and all that is in them; . . . and the host of heaven worships thee. Thou . . . didst choose Abram . . . and didst make with him the covenant to give to his descendants the land of the Canaanite, . . . and thou hast fulfilled thy promise' (Neh. 9.6ff.). A melodious continuation of this is found in the prayer of praise to the psalms in the Jewish Eighteen prayer (*shemone 'esre*). An echo to the Jewish (and Christian) praise is found in the *suras* of the Qur'ān and in Persian poetry.

The Hebrew psalm prayer is continued in the *eucharistia*, the central prayer in the celebration of the Lord's Supper, the 'great prayer of thanksgiving': 'Lift up your hearts (*sursum corda*), let us give thanks unto the Lord our God'.' This high prayer is originally a thanksgiving not only for creation but also for the saving events in history. In its emphasis upon creation there lies a protest against the Gnostics and Marcion who were hostile to creationism. The culmination of saving history is the miracle of the incarnation, the Infinite implanting itself in the finitude of space and time. Besides the liturgical prayer of thanksgiving stands the free hymnody in which Christ is spontaneously glorified. The earliest traces of these praise songs are found in the Apocalypse of the New Testament: 'Worthy is the lamb who was slain, to receive power and wealth and wisdom and might and honour and glory and blessing!' (Rev. 5.12). About the same time Pliny writes of the 'singing to Christ as God' in early Christian services. The treasury of hymns from the early period has been lost apart from fragments including, for instance, the Greek evening hymn 'Hail gladdening light' (*Phos hilaron*); but many hymns of the post-Nicene period have survived. Latin hymnody took its departure from Ambrose and Hilary of Poitiers (*RGG* 3, 501f.).

The hymn of praise occupies a central place in the liturgy. To every psalm the 'little doxology' (Glory be to the Father and to the Son and to the Holy Spirit . . .) is added. Whole sections of the canonical hours have largely hymnic character, thus Matins and Lauds have the *Ainoi* which have taken their name from the last three praise psalms of the Psalter (148–150); the same with Vespers. At the end of Matins there resounds in the West the Ambrosian canticle, the so-called *Te Deum* (Burn, 1926; *LThK* 9, 1027ff.; *RGG* 1, 306f.); the church in heaven praises God in company with that on earth: '. . . To thee all angels cry aloud . . . to thee Cherubin and Seraphin continually do cry . . . The glorious company of the apostles . . . the prophets . . . martyrs praise thee. The holy Church throughout all the world doth acknowledge thee' (BCP). In the Western Lauds there is frequently sung the *Benedicite* (Bless the Lord . . .) of the three men in the fiery furnace (Sus. or Dan. 13), a nature hymn similar to Psalm 148, while the *Benedictus* of Zacharias (Luke 1.68ff.) is constantly sung. In the monastic orary prayers the praise of God never ceases. The word of the psalmist applies to these canonical hours: 'Seven times a day I praise thee' (Ps. 119, 164; *Rule* of St Ben. 16). This liturgical praise has entered also into individual piety. The *Confessions* of Augustine are a single great prayer of thanksgiving. Francis of Assisi lived in the constant praise of God; his prayers are for the most part prayers of praise; their culmination is in the *Hymn to the Sun* (see above, Chapter 1). Henry Suso invited the whole world to praise its creator in a great *Sursum Corda*. The solemn prayers of praise of the early Church are embodied in such hymns as: 'Praise to the Lord, the Almighty, the King of Creation' (*Lobe den Herren*) or John Henry Newman's 'Praise to the Holiest in the height' (*CH* 32).

(5) Confession of faith, sacrificial formula and vow

The *confession of faith* also belongs to the genre of praise and thanksgiving, and here too Christianity participates with the other religions. In early Buddhism such a confession appears in the threefold formula three times repeated: 'I take my refuge in the Buddha, I take my refuge in the doctrine of salvation (*dharma*), I take my refuge in the Community (*sangha*)'; in Mazdaism also, similar confessions are features of daily prayers and the liturgy of the *Yasna*. The confessional formula of Judaism is the word of Yahweh preserved in Deuteronomy: '*Shema' Yisra'el* (Hear O Israel), Yahweh our God, Yahweh is one' (alt. rdg.); 'and you shall love Yahweh your God with all your heart, and with all your soul, and with all your might' (Deut. 6.4). As with Buddhism, Mazdaism and Judaism; and as with Islam which was to follow with the *Shahadah*, and the opening and 112th *suras* of the Qur'ān, so Christianity has also made use of the credal formulary. The Eastern Church uses the Nicene-Constantinopolitan Creed as baptismal confession and confession of faith during the Mass (see above, Chapter 8). The Western Church employs the same Creed with the addition of the *Filioque* clause ('and from the Son') in the Mass on Sundays and feast days. For baptism, in the Divine Office and in private prayers the Apostles' Creed is used as a prayer (see above, Chapter 8). Both confessions of faith were passed on to the Anglican Church and to Protestantism. Besides these the Athanasian Creed was used in Morning Prayer on Sunday, both in the Roman and Anglican Churches. There came into use in the Roman Church also the Tridentine confession which was directed against the Reformation and prescribed for conversions from Protestantism. Characteristic of the Christian confession are: (a) confession of the triune God, (b) in opposition to the cosmological speculations of the Gnostics, the affirmation of salvation history in the centre of which are the incarnation, saving death and resurrection of Christ; and (c) the confession of the catholic and apostolic Church.

The creed serves as the confession of true and correct belief, of orthodoxy. The original meaning of the word orthodoxy, however, is 'true glorification'. For many Christians the creed is less an outline of theology than a 'poem of the Holy Spirit', 'hieratic poetry' (Söderblom). Said in this context it is not so much a case of binding oneself to the literal acceptance of individual clauses, whose symbolic and mythological character often emerges quite clearly, e.g. 'descended into hell' and 'ascending into heaven'; but rather of confessing one's faith in the creation, the history of salvation and the work of the Holy Spirit. In the liturgy also the confession bears the character of a spiritual sacrifice (see above, Chapter 6). This becomes especially clear in the introductory rubric of more recent Protestant liturgies.

With the confession of faith is associated the *sacrificial formula*. The sacrifice is offered with a commentary, a formula, making clear that the gift sacrifice is the property of the Deity. With all thank-offerings God is expressly recognized as the giver: man repays to God what God has given to him. The primordial sacrificial prayer lives on in the Christian liturgy. Here the traditional formulae of sacrifice occur again and again: 'take', 'receive', 'we offer unto you'. Particularly is this the case in the offertory prayer. In personal devotion self-offering takes the place of the external offering. This occurs in the sacrificial prayer: 'I bring thee in me and me in thee as a sacrifice of praise, I have nothing more; that which I am and lives in thee, all of that I give unto thee' (Gertrude von Helfta). 'I bring myself as a burnt offering on the altar before thy feet. Receive the sacrifice as thou dost wish. Use me as it pleases thee' (Sundar Singh). 'Take, Lord, all my freedom, take my memory, my understanding, my will. All I have and own hast thou given me, all this I give back to thee and yield myself wholly to the guidance of thy will' (Ignatius Loyola). 'All that I think and plan is before thee. Doing and not doing, joy and sorrow shall be offered up to thee' (Tersteegen). Sacrifice and prayer have here merged together into one (see above, Chapter 6). Sacrifice is no mere metaphor ('the sacrifice of the lips'). It is a reality acted out by the will: the word of prayer is simply its means of expression.

A special form of the sacrificial prayer is the *vow* (*ERE* 12, 644ff.; *RGG* 2,

1822f.; Heiler, 1923, 78ff.; *ER* 15, 301ff.). Here the sacrifice is usually promised for when the prayer is heard. The content of the vow is as diverse as the object of the sacrifice: from food and drink up to the real or symbolic sacrifice of human life (see above, Chapter 6). The unconditional vow has won a firm place in the 'profession' of monks and nuns who take vows of poverty, chastity and obedience (see below, Chapter 11). Some vows are temporary, others life-long; one speaks accordingly of 'temporal' and 'eternal' vows. The nun's vow stands for a solemn 'Yes' to the heavenly bridegroom. According to Roman canon law, the pope can release those concerned from all vows. In African Churches the vow was frequently taken over from African traditional practice. Members of Aladura Churches meet 'to pay their vows' (*The Church in a Changing Society*, 1978, 373).

(6) Supplication and intercession

The *petition* or request is as universal as religious thought and aspiration. There is neither a good nor a bad wish that has not been uttered in prayer. In traditional religious prayers the request for the good things of life comes through clearly: material goods, prosperity, happiness and longevity both for oneself and for others. Such requests are profoundly spiritual because they presuppose a world view in which the spiritual is prior to and interpenetrates the material. Traditional prayer requests are documents of *sola gratia* (by faith alone). Under the influence of moral ideas, ethical values have more and more become objects of prayer. Philosophical and ethical reformers pressed for such values as : wisdom, obedience to the law, peacefulness, purity and righteousness. But such ethicizing often leads eventually to the weakening of prayer.

The moral dimension forms but a part of petitionary prayer. Object of the deepening of prayer is the Deity, his grace and kingly rule. 'Whom have I in heaven but thee? And there is nothing upon earth that I desire besides thee' (Ps. 73.25). In the piety of prophetic faith objects of petition include: forgiveness of sins, justification, sanctification and union with the divine will. The same series is also found with other nuances in the prayer of Christian mysticism: purification, illumination and union (see above, Chapter five). At the centre of all requests in both prophetic and mystical piety is the request for God himself. 'Do not seek anything from God except God himself' (Augustine). Similar expressions are prominent in Indian *bhakti* and Islamic sufism.

Biblical, Christian prayer is marked by four characteristics: (a) the central request for the Kingdom of God. The Lord's prayer is a prayer for the Kingdom (Lohmeyer, 1953); the hallowing of God's name, the doing of his will, and the deliverance from evil are only variations of the request for the Kingdom. Also related to God's kingly rule are other requests: the plea for forgiveness and the request to be kept from temptation which includes all tribulation. Even the request for bread was originally an eschatological one: 'our bread for tomorrow, our supernatural heavenly bread give us already today', i.e. let us soon participate in thy heavenly banquet. In the early Church, the plea for the Kingdom became one for the return of Christ: 'Come, Lord Jesus' (Rev. 22.20). Later it became a prayer for the expansion of the Kingdom of God on earth and for inner peace and joy.

Christian prayer also includes (b) *universal intercessions*. The way to these had been prepared in the Jewish Scriptures. Such intercessions have their parallel in Buddhism where the meditation of love embraces all creatures, even the animals. The objects of Christian intercessions in the liturgy are the Church, the state and its rulers, 'the peace of the whole world', the fruitfulness of the earth, and all the needs of Christendom and humanity. Examples of general intercessions are the *ektenia* of the Oriental liturgies, the litanies of the Western Churches, the great intercessory prayer of the Roman Good Friday service and the general intercessory prayers in Protestant Sunday services.

The petitions are supported by (c) the appeal to God's promises. In this way revelation from the Deity and prayer, the word from God and the word to God are joined together. The appeal to God's promises is summed up in the phrase 'in the name of Jesus' (John 16.23) and in the concluding formula in the liturgy, 'through Jesus Christ our Lord'. There is no relationship that is not first established by God, and no access to him except through the *Logos*, the Word, Christ.

The prayer of intercession ends in (d) an expression of unshakeable confidence or complete surrender. 'For thou, O Lord, art my . . . trust, / upon thee have I leaned from my birth' (Ps. 71.5f). 'Not my will, but thine, be done' (Luke 22.42). Such surrender is also found in traditional African prayers (Mbiti, 1975) and among the mystics.

In petitionary prayer a distinction may be drawn between individual and communal forms. In traditional religions individual forms are evident especially during the time of initiation when the initiate withdraws to a secluded place to find a new and more personal relationship with the Deity. Through daily prayers and simpler, personal forms of divination, profound exchanges with the Deity may take place. The tradition of solitary prayer in Christianity grows out of Israelite religious experience. Elijah talks with Yahweh in solitude (1 Kings, 19.9). Jesus also withdrew into solitude for prayer with God; he advocated praying in a room alone (Matt. 6.6). The withdrawal of the devotee to a solitary place is found with many, such as Benedict and Francis of Assisi. African prophets are driven into solitude after their inaugural experience; the same impulse to seek solitude for meditation and prayer is seen in Indian religions also.

While no one can ever really know the extent of solitary prayer, common prayer is characterized by its visibility. In traditional religious cults, common prayer occurs at the sacrificial rites. The clan head, chief, king, priest or official acts as prayer leader and represents all present. It was in the temple and synagogue that the people approached Yahweh. In the early Christian Church it is said, with reference to prayer, that they praised God 'together with one voice' (Rom. 15.6). The Church is *ecclesia orans*, a praying Church; the individual joined in congregational prayer at worship services in fellowship with the whole of Christendom. This theme was taken up into Islam where the common *salāt* prayers led by the *imām* in the mosque are enacted in the awareness of the unity in prayer of the whole world-wide house of Islam. The liturgical prayer of the Christian Church went through a troubled time in the medieval period through the one-sided elevation of the priest and the passivity of the lay congregation. In the Reformation the congregation's activity was renewed but the link with the early Church's liturgy was weakened. The liturgical movements of the nineteenth and twentieth century have directed their attention to the restoration of early Christian congregational prayer.

The spontaneous free prayer of the individual represents the original form of all prayer, approaching as it does the unreflecting responsive nature of the human person. Free individual prayer consists of one's own impulsive words and is a completely personal outpouring of one's needs. We find it at all times and among all peoples. It received powerful impulses in Jewish-Christian piety under the influence of Israelite prophecy. In the liturgical life of early Christianity free charismatic prayer was dominant for a long period, after which it became fixed in set prayers. In Protestant Free Churches we find a revival of extempore prayer partly through the rejection of all set prayers. Yet the set prayer has its place in the cultus of the congregation, even if reduced to the repetition of the Lord's Prayer; and also as the prescribed prayer for individual devotions. For the latter the set prayer is an important pedagogical aid. In Islam we find prescribed *salāt* prayer and free *du'ā* prayer in an ideal combination.

Prayer is also seen as a divine gift of grace in both mystical and prophetic piety. 'I will pour out on the house of David and the inhabitants of Jerusalem a spirit of compassion and supplication' (Zech. 12.10). 'God has sent the Spirit of his Son into our hearts, crying, "Abba! Father!"' (Gal. 4.6). 'We do not know how to pray as we ought, but the Spirit himself intercedes for us with sighs too deep for words' (Rom. 8.26). Nilus Sinaita, the father of monastics, says: 'If you want to pray, you need God for it. He gives prayer to those desiring to pray.' Augustine explains with reference to the cry 'Abba! Father!' (Rom. 8.15): 'That is exactly the divine gift, that we call to God with true heart and in a significant manner.' 'Only the prayer which comes from God ascends to him again', says Charles Spurgeon. The character of prayer as grace is also emphasized in Hinduism and Islam, especially in Sufism. Jelal-ud-din Rumi tells of a Muslim who doubts whether God hears prayer because his call, 'O Allah', receives no answer, 'Here am I'; and who received from God this reassurance: 'In every one of your calls of "O Allah" there are a hundred "Here am I's".'

(7) The word to and from the Deity

Here the ring closes. The *word from the Deity* and the *word to the Deity* form a final unity. The nature of Christianity, indeed of religion, becomes visible at this point. It is not simply human experience, not Titanism, snatching at Deity, stealing fire from heaven, but rather the operation of prevenient grace. The word is something divine. This is the profoundest meaning in the magic formula which still lives on in popular religion. Whether one speaks of magical formulae or 'real prayer', it is clear that in Christianity the highest status is given to the word. 'In the beginning was the Word, and the Word was with God, and the Word was God', says the prologue of John's Gospel (John 1.1). In the religions of antiquity the word appears to possess the capacity of creating the cosmos (*ERE* 12, 749ff.; *ThWNT* 4, 80ff.; Mensching, 1937); and in the Genesis creation story we find: 'God said, "Let there be light"; and there was light' (Gen. 1.3). Brahman also speaks and the cosmos comes into being. From the creative word it was only a short step to the word as a divine hypostasis, whether in the sense of a more or less impersonal cosmic reason (*brahma, logos*) or a force subordinate to God (*Heb. memrā*) or a personal Deity, such as the Vedic *Vāc* (speech, Lat. *vox*). As the prologue of John's Gospel puts it: 'God was the *Logos* (or Word)', so also in the Brahmanas: 'Brahman is the *Vāc*'. The Johannine 'all things were made through the *Logos*' is anticipated in the same priestly book where it states: 'From *Vāc* (speech) the deities live, from *Vac* the Gandharva, animals and men . . .'

Besides the divine, creative word there stands, above all in prophetic religion, the word of revelation. Like the creative word, the word of revelation is also more than an announcement of God to man, it is a divine hypostasis. 'For ever, O Lord, thy word is firmly fixed in the heavens', the Psalmist prays (Ps. 119. 89). The Hellenistic *Logos* embodied in the figure of Hermes was described as saviour, herald and messenger (*angelos*). This Hellenistic *Logos* speculation was taken over by Philo and combined with a biblical train of thought (*Th WNT* 4, 71, 86ff.). In the prologue of the Fourth Gospel, the *logos* appears as the principle of God's universal revelation: 'the true light that enlightens every man' (John 1.9), and as the word which 'became flesh', the fulness of God's revelation (John 1.14); the name of the coming judge of the world is, according to the New Testament Apocalypse, 'the Word of God' (Rev. 19.13). In the Reformation of the sixteenth century, faith in the hypostatic Word of God broke through with an almost magical power. Since 'the Word' alone is the 'vehicle of grace' for Luther, it is therefore 'the highest and the greatest thing in the whole of Christendom' (Aland, 1983, 393ff.) In the dialectical theology of the twentieth century this apotheosis of the word was revived in an even sharper form (Barth, 1963).

Whereas Luther placed the emphasis on the 'external', 'oral' word, mystics such as Tauler remind us of the 'inward hearing of the inner word and the inner ground (of being)'. In contrast to Luther Protestant spiritualists of the sixteenth and seventeenth century (Denk, Sebastian Franck, Schwenkfeld) tirelessly maintained the precedence of the 'inner' word over the outer one (R. Jones, 1914).

(8) Sacred silence

However great the significance of the sacred word, it remains only one manifestation of the divine, it cannot comprehend the whole of Deity. As Euripides says: 'There is a place where silence is better than the word.' Ignatius of Antioch speaks of 'the word which has proceeded out of silence'. Behind the Deity who is revealed in the Word, *deus revelatus*, there stands the hidden God, *deus absconditus*, in his impenetrable silence. There are many forms of *sacred silence* (*HWDA* 7, 1460ff.; *LThK* 9, 374ff.; Mensching, 1925; Van der Leeuw, 1964, 432ff.; *ER* 13, 321ff.).

(a) *Cultic silence*: a religious specialist may often not pronounce the name of the Deity and the sacred formula, lest their power be lost. Silence serves as a means of concentration analogous to the practice of temporary celibacy before the performance of the rites (see above, Chapter 5). Silence also has importance in the cultic action which has to be carried out in an undisturbed and effectual way. In the cults of antiquity, the warning was given: 'Keep silence'. The motive was concern lest a chance word should bring to nought the cultic action and the blessing flowing from it. Linked to this is silence concerning the cultus outside cultic meetings. Some traditional cult-groups are prohibited from communicating cult secrets to non-initiates. The same requirement of 'secret discipline' was binding for initiates of the mystery cults of antiquity, as also for early Christianity (*RAC* 1, 667ff.) and the Freemasons' lodges of modern times.

In the cultus itself silence is the expression of the deepest reverence. God is ineffable, greater than all speaking; before his majesty mankind is dumb. Silence reigns in the ancient Chinese cult of heaven. In the Eleusinian mysteries as in those of Isis and Mithras, silence forms part of the cultus. In the Israelite cultus the prophetic word applied: 'The Lord is in his holy temple; let all the earth keep silence before him'; a word which, said or sung, has lived on down to the present in Christian services, and testifies to the place of silence in the Christian cultus. Commodian interprets the *Sursum corda* (Lift up your hearts), which precedes the great prayer of thanksgiving, as an appeal for silence. In the silent Masses the whole canon is prayed softly. In the Good Friday liturgy, silence reigns during the adoration of the cross. Beloved in Roman piety is the silent devotion before the most holy, the 'eternal devotion'. Corpus Christi chapels in which the host is displayed for silent worship (see above, Chapter 2) are a reminder of similar Isis chapels in Hellenistic times. The divine service of the Society of Friends is *silent worship* (Hodgkin, 1919; Hepher, 1924; Bauman, 1984). The 'expectant silence' in it is the basis of charismatic prophecy and eucharistic prayer. Rudolf Otto called for the introduction of a 'sacrament of silence' which should form the numinous high point of Protestant worship (Otto, 1932b and 1972). A distinction can be drawn between cultic silence with the inner concentration of Quaker worship, and that with an external object or objects upon which to focus one's worship.

(b) *Ascetic silence* is connected with fear of the disturbing effect of the word, also the avoidance of sin; in addition is the recognition that silence is part of the

Deity. The vow of silence is widespread among the ascetics of India; 'noble silence' is a traditional practice of Buddhism. Islam is also a way of silence, particularly in parts of Africa where, in the midst of a bustling, noisy environment, groups at *salāt* prayers in open-air mosques impress others by their total silence. In Christian monasticism silence is also an important practice. The *Rule* (42) of Benedict prescribes silence from evening prayer to after the morning prayer (Prime). The motives for silence here are to preserve oneself from sins and idle speech, and to enable inner concentration. Silence is practised especially by the Carthusians, the Camaldulensians and the Trappists; it is only interrupted by the greeting: '*Memento mori*' (Remember . . . you must die, cf. Ps. 89.47). On the wall of a Franciscan hermit are the words of Isaiah: 'In quietness and confidence shall be your strength' (Isa. 30, 15). Temporary silence prevails in the zealously spiritual exercises of Roman Catholics and Anglicans, whether they be of forty days, eight days or three days.

(c) *Wordless prayer*: the devotional silence of personal piety has a yet deeper significance. For the ineffability of the divine, beyond all understanding, there is no other language than silence. Silent prayer is especially practised by Neoplatonist mystics and lives on in early Christianity. Gregory of Nazianzus speaks of the 'silent hymn'. Pseudo-Makarios glorifies silent prayer. John Cassian in the West, praises the 'inexpressible' prayer that has 'nothing to do with the tone of voice or the movement of the tongue'. The most wonderful praise-song to contemplative and ecstatic silence was uttered by Augustine in his *Confessions* (9, 10): 'If . . . the tumults of flesh be silent, if fancies of the earth, and water and air be silent also; if the poles of heaven be silent also; if the very soul be silent to herself, . . . if all dreams and imaginary revelations be silent . . . , if whatsoever is transient be silent to anyone – since if any man could hearken unto them, all these say unto him, we created not ourselves, but he that remains to all eternity: if then . . . they also be silent, . . . and if he speak alone, not by them but by himself, that we may hear his own word . . . could this exaltation of spirit ever have continued . . . , were not this as much as "Enter into the master's joy"?'

The praise-song of silence resounds further in medieval and more recent mysticism. Tauler exalts inner prayer above the set prayer: 'All prayer of the mouth is like hay and straw compared to the pure corn.' Angelus Silesius sings: 'God is so much everywhere that one cannot really address him. It is better then that you pray to him with silence also.'

(d) The silence of prayer leads up to *theological silence*, the 'negative theology' of the Neoplatonists. The nature of the Deity admits of no statement about it; the Wholly Other is exalted above concept and word. Contemplative and ecstatic silence form the basis of this. In the ecstatic state what cannot be told arises in the mystic. Plotinus says: 'We say what God is not; what he is, however, we do not say.' Similarly Dionysius the Areopagite, whose influence on Christian mystics was immeasurable: 'In that we say what he is not, we know who he is.' Further than the theology of total denial is that of total silence. In the theology of early Buddhism we find this silence consistently maintained right to the end and beyond. Gautama Buddha refrained from every metaphysical statement about the final secret of the divine. Where other religions, philosophies and theological systems set their concept of the Deity, early Buddhism sets an empty space. *Nirvāna* is the totally inexpressible. For Lao-Tzu, the *Tao* is similar, and for the *Upanishad*, the *Brahman*. Proclus even adds that the Deity is 'more ineffable than all silence'. Christian mystics, in common with others, do delineate the divine in positive terms but they return again and again to a near-Buddhist stress on the ineffable and inexpressible.

Linked with theological silence is (e) *metaphysical silence*. Silence appears in the Hermetic literature as a primordial hypostasis. In the chain of aeons of Valentinus, the highest pair are made up of Abyss and Silence. Proclus emphasizes that before the word there must be the silence that constitutes it. In agreement with him is Ignatius of Antioch. An earthly and ethical analogy is provided by the silence in the face of the person in need. The friends of Job sat 'with him on the ground' and kept silence, 'for they saw . . . his suffering was very great' (Job 2.13). Only after seven days do the words come.

There is a certain parallelism between the sacred word and sacred silence. Prophetic piety lays the stress upon the word. As the expression of God's revelation; the mystic considers silence as the only adequate expression of the divine. The difference between the prophetic and the mystical appears at this point in all its sharpness; the prophet is the one speaking in the place of God, the mystic is the one 'closing mouth and eyes'.

10
Christian Sacred Writings

(1) The sacredness of the written word

Not only is the oral word sacred; so too is the written one. The written word is sacred in and through its greater permanence. *Sacred writings* (Lanczowski, 1961; Bouquet, 1962; Browne, 1945; *RGG* 3, 774f.) have become basic constituents of many religions including Christianity. Although such religions may have begun as oral traditions, they sooner or later become 'religions of the book'.

To the peoples of antiquity the very possibility of preserving and passing on thoughts and words through writing appears miraculous. For them the pictures and signs through which the thoughts are expressed are supernatural and filled with power (*HWDA* 9 App. 293ff.). The Egyptian hieroglyphs or sacred incisions were regarded as magical and called 'deities'. The written word had the same magical power as the spoken one. Their close connection is especially apparent in the Germanic runes (Arntz, 1944; *ER* 12, 486); *runa* is the magical word whispered softly which goes back to Odin, master of runes. Runes are magical words which have become magical signs. In the Gothic Bible of Wulfila, the gospel itself is called a *runa galaubinais*, a rune to be believed (1 Tim. 1.11; *KüG* E, 6).

Belief in the sacredness of writing lives on in *magic letters* (*RAC* 2, 775ff.; *RGG* 1, 246), above all those found in the Greco-Roman world. In Hebrew and Arabic, Greek and Latin, the letters served at the same time as numerals. They therefore took on additional sacredness as numbers (see above, Chapter 4). The Greek vowels formed the mystic word 'a e ē i o u ō'. It assumed virtually metaphysical and cosmic significance. The letters (*stoicheia*; *ThWNT* 7, 666ff.) became elements, primordial matter, cosmic powers and star systems (see above, Chapter 1). In Greek magical literature, Gnosticism (*ER* 5, 566ff.) and Jewish *kabbalah* (*ER* 12, 117ff.), a widespread letter-mysticism is found; so too in the New Testament, followed by Shi'ite Islam. The Greek letters Alpha and Omega feature in the New Testament Apocalypse as signs of Christ and have passed into Christian art as a symbol of him. The ancient power of letters lives on today in the Roman rite for the consecration of churches (*LThK* 5, 1053ff.; Muncey, 1930): with his staff the bishop writes the Greek and Latin letters on a cross of ashes which has been laid out on the ground. The Greek alphabet also appears as an inscription on bells; like other sacred signs and words it is intended to increase the bell's power to drive away demonic forces (see above, Chapter 5).

If writing is sacred and magically powerful, even more is this so in the written, magical formula as this appears on scraps of paper, bands and potsherds; on walls of houses or worn around the neck they serve as talismen (*telesma*, consecration or initiation) and amulets (see also above, Chapter 2). On Jewish phylacteries the *shema'* is written and on Muslim amulets Quranic passages. On Christian amulets are found the names of saints or bible passages, especially the first verses of the four Gospels. Pictures with captions and letters served as protection against dangers and sickness for Irish monks. There are also the petitionary notes written down by devotees and left at sacred places and shrines, as for instance in pilgrim chapels in parts of Europe. In Africa, amulets are popular in the Ethiopian Church; while in West Africa bible verses such as parts of Psalm 23 and pious slogans ('Go with God', 'God first') feature on motor scooters, mammy wagons and mini-buses.

Wall texts (see above, Chapter 2) are also a form of sacred writing. In Catholic houses pictures and images of Christ, Mary and the saints are fixed to the wall, in Protestant ones it is scripture texts, although among Swedish Lutherans there used also to be pictures of the sacred heart of Jesus. In Islamic houses, similarly, Quranic passages are written, painted or burnt onto the wall. Just as the saints' images are more than a mere representation, so too the scriptural verses are more than written words: they are filled with supernatural power.

(2) Forms and bearers of canonical writings

Prayers, hymns, oracles, omens, myths, laws, genealogies have been handed down for millennia only by *oral tradition* (Nielson, 1954; Vansina, 1965 and 1985; Hollenweger, 1977; *ER* 11, 87ff.). This has been achieved on the whole with a remarkable degree of accuracy. Students of the Brahmanas, Parsi *mobeds*, and Muslims still learn the sacred texts today by reciting them, and are able to retain large portions of such texts in the memory. Despite the advantage of the religion based on oral tradition, there remains the danger that it may die out, and with it the sacred texts as well.

The emergence of a written sacred literature creates a watershed in the history of religions. A cleavage develops between religions without written sacred traditions and the scriptural religions. For the latter, something valuable has been lost: the fluid adaptability of their myths and genealogies to historical circumstance. In return for this loss they become stronger and able to compete with rival faiths. Amongst the scriptural religions a further distinction emerges. There are those with sacred texts used in common worship and private devotions; and there are others which, over and above such uses of their sacred texts, have produced *canonical* scriptures, those which are normative, authoritative and infallible, and stand out in contrast to other, non-canonical writings. It is of course true that every written religious text is sacred in the sense of being borne by the sacredness of the words which form it. Yet the canonical scriptures are sacred and binding to a pre-eminent degree; they are considered to be of divine origin and to partake of eternity.

Mankind's canonical scriptures or bibles (Lanczkowski, 1961; *ER* 13, 133ff.) may be divided into two types: first, those which arose anonymously in prehistorical times where the bearer was an ethnic community. The oldest of these is probably the threefold *Veda* of early India, the *Rigveda*, *Sāmaveda* and *Yajurveda*. These found their continuation in secondary but likewise canonical texts, the priestly *Brāhmanas* and the esoteric, mystical *Upanishads*. The other bible of this kind is younger. It was edited by K'ung-fu-tzū, but its earlier parts go back to the second millennium. The five canonical books of Chinese imperial religion were continued in the four classical works of K'ung-fu-tzū's pupils. All other bibles have arisen on the basis of religions which have been founded and are the work of individual personalities of outstanding creativity. The bibles of religions with founders again may be divided into two categories. On the one hand there are the canonical scriptures of the mystical religions of salvation from India: Jainism, Buddhism and through Buddhism (in China) the *Tao-te-ching* of Lao-tzu. Of a different kind are the bibles in the prophetic religions of revelation, where is found the *Christian Bible* (Barr, 1973 and 1984; Barth, 1957; Black, 1962; Bruce, 1968; Dodd, 1956; Grollenberg, 1979; Nida, 1972; Nineham, 1976; *ERE* 2, 562–615; *ER* 2, 152ff.). Also included are: in Iranian Mazdaism the *Avesta*, in Judaism the *Torah* with the prophets and the writings, more narrowly considered the Christian *New Testament* (*RGG* 1, 1130–41; Perrin, 1982; Collins, 1983; Finegan, 1975; Kee, H. C., 1983) together with the Old Testament (Eissfeldt, 1974); in Islam the Qur'ān (*ER* 12, 156ff.), in Babaism the *Bayān*, written by its founder Mirza Ali Muhammad; in Mandaism, an Iraqi baptist sect, the *Ginzā* (treasure) and the book of John; in Manichaeism the seven works of Mani; in the Tenrikyō movement of nineteenth-century Japan, the seventeen revelations of the founder Nayakarna Mikiko, and other writings; in the Church of Jesus Christ of Latter Day Saints, the *Book of Mormon* revealed to Joseph Smith; *Christian Science with Key to the Scriptures* of Mary Baker Eddy; in the recent Unification Church, the *Divine Principle* of its founder Sun Myung Moon; and many more.

To these canonical scriptures are added the deutero-canonical ones. These secondary writings possess a lesser degree of authority than do the canonical ones, but may also achieve the same or even a higher level of appreciation. This is the case with the Hindu *Mahābhārata* together with the *Bhagavadgītā* and the *Rāmāyana*, or in Mazdaism the Pahlavi writings, and in Judaism the *Mishnah*, *Talmud* and the work of *kabbalah*, the *Zohar*. It is also no different with Christianity: its deutero-canonical writings include those of the apostolic Fathers (the letters of Clement, Barnabas, Ignatius, Polycarp, the Shepherd of Hermas and the *Didachē*, which in part were regarded as belonging to the New Testament canon) and the works of the church Fathers (Altaner, 1966; Richardson, C C., 1953; Schopp, 1962; *RGG* 1, 280ff.). In this process Islam too was no exception: its collections of *Hadīth* take their place as deutero-canonical literature as well.

Besides the authoritative writings of the first and second degree must be placed the *apocryphal* scriptures which the religious community has excluded from use in services of worship and as doctrinal sources because they were held to be of less value and heretical. These works originally stood on the same level as those later declared to be canonical. They were eliminated by accident or for more fundamental reasons, or else they represented imitations of the latter and served to promote the doctrines of special groups within the religious community. Of such are the Jewish writings which later were regarded by a part of the Christian churches as canonical (Charlesworth, 1983; *RGG* 1, 472f.); also the scriptures of the Qumran community (Dupont-Sommer, 1961; Stendahl, 1975) which were concealed in time of persecution; and similarly, those early Christian writings: gospels, acts of apostles, letters of apostles and apocrypha (James, M. R., 1983; *RGG* 1, 473f.). The majority of Christian churches came in the course of time to regard these as heretical. Individual ones, such as the gospels of Jesus' childhood (*RGG* 3, 1294f.) and the book of the Assumption of Mary, lived on in popular piety and have exerted a strong influence upon Christian art and literature. It is true that the greater part of this genre was lost as a result of its condemnation by the Church; but many apocryphal writings have recently been discovered and help to throw light upon early developments in Christianity (Pagels, 1982).

Sacred scriptures are borne by a political or religious community. Insofar as they have not grown up naturally, like the Vedas apparently, they are based on a conscious process of selection and definition. Jaina and Buddhist councils of monks defined the canon of their respective religions. Organs of the state church determined the canon of Zoroastrian Mazdaism in opposition to other religions of the book, including Christianity. Councils of rabbis drew up the Jewish biblical canon, deliberately excluding works written or circulating in Greek and used in part by the Christians (*RGG* 1, 1123ff.). After Marcion had created a New Testament canon out of the Gospel of Luke and the Pauline writings, the major Christian communities, which regarded Marcion as a heretic, agreed upon the compilation of a larger canon (Knox, 1942; *RGG* 1, 1130ff., 1119ff.). This they selected from a mass of gospels, acts of apostles and letters that were then in circulation. The canonicity of individual writings, such as the Epistle to the Hebrews, the catholic Epistles and the Apocalypse, long remained in doubt. As a result, some small national Churches in the East today possess a canon which diverges from the majority churches of East and West. Mani marks a fresh development in that he created his own canon. This was in the belief that to restrict oneself to oral preaching and oral tradition, as did Zarathustra, the Buddha and Jesus, would have an adverse effect upon the religion concerned. Muhammad also at least began the collection of the inspired oracles he had been receiving. This collection was continued by his secretary Zaid and completed under the first caliphs. Crucial for the establishment and acceptance of canonical scriptures is the value placed on them by the religious community, even where the founder provides the initial impulse in the direction of the canon's formation.

(3) The divine origin of sacred writings

Where a canonical scripture has come to prevail, it becomes regarded as divine, sacred, eternal and unalterable. Such applies in large measure to the secondary sacred writings as well. Where a concept of Deity is prominent, these scriptures were derived from a divine origin. This divine origin is made apparent in different ways which can be grouped together into two main types: the mechanistic, materialist and mythological modes; and the psychological one.

The first way of conceiving the divine origin of scripture is in terms of various complex images. It may be through an act of creation, as in early India with Prajapati as creator, or the Iranian *Avesta* according to the *Yasna* (55, 3). Alongside this theistic conception stands a pantheist one whereby the sacred scriptures are said to have emanated from Brahman. Besides these conceptions of a materialist inspiration stands the mythological idea of a personal inspiration. Thus the authors of the *Vedas* are begotten by deities in a supernatural way, e.g. by Mitra and Varuna at a *soma* sacrifice. Fourthly, sacred scriptures are described as pre-existent. The Vedas are pre-existent, indeed eternal. Early Buddhism regarded its scriptures as sacred and unalterable without, however, relating this to a theistic concept. The theistic religions of revelation such as Christianity tended to ascribe to their canonical writings pre-existence in heaven. Already the Book of Enoch and that of Jubilees speak of heavenly books, tablets and scriptures (Jub. 1, 27ff.; 16.28; 23.32; Enoch 93.2). According to rabbinic ideas, God himself created the *Torah* a thousand years before it was proclaimed. He loves it as his daughter and puts into effect its decrees (*UJE* 10, 267ff.). The Jewish concept of the heavenly primordial original was taken up into the early Christian world of thought. The *Shepherd of Hermas*, an early Christian work on penance which was sometimes included early on in the New Testament canon, sees itself as the copy of a divine original (*Vis.* 2, 1). The heavenly book also became a favourite image in early Christian language (Koep, 1952), just as recent spirituals love to sing about John the Divine's 'book of the seven seals'. The conception of the heavenly book in Judeo-Christianity then found its way into Islam. The *Torah* and Gospel are fragments of the heavenly book; the Qur'ān is the book sent down from heaven upon the prophet.

Besides these mechanistic and mythological conceptions which stress the significance of scriptures may be set the psychological ones which come closer to the actual circumstances of their composition. The writers of the sacred book have received its contents in visions and auditions or in a state of inner illumination. First, they have heard, they believed, the sacred words from the very mouth of God or from his messenger. The Vedic *ṛṣi* spoke with the deities over the sacred truths. The Israelite prophets heard Yahweh's words and wrote them down. 'Then the Lord said to me: "Take a large tablet and write upon it" ' (Isa. 8.1). According to the Yahwist narrator: 'Moses wrote all the words of the Lord' (Exod. 24.4). The New Testament apocalyptist received the command from Christ: 'To the angel in Ephesus write' (Rev. 2.1). Muhammad hears the Qur'ān from the mouth of the angel Gabriel.

1.
SACRED OBJECTS:
natural

In this contemporary
German wall-hanging
by Rudolf Koch the
Christogramme is
surrounded by therio-
morphic represent-
ations of three of the
evangelists, 'The *lion,
ox* and *eagle* are
symbols of Mark,
Luke and John' (p.30).

2.
SACRED OBJECTS:
artefacts

A Russian icon of the
eighteenth century
depicts saints
venerating an icon of
the Virgin's Present-
ation in the temple.
'The veneration of
the icon arouses
a longing for the
"prototype" which
the icon represents'
(p. 41).

3a.
SACRED SPACE:
the open space

An independent
church's open air hill
shrine and praying
ground at Oke Ado,
Nigeria. 'The open
space is one of the
oldest forms of sacred
space' (p. 48).

3b.
SACRED SPACE:
the covered space

Sainte-Chapelle, Paris
(thirteenth century):
'Gothic architecture
was seized by a
boundless urge
towards infinity. The
walls dissolved into
soaring pillars . . .'
(p. 55).

4. SACRED TIME

An ivory diptych or tablet dating from the fifth century, kept in Milan cathedral, shows the Christian view of sacred time. Christ the Passover Lamb stands here surrounded by the annual cycle of seasons shown as a wreath of greenery, grain and fruits above two chthonic serpents. Enclosing the natural cycle is a second series of panels. For 'although the link with the nature festivals remains, a distinction is introduced by the representation and commemoration of a saving event. The birth and other events of the life of the religious founder and saviour figure are now celebrated' (p. 63).

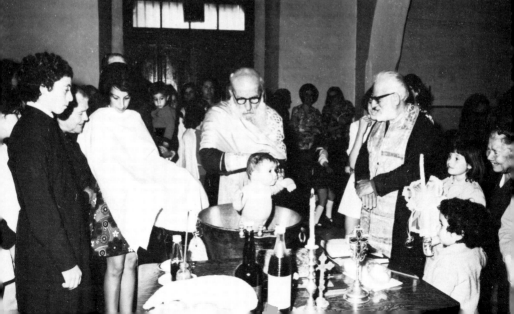

6. SACRED ACTION:
sacrifice

SACRED ACTION: purification

opposite, above)
Christian baptism in Zimbabwe. 'Baptism
total immersion has found support among
e independent churches of Africa' (p. 84).

opposite, below)
Greek Orthodox baptism. 'The Eastern
hurch has retained the practice of
mmersion down to the present day' (p. 84).

Martyrdom (seen here of Japanese
Christians in 1614) was considered
by the early church as being 'the
highest form of self-sacrifice with
Christ' (p. 104).

SACRED ACTION: unification

7a. (*top*)
Two groups of early Ethiopian clerics, facing each other, are performing a religious dance. 'Down to the present day, a dance of priests is customary in the Ethiopian Church' (p. 116).

7b. (*middle*)
Lines of Ethiopian chanters execute a ritual dance on the Saturday before the Palm Festival (p. 116).

7c. (*left*)
An Ethiopian saint (with the Christ child) being suckled by the Virgin Mary (p. 114f.; cf. p.37).

8. THE SACRED WORD: from the Deity

A Javanese Islamic representation of one of Jesus' example stories, that of the Rich Man and Lazarus (Luke 16. 19-31; p. 150).

9. THE SACRED WORD: to the Deity

In Poland, a Catholic priest hears private confession. 'Private confession was zealously promoted in the early days of the Reformation' (p. 162).

10.
SACRED WRITINGS:

The divine origin of
sacred writings is shown
in this medieval
representation of the
evangelist Matthew who
waits, pen in hand, for
inspiration, 'under the
compulsion of a higher
power' (p. 179).

THE SACRED PERSC
The Pr

A priest of the Russ
Orthodox Chu
administers
Sacrament. 'To be pri
means . . . mediat
between God and
people. The priest
distributes to n
sacramental divine gra
(p. 1ζ

12. THE SACRED PERSON: Woman as sacred

'Woman . . . became herself the object of veneration. Luther himself described Mary as the "woman above all women", "the princess of the whole human race" . . .' (p. 218f.). This fifteenth-century painting by Jean Mirailhet shows the Virgin Mary as protectress of mankind.

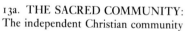

13a. THE SACRED COMMUNITY:
The independent Christian community

One such group 'in which free rein was given to the development of ... spiritual gifts' (p. 232) was this revivalist pop festival combining biblical slogans with country music.

13b.
THE SACRED COMMUNITY:
The spiritual church

A small group of 'the spiritual ones' (p. 233) is shown here at Rorke's Drift, South Africa. They stand before their drums holding their staffs upright, singing until the presence of the spirit comes over them.

13c. THE SACRED COMMUNITY: The unification of the Church

'The movement for unity between Roman and non-Roman churches received a strong
impetus through Pope John XXIII, who saw the unity of Christians as one of the main
goals of his pontificate and who created a secretariat for this purpose. The latter has
carried out intensive bilateral conversations with other Christian confessions following
Vatican II ... which marked the entry of the Roman Church into the ecumenical
movement' (p. 235). Shown here is the opening of the Council on 11 October, 1962,
attended by 2,600 bishops and abbots, with non-Roman observers also in attendance,
and Pope John presiding.

14. THE DEITY (*above*)

This nineteenth-century
Ethiopian icon of the Trinity
is far removed in intention
from any idea of 'tritheism'.
It suggests rather that 'all
three persons are . . .
co-equal' (p. 248).

15. CREATION (*right*)

Depicted in this
twelfth-century icon is man's
predicament as a created
being (255ff.) who climbs a
ladder towards the angels,
but is prey to evil spirits and
demons.

16. REVELATION (*left*)

Detail of stained-glass
window in Lincoln Cathedral
showing the head of Christ;
thirteenth century.'The
incarnation is understood as
the divine glory . . . shining
through the person' (p. 262).

17a.
SALVATION
Christ in peasant clothes, on the cross, depicted in the direct style of Nicaraguan folk art as the bringer of life (p. 270).

17b.
SALVATION
A Peruvian folk painting shows the exalted Christ as the bringer of salvation, amid scenes of rural life.

18. ETERNAL LIFE

The last judgement depicted on the east face of the eighteen-feet high Celtic cross of Muiredach, Monasterboice, County Louth, Ireland. 'The original form of the Christian doctrine of the beyond is the universal eschatological one' (p. 286).

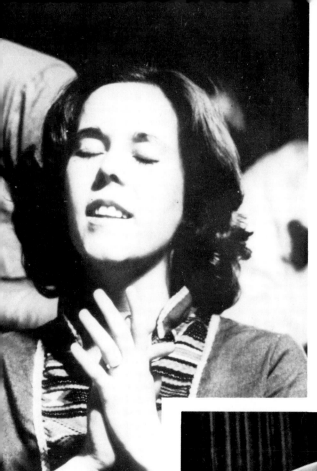

19.
CHRISTIAN EXPERIENCE:
joy

A member of the Jesus People, with
eyes closed and hands clasped, in a
state of joyful devotion. 'The
Christian worship service is a
constant source of joy' (p. 300).

20.
CHRISTIAN EXPERIENCE:
ecstasy

Saint Teresa of Jesus depicted
by Bernini in a state of rapture.
'In the remoteness of this
unitive experience from all
normal experiences, ecstatics . . .
apprehend their own being as
identical with universal cosmic
being' (p. 305).

An analogous concept holds that the writer of sacred scriptures saw the words in a vision. The Vedic hymns were seen in visions. One should probably understand the 'vision of Isaiah', referred to in the first pages of the Book of Isaiah, as the words which he saw before him. To the New Testament seer Christ says: 'Write what you see in a book' (Rev. 1.11).

Inspired writing forms an analogous process to inspired speaking. The author finds an inexplicable impulse to write. He does so in a passive state, automatically so to speak, under the compulsion of a higher power. This psychological phenomenon underlies the concept of *inspiration* (*ERE* 7, 346ff.; *RGG* 3, 775ff.; *LThK* 5, 703ff.; Sanday, 1908). This term has been used by the Christian Church to make clear the divine character of the Scriptures of the Old and New Testament. Not simply a person but God himself is the primary author of sacred Scripture. The measure in which the divine and human participate in this act of inspiration is differently estimated. There can be little doubt that a not inconsiderable part of the Hebrew Scriptures and New Testament writings was set down in a psychological state of inspiration; for instance, numerous portions of prophecy, many psalms, mystical and meditative pieces of John's Gospel, poetic sections of Pauline letters such as Romans 8, 1 Corinthians 13, Philippians 2, and Revelation. The authors wrote 'moved by the Holy Spirit' (2 Pet. 1.21). The same thing applies to the sacred writings of other religious traditions. Vedic hymns, words of the Buddha, the Gathic hymns of Zarathustra, individual *suras* of the Qur'ān, Lao-Tzu's *Tao-te-ching* and Plotinus' *Enneads*. There can be equally little doubt that part of the Judeo-Christian Scriptures, indeed of the canonical scriptures of all the major religious traditions, is not inspired in the sense of this special experience. The majority of authors did not hold themselves to be inspired at all. Only through the value judgement of church communities was the concept of inspiration extended to the whole of the canonical Scriptures, as is claimed in an early church document, the Second Epistle of Timothy (3.16): 'All scripture is inspired'. The plainly uninspired character of many canonical writings has led individual theologians to the view that these writings came to be part of Scripture only through some subsequent pronouncement by the Church that such was the case.

(4) The inerrancy of Scripture

For dogmatic theology it was not so much a matter of the psychological phenomenon of inspiration but rather the authority and *inerrancy* of Scripture. The inerrancy of the Scriptures was not limited to their religious and moral content but was extended to its assertions about the profane world of science and history as well. This teaching of the complete inerrancy of Scripture was still being stressed in the encyclicals of recent popes such as Leo XIII, Benedict XV and Pius XII (*RGG* 3, 262). However, increasing recognition of the modern world view and theory of evolution forced theology to acknowledge that the biblical writers had to work within the thought-forms of their own day.

Yet despite all the upheavals brought about by science and biblical criticism, faith in the divine origin and inerrancy of Scripture remains strong. This may be seen not only in Islam but also in Protestant *fundamentalism* (Barr, 1977; *ER* 5, 190ff.). For some, every sentence, every word, comma and full stop is inspired. Faith in sacred writings sees in Scripture God's word and revelation alone; indeed God's revelation in nature often appears recognizable only when mediated by the Bible. Hence the well-known Islamic saying: 'Everything between the two covers is God's word.'

Biblicism has again and again led to cultic veneration of the sacred book, or *bibliolatry* (*ERE* 2, 617ff.; *HWDA* 1, 1207ff.). Many instances of this may be found. An example taken from Burmese Buddhism shows scripture's sacredness enhanced in conjunction with sacred objects and sacred space. The Kuthodaw's pagoda with 729 stupas contains thousands of slabs on which the entire Buddhist canon has been engraved from the recitations of 2400 monks. Cultic veneration of Scripture is also found in the Eastern Orthodox Church as in the Western Church. In the Eastern Church the Scriptures are brought in solemn procession into the nave of the church preceded by the carrying of lights and the censer. In the Western Church the Bible is censed and kissed after the reading of the gospel. In the Syrian Church near lake Urmia in Iran, an ornate Bible is kissed by the faithful; dust from it is baked in bread which is then enjoyed as sacred food. In the Little Entry in Protestant churches, the Bible is solemnly carried into the church and placed on the lectern or pulpit (see also above, Chapter 7). Otherwise it remains on the altar or communion table under the cross. Because the sacred book is laden with secret power persons taking an oath place their hand upon it so that it will impart power to their words and in the event of an untruth have the effects of a curse (see above, Chapter 9).

The sacred scriptures have also long been used in oracular and divinatory forms of the sacred word. The Greeks used Homer for oracular purposes, the Romans used Virgil. As early as Augustine's time the custom which is still found today among Christians makes use of the Bible for divination: with eyes closed, the thumb or forefinger is placed at random on some verse in the Bible (likewise opened at random) which is taken as the answer to some particular problem. A variant used in Africa is to have a pointer that spins over the open Bible or to have the Bible itself suspended so as to give a yes/no answer (see also above, Chapter 8). There is also the custom of placing the Gospel on the head in the case of a headache or some other affected part (Zellinger, 1933; Van der Meer, 1961). In the twelfth century the Church even took over the popular custom of 'praying' the prologue of John's Gospel (1. 1–18) at the time of a thunderstorm. It forms the introduction to the blessing of the weather and probably this was the occasion for its inclusion in the Mass.

Bibliolatry however applies not only to some forms of sacred word and action including the employment of the material book for divination and healing. It also applies to its being given a position so exclusive that every other revelation of Deity is denied. Protests have been raised against such biblicism within

Christianity as well as outside it. In the Christian world opposition to the over-valuation of the written sacred word has been voiced time and again, beginning with the warning cry of Paul: 'The written code kills, but the Spirit gives life' (2 Cor. 3.6). Alfred Bertholet, a leading historian of religion and biblical scholar of this century wrote: 'It may sound harsh, but with reduction to writing there begins a process of fossilization of that which as spoken (or thought and often also written) once had a share in the spontaneous life of living religions.'

(5) The dogmatic interpretation of Scripture

Such spontaneous encounter with the living Deity is stronger in the final analysis than the authority of the sacred book. Individual believers who do not want to bring down this authority even if they could, find a means of escape in the *interpretation* of Scripture. The sacred scriptures of the different religions are in large measure expounded differently from what their author intended. Religious and theological exposition interprets Scripture according to the present not the past. Sacred writings, especially the Christian Bible (*RGG* 3, 242–62; Grant, 1984; *ER* 6, 279ff.) have been interpreted in widely different ways. Often indeed this interpretation was a travesty of the original meaning of the text. The saying of Samuel Werenfels of Basel (d. 1740) applies here: 'This is the book in which each looks for his own doctrines; and in it similarly he finds them.'

All great religious figures, church Fathers, Reformers, founders of orders, preachers of repentance, founders of religious movements, apocalyptic enthusiasts, mystics, humanists, spiritualists, rationalists, even enemies of Christianity, all alike appeal to the Bible. The Church of Jesus Christ of Latter Day Saints found in it the justification for polygamy; then, following a revelation, it was held to justify monogamy. For the Christian Scientist it justifies the non-existence of the material body, to the Adventist and Jehovah's Witness it provides the date for the imminent return of Christ. Similarly in Islam Muslims of different tendencies find confirmation of their version of Islam in the Qur'ān.

In the 'religions of the book' three main forms of interpretation may be distinguished: dogmatic, mystical and critical. These may be considered in order. Dogmatic exegesis (*exēgeomai*, to expound) became part of the earliest Christian community which held the Jewish Scriptures, their lectionary for services, to be an arsenal for proofs of Jesus' messiahship. They consolidated their belief in the crucified and exalted Lord by the interpretation of biblical sayings which constituted in large measure a reinterpretation. The classic example is the Isaianic prophecy of the birth of Immanuel (Isa. 7), the birth of a child from a virgin in the near future, applied to the fatherless birth centuries later of the child Jesus from the virgin Mary; with the aid of a mistranslation of the Hebrew word '*almā* (young woman) to read 'virgin'. By means of this apologetic method, early Christianity succeeded in projecting the New Testament back into the Old in the sense of Augustine's famous saying: 'In the Old Testament the New is latent; in the New Testament the Old is patent (or obvious).'

The Church later used the Bible as a quarry of proof texts for the truth of her dogmas of the Trinity and the incarnation; in the West, additionally, those of the fall, grace and the sacraments. The dogmatic teaching, which had been elaborated in a complex process over the centuries under the influence of Greek philosophy and other Greco-oriental teachings, was read back into the New Testament, and where the New Testament reference was lacking, into the Old Testament. This was the case with Mariology, which was achieved only through the allegorical reinterpretation of the Song of Solomon. Here too it did not succeed without mistranslations, for instance when the belief that Mary was kept free from original sin was proved by the false translation of Genesis 3.15: 'He (Heb. *hū*) shall bruise your (the serpent's) head', by (Lat.) *ipsa conteret*, 'she herself shall bruise ...'. Another mistranslation is found in Romans 5.12: 'because (*eph hō*) all men sinned' is rendered by 'in whom (Adam) all men sinned' (*in quo omnes peccaverunt*). This served to reinforce the Augustinian doctrine of original sin. The dogmatic interpretation of Scripture, according to the Council of Trent, should follow 'the unanimous consensus of the Fathers'. Such a consensus, it must be admitted, has never really existed.

The Reformers interpreted the Bible from that part of the gospel message which appeared to them to be central from their own experience, rather than from the standpoint of traditional dogma. For Luther this was the experience of justification. From this point of view certain central passages emerge, the ones italicized in the Luther Bible. Starting from these central passages Luther interpreted the whole Bible in sovereign fashion. Writings which are at variance with his over-view are devalued, as in the case of the Epistle of James, called an 'epistle of straw'. The individual writings are arranged in order according to their value: Romans and Galatians, First Peter and Isaiah 53, the suffering servant song which is described as a better gospel than the writings called Gospels. Among the latter, not only is John's Gospel 'to be preferred to all others', but the Synoptic Gospels which appear as 'gospels of works' are reduced to an appendix of the former, 'the gospel of faith'. However the other elements overlooked or suppressed by Luther demanded their rightful place. These were raised up by other Reformers to the status of a principle of scriptural interpretation. Central to Calvin's exegesis stands the glory and kingly rule of God, his holy community and the fulfilment of the law. Every Protestant group has its 'Key to the Scriptures' (Mary Baker Eddy): Baptists, Methodists, Pietists, Spiritualists, Adventists. Yet the prospect of differing interpretations of Scripture is not confined to the Christian tradition alone. On Indian soil the Vedas and Upanishads are very differently interpreted by Shankara and Ramanuja; while the Qur'ān is expounded with a similar degree of divergence by the Mu'tazilites and their orthodox opponents.

(6) Mystical exegesis of Scripture

Still more closely akin are the different 'religions of the book' in their *mystical* exposition of scripture. The mystics have all sought salvation, union with the highest good. Often they seem to be speaking the same language and even to be making use of the same illustrative images and abstract concepts. This does not mean that there were not also considerable differences of religious context (Katz, 1978); but it meant that for the mystics who found themselves in the sphere of prophetic religions such as Christianity there was a good deal that was alien or hard to assimilate in the sacred records. In their peaceable way, however, they understood how to transform these texts into graphic testimonies to their mystical experiences. This art of *allegorēsis* (*ERE* 1, 127ff.; *RAC* 1, 282ff.; MacQueen, 1970) goes back to the reinterpretation of Homeric stories of the gods by Greek philosophy. It was to serve as an 'antidote', as the 'healing of the myth'. From Aristobulus it was taken up into Jewish exposition of Scripture where it was employed in a masterly way by Philo to insert into the *Torah* the basic ideas of his Platonic mysticism. Paul and the writer of Hebrews follow in his steps (as do later Jewish mystics). John's Gospel transmits this allegorical vision also to stories of the life of Jesus, including the marriage at Cana and Christ's death on the cross. Through Clement of Alexandria and Origen (Hanson, 1950) *allegorēsis* was adopted into Christian theology and piety. Jericho (Josh. 6), for example, stands for heathendom, the walls for idolatry, the trumpet-blowing priests who bring down the walls, the apostles (Origen, *Hom.* 7/1). In Jesus' parable (Luke 10.30ff.) the good Samaritan is Christ, Jerusalem paradise, Jericho the world, the man fallen among thieves Adam, the robbers are the demons, the wounds are sins, the animal to ride on is the body of the Lord, the inn is the Church, the innkeeper the apostles (*Luc. Hom.* 34). Origen it was who also transformed the Old Testament Song of Solomon, a collection of Jewish love and marriage songs, into the text book of Christian mysticism (see above, Chapter 7). Methodius of Olympia and Bernhard of Clairvaux followed him in this. The greatest teachers of the Western Church, Ambrose (Dudden, 1935) and Augustine (Battenhouse, 1956) also practised allegorical exegesis.

The two sisters, Martha and Mary (Luke 10.38ff.), became the archetype for the twofold mystical life of contemplation and action (Butler, 1922). The same approach was taken by the mysticism of the Sufi in their exposition of the Qur'ān when they distinguished between the outer and the inner word of scripture. The Sufi even read into a Quranic verse, 'wherever you turn is the face of Allah' (*sura* 2), their indifference to all confessional differences. In such allegorical exegesis Christian mystics and others freed themselves inwardly from the constraints of external religious observance. Whatever they touched with the magic wand of their mystical view was bathed in the golden light of their divine inwardness.

(7) Biblical criticism

Alongside both of these methods of expounding sacred texts may be set as a third form the scholarly, historical and critical exposition of the Bible (Kraus, 1956; Hunter, 1950; Davidson, 1970; Soulen, 1977; *RGG* 1, 1184ff., 1127ff.; *ER* 2, 136ff.). It has its stronghold in Christian theology. The Antiochian school made the first beginning; but Alexandrian exegesis, although more inclined towards allegorizing, advanced the textual exegesis of the Bible as shown by the *Hexapla*, Origen's work on the Bible with six columns arranged in parallel. The fathers of modern biblical criticism are Erasmus, who prepared the way for the advance of New Testament textual criticism, Spinoza who practised biblical criticism in an unprejudiced fashion, Richard Simon the Catholic priest who showed an astonishing freedom in his approach, and Semler who brought biblical criticism into Catholicism after its condemnation in the Protestant form. From there it penetrated into Catholic modernism. Often enough it has been damned as a sacrilegious and heretical attack on God's word, yet it constitutes one of Christianity's greatest titles to fame. It is the strongest proof of the strict self-criticism which was already the object of praise by Schleiermacher (*Speeches*, 5, 148f.). Christian biblical criticism prepared the way for the textual and historical criticism of the sacred texts of other religions as well. These were investigated with the same methods and similar problems and inter-relationships were discovered. It also ran up against the same difficulties.

The task of biblical criticism in Christianity as in other religions is sixfold: (a) The foundation is laid by *textual* criticism which tries to determine the original text from the numerous variant readings. (b) This is followed by the *history of the canon* which uncovers the process, extending over hundreds of years, which led to the divine character of these texts being recognized. (c) The next step is *literary* criticism which unravels the tangled strands of the documentary sources and tries to identify the real author behind all the pseudepigraphical disguises. (d) The task that follows is *historical* criticism: the investigation of the historical character of the biblical narratives. Large sections of the sacred writings, above all of the Hebrew Bible but also of the New Testament, contain, as do other sacred texts (the Buddhist *Tripitaka*, for instance) legendary and mythical elements. (e) The most important task is to uncover the major lines of development in the history of religions that are reflected in the individual bibles. The Judeo-Christian Bible leads from the dawn of an early traditional cult of '*El* and Yahweh through the Israelite prophets and the age of Jewish law and the expectation of the end, to the gospel of Jesus and the gnostic salvation history of Paul and John, and finally to the strongly-established ecclesiastical structure of the Pastoral Epistles. A historical span no less wide is discernible in the case of the Vedic bible. Each bible, however, leads beyond its immediate circle into the wide expanse of the universal history of religions. In the case of the Jewish Bible close connections are apparent with the religions of the entire Near Eastern world, especially the Egyptian and Mesopotamian religions but also Iranian and Hellenistic religion;

the New Testament for its part cannot be understood without the links with Hellenistic philosophy, Gnosis and mysticism, as well as the oriental and Hellenistic mystery cults, for knowledge of which we are indebted to the *Religionsgeschichtlichen Schule* of Jeremias, Gunkel, Gressmann, Heitmüller and Bousset. (f) The last task of the historical exposition of the Bible is the history of biblical exegesis and piety (*ERE* 2, 601ff.; Deanesley, 1920; Smalley, 1983), the beginnings of which are found in the work of Richard Simon. The sacred Scriptures including the Judeo-Christian ones, not only reveal in themselves a variegated religious life, but they also have engendered throughout the centuries a religious life of unimaginable richness and depth. From their fulness the generations, simple believers and religious specialists alike, have drawn life and power.

11

The Sacred Person in the Christian Tradition 1

(1) The person as sacred

Another important way to approach the practices and beliefs of Christians is through the category of *sacred person* (Van der Leeuw, 1964; Wach, 1964; Eliade, 1979; *RGG* 3, 2100f.). For Christians as for those of other religions, the human person bears a certain sacredness. The sacredness of the human person is similar to that of natural objects and images, of space, time, actions, words, and writings. In traditional religions and in antiquity the *sacred person* is the human person as such, filled with power in particular parts of the body (*ERE* 2, 755ff.; *ER* 6, 499ff.), the *soul* (*ERE* 8, 9–44; 11, 725–55; *RGG* 2, 1268ff.; Bonnet, 1971, 357ff.; *ER* 13, 426ff.), and certain psychological states. Certain persons are sacred because of their calling or personal gifts. Finally, larger and smaller groups share in this sacredness and not simply individual persons.

There is sacredness in human hair, even that which has been cut off, nail parings likewise, spittle, breath, even faeces and urine, blood especially, and objects associated with the person: clothes, weapons and tools (see Chapters 2 and 5 above). The sacrifice of hair communicates power to the Deity (Chapter 5). Touching with spittle (*ERE* 11, 100ff.) is effective in healing. Jesus heals the deaf-mute through his saliva (Mark 7, 33). Following the example of Jesus, but also that of the early Roman custom of smearing newly-born children with saliva, the Christian priest according to the Roman rite of baptism, touches the nose and ears with saliva. The kiss is, traditionally, the exchange of soul-substance in the form of saliva and breath (see above, Chapter 7). The *breath* (*ERE* 2, 838ff.; *ER* 2, 302ff.) is likewise the bearer of soul-power, hence the blowing on the baptismal water at the Roman consecration of the latter, and on the baptizand during the Roman baptismal ritual. A theology of the breath (German: *Atem*) is contained in early Indian *Yoga* (Eliade, 1958; *ERE* 12, 831ff.; *RGG* 1, 668f.), now increasingly popular in the West. *Ātman* as bearer of the soul became the immanent Deity, the ground of the soul. Human (and animal) blood also contains soul substances (see above, Chapter 6). Like the kiss it joins people to one another and creates 'blood brotherhood'. The name is traditionally a person's alter ego; whoever is in possession of the name has power over the particular person.

Besides the different 'body-souls' (blood, breath, shadow, name, etc.) are the subtler 'spirit-souls': the dream soul, the soul in the thumb (*Purusha* in India, *ka* in Egypt, Tom Thumb in Eng. mythology), the bird soul (*ba* in Egypt, the dove in the legend of Semiramis and St Scholastica: see above, Chapter 1). According to the Greek view, the personal *daimōn* (guardian spirit) dwells in man from birth onwards and accompanies him throughout the whole of his life.

Regular sacrifices are made to it, a cult which resembles that made to the *tondi* of the Batak, the *orí* of the Yoruba or the *chi* of the Igbo. The Roman *genius* is originally the man's power of procreating; the *juno* is the woman's power of giving birth.

In particular states persons are also considered to possess a marked degree of sacredness: in war, hunting and fishing men are filled with mysterious power. This power-substance must not be disturbed through another power such as that of sexuality (see above, Chapter 5). Later the whole area of sexuality (coitus, menstruation and birth) was regarded as 'polluting'. Its 'impureness' is nevertheless only a change of emphasis from its previous 'sacredness' (see Chapter 1). For the return to the normal state isolation is necessary, as also are special rites of purification and protection (see above, Chapter 5). The sphere of *death* (*ERE* 4, 411–511; *HWDA* 5, 1023ff.; 8, 970ff., 1019–34, 1051–1100) is also governed by ideas of *mana* and tabu. The dying person and the body of the dead are imbued with mysterious power. The blessing and curse of the dying possess even greater power. The corpse is tabu and contagious; all who have to occupy themselves with it must undergo rites of purification.

Above all, however, sacredness is a characteristic of particular persons or groups of persons. In matriarchal cultures it is the *mother* (Neumann, 1972; James, E. O., 1959; *ERE* 8, 851ff.; *RGG* 4, 1228f.). She is the centre of the family and kinship group. She represents the 'great mother' (earth mother, moon mother; Chapter 1 above), and as such is filled with special sacredness. In the patriarchal cultures on the other hand, the father is the family and clan head, the chief of the village or ethnic group, and surpasses all other members of the group in sacred power.

(2) The sacred ruler

Traditional concepts of the person's sacredness form a constant background to the beliefs and practices of Christians; with the sacred ruler, however, the sacred person moves into the foreground and that not only in the past but down to the present. The sacred powers inherent in the family and kinship head are increased in the chief and king (Sacral Kingship, 1959; *ERE* 7, 709ff.; *RGG* 3, 278ff., 1709ff.; *ER* 8, 312ff.). His power is concentrated in a weapon, staff, fly-whisk, or sceptre (see above, Chapter 1). As the bearer of sacred power the ruler is subject to tabus and requirements. Because the sacral powers of the ruler were held to decline in the course of time, it was the practice in many ethnic groups for the king to be killed (regicide) or to commit suicide. A reform of this rite is the *regifugium* or driving away of the ageing ruler (see Chapter 5 above).

The traditional sacred king is not only a power-filled person, he is also in many cases in close relationship with the Deity. In the religions of antiquity this is also the case, as, for example, in ancient Egypt, Mexico and Peru, Mesopotamia, Syria and Persia, India, China and Japan, Ashanti and Benin. In sacral kingship two lines of thought come together: the ruler appears partly as the Deity made visible, as the incarnation or emanation of Deity; and partly as the commissioner, representative and viceroy of Deity, the feudal lord of God's possessions and the executor of the divine will, subject himself to it, raised up by it, endowed with gifts by it, but also under its scrutiny and judgement. In the first line of thought the numinous element predominates, in the second the ethical one. Monotheistic religions are linked with the second. Darius, for instance, confesses: 'Through the grace of Ahura Mazda am I king. Ahura Mazda gave me the kingdom' (Kent, 1953). The relationship of the king to the Deity is often seen as one of sonship. In the Hellenistic world the cult of the ruler experienced a powerful increase with the king being addressed as the Deity. A series of Roman emperors beginning with Diocletian – who called himself 'Lord and God' – forced their subjects into the cultic veneration of their living person; others allowed such an apotheosis only after their death.

The young Christian community took over the terminology of the emperor cult in 'polemical parallelism' (Deissmann, 1911), for instance, the predicates 'God's Son' and 'Lord' (*kurios*), 'ruler of all' (*pantocratōr*), 'saviour' (*sōtēr*); and spoke of Christ's 'epiphany' (manifestation), 'appearance' (*parousia*), 'authority' (*exousia*) and his gospel (*euangelion*). At the same time, however, they refused to recognize the divinity of the emperor, whether by bowing the knee before the emperor's sacred image, through the offering of incense or by taking an oath on his genius (*tuchē*). Although over three long centuries the Christians demonstrated their rejection of the emperor cult to the point of accepting martyrdom, the cult itself persisted after the victory of the Christian religion even though in a Christian guise. Constantine (A. Kee, 1982) allowed the offering of a cult in temples dedicated to him and received apotheosis after his death as Constantinus the Divine. The Byzantine emperors who followed him bore the honorific titles of the traditional Roman rulers and were described as 'most divine' (*theiotatos*), 'most holy' (*sanctissimus*), 'Deity' (*theotēs, divinitas*), 'the eternal one' (*aiōniōtes, aeternitas*). They spoke as the traditional Roman emperors did also of their *tuchē*, their *numen*. Panegyrics celebrated the emperor as nothing short of 'the present and visible God'. Subjects took the oath on the *tuchē* of the emperor as in traditional Roman times they showed their veneration for him by prostration and kissing his foot. Again as in traditional Roman days they venerated the emperor's sacred image through prostration, acclamation and the offering of incense. Christian theologians justified this cult by referring to the divine 'providence' and 'grace' through which the emperor was called to be 'vicar of Christ' and 'co-ruler with Christ'. The Church bestowed its approval on the emperor's sacredness through the ceremony of blessing, coronation and anointing with myrrh (see above, Chapter 7). Thereby it elevated him into the ranks of the clergy and to the office of priest-king.

Following the Byzantine example the peoples of the West also regarded their king as sacred, divine, vicar of Christ and the 'Lord's anointed'. Poets address the rulers as nothing short of God himself. In the West the sacrality of kingship found its most powerful expression in the solemn coronation of the king at which, according to Germanic custom, the insignia of office were handed over to the king and he was anointed like the bishop following the Jewish example.

The sacredness of the king appears in a more intense form in the emperor, who was regarded as 'vicar' of God and Christ and also 'bishop of bishops'. At the sacramental coronation, he received as world ruler the 'mantle of heaven' with sun, moon and stars which has been the vestment of deities and rulers of antiquity (see above, Chapter 1). The increase of papal power in the struggle with the imperium led to a decrease in the latter's sacrality. A part of the terminology of sacred kingship and of the emperor cult passed to the pope, for example, the title 'vicar of Christ', also the threefold prostration and the separation at meal-time as was required by traditional kingship tabus.

The concept of the ruler's divinity has also entered into Reformed Christianity. For Luther the rulers are established as gods by God and are the latter's collaborators. The reigning prince became the supreme bishop in German Protestant Churches. The English monarch was described as head or supreme governor of the Church of England. In England the sacramental medieval coronation rite has been maintained down to the present day whereas it has disappeared from most other Christian lands. Today there are sacred kings still in parts of Africa, Nepal, Thailand and in Japan, where the *tennō* or heavenly majesty, whose ancestor is the sun goddess, was forced by the victorious Americans after the Second World War to confess to his people that he is of human not divine origin. Many Christians today may give sacred kingship scarcely a thought, some indeed such as the Jehovah's Witnesses, Brethren and groups of pacifists are deeply distrustful of earthly rulers, and yet the sacredness of the ruler lives on among the mass of Christians in the uncritical willingness to believe that their rulers automatically 'know what is best'. Others struggle against such credulity.

(3) The priest

Even more important than sacred kingship for most Christians has been the sacred person of the priest. Kingship and *priesthood* (*ERE* 10, 278–336; *LThK* 8, 462ff.; *HWDA* 7, 307–29; *RGG* 5, 570ff.) were originally bound up with each other: the king was at the same time the priest. The Peruvian Inca kings and the Sumerian priest-kings were at the same time the chief priests. Melchizedek was a western Semitic priest-king (Gen. 14.18). The ancient Athenian king, the Japanese emperor and the ancient Roman king also had the office of high priest though the last named was so restricted by tabus that the office of priest was transferred to a high priest (*rex sacrorum*). In the year 12 AD the priestly office of pontifex maximus was nevertheless added to the political imperium. Yet the tendency was clear: priests were set apart for the professional exercise of the relationship with sacred powers. The *shaman* (*ERE* 11, 441ff.; Eliade, 1970; *ER* 13, 201ff.) similarly is a traditional priest with wide powers of divination and sorcery, healing, and communication with the spirit world. The professional diviner was very often also a priest inasmuch as he or she exercised the role of mediator between the people and the powers of the spirit world. From the twin sources of sacred kingship and the shaman-diviner the priesthood developed in terms of a regular and ordered communication with the divine world. Priesthood thus becomes related to the cultus. Cultic activity increases the tendency for a separate priesthood. The priesthood increased perceptibly in the cultic religions of antiquity, in India, Egypt, Mesopotamia, Japan, Mexico and Peru, and in later Israelite religion. In China, and partly also in Greece, a professional priesthood was lacking inasmuch as officials carried out priestly functions (as for instance today in registry-office weddings).

As with the sacred ruler, so also the priest became separated from the people by tabus and restrictions designed to preserve their sacredness. Only the priest was qualified for immediate intercourse with the Deity, for worship at the temple, altar and image of the Deity. To be priest means being with God, seeing and touching him, mediating between God and the people. The priest like the king represents the Deity and conveys the divine will through oracles and divination (see above, Chapter 8), distributes to men sacramental, divine grace; confers the divine blessing (see Chapter 8), pronounces the sacred formulae, is also healer and physician. The priest in short is the Deity made visible. He bears often a theophoric name and a special mark of the Deity. He wears a special vestment, usually but not always, white (see above, Chapter 2). At the same time the priest is the people's representative before the Deity, conveying their sacrifices and prayers. The belief becomes widespread that man cannot come alone or directly to God but needs the priest for this. Further cultural functions consolidate the priest's position: the custody of the law, responsibility for the sacred scriptures, which priests know and also partly make up, and the promotion of the sciences, astronomy, education, theological sciences, history etc. Such comprehensive sacral and profane priestly functions led to the laity being deprived of their rights. There arose whole priestly castes which formed 'a state within a state' as in Central America, India, Egypt, Mesopotamia, early Rome, among the Celts (Druids), and in later Israelite religion. In the mystical religions of salvation the priesthood grew out of monasticism. The prophetic religions (to which Christianity also belongs) are, as the name suggests, either without priests or in a state of tension with the priesthood. All the same a priesthood developed on its soil as well, or at least a substitute for it. A priesthood developed in Zoroastrian Mazdaism, and was deliberately created in Manichaeism. Islam, originally priestless, never developed a priesthood apart from the prayer leader (*imām*) and the lawyer ('*ulamā*). The Sikhs have biblical scholars (*Granthi*) not priests.

Early Israelite religion had priests who looked after an oracular shrine (see above, Chapter 8); sacrifices were a matter for family heads, the administration of justice went to the elders. In the eighth century BC the priests began to organize more strongly. Israelite prophetism confronted the priesthood of the existing cult in a critical way, although individual prophets such as Jeremiah and Ezekiel came from the priesthood. In the post-exilic period the Israelite priesthood became a caste-like hierocracy which on the political level achieved a position of pre-eminence over the laity. Following the text of the Deuteronomic reform, the priesthood at Jerusalem became sole rulers, whereas the priests at the shrines of Yahweh in the provinces were downgraded to a lower clergy which henceforth bore the name of 'Levites'. With the destruction of the temple the priesthood ceased. The place of the priests was taken by teachers of the law, the 'wise ones' (*hākām*), later called rabbis, who soon took over the preaching and later also the leading of services of worship. In the nineteenth century their position was made similar to Protestant ministers.

Christianity (Swete, 1921; Campenhausen, 1969; *RGG* 5, 578ff.) was originally without priests. It possessed only an apostolate and a prophethood. The latter formed the basis of a charismatic priesthood. Prophets according to the *Didache* (13, 3) are the 'high priests' of the congregations. With the demise of the apostles and the fading of early Christian charismatic gifts, the presbyterate, i.e. the office of elder, originally honorary, and the episcopate, director or overseer, became an official priesthood. The influx of ideas emanating from the mystery cults and the development of the concept of sacrifice enabled the assimilation of this priesthood to the idea of the priesthood current in the ancient world. Given that, a difference still persists between the attitude to priests in the Eastern and Western Churches. The priesthood of the Eastern Church represents a mystagogy and at the same time a people's priesthood; the priesthood of the Western Church gives a more juridical and military impression. The priest in the contemporary Roman Church, the greatest priestly Church of all time, is an officer of a militant spiritual host. The separation of clergy and laity is more sharply drawn than in the East. The sacramental consecration raises the Catholic priest to special dignity above the mass of the laity. He stands in an immediate relationship to God through the celebration of the Eucharist; he alone may touch the holy of holies, have daily intercourse with the present saviour-Deity in sacramental form. The priest stands closer to God than the ordinary believers. In the Middle Ages, immediate contact of the faithful with the Deity was seldom, whereas the priest could experience this daily. The priest has not only stood in a continuous relationship to God; he has, through the transformation of the bread and wine into the Body and Blood of Christ, 'power over the Creator himself, and indeed, whenever he wills. A word from his mouth forces the Creator of the cosmos and of heaven down to earth' (Haggeney, 1921).

The Catholic priest is a mediator between God and man, distributing divine grace: he transfers the sinner into the state of sanctifying grace through absolution and extreme unction; he offers the sacrifice of the Mass for the living and the dead. In the canonical hours he prays vicariously for the many who are unable or unwilling to pray themselves. The priest, in addition, is physician, helper and pastor; as confessor he practises individual pastoral care. The one going to confession is pledged to obedience. The priest in the confessional is also judge. He has the power to bind and loose (Matt. 18. 18); he can forgive and retain sins (John 20. 23).

The power which the priesthood possessed in the history of religions and in Christianity is explained by the permeation of (a) the impersonal, cultic and magical element on the one hand, and (b) the personal, religious and ascetic one on the other. Priestly dignity and authority do not rest on personal, individual qualities, nor on some psychological disposition. Authority and holiness are *objectively* communicated: first through blood relationship – the priesthood is inherited through certain families, as in India, Persia, Israel and partly also in the Eastern Church, especially in the Nestorian Church; secondly, through call and lot – in the early Church, and in the nineteenth century in the Catholic Apostolic Church, priests were designated by prophets with charismatic gifts, and in this century in spiritual African Churches pastors are often directly called by the Spirit, through whom God makes known his choice; thirdly, through consecration. Consecration frequently consists of cultic purification. Mostly, however, inheritance and consecration are bound up with each other. In the Israelite religion consecration was conferred through anointing (see above, Chapter 7). In post-biblical Judaism ordination of rabbis took place through the laying on of hands (see Chapter 7). The laying on of hands passed into the consecration of Christian deacons, priests and bishops. In the West came in addition anointing according to the Old Testament example and also, later, the handing over of liturgical objects following Germanic custom. At the consecration of priests these consisted of the chalice and the host.

Through consecration a spiritual lineage was established. In many religious traditions unbroken succession is an important basis of spiritual office. Such a succession was instituted in Buddhism through the ordination of monks. The succession of the Indian patriarchs was transplanted to China through Bodhidharma. Jewish rabbis assumed that an unbroken chain of the laying on of hands reached back to Moses who had transferred his spirit and position by this means to Joshua (Num. 27.18ff.; Deut. 34.9) and so down to themselves. This chain was a guarantee of the tradition for them. This Jewish succession became in turn the pattern for the succession of the Christian bishops which went back to the apostles and was seen in the same way as a guarantee that the tradition's purity had been preserved.

This cultic and magical element becomes enhanced by the *personal and ascetic* one, temporal sexual abstinence for the period of the cultic functions or permanent celibacy (see above, Chapter 5). As the bearer of this twofold form of sacred power the priest is the object of veneration for the laity; even when accompanied by moral deficiencies, the awe before the priesthood remains intact. An example is Francis of Assisi who always felt deep respect for country priests lacking in education and piety and required his followers to venerate them for their authority. In the form of address, 'Reverend', primordial numinous overtones are discernible. If farmers of upper Bavaria inveigh against the faults of their priest, they add the words, 'saving the holy consecration', and thus protect themselves from the cursing power of the priestly tabu. A greater veneration is shown to the newly consecrated priest whose sacred power is still effective in its entire freshness and immediacy. The blessings of a priest at the time of his first Mass counts as especially powerful and effectual (see above, Chapter 8). Even the hatred of the priest (anticlericalism) is a reaction against the impersonal, numinous value placed on the priesthood.

The arranging of the priesthood into degrees and a hierarchy is seen in many religious traditions including the Vedas, early Rome, Zoroastrianiam, Mithraism and Manichaeism. In Israel the separation of a lower from a higher clergy followed the Deuteronomic reform. Priests performed the real cultic acts, especially the sacrifice (see Chapter 6); Levites carried out the door duties and assisted as singers. The gradations of the *Christian hierarchy* (*RGG* 3, 313f.) include deacons, priests and bishops. The preliminary grades are more elaborate in the West than in the Eastern Churches. They consist of the minor orders and the subdiaconate. The bishops again are arranged into country bishops (*ODCC*, 277), assistant bishops, metropolitans, archbishops, primates, patriarchs. Added to these, in the Roman Church, are the titular prelates and cardinals.

In many religions a high priest stands at the head of the priests: in Egypt, in early Mexico, in Roman traditional religion, at the head of the cult of Mithra, in early Phoenicia and Syria (Ugarit) and in Tibetan Lamaism. According to the priestly codex (Lev. 21. 10ff.) the diadem and anointing were owing to the Israelite high priest (*RGG* 3, 427f.). These qualified him for the highest political leadership of the Jewish community. In its way of allegorizing the Jewish cultus, the Epistle to the Hebrews transfers the idea of the high priest to Christ, although it does not place him in the Aaronic order of succession but praises him as following the western Semitic priest-king Melchizedek following the messianic psalm (Ps. 110.4). The conception of the high priest lives on also in the Christian idea of the bishop (*RGG* 1, 1303). According to Cyprian, as the 'vicar of Christ' every bishop is sovereign, responsible only to Christ. The collegium of bishops is held together only by the bond of love. In the Roman Church since Vatican II, the college of bishops has taken an institutional form, meeting together every three years. In all the early Christian Churches a superintendent episcopacy arose: the office of patriarch or catholikos. Political considerations influenced the rise of the patriarch of Constantinople to the status of ecumenical patriarch or imperial bishop.

The most imposing form of the high priesthood is the *papacy* (J. L. McKenzie, 1969; *ER* 11, 171ff.) which lays claim to the fulness of power (*plenitudo potestatis*) in the Church. It has undergone a most complicated history. Peter was the first disciple to whom the risen Christ appeared. The universal episcopacy of Rome developed slowly in the Church. It had as its New Testament basis the pre-eminence of Peter in the circle of disciples; and received further support from the tradition of the martyrdom and tomb of Peter in Rome. The influence of early Roman religion is shown in the pope's designation of himself as *pontifex maximus*; while the persistence of the ancient Roman *imperium* is apparent in his assuming the official imperial style of letter writing. All the great Western dioceses: Carthage, Milan, Aquileia, Lyons, Toledo and Braga (Port.) lost their original independence; their ecclesiastical territories (Italy, Spain, Portugal, Gaul, also Ireland and Scotland) were subordinated to Roman jurisdiction. Secular power was added to spiritual, based on the fictitious Donation of Constantine (Bettenson, 1975). The spiritual power was supported by the great forgery of the Pseudo-Isidorean decretals (*ODCC* 501f.). Gregory VII proclaimed that Christ made Peter to be 'leader over the kingdoms of the world' and thereby also judge over all kings. What for Gregory was still an idea and a demand, became through Innocent III a reality. Boniface VIII declared in the bull *Unam Sanctam*: 'We declare, state, define and pronounce that it is altogether necessary to salvation for every human creature to be subject to the Roman pontiff' (Bettenson, 116). In 1303, as he prepared to proclaim the messianic plenitude of the pope's power in a new bull, he was taken prisoner by the troops of the French king. Thus began the decline of the papal world imperium. The struggle against the worldly papacy was taken up by the saints. Bernard of Clairvaux preached *ministerium* (service) not *dominium* (rule) as the gospel's idea for the papacy. The Conciliar movement sought to subordinate papal power to the united episcopate. Dissident movements like the Waldensians, spiritual Franciscans and Wyclif- fites inveighed against the papacy. More and more openly the pope was considered to be the Antichrist, and this polemic reached its zenith in Luther. All the same, the papacy emerged from the Counter-Reformation with its spiritual power strengthened. A renewed advance by episcopalianism followed through Gallicanism and German Febronianism in the eighteenth century. It was overcome in the Vatican Council of 1870 which put into dogmatic form the pope's primacy of jurisdiction and universal episcopacy, also the infallibility of his *ex cathedra* decisions in matters of faith and morals. In 1917 the papacy reached a new high point with the promulgation of the code of the canon law in which the centralizing of the whole of church life is sanctioned: episcopalianism and laicism were now uprooted. In the Lateran treaties of 1929 the pope obtained a token state and once again became a political sovereign. However, influenced by the ecumenical spirit the Second Vatican Council (1962–5), called together by John XXIII and concluded by Paul VI, showed renewed support for the collegiality of the bishops and the apostolate of the laity. Since then bilateral talks between the Vatican secretariat for unity and representatives of other denominations including the Anglican Communion have put forward the idea of ecumenical recognition of the pope as the 'bishop of unity' whereby he would become (if invited) titular head of other denominations while remaining executive head of the Roman Communion. This idea goes back also to one that runs parallel to the imperial papacy, namely, the evangelical papacy. It arises with the self-designation of Gregory the Great (590–604) as 'servant of the servants of God', and continues in the warning of Bernard of Clairvaux to Pope Eugenius III in which the pope is described as the 'chief among servants' and summed up his task in the call to 'do the work of the evangelist' (*De consid.*). It lives on above all in the longing for a *pastor evangelicus* which from the time of Joachim of Fiore and the Franciscan spirituals has seized the imagination of far-sighted Catholics.

The history of religions and especially that of Christianity records not only the high esteem in which the priesthood is held, but also the struggle carried on against it. Several movements broke with the Brahmanic priestly cult including the ascetics, the Jains and early Buddhism even though the last named developed a priesthood on the soil of Mahāyāna, especially in Tibet, China and Japan. In early Christianity in place of the Jewish priesthood there entered a new form: the *priesthood of all believers* (*RGG* 5, 581f.). Christ is the high priest (Heb. 5.1); those who believe in Christ represent the 'royal priesthood' (1 Pet. 2.9); they have the task of offering 'spiritual sacrifices' (1 Pet. 2.5). 'He (Christ) made us priests to his God' (Rev. 1.6; cf. 5.10). Tertullian advanced the view that any layman can dispense the sacraments if necessary, though he also made the fundamental distinction between the ordained and the laity encountered in the later Church.

Out of this priesthood of all believers there emerged, firstly, the prophets and charismatics. With them were numbered also the martyrs and confessors, the first being accorded priestly functions without ordination, the latter receiving the laying on of hands but without the invocation of the Holy Spirit who had already given his testimony in their good confession. For centuries there were monks in the Eastern Church, priests and laymen, who were 'spiritual fathers', confessors (see above, Chapter 9) and pastors. There also emerged, secondly, the office-bearers: deacons, presbyters and bishops. These filled the gap, previously occupied by the charismatics, which arose with the fading of the primitive Christian charismata. They took over from the latter the functions of preaching and the celebration of the sacrament. Whereas the charismatics were spontaneously seized by God's Spirit, the office-bearers received it by consecration conferred by the laying on of hands and the calling down of the Spirit. Later the bishops and also the presbyters were described as priests in the real sense. A new separation of priests and people had come about. There arose 'sacerdotalism' in the sense understood in antiquity. Its sharpest form is found in Canon 1342 of the 1917 code of canon law: 'The laity are totally forbidden to preach in church even when they are religious (monks)', a sentence which marks the complete break from early Christian prophetism (1 Cor. 14), until its reversal in the post-Vatican II revised code (1983, c.766).

Over against the traditional official priesthood there arose the protest of the medieval dissidents: firstly the Waldensians. They created a new lay priesthood (*barbas*) and a threefold ordination. Following Joachimite prophecy, the Franciscan spirituals expected the abolition of the official priesthood and the hierarchy in the kingdom of the Spirit and their replacement by monks as the bearers of the Spirit (Benz, 1934). Wycliffe's revival (*RE* 21, 225–44; *ODCC*, 1502f.; Workman, 1926) resulted in 'poor priests' called Lollards travelling through the land as popular preachers. According to Wycliffe there is no priesthood which mediates between God and man, no capability for office supplied by the ordination of the bishop, no indelible character conferred by the consecration to the priesthood.

In the Reformation the barriers between the sacred and profane were destroyed. As there were no exclusively sacred places, no cultus which provided a special nearness to God, so also no person was the exclusive bearer and mediator of the sacred. In the affirmation of the priesthood of all believers

Protestantism is united. And yet Luther fully recognized the greatness of the priesthood: 'Before God and man there is no higher name and honour than to be a priest.' The young Luther drew the conclusion from this 'that we are all in the same way priests, that is have the same authority in respect of the word and sacrament'. Every baptized Christian may therefore teach, preach, proclaim God's word, baptize, consecrate or dispense the Eucharist, bind and loose sins, pray for others, sacrifice and judge all doctrines and spirits.

Although the church Fathers had also praised the priesthood of all believers, the Catholic Church rejected these views and insisted on continuing a special priestly office and hierarchy. The struggle against the priesthood of all believers proclaimed by Protestantism occasioned in the Roman Church a further increase of sacerdotalism and a retreat from the priesthood of all believers, e.g. the complete disappearance of lay confessors who had been widespread in the Middle Ages. In the period after the First World War, however, there occurred a renewed break-through of the priesthood of all believers in the Roman Church through men like Joseph Wittig and Ernst Michel. 'Catholic Action' (*RGG* 3, 1197f.), promoted by more recent popes, signifies the 'participation of laity in the hierarchical apostolate'. The liturgical movement also called for an activation of the priesthood of all believers. The sacrament of confirmation was given a new value as consecration to the priesthood of all believers, and the way was opened for a new understanding of the liturgy, in which the whole community of the faithful celebrated, prayed and acted *with* the priest. The idea of the priesthood of all believers was, it must be admitted, rarely put fully into practice even in Protestantism, although this did occur in the case of the Quakers. Its most enthusiastic champions were found in the Free Churches.

In Protestant Churches a new type of spiritual office arose in the Church, that of the pastor or minister. The understanding and appreciation of the pastor's position was, however, by no means a unified one. In later life Luther came to recognize a special spiritual office, and advocated the ordination of those called to it by the congregation (Brunotte, 1959). Through ordination the authority to preach and dispense the sacraments is conveyed. But the Protestant ministry of preaching the word and dispensing the sacraments is not seen as performing a sacrifice. In early Lutheranism a strong conception of pastoral office began to develop. The pastor in Lutheran Scandinavia is called *präst* (priest). The view of the ministerial office in Calvinism has been equally strongly developed, distinguishing a threefold office of deacons, elders and pastors. Here the idea of following the practice of the apostles is stronger than in Lutheranism. In recent Protestantism, Luther's early view that ordination is not a consecration but a delegation has recovered lost ground. In it for the sake of good order congregations transfer to a particular group, by ordination, the rights which belong to all Christians on the basis of the priesthood of all believers. The strongest concept of priestly office is found in Anglicanism. Here the threefold office of deacons, priests and bishops is maintained on the basis of the apostolic succession. This view of the ministry received renewed emphasis in the Oxford Tractarian movement (Wand, 1961; Neill, 1965; Yates, 1983).

The ministerial office is not a creation of the congregation but rests on its institution by Christ; the office of apostle is continued by the ecclesiastical office-bearers. This idea was proclaimed anew by the high church movement and has become increasingly influential in recent days (*RGG* 4, 1673ff.). A counterweight to the stronger emphasis placed on the ministerial office was provided by the increased participation of lay people in church bodies especially in legislative synods, and also the giving of authority to lay people to preach (especially in the Methodist, Anglican and Swedish (Lutheran) Churches). The same also happens in Orthodox and in other Eastern national Churches; with many new developments appearing in the Roman Church after Vatican II. Between both extremes of sacerdotalism and the radical egalitaria-nism of laicism are many different stages that are represented in the different communions of Christendom.

(4) The ascetic, monk and nun

Besides the priest, the *monk* and *nun* are also held to be the bearers of sacredness. A person becomes a priest through birth or consecration, the *ascetic* – monk or nun (*RGG* 4, 1070ff.; *ER* 1, 441ff.; 5, 137ff., 10, 35ff.) does so through a free decision, heroic renunciation and personal sacrifice. The priest is the bearer of a material, substantial sacredness, the ascetic a personal one. The classic land of monachism is India (*ERE* 8, 797ff.; 10, 713ff.). Originally there were only individual ascetics in India. Towards the end of his life the Brahmanic household head would become a hermit in the forest. He would still keep up limited sacrificial rites before finally becoming a *sannyāsin* (*ER* 13, 51ff.), one who renounces the world, no longer performs the rites, and wanders about as a beggar. There were in addition ascetics who became homeless, wandering monks already in their earlier years. The first founder of a monastic organization was Parshvanātha (d.*c.* 720 BC), a king's son who renounced the world at the age of thirty. He established an order (*sangha*) embracing those men and women who were 'liberated from the shackles of *karma*'. He required no injuring of any living being (*ahimsā*; *ER* 10, 463ff.), truthfulness, sexual abstinence, and poverty. Around the order a lay community of men and women gathered. Reformed in the sixth century, this order became the *Jaina*, whose members are obliged to observe the five 'great vows': *ahimsā*, including a strict vegetarian diet and avoidance of inadvertent killing of insects; truthfulness; sexual abstinence which excludes all association with the other sex; respecting the possessions of others; and complete absence of possessions. Lay people of the order have only to observe the 'lesser vows'. The fifth vow disappears; the third vow becomes the avoidance of adultery. The laity assume responsibility for the monks' and nuns' subsistence. The Buddhist *sangha* (*ER* 13,36ff.) which arose about the same time is organized similarly. Around the community of mendicant monks (*bhikshu*) and nuns (*bhikshunī*) there gathered the tertiary order of lay devotees. The monks observe ten commandments: to the five Jainist ones are added – to eat only once a day; to avoid dancing, music and plays; to despise wreaths, sweet smells and jewellery; to sleep on the earth; and to touch no gold or silver. The original order of nuns ceased in the lands of Theravāda Buddhism after the succession of ordination was broken. In its place came a sisterhood half-way between the nuns and the lay women devotees. Mahāyāna Buddhism placed above the ten commandments of early Buddhism the obligation of the *bodhisattva* ideal, according to which the monk must lead all beings to liberation and prepare an end to all their sufferings. Through this ideal the difference between monks and laity was levelled down. Mahāyānist monachism conquered Tibet and the Far-eastern lands of China, Korea and Japan. In Tibet, the obligation of monastic celibacy was given up; the reformer Tsong-kha-pa (1357–1418) restored it for a part of the monks ('the sect of the yellow caps') whereas in the 'sect of the red caps' the monks are married. In Japan, Shinran, the protagonist of the doctrine of *sola fide* (by faith alone), gave up celibacy for the 'sect of pure land Buddhism' founded by him, and so transformed monachism into a secular priesthood. The other sects held firmly to celibate monasticism. In the national restoration of the nineteenth century, however, celibacy was prohibited and the monks were compelled to resume their duties as secular priests. After this ban had ended, only a few Buddhist monasteries renewed the vow of celibacy. Reformed Buddhism of the Cao Dai sect, on the other hand, reintroduced the vow of celibacy after its initial toleration of the priestly marriage. Taoist monachism conforms to the pattern of the Buddhist one.

In Hinduism, to complete the picture of the homeland of asceticism, coenobitic monastic life remained far behind individual asceticism. Most of the Indian monks lead their spiritual and ascetic life wholly for themselves as *yogin*, *sādhu* (wandering monk) and *sannyāsin*. At the Indian census of 1901, 2,755, 900 ascetics were counted. Many of them embrace the self-torment which was rejected by the Buddha as extreme. Some may go round naked, sit between fires in the heat of the sun, hold their arm straight up, allow the clenched fist to grow into the flesh or feed on the flesh of dead bodies. There are also individual monastic orders, but only a minority of the monks live together in ashrams. The order founded by Shankara the philosopher and theologian in the eighth century CE bears the name 'Ten-named' from its elaborate hierarchy; its leader takes the title of *Shankarācārya*. Whereas this order is devoted to the cult of Shiva, other orders, such as those of *Bhakti* theologians Rāmānuja and Madhva, venerate Vishnu.

Whereas all this widespread ascetic monasticism was developed in India during the middle of the first millennium before Christ, the Mediterranean world, in which Christianity later arose, did not get beyond the beginnings of monachism and of monastic orders. The Pythagoreans, the Cynics, and the *katochoi* (possessed) of Serapis all established forms of ascetic community life. The spread of ascetic ideals in the Hellenistic world influenced the *Meditations* of Marcus Aurelius and above all Plotinus' mystical and philosophical writings. On Israelite soil the Rechabites represent an asceticism which Jerome regarded as the precursor of Christian monasticism. The Essenes (*ERE* 5, 395–401; *RGG*

2, 701ff.; *LThK* 3, 1110f.) and *Therapeutae* (*RGG* 6, 847), communal orders described by Philo and Josephus, led an ascetic life with community of possessions, celibacy, work and prayer. The Qumran community (Sutcliffe, 1960) which has become known through the discovery of the Dead Sea Scrolls, is clearly identical with the community of the Essenes.

Earliest Christianity already showed strong ascetic tendencies, although a real monachism was foreign to it. Jesus and the disciples sent out by him (Matt. 10.5f.) resembled the Buddha and his mendicant monks, in their wandering life. Jesus' words that the Son of man has nowhere to lay his head (Matt. 8.20) recall the Buddha's word of going out of the home 'into homelessness'. Jesus' instructions to his disciples about having no possessions (Matt. 10.9f.) recall the complete poverty of the Buddhist monks. Paul specifically recommends celibacy (1 Cor. 7). Early on a privileged class of male and female ascetics arose who in part lived alone and in part lived together in convents (*askētēria*). One of the principal advocates of ascetic ideals was Origen whose writings were eagerly read by later Christian monks. Real Christian monachism (Knowles, 1969; *ODCC*, 930) begins with Antony. The earliest form is marked by a radical separation from the world, and even from the Church, through the retreat into the desert. As the name *monachos* (living alone) already signifies, Christian monachism was originally solitary or eremitical in character. Soon however communities of hermits (*monai monastēriai*) were formed which placed themselves voluntarily under the leadership of a spiritual father. The communal life was even stronger in the eremitical colonies. Besides these there were, as in India, solitary wandering monks. The former Roman soldier Pachomius became the father of coenobitic and conventual monasticism. He set up many houses for monks with a wall around them and a church for common worship. He composed also the first monastic rule which made obedience to the leader or abbot a duty, and regulated matters of dress, diet, daily programme, prayers, work, and separation from the world. Basil of Caesarea sought to suppress entirely the old eremitical pattern through a still stronger form of community life. The community of monks was to be an image of the early Christian congregation. In place of the different monks' houses came the unified convent with one roof, one table, one leader and one oratorium where the canonical hours were observed. Through Basil's rule entry into monastic life became irrevocable. Yet the old eremitical life in the Eastern Church never died out; the community life (*koinobion*) was held to be rather like the elementary school for an anchoritism which saw itself as the final stage of monastic perfection. Whereas in the earliest stages monasticism stood in a state of tension with the priesthood, the necessity for the celebration of the sacrament led to the creation of a monastic priesthood. Even so lay monks remained for centuries the 'spiritual fathers' – confessors and pastors of the Eastern Church (see Chapter 9). If in the first period Egypt, Palestine and Syria were the main areas of Eastern monasticism, later on Mt Athos (Riley, 1887/1982; *LThK* 1, 1008ff.) and the cave monastery in Kiev (Smolitsch, 1953) also became leading centres.

Western monasticism (*ERE* 10, 693–713; Workman, 1927) was inspired by that from the East. Through the mediation of the Gallic monastery of Lérins, strict Egyptian asceticism was brought into Celtic (Iro-Scottish) Christianity. This took on a special character through the latter's missionary journeying (Duckett, 1959). In contrast to this pilgrim monasticism, Benedictine monasticism (*LThK* 2, 184–92; *ODCC* 154–6g.; McCann, 1938) stood for the *stabilitas loci*, remaining in one place. In it the Christian monastic tradition was linked with ancient Roman military order, and so monasticism was formed into a *militia Christi*. In distinction from Celtic monasticism the Benedictine form was also at first a lay monachism where the convent priests did not take precedence over the lay monks. Common to both these types of monasticism is their activity in the service of the Church and culture. Alongside these, however, there arose purely contemplative ascetic orders of the Carthusians and Camaldulensians, and also the mendicant and preaching orders of Dominicans (*LThK* 5, 483ff.; *ODCC* 417f.) and Franciscans (*RGG* 2, 1057f.; 2, 1061ff.; *LThK* 4, 274ff.; *ODCC* 530ff.) who revived the early Christian peripatetic preaching. Although Francis of Assisi desired simply to found a free brotherhood to imitate the ascetic life of Christ and his apostles, this was soon transformed into an ecclesiastical order. The early Franciscan spiritual movement (Benz, 1934; *ODCC* 1301) was expelled as heretical. A quite new form of order arose in that of the Jesuits (*RGG* 3, 613ff.; *ODCC* 734ff., Hollis, 1968; Mitchell, 1982), who combined an outspoken individualism with the service of the hierarchical papacy, training in contemplation with the greatest activity in parishes, schools and scholarly pursuits. With most of the male orders female ones are affiliated. The Western monastic activity also manifested itself in the numerous new foundations of female orders and congregations which work in school teaching and in the care of the sick.

The champions of the Reformation believed they had eradicated monasticism and the convent. But in the nineteenth century there arose not only Protestant orders of deaconesses in imitation of the female Catholic orders (*RGG* 2, 162ff.; *ODCC* 380f.), but also a call for the restoration of monks and nuns (*RGG* 1, 1430ff.; Moore, P. C., 1970). A series of male orders and a great number of female orders were established in the Anglican Church. Recently, orders were found also on Lutheran soil. Of significance in Europe have been the Taizé community in Burgundy, the sisterhood of Pomeyrol and the sisterhood of Mary founded by Mother Basileia Schlink in Darmstadt. Alongside these arose a series of tertiary orders, amongst others the 'Tiers ordre protestant des veilleurs', the Protestant Franciscan tertiaries and the *Michaelsbruderschaft*, the Norwegian *Ordo crucis* and the Swedish *Societas Sanctae Birgittae*.

The parallel experience of monasticism in Islam is instructive. Islam as a strongly prophetic religion was originally hostile to monasticism although signs of the veneration of Christian monks may be found in the Qur'ān. From Muhammad have been handed down the words: 'There is no monachism in Islam', and 'The monasticism of this community is the holy war.' Nevertheless the strong eschatological expectation, which predominates in the Qur'ān's early *suras*, led to a strict asceticism in which pious Muslims surrendered themselves wholly to prayer, fasting and Quranic reading. In the course of the ninth century a number of mystics arose who gathered round themselves loose circles of disciples. The first community-like orders arose with strict forms under the Baghdad mystic Abdul-qādir al-Jīlānī. The brotherhood founded by him, the Qādirīya, has remained of significance down to the present especially in the Indian sub-continent. The number of orders in Islam (*ERE* 10, 719–26; *HWI* 78ff.; Trimingham, 1973) varies considerably as orders cease or branch off. In addition to the Qādirīya, the most important role has been played by the Mevlevī, described by Europeans as 'dancing dervishes' (*dervish*, Arabic *fakir*, 'beggar'). Founded by Maulānā (Turk. *Mevlana*) Jelāl ud-dīn Rūmī, whose mausoleum in Konya is the spiritual centre of the order, it was, with other orders, abolished in 1925. Recently, however, Turkey has somewhat relaxed such restrictions. Another order, the Rifā'iya, have been described in the West as 'howling dervishes' on account of their remarkable mystic rite, the *dhikr* (remembrance). The Chishtīya were founded in India according to tradition by Mu'in ad-dīn Chishtī who died in 1226. The Bektāshīya arose in Turkey, incorporated remarkable heterodox elements and became significant through their association with the Janissaries. The Naqshibandiya have been numerous mainly in Turkestan and in Turkish territory where they distinguished themselves through the power of their meditation. In North Africa the Sanūsīya sought a spiritual and political renewal of Islam in the form of an *imitatio Muhammadi*. Common to all orders is a special rite of reception; around the real members of the order who only in part observe a celibate life, are the tertiaries who take care of the monks' necessities of life. The various degrees in the monastery hierarchy are strictly regulated. The importance of the Islamic orders for Islamic culture and also for missionary work can scarcely be overestimated. Their mystical piety made them better preachers than the *ulamā* of *shari'a* Islam. Despite the relatively large numbers given for the Islamic orders, it should be remembered that it is not a matter of a *closed* monasticism in the Christian or Buddhist sense.

Despite the great differences in the orders within Christianity and even more so within the different religions of the world, there remains a remarkable conformity to the basic features of monastic life. Monastic life begins with taking leave of the world. Associated with this is the putting on of the monk's dress (mostly, at first, a special novice's clothing [Oppenheim, 1932]). The transition to full monkhood follows in an act of ordination, consecration and vow-taking. In Christian and in Mahāyāna Buddhist monachism a ceremonial profession of vows or taking the veil takes place. Common to all full members of the order is the threefold ideal of povery, celibacy and obedience; in the Christian Church these are called 'evangelical counsels' with reference to the example of the apostles.

The basis of monastic life is the absence of possessions. The most radical form of this is mendicant monachism as represented, for example, by the Jainist, early Buddhist, early Christian wandering apostolate (Matt. 10.5ff.) and the first Dominicans and Franciscans. This ideal of complete poverty is so strictly observed that in the East as in the West the touching of a coin is strictly prohibited. The daily round of begging practised in the Buddhist lands of Thailand, Burma and Kampuchea is paralleled in Western Catholic lands by the practices of Franciscan and Capuchin lay brothers. However, most monasteries, Christian and otherwise, have acquired property in house and land; the individual monk, it is true, remains poor and receives what he needs from the monastery. Complete poverty is praised by Christian monks as well as others, as the source of the highest spiritual freedom and the profoundest peace of mind. For Christian monks the Pauline 'having nothing, yet possessing everything' (2 Cor. 6.10) is a favourite expression.

The second basic form of monastic life is complete sexual abstinence and the renunciation of marriage. To safeguard this abstinence every association with the other sex is frequently avoided or else the greatest reserve is to be shown towards it, as in Jainism, early Buddhism and in Christian monasticism. This reserve leads often to downright hostility towards women (see below). The motives for celibacy are many: as with poverty, so celibacy and sexual abstinence are also seen as a source of spiritual freedom. The second motive is the gathering of spiritual powers, the concentration on the attainment of salvation. The third is the complete surrender to God as the highest good. 'The unmarried man is anxious about the affairs of the Lord, how to please the Lord; but the worldly man is anxious about worldly affairs, how to please his wife' (1 Cor. 7.32f.). The fourth motive is the anticipation of the position at the end, when men, according to Jesus' words, 'neither marry nor are given in marriage, but are like angels in heaven' (Mark 12.25). This is the imitation of the 'angelic life' as early Christian monachism liked to call it. The fifth motive is the possibility of works of love on a broad basis: the celibate are able to attain not only to perfect love of God but also to perfect love of their brethren because their love and concern is not restricted to a limited family circle (however demanding such may be). Besides all these motives there persists still the traditional tabu, the idea that all that goes with sexual life has the power to cause pollution (see above, Chapter 5).

The third monastic ideal is total obedience to the spiritual leader, be he *guru*, abbot, teacher, leader, sheikh, prior or guardian. According to Thomas Aquinas, obedience is the greatest sacrifice that a person can bring because he is not going without external things as in the case of voluntary poverty, and not without simply the bodily needs as with sexual abstinence, but is deprived of his own free will. This last is compared to the complete passivity of a corpse.

The most important task in the daily life of the monk is the exercise of the spiritual 'art' and 'discipline', the mental training or exercises, meditation or contemplation. Parallel to *yoga* and Buddhist *jnāna* and *zen* runs in Christian monasticism of East and West a technique of inward prayer called *proseuchē*, *noerā* or *kardiakē*, *oratio mentalis* (Heiler, 1923, 287ff., 594). The prayer technique of the monks of Mt Athos is probably influenced by Indian *yoga* (Ammann, 1938); just as the Eastern *mnēmē theou* ('remembrance of God') may have passed over into the *dhikr* ('remembrance') of Islam. The individual prayer is accompanied by common prayer (choral prayer, horary prayer, the canonical office) which is practised in Eastern and Western monachism. In the Benedictine rule it is even given pre-eminence over all other monastic exercises, being described as *opus Dei* or *opus divinum*, the service of God in the highest degree (c.43).

In Christian monasticism the link between prayer and work (*ōrā et labōrā*) becomes the rule. Pachomius, Basil, Benedict and Francis of Assisi all require manual work. Christian monks achieved a great deal through the cultivation of the soil, but also in the areas of learning and the arts, especially in the copying of biblical, religious and profane texts. It is true that with the predominance of priestly monasticism manual work was relegated to the lay monks; recently in Benedictine abbeys manual work has again been required of the priest monks also. (The monks of Theravāda Buddhism on the other hand were purely contemplative: manual work even incurred punishment.) The zealous copying of sacred texts fell away with the advent of printed versions. Japanese *zen* monks are also required to work: their zeal for working in the rice-fields is proverbial.

Monasticism in Christianity just as in early Buddhism and in Hinduism is regarded as 'the state of perfection' (*status perfectionis*) or simply as 'religion' itself (*status religionis*). In Christianity the monk was described as the perfect one (*teleos*). Thomas Aquinas modified the doctrine of monachism as a state of perfection inasmuch as he considered perfection simply in terms of the love of God and one's neighbour. This is of course possible to achieve in the lay state also but Thomas considered the 'three evangelical counsels' of poverty, chastity and obedience to be the best 'instruments of perfection'.

Against monasticism, there arose in the East as in the West the protest of a religious piety at whose centre lies faith in the divine gift of grace. Shinran, the 'Japanese Luther', broke with the monastic tradition of Far-eastern Buddhism from his stand of piety based on faith, and set the example for others by marrying. Luther rejected his monastic vows and led a passionate struggle against the 'hellish, sugar-coated, poisoned cake' of 'monkery'. He rated the service of a stable girl higher than the ascetic achievements of a Carthusian. The renewed Protestant monasticism held fast to the Reformers' faith but saw in a life conformed to the evangelical counsels an aid to the proclamation of the gospel in the modern world. Even Indian Christians who were imbued with the idea of grace, such as Sundar Singh and Nārāyan Vāman Tilak (Winslow, 1923) chose the life of a poor and celibate *sādhu* and thereby exercised a strong missionary influence on their contemporaries.

12

The Sacred Person in the
Christian Tradition 2

(1) The prophet as sacred person

A person becomes a priest through birth, training and consecration, a monk through constant inner training; the *prophet* (see above, Chapter 8; Fohrer, 1953; Greschat, 1974; *HWDA* 7, 338–66; *RGG* 5, 608–38; *ER* 15, 294ff.) on the other hand, is called to prophethood by being seized, overwhelmed and forced into it by the divine spirit or, psychologically speaking, through inspiration which is based on religious gifts and creative talents. Forms associated with that of the prophet include those of the ecstatic seer and diviner. Siberian shamans often receive no instruction; the power to be a shaman comes upon them suddenly even though the vocation of shaman is often hereditary. If he refuses the call to become a shaman he must suffer fearful torments, loses his senses, and often dies after a short period.

Ecstatic prophethood is also found in the religions of antiquity, especially in Syria and Asia Minor. Through the cultic dance, especially the flute dance, a state of ecstasy and excitement is induced, especially in the Canaanite cult of Ba'al. From there it passes to the Israelites. From the cults of Ba'al divination through ecstatic states made its way into the cult of Yahweh. The God of the desert now becomes the originator of the sacred trance. Yahweh's 'spirit' or 'hand' falls upon the prophets. Whole prophet associations practised such ecstatic divination. In a state of trance fragmentary sounds are uttered, words that are thought of as having power to shape the course of future events. The prophet thus becomes proclaimer and announcer (*nābī*), one who speaks in place of another (*prophētēs, hypophētēs*). Ecstatic divination also made its way into Greece. Plato refers to the prophetesses of Delphi, Dodona, the Sibyls and also many other ecstatic diviners.

Out of such ecstatic divination later Israelite prophecy emerged. Some of the prophets resembled ecstatic diviners in being prophets by profession; a few, like Amos the shepherd of Tekoa, were lay persons. The psychological phenomena of ecstatic divination come to expression here as well: ecstasy with paralytic cramps and lameness, anaesthesia, visions and auditions in a waking state, in dreams and in a state of hypnosis, clairvoyance, compulsive movements, actions and speech. Common to everything is an irresistible compulsion. The prophets may resist this compulsion: 'Ah, Lord God! Behold, I do not know how to speak, for I am only a youth' (Jer. 1.6); but he is compelled or persuaded by God and he can do no other than proclaim: 'If I say, "I will not mention him or speak any more in his name", there is in my heart as it were a burning fire shut up in my bones, and I am weary with holding it in, and I cannot' (Jer. 20.9).

There remain, however, important differences from ecstatic divination: (a) Clear verbal revelations appear alongside the ecstasies and visions. The prophet receives a specific commission to proclaim the word of God. God reveals to the prophet his will, his intention, what will happen in the future, and he requires him to declare his message. (b) The revelations of God are related to the destiny of God's elect. The prophet is forced into politics. He receives the commission to declare God's message before the powerful and mighty of this world. 'See, I have set you this day over nations and over kingdoms, to pluck up and to break down, to destroy and to overthrow, to build up and to plan' (Jer. 1.10). It is political action derived from faith, out of the overwhelming experience of God. (c) The revelations bear a religious and moral character. The central religious idea here is, first, the unique power and unity of God; second, faith in God as the controller of history. Historical events are seen as the revelation of God (Pannenberg, 1963). The central idea is that God requires obedience to his moral demands; he requires from men truth and righteousness, mercy and love. Cultic prescriptions are secondary, indeed, without moral integrity are not pleasing to God. (d) A twofold form of prophecy is to be distinguished: a prophecy of salvation and one of doom. This distinction was already drawn by Jeremiah, confronted with the false prophet Hananiah. True prophets for him are prophets of evil: 'They have prophesied war against many countries and great kingdoms.' In contrast to these were the false prophets who 'prophesy peace' (Jer. 28.8f.); 'They have healed the wound of my people lightly, saying, "Peace, peace," when there is no peace' (Jer. 6.14).

The gigantic tragedy of the prophets of doom meets us in the figure of Jeremiah. He loved his people, he believed in its election and yet he must proclaim doom and destruction, not because it was a matter of God's eternal decree, but because the people was disobedient, served foreign gods, violated justice and righteousness. 'My people have committed two evils: they have forsaken me, the fountain of living waters, and hewed out cisterns for themselves, broken cisterns, that can hold no water' (Jer. 2.13). In the face of the intensive preparations for war which could only lead to the outbreak of hostilities and collapse, Hosea cried: 'Because you have trusted in your chariots and in the multitude of your warriors, therefore the tumult of war shall arise among your people, and all your fortresses shall be destroyed ... Thus it shall be done to you, O house of Israel, because of your great wickedness. In the storm the king of Israel shall be utterly cut off' (Hos. 10.13ff.). This prophecy of doom was unwelcome to the people in the highest degree; hence the fearful isolation of the prophet. The people followed the prophets of salvation who deluded them with phrases and suggestions and unveiled before their eyes glorious visions of the future. They plunged into a delirium of power. The false prophet Hananiah took the wooden yoke from the neck of the prophet Jeremiah and broke it as a sign that Yahweh would break Nebuchadnezzar's yoke (Jer. 28.10). Jeremiah hurled at him a fresh word of Yahweh: 'You have broken wooden bars, but I will make in their place bars of iron' (Jer. 28.13). The prophet remained faithful to Yahweh's warning at his call: 'Do not be dismayed by them, lest I dismay you before them . . . I make you this day a fortified city, an iron pillar and bronze walls, against the whole land, against the kings of Judah, its princes, its priests, and the people of the land. They will fight against you; but they shall not prevail against you, for I am with you, says the Lord, to deliver you' (Jer. 1.17ff.). In this loneliness there remained for the prophet nothing else save prayerful communion with his God. In the history of Israelite prayer, nothing has had a comparable significance to the tragedy of the prophet Jeremiah. Martyrdom, dishonour and suffering were the reward for bringing the message of God. Jeremiah was thrown into prison. But the prophets of doom were proved right. Israel collapsed as a people and as a state. Its kings were killed or blinded, the people led captive to Babylon, the country devastated.

Yet the prophets were not simply prophets of doom. They believed in a 'remnant' being saved, in a final acceptance of the chosen people. The prophecy of doom ends in a prophecy of salvation, though of a higher and more spiritual kind. After the prophecy of doom was fulfilled, the prophecy of salvation was unfolded. No more did it suffice to speak about God's wrath; now comfort had to be given and salvation proclaimed. So the exile is the victory of the prophecy of doom, but at the same time the hour of its demise. The prophecy of salvation had plunged Judah into destruction, but now it raised its head proudly. The prophecy of doom experienced a dreadful fulfilment. The dream of Zion's transfiguration never became a reality. The greatest thought of these prophets of salvation was, however, that Yahweh's religion would become a world religion, and that was fulfilled when the time came..

Judaism of the second century before the Christian era had no more prophets of the old style. In their place came the writing prophets, the apocalyptists (see above, Chapter 10). Their writings are pseudonymous. They put forward a dualism in a double sense: of this aeon and that to come, and of the struggle between good and evil. Babylonian and Iranian influences are discernible. We find history divided into periods in the prophecy of the four world empires (see above, Chapter 4). The future passes into transcendence, into 'a new heaven and a new earth' (Isa. 65.17; Enoch 91.16; Jub. 1.29; 4 Esd. 7.57; 2 Pet. 3.13; Rev. 21.1). This apocalyptic message exercised a deep influence upon early Christian preaching.

The prophecy of doom lived on in John the Baptist. He is the preacher of judgement in classical style. Jesus was a preacher of judgement but also at the same time a preacher of salvation. The early Christian prophets testified to the great and mighty deeds of God in history and proclaim the early return of Christ. Paul and Barnabas were numbered among the 'prophets and teachers' of the congregation in Antioch (Acts 13.1). Prophets, according to the *Didache*, provided the leadership in early Christian services of worship (*Didache* 10.7; see also above, under priests). In Rome, Hermas emerged as a preacher of repentance. Montanism represents a revival of early Christian prophetism with a substratum of Phrygian traditional religion (Strobel, 1980).

In the imperial Church the awareness that prophetic gifts were continuing lived on in the sacrament of confirmation, which is interpreted in the liturgical texts as the consecration to prophethood. Christians are anointed with the same oil with which God has anointed the prophets (see above, Chapter 7). Real prophecy also lived on in the medieval Church, for instance in great women such as Hildegard of Bingen, Birgitta of Sweden and Catherine of Siena. Many similarities may be found between them and the Hebrew prophets. They come before kings and princes, cardinals and popes. An immense impact was made by the prophecy of the Cistercian abbot Joachim of Fiore (see above, Chapter 4). He proclaimed the coming of a 'Church of the Spirit', the passing of the official Church into the spiritual Church. This prophecy influenced above all the Franciscan movement. The prophecy of the Florentine Dominican Girolamo Savonarola aimed at a moral renewal of the people, the setting up of a 'city of God' in Florence.

The Reformers' proclamation of the gospel, Luther's first and foremost (Söderblom, 1962), bore a truly prophetic character. With the message of justification by faith they associated the struggle against all concepts and institutions which diminish that faith. The demand for a city of God was raised by the Baptists and for one in a more spiritual form, by Calvin; the demand for freedom of the spirit was raised by the father of the Quakers, George Fox (*RGG* 2, 1010), who joined with this a sharp polemic against the Anglican Church. Prophetic figures in Christianity in the twentieth century were Nathan Söderblom (Sundkler, 1968), Dietrich Bonhoeffer (Bethge, 1970); William Temple (Iremonger, 1948), John XXIII (*NCE* 7, 1015ff.); and among living contemporaries Helder Camara and Desmond Tutu. Streams of genuine prophecy have flowed through the Christian Church. The institutional Church, it is true, sought to dampen down prophecy or to steer it into its own channels. The conflict between prophetism and the main institutional Church began in Montanism; it continued in Franciscan spirituals and in the Reformation and was repeated in the contest between the prophetic sects and the established Protestant Churches. In the Roman Church prophethood becomes subordinated to the canon law (see under *Priest*, above). The developments in the Roman Church, however, make light of its paragraphs. In recent days concern for the lay apostolate has led to the call for the revival of the prophetic office as it existed in the early days of the Church. Priests have led the way: Camara; even a Pope, John XXIII. Prophets have also tended to arise throughout the world in areas where the traditional cosmology has been challenged by a universal faith such as Christianity or Islam. One can speak of a veritable universal revival of prophetism (H. W. Turner 1977, 1978), and with the aid of hindsight find throughout the history of religions prophetism featuring as the attempt to formulate a new religious synthesis and thus provide the initial vision out of which a new religion grows. Prophetism is a universal motif in the history of religions just as shamanic motifs also run through the later developments in the history of religions as well (Cohen, 1974). At least as early as the Hebrew prophets and bearing some shamanic traits was the prophet of Iranian Mazdaism *Zarathustra* (*ER* 15, 556ff.). In Iranian Mazdaism Zarathustra undertook a similar reformation of the tradition, following revelations of a shamanic character received from Ahura Mazda. Out of the Iranian tradition Mani emerged. *Mani* (Widengren, 1965; *ER* 9, 159ff.) felt called as prophet to unite East and West. He was the unveiler of a gnostic system; but he regarded himself as a prophet with a missionary's commission. He called himself an apostle of Christ, but placed himself above him at the same time. Whereas all prophets, according to Mani, had only a limited area of activity, the Buddha, for instance, in the East, Zarathustra in Iran, Christ in the West, Mani felt himself to be 'although at first called to be prophet of Babylon' also prophet of humanity and the 'seal of the prophets'.

Muhammad (Andrae, 1960; Watt, W. M., 1969; Parrinder, 1965) underwent experiences similar to those of the Hebrew prophets. He was called through a vision: he saw Gabriel with crossed legs in heaven. He felt a touch: he was pressed with a cloth and was afraid he would die. He heard a heavenly voice which ordered him to 'read' (*sura* 96, 1–4). The prophetic consciousness of Muhammad underwent an important development. Originally he considered himself only as a local, people's prophet who was sent to the traditional Arab religionists as Moses was to the Jews, Jesus to the Christians. This awareness was later widened: Muhammad saw himself as the restorer of the pure religion of Abraham as *hanif* (monotheist) and *muslim*, as the last and greatest prophet, as the 'seal of the prophets' (*sura* 33, 40).

A prophetic element is already found in the preaching message of Gautama Buddha: 'Open your ears, the salvation from death has been found.' Thus begins the Buddha's first sermon. A prophetic movement arose in Japanese Buddhism begun by Zen-nichi-maro (b.1222; De Bary, 1958). He became monk and priest as a youth and was called after his first appearance Nichi-ren, 'sun lotus'. In 1253 he appeared as a preacher in the temple of his home monastery Kiyozumi, savagely criticizing the existing Buddhist sects which he believed had widely diverged from original Buddhism. He had to flee from his home land. In 1271 he was condemned to death by beheading but was reprieved at the last moment. In 1274 he received a pardon and was able to proclaim his message undisturbed for the remaining eight years of his life.

(2) The teacher

Besides the ruler, diviner, priest, monk and prophet the *teacher* (Wach, 1925; Fascher, 1954; *ThWNT* 2, 150ff.; Riesner, 1984) is found, importantly in Christianity as well, as a further manifestation of sacred person. Like the prophet he receives a spontaneous call, yet not with a vehemence beyond the normal and customary; but in light, clarity and stillness profound insights illuminate his soul in lightning flashes and are communicated in similar fashion. Such teachers are K'ung-fu-Tzū, Mo-ti, Gautama Buddha, Heraclitus, Pythagoras, Socrates, Apollonius of Tyana, Seneca, Plotinus, in a certain sense Jesus, and rabbis such as Hillel and Gamaliel. Israelite literary teachers of wisdom were the authors of the Wisdom of Solomon and Jesus Sirach (Ecclesiasticus).

In the early Christian community the teachers (*didaskaloi*) were clearly distinguished from the prophets (1 Cor. 12.28). The teachers of the Alexandrian catechetical school occupied an important position as 'teachers of the holy word' or of catechesis (Eusebius, *H.E.* 5, 10, 1; 6, 26; *LThK* 1, 323ff.). Such included Pantaenus, Clement and Origen, and later the great Greek and Latin church teachers. *Medieval scholastics* (Grabmann, 1910/1911; *ER* 13, 116ff.) taught with strict dogmatic methodology. They included Albertus Magnus, Thomas Aquinas, Bonaventura, Meister Eckhart, Duns Scotus. *Doctor ecclesiae* (church teacher) is an honorary title of the Western Church which is still being conferred. The greatest Indian teachers are Shankara and Rāmānuja, Pillai Lokārya, Madhva. A special form of the teacher, the Indian *swāmi* or *guru* counts as an *avatāra* (incarnation) of God. To him divine honours are paid by his pupils. Unlike the prophet and missionary the teacher's circle of hearers is usually restricted to an élite. But in their Western activities, many contemporary Indian *gurus* including the Maharishi, the Maharaj Ji, and Rajneesh, have sometimes taken on features of the prophet and missionary as well.

(3) The mystic

The teacher can be at the same time not only prophet but also a *mystic* (*ERE* 9, 83–117; *RGG* 4, 1237–62; *LThK* 7, 405ff.; Underhill, 1961; Hügel, 1923; Ellwood, 1980; *ER* 10, 245ff.). Between these two (prophet and mystic) are both connections and also divergences. In mystical life we find the same irregular psychological phenomena as in the prophetic: ecstasy, vision, auditions, etc. Like the prophet also, the mystic becomes possessed by *enthousiasmos* (concentration on God). The special form of the mystic is well described by Augustine in words from his earlier Neoplatonic period: 'I desire to know God and the soul. Nothing more? Nothing more' (*Solil.* 1.7). His goal is the silent contemplation of the inconceivable and ineffable, be it in absolute restfulness or in holy intoxication. The high point of mysticism is in the Tabor experience (cf. Mark 9.2ff.). Many mystics persevere in continual isolation from the external world, if not also in inner isolation as well. To the mystical union with God belongs union with the cosmos as well. The mystic feels at one with the whole of humanity, indeed with the whole of creation. He is the great intercessor, as we see in Athos anchorites and the Buddhist monk alike. The majority of mystics however return from Tabor to the lower slopes of life; they communicate the mystical experience to others. The communication takes place in different ways: (a) It occurs as an *esoteric* or private report to individual disciples and seekers: we see this in the Vedic *Upanishads* (*Upanishad* means literally the disciple sitting beside the teacher); or to a circle of disciples, as with the Pythagoreans, Gnostics and Sūfīs. But there is also the written account for those of like mind, be it in the form of a personal confession or instruction on the inner life. (b) It may be as *exoteric* communication, of which the classic example is Gautama Buddha. Out of compassion he refuses the peace and blessedness of Nirvāna in this life and preaches the saving doctrine publicly.

Numerous *Christian mystics* (Capps *et al.*, 1978) such as Bernard of Clairvaux, Hildegard of Bingen, Catherine of Siena and Teresa of Jesus have intervened actively in the ecclesiastical and political life of their time. Others such as Francis and Elizabeth have built up a caritative enterprise. Not a few mystics have become great writers and poets and are part of national, church or world literature, as for instance the writer of the *Bhagavadgītā*, the Persian poets Attar and Rūmī, the Byzantine mystic Symeon the New Theologian, the Spanish mystic John of the Cross, and the German mystics Angelus Silesius and Tersteegen. Others again have become politically active, such as Lao-tzu, Plato and Plotinus; Lao-tzu outlined virtually an ideal state on mystic, quietist lines. The mystics always allow their contemporaries to share in their own vision. The final goal is twofold: either solitariness, and indeed the twofold solitariness of the *unio mystica*, 'the flight of the alone to the alone', as the final words of the *Enneads* of Plotinus have it; or it is the community of life, commensality, which lies beyond this. Christian mysticism would appear to favour the latter alternative (Heighton, 1980).

(4) The martyr

The prophet is also constantly a *martyr* (*martus*), one who openly confesses his faith, carries out his commission, fulfils the divine law and who must often suffer or even die for his witness (Campenhausen, 1936; *LThK* 6, 995ff.; *RGG* 4, 587ff.; *ThWNT* 4, 477ff.; *ER* 9, 230ff.; 11, 247ff.). Prophecy is linked with *marturion* because the prophetic witness again and again meets with the resistance of men. Jeremiah is the Hebrew martyr-prophet. Further examples are the Maccabean brothers (2 Macc. 7). John the Baptist was beheaded by Herod. Jesus became a martyr through his preaching about God's Kingdom, Stephen a martyr for his faith in Jesus' messiahship and his sermon on the gospel of freedom from the law. Beside the prophets stand the many simple believers who on account of their faith took upon themselves persecutions, expropriation of property, exile, torture and even death. Countless martyrs there were during the persecutions of Christians in the Roman empire; they were condemned *ad metalla*, to forced labour in mines, most however *ad leonem*, to the lion, or to beheading, frequently also to crucifixion, and to burning. After the end of the Roman persecutions of Christians many more became martyrs: in the fifth century in the Persian empire, in the sixteenth century in Japan, in the nineteenth century in Africa, in the twentieth in individual Communist and Latin American countries. In the Middle Ages, on the contrary, the Christian Church assumed the role of persecutor, especially through the agency of the Inquisition (Lea, 1963). Martyrs were on the one hand the Jews, on the other those Christians who followed their conscience in their conflict with the church hierarchy. The *heretics* (*RGG* 1, 633f.; Dunham, 1965) of the Middle Ages and the Reformation period suffered just as much and died with the same joy as did the early Christian witnesses. For their part the Protestant Churches and princes made martyrs of the Catholics, especially in England.

Other religions have also known martyrdom. Buddhism in India (when Islam stormed in) and in China (from Confucian rulers), Sufism (al-Hallāj), Babāism and Bahāism. The history of religion including Christianity is written with blood.

(5) The saint

The person embued with mysterious power was originally described simply as 'sacred'. In the hagiographic legend this magical conception of saintliness lives on (see Chapter 8 above). This idea of saintliness or sacredness was personalized and ethicized (*ERE* 6, 147ff.; *ER* 13, 1ff.). The person who served the Eternal and fulfilled the divine law became holy even when he (or she) was not a priest, monk, prophet or mystic. In Israelite prophetic religion the call for saintliness is directed to all who belong to God's people: 'You shall be holy; for I the Lord your God am holy' (Lev. 19.2). Man shall be an image, a herald of the holy God. This ideal of holiness appears too in the New Testament (*ThWNT* 1, 87–116): 'You must be perfect, as your heavenly Father is perfect' (Matt. 5.48). Perfection means first truth and purity but then finally love and mercy. Holy is the person filled with love. 'God is love, and he who abides in love abides in God, and God abides in him' (1 John 4.16). Holiness is heroism in being patient and forgiving.

In early Christianity *hagios* (holy) is a universal concept. The Christian congregation is a community of 'saints' (Rom. 1.7; 1 Cor. 1.2; 2 Cor. 1.1; etc.). Saintliness is a religious and moral ideal of general validity: 'Strive for . . . holiness without which no one will see the Lord' (Heb. 12.14). Nevertheless, there is also in Christianity a living awareness that the saintly person has power from God over his own soul, over other souls, over his own body and that of others and over nature (see Chapter 8 above). Through one-sided stress on extraordinary side effects the conception of saintliness was again narrowed down. Supernormal ascetic works and miracles count as demonstrations of sanctity; especially characteristic of this are the saints' lives in the *Roman Breviary* (1964). The martyrs, confessors and ascetics are also holy. Holiness was especially brought into connection with monasticism. In his work on beatification and canonization (1745), Pope Benedict XIV gave heroic acts of virtue and continual joyfulness besides the three miracles which such a person should have performed.

According to the Protestant notion of saintliness they are holy who out of faith practise love. Holiness does not mean conforming to a pattern of asceticism but testimony to the living God. Söderblom says: 'The saints are those who proclaim in their nature and life that God lives.' 'A saint does not mean living up to some pattern of perfection but revealing God's free, creative power' (Söderblom, 1962, ch. 10). Corresponding notions of saintliness are found in other religious traditions, for instance the Buddhist *arhat* and *bodhisattva*, the *saddīq* of Jewish Hasidism and the 'perfect one' of Islamic Sufism. In the traditional religions of Africa and elsewhere, the truly saintly devotees are well known to cult members.

(6) The person in need

Not only the loving, serving, helping person is holy, but also, on the contrary, the one who is helped and served, the person in need. In this Christianity affirms what is already a general tradition. In the religions of antiquity those imploring help are sacred: they should not be harmed nor turned away. If they are, they are able to revenge themselves on the loveless person through the power of their curse. Sacred in this way is the *stranger* (*ERE* 11, 883–96), the one in need of *hospitality* (*ERE* 6, 797–820), the one imploring protection. Sacred are widows and orphans; the beggar is likewise sacred. The one imploring help was frequently seen as an incarnation of Deity. In early Greece Zeus appears as the one seeking help, the refugee, the sojourner, the guest. The Buddha exhorts his disciples: In the sick brethren you shall care for me (*Mahāvagga* 8, 26). This thought is also developed in Christianity: 'Whoever receives one such child in my name receives me' (Matt. 18.5). 'As you did it to one of the least of these my brethren, you did it to me' (Matt. 25.40). This saying of Jesus is later paralleled in a *Hadīth* of Islam where help of one's fellow is praised as help to Muhammad. Besides the canonical saying in Matthew 25, there is the *agraphon*: 'Thou didst see thy brother, thou didst see the Lord.' The thought of the secret identity between the person in need and Christ was restated by distinguished Christian believers in ever new forms. Martin of Tours clothed a beggar with half of his mantle: in the following night Christ appeared to him clothed with this piece of mantle. Benedict says in his *Rule* (36, 53): 'All strangers who come this way should be received as Christ'; 'When they are coming and going Christ should be venerated in them.' Francis of Assisi emphasized: 'If you have a poor person before you, you must see in him him in whose name he comes, the Saviour, who took our infirmities upon himself' (*Mirror of Perf.* 37). Elizabeth of Thüringen cried out: 'How delightful it is for us that (in the sick) we can bathe and cover our Lord.' According to the legend the leper whom she laid in her own bed was transformed before her husband's eyes into the crucified Christ. Vincent de Paul (*LThK* 10, 633ff.) required of the daughters of charity that they should care for the needy, afflicted and destitute of all kinds regardless of calling or confession because in them they see Christ himself. Luther proclaims tirelessly: 'The world is full, full of God, in every alley, before your door you find Christ'; while social concern was equally a feature of Calvin's Geneva (Innes, 1983).

'Man is God to man' (*homo homini Deus*): not only are individual persons sacred through their profession or consecration or through special gifts of grace or through extraordinary experiences and deeds, but every person is sacred, a revelation of the invisible God who enters into lowliness and wretchedness. The Stoic ideal was expressed in the words of Seneca: 'Where a person is, there is the chance to do good.' The suffering person above all is a form of God's appearing. The mysticism of the passion and the cross places a bond which cannot be loosened around the crucified's head and that of every suffering person. The mystic Jean Crasset says : 'As man God suffers with and in all suffering people; hence every affliction is like a sacrament for me.'

Humanism (ER 6, 511ff.) must consequently be seen as a religious phenomenon: *anthrōpismos, philanthrōpia* and *humānitās* are religious terms. All true religion is humanity and all true humanity is religion (Krüger, 1953, *RGG* 3, 482ff.). Every human countenance should be respected, no matter how this veneration is justified: whether in terms of man made in God's image (Gen. 1.27), the immortality of the human soul, the unity of all living beings (*Chandogya Up.* 6, 8ff.), the redemption of mankind through the blood of Christ, or the predestination to eternal salvation. However great, also, the differences between people may be in every respect, before the face of the Eternal all are equal. Before God there is no *prosōpolēmpsia*, no 'partiality' (Rom. 2.11), whether of race, of confession, of education, or of possessions. Here the religions and moral teaching are one: Christianity, Buddhism and Islam, Hindu *bhakti*, Sikhism, Taoism, Confucianism and the Stoics. Under the influence of the classical Greek ideal of humanity, Cicero placed *homo humanus* over against Cato's *homo romanus*. So the *imperium Romanum* was changed: there is no longer victor and vanquished, rulers and ruled, but only people; Roman law proclaimed the equality of all people, the state was broadened out to include humanity. The Christian idea of the 'mystical body of Christ', the world-embracing *ecclesia*, deepened this classical idea of humanity. In Christianity, the Greek ideal of humanity and the prophetic call for the love of one's brethren, which Jesus had uttered, come together. Through the Renaissance of the world of antiquity at the close of the Middle Ages, the bond between Christian love and classical *humānitās* was cemented afresh. Erasmus, Reuchlin and Melanchthon were the great teachers of humanity in Germany, John Colet and Martin Bucer in England. Pietism and Methodism translated this idea into social action. The Enlightenment gave it a rational basis. In the human rights of the French Revolution it was secularized. The greatest German spirits Lessing, Herder, Schiller, Goethe, Wilhelm von Humboldt, and in Britain and America the Quaker Tom Paine gave the ideal of humanity its complete form. Modern French philosophy and sociology proclaimed humanity as the highest ideal of mankind; August Comte and Alfred Loisy were heralds of a religion of humanity. In this idea of humanity religion and society become virtually identical (Durkheim, 1976).

(7) Woman as sacred

Not only does man appear as bearer of the sacred but also *woman* (Briffault, 1927; Heiler, 1939; *HWDA* 2, 1732–74; *RGG* 2, 1065ff.; *LThK* 4, 294ff.; De Beauvoir, 1976; Carmody, 1979; Daly, 1977; Daly, 1979; Ruether, 1979; Dowell *et al.*, 1981; Giles, 1982; Garcia *et al.*, 1983; *ER* 5, 302ff.). She does so, indeed, in similar forms as diviner, healer, sacred ruler, priestess, seeress, prophetess, mystic and simply as woman. Her service to religion is not the same in the different religions and among different peoples. On the one hand we find a high regard for woman; while on the other she often is assigned a lowly place and even excluded from the life of the religious community, being confined to the narrow circle of private piety.

The function of woman in religion was connected with the institutions of *matriarchy* (Bachofen, 1967; Davis, 1971; *ERE* 8, 851ff.; *RGG* 4, 1229). Bachofen believed he had found here the original form of human society. The mother appears in primordial society as the key member, indeed the predominant one. Gradually she was forced out of this position by the father. This view has been confirmed by subsequent research. Along with the matriarchal institutions went the veneration of the Deity in the form of mother earth (see above, Chapter 1). The high social and constitutional position of woman involved as well as the exercise of the priesthood, a priesthood linked with magical powers and divination. Besides this other motifs are operating: woman is closely related to valuable and dangerous powers. In her female functions of menstruation, conception and birth miraculous, magical powers are at work which fit woman for religious service. In addition there are the special psychological traits: stronger suggestibility and sensitivity enable her to experience the ecstatic, the visionary, especially ecstatic divination.

(a) The woman is medicine-woman and magician. Woman is the midwife and helper and has kept this vocation through the ages. She knows the secret potencies and actions, the magic formulae and sayings (see above, Chapter 9). (b) In connection with her role as magician and diviner, woman is also singer and musician (see above, Chapter 8). Woman is therefore to be regarded as the creator of music (Drinker, 1948). (c) Oracles and divination are closely linked with magical powers: women are seeresses and prophetesses. They prophesy, however, less with the aid of a divining apparatus than in the state of ecstatic trance. Mention has been made earlier (Chapter 8) of the great significance of the Sibyls. The messianically interpreted prophecy of the saviour in Virgil's fourth *Eclogue* was regarded as the prophecy of the Cumaean Sibyls. This has had the effect that not only they but also their Eastern sisters were placed on a par in medieval piety with the Old Testament prophets. Their importance was also enhanced by their number of twelve. From the eleventh century onwards the Sibyls made their way into Christian church art where they appear on floors and ceilings, portals and walls, choir stalls and windows – most beautifully in Michelangelo's paintings in the Sistine Chapel and those of Raphael in Santa Maria della Pace. In the Latin Roman Mass for the dead the Sibyl is called on as witness: *Dies irae, dies illa . . . teste David cum Sibylla.* (d) With the office of seeress is frequently associated that of female priesthood in the cult. Germanic religion knows of priestesses who officiated at sacrifices. The greatest extent was attained by the female temple priesthood in the great religions of antiquity (Egypt, Sumeria, Babylonia, Phoenicia and Syria). The priestess was recognized as the earthly image of the queen of heaven. Especially widespread was the female priest in Greece; and it still is (though less so than formerly) in Japanese Shinto and in certain traditional religious cults, such as Oriṣa-Oko in West Africa. (e) Women counted as the guarantors of the life and fertility of the people (i) through offering their virginity as hierodules or temple prostitutes of the great fertility goddess (see also above, Chapter 6), whereas the priests were representatives of the male deity. The other form of guarantee for the vital power of people and state was (ii) the virginity of the priestesses. Virgin temple priestesses served in pre-Columbian Central America, in Babylonia and in Rome where the Vestal Virgins enjoyed the highest honours.

In its original form the institution of seeresses and priestesses of the early religions has largely disappeared; although in the traditional cults of Africa and elsewhere it has continued to the present day. In the West particular survivals, mostly not understood, have persisted in custom and folk-lore. Besides this, however, it has lived on under the cover of other religions and mostly in secret. These other religions, especially Christianity, led a violent struggle against the secret priesthood of women and sought to brand its bearers as sorcerers and witches (Parrinder, 1968; *HWDA* 3, 1827–1920; 6, 293–351; *RGG* 3,307ff.; *LThK* 5, 314ff.; *MMM passim*) and to call for their eradication. Nevertheless this age-old priesthood proved to be indestructible. The medieval witches were the protectors of old traditional forms of faith repressed by new ones in which men were the determining influence. These seeresses lived on into the present century in Catholic areas of southern Germany. The Catholic priesthood was not able to suppress this grass-roots woman's priesthood from Germanic prehistory. The Catholic population does indeed attend the services and call the priest to the dying; but in the troubles of everyday life (sickness, rinderpest, crop failure, enmities) they go by preference to men (mostly shepherds) and women skilled in the traditional rites, who help and heal according to age-old half-secret or wholly-secret remedies, put a spell on wounds, pray away melancholy, ensure the fertility of the land and the livestock, prophesy the future from palmistry, a magic mirror or cards. Even faith in the magical power of virginity or celibacy has not been extinguished. Many magical actions can only be performed by virgins or by widows. Even sacred prostitution has been maintained in certain particular fertility customs which can only be carried out by naked girls and women (see above, Chapter 5). Here, too, the saying of Franz Cumont, the great scholar of ancient religions, is applicable: The piety of the masses is as unchanging as the water in the ocean depths; it is neither moved nor warmed by surface currents (Cumont, 1956, 231).

In the course of time the world religions became the religions of men. The old priestly services of women were repressed, in Persian Mazdaism and the related cult of Mithras, in Brahmanism, in Israelite religion, Islam, and above all Christianity. Even so, in their early days wide scope was given to women, and subsequently woman's religious power broke through victoriously again and again. This happened in Vedic India, among the ascetics, in Hindu *bhakti*, in Jainist orders, and in Buddhist orders. The Buddha himself associated freely with women, even courtesans, and was invited to meals by them. He showed thus the same freedom as Jesus. In turn women showed themselves to be the religious equals of men in the knowledge and practice of the Buddhist way of salvation and meditation, and also as lay devotees. In early Israelite religion (Peters, 1926) we find traces of a female priesthood. Women make sacrifice with their husbands (Judg. 13.23; 1 Sam. 1.3ff.) or, in the shrine of Yahweh, alone (Lev. 12); women perform duties in the temple (Exod. 38.8; 1 Sam. 2.22);

women beat the drum even in the temple of Yahweh in Jerusalem (Ps. 68.25). Above all Israelite religion features a female seerhood. Moses' sister Miriam leads off as prophetess (*nebī'ā*) into the triumph song of the Egyptians' downfall. Deborah the judge and prophetess directs the battle against Sisera and sings the victory song (Judg. 4.4ff.; 5.1ff.). The prophetess Hulda prophesies like the great prophets (2 Kings 22.14ff.). This female prophethood persisted even into New Testament times, as is shown by the example of the aged Anna in the infancy narrative (Luke 2.36). Only in 'late' Judaism was woman repressed in the worship service. In the synagogue she is accorded only the role of passive participant in a separate room. The reciting of the *shemā'* and the wearing of phylacteries are the exclusive right of men. Only in nineteenth-century Reformed Judaism was the right of active participation in services extended to women. Although Islam followed Christianity, it may simply be noted at this point that its history also shows a repression of women. (Hartman, 1909; Ameer Ali 1912; Hussain, 1984). Muhammad owed it to his wife's help that he became prophetic proclaimer of the revelations vouchsafed to him. In the initial period of Islam women took part in the services. Great female saints, such as the mystic Rabī'a (M. Smith, 1928) worked as pastors, others such as Suhda and Bint al-Kamāl were active as teachers of the law and taught men, others again were transmitters of the *hadīth*, preachers, abbesses of convents, builders of mosques and madrasas. In Shī'a Islam Muhammad's daughter Fātima was regarded as handing on the divine light-substance to his followers. There was even a tendency to see her as the incarnation of the divine in female nature. The shutting up of women in the harem stems from Byzantium, and the hostile remarks about women placed in the mouth of the Prophet apparently comes from Christian monasticism.

In Christianity itself (Leenhardt *et al.*, 1949; *ThWNT* 1, 776–90; Clark, 1977; Carmody, 1982; Weidman, 1984) the position of the woman underwent a development full of changes. A virgin conceives the world's redeemer by the Holy Spirit. The angel greets her as blessed, full of grace; she humbly receives God's message and says: 'Behold I am the handmaid of the Lord; let it be to me according to your word' (Luke 1.38). Women (Moltman-Wendel, 1982) shared the wandering life of Jesus and served him, amongst others Mary Magdalene (Luke 8.2ff.). Besides the tax-collectors, Jesus proclaims the good news of the forgiveness of sins to prostitutes also. Jesus says of the woman who was a sinner: 'Her sins, which are many, are forgiven, for she loved much' (Luke 7.47). In contrast to the busy Martha, Mary who listened to his words is praised as the one who has chosen the 'good portion' (Luke 10.42). The women stayed on, at some distance from the cross, after the disciples had fled. Women including Mary Magdalene shared in the burial of Jesus (Mark 15.47); they hurried to the grave when the Sabbath was past and found it empty; from the angel's lips they received the news of the resurrection and the command to tell it to the disciples (Mark 16.2ff.). Mary Magdalene is therefore called 'the apostle to the apostles'. According to Augustine the whole Church was represented in her person (*Smn.* 243, 2). In Christian Gnosticism Mary Magdalene became the bearer of a secret Christian tradition.

In the earliest Church the Pauline principle applied (Gal. 3.28) that 'there is neither male nor female; for you are all one in Christ' (Michaelis, 1931; Foster, 1936; L. Hick, 1957; Kähler, 1957). Woman stood beside man with equal rights in church life. Her service embraced four areas: (i) the prophetic office: women such as the four daughters of the evangelist Philip served as prophetesses (Acts 21.8ff.). As such they made their appearance in services, prophesied and prayed (1 Cor. 11.5; Justin, *Dial. with Trypho*, 88), and even spoke the eucharistic prayers. Early on, however, an opposing movement set in which made it a rule: 'Let the woman keep silent in church' (1 Tim. 2.12; 1 Clem. 21.7; and the manifestly interpolated passage 1 Cor. 14.34f.). The controversies between the opponents and advocates of female preaching in the Church found expression in the *Streitgespräche* of the disciples with Jesus, which were reported in the gnostic writings. According to the *Pistis Sophia* Jesus places himself on the side of Mary Magdalene in this battle. (ii) Teaching, mission and catechetical work: Paul names a series of women as his 'fellow workers' (Rom. 16.3; Phil. 4.2f.); he praises above all Phoebe the 'deaconess ... at Cenchreae' (Rom. 16.1f.). Thekla, Paul's pupil of legendary fame taught the baptized and healed the sick. But early on women were also excluded from catechetical work. (iii) Caritative work: originally this activity fell to widows who formed a kind of separate community in the congregation. Out of these, suitable women over sixty were called to a special office, the female counterpart to the office of presbyter. They were called *presbyterides, kalogriai* (beautiful old ones) or *diākonissai*. Soon however these widowed deaconesses were being supplanted by the virgin deaconesses. (iv) To the tasks of the *deaconesses* (Kalsbach, 1926) belonged liturgical duties also, including supervision at the service, assisting at baptism and confirmation, and taking the Eucharist to the sick. The ordination to the office of deaconess followed that of the male presbyter and deacon, being performed by the bishop through the laying on of hands and calling down of the Holy Spirit, later also through the putting on of the stola and the taking up of the chalice. With the cessation of adult baptism the deaconess disappeared from the congregational service and lived on in Eastern Churches to the present day only in isolated cases in convents. In the West the office of deaconess ceased early on and was retained only in the form of the half-monastic *canoness* (*ODCC* 233). Apart from such foundations, only dissident communities apart from the main Church, such as the Marcionites and Montanists, held firmly to the early Christian female office.

The repression of woman's service in the Church is accompanied by a progressive disparagement of her. She was seen to be incapable of assuming ecclesiastical office and of receiving ecclesiastical consecration, as a seductress not only of man but also of the angels (Tertullian). In monasticism, especially, there existed an unnatural contempt of women, even with great church teachers like Augustine, Anselm of Canterbury, Albertus Magnus and Thomas Aquinas.

The last mentioned describes man as the 'principle and goal of the woman' who aspires to the procreation of a complete male nature; if however a female is born it is something deficient and accidental. The woman finds herself therefore in a 'state of subjection' to man by nature, and thus incapable of ecclesiastical office and consecration. This principle was decisive for the canon law of the Roman Church (Borsinger, 1930). Under the influence of such ideas there arose in the Middle Ages a widespread literature hostile to women.

In contrast to the denigration of natural woman stands a boundless veneration of the untouched virgin. Paul already places virginity above marriage (1 Cor. 7). Almost all church teachers glorified virginity in an extravagant fashion (see above, Chapter 6). The early Church accorded the virgin ascetics a privileged place after widows and deaconesses (Metz, 1954). The church consecration of virginity (see above, Chapter 7) bore the character of a wedding. In the Middle Ages, with the handing over of the veil came the bridal crown and bridal ring as well. But this appreciation of ascetic virginity formed a preliminary step towards the valuing of woman as an independent religious personality. The sisterhood of nuns (Eckenstein, 1896) developed strongly creative forces despite the restrictions of the canon law. Examples are Lioba in the field of missions, Bride (Brigit) of Kildare in the area of church leadership, in the reform of monastic orders, Teresa of Avila; in charity, Elizabeth of Thüringen; Mary Ward in school teaching (Köhler, 1984), Gertrude of Helfta and Catherine of Genoa in the mystical vision, Mechthild of Magdeburg in creative language, Hroswitha of Gandersheim in poesy, Caritas Pirkheimer in humanistic education. Nuns have created forms of devotional worship which have become the common heritage of the Roman Church. The most universal nun is Hildegard of Bingen (*LThK* 5, 341f.) who was simultaneously mystic visionary, prophetess, natural scientist, physician, poetess and composer.

Woman was not only active in church life but became herself the object of veneration as well. *Mary* was venerated not only as mother of the eternal Son of God (Heiler, 1934; *RGG* 4, 763ff.; *ER* 9, 249ff.), but also as the archetype of virginity and motherhood. The poet of the *Heliand* and Otfried of Weissenburg praise her as 'the maid, the very beautiful', 'the most beautiful lady', 'the most precious mother of all', 'the woman nobly born', as *the* maid, woman and mother. In the *minne* songs the veneration of Mary was extended to that of woman. Henry Suso the spiritual *minne* singer declared: 'It is my custom to show respect willingly to all woman for the sake of the gentle Mother of God in heaven.' In this sense the great Protestant poets and writers have also been devotees of Mary. Erich Bockemühl says before the picture of Mary: 'Every mother with child art thou, Mary, virgin thou.' The Reformation campaigned for marriage as willed by God over against the Catholic glorification of virginity. It destroyed many communities of nuns but laid the foundation for a new ideal of the home maker (Stricker, 1927). In Lutheranism, nevertheless, veneration of Mary was retained (Schimmelpfennig, 1955). Luther himself described Mary as the 'woman above all women', 'the princess of the whole human race', 'the highest, the noblest, holiest mother', 'no woman gives a man such pure thoughts as the virgin'.

After the principle of 'equal rights' gradually began to prevail in public life, the way was opened up in the church sphere also for women's services in the Church. Under the influence of the general women's movements, there arose a church ministry and orders for women (Bliss, 1952; Ryrie, 1958), partly a limited ministry as the deaconess office in the Anglican and other Protestant Churches and the office of female curate or assistant minister in different Protestant Churches, partly a full female ministerial office, in different Congregational, Methodist, Baptist Churches, in some Anglican Churches (except in England), in individual German Protestant Churches, in Danish, Swedish, Norwegian Lutheran Churches, and in Reformed and Presbyterian Churches. Some Churches, including the Polish Mariawite Church, admit women to all levels of the hierarchy, not only to priestly office, but also to the office of bishop.

Thus the place of woman in the Church shows a continuation of the different functions she enjoyed during early times: she continued to be helper and healer in the care of the sick, diviner and *rune*-knower, seeress in mysticism and prophecy, *hierodule* in the dignity of bride of Christ, and sacrificial priest in the works of charity (of a Mother Teresa). The age-old thought of woman as divine being prevails again and again despite all the tendencies to the contrary which have issued from the patriarchal institutions of society. However, the resurgent women's movement of the seventies and eighties has greatly accelerated the momentum towards equal rights in state and Church besides developing a critique of the patriarchal ideology, still strongly entrenched there, on an unprecedented scale (Daly, 1977, 1978, 1984; Ruether, 1983).

(8) The dead

Not simply the living person but also the dead one is regarded as sacred and powerful (*ERE* 1, 425–67; *RAC* 1, 190ff.; *HWDA* 8, 1079ff., 1095ff.; *ER* 1, 263ff.)—both in the history of religions from the remotest times and, equally though with large variations, in Christianity in particular. Traditionally, belief in the life of man beyond the grave is linked with the fear of harmful influences, especially those causing sickness. Protection against the dangerous effects of death is offered by apotropaic actions (see above, Chapter 5), compulsive prayers (also Chapter 9), the sacrifice of food and drink (Chapter 6) especially blood offering (Chapter 5). Amongst the host of anonymous spirits of the dead certain ones that are specially named are to be distinguished: (a) the *ancestors*, who are thought of as predominantly, although not exclusively, friendly and protective spirits. However, if they are not venerated or are generally angry, they can produce the same harmful influences as other spirits of the dead. They are honoured mostly as helpers and givers. Ancestor veneration is marked by regular food offering and libations at their graves or before their images and symbols and by regular intimate fellowship. Help will be given to them in the form of magical verses for the dangerous journey to the spirit world. Veneration of the dead is a practical religious cult of varying importance for many traditional religions, and among the religions of antiquity (Chinese religion especially, also in India, Greece and Rome, Iran and among the Celts). The cult of ancestors ensures the continuity of family connection even after death. (b) Above the ancestors emerge the dead rulers. The *mana* of the chief continues after death. As families honour the fathers and mothers, so the ethnic group and people honour the chief and king. This veneration was widespread especially in Egypt; the giant pyramids served also to preserve the wellbeing of the dead kings. Following the pattern of the Hellenistic rulers the Roman emperors were accorded apotheosis after death, as were also the Byzantine emperors even though in a Christianized form (see above, Chapter 11). (c) Besides the rulers heroes (*RGG* 4, 270f.) are accorded special veneration, particularly persons who have acquired power, perhaps through war, in their earthly life. The cult of heroes formed one of the pre-conditions for the rise of the early Christian cult of martyrs.

(d) In an important group of religions there enters in place of, or alongside, the cult of ancestors, rulers and heroes, the veneration of religious personalities (*ERE* 11, 49–82; *RGG* 3, 168ff.). In Taoism, the 'god-man', the 'true person' is the bearer of the *Tao* (the way); In Confucianism, K'ung-fu-tzu was deified, though only after centuries had passed. In Jainism, the Jina (conquerors i.e. liberated ones) are so honoured; in Buddhism, the Buddhas. Hinduism honours its *avatāra*, Mazdaism its heroes and *fravashi*. In Islam, coming after Christianity as a religion of strict monotheism, *shirk*, associating other beings with Allah, counted as the greatest blasphemy. All the same in popular Islamic piety and theology, Muhammad (Royster, 1981) became the intercessor for men and women at the last judgement. In the course of time he became the 'perfect person', the ideal image of the person bound to God. Early on, individual mystics became honoured as *aulia* (plural of *walī Allāh*, friend of God), and their miraculous powers were seen as enduring after their death. Early cult places were associated with the name of a *walī*; and in this way many local deities from pre-Islamic times entered into Islam as saints, a phenomenon common in North Africa, Anatolia and India. Numerous women are found among these saints to whose graves the faithful make pilgrimage to implore their intercessions. In Shi'ite Islam the Prophet's grandsons and sons of 'Ali, Hassan and Husain, occupy a special place among the *aulia*; they are regarded as having transmitted a secret light-substance. The Wahhabis, champions of a puritanical Islam, fight against the veneration of saints as *shirk*, threatening the uniqueness of Allah.

In Christianity also there developed a *cult of saints* (*ERE* 11, 51ff.; *RGG* 3, 171ff.; *ODCC* 1227f.; *ER* 4, 172ff.) which arose as a cult of martyrs. The *martyrs* (Campenhausen, 1936; Frend, 1965; *ThWNT* 4, 477–520; *ODCC* 881ff.) were reckoned to be similar to Christ because like the Redeemer they give their blood and through 'the seed' of their blood made the Church blossom. 'The blood is the seed of Christians' (Tertullian, *Apol.* 50). Martyrdom signified a continually renewed revelation of the mystery of Golgotha; Christ suffers, dies and triumphs in the martyrs. The devotion to martyrs by the people occurred in forms similar to those of the cult of heroes in antiquity. It consisted in keeping sacred the graves and relics of the saints and the invoking of them (first witnessed to in the acclamations on inscriptions). The Church was at first hesitant about the liturgical veneration of saints; it confined itself to the mentioning of their names during the celebration of the Eucharist. 'Martyrs are named, not yet invoked', Augustine emphasizes (*CD* 22, 10). In many early liturgies prayer is not offered to the saints but *for* them, for their being perfected at the resurrection of the dead (Brightman, 1896, 128f.; Férotin, 1904). The cult of martyrs lives on in the remembrance of the fallen in two world wars. A popular hymn of remembrance, 'O valiant hearts' by John Arkwright, includes these words: ... 'The Victor's pitying eyes/look down to bless our lesser Calvaries ... These were his servants, in his steps they trod/ following through death the martyred Son of God.' (See also on the war memorial, in Chapter 3 above.)

With the martyrs were associated confessors, bishops, monks, teachers, ascetics, virgins and widows. There developed in this way a whole heaven full of saints. Characteristic is the emergence of the litany for *all saints* (*LThK* 1, 348) analogous to the litany of the gods of antiquity. The pantheon in Rome was transformed into a church consecrated to all the saints. In the Eastern Church as in the West an All Saints' festival is celebrated (*LThK* 3, 348f.; *ODCC* 36f.).

Later than the veneration of martyrs and at the same time as that of confessors and virgins there arose the devotion to the Mother of God. It developed gradually into a cult of the Madonna (see above, section seven). The first stage was the recognition of Mary as an ascetic virgin; Mary is virgin before, during and after the birth (of Jesus); she is therefore the archetype of all virgin souls. At the second level she is praised as *theotokos*, bearer of God, an expression already used by Hippolytus and Origen. The latter theologians followed in an analogous way descriptions of Isis as the mother of Horus. The ascription became a dogma at the Council of Ephesus in 431. At the third stage she became *coredemptrix*, who actively participated in the redeeming work of her son. Thereby a complete parallelism of Christ and Mary ensues (see above, Chapter 8). On the fourth level she is raised to queen of heaven whose body is preserved in heaven or was taken up into heaven, to become queen of the angels and saints. As the queen of heaven she becomes, fifthly, universal mediator and intercessor, helper for every need of body and soul. Through this development the influence of the cult of the mother goddess is clearly apparent (Neumann, 1972; James, E. O., 1959; *RGG* 4, 1227ff.). Sixthly, Mary became early on the symbol of the Church, already in Revelation (12.1ff.), and in the medieval German veneration of Mary (for the first time in the *Heliand*) as the prototype of all virgins and women (see section seven above).

The Church's veneration of saints embraces two spheres: firstly: the *imitation* of the saints because of their religious and moral example. Christ takes shape in the saints; the veneration of saints is part of the imitation of Christ. Secondly: the *fellowship of prayer* with the saints. Its oldest form is the prayer *for* the saints who want to be perfected at the coming of the Lord. The second form is the prayer *with* the saints, the prayer in the great communion of saints (*communio sanctorum*). In prayer to God reference is made to the prayer with and for the saints: 'Grant us by the blessed intercession of NN . . .' The third form is the direct invocation of the saints and the request for them to make intercession with God: 'Pray for us.' With this direct invocation belief in the special deity of antiquity made its way into the Church: the individual saints received different areas of human professions and needs (*LThK* 8, 1ff.). Joseph became the patron of craftsmen, Florian and Sebastian the soldiers' patron, Magdalene the saint of prostitutes, Wendelin and Leonhard the patrons of herdsmen, Laurentius the protector of bakers and cooks, Florian helper against fire, Peter a weather saint, John Nepomuk saint of bridges, Rochus help against the plague, Apollonia against tooth-ache, Lucia, Otillia and Clara against eye trouble, Blasius against throat infections, Antony patron of those wanting to marry and the slovenly, and Jude patron of hopeless causes. Many figures of the saints conceal the traits of ancient deities: Michael that of Odin, Peter that of Donars, Nicholas that of Poseidon; Mary has absorbed traits of the mother goddess of Mediterranean religions and also Celtic and Germanic goddesses. This process extended later on beyond Europe to Latin America where Christ, Mary and the saints were associated with native Indian deities and above all with the deities (*vodun, òrìshà*) of the West African slaves. Thus in Umbanda, a new religious movement, Mary has become the mother goddess Yemoja (Brazil: Yemanja), Jerome represents Shango, god of storms, Barbara is Oya, wife of Shango, Christ is the great *òrìshà*, Òrìshà-nla (Brazil: Oshala), George is Ogun the god of iron and transportation, Sebastian is Oshosi, god of hunters, and Anna is Oshun a river goddess (Fischer, 1970).

It was Luther who already recognized that the saints had been made into gods. Even so Lutheranism retained for a long time elements of the Catholic veneration of saints, for instance the veneration of the biblical saints, and in Sweden and Anglican England, that of all saints. Recent Protestant theologians have fought for the necessity of the veneration of saints, albeit in a deeper and purer form. Nathan Söderblom and Walter Nigg (Nigg, 1962) have stood up for a universal 'communion of saints' in all religions, as the humanists and Zwingli already dimly perceived in their recognition that the heroes, rulers and thinkers of antiquity were one with the witnesses to the Christian faith. There are many in the consortium of the saints, said Erasmus, who are not in our catalogue.

A special feature of the devotion to saints in many religions is the *cult of relics* (*ERE* 10, 650–62; *RGG* 5, 1044ff.; *ER* 12, 275ff.). Amongst traditional peoples and in the world of antiquity the cult of relics became widespread. We find also a cult of relics in Jainism and Buddhism. The *stūpa* (Dallapiccola, 1980) are reliquaries, containers of ashes, originally round hills, later tower-like temple buildings called Pagodas (from *Dagoba*, Sanskrit *dā-tu-garbha*, 'relic holder').

In Christianity, too, there arose a cult of relics (*LThK* 8, 807ff.; *ODCC* 1170), because the bones of the martyrs who had given their lives for Christ were regarded as sacred. The Eucharist was dispensed over the graves of the martyrs and later whole churches were built over them. In the Western Church, from the fifth century down to 1969, no church altar could be built without a sepulchre with a relic in it. In the Eastern Church there can be none without an *antiminsion*, a cloth with a relic sewn into it. The belief in the healing and protective power of relics led to the dismemberment of sacred bodies so that as many churches and believers as possible might receive a share. The cult of relics assumed immense proportions during the Middle Ages, especially during the Crusades. Apart from the relics of bodies the clothing of saints was preserved, as in Islam their turbans. Besides the genuine relics are the numerous false ones, in all the world religions including the Christian: the tooth of the Buddha in Kandy, the beard of Muhammad and the shroud of Christ (I. Wilson, 1979). The countless Buddhist *stūpa* exclude the authenticity of the vast majority of the relics of the Buddha; the same goes for the numerous heads and arms of individual Christian saints which are venerated at different places, or the great number of 'sacred mantles' of Christ (*RE* 17, 58ff.) of which no fewer than 120 have been counted, as with the girdles of Mary. In the Middle Ages relics were frequently stolen, indeed wars were fought to gain possession of them. They were, and still are, kept in magnificent reliquaries (Braun J., 1940) and carried about in procession. Chapels for relics, especially pilgrimage churches, became centres of popular piety. But through its popular and magical character, as through its fictions, the cult of relics has tended to divert the faithful from the deeper meaning in the veneration of saints. Against the cult of relics, therefore, voices have been raised in criticism from the viewpoint of a purer piety: Vigilantius of Aquitaine (*c.*400), individual critics in the Middle Ages, and in a comprehensive way in the Reformation, particularly through Luther and Calvin. The Council of Trent answered this criticism with the observation that the bodies of the saints were 'living members of Christ and a temple of the Holy Spirit and were raised by Christ to eternal life and glorified' (Session 25). The modern cult of the saints in the Roman Church is regulated by the canon law (can. 1186–90).

13

The Christian Sacred Community

(1) Forms of sacred community

(a) Marriage, family, ethnic group

The community like the individual is also the bearer and transmitter of the sacred. Every religious tradition, including Christianity, is born by a *community* (Wach, 1964; Weber, 1966; Yinger, 1957 and 1970; O'Dea, 1966; Robertson, 1969; *ER* 3, 556ff.; 13, 376ff.). The significance of the community for religion is so great that the social and the sacred could be regarded as interchangeable terms. Durkheim's sociology (Durkheim, 1976) considered the origin of religion to be keeping society sacred. On the other hand, individual religion is also found in early religious forms. Religion may separate itself from existing social forms and frequently creates new forms of community out of its own resources.

The smallest cell of all religious community is *marriage* (Westermarck, 1922; *ERE* 8, 432–72; *RGG* 2, 314ff.; *LThK* 3, 675ff.; *NDLW* 349ff.; *ER* 9, 218ff.). Marriage, above all monogamous marriage, counts as a sacramental community which is constituted through special marriage rites (Van der Leeuw, 1964). In early India, as in Rome, marriage was sealed by a communal eating of sacred sacrificial cakes. The most important act of the early Indian marriage rite was the leading of the bridal couple round the sacred fire. The sacramental character was shown by the fact that in the Indo–Germanic sphere, for instance, earthly marriage was a re-enactment of the heavenly marriage between a male and female, ouranic or solar deities. According to the word of Jesus (Mark 10.5ff.) marriage is based on the order of creation and is indissoluble. According to the Epistle to the Ephesians (5, 23ff.), marriage represents an image of the mystical union between Christ and the *ecclesia*. In the Eastern Orthodox Church, as in the Roman Church, marriage is regarded as *mystērion (sacramentum)*. According to the contemporary view of the Eastern Church its sacramental character rests upon the priestly actions in the marriage rite (leading around the altar, bridal wreaths). In the West the consecration of the marriage is only preparatory, the sacrament itself is performed in the sexual union, hence the grounds for nullity in the case of non-consummation. The Roman Church as distinct from the Eastern Church holds fast to the indissolubility of marriage. The Protestant and very recently the Anglican Churches are prepared under certain circumstances to remarry divorced persons. But the widespread and increasing practice of cohabitation represents a common perplexity for all the Churches.

Marriage widens out to include the *family* (*ERE* 5, 716ff.; *ER* 4, 400ff.; 5, 277ff.) and clan as living religious communities. The religious family community manifests itself amongst the Greeks and Romans in the family festivals. With the Germanic peoples the clan attains great significance as a religious community. The significance of the family as a cultic community is especially clear in the Jewish religion. The *kiddush* rite on the eve of the Sabbath is a family celebration (see above, Chapter 7). As a religious centre, the family revived again in Protestant Christianity in the form of family devotions.

(b) Caste

To the kinship group is related another form of sacred community, the caste (Cox, 1948; Hocart, 1950; Lyttleton, 1982; *ER* 15, 188f.). It attained its most elaborate development in India. It arose there on the basis of the racial differences between the Indo-Aryan conquerors and the conquered (*varna*, caste, means colour, race); and also according to Aryan tripartite social functions (explored by Dumézil). The later differentiations follow according to professions: *brahman* (ruling and priestly), *khshatriya* (warrior) *vaishya* (economic: pastoral and agriculture) and *shūdra* (lowest level). These differences of profession continued to proliferate so that countless castes arose. The caste system was regarded early on as 'the divine order of creation', and firmly anchored in the cosmogonic myth of *Purusha* (Eliade, 1979). In the twentieth century, however, it has become the great problem of India. Gandhi justified it on the one hand as a 'division of labour', on the other hand he led a holy war against the isolation of the classless 'untouchables'. In the present Indian state there is complete equality before the law, even of those without a caste. Nevertheless, amongst the Sikhs, a religious movement which grew up in opposition to caste, concern has been expressed at their internal caste differences. Similarly in Christianity, Jacobite Christians and village Catholics have over the centuries become influenced by the caste structure of southern India despite the anti-caste policies of the Churches themselves.

(c) The state

As on the stateless and traditional level the public cult is linked to the ethnic community, so also in the greater political constitutions of antiquity the public cult is likewise linked to the public community organized in the state. Even where the priesthood made itself independent from the rulers and their officials, it stood in close relationship to the state. At birth a person is born not only into the political community but at the same time also into the religious community. In view of the sacredness of the ruler (see above, Chapter 11), the recognition of his or her political power is at times a religious act. The rejection of the cult of the ruler counts as religious sacrilege. Christians who refused to show veneration to the Roman emperor's image, to sacrifice for the emperor's well-being and to swear by his genius or his *Fortuna* made themselves guilty of anti-religious activity, indeed 'godlessness' (Schütz, 1933). Whoever excluded himself from the religion of the state showed himself or herself to be thereby an opponent of the state. Early Christian converts in West Africa and elsewhere were to relive the experience of the first centuries (McKenzie, P. R., 1977).

(d) Men's and women's societies and cult groups

Already in traditional societies there arose independent religious groups within the ethnic religious community, to balance the power of the chiefs. Men's societies (*ERE* 11, 287ff.; Van der Leeuw, 1964, 282ff.; Wikander, 1938; *ER* 13, 151ff.) and women's societies have flourished along with cult groups of men and women (Bascom, 1969). The reception of the young man or young woman into the cult group occurred in a solemn act of *initiation* (*ERE* 7, 314ff.; Eliade, 1958; *RGG* 3, 751ff.). In these societies and cult groups there was often a strict command to maintain silence over against those outside the group.

The traditional societies and cult groups are the precursors of the Greco-Roman mystery societies alongside of which Christian churches grew up in the first centuries. With the national mystery societies were associated ecumenical mysteries which flourished with the decline of state and ethnic religion in the Hellenistic age (Cumont, 1956; Reitzenstein, 1927). The profoundest motif of these mystery societies is the yearning for personal assurance of salvation and closer fellowship with other members. Very often entry followed on the basis of a 'divine call' (Apuleius, *Metam.* 11, 21). The Hellenistic mystery cults of Cybele and Attis, Sabazios, Atargatis, Isis and Osiris, and Mithras rest on a basis, often, of earlier popular religion, but they have gone beyond the boundaries of race and become ecumenical communities which embrace followers of different peoples. The individualization and narrowing down of the mystery communities contributed at the time to their expansiveness and tendency towards universality. The cult of Mithras (Vermaseren, 1956 and 1963; Bainchi, 1979; *RGG* 4, 1020ff.) achieved the greatest expansion, with monuments extending from Persia to Spain and the British Isles. Mithraism stood in sharp competition with youthful Christianity. Besides the former the Egyptian Isis cult achieved the widest extent. As world religions the mystery cults were of great significance for Christianity's own growth.

(e) Religious orders

Religious groups cut loose from ethnic religion in another form, that of the heterodox *religious orders* (*ER* 12, 302ff.). Jainism rejected completely the traditional Vedic and Brahmanic religion. It broke with the sacrificial cult, with the sacred scriptures of the Vedas and with the caste system, and in this way an independent ascetic religion of liberation came into being. Buddhism was originally a heterodox community of ascetics as well. It was a *sangha* of monks and nuns, the third of the 'jewels' besides the Buddha and the Dharma. Entry into the orders meant both for Buddhism as for Jainism complete emancipation from the caste. As the sign of this renunciation, both monks and nuns had to put off their head-dress, the symbol of caste membership, and have the head shaved. The order of tertiaries was of still greater significance in Buddhism. Whereas Jainism remained confined to India, Buddhism became a world religion. Missionary monks carried it to all the countries of eastern and central Asia. In a number of countries Buddhism became the official religion: Sri Lanka, Burma, Thailand, Kampuchea, Tibet, temporarily in Korea and Japan. There arose in China a series of independent departments (*tsung*); the most important of which are the 'T'ien-t'ai-school' which stressed the importance of scriptural studies, 'the school of discipline' which held fast to the early discipline of the order, the 'school of secrets' which possessed an esoteric cult, 'the school of meditation' which practised contemplation, and 'the school of pure land' which made known the alone effective grace of Amitabha Buddha. However, the schools are not sharply separated from each other; indeed not even from the other religions of China, Confucianism and Taoism. From China these schools were transplanted to Japan. There they became, however, separate churches or sects. Both the Chinese schools and the Japanese sects are independent of the state, as is the Cao Dai church in Vietnam which was a reformed Buddhist creation of the twentieth century. The contrasts which have developed over the centuries between *Theravāda* Buddhism and *Mahāyāna* Buddhism remain extraordinarily sharp to the present day. There are equally movements within Buddhism this century which seek a coming together across all these divergences of all who make confession of the Buddha. The most significant of these is the World Fellowship of Buddhists founded by the Sinhalese scholar G. P. Malalasekera.

Manichaeism is similar to Jainism and Buddhism in its communal structure.

(f) The prophetic religions

The prophetic religions, to which in many respects Mani's religion also belongs, have a strong expansive power. Mazdaism, out of which Manichaeism was later to emerge, was predestined to be a universal religion with its own philosophy of history, its concept of progress and its eschatology. Following the Achaemenid and Arsacid empires, Mazdaism became more narrowly a Persian state religion under the Sassanians. But individual elements such as the belief in light attained universality through the cult of Mithras and Manichaeism. As a religion of the state, Iranian Mazdaism was swept away by Islam. A small community remains in eastern Iran and in Bombay and Gujerat. Recently, however, it has spread to other countries and faces a renewed challenge to allow conversion and a renewed universalism.

The *Israelite* religion (De Vaux, 1965; *RGG* 3, 978ff.) was clearly an ethnic religion; Yahweh was an ethnic deity. But Israel's exclusive monolatry was the nucleus of an authentic monotheism and thereby of a world religion. Through prophetism (see above, Chapter 12) this universality was gradually unfolded. The detachment from nationalism was effected first through the prophecy of doom: Yahweh rejects his disobedient people and retains a remnant of believers. The prophecy of doom was succeeded by the prophecy of salvation: Israel faced a time of joy, the other peoples recognize Yahweh as the only God; Zion becomes the central shrine of the world (Isa. 2.3). In the exilic period there arose a Jewish religious community, and after that came to an end, a

Jewish state church. Diaspora Judaism developed a mission for Yahwistic monotheism. Through the translation of the Hebrew Bible into the universal language of Greek, the ethical monotheism of Israel broke into the Greek world. Conversely Hellenistic Judaism took into itself Platonic philosophy and mysticism. But the period of expansion was only temporary. After the destruction of the temple a reaction followed in rabbinic Judaism. The universalistic forces of Judaism were interrupted by a youthful Christianity. Judaism itself went into isolation over against the Greco-Roman world and became a religion of race and law.

The *bene-haggōlāh* (sons of banishment) were scattered all over the world. They had lost their religious centre in the homeland together with its priesthood and cultus. The Torah, of whose regulations only a small fraction could be fulfilled, together with the Talmudic interpretation and synagogue worship, remained the only bond by which the Jewish community was held together through centuries of oppression and persecution. Through the emancipation from the ghetto the universal powers broke out afresh in liberal or reformed Judaism (*ERE* 7, 900ff.). By the suppression of the Talmud the universal ethical monotheism of prophetic religion could be proclaimed as the essence of religion (Buber, 1960) and the way opened for a denationalizing of Judaism. But also outside the field of religion the ecumenical forces of Judaism had their effect; the modern idea of humanity in its socialist form especially, has received a strong impetus through one who came out of Judaism, namely Karl Marx. Over against liberal Judaism Zionism (*EJ* 16, 1031ff.; *ERE* 12, 855ff.; *ER*, 9, 240ff.) strove for the recovery of the Palestinian homeland. Its dream was fulfilled, at least in part, with the setting up of the state of Israel; the old central shrine, it is true, cannot be erected again. Christian theology since Paul seeks to solve the puzzle which this 'God's people of mankind' represents, in an eschatological perspective. Paul believed in the conversion of Israel, that is, the recognition of Jesus' messiahship by the Jewish people at the end of history. 'A hardening has come upon part of Israel, until the full number of the Gentiles come in, and so all Israel will be saved' (Rom. 11.25f.). But this Christian theology of history like its Jewish counterpart (Rubinstein, 1966) has been radically called into question by the Holocaust of Auschwitz and elsewhere in recent days.

As with Judaism so also with *Islam*: it was originally linked to a nation; Muhammad saw himself at first as the special prophet for his traditional Arab people; he held his message to be identical with that of Moses and Jesus. The Jews' attitude effected a change in his awareness of vocation; he saw himself as the restorer of pure Abrahamic religion which had been distorted by Judaism and Christianity. Islam thus became a world religion. The *umma* or community is a world community. Islam has sought to draw the whole of mankind into this community and in this has made use of a double method: the traditional religionists were compelled to accept Islam as a religion by force of arms, 'the people of the book' had only to recognize the political authority of Islamic princes; they retained the right to practise their religion freely. The patriarch of

Constantinople exercised political power over all Christians in the Turkish empire. As a world community Islam possessed an immense drive: it had *one* confession of faith, *one* prayer in gesture and word, one sacred language, one sacred scripture. Despite the divisions (Mu'tazilites, Wahhabis, Shi'ites and splinter movements (Babites, Bahais), Islam formed a unified, virtually closed, ecumenical community, which is only comparable with the Roman Church as it was before Vatican II. This is all the more astonishing as Islamic unity is not organized as is the Roman one. The caliphate had not the same significance as the papacy; it had only judicial, military and administrative powers, but no authority to define doctrine; this last was assured in the validity accorded to the canon law (*shari'a*) and the consensus (*ijma'*) of the legal scholars (*ulamā*).

The same closed community is shown in the *Khalsa* of the *Sikh* which combines the exclusiveness of the Hindu idea of caste with the closed nature of the Islamic community: Gobind Singh united the followers of Guru Nanak's religion into a high caste. Their warlike spirit was shown in the surname *Singh* ('lion') which every Sikh bears. As Islam expanded through *jihad* (warfare of faith) so also was the Sikh community a community of war, and as such political tendencies were mixed with religious ones. At the same time, however, universalistic tendencies in Sikhism broke out again and again, based on the imageless monotheism of Guru Nanak.

(2) The Christian Church as sacred community

More comprehensive even than these other religious communities, yet exhibiting many of the same basic themes, is the Christian Church (*RGG* 3, 1296ff.; 1531ff.; *LThK* 3, 781ff.; Troeltsch, 1931; Stark, 1966ff.; Carrier *et al.*, 1964; *ER* 3, 473ff.). Christianity is not only the greatest of the world religions in numerical terms (Barrett, 1982), it also manifests some of the deepest and most comprehensive conceptions of community. The Christian Church, it is true, did not fall from heaven, it also was not 'founded' in the juridical sense. It proceeded out of the Jewish ethnic community which had become a religious one through the loss of its national independence. In this community there arose the 'little flock' of disciples which gathered about Jesus. To it Jesus promised his Kingdom (Luke 12.32). After his death and resurrection it became the *ecclēsia* (*kāhāl, kenishtā*) which the 'powers of death' would not prevail against (Matt. 16.18; Theissen, 1978; Gager, 1975; Richter, 1984).

The Church in its original sense is an eschatological community, a community of the last days. Jesus' sermons were directed to the Jews only (Matt. 10.5f); those who were not Jews, however, should, according to his expectations, come spontaneously from the east and west, north and south and sit down with the patriarchs of Israel at table in the Kingdom of God (Matt. 8.11). As an ecumenical magnitude the Church is vividly portrayed in the story of Pentecost (Acts 2); 'Jews and proselytes' make up the Jerusalem congregation. The first Hellenistic-Jewish congregation of Christians arose in Jerusalem; the leading Gentile-Christian congregation arose in Antioch. Barnabas and Paul took over the mission to those who were not Jews. The strong differences between the Jewish Christian community and the traditional Greco-Roman Christian community were reconciled through Paul. There arose a new community of the dispersion analogous to the Jewish one, which was linked with the first congregation at Jerusalem through 'the collection' (Georgi, 1962).

After the break with Judaism, Christianity took on the form of ecumenical mystery societies. Out of a gathering which lived in messianic expectation of the last days the Church developed into a brotherhood of mysteries (Angus, 1925). In its services only the initiated could take part: the catechumens and penitents only in the service of the word, the baptized also in the eucharistic meal. Early on the eschatological view of revelation and the sacraments passed over into that based on the history of salvation. After the outward, external victory of Christianity the esoteric character disappeared; it was retained only in the terminology of the cultus and of mysticism, especially in the writings of Dionysius the Areopagite (*RAC* 3, 1075ff.).

The specific sociological character of the Christian Church lies in a manifold tension: firstly, between the visible and the invisible Church (McKenzie, P. R. 1953). The Church as the Body of Christ (Mersch, 1949) is the invisible community of all those who have become 'members of Christ' (1 Cor. 12.12ff.) through faith and mystical union with him. The community becomes visible in the service, in common listening to the preached word and in common prayers, as also in the receiving of both the sacraments of baptism and the Lord's Supper. Through the former, this visible community is constituted, through the latter it is sealed again and again. All the same, the invisible and visible Church are not coextensive: even without membership of the Church of Christ and without participation in the sacraments, membership of his body is possible: 'Many, who appear to be outside are in reality within and many who appear to be inside are in reality outside' (Augustine).

The second tension exists between the world Church and the popular Church (Vrijhof *et al.*, 1979). The Church of Christ is universal, 'catholic', i.e. including the whole. It includes Jews and Gentiles, all nations; it is the 'great multitude which no man could number, from every nation, from all tribes and peoples and tongues, standing before the throne and before the lamb' (Rev. 7.9). But because, as the peoples' apostle puts it, the Church has the task to 'become all things to all men', 'to the Jew . . . a Jew . . . to those outside the law . . . one outside the law' (1 Cor. 9.20.22), this universality is combined with the most varied national characteristics and cultural forms, indeed, brings these to their fulfilment. The type of church appears conformed to the nation in each case, whether as Jewish, Greek, Syrian, Egyptian, Armenian, Georgian, Ethiopian, African, Roman, Spanish, Celtic, German, Slavic, Indian or Chinese. Many peoples have only acquired a national literature and culture through the Christian Church. Yet in overstressing the ecumenical dimension of the Church the Greco-Byzantine Church, and still more the Roman one, sought to make the whole Church conform to its own pattern. The former restricted the tendency to make all uniform and finally gave it up and so made possible a series of national churches – a Greek, Bulgarian, Serbian, Russian (Lane, 1978), Rumanian, Albanian, etc. The Roman Church, however, succeeded in completely absorbing the old independent churches of the West into its own canon law and its own liturgy apart from some insignificant liturgical elements. Connected to this are not only the subordination of the episcopal order by the papal one, but also the diminishing of the secular rulers' influence on the Church in their country. In the Reformation the repressed national Church raised its head anew: there arose on Lutheran as on Calvinist soil a series of independent national or provincial Churches (*RGG* 4, 222f.; *ER* 12, 238ff.). In most of the Lutheran Churches the princes possessed the power of supreme oversight; the Anglican Church had its 'supreme head' in the English king (Wand, 1961; *ER* 1, 286ff.). Through the colonial expansion of the British empire the Church of England developed into an ecumenical Church within which the individual daughter churches attained autonomy. It was similar with world Methodism. World Reformed Churches were less exclusively Anglophone; while the world Baptist alliance had a strong base in North America.

The third tension is that between inclusiveness and exclusiveness. The Church has on the one hand the tendency to take into itself in catholic fashion everything true, good and beautiful that it finds in the piety, cultus, morality, politics, philosophy and arts of the different cultures, and thereby to grow continuously in their richness. On the other hand the Church has also the tendency to fix its institutions and theology in an absolute way and expel as heretical everything that goes against these, indeed, not only condemning different views, but also the people who think differently. The Cyprianic formula, 'outside the Church there is no salvation' (*Ep.* 73, 21), in which under 'church', indeed, only the external church institution is meant, led in its consequences to the assertion of the Council of Florence (1439) that all Jews, pagans, heretics and schismatics are condemned to the eternal torments of hell if they do not join the Roman Church before their death (Denzinger, *Ench.* No. 714).

The fourth tension is between the spiritual attainment of salvation and the secular striving after power. The churches want on the one hand to tear mankind out of the power of the demons and to mediate eternal salvation in Christ. On the other hand they are often themselves made subject in varying degrees to the demonic power of the world. This striving after power induced the Church again and again to suppress the quest for truth and the call for holiness, by using the means of secular power for the prohibition of books and the burning of them, the hunting down, torturing and killing of heretics (Lea, 1963; *RGG* 3, 769ff.), indeed also pious frauds such as the fictions of the Donation of Constantine and the Pseudo-Isidorean decretals. The repressive means of the medieval Roman Church were also used, if on a reduced scale, in the various national Protestant Churches.

(3) Independent Christian communities

The dogmatic exclusiveness of the churches on the one hand and their secularization and demonization on the other, led again and again to the detachment of parts of its members and to *the formation of new communities*. The latter were described as schismatic and heretical, the former, however, were confessed to be the true Church, as Orthodox and Catholic Churches (*RGG* 3, 13ff.; Bauer, 1971; Stark 2, 1967; *ER* 13, 154ff.). The main Church imposed the ban on the separate communities; frequently, however, they hurled anathemas at each other. With the dogmatic condemnation it was often a question of nuances in formulation as with the battle over the two natures of Christ or over the title of Mary as *theotokos* or *Christotokos*. Even modern Catholic history of doctrine has reached the view that not only the Christology of Nestorius but also the so-called Monophysite Churches are not material heresies but only 'verbal' ones. Sometimes they were not genuine conflicts at all, but ecclesiastical and political intrigues and struggles for power, as with the controversy between the two patriarchs Cyril of Alexandria and Nestorius of Constantinople which led to the Council of Ephesus (431).

Besides the dogmatic grounds for separation from the main Church are to be numbered the religious and moral ones. Over against the secularization, indeed the demonization of the main Church, smaller groups felt themselves compelled to put into practice the ideal of the original 'congregation of the saints' in which free rein was given to the development of charismata, spiritual gifts. This took place partly in complete separation, indeed sharp opposition to the main Church, and partly in continuing association with it. In the first instance this community of sanctification achieved the sociological form of the *sect* (Troeltsch, 1931; Stark, 1967, v, 2; *ERE* 11, 315–29; Wach, 1964; *RGG* 3, 1325f.; Neve, 1952; Turner, B., 1970; *ER* 13, 154ff.), in the latter case that of the *church order* (see section (e) above; Troeltsch, 1931; Wach, 1964). Both forms served the renewal of original Christianity. Regarding sects, the will to renew early Christianity is impressively depicted in the pioneering work of Gottfried Arnold (*RGG* 1, 633f.). In the history of monasticism this will for renewal emerges in successive movements, but especially clearly in the Cluniac movement which proceeded out of Benedictine monachism; also in the Cistercian and Franciscan movements. Francis of Assisi sought nothing else save 'to live according to the form of the holy gospel' (*Anal.* 37) the life of the mendicant wandering apostle. Admittedly it failed inasmuch as the Church made an ecclesiastical order out of Francis' free brotherhood, an order in which his ideal of poverty was weakened and distorted, whereas the Franciscan group which had remained true to this ideal were driven towards sectarianism (Benz, 1934), as before them the Waldensians were and after them the Wycliffites and Hussites. But also on the soil of the Reformation 'Free Churches' (*RGG* 2, 1110ff.) broke loose from the established Churches – not only the spiritual holiness movements: Baptists, Methodists, Mennonites, and the Moravians; but also the more ecstatic communities: the Quakers, the Pentecostalists (*ER*

11, 229ff.), the Salvation Army, and recently the charismatic and house-church movement.

Related to them are the eschatological and apocalyptic sects whose archetype was the early Christian Montanists (see above, Chapter 8). In the nineteenth century this type is represented by the Catholic Apostolic Church (Irvingites) with their offshoots the new Apostolics, the Adventists and the Latter Day Saints. A final form of the separated communities is manifested by the rationalist and latitudinarian groups such as the Arminians or Remonstrants (*ERE* 1, 807ff.; *RGG* 1, 620ff.) and Unitarians, who admittedly remained numerically small though often influential and creative. The separation of the Russian sects (*ERE* 11, 332ff.; Lane, 1978; *ER* 13, 187ff.) from the Orthodox Church had different grounds: the liturgical hyper-conservatism of the 'Old Believers', a mystical and ecstatic enthusiasm in the case of the Chlysty, a Manichaean asceticism with the Skoptsy, an evangelical pietism with the Stundists. The majority of these sects, apart from the Quakers—and perhaps even there as well—moved in the course of time towards a more churchly form. The evidence tends to show that a sect achieves permanence and extent only if it can consolidate and crystallize into an ecclesiastical institution, even if this may take on a looser organizational form than that of the main Church or national Church, especially in African independent Churches such as the Cherubim and Seraphim (Barrett, 1968).

(4) The spiritual church

Besides the Church and the independent religious movement or community stands mysticism or the *spiritual church* (Jones, 1914) as the third sociological form of the sacred community. At the turn of the twelfth century Abbot Joachim of Fiore had prophesied the coming of a Church of the Spirit in which the hierarchical and sacramental institutions are replaced by the charismatic works of the bearers of the Spirit, namely the monks. This spiritual church becomes actualized in the mystics as a community of 'the spiritual ones'. For them the external church community is secondary; the community in which they live is the invisible *communio sanctōrum*, the union of all who love God and are united with God throughout the world regardless of the external community to which they happen to belong. Among them, some find a place in the external community of the main Church. In the event of condemnation they offer the sacrifice of obedience. But within the Church they live their own spiritual life. In sovereign fashion they make use thereby of the external dogmatic and cultic forms but reinterpret them into aids and illustrations of the mystical union with God. The others, including radical spirituals, such as Sebastian Franck and Gerhard Tersteegen, have moved beyond all confessional Churches. Their community with God suffices, in whom all things are one. Insofar as the spiritual mystics seek concrete human fellowship, this consists in friendship with individual souls of like mind, for example, Hildegard of Bingen and Ricardis (Heiler, A. M., 1972), Suso and Elsbeth Stagel, Heinrich von Nordlingen and Margareta Ebner, Francis de Sales and Madame Chantal; or else in the formation of informal groups such as the 'friends of God' of the upper and lower Rhine (Jones, 1939) who had been awakened through the preaching of Meister Eckhart, Tauber and Suso, or the Society of Friends which was gathered together out of 'seekers' through the prophetic enthusiasm of George Fox (*ERE* 6, 142ff.; *RGG* 5, 728ff.; Russell, 1942). Yet above all human relationships there stands for the mystic the aloneness with the solitary God (see above, Chapter 12).

(5) The splitting and unification of the Church

The history of Christianity bears witness to a continuing *splitting* and differentiation (*ER* 13, 98ff.). The separation of the national Churches from the Eastern imperial Church followed the great schism between Rome and Byzantium in the eleventh century, just as in the West there occurred the separation of the medieval dissident movements from Rome and the formation of the different Reformation Churches in the sixteenth century. These fissiparous tendencies were greater in North America and other countries of the New World where even denominations with a unified confession, such as the Lutherans, fell apart into a great number of separate Churches (Barrett, 1982). The motives for this American fissiparation were partly dogmatic, partly ethical and ethnic in nature. Events such as the American civil war also led to fresh divisions. The greatest proliferation of independent church movements has occurred in the twentieth century, notably in Africa but also world-wide. This development has brought to light a further factor which has been present in Christianity since its inception, namely, the new movement seen as the product of the impact made by an invading church (and state) upon a traditional society and religious cosmology. The prophet-founder, under conditions of strain, formulates a new cosmology incorporating aspects of Christianity, or another major religion, and traditional religion, following an inaugural revelation of basically shamanic character. In this light, Buddhism, Christianity itself, Montanism, Manichaeism, and Islam, to name but a few historic religions or religious movements, may be seen as, initially, independent religious movements.

In opposition to this process of splitting or formation of new religious movements, *unifying forces* have emerged again and again (Rouse and Neill, 1954). In the fifteenth century, for instance, the Council of Constance was concerned to heal the breach between the Eastern and Western Church (Gill, 1959). The unity restored there was only apparent, however. Soon afterwards it broke up. Through the Augsburg Confession with its stress on catholicity and in other ways (McNeill, 1930) the confessors of the Reformation faith sought to restore the unity broken in the Reformation. Only after such attempts had failed did the Augsburg Confession become a confessional creed in the denominational sense (Schlink, 1947, *RGG* 1, 733ff.). In the Marburg colloquy

(1529) Landgraf Philipp sought to create a united Protestant front; it failed, however, through the controversy concerning the question of the Lord's Supper (*RGG* 4, 738). As had already happened with the Lutheran and Roman conversations of the sixteenth century, so also the efforts for unity of a Calixt, Molanus and Leibniz in the seventeenth century remained without success. Even the strong approach of the Anglican Oxford Movement to the Roman Church in the nineteenth century did not lead to unity; nor did the Malines talks on unity in the twentieth (Halifax, 1930). The great ecumenical endeavours of the Faith and Order, and Life and Work movements included only the non-Roman Churches. The first sought on the basis of a minimal programme to reach an organic unity of the Church, the unity of the faith through the recognition of holy Scripture and the Nicene-Constantinopolitan creed, the unity in church order through the recognition of both sacraments (baptism and the Lord's Supper) as also the office of bishop on the basis of apostolic confession. Life and Work was restricted to the celebration of common services of worship and co-operation in questions of social ethics affecting mankind. The *Una Sancta* movement which went back to Protestant suggestions but was mainly borne by Roman circles, again sought to prepare the way to unity through conversations on matters of faith between Roman and non-Roman Christians. This movement received a strong impetus through Pope John XXIII, who saw the unity of Christians as one of the main goals of his pontificate and who created a secretariat for promoting 'the unity of Christians'. The latter has carried on intensive bilateral conversations with other Christian confessions following Vatican II (*ER* 15, 194ff.) which marked the entry of the Roman Church into the *ecumenical movement* (*ER* 5, 17ff.) at every level from that of the local parish to the World Council of Churches' co-ordinating committee, where it has six of the fourteen places. Subsequent popes, especially John Paul II, have also done much for the cause of unity through their world-wide pastoral visits.

(6) The union of all religions

Beyond these movements towards unity within Christianity are those efforts on the part of Christians and others which aim at a union of all religions of the world. Embued with the belief that all religions are only different forms of expression of the one divine logos, Cardinal Nicholas of Cusa in 1453 made the proposal that efforts be made through a free religious dialogue towards the *one* religion and *one* cultus that alone corresponds to the divine unity. A century later the Indian Mogul emperor Akbar, a Muslim with mystical leanings, had 'a house for divine worship' erected in which representatives of the different religions gathered every week for conversations; indeed, he was bold enough to found a 'religion of God' (*RGG* 1, 208f.). The achievement of a higher synthesis between Christianity and Hinduism was also sought by the *Brāhma Samāj* ('city of God') founded by the Brahman Ram Mohan Roy in 1815. Keshub Candra Sen led this community further in the 'Community of God of

the New Covenant', named anew in 1881, in which the different religions were
to find a higher unity. What he envisioned was a universal church of the future
in which, at the same time, the characteristics of every nation should find
expression. Emerging in Persia from Islam, the Bahai religion (Esslemont,
1974; *RGG* 1, 843f.) spread more widely than the Brāhma Samāj. The Bahai
faith also proclaimed the unity of all religions but had a tendency to become a
new religion, a 'super Islam', and to consolidate itself into a theocracy. The *Sūfī
society* (Inayat Khan, 1949; 1978) which goes back to Inayat Khan, is marked
by a much looser social structure although it vividly depicts the unity of
religions in its liturgical symbolism and scripture readings. The *Cao-Dai church*
(*RGG* 1, 1611f.; *LThK* 2, 924) of Vietnam, on the other hand, combines
Confucianism, Buddhism, the Jewish Kabbalah, Spiritualism and Christianity,
but has built up an elaborate hierarchy after the pattern of the Roman Church.

As with the independent religious movements within Christianity (see above,
section five), in all these experiments it is a question of the creation of real
religious communities in the sense of religious communities hitherto, but there
is the important difference that they seek to combine the different world
religions in a larger synthesis. In this century, however, there has arisen a series
of movements which reject the mingling of the different forms of cultus and
belief while at the same time striving after an encounter of the religions on a
higher religious and moral level (*RGG* 4, 876; Peacock, A. R., *c.* 1938). Such an
encounter assumes the awareness of some ultimate common ground; it seeks
this, however, only in occasional common services, but above all by co-
operation in ethical goals affecting all mankind, social and educational ones and
the question of *peace*. The *World Parliament of Religions* (Barrows, 1893)
exercised a pioneering influence in this direction. It came together at the same
time as the Chicago World Exhibition in 1893. The *International Association for
Liberal Christianity and Religious Freedom* pursued a similar aim. There
followed the *Universal Religious Alliance*, founded in 1912, which strove for a
permanent world parliament of religions, the *Religious Federation of Mankind*
founded by Marburg theologian Rudolf Otto, the *International Religious Peace
Conference*, which was held in Geneva in 1929, the *World Congress of Faiths*,
called into being by Francis Younghusband in 1936, the *World Fellowship of
Religions*, founded by Indians in 1958, and the *World Harmony of Religions*
created by Iranshah, an Iranian living in Switzerland. To these we add the
East-West meetings of the Christian Peace Conferences founded by the Prague
theologian, J. L. Hromadka and the inter-religious dialogues held in recent
years by the World Council of Churches and members of individual Churches.
(On another level there is an almost endless number of new religious
movements aspiring to transcend existing religious divisions with the aid of
some new synthesis [Matson, 1979].) All these loose associations appear as a
fulfilment of the historian of religion's prophecy (Müller, 1878) that an élite of
followers of all the world religions would join together in an esoteric
brotherhood, comparable to a medieval crypt, which is the nucleus of the future
Church.

All these religions of unity and movements of religious unity pursue a single goal: to make 'mankind' a reality (Heiler, 1951). In his fourth *Speech on Religion* Schleiermacher said that as each one approached the *Universum* the other comes closer in a unity not of men but of mankind. There is no lack of personalities who have wanted to substitute a new religion, that of humanity for existing ecclesiastical religion. Arising in eighteenth century England, Freemasonry (*RGG* 2, 1114f.; *LThK* 4, 342ff.; *ERE* 6, 118ff.) sought in the external form of an esoteric brotherhood to realize the ideal of humanity and humaneness, of universalism and tolerance. It created a ritual that followed on from the medieval orders and required a secret discipline like the mystery cults of antiquity. But its goal is not a religious one in the sense of salvation but an ethical one in the sense of the service of humanity world-wide. This esoteric universalism led to the sharpest condemnation by the Catholic Church, also by individual Protestant groups, for example the North American Lutherans and, more recently, British Methodists. But the Masonic ideals of universality, tolerance and humanity found enthusiastic support from philosophers, scholars, poets and musicians (Haydn and Mozart). The religion of humanity which Auguste Comte proclaimed venerated mankind as the supreme being. He was followed by the Catholic modernist Alfred Loisy, who in his most radical period approved of Comte's cult as the highest revelation of God. Also a conscious representative of modern Christianity such as Albert Schweitzer stands close to these advocates of a religion of humanity when he describes the future goal of all religion and ethics in the realization of the oneness of humanity. In more recent times Karl Rahner's notion of 'anonymous Christians' or John Hick's of a 'second Christianity' (Hick, 1984) also contain strongly universalist implications that go beyond the confines of ecclesiastical Christianity.

Over against this ecumenical tendency stands an opposite one which aims at a form of religion which conforms to a particular people or race. In a series of Christian countries (Poland, Latvia, Hungary, Brittany and Celtic Britain) smaller groups have attempted to renew the religion of their pre-Christian ancestors and to adapt to serve modern needs. These tendencies on German soil in the context of the nationalist and racialist movement acquired an impetus through Ludendorff, Bergmann (Bergmann, 1934) and, in more refined form, in Jakob Hauer's *German Vision of God* (1934). The efforts of the German Christians (*Deutsche Christen*) were also directed towards this ideal of a national religion. They believed they could give Christianity a form that was suited to the German nation and Aryan race. With the collapse of National Socialism in Germany all these endeavours received a set-back, but they are still to be found in small groups such as the English Odinists. Perhaps the most significant renewal of an ancient national religion was the raising of Japanese Shinto to be the state religion in connection with the nationalist revival under the Meiji dynasty in 1868. Later on the rites of emperor veneration were interpreted as simply an act of loyalty. In 1945 when state Shinto had to be given up again at the request of the victorious American forces, Shintoism became a religious community. It underwent further renewal along with the Japanese independent religious movements or new religions which came out of it, under the influence of Buddhism and Christianity. There was even a tendency in the direction of monotheism.

The development towards ecumenicity cannot be held back. God is either God of the world and the worlds, God of mankind and the cosmos or no God. The national God who arises, lives and dies with a people is no God for a follower of a world religion such as Christianity. Belief in God suffers no restrictions; God is infinite, eternal, he embraces all creatures with the same righteousness and love. In saying this we have gone on beyond the world of religious manifestations to that of religious concepts, indeed to the very object of religion including the Christian religion.

The world of Christian religious manifestations is the most important for the understanding of that religion because it shows it in action in its concreteness. Religion including the Christian is no mere conception of God but intercourse with the God of the present in manifold appearances. All relationships with God, however, are accompanied by definite conceptual forms, the notions of God, the world, man, revelation, salvation, the beyond and final fulfilment.

PART TWO

The World of
Christian Concepts

14

The Deity

(1) The many and the one: the way of causation

Supra-sensory, infinite, ineffable is *The Deity* (Söderblom, 1962; Otto, 1972; James, E. O., 1950; Prestige, 1952; Gilson, 1940; Watson, 1948; Parker, 1952; Baillie, 1939; Temple, 1949; *ER* 4, 264ff.; 6, 1–66; 14, 166ff.). People can therefore have no relationship with the Deity except by symbolic conception. Such symbols are formed in a threefold way. A scholastic formula of Thomas Aquinas calls this the way of causation (*via causālitātis*), the way of eminence (*via ēminentiae*) and that of negation (*via negātionis*).

The thought of causation is a point of departure towards ultimate reality. For religious causality is no mere category of thought but a way to the knowledge of God. For the pious God is the originator of all that occurs in nature, all human doings, the source and the norm of social, moral and religious life, and of artistic creation and enjoyment. The causal conception of God is shared by Christians with those of many other religious traditions. It is found with astonishing clarity in many traditional religions as also among the peoples of antiquity. One of the discoveries of the Study of Religion this century, which began with the Scottish folklorist Andrew Lang, is that of the god of heaven, the primordial father. The ethnologist Theodor Preuss, the Swedish theologian Nathan Söderblom, the Indologist Leopold von Schröder, the Islamist Carl Brockelmann, the Italian historian of religion Raffaele Pettazzoni and the Swedish scholar of Iranian religion Geo Widengren all brought into clearer focus this concept of Deity which was seen by the ethnologist P. Wilhelm Schmidt as testifying to a primordial monotheism. The dwelling-place of the Supreme Being is in heaven; he is closely linked with thunder and lightning. He is thought of as invisible or a form of light, partly endowed with anthropomorphic features, e.g. conceived of as a venerable old man with a long beard. His names include: Father, my Father, our Father, Maker, Creator, Heaven, Chief of heaven, Lord of the heavens, the Old One, the Primordial Old One, the Master up There, the One, the Power. His attributes include: creative power, omnipotence, omniscience (which is linked with his dwelling-place in heaven), righteousness and goodness.

He is the creator of the world and of men, sustainer of what he has made but also 'Destroyer', Lord over life and death. He is the provider of weapons and tools, creator of human social institutions, originator of religious rites, promulgator of the moral law, rewarder and punisher. Whereas individual traditional peoples have a living relationship with him through prayer, the sacrifice of the first-fruits and sacramental consecration of the ethnic group, for others he is a creator who has handed over his work to itself and has gone far away, which is why people in their need turn powers closer at hand – nature deities, 'social' deities, spirits and numina, ancestors. The form of the God of heaven lives on in Chinese religion, in Sumerian and Babylonian religions, in Indo-European and Indo-Iranian ones, and in the religions of the central and western Semites including the Israelites. The function of creating, giving laws, etc. is also ascribed by particular peoples to primordial beings of a partly human, animal or plant form which, in contrast to the being from the highest heaven, die and may be dismembered. Jensen introduced for these the term *Dema* deity used by the Marind-Anim of New Guinea.

In matriarchal cultures, in place of the Deity as Father there stands the Great Mother from whose womb all things and beings have proceeded and into whom they all return (see above, Chapter 1). In the different forms of the mother goddess and fertility goddess this great expression of Deity has maintained her place in the Near East, Egypt and India. If matriarchy is older than patriarchy it must be assumed that the cult of the mother goddess has preceded that of the male 'high god'.

Plurality has entered into the concept of Deity through differentiation: causation becomes thought of as multiple. It becomes split and fragmented (Bertholet, 1932); special functions of the Supreme Being become associated with sacred objects (natural objects and phenomena or else images and symbols made by hand), with living and dead persons (especially ancestors), with local and territorial deities who often are linked with specific cult objects, and abstract deities who personify a divine function or quality. Abstract functional deities are especially numerous among the Greeks, Romans, and Baltic peoples (Usener, 1948). Every aspect and phase of the life of nature and people is regarded as being caused by a special deity, a patron deity or one who controls a particular activity. The whole life of nature and people dissolves into a host of momentary deities. Among the western Semites, every village, every town, every altar on a high place, every house had its local form of deity. Frequently they had no names but were simply known as '*El, Dān, Melekh, Ba'al* (Power, Judge, King, Lord) or combined with the place-names: Ba'al-Pe'or or Melkart (King of the city). Among the Romans, local and protective (tutelary) spirits were called collectively *lares*; in Mazdaism, *fravashi*.

Behind the proliferation of personal deities there arises an impersonal power, that of cosmic order and uniformity, the moral world-order, destiny or *fate* (*ERE* 5, 771–96; 6, 88–104; *HWDA* 7, 1045ff.; Mensching, 1942; *ER* 5, 290ff.). This power is often not independent but is regarded as the expression of a higher or the highest Deity's will. People receive their destiny in absolute impartiality from heaven. Fate in this sense is also divine providence. It is quite relentless: it can cast down the gods from their thrones. It may also be given a secondary personification: *Moira* is the Greek goddess of fate. In early Germanic religion belief in fate is strongly developed. As in Greek religion there occurs a remarkable oscillation between the decree of fate through a personal Deity and an impersonal power. The *Völuspa*, an ancient Germanic epic, shows the gods going to meet an inescapable fate (the *Ragnarök*).

The process of splitting apart, the fissiparous tendency in the concept of Deity, is confronted by another, that of reunification (*RGG* 4, 1109ff.); in both processes Christianity has been involved. The tendency towards unity is directly shown in prayer. The worshipper is inclined to recognize the Deity called upon as the only one. The emphasis upon the Deity's uniqueness is especially characteristic of the poetic hymns of antiquity; it may be often flattery, but behind this is concealed a longing for the oneness of God. One may speak here of a subjective theism (henotheism). This subjective theism helped to prepare the way towards an objective monotheism. The coalescing and re-unifying of deities of different genres was especially promoted by the expansion of kingdoms and empires; they reached their zenith in the Hellenistic syncretism of the Roman empire. Particular deities attracted to themselves attributes, symbols and cult forms of other deities. Thus the deity of the city of Thebes, *Amun*, joined with the sun deity *Ra; Marduk*, the deity of the city of Babylon with older Sumerian and Babylonian deities; and numerous local Semite deities coalesced with the great deities *Anu, Ea, Shamash*, and *Nabū*; Greek local deities did likewise with Zeus; local deities in the Empire, with Jupiter, e.g. Jupiter Dolichenus.

Monotheism proper (*ER* 10, 68ff.) arose in a threefold way. (a) Theology worked to unify the manifold deities in a logical and rational manner. We find such theological speculation in Egypt, Mesopotamia, India and Greece. It regards the plurality of the deities as functions of the one Deity. Isis is described as the many-named and the thousand-named; there are many names of deities, but only one single Deity. (b) The mystical theophanic experience embraces both oneness and the cosmic all. In the Upanishads the deities are part of the great process of the emanation of the *Ātman*. Mystical unification remains down to the present the norm in Hinduism. This form of belief in one God is marked by a boundless tolerance (Mensching, 1966). (c) Completely different from this is the prophetic experience of God's uniqueness in Iran, Israel and Arabia on the part of Zarathustra, Moses and Muhammad. The prophets of Israel were seized by a God who is 'jealous' (Exod. 20.5. cf. 34.14; Josh. 24.19) and suffers no other deities besides himself. 'I am Yahweh your God . . . You shall have no other gods before me', God says through Moses to Israel (Exod. 20.2f). Originally the existence of other gods was not denied; they are mighty beings, but Yahweh is mightier still. Here also one cannot speak of a theoretical monotheism but only of a practical one, a monolatry (*RGG* 4, 1113ff.). Out of this real monotheism developed; the other gods either are reduced to powerless figments of the imagination, simply 'nothings' (*elīlīm*, Isa. 2.8); or else are degraded to bad demons or fallen angels. The reality of the one God crowded out the other gods. The first attitude is that of later Israelite prophetism; the second, which assumes the dualism of God and Satan, is that of Mazdaism, 'late' Judaism and early Christianity. This prophetic monotheism flowed together with speculative monotheism in the Hellenistic world and thus led to the confession of one God, *heis theos*, (*RGG* 4, 1115f.; Pannenberg, 1959).

(2) The supreme good: the way of eminence

The second way to the knowledge of God is the *via ēminentiae*. Besides the ascent from creation to the Creator there follows the ascent from values and value systems to the supreme good (*summum bonum*). Everything that is of value to people: the logically true, the morally good, the aesthetically beautiful, the religiously sacred is summed up in God as their source and norm. The Divine is the measure of all value and disvalue. The highest values are regarded as attributes of God which become identical with God:

(a) God is *power*. *Wakanda, manitu, ngai, mana, ashe* (Dye, 1984; *ER* 11, 467ff.; see above, Chapter 1) are not only names for the object full of power but also refer to the source of that power, the Originator. *Brahman*, the power in the sacrificial formula and in the sacrificing priest, becomes the description of the Deity who is infinite and permeates the cosmic all. Power becomes also the Absolute's manner of operation (*shakti, dunamis*), or the divine gift of grace (*charis, charisma*) from which it comes to characterize the Deity as 'the God of all grace' (1 Pet. 5.10).

(b) God is *beauty*. Traditionally the concept of beauty is associated with light. The original significance of the Vedic Brahman is 'shining', of the Avestan *xvarenah* the 'radiance of the sun', royal glory, often linked with *raya* (might). The primordial significance of the Hebrew *kābōd* is light, radiant glory (of light), the light of Yahweh who descended upon the shrine in the cloud (Exod. 40.34ff.). The Greek *doxa* also is equivalent to radiance and signifies splendour, exaltation, glory, majesty (*ThWNT* 2, 236ff.). There are goddesses of beauty such as the Indian Shrī or Lakshmi. In Neoplatonism the Divine appears simply as beauty. Under its influence Augustine describes God as 'ineffable beauty' (*CD* 9.22). A mystical *hadīth* of Muhammad also declared God to be beauty – one of the 'ninety-nine names' of the Deity.

(c) God is *wisdom and reason*. Closely linked with the Deity is the great regularity and orderliness of the cosmos (*tao, rta, asha*). Wisdom often becomes conceived of as an independent Deity, as in the case of the Babylonian *Marduk* son of Ea, the Egyptian *Thoth* and the Greek *Hermēs*. Wisdom is also thought of as a hypostasis under God, as with the Hebrew *chokmāh* (Baumgartner, 1933) and the Greek *sophia*. The gnostic speculations which fastened onto this concept live on down to the present day in the Russian philosophy of religion of Soloviev and Bulgakov (Bulgakov, 1937). The closest association that God entered into with reason was: 'The *logos* was God' (John 1.1; *ThWNT* 4, 76ff.; *RGG* 4, 434ff.), a connection which reached back to Heraclitus and continued in the Stoics, Plutarch, Philo and Neoplatonism; as well as the Western tendency to interpret religion in terms of its *theo-logy*.

(d) God is *the quintessence of moral values*, the *truth*. The divine truth appears as hypostasis in the Egyptian *ma'at*, the divine righteousness or justice appears similarly in the Greek *Dikē* and the Roman *Justitia*; similar hypostases in Rome are *Fides* and *Fidius* (truth and faithfulness), *Pietas, Pudicitia* (piety, chastity). Mazdaism knows the holy immortals associated with Ahura who is *Mazda* (the wise Lord), Good Mind, Righteousness, Dominion, Devotion, Healing and

Immortality. In Western Christianity the 'cardinal' virtues of prudence, temperance, fortitude and justice were taken over from Plato and Aristotle by Ambrose, Augustine and Aquinas and were widely personalized in medieval art. To these 'natural' virtues were added the 'theological' virtues of faith, hope and love (1 Cor. 13.13; cf. 1 Thess. 1.3; Gal. 5.5f.).

(e) God is *spirit*. Traditionally, the spirit-soul is the power of life, the power of knowing and wanting. *Ātman* becomes identified in the Vedic Upanishads with *Brahman*. The spirit from a numinous soul power becomes a divine hypostasis as in the Hebrew *ruach Yahweh*, the *ruh allāhī* in Islam, and the *pneuma theou* in Hellenism. The *pneuma* is considered the divine or heavenly part of the human being.

(f) God is *love*. In the Greek world God appears as *Erōs* (*RGG* 2, 603ff.; Nygren, 1953). This fertility *daimōn*, son of Aphrodite for the Greek poets, became in Orphic theology the cosmic principle of generation, for Plato the essence of the soul's striving towards primordial beauty. From Neoplatonism this concept made its way into Christianity. Love for the mystic is a power implanted in people by the Deity which draws them back to the primordial One. As the embodiment of compassion and love the great mother Deity appears in the ancient world. In the New Testament God is described as love (*agapē*, 1 John 4.26; *ThWNT* 1, 20ff.; Nygren, 1953). Related to this is the description of the Divine in Mahāyāna Buddhism as the 'Heart of Great Compassion'.

(g) In the description of the Divine as the 'highest good' (*summum bonum*) all values are brought together. This ascription is found among mystics the world over: with Lao-Tzu, in early Buddhism, in the *Bhagavadgītā*, with Plato and Plotinus. It was introduced into Christian theology and piety by Augustine. The view of God as the highest good is expressed most clearly in the prayers of Augustine and Francis of Assisi.

(h) Divine power and love are also expressed more concretely and anthropomorphically in terms of human social relationships (Bertholet, 1934). The oldest of these expressions, that of the mother, derives from the matriarchal culture. The priority of the symbol of the mother is shown especially clearly in the early Greek prayer to Mother Earth and to Zeus: 'Mother Earth, Mother Earth ... O Father, Son of the Earth, Zeus' (Aeschylus). The Deity is addressed as 'Our Mother', also as 'Grandmother' and 'Mistress'. The appellation of Mother has been retained in Hinduism until today for the successors of the pre-Aryan mother goddess who appears under the names of *Mahādevī, Kalī, Durgā, Candī, Pārvatī*, etc. Great mystics also make use of the mother symbol, as with Lao-tzu and Julian of Norwich, Indian Christians such as Nārāyan Vāman Tilak and Sadhu Sundar Singh, indeed, even Israelite prophets of salvation (Isa. 49, 15; 66.13).

From early patriarchal culture has proceeded the ascription to God of 'Father', 'Our Father', occasionally also 'Grandfather', as also with different ascriptions of dominion: Chief, Lord, King. Besides these may be set the descriptions of Deity as Beloved, Bride and Bridegroom (see above, Chapter 7), as also the ascription of Friend (Zarathustra). The double ascription of God (often the cosmic all Deity) as 'Father-Mother' is found especially in India, in West Africa (Mawu-Lissa of the Fon people), and also in the Hellenistic area, as in the hymns of the Christian Neoplatonist Synesius: 'Thou art Father, art also Mother, a male and also a female.' Indeed, mystical worshippers link together in their invocation of Deity all social relationships, as with David of Augsburg: 'Thou art (the soul's) Lord, thou art her servant, thou her father, thou her mother, thou her child, thou her brother, thou art her most chaste and sweetest loving divine Spouse.'

In many religions, in Judaism, in early Christianity and in Islam the Deity becomes conceived of in male symbols. Even so as late as the fifth century BCE the Jewish community of Elephantine in Egypt still venerated two consorts of Yahweh. In the Christianity of East and West the one-sided male concept of Deity was expanded through the veneration of the Mother of God (see above, Chapter 12). The latter becomes addressed as 'My Mistress' (Madonna), 'Our Mistress', 'Our Queen', 'Mother of Heaven', 'Our Mother', 'Our Lady'. Primordial religion breaks through in Catholic hymns to Mary. For example: 'Our tears and prayers the Son will heed, If Mother for us intercede' (*RB* 1087). In medieval piety Christ is portrayed as a strict judge, Mary as a mild intercessor beside him. In the Middle Ages the faithful were not afraid to call Mary 'Goddess', as in the case of Mechthild of Magdeburg (see also above, Chapter 12).

Although the Reformation opposed every tendency to turn the Mother of God into a divine figure, a biblical and purified veneration of Mary still obtained in Lutheranism. The Apology of the Augsburg Confession (a. 21, 21) names Mary as 'most worthy of the greatest honour'. The cult of the mother goddess returns in Protestant poetry as when Goethe places in the mouth of the heavenly chorus the words: 'Virgin, Mother, Queen, Goddess have mercy on me'. Modern religious movements such as the Germanic piety of a Bergmann (Bergmann, 1934) sought to renew the ancient religion of the mother. They required that no god should be worshipped save 'the eternal Motherhood which bore us'. Modern feminist writers have also sought to uncover the religion of matriarchy (Davis, 1971) and to explore its revolutionary accents (Daly, 1979).

The mystics were aware that the nature of the Divine could not be exhausted either in causally related concepts or in ascriptions of value. They were never tired of stressing that God is exalted above everything of value and is beyond all value systems. The prepositions 'other than', 'beyond' and 'above' belong to the favourite expressions of the mystics. A hymn of Gregory Nazianzus begins: 'O thou beyond all that is, how could I name thee differently?' God is 'above beauty', 'above that which is' (Dionysius the Areopagite). In another way the mystics bring to expression the inadequacy of all ascriptions of value, namely through bringing together contrary statements. God is the 'coincidence of opposites' (Nicholas of Cusa), always active always quiescent (Augustine); 'His working is his resting and his resting his work' (Angelus Silesius).

(3) The wholly other: the way of negation

An even stronger form of expression than the way of eminence is that of negation. God is the wholly other (Otto, 1932[a] and 1937), 'different, totally different from anything we know on earth' (Augustine), the complete 'emptiness' in Buddhism, indeed the 'Not God' of Meister Eckhart. Through 'not-knowing' God becomes known (Augustine). 'Through the uttering of that which God is not we come to know what God is' (Dionysius).

Prophetic piety similarly stresses the absolute exaltation and unapproachableness of God: 'God dwells in unapproachable light' (1 Tim. 6.16), yet it does not seek to circumscribe the nature of God through negation or by going beyond comparisons. Instead it expresses this in positive statements. The prophetic conception of God is above all marked by the stress on his activity. God is effectual will, and indeed moral will, which is made known in a twofold manner: in wrath and compassion, in judgement and grace. Wrath and grace are, it is true, in the final analysis only personal paraphrases of the *tremendum* and *fascinans* which are the two sides of the numinous power (Otto, 1972).

(4) Personalism and impersonalism in the concept of deity

In all religions including Christianity the concept of God manifests a double tendency: towards personalism and impersonalism. According to Thomas Aquinas the person is the most perfect being that exists in the whole of nature and indeed of rational nature. Over against this must be set the mystical thinkers' assertion that the notion of the person presupposes a twofoldness whereas perfection consists in oneness. The struggle between personalism and impersonalism extends throughout the entire history of religions. In the traditional religions of antiquity already, the belief in an impersonal power, the *numen* (see above, Chapter 1), and a personal spirit-being continually intersect. The Germanic word for God (OHG *got*, Anglo-Saxon *god*, Old Norse *gud*) is neuter and possibly goes back to an original Indo-Germanic *ghu-tóm* (Sanskr. *hutám*), meaning a being called on or the being to whom one sacrifices. It first became masculine under Christian influence.

One of the most remarkable endeavours devoted to working out the impersonal elements of the Divine is found in India. The *brahman* of the Upanishads is neuter, it is called 'the one without a second'. Shankara describes the Absolute as *advaitam*, simply the 'secondless'. The personal concept of God (*Ishvara*, Lord) is, it is true, also indispensable to him as a preparatory pedagogical step towards the pure knowledge of God, but it is only a part of *māyā* (the world of illusion). Over against this pure monistic concept of God Rāmānuja fought for the personality of God: *brahman* is indeed 'secondless' but 'characterized secondlessness', his personality is reality not the illusion of imperfect recognition. In a still more extreme form impersonalism appears in the idea of God in early Buddhism inasmuch as here every statement about the

Absolute is rejected; all the same, as the goal of salvation *Nirvāna* is a metaphysical absolute which is described in very similar terms to the Divine of the mystics (Glasenapp, 1954). Mahāyāna Buddhism has nevertheless returned to a metaphysical notion of God similar to the Vedantic one; the absolute appears indeed in personal form as 'Primordial Buddha' or 'Great Buddha' or 'Sun Buddha' (*ERE* 1, 47f.; 93ff.).

In Christian theology and mysticism a continuous, secret contest took place between personalism and impersonalism. The tendency to impersonalism in it is very strong; Dionysius the Areopagite speaks of 'the Deity' which is above all things and above all beings. A church Father such as Augustine, indeed even a naive saint like Francis of Assissi, make use in their prayers of neuter terms which make reference to God, such as 'truth', 'goodness', 'justice', 'wisdom', 'quietness', 'beauty', 'all good'; and a mystic like Catherine of Siena describes God chiefly with images taken from nature such as: 'sea', 'ocean', 'abyss', 'wilderness', 'fire', 'light' and 'sun' (Hügel, 1923, 1, 245). These expressions had been employed by German medieval mystics as well. The *doyen* of the scholastics defined God as Being (*esse*); Meister Eckhart repeated this 'teaching of the great master that God is pure being' but goes beyond it to: 'He is high above all being.'

In the doctrine of the Trinity the personal and impersonal elements were brought into harmony through the work of Greek and Latin theology (Kretschmar, 1956). The Greek liturgy ceaselessly praises the 'triad equal in substance and indivisible'; The 'Athanasian' Creed used in the Latin liturgy sees the nature of the catholic faith in the veneration of 'the one God in trinity and the trinity in unity'. This trinitarian theology was not only developed under gnostic and Neoplatonist influence, it also had as its background the belief in triads shared by the history of religions as a whole (see also above, Chapter 4; Gerlitz, 1960). Closest to it stand the metaphysical triads in Lao-Tzu, in the Upanishads and in Plotinus. The earlier Christian belief in the Trinity is predominantly soteriological and subordinationist (the Father is greater than the Son who again is greater than the Spirit). But later it becomes metaphysical and homoousian: all three persons are co-eternal and co-equal (Athanasian Creed). Originally an own activity was ascribed to the individual divine persons, but in the later theology of the Trinity its activity, viewed externally, was taken as a unified whole and the works declared to be of the individual divine persons were now explained as being simply 'appropriations'. Both the great church Fathers and medieval theologians (Augustine, Thomas, Bonaventure and Meister Eckhart) and also modern theologians have sought to explain the mystery of the Trinity in a special way, as with the Eastern Orthodox philosopher Soloviev, the Roman Catholic theologians M.-J. Scheeben and Karl Rahner, Anglican scholars (Hodgson, 1946; Brown, 1985) and also the Christian Brahmin Sannyāsi Brahmabandhav Upādhyāya.

The meaning of the Christian belief in the Trinity lies in the fact that God is endless fulness and that he bears within himself his own life. Consequently he does not necessarily need the world and mankind. The Trinity lies in the middle between an unco-ordinated plurality of deities, diffused monotheism and pantheism on the one hand, and a rigid monotheism on the other. It also lies between a deism which would separate God from his creation, and an anthropomorphism which sees in God only the one who ministers to human needs.

15

Creation

(1) Concepts of creation

The transcendent reality enters in a manifold way into the immanence of space and time: in creation, in revelation and in salvation; in nature and in human life, in history and in the individual's religious life.

In the religious sphere the *creation* (*ERE* 4, 226ff.; *LThK* 9, 460ff.; *RGG* 5, 1496ff.; Bavink, 1950; Barbour, 1968; Peacock, 1979; Moltmann, 1985; *ER* 13, 121ff.) is not simply a philosophical explanation of the world but an experience of faith: the Christian creed begins with the words: 'I believe in God the Father, maker of heaven and earth'. Creation is the subject of numerous myths of traditional peoples and those of antiquity (see above, Chapter 8). The first book of the Bible contains two creation narratives: the older which stems from the Yahwist source and the beginning of which has been broken off, manifests a simple poetic character (Gen. 2), the later one from the Priestly codex (Gen. 1) a more abstract theological character.

The creation is presented in at least four different ways: (a) as a spontaneous formation. According to the Vedic cosmology the cosmic egg divides into two parts; the golden half becomes heaven, the silver one earth, the yolk the sun (Eliade, 1979). According to Egyptian cosmology the sun god Ra also comes out of the cosmic egg, likewise according to Orphic cosmology the gold-winged *Phanes* of the Greeks. Also under the concept of spontaneous formation falls that of a differentiation of the one Divine One into the plurality of individual things and beings. According to the Upanishads all worlds and beings proceed out of the *Brahman* like a spider's web out of the spider and the sparks out of the fire. A second way is (b) as giving birth or begetting through deities. According to the Japanese myth (Eliade, 1979) *Izanagi* and *Izanami* (heaven and earth) climb down to the ocean island which had risen out of a drop of salt; there they copulate, *Izanami* gives birth to the eight islands of Japan together with mountains and rivers, and also the gods at whose head are the sun goddess *Amaterasu* and the moon god. Then she dies 'in childbed' and disappears into the underworld. Besides begetting in the normal way may be set generation in the form of self-copulation by an androgynous creator deity, as in the case of *Prajāpati* in the Upanishads or *Zurvan* in the Iranian tradition. In a more spiritualized form the idea of begetting the world lives on in the doctrine of emanation; in Neoplatonist metaphysics which has influenced Christian thought, the *nous* proceeds from the primordial oneness (see above, Chapter 4), out of the *nous* the *psuchē* (world soul) and out of it, finally, *hulē* (matter). According to Ramanuja creation consists in the unfolding of the body of God into the plurality of name and form.

A third way is (c) as the fashioning of existing primordial matter, as victory over the dark primordial powers, as the forming of chaos into cosmos. The Babylonian Marduk conquers the abyss (*Apsu*), kills the primordial serpent *Tiāmat* and forms the world out of it (see above, Chapters 1 and 8). According to the Mithraic cosmology the world is fashioned out of the dead primeval ox, according to the Germanic cosmology out of the giant *Ymir*, according to the Platonic view the Demiurge creates the world out of primal stuff according to the pattern of the world ideas. Finally, there is (d) the way of creation out of nothing through divine magical power, be it by means of asceticism of will, of sacrifice, of thought, word or song. This idea of *creatio ex nihilo* ('Let there be light; and there was light') was adopted into 'late' Judaism through the Priestly codex (Gen. 1) and in this way became a Christian doctrine. No second independent principle is ranged here alongside God (but see under (3) below). Early on this biblical view of the Creator became linked with the Platonic idea of the Demiurge and the Neoplatonic idea of emanation. The spiritual creation in pre-existence or eternity precedes the creation of the visible world. The self-knowledge of the eternal God is at the same time the knowledge of all possible worlds; in the creation the eternal cosmic plan of God is realized. The created world is therefore bound up with the Creator by the 'analogy of being' (*LThK* 1, 468ff.). The creation is thus not God but a likeness of his eternal wisdom and beauty; the individual creatures are shadows, resonances, pictures, vestiges, images and plays (Bonaventura).

According to views inclining towards pantheism the reason for the creation lies in a dark impulse, an illusory thought (*maya*), a game (the *līla* of the Indian *bhakti*), an overflowing of the fulness of the primordial unity (Neoplatonism). Theism sees in the creation a free act of God which springs from an inexplicable act of the will (Augustine) or from the desire to manifest his glory and permit other beings to participate in his own beatitude and blessedness. According to Thomas Aquinas the objective goal of creation is the honour of God, the subjective motive is the communication of his own perfection. In Islamic theology the will to self-communication as the motive for the divine creation also apears. A *hadīth* on which pantheistic mysticism is fond of relying has Allah say: 'I was a hidden treasure and wanted to be known, so I created the world.'

The creation of *man* is seen as a special divine event. It is thought of like the cosmic creation, partly as proceeding immediately out of a sacred object (a stone, living being, a tree, an animal), partly as the shaping of some existing material by a divine originator, the earth in the biblical creation myth (Gen. 2.7), congealed blood in the Quranic one.

Individual religions of salvation such as Jainism and Theravāda Buddhism have indeed a world view, but know of no creator either in the pantheist or the theistic sense. Full of suffering the world of the cycle of births and rebirths stands beside the sphere of Nirvāna without any relation to it. The former is symbolized by a monster which holds the world tablet in its claw, the latter by paradise on the mountain top of the universe, the further bank of a river and the solitary island in the midst of the cosmic flood. Early Christian Marcionism separates creation and redemption by ascribing creation to an inferior demiurge and redemption to the 'strange God' who simply wants to save mankind (Harnack, 1921).

(2) Spirit beings and angels

Besides the Deity stand spirit beings or angels (*RGG* 2, 1298ff.; *ER* 1, 282ff.) which are often subject to the Deity but mostly are superior to people. The Supreme Being, for traditional societies, is already surrounded by a family or court. The Holy Immortals who surround Ahura Mazda are limited to six. The *deva* similarly occupy a special place in Buddhism. They are higher spirit beings which lead the life of the blessed in the different heavens and participate also in the life of mankind, especially in that of the Buddha, but are not deities who hear prayers in the sense of other religions.

In addition to the angels who belong to the proximity of the Deity there are the protective spirits who give help to people. Besides their presence in Amerindian religions, Germanic religions, African religions, Babylonian, and Iranian religion where the *fravashi*, originally spirits of the dead, defend not only the living but also the whole sacred cosmos against hostile demons, a striking development in the belief in angels occurred on Jewish, Christian and Islamic soil. The angels are assistants at the throne of God, as such they are God's 'sons' (Job 1.6), at the same time they are his messengers, companions and helpers of men (protective, escorting, servant angels) and also intercessors with God on their behalf. The increase in the transcendence of God led to the development in 'late' Judaism of an elaborate doctrine of angels; one began to distinguish different angelic choirs and to ascribe to prominent individual angelic beings theophoric names such as Michael, Gabriel, Raphael and Uriel (*RAC* 5, 239–58; *ODCC ad loc.*). In the New Testament (*RGG* 2, 1301ff.; *RAC* 5, 97ff.; *ODCC* 52f.; Langton, 1937; Caird, 1956) the angels received the further function of accompanying the Messiah at the last judgement. This *parousia* of the *Kurios* is anticipated in the Christian service of worship. Consequently, in the prayers and hymns the angels are praised as the companions of Christ who is making his appearance. This is especially the case in the 'hymn of the cherubim' which is sung in the Eastern Orthodox liturgy at the Great Entry with the prepared eucharistic gifts, as also in the Isaianic threefold 'holy' (Isa. 6.3) with which the congregation receives the great prayer of thanksgiving.

The angels also receive the soul at death; they are therefore especially called upon in the Western Church's prayers for the dying. Since as heavenly beings 'they neither marry nor are given in marriage' (Mark 12.25) they are an example for the monks (see above, Chapter 11). Christian piety developed a cult of angels analogous to the cult of saints (*RGG* 2, 465f.), Christian theology an entire doctrine of angels (*LThK* 2, 867ff.; *HWDA* 2, 823ff.). In conformity to the Jewish tradition the angels were at first thought of as being not completely without a body and as late as Augustine, as being clothed with a fine astral body. This was because of their relation to the stars. They were also thought of as having a body of fire, hence their red vestments in Greek icons. The division of the angels into nine choirs: Angels, Archangels, Powers, Forces, Rulers, Principalities, Thrones, Cherubim, Seraphim, came about through the Pseudo-Dionysius Areopagite and was firmly established in the West through Gregory the Great. Angels became favourite figures in Christian legend and art (*RGG* 2, 467ff.; *LThK* 2, 872ff.; *RAC* 5, 258–322).

The veneration and invocation of angels as practised in the Eastern and Western Church was abolished by the Reformation. But Luther thanked God that he had created them for our benefit. In this sense angels are often mentioned in Protestant hymns. The Enlightenment believed it had to declare as superfluous the existence of angels along with its denial of the devil. Classical and Romantic poetry, however, held firmly on the idea of angels, as the prologue to Goethe's Faust makes clear. Neo-orthodox theology has once more conceded an important place to the doctrine of angels (*RGG* 2, 467ff.; Barth, *KD* III, 3, Sn.51), as have also the independent African Churches (Turner, H. W., 1967). The Jewish and Christian doctrine of angels was taken up by Islamic teaching and developed further. The angels, made of a fine light substance, are divided into seven classes and praise God from eternity to eternity. They remain in a certain attitude of prayer and have no free-will of their own. Nineteen watch over hell; two of four angels serve people as guardian angels, while both the recording angels, seated at their shoulders, write up their good and bad deeds. At the head of the angels stands Gabrā'īl who brings God's revelation to the prophet. Beside him Mikāl, lord of the powers of nature, Isrāfīl, the angel with the trumpet at the last judgement, and the angel of death with four thousand wings.

(3) Evil spirits and demons

Besides the good spirits there are the evil ones or *demons* (*ERE* 4, 565–636; *LThK* 3, 139ff.; Bamberger, 1952; *ER* 4, 282ff.). In traditional societies and in antiquity these include fearful spirits of the earth and forest, spirits of the dead who wander about without rest, partly also evil powers causing sickness and disease, madness and death, also natural disasters, floods and earthquakes; finally sex demons, embodying the tabu power of sexuality, called in the Middle Ages *incubī* and *succubī*, who give rise to sexual dreams, threaten bridal couples, disturb nuptials and pregnancy. (The Tobias nights after the wedding are helpful as a protection against these spirits.) The fear of demons is pronounced in traditional religion and in the religions of antiquity, including the Babylonian, Vedic, early Iranian, Arabian traditional religion and Islam (*jinn*).

The evil powers are summed up in a concrete personal figure, the *devil* or *Satan* (*HWDA* 10, 347ff.; *RGG* 6, 704ff.; *ThWNT* 7, 151ff.; Russell, 1977; *ER* 4, 319ff.; 15, 81ff.). Amongst some traditional peoples the devil is regarded as the originator of evil who disturbs the good works of the Supreme Being (Amerindian Algonquin, Bulgarian creation myths); in India *Māra*, god of death, god of desire, lord of this world and the tempter who sought to hold the Buddha back from enlightenment and from proclaiming the way to it. The strongest dynamic is shown by *Angra Mainyu* (*Ahrimān* of the later Avesta) the evil spirit in Zoroastrian belief who sets something evil over against the good that Ormazd creates. In early Israelite religion belief in demons (Langton, 1949) is not so strongly developed as in Babylonia or Iran. Besides the good angels there are bad ones, such as the destroying angel; the *shēdīm* are alien deities; *Līlīth* (spirit of the night) is a female demon (Bab. *ardat līlī*). The idea of the devil entered into Judaism from Persia; it received different names: Beelzebub (God of flies or dung; *ThWNT* 2, 69ff. (*diabolos*)), Belial (*RGG* 1, 1025f.); his most common name is *Satan* (*ThWNT* 7, 151ff.). The latter was originally considered as one of the 'sons of Yahweh' from his court (Job. 1.6ff.). His task is that of an accuser, 'a heavenly attorney general', a seducer and executor of the blows of fate. Under Iranian influence late Jewish faith received a strongly dualistic character. The dualism of God and Satan is shown with immense vividness in the case of Jesus and in the whole of earliest Christianity. Christ has come 'to destroy the works of the devil' (1 John 3.8). Jesus struggles against Satan in the desert (Matt. 4, Luke 4). His driving out of devils is a constant attack on the rule of the Evil One, works for the setting up of God's Kingdom (Luke 11.20). Exorcism became an essential part of early church ritual (see above, Chapter 9). Satan also occupied an important place in Christian thought and life. Hermits in the desert and monks in their cells believed that they were persecuted by him. Theologians created a whole *demonology* (*LThK* 10, 10ff.): devils are fallen angels who revolt against God, Lucifer who aspired to equality with God at their head, and were cast by Michael into hell. The angels' sin is pride. In popular piety belief in the devil was bound up with pre-Christian belief in the spirits. Poetry and art provided symbols for belief in the devil and kept it alive. The devil also made his appearance in mystery plays and masked processions. Belief in the devil took on its worst forms in the persecution of witches (Lea, 1939; *RGG* 3, 308ff.) who were seen as brides of the devil (see also above, Chapter 12). Luther defended the realistic belief in the devil. The three forces hostile to God are the world, the flesh and the devil. In Protestant hymnody, beginning with Luther, the devil appears quite realistically: 'The ancient prince of hell/hath risen with purpose fell . . ./on earth is not his fellow' (*CH* 526).

A reaction arose in the Enlightenment (*RGG* 5, 1066) against the exaggerations and the crudities of the belief in the devil. The latter appeared to it as a pathetic form of madness on the part of an unenlightened age. With the philosopher Kant, out of a person came a principle: 'radical evil'. Schelling followed Jacob Boehme by transferring evil into the primary cause of the world itself. Modern Protestant theology (Schleiermacher, Ritschl) went further along the way of the Enlightenment inasmuch as they recognized the reality of the power of sin working against God but not the existence of a personal devil. In recent days a deeper understanding has been reached of the 'mystery of lawlessness' (2 Thess. 2.7). For many modern people the reality of the Satanic has emerged in the totalitarian powers of the twentieth century in whom megalomania, cruelty and sadism were covered with a mantle of deceptions and nationalist, superficiality humanist, pseudo-morality (Tillich, 1926; Bernhart, 1950). Also widely seen as Satanic is the constant possibility of a nuclear holocaust.

Islam took over Judaism's view of Satan together with the word (*Shaitan, iblis = diabolos*) and linked it to the early Arabian concept of *jinn*. The legend of Satan found its way into the Qur'ān out of the apocryphal Life of Adam and Eve (15). According to this legend Satan, alone among the angels, refused to worship Adam because he had been created out of earth and not like himself out of fire (*suras* 7, 11; 38, 77). Islamic mysticism gave this idea a spiritual interpretation: Satan is the infinitely loving one who did not want to worship a second person beside God, he is the one true monotheist, the representative of absolute reason who was incapable of recognizing the divine spark in the form of man; he is also the prover and tester of man in the sense of the original Jewish conception.

With belief in the reality of the demonic is bound up the concept of demonic possession, i.e. a person's being filled with the power of Satan (*RGG* 1, 1093). On the one hand the possessed is deprived of freedom, on the other hand such persons possess the power to effect miracles. In his portrayal of demonic man, Goethe makes clear that Zoroastrian and early Christian dualism correspond more to reality than the monism of the Enlightenment: 'An immense power emanates from them, they exercise an incredible power over creatures, indeed even over the elements ... Nothing can overcome them except the universe itself against which they have taken up arms' (*Dichtung und Wahrheit*, Bk 20).

(4) Human beings

Besides the invisible spirits, good and bad, there stand in the visible order – *human beings* (Wach, 1932; Stevenson, 1979; Dodd, Bultmann et al., 1952; *RGG* 1, 414ff.). With body and soul they belong to the two worlds of the visible and the invisible. Precisely because of this joining of nature and the spiritual they are called the 'crown of creation' (*kosmos kosmou*; Brightman, 1896, 16). Human persons unite in themselves, however, not only the visible and invisible world but also the divine and the demonic. Their divine and demonic nature is vividly depicted in the Orphic myth where the human person is created with a divine and a titanic element.

The invisible, divine element in human beings, the *soul* (Van der Leeuw, 1964, 311ff.), appears at first as magical power in numerous power-laden parts or functions of the human body, the blood, the breath; also in the head, toes, etc., and in the shadow and name; and in animals who are associated with humans, familiars such as the snake, wolf, dove; and in wraiths or doppelgangers as in the Egyptian *ka*, the Roman *genius*, the Germanic *fylgya* and Yoruba *orí*. Animals and guardian souls fall under the concept of 'external soul'. Frequently human persons are thought of as bearers of many souls (as with the plurality of souls in Yoruba traditional anthropology). The soul is also conceived of as capable of transformation (*HWDA* 8, 1623ff.); it takes on the form of an animal temporarily, for example, that of a wolf (lycanthropy), or migrates after death into a new body, and that of a human, animal or plant (metempsychosis, transmigration of souls, reincarnation). Because the power and divinity are transferred from the body's soul to the spirit soul, the body tends to be devalued and there arises that dualism of body and soul where the soul takes its rise in the heavenly world and as a result of a fall sinks down into the material world; it languishes there as in a prison or in a grave.

In mysticism the view of the soul's divinity reaches its apogee. According to the teaching of the Upanishads the $\overline{A}tman$ is identical with the *Brahman* that governs the cosmic all. The Neoplatonic doctrine of the divine or middle point of the soul was made a part of Christian mysticism above all by the church Father Augustine. The innermost part of the soul is described by the medieval mystics as the 'holy of holies'. Meister Eckhart speaks of the ground of the soul which 'blooms and greens as God in all his Deity and the Spirit in God'. Not only mysticism but also the prophetic traditions know of the soul's likeness to God. According to the older Israelite creation myth, which the Qur'ān (38, 72) took over, God breathes into man his breath of life (Gen. 2.7); according to the later, more abstract account God created man 'in his own image' (Gen. 1.27). Christian theology erects on this the doctrine of the *imāgo* and *similitudo Dei* in man (Niebuhr, 1947, 1, 161ff.). Thomist theology interprets the *imāgo Dei* as a gift of grace which is added to man's natural endowment (*dōnum supernāturāle, superadditum*; Troeltsch, 1931) whereas according to the view of the Reformers it is given already at the creation of man.

With human beings' power and divinity is contrasted their sinfulness, lostness and mortality. The sense of their depravity is often stronger than that of their likeness to God. The *concept of sin* (*ERE* 11, 528ff.; *ThWNT* 1, 267ff.; Otto, 1932b; Thomas, E. E., 1926; *ER* 13, 325ff.) is a universal one. As with the concept of Deity and that of sacred action there intersect constantly in the idea of sin, personal and impersonal elements. On the one hand sin appears as dangerous, 'contagious fuel', as pollution, staining or magical chaining, as tabu (*ER* 14, 233.); on the other hand it appears as the anger of a personal Deity through the transgression of his or her commands, be they ethical, social or cultic. The tabu character is especially clear in sexual sin which early on became, with cultic sin, counted among the chief forms of sin. Both these strands are taken further in the world religions. The concept of sin as a powerful substance lived on in the early Indian doctrine of *karma* (*ERE* 7, 673ff.; *RGG* 3, 1155f.; *ER* 8, 261ff.) which was created through the act of sinning and was expressed in rebirth after death (reincarnation); also in the Manichaean concept of sin as a substance of which all subsequent anti-Manichaean polemic, even that of Augustine, remained a prisoner, when it is taught that sin is inherited through the act of copulation (Adam, 1958). The personal view of the excitation of God's wrath through the breaking of his commands finds its complete form in the Judeo-Christian-Islamic doctrine of sin: sin is wilful disobedience of God, renunciation of God and immediately directed against God: 'Against thee, thee only have I sinned' (Ps. 51.4). In Jainism and Buddhism, where the personal concept of Deity is lacking, sin is seen as disturbing the eternal moral order, the *dharma*. Ethical refinement also moves sin from the external action to the inner intention and places the sinful thought on the same level as the sin in word and deed, for example, with particular sharpness in Jesus' Sermon on the Mount (Matt. 5.21–8). The ancient division of sins into deeds, words and thoughts is central to the Zoroastrian 'good thoughts, good words and good deeds', and is the formula of the Christian confession of sin: 'I have sinned much in thought (in) word and (in) deed'. While prophetic piety regards sin as a reality albeit a purely spiritual, volitional one, Neoplatonic mysticism considers sin to be something 'negative', a 'deprivation', 'absence of the good', hence 'nothing belonging to the external world', but 'something present only in the soul', something 'accidental', indeed, as something virtually 'non existent'. This view of Plotinus (*Enn.* 1, 8, 11; 9, 8) returns with Origen (*Joann.* 2, 7; 20, 9, 2) who with Dionysius the Areopagite and also with Augustine describes evil as 'without nature' and as 'turning away from God'. The last defines evil as 'being far from God', as 'perversity of the will' and as 'absence of good', or, expressed in a metaphor, as darkness in the sense of the absence of light.

The origin of sin is one of the most difficult problems with which the religions have been occupied, in conjunction with the question concerning the origin of suffering and death. The concept is widespread of a paradisal state, originally without suffering and death, which was brought to an end by the *fall* (*ERE* 5, 701–16; *RGG* 6, 476ff.; *NCE* 5, 814ff.; *ER* 5, 256ff.). Sin is ascribed to evil spirits or animal demons such as the serpent (Gen. 3.1ff.; see above, Chapters 1 and 8). According to the myth recounted in the Buddhist Pāli canon, people lived originally as spirit beings, formed out of light, sexless, in innocence and blessedness in the earth's atmosphere. Because they tasted the sweet cream that was being formed on earth they were seized by 'thirst'. They descended to the earth, became ever more material and lost their power of light. They became differentiated into both sexes and allowed themselves to be led astray into sin through concupiscence. In this way suffering came into the world. According to the Platonic view also mankind fell out of the heavenly world of ideas into the material world because of desire. Hermetic mysticism developed Platonic thought further: inflamed by *erōs* man descends from heaven to the earth and water and embraces unreasoning nature; the latter draws him to himself, and he begets humankind. The creator God says to man these words: 'The man with reason should know that he is immortal and that the origin of death is *erōs*' (*Poimandres* 1, 18).

The biblical myth of the fall became the basis for the theological speculation of Romans, chapter five, according to which sin came into the world, and through sin death, through one man. In developing this line of thought the church Fathers assumed a primordial sin of Adam and death through inheritance. But it was Augustine, who for many years was a follower of

Manichaeism, who created the doctrine of inherited or 'original' sin (Williams, 1927). This original sin is transmitted from one generation to another through the desire which expresses itself in sexual union. It is interpreted as one's own culpable sin, therefore children who have died in original sin without baptism are like active sinners damned to eternal punishment in hell, though of the mildest kind. The Augustinian doctrine of the radical depravity of man was moderated by medieval scholasticism whereby the effect of original sin was limited to deprivation of the supernatural gifts of grace and weakening of man's natural capabilities of reason and free will (Aquinas). The Augustinian view was renewed, indeed made even more one-sided in Lutheranism and Calvinism, and also in Jansenism. Luther even denied to mankind freedom of the will; the latter is like a mount on which sits either God or the devil. The Eastern Church has remained free of the Augustinian doctrine of original sin; and even a Western humanistic theologian such as Erasmus called it a mere theological hypothesis. Islam which was under the influence of Judaism and Eastern Christianity, also knows nothing of a doctrine of original sin.

16
Revelation

(1) Mystical and prophetic forms of revelation

The belief in creation contains within it the belief in *revelation* (*RGG* 4, 1597–1611; Söderblom, 1962; Arberry, 1957; Bultmann, 1962; Baillie, 1956; Brunner, 1946; *ER* 6, 313ff.; 12, 356ff.). On the soil of an optimistic world-view such as the Confucian such a belief in revelation is considered sufficient. According to K'ung-fu-tzu heaven does not 'speak', it reveals itself only in the constant order of nature. Where evil and suffering, sin and death are experienced as painful questions about the meaning of existence people may find the 'basic revelation' insufficient; they then yearn for a renewed and continued revelation of the Deity's power, wisdom, justice and goodness.

In oracular divination continuous revelation ensues in which the Deity discloses the future or the divine will through the mouth of seers and seeresses or by mechanical manipulation of the divining objects (see Chapter 8, above). Another form of revelation is the acts of fate and destiny, whether of suffering or joy, which are allotted to people by divine predestination (see above, Chapter 14). Of special importance is the manifest intervention of Deity to reward the good and punish the wicked. According to Hindu belief Vishnu assumes visible form when evil threatens to gain the upper hand in the world. These forms of appearance—the expression incarnation is misplaced—are described as *avatāra* (descents). The most important of these are the forms of the fish, tortoise, boar, lion, dwarf, *Rama* with the hatchets, *Ramacandra*, Krishna, Buddha and *Kalki* who rides on the white horse with a sword of lightning (cf. Rev. 19.11, 15).

Distinct from these external forms of revelation is *inner revelation*. It may consist of an inner voice as in the intervention of the *daimonion* which Socrates experiences (Söderblom, 1962, 225ff.). Such an interior revelation is represented above all by mystical illumination. In a state of ecstasy, the seers of the Vedic Upanishads have visions in their innermost souls of the *Ātman* and its unity with the cosmic *Brahman*. In the *sammā-sambodhi* ('perfect illumination') Gautama Buddha had a vision of the four sacred truths of suffering, the cause of suffering, the overcoming of the cause of suffering and the way to its destruction. After the illumination Buddha resisted the temptation to keep this saving knowledge for himself; out of sympathy with the beings who would perish without the proclamation of the sacred knowledge, he decided to engage in public preaching. In Mahāyāna Buddhism this sympathy is projected into the metaphysical realm as the eternal 'heart of great mercy'. This eternal compassion has endless manifestations. Just as the radiant moonlight is revealed in every body of water, in the muddy rain-pool as in the crystal clear mountain lake and in the oceans of the world, so the endless divine love is revealed in every stage of religion (Suzuki). These manifestations bear, it is true, an illusory, docetic character. According to the teaching of Mahāyāna the primordial Buddha has a threefold body (*trikāya*); in the *dharma-kāya* (body of salvation) he is the absolute, eternally real in his pure spirituality; in the *sambhoga-kāya* (body of blessedness) he appears in the paradise of bliss beyond this world, and in the many *nirmāna-kāya* (bodies of transformation) he shows himself on earth. Both the last forms of appearance are not, however, as real as the first one, but are part of *māyā* (world illusion).

Basically different from this mystical idea of revelation is the *prophetic* view. According to it, the Deity, rather than simply assuming changing forms, reveals his will, proclaims righteousness and judgement, compassion and grace through the mouth of chosen prophets. Thus Ahura Mazda calls Zarathustra and commands him to proclaim his moral demands: protection of the cattle, purity, holiness, right-mindedness, assuming the struggle against the powers of the Druj (the Lie), and announcing the coming of the world judgement, of a final decision (Söderblom, 1962; Duchesne-Guillemin, 1963). An equally strong dynamic is shown by the idea of revelation in Israelite prophetism. It is true that theophanies are also mentioned here, as in the appearance of God in the burning bush (Exod. 3.2), in the volcanic eruption of Mt Sinai which is followed by a 'descent' of God onto the summit (Exod. 19.16ff.), and in the cloud in which the 'glory' (*kābōd*) of Yahweh comes down upon the tent of meeting and the tabernacle (Exod. 40.34ff., Priestly source). But the decisive revelation follows through the word of God to his prophets (see above, Chapter 8). Through it Yahweh as lawgiver and judge discloses his will in clear concrete demands. Through the oracular proclamation of his will he interprets those external events in history through which he accomplishes his judgement and his grace. Every single event is willed and effected by God: the freeing of the Israelite people from bondage, the victory and defeat in the battle against enemy peoples and finally the destruction of both the kingdoms of Israel and Judah, and the exile and return. The most important facts, the deeds of saving history, are the exodus from Egypt and the conquest of Canaan. The further the distance in time from these saving actions, the more wonderful the light in which they appeared. With the prophets of doom, the revelation of God's judgement stands in the foreground. They were succeeded during the exile by the prophets of salvation (see above, Chapter 12).

The Deuteronomic historiography (*RGG* 2, 100f.; Eissfeldt, 1948) regards the various revelations of God in history as a unity and thus establishes the history of salvation. All instances of natural calamity it interprets as Yahweh's punishments for back-sliding from the worship of one God. A more comprehensive concept of history is created by the post-exilic Priestly legend which begins with the creation and the flood. The whole picture of the history of creation and salvation entered into the liturgical prayers of the post-exilic period, as is shown in Psalms 105 and 106, and Nehemiah, chapter 9.

With the retrospective view of the mighty deeds of God in the past is finally linked the prospect of the future. The God who has done great things for his people, who called Israel, led it and liberated it again and again from its enemies, this God will restore the glorious age of the Davidic and Solomonic kingdoms. This future vision was at first conceived of in a this-worldly sense. But to the degree that tension increased between this hope and its realization, so the Kingdom of God became spiritualized. Under the influence of the Mazdaist doctrine of the other world and the final fulfilment of the cosmos, 'late' Judaic piety attained a position of hope in a transcendent, glorious kingdom which will descend to earth from heaven when earth's kingdoms are broken in pieces and the present world is destroyed.

(2) The Christian revelation

The eschatological and apocalyptic concept of revelation achieved its fulfilment in the preaching message of Jesus (*RGG* 3, 619ff.; Bultmann, 1934; Schweitzer, 1948; Perrin, 1963). The Kingdom of God stands before the door. The present generation will experience its coming in glory. For Jesus the working of miracles is the confirmation that the Kingdom is coming 'now', that the bringer of the Kingdom sojourns among his people. Jesus appears to have been conscious of himself as the predestined Messiah from the moment of his baptism. To hasten the coming of the Kingdom, he decided at the risk of a catastrophe to go to Jerusalem, and thus brought about the conflict with his Jewish opponents. He suffered death by crucifixion as a political criminal. He died abandoned by those who had acclaimed him at his entry into Jerusalem, by his disciples who fled at his arrest, and even by his heavenly Father who did not rescue him from the cross. The grandiose belief in the Kingdom of God appeared to be shattered.

There then took place that which no criticism could demolish by its denials, but also no apologetics could explain: his disciples who had fled back to their Galilean homeland after his death saw him again, at times alone, Peter at first, at times the twelve, at times a greater number (*RGG* 1, 698ff.; *LThK* 1, 1028ff.; Grass, 1962; Geering, 1971). Their encounters with their risen master gave them unshakeable certainty that he had not remained in the kingdom of the dead, but lived, raised to the right hand of the Father, and would shortly return in glory to establish the Kingdom of God on earth. Later tradition found tangible proofs for the reality of the resurrection in the narrative of the tomb found empty despite its being sealed and guarded by the authorities (Matt. 27), and also by the touching of his body by the disciples (Luke 24.39).

The apostles' visionary experience of the resurrection and ascension of the master found their continuation in common ecstatic experiences which appear in condensed form in the narrative of Pentecost (Acts 2). This enthusiasm helped them to overcome their inhibitions and turned them into witnesses to the crucified and risen one before the whole world. The entire life and work of Jesus now took on a new perspective, but so also did the whole of Scripture and the Israelite history of salvation contained in it. The history of salvation as interpreted in the exile and post-exilic periods now receives a profound reinterpretation. The revelation of God in the Old Covenant is combined with the revelation of God in Christ into a fresh unity. The whole of Scripture appeared as a chain of prophecies pointing to the messianic event in Jesus (see above, Chapter 10). It is true that this messianic apologetic did violence to the literal sense of the Old Testament narratives and prophecies.

The history of salvation experienced a widening and deepening through Paul and the deutero-Pauline writers (*RGG* 5, 166ff.; Schoeps, 1961; Stendahl, 1977; Dassmann, 1979). The historical Jesus whom he had known personally was placed in the background. The history of Jesus was compressed into the great facts of saving history: the kenosis and self-humiliation of the pre-existent Son of God, his death on the cross for the salvation of the world which is 'a stumbling block to Jews and folly to gentiles' (1 Cor. 1.23), his resurrection and exaltation, his continued life in the Church (Phil. 2.5ff.). With a sense of immediacy Paul directed his gaze upon the living Christ who had met him on the way to Damascus. He reckoned the mere historical Jesus, 'Christ from a human point of view', to belong to the 'old' which has 'passed away' (2 Cor. 5.16f.).

The Fourth Evangelist (Bultmann, 1971; *RGG* 3, 840ff.) viewed this history of salvation along with the older Synoptic tradition as a unity. In this way there arose the 'spiritual Gospel' which is at the same time a kind of historical narrative and a theology of history. The incarnation is understood as the divine *doxa* ('glory', see above, Chapter 14) shining through the person, miracles and preaching of Jesus, rather than as the mere self-humiliation of the one dwelling in divine glory. Through John the belief in the incarnation, an idea widespread in the Hellenistic world, became rooted in Christianity (John 1.14).

(3) The virgin birth

The Pauline and Johannine belief in the incarnation found further anchorage in the concept of the virginal conception of Jesus which secured a place in the infancy narratives of Matthew and Luke (*RGG* 3, 1068f.; Machen, 1932; Edwards, D., 1943; *ER* 15, 273ff.). Paul, Mark and John know nothing about it. The genealogy of Matthew excludes it; the end (Matt. 1.16) can only have been 'Joseph, the father of Jesus', as it actually was in the Syriac manuscript *Codex sinaiticus*. The numerous variants of this passage point to a correction being made at this place.

The concept of *parthenogenesis* (*RGG* 3, 1068; *ThWNT* 5, 825ff.) is found throughout the whole of mankind. It goes back ultimately to the idea that procreation occurs in a supernatural, magical way, not during the natural act of sex. Added to this was the idea of pollution caused by natural procreation. This explains the fact that numerous outstanding persons (saviour figures, kings, heroes, wise men, prophets and saints) are deemed to be supernaturally conceived, that a deity makes pregnant a human virgin or in some other miraculous way a virgin conceives her child. The culture bringer of North

American Indians was conceived by pebbles, pine needles, etc. The Mayan heroes Hunahpu and Hbalanque were conceived from saliva of a dead person and a virgin. Chih the ancestor of the Chinese Chou dynasty was conceived by his pious mother Chiang Yuan after the sacrificial rite when she trod in the toe-prints of the Deity. Lao-tzu was conceived by a virgin under a plum tree when a tiny ball of light from the gods, made up of sun-substance, settled on her lips. The Egyptian kings were conceived by the queen with whom Amun-Ra, in the form of the king, united as *Ka-mutef* (steer of his mother). Heracles, Asklepios, Perseus, Pythagoras, Plato, Augustus were considered sons of God. Alexander was conceived when lightning struck on his mother's wedding night and entered her womb. The Irish king Conchobuir was conceived when his mother drank water in which were two worms. The Buddha, according to a later but still pre-Christian tradition, enters into the womb of the virgin mother Maya in the form of a white elephant (Thomas, E. J., 1952). Kabir was conceived supernaturally by a Brahman widow as the holy Ramananda blessed her. Ramakrishna is conceived by his mother Chandramani in visionary embrace with Shiva while the father was away on a pilgrimage. The monk Padma Sambhava who carried Buddhism to Tibet emerged at the age of eight from the sepal of a lotus flower which grew in the delta of the Indus. Krishna the god of the shepherds entered into the spirit of his father Vasudeva who transferred the child into the spirit of Devaki who bore it in prison which was now full of light. The eschatological saviour of Mazdaism, the Saoshyant, will be conceived by a virgin who conceives as she bathes in a lake in which is the seed of Zarathustra, lost there and preserved through the centuries.

The miracle of the virgin conception (*virginitas ante partum*) is further heightened by the virgin birth with the exclusion of the genitals (*virginitas in partu*). The mother of Lao-tzu became pregnant with her child at 81 and then bore it under a plum tree out of her armpit. Maya gives birth to the Buddha standing. The latter emerges out of the right side of her body. According to the narrative of the *Protevangelium* of James, Mary bears Jesus without injuring her womb. This legendary story soon became a theologoumenon and later even a dogma of the Church at the Lateran Council 649 (Denzinger, no. 256). According to this view, reminiscent of gnostic docetism, Mary's son passed through her womb like the risen one through closed doors (Jerome, Augustine) and the sun's rays through glass.

Besides the assumption of a fatherless conception and birth stands the rarer view of an origin without any mother. Pallas Athene rises fully armed out of the head of Zeus; Dionysos was born out of the ankles of Zeus; Aphrodite rises out of the foaming sea; Mithra is born out of the generative rock. In the Epistle to the Hebrews (7.3), Christ also is described as, according to the manner of Melchizedek, 'without father or mother or genealogy'.

There are few New Testament concepts where so many parallels exist outside of Christianity as in the case of the virgin birth. Three different explanations may be given for this; (a) that of the history of religions points out that in this case a religious symbol of mankind especially widespread in the

Hellenistic world was applied with a measure of inevitability to Jesus as the incarnation of God. It is an attempt to explain the origin of genius and the extraordinary appearing in the midst of the chain of human generations (Söderblom). Liberal Protestantism and Catholic modernism see in the virgin birth of Christ an ancient transparency of it, not the incarnation itself, but a helpful interpretation of the real belief in incarnation. (b) From the parapsychological viewpoint: a psychic power takes over the function of male sperm. Parapsychology points to the extraordinarily far-reaching effects of the psychological in the religious sphere. Nevertheless, scientific proof of human parthenogenesis has not yet been forthcoming. (c) From the theological, apologetic standpoint, the countless parallels in the history of religions are presentiments of that event which once happened as an extraordinary miracle in the womb of Mary. 'And was incarnate by the Holy Spirit of the Virgin Mary, and was made man' (Nicene-Const. creed).

(4) The idea of a universal revelation

The story of revelation was further eleborated in the theology of the Christian Apologists and Alexandrians who also combined it with Greco-Roman philosophy. The latter for Clement of Alexandria is a teacher (*paidagōgos*) to lead one to Christ, as is the law and prophecy of the Jewish Scriptures. While the concern of Alexandrian theology lay with the history of culture, Augustine in his work *City of God* moved further towards a philosophy of world history. He traces through traditional Roman civilization and Judaism and also through the first Christian centuries the struggle of the city or state of God against that of the devil, a struggle which must end with the final victory of the *civitas Dei*.

The idea of a universal revelation is also an essential part of Islam. According to Muhammad Allah sent a warner to every people. God has given one and the same revelation to a chain of prophets: Adam, Noah, Abraham, Ishmael, Isaac, Jacob, Moses and Jesus. The different revelations are in agreement; each successive revelation is a confirmation of the preceding one. Muhammad is the seal of the prophets, the *paraklētos* prophesied in the Johannine Gospel (14, 16 and 26). This universal view of revelation Muhammad had received from the Ebionites and Manichaeans. The same idea lives on in the Bahai religion which proceeded from Islam (see above, Chapter 13). But here Baha-Ullah takes the place of Muhammad as the greatest bearer yet of the revelation of God and as the promised paraclete. Yet Baha-Ullah recognizes that further prophets could arise after a certain time who will adapt religion to the circumstances of the age.

While all these systems of revelation possess a valid insight, modern Hinduism recognizes the different major revelations as equal in value (as did also the emperor Akbar in the sixteenth century) especially the *Brāhma-Samāj* of Ram Mohan Roy, the *Nava-Vidhāna-Brāhma-Samāj* of Keshub Candra Sen, and the *Rāmakrishna* mission which goes back to Rāmakrishna and Vivekananda. Rabindranath Tagore also is wholly permeated by the universality of God's revelation. The idea of universal revelation has found representatives in the West as well, for example, in the Middle Ages in the work of Nicholas of Cusa, *Concerning the Peace of Faith*; at the beginning of the modern period the humanists Erasmus and Zwingli, and Spiritualists Sebastian Franck and Robert Barclay, Quaker advocate of 'an inward and immediate revelation' (1686); and the advocates of the Enlightenment and Romanticism. Schleiermacher's speeches are likewise testimonies to this universalism, as are Max Müller's works on the history of religions (*RGG* 4, 1142; Chaudhuri, 1974). According to Max Müller there is only *one* revelation, the 'revelation in us'. For him, the 'worst heresy' is to believe that God has only revealed himself to a single people, the Jews in Palestine, during all the centuries that have passed and in all the countries of the world. The greatest advocate of universal revelation in this century has been Nathan Söderblom who declared (Söderblom, 1962) that God reveals himself in history again and again, in the creative genius and in the individual seeking God. At Worms in 1521 Luther declares: 'It is revealed to me that God's revelation goes on and on.'

(5) Miracles

In addition to mystical and prophetic forms of revelation, the revelation of the divine is accomplished in *miracles* (Mensching, 1957; Richardson, A., 1952; Grant, 1952; *ER* 9, 541ff.). For traditional believers, the divine is miraculous not only in its being but also in its effects. Every successful act of divination is for them a miracle, every hearing of prayer, every rescue in time of need, every good fortune which they believe they must thank God for. But the more people become conscious of orderliness in the events of nature, the more only an extraordinary work of God appears to them as a miracle in a particular instance.

In the 'world' religions, and not only these, the divine work of salvation is especially accompanied by miracles. The life of the Buddha is full of wonderful events occurring at his birth, enlightenment, first sermon and entrance into *Nirvāna*. The whole world of gods and nature takes part in these world-shaking events and is there to serve him. Miracle also occupies an important place in the life of Buddhist and Hindu saints, though to a lesser extent than with the Buddha himself. In particular it is the birth of the great proclaimers of salvation which takes place in a miraculous way (see section one, above). The same goes for their death. Here the prophetic religions are no less rich in miracles. The history of the Israelite people beginning with the patriarchs, above all the works of Moses and Joshua, Elijah and Elisha, is a long series of miracles. In the Psalms, Yahweh is praised again and again as the God who alone works wonders (Ps. 72.18 etc.). In the Talmudic literature the Jewish miracle stories are continued. The Gospels are full of miracles, as are the Acts of the Apostles according to which book 'many wonders and signs were done through the apostles', and Stephen 'did great wonders and signs' (2.43; 6.8). The miraculous happening continues from post-biblical times down to the present according to the sources of church history and hagiography.

Not only is miracle the 'dearest child of faith' and thus an indestructible part of popular religion, it is also an essential part of church doctrine. The Roman Church attested miracles as one of the essential prerequisites for canonization and thus as a criterion of sainthood (see above, Chapter 12). Catholic dogmatics and apologetics place great value on the proof from miracles. Every Roman priest must swear in the oath against modernism that miracles and prophecies are to be regarded as 'external arguments for revelation', as 'certain signs of the divine origin of the Christian religion (Denz., no. 2145). Even if not going so far, Protestant Churches still hold fast to the miracles of the virgin birth and incarnation, the miracles of Jesus' ministry, the resurrection and the miracle of Pentecost. Officially at least, Islam is more sober than Judaism and Christianity in its belief in miracles; but the figure of the prophet is still surrounded by a circle of miracle stories as are the Islamic saints' lives (see above, Chapter 8).

All the same, an equal place to that occupied by miracle in world religions is taken up by the process of spiritualizing and transposing the concept of miracle. The Vedic *Upanishads* already know of no other miracle than the knowledge of the *Ātman*'s unity with the *Brahman* which possesses saving power. Early Buddhism places the liberating knowledge through which the perfect one enters into Nirvāna above all miraculous knowledge and spiritual powers. the enlightened one confesses that as a blind man finds a pearl in a heap of dung so also has the thought of enlightenment arisen in him, as he knows not through which miracle (Shantideva). The great prophets of the Hebrew Scriptures proclaim no external miracles in their preaching. The only miracle for them is Yahweh's righteous judgement and forgiving grace. Jesus rejects the demand of the Pharisees and scribes for miracles as proofs and declares that those who crave miracles will be given no other sign than the sign of the prophet Johah, i.e. his sermon of judgement (Matt. 12.38ff.). And to his disciples who are proud of their exorcism of demons he says: 'Nevertheless do not rejoice in this, that the spirits are subject to you; but rejoice that your names are written in heaven' (Luke 10.20). Also, for the poet of the 'hymn to love' (1 Cor. 13) all the miraculous events of the early Christian Church (speaking with tongues, the faith that moves mountains) are not comparable with everyday brotherly and sisterly love. In the story of doubting Thomas the Fourth Evangelist makes plain his critique of the massive belief in a materialistic, miraculous resurrection: 'Blessed are those who have *not* seen and yet believe' (John 20.29).

For Augustine the daily wonders of nature are greater than those related in the Bible. The sprouting of the wheat out of the insignificant seed corn is a greater miracle for him than the feeding of the five thousand. Indeed, the creation of mankind is a greater miracle than the resurrection and that of the cosmos a greater miracle than all the biblical miracles put together. Similarly the spiritual miracle of the awakening of numerous sinners to new life is a greater miracle than the awakening of the dead in the gospel stories. The biblical miracles for Augustine have only the function of opening people's eyes to the 'daily miracle' which 'people are blind to'. Luther also considered the 'bodily' or 'external' miracles related in the Bible as 'signs for the uncomprehending, unbelieving mass of people'. These must give way to 'the great, glorious, miraculous deeds' which Christ performs daily in the souls of men, namely the overcoming of the devil's power through the preaching of the gospel and the dispensing of the sacraments. The greatest of all miracles is simply faith, exemplified in the centurion of Capernaum. Modern theology has also accepted this spiritualizing of the miracle. An Indian evangelist like Sadhu Sundar Singh who had experienced many extraordinary things in his wanderings, was never tired of saying that 'the greatest, indeed the only miracle' is the rebirth of the sinner to new life and the peace of Christ. The spiritual piety of Christians frees itself from the view that miracle is an external event which breaks through the laws of nature, and returns in a measure to the traditional religious view that all things are signs and wonders. 'The more religious you were', said Schleiermacher, 'the more you would see miracles everywhere' (*Speeches* 2, 60f.).

17

Salvation

(1) The saviour

Most closely bound up with revelation is *salvation* (*ERE* 11, 109–51, 694–725; *RGG* 2, 576–99; Wach, 1922; Rall, 1953; Deursen, 1936; Reitzenstein, 1921; Hahn, 1963; McIntyre, 1954; Brandon, 1963; Davies, D. J., 1978; Enang, 1979; Okafor, 1984). The point of view of each, however, is different. Revelation is related to that which is independent of people, transcendent, wholly other, overwhelming; its final goal is the glory of God. Salvation is related to people, their liberation from evil powers, the forgiveness of sins, participation in eternal, divine life. The benefits and possession of salvation are to be distinguished from the carrying out and transmission of salvation and also from the mediator and saviour.

In traditional religions the saviour figures are related to the divine Originator and bring cultural goods, religious values, tabus, ethical norms and essential rites (see above, Chapter 14). The great bringers of salvation in the religions of antiquity free people from sin and sickness: The Vedic *Varuna*, Babylonian *Ninib*, Syrian *Eshmun*, Greek Zeus with the associated names of saviour (*sōtēr*) and liberator (*eleutherios*); Apollo the sacred physician, and turner-away of evil, the god of purification and expiation especially of blood-guilt. The great dying and rising vegetation deities Osiris and Attis also became saviours (*RAC* 1, 919ff.). Gnosticism created the figure of the 'redeemed redeemer' (Reitzenstein) who himself languished in the bonds of matter and the body before finding 'the ascent to the world of light'. This figure is related to the Indian *Tirthankara*, *Jina* and *Buddha*, persons who find the way out of the cycle of births full of suffering and so become the teacher and example for all other persons and living beings. They are ranked higher than the deities who must find their way to salvation along with those subject to rebirth. The creator God *Brahmā Sahampati* bows the knee before Buddha and beseeches him to proclaim his teaching out of compassion for the world. There is not *one* Jina or Buddha but infinitely many in the different cosmic aeons. In Mahāyāna Buddhism there step into the place of the Buddha the ones who have found salvation themselves and then become proclaimers of the sacred doctrine, who are prepared to forgo their own salvation until all other beings have attained it, indeed have forfeited all their own merits for the sake of rescuing others (*ERE* 2, 739–53). To the Buddha and Bodhisattva the believers turn with fervent prayers. Those mostly invoked are *Buddha Amitābha* (Buddha of the clear light of bliss) and the Bodhisattva *Avalokiteshvara* (Lord of compassion) who has become in China a goddess of mercy (*Kuan-yin*, Jap. *Kannon*). *Amida* is a 'redeemed redeemer', a monk who took an early vow not to receive enlightenment himself if even one of the living beings in his land who yearns for rebirth and believes in him, has not yet been reborn. With the saviour figures of Mahāyāna Buddhism contact is made at various points with the Hindu saviour deities Vishnu, Krishna, Narāyana and Shiva. These also save people from the cycle of births and rebirths through their gracious assistance. Also to them the faithful direct fervent prayers.

Besides the saviours of the present must be set the *coming saviours.* According to the Pali canon Buddha himself prophesied the coming of a further Buddha, *Maitreya* (Pali *Metteya*), who would lead many beings to salvation and peace. *Maitreya* attained such significance in Mahāyāna Buddhism that he sometimes appeared to be the central figure of the Buddhist pantheon. In China he was venerated as *Mi-lo-fo.* In Hinduism there corresponds to Maitreya *Kalkī* the future avatar of Vishnu who will restore the moral order on earth. According to the Avestan doctrine of world aeons a *Saoshyant*, 'saviour', will be born in each millennium and will take up the struggle against the *daeva* and the *Druj.* The last *Saoshyant* of the three is conceived in miraculous fashion (see Chapter 16 above) and will effect the resurrection. After the great purification he will dispense to all mortal beings the elixir of immortality.

Faith in the future saviour also attained the greatest significance in Judaism. Out of the misery and disgrace of the exilic period was born the faith in a saviour who as *mashiah*, 'anointed' (*RGG* 4, 901ff.; Bentzen, 1955), renews the Israelite kingdom and brings about an era progressively spiritualized into an eschatological expectation, above all by being blended with the concept of the heavenly son of man in the prophecy of the Book of Daniel (7.13ff.). The Messiah–Son of Man comes after the cosmic catastrophe on the clouds of heaven to establish the kingdom of righteousness and blessedness on the earth where all is renewed.

In this sense Jesus (*ER* 8, 15ff.) appears to have been conscious of himself as *Messias praedestinatus* (Schweitzer, 1948) who has God's commission to set up the Kingdom of God. He appears to have foreseen his death in advance as a means of hastening the breaking in of this Kingdom and in this sense as 'a ransom for many' (Mark 10.45). The early Palestinian Church saw in his death the indispensable passage to his installation in messianic dignity through 'exaltation to the right hand of the Father'. On Hellenistic soil there was added to the Jewish concept of the Messiah the idea of *Theos sōtēr*, 'divine saviour', which was widespread in the religious world of antiquity, especially the concept of the *sōtēr* stemming from the Hellenistic cult of the ruler (*RGG* 3, 143ff.; *ThWNT* 7, 1004ff.; Arndt and Gingrich, 808) who establishes an empire of peace on the earth.

While his death on the cross had eschatological significance for Jesus himself and the Palestinian Church, as the means for bringing about the Kingdom of the last days, for Paul on the other hand it becomes the factual basis for the salvation of people from their sins. This salvation is represented by the most varied images: as *ransom* analogous to the sacral ransoming of slaves (1 Cor.

6.20), as the *judgement* on sinful flesh which Christ took upon himself (Rom. 8.3), as *freedom* from the law (Col. 2.14), above all, however, as the *quenching* of the divine wrath through the numinous power of the blood sacrifice (Rom. 5.9; see above, Chapter 6). Linked to the concept of salvation is that of the *second Adam* (*ThWNT* 1, 144ff.; Arndt and Gingrich 15). The latter restores the benefits forfeited through the fall of the first Adam and the lost filial relationship with God (Rom. 5.12ff.; 1 Cor. 15.45). The Epistle to the Hebrews (*RGG* 3, 106ff.) goes on to develop a comprehensive, speculative soteriology. Christ appears, according to Hebrews, as high priest of the new covenant who through his death offers the sacrifice of expiation in a still higher sense than the high priest of the Old Testament who makes expiation to the most high on the Day of Atonement (see above, Chapter 6).

The Fourth Gospel is based on a completely different concept of the saviour (see above, Chapter 16). At its central point stands not so much the death of the saviour for the forgiveness of sins but rather the breaking in of the divine glory in the victory of light over darkness, truth over the lie and life over death. Christ's death is the revelation of divine love, the cross the exaltation of the Son of God. The last word of the crucified one is not a despairing cry of dereliction but the victorious shout: 'It is finished' (John 19.30). According to Marcion (Harnack, 1921) the benevolent Saviour God buys people out of the rule of Yahweh the world creator and God of law. The ransom theory that Christ paid Satan with his death for the redemption of mankind, whereby he finally tricked his adversary, lived on with Origen, Amphilocius, Gregory the Great and even with Luther (Aulen, 1950). A new motif in the interpretation of salvation was introduced into Christian theology through the satisfaction theory of Anselm of Canterbury (*Cur Deus Homo*; McIntyre, 1954). The death of Christ is here arguably a necessity inasmuch as the injured honour of God has to be made good. This satisfaction could not however be carried out by a human being; it could only be made by a person of the Deity. It is possible that Germanic juridical views lived on in this theory.

Medieval mysticism (Weymann, 1938) sees in the crucified saviour the archetype of humility and love, the pattern for the 'imitation of Christ' in suffering with him and dying with him. The idea of the moral effect of Christ's death, sketched out at the time by Peter Abelard (Franks, 1962), revives again in nineteenth-century liberal views of the atonement. To a pre-eminent degree the Reformers (Loewenich, 19) again place the cross of Christ in the centre of faith in Christ the Saviour as the basis of salvation. The cross is the unity of divine judgement and divine grace; it is the guarantee for the certainty of the forgiveness of sins. The Reformers' theology sees itself as a 'theology of the cross' in conformity to the Apostle's words in 1 Corinthians (2.2).

All these different images and theories of salvation are merely illustrations of a mystery which in the last analysis is as ineffable as the mystery of God himself. The sacrificial death of Jesus in space and time is simply the window through which is manifest the eternal, loving self-giving of God to sinful people. Because it is a question of a supra-historical, eternal event, the death of

Christ is counted as being effectual unto salvation even before it took place as a historical event.

(2) The benefits of salvation

Salvation in early traditional religions is something substantial, magical and eudaemonistic. The early Nordic word *heill* (whole) means as adjective, 'whole, unbroken, in a bodily and spiritual sense, without weakness'. As a substantive it means 'luck' (see above, Chapter 1). The Egyptian formula 'life, luck, strength' also has magical significance. The last term (*shnb*) is related to the Hebrew *shālōm*. *Charis* (Gr.) was likewise at first of a magical character (see Chapter 1). The concept of grace and salvation therefore belongs originally to the sphere of *mana*. Moreover this *Heil* is a free, divine gift. Grace means favour, the mercy shown by the personal Deity. The forgiveness of sins is originally thought of eudaemonistically, be it as the elimination of a substantial sin-tabu and its malefic consequence (sickness, misfortune), or as appeasing the wrath of the injured Deity which has imposed misfortune as a punishment (see above, Chapter 14). This becomes manifest in the Babylonian lamentations and the Vedic penitential hymns (see above, Chapter 9). The more spiritualized concept which we encounter in Egypt and the mystery cults of antiquity aims at immortality and participation in the life of Deity. Here the concept of salvation is already directed to the other world even though still remaining somehow bound to this one.

A purer, more individual view of salvation grew up on the basis of the pessimistic valuation of earthly life in India and Greece. The early Indian concept of *karma* (*ER* 8, 261ff.) gives the possibility for an improvement in life: whoever brings forth good works will be reborn in a good life, be that as warrior, brahmin or God. But this improved life is not the real salvation because it does not lead a person out of the cycle of births and rebirths full of suffering, again and again to be born and to die. The profound pessimism, which the *karma* doctrine evokes, is symbolized by the monster which holds in his claws the Tibetan wheel of life. Salvation (*moksha, mukti*) means freedom from being bound to *karma*, freedom to step out of *samsāra*, the cycle of birth and rebirth. The seers of the Upanishads teach that this salvation is attained through the knowledge of the identity of *Ātman* and *Brahman*. For Gautama Buddha salvation consists of the knowledge of the sacred truths and the connection of causes. He who has recognized the origin of suffering, the thirst for life, has escaped from the omnipotence of karma; he goes first into the visible Nirvāna and at death into perfect Nirvāna after the karma acquired in life up to that point has been completely consumed. Nirvāna is by no means nothing or even partly negative inasmuch as it signifies the cessation of all passion and attachment; it is truly positive: peace and blessedness in absolute detachment. Nirvāna is the highest good and basically the same as the unity of *Ātman* and *Brahman*.

Similar ideas of salvation are found among the Greek Orphics. Salvation for them is also to escape from the cycle of birth and evil. Orphism reflects the Platonic conception as a liberation from the chains of the body and of the material world, the sloughing off of the husk, foreign in nature, and the return to the original purity and freedom in the heavenly home, the world of ideas. In Orphism, thus, are already fused together the thought of the mystical union with the Deity and the divinization which stems from the ecstatic cult of Dionysus. For *Gnosticism* salvation is the ascent of the soul which has been freed from all bondage to the material into the heavenly world of light; for *Neoplatonism* it is the return of the soul loosed from the bonds of matter to the primordial unity out of which it has emanated. *Manichaeism* (Widengren, 1965) sees salvation in the liberation of the light particles and their return to the kingdom of light. Traces of this Orphic-Platonic view of salvation are also found in the Pauline writings of the New Testament (2 Cor. 5.1–8).

In contrast to this pessimistic, mystical view of salvation, prophetic religion seeks salvation in personal and loving fellowship with God. Because this relationship is disrupted by sin, salvation means forgiveness of sins which is reached through repentance and returning to God (*ThWNT* 4, 976ff.). This view of salvation found its strongest expression in the penitential psalms, above all in the Psalm *Miserere*: 'According to thy abundant mercy blot out my transgressions' (Ps. 51.1).

However salvation is not only forgiveness of sins but also sanctification, filling with divine power, and communication of the holy spirit. The radical change in the soul is expressed in the words of the Psalm: 'Create in me a clean heart, O God' (Ps. 51.10). According to the prophecy of Ezekiel the 'stony' or sinful heart of man is to be taken away and to be replaced by a 'fleshly' or holy heart given by God (Ezek. 36.26). In the preaching of Jesus, salvation for the individual person consists in the forgiveness of sins. Jesus' gospel is good news for the tax-gatherers and other transgressors of the law. According to the parable of the Pharisee and the tax-collector, the one ejaculatory prayer, 'God, be merciful to me a sinner', sufficed for justification before God (Luke 18.13f.). The simple confession of the lost son, 'Father I have sinned', opens the father's heart to him and causes him to be taken back into the father's house (Luke 15.11ff.). This view of salvation is strictly personal; it signifies nothing else than the restoration of friendship and sonship between man and God.

Upon Jesus' message of the forgiveness of sins Paul builds a formal doctrine of justification (*ThWNT* 2, 199–229). Justification is nevertheless by no means restricted to forgiveness of sins as a divine judicial act, but is bound up with rebirth, sanctification and union with Christ. In the Fourth Gospel (*ThWNT* 2, 833ff.) the forgiveness of sins recedes into the background. Salvation here lies in the communication of the knowledge of God and of eternal life which takes place in the union with Christ: 'You in me and I in you' (John 15.4, 7).

For the Greek Fathers salvation consists in 'deification'. The object of the incarnation of God in Christ is the deification of those believing in him. God is God by nature, man becomes God through 'adoption and grace', according to Symeon the New Theologian. Along with deification man receives immortality.

The seed of the resurrection is implanted in the body and soul of the believer in Christ through the Eucharist (see above, Chapter 7).

In contrast to the doctrine of grace in the Eastern Church Augustine emphasizes the forgiveness of sins more strongly without weakening the link between justification and union with Christ. In the doctrine of grace of Thomas Aquinas, on which the doctrinal definitions of the Tridentine Council are based, justifying grace and sanctifying grace are harmoniously joined. The Lutheran doctrine of grace follows Paul and Augustine in making forgiveness of sins central. Salvation and forgiveness are the restoration of the fellowship with God destroyed by sin. This includes in itself, however, union with Christ and deification. The Lutheran scholastics, especially Hollaj, describe justification as 'mystical union' and as 'approximation to the divine substance'.

Schleiermacher developed this Lutheran doctrine further when he stressed that forgiveness of sins is at the same time the indwelling of Christ. This mystical interpretation of justification stands over against the forensic theory according to which justification takes place outside of us not in the heart but in heaven (*LThK* 8, 675ff.). The emphasis upon forensic justification runs from Melanchthon on the one hand and Calvin on the other down to the dialectical theology of the twentieth century. In Calvinism where it predominates, this theory was nevertheless softened through pietism and mysticism (*RGG* 4, 193).

(3) The way of salvation

In the interpretation of the way salvation is appropriated, the same series of steps may be observed in the history of religions as with the saviour and the benefits of salvation. In traditional religions salvation is attained often in the context of festivals and other rites, through divination and dance, sacrifice and prayer. Vedic Brahmanism speaks in this context of *karma mārga*, the way of works.

In the salvation religions of India salvation is attained through knowledge, not of course in the rational but in the mystical sense of this term. This way is called *jnāna mārga*, the way of knowledge. According to the teaching of the *Upanishads* he who knows the unity of *Ātman* and *Brahman* attains liberation from the pitiless law of *karma*. This knowledge is expressed in the mystical formulae: 'I am Brahma', 'that thou art' (*tat tvam asi*). The way to such knowledge is prepared through asceticism, instruction and *meditation* (*ER* 9, 324ff.). But in the final analysis it is amazing grace; it flames up without warning in the human spirit; it is governed by divine election: 'Only him whom the Ātman chooses is capable of grasping him' (*Kathaka Up.* 2, 23). In early Buddhism too, salvation is attained in visionary knowledge, perfect illumination, which is prepared through ethical and ascetic discipline and contemplation (*samādhi*). Enlightenment cannot be forcibly brought about by ascetic works, neither by fasting nor by mortification of the flesh. It arises in silent contemplation in an inexplicable way. Nirvāna is the divine without God (in a personal sense); it is the gift (of salvation) without the Giver (Söderblom).

The idea of grace hinted at in Upanishadic mysticism and in early Buddhism, breaks through unreservedly in Bhakti mysticism. To the two early Indian ways of salvation already mentioned a third must be added: *bhakti mārga*. *Bhakti*, the believing, trusting love of the saviour God and the selfless surrender to him, possess saving power. *Bhakti* appears in a twofold form: on the one hand as faith alone (*sōla fides*) to the exclusion of all good works; and on the other, as faith in a 'synergistic' sense, associated with a person's own actions. Both ways were appositely illustrated in southern India theology: synergism, linking grace and good works, is the 'way of the monkey'. The monkey's child actively grasps hold of its mother who is rescuing it from mortal danger. Faith alone is the 'way of the cat'. The mother cat lifts up its young in its mouth and so brings it out of danger. The *sōla fides* doctrine of faith alone appears again in Mahāyāna Buddhism, especially in the Chinese 'school of pure land' and in both the Japanese sects, *Jōdo-shū* and *Jōdo-Shin-shū*. Here good works possess no saving power. Only unshakeable trust in the Buddha's saving grace has it. This trust finds expression in the ever repeated formula of invocation: 'Glory be to the Buddha of immeasurable radiance'. *Jōdo-Shin-shū* goes further than *Jōdo-shū* in its emphasis on *sōla grātia* (grace alone). Every ejaculatory prayer is simply a prayer of thanksgiving for God's free gift of grace. The similarity of this Buddhist doctrine of grace to the 'Lutheran heresy' was apparent to the Catholic Jesuit missionaries in Japan in the sixteenth century. In turn a Buddhist *Amida* priest described Luther as the 'Shinran of the West' (see above, Chapter 11). This doctrine of faith alone stands in Chinese and Japanese Buddhism over against the call for activity and practice in other schools of meditation, notably the Ch'an-tsung and Zen-shū schools.

The Hebrew prophets (Gelin, 1955) also call for unlimited reliance on Yahweh (*RGG* 2, 1588ff.): 'If you will not believe, surely you will not be established' ('*im lō ta' amīnu kī lō ta' amēnu*), as Isaiah's play on words has it (Isa. 7.9). At the same time, however, they demand moral action. Without righteousness and compassion all presuming upon Yahweh's presence and assistance is in vain. Jesus' preaching shows the same double attitude (*RGG* 2, 1590ff.; *ThWNT* 6, 174–230ff.; Braun, H., 1957). The sinner is justified, through repentance and trusting faith. The heavenly reward is measured not on the basis of achievement but the gracious promise of God—as the parable of the workers in the vineyard makes clear (Matt. 20). And yet, without the fulfilling of what God requires, without the 'doing of the will of God', the 'I ought', all the saying of 'Lord, Lord' is in vain (Matt. 7.21). At the last judgement the decision concerning one's salvation or damnation is taken only in terms of the works of love (Matt. 25, 34ff.).

Paul's doctrine of justification rests on quite different premises. Through the collapse of his Pharisaic righteousness, built up in terms of good works, he was led to the knowledge that a person 'is justified by faith apart from the works of law' (Rom. 3.28). Good works are thereby not excluded, they are much more the natural 'fruit' of faith: 'faith working through love' (Gal. 5.6; Bornkamm,

G., 1961). This Pauline doctrine of grace finds an echo in John's Christ-mysticism (Schnackenburg, 1937): 'Apart from me you can do nothing' (John 15.5). Still, in terms of the divine love made manifest, brotherly love is even more strongly emphasized in the Johannine writings than in the authentic parts of the Pauline ones (John 13.34f.; 1 John 3.14ff.; 4.7ff.).

The Jewish emphasis on works penetrated afresh into Christianity through the Epistle of James and, in the West especially, through Tertullian and Cyprian. Augustine renewed the idea of grace, linking up with Paul, and became the teacher of grace (*doctor grātiae*) of the Western Church. In his *Confessions* he sang the most wonderful hymn to God's unmerited grace; works (*opera*) are for him basically gifts (*munera*). Still, Augustine avoids the extreme position of a passive view of grace; the activity of man is not excluded by the receiving of grace. Under the influence of the Augustinian train of thought Thomas Aquinas developed a balanced synergism. Grace is an undeserved and free gift of divine love preceded by no works on the part of man. But the act of faith is not itself passive but rather active. Whoever has received grace must co-operate with grace, just as the man in the parable who had received the talents from his master had to put them to use (Matt. 25.14ff.). Grace is thus the foundation for good works. The latter are meritorious because those that perform them are co-operating with grace.

Over against all such synergism, Luther fought for grace alone and faith alone (Bring, 1955). The human person, he argued, is completely incapable of doing anything good. One attains grace and salvation only by means of the simple act of trust in God's promise of grace and God's act of salvation. It is not a question of performing good works in order to be saved and go to heaven but the other way round: the good person must already be saved and have heaven himself before he can achieve any good works. Faith and works are related to each other as burning and shining are to light. The works of love are the expression of gratitude for the gift of divine grace received in faith.

The theology of the Enlightenment (*RGG* 1, 723ff.) advocates afresh a form of religious moralism; not faith but virtue is the decisive thing in Christian life. Neo-Lutheranism (*RGG* 4, 535ff.) renewed for its part the Lutheran doctrine of grace. Then this century came dialectical theology (*RGG* 1, 894ff.; 2, 168ff.) through which the Reformers' view of the sovereignty of divine grace came into its own in an even sharper and more uncompromising way. The liberation theology of Latin America by contrast sees the operation of divine grace more in terms of God's social justice on the plane of history (Gutierrez, 1974; Bonino, 1975; Boff, 1985).

Sometimes Islam is unjustly described as a religion of righteousness through the performance of good works. Yet for Islam the basis of all good works is faith. This is itself an act of God. 'To no soul is it given to become a believer except when Allāh permits' (*sura* 10, 100). Faith is not the holding of Allāh's revelations to be true in an external way, but a hearing of God, a resting in God and a surrender of oneself to him. Thus the prophet prays: 'Lord, stir me up that I thank thee for the grace that you have shown me and my parents, that I may perform good works to those with whom thou art well pleased' (*sura* 46, 14).

Faith in the nature of salvation as sheer grace draws with it the idea of *election and predestination* (*RGG* 5, 479ff.; *LThK* 8, 406ff.; Pannenberg, 1954). Such faith differs from the notion of the determining of human life by fate (see above, Chapter 14) because it is directly related to eternal salvation. As the *Kāthaka Upanishad* speaks of the *Ātman*'s election of grace, so the *Bhagavad-gītā* (16, 5) speaks of a 'divine predestination', 'God's lot cast for salvation', which stands over against a 'demonic predestination' and a 'demons' lot for enchaining'. The idea of grace which dominated Paul's doctrine of salvation includes a double predestination to 'glory' and to 'damnation'. It comes to expression in the classical parable of the potter who forms out of *one* lump vessels both 'for beauty' and 'for menial use' (Rom. 9.21ff.). In Christian theology (Augustine, Gottschalk, Thomas Aquinas, Duns Scotus, Luther, Calvin and Cornelius Jansen) the problem of double predestination has remained unresolved to the present day. According to the milder theory, predestination to be rejected is interpreted as 'infralapsarian', that is, God condemns man only in the light of the fall of man. According to the harsher, 'supralapsarian' view, God predestines people to damnation regardless of human blameworthiness. Islamic theology also occupied itself with the same problem. Muhammad in his later years seems to have been inclined to favour the doctrine of predestination. Later theologians in part advocated absolute predestination while the Muʿtazila (Kadarīya) fought for the freedom of the will. Islamic orthodoxy laid emphasis on the complete sovereignty of God using the same simile of the potter as Paul had done. According to Rudolf Otto the idea of predestination is an ideogram for the totally irrational relationship between the creator and his creature; for Tor Andrae it is the expression of a purely religious interpretation of the world and of human life.

18
Eternal Life

(1) Continuation of earthly life

Salvation is fulfilled and completed in *eternal life* (*ERE* 5, 373–91; 8, 1–47; 4, 411–511; 11, 817–54; 2, 680–710; *HWDA* 8, 1465–83; *RGG* 2, 650–89; *LThK* 3, 1083–98; *NDLW* 117ff.; Andrae, 1940; Edsman, 1946; Leeuw, 1950; Schilling, 1951; Brandon, 1963; Farnell, 1922; Cumont, 1959; Evens-Wentz, 1949; Charles, 1970; Benz, 1967; Hick, J., 1976; *ER* 1, 107ff.; 5, 149ff.; 11, 133ff.; on Christianity, see further under section five, below). Mankind is embued with the belief that death is not the end of life. The individual forms of belief in an after-life are extremely diverse; and Christians have not remained uninfluenced by many of these even while developing characteristic forms of their own.

An early form of this belief is acceptance of *a continuation of earthly life* (a) in the realm of the *grave* (*ER* 5, 450ff.). Already in prehistoric times people were buried with gifts of food and drink, weapons and ornaments, also spouses, followers and slaves. The last named were often replaced by figurines and images. Nordic megalithic graves, like the Egyptian pyramids and mastabas, bear witness in stone to the belief in this kind of continuation of life. Besides the equipping of the dead at burial was also their continued feeding at special festivals; in hot climates cooling water especially was offered to the dead. An important motive for this offering for the dead was the belief in the intervention of the dead in the life of their descendants. The burial in family graves had the aim of securing the continuation of communal fellowship for deceased members of the family. For many peoples, such as the Chinese, Romans and Israelites, the idea of individual immortality receded behind that of the immortality of family and clan. The burial of a dead person in early Israel is described as being 'gathered to his people' (Gen. 35.29; 49. 33). The Germanic peoples believed in a continuation of life for the clan in the city of souls (*Seelenheim*) or mountain of the dead under the leadership not of a deity but of a clan leader.

Another form of belief in the continuation of life after death sees (b) an *enhancement* of that life. In the first variety of this belief the dead acquire *power over a particular sphere of earthly life*. Deceased individuals who already in this life possessed extraordinary and magical powers: chiefs, healer-diviners or heroes, achieve enhanced power after death and can intervene all the more in the life of their descendants. The dead even become deities; in early Israel they were called *'elohīm*, 'gods' (1 Sam. 28.13f.). The conjuration of the dead serves the purpose of oracular divination; an example being offered by the seeress of Endor who had the power to call up Samuel (1 Sam. 28.7ff.). The cult of heroes and ancestors scarcely differs from that of the deities; both are called upon in prayer and venerated with sacrifices. The motive is fear of the mighty spirit of this dead hero who through separation from the body has become mightier yet.

According to another view the enhanced earthly life is continued in a paradise or kingdom of the dead. The dead lead a happy existence through continuing pleasant earthly occupations such as fishing, hunting, banquets and feasting. North American Indian peoples know of a land of souls in the west under the earth. It is a warm land with flowers and plenty of everything, without sickness, where people go naked, sing and dance. The Egyptians know of a green, fruitful place called *Aalu* (*Earu*) where one sows, reaps, hunts and plays. The *Rigveda* (10, 135) speaks of the fathers' heavenly place where they are banqueting and feasting, singing songs and playing the flute. There is a widespread idea of the island of the blessed which is surrounded by sea (Algonquins, Egyptians, Celts, Greeks). The Elysian Fields lie on the boundaries of the earth where the pleasantest kind of life is assigned to the dead. The Irish island of the blessed is called the 'land under the waves', the 'other world', the 'radiant land', a land of wonderful people with amazing fruit trees and music, luscious food and drink that give immortality, where the departed enjoy eternal youth and beauty. In many images, traditional religions depict the glories of paradise or the realm of the dead in which people find again all that is dear to them.

Some people believe (c) *in a change for the worse*, the deterioration of earthly life after death. One form of this is when departed souls wander about as spirits and endanger the living on earth, especially if their bodies are not buried or if no sacrifice has been offered to them. Another widespread supposition is that the dead lead a shadowy existence in the underworld. The Babylonian realm of the dead is a city surrounded by seven walls. It is the land without return, the house of darkness where the inhabitants are fed on dirt and dung. According to the Homeric view, the shades in Hades (derived from *a-idēs*, the invisible kingdom) lead an unconscious half-life without striving and desire, without influence upon the world above. They remain therefore without veneration and the sacrifices offered by the living. There is no means of conjuring or attracting them up. Only through the blood gift of Odysseus is the remembrance of their earlier life awakened in them (*Odyss.*XI). No compelling of the dead occurs; there is also no oracle of the dead. An enlightened rationalism has made the once mighty and living dead into shades and thus banished all fear of them. We find a similar development in early Israel where the cult of ancestors and the dead and the conjuration of the dead were commonly practised. The departed are called *rephā'īm*, the 'languid', the 'feeble' (Isa. 14.9f; Ps.88, 10, etc.); their state is a 'sleep', 'eternal sleep'. Even so they still have some connection with their earlier life. In the shadows the outlines, so to speak, of their earlier form are recognizable.

The cause of this depreciation and devitalizing of the departed, this weakening of the early belief in the dead is twofold. There is (1) the belief in the overwhelming might of Yahweh behind whom the power of the dead as that of magical objects and nature spirits has to be suppressed. The intensity and energy of Yahwism led to the paralysing of powerful early conceptions of the state after death. In place of the cult of the family grave came the conception of the realm of shades in which all are equal. There is also (2) the strongly collective character of Israelite religion.

Many peoples know of a continuation of life after death (d) *on this earth* (*ERE* 12, 425ff.; Moore, G. F., 1914; Eliade, 1959). The soul is separated from its present body and enters into another one, be it human, animal or plant, occasionally also into inorganic objects, snakes poisonous and harmless, lizards, the falcon, the lotus flower, the phoenix and heron (Mexico, Zululand, New Zealand, Germanic peoples, Egypt). Especially widespread is belief in rebirth among the Indo-Germanic peoples, the Indians, Thracians, Greeks, Slavs and Celts. The Celtic druids taught reincarnation. The Lithuanians believe that animals return after death. The Greeks coined several expressions for rebirth: *metensōmatōsis*, *metempsychōsis* and *palingenesia*. Basic here is the belief in the homogeneity of all living beings.

(2) The idea of recompense

The idea of the continuation of earthly life was early on linked with the moral idea of recompense. The sense of justice requires the harmonizing of moral deeds with a person's destiny. Experience shows that here on earth life often goes badly for the good and well for the wicked. This contradiction the belief in recompense seeks to eliminate in a twofold way: (a) by *compensation* in the life to come. First of all, in the other world *some form of judgement* (*ER* 8, 205ff.; 15, 126ff.) may decide upon the form of continued life. This judgement may be *immanent and automatic*. The idea is widespread of the narrow bridge which leads over an abyss and links this world with that to come. The good complete the crossing without difficulty and reach the land of the blessed. The wicked fall down from the bridge. We find this concept among the traditional peoples of North America and Asia and in the *Chinvat* bridge ('bridge of separation', *Yt.* 19, 6; *Y.* 50, 7) of the Mazdaist doctrine of the after-life, also in Islam. Especially characteristic for the automatic judgement is the other Avestan concept: in the third night after death the conscience (*dāenā*) appears to the good in the form of a beautiful fifteen year-old girl, but to the wicked as an ugly old woman.

The compensation may, however, not be automatic but carried out by a judicial deity in a duly constituted court (*RGG* 2, 1415ff.; *LThK* 4, 726; Brandon, 1967). The Melanesians know of a judge of the dead, Nedengei. In Egypt Osiris is 'Lord of judgement'; the court is depicted in chapter 125 of the *Book of the Dead*. In the judgement hall Osiris sits on the throne surrounded by forty-two terrifying judges. The deity of truth (*Maʿat*) receives the dead, Horus and Anubis stand ready to take the heart of the dead and lay it on the scales. The deceased utters a long prayer before his judges in which he swears that he has committed none of the forty-two sins against the gods and men but has lived according to the truth and done what is right. He implores them to rescue him from the monster *Babi* that eats the dead. In early Indian religion the image of the scales is also found. Yama, king of the other world, is judge. He has also entered into the Buddhist pantheon, appearing in China as *Yen-lo* and in Japan as *Emma-O*. The Greek concept of the other world knows of three judges for Hades: Minos, Rhadamanthos and Aeakos. That of Iranian Mazdaism knows of Mithra (god of the Sun), Sraosha (Obedience) and Rashnu (Justice, an ancient god of ordeals).

The separation of the good and the bad follows in accordance with the automatic or formal decision reached. The righteous come to a place of light and happiness, the others to a place of darkness and torment (*ER* 6, 237ff.). The abode of bliss is heaven where the Creator lives, or the underworld or the land in the west; sometimes it is a special part of the realm or city of the dead. The abode of the outcast (*LThK* 5, 450ff.) is situated variously in the underworld, in the interior of the earth or in an area of the city of the dead which has been separated off from the remainder. It is a 'loathsome horrible place' on the coral island Wuwulu, a 'stinking cesspit' on Tahiti. The Eskimo hell is a sunless land of ice and snow where the storm winds howl. In the Tartar hell the wicked soul has to consume objects which it cannot get down; the quarrelsome are cooked in boiling pitch, the unfaithful women must embrace thorn bushes. In the Ewe hell the miser has to starve miserably because he can buy nothing for his money. Many more punishments have been depicted by the religious imagination (extrapolating often from early punitive measures): drowning, dying of thirst, being eaten by a monster, or dashed to pieces on the rocks. In the Chinese Taoist temples and the Japanese Buddhist ones pictures are hung in which the punishments in hell for the various sins are represented with terrible clarity. Devils tear out the tongue of slanderers with a cord; lecherous men are embraced by women of fire or driven along barefoot on sharp, cutting swords; the greedy suffer the tantalizing torments of hell when they see food and drink change into fire before they can eat it.

According to the Mazdaist view, the souls of true believers go to the golden throne of Ahura Mazda and the 'immortal spirits' and the other true believers, in paradise, the 'House of Song'. The wicked souls are brought by evil spirits into the 'darkness without beginning' where food of poison and poisonous stench is brought to them. In the Orphic-Platonic doctrine of the after-life the contrast between reward and punishment is especially emphasized. A fearful punishment in the deepest mire of the abyss of Tartarus awaits the transgressor.

The idea of compensation for moral actions in a subsequent destiny also leads 'late' Judaism, under Iranian influence, to belief in the *resurrection of the body* (*LThK* 1, 1042ff.; *ER* 12, 344ff.). Until then, the Israelite expected the rewards and punishments for actions whether of individual or of the whole people, to take effect in this world alone. Belief in God's universal power (which even reached down into the underworld) created the basis for the belief in resurrection. The first real impulse towards this was provided at the time of the Maccabees by the martyrdom of the pious and those faithful to Yahweh. 'The

King of the universe will raise up to an everlasting renewal of life, because we have died for his laws', declares one of the Maccabaean brothers before his torturer (2 Macc. 7.9). The resurrection is the prerogative of martyrs. For persecutors 'there will be no resurrection to life' (2 Macc. 7.14). This belief was later widened through the supposition of a parallel resurrection of persecutors, not however to life but to torment. Finally, this partial resurrection was broadened out to belief in a resurrection of all people at the final judgement (Enoch, 50).

A second kind of equalizing the destiny of good and bad has its place not in the other world, but rather through *the return to this world*. In India and Greece the moral ideas of rewarding and punishment were closely linked with the transmigration of souls (see above, section one). The great law of *karma* states that 'good will come to one through good work, bad through bad'. Moral action forms a kind of sublime power-substance which condenses after death into a new bodily form (see above, Chapter 15). A rebirth is possible as god, as man in the different castes, as animal 'be it as worm, as fly, as fish, as bird, as boar, as a savage animal or as a tiger'. Later the exact correspondence between the form of sin and its punishment was worked out more specifically: whoever steals jewels will be reborn as a goldsmith's bird; whoever steals gold, as a rat; elephants, as a wolf; horses, as a tiger; whoever kills a Brahmin, as a dog or a pig after long being tormented in hell; whoever commits adultery with the wife of a Brahmin, becomes reborn as grass, a bush or a reptile.

The idea of rebirth is the basis for the Upanishads' mysticism and also for the Jainist and Buddhist doctrine of salvation (see above, Chapter 17). According to the Indian view the possibility exists in meditation of remembering earlier existences. The doctrine of rebirth has remained Hindu dogma down to the present. Very few spirits, such as the followers of the Brāhma Samāj, have, under European influence, emancipated themselves from it.

Orphism has a similar doctrine of rebirth. Stressed here also is the balancing of the moral act with one's destiny in life, the symmetry of body and soul with the psychic and ethical character of the preceding existence. The same possibility is also recognized of remembering earlier existences. Pythagoras could give the place in the temple of Hera where the shield hung which he had carried in an earlier existence, as Euphorbos, during the siege of Troy, at the time Menelaus killed him. Empedocles developed the ethical doctrine of reincarnation: 'If someone stained his hands with the blood of a murder victim and . . . in addition . . . commits perjury . . . the same must stray for three times ten thousand seasons far from the blessed and wander through weary paths of life, so that in the course of time he becomes born into every possible kind of mortal being. I was already in the past boy, girl, plant, bird and fish . . . Nature . . . rings the changes . . . Men obtain the best protection in the transmigration of souls amongst the animals, lions sleeping on the earth and among the trees . . . Finally they become seers, singers, physicians and princes . . . and grow to be gods, richest in honour.'

Plato also stood under the influence of Orphic reincarnation doctrines (*Tim.*

41f.). The powerful influence of Platonism on the one hand and the age-old Indo-German inheritance on the other explains the firm persistence of the doctrine of reincarnation. The latter has had a far greater significance in the history of Western thought than is commonly realized. Virgil explains that after a thousand-year stay in Elysium the soul drinks from the waters of Lethe and returns to the earthly world to be reincarnated. It is debatable whether the Old Testament (Job and Ps. 90.3) contains signs of the presence of the doctrine of the transmigration of souls. Clear traces of it, however, are found in the New Testament, e.g. in the story of the man blind from birth: 'Who sinned, this man, or his parents, that he was born blind?' (John 9.2). The Gnostics, including Basilides and the followers of Carpocrates, taught transmigration of souls. Epiphanes interpreted Jesus' saying about the prison in which one must pay the last penny (Matt. 5.25f.) in terms of the body in which a soul again becomes imprisoned. According to the Manichaean view, the 'hearers' who belong to the lowest class of members pass into the body of one of the 'elect' or into plants and trees, especially melons and cucumbers which the true believers eat; this is the way of purification. The souls of non-Manichaeans pass into the lower inedible plants or into the bodies of animals. For this reason the killing of animals was forbidden to Manichaeans. The medieval Cathari who go back to dualist Eastern religious groups taught the transmigration of souls and affirmed that it was possible to remember earlier rebirths. Individuals declared that as a horse they had lost at a particular place a horseshoe which then was really found. Also in rabbinic Judaism and in the Kabbalah the transmigration of souls is found, likewise in individual heterodox sects in Islam.

Reincarnation doctrine was also revived in the modern period. In the seventeenth century Franciscus Mercurius of Helmont faced the Inquisition (*ER* 7, 251ff.) in Rome because of his belief in the transmigration of souls. Lessing and Goethe referred to it in the eighteenth century, Schopenhauer in the nineteenth. Even at the present time it is widespread among educated people old and young, in Catholic lands (Poland and Italy), amongst the followers of Theosophy and Anthroposophy, in Anglo-Saxon Christianity among the laity. Conservation groups have absorbed its ethic of reverence for all forms of life and nature. The myth of the transmigration of souls has the advantage that it contains no elements except those which lie before our eyes. Hence, all its concepts can be illustrated with examples. For some it is the only explanation which gives life meaning.

(3) Life with God and in God

All ideas of immortality in terms of a continuation of life after death and also of the moral reward following therefrom, have left some unsatisfied. For some people are aware of their relatedness and similarity to God; they also know in themselves the longing for *a life with God and in God*, for deification (*ER* 4, 259ff.; 7, 123ff.). It comes to expression already in the *Rigveda* (9, 113): 'Where uncreated light, the world in which the sun is set, into this set me, Soma, in imperishable immortality ... there ... where bliss and joy, desire and enjoyment dwell, where ... wishes are fulfilled, there make me immortal.' The longing for immortality lived also in the Semitic world. In the Gilgamesh epic the hero is in search of eternal life. Finally he finds the plant of immortality but a demon snatches it from him (see above, Chapter 8).

Both the Israelite and also the Greek sagas know only of the gathering up of individuals blessed with a life similar to God's, such as Enoch, whom God took away after a life 'in fellowship with God' (Gen. 5.24), and Elijah, who went up into heaven, to Yahweh, in a whirlwind (2 Kings 2.11). The Greek gods give only certain individual mortals the food of immortality and thereby immortality itself. Ganymede the most beautiful of the children of men becomes caught up to Olympus by the gods and there made a cupbearer (*Iliad* 20, 231ff.). Telemachus prophesies to Menelaus that gods will send him to the Elysian Fields at the end of the world (*Odyss.* 4, 561ff.).

The yearning for divine life leads people to create the certainty of immortality in cultic ways, through sacred consecration. All the mystery religions of antiquity constitute ways to immortality and resurrection. The union with the dying and rising vegetation deities guarantees people eternal life beyond death. Such is the case with the mysteries of Osiris, Isis, Attis, Dionysus, Eleusis and the mysteriosophic Mithras (see above, Chapter 7). Sophocles says: 'Thrice blessed are they who beheld these consecrations and then went into the kingdom of Hades; then among mortals only these live, all others meet with suffering.' The Cynic Diogenes mocked: 'Pantaikion the thief will have a better lot after death than Agesilaos and Epaminondas because he was initiated into the mysteries.' But a profound thought lies at the heart of the mysteries: immortality is not an entitlement nor an achievement of a person, but the free gift of love whose outward symbol is the sacred act of consecration.

(4) Salvation religions' concepts of the beyond

Over all traditional, ethical, mystical and cultic concepts of the beyond rise the different concepts of the beyond of the salvation religions. The beyond for them is the fulfilment of the salvation which is already attained on this earth. According to the Orphic Platonic idea the soul at death is freed from the bonds of the body and of matter, which it can only loosen through asceticism (see above, Chapter 16). It is allowed to return to the heavenly home of the Father to live forever in the world of light and of ideas. The whole Hellenistic world, above all Gnosticism and Neoplatonism, follows this Platonic idea of the beyond. According to Orphic teaching people step out of the cycle of births through the grace of Dionysos and attain after a series of rebirths to a life like the God. According to Pindar, at least a threefold migration on earth without lapse is necessary before the soul is freed from the cycle of births. The Cathari believed that the soul migrates until it comes into the body of a fellow-member and, freed from all guilt through the sacrament of the laying on of hands (*consōlamentum*), enters into paradise after death (*RE* 13, 765f.; Söderberg,

1949). According to the teaching of the Upanishads the soul which has attained the saving knowledge of its unity with Brahma enters after death everlasting Brahma. It is in this case a matter of the complete dissolution of individuality in the divine infinity as salt dissolves in water and can no longer be discerned as something separate: 'After death there is no consciousness', Yājnavalkya teaches; for where unity rules there can be no more twofoldness of knower and known, but only the undifferentiated unity of the individual self with the endless divine *Ātman*. The early Buddhist idea of *Parinirvāna* (see above, Chapter 16) corresponds to this Upanishadic concept of the beyond. It is a state of endless peace and perfect blessedness, but an unconscious blessedness.

Crucial for this concept of the beyond of the mystical salvation religion is that there is no fundamental difference between this-worldly salvation and that of the world to come. The perfect one according to the Upanishads attains 'the Brāhma already here' and enters daily into the world of Brāhma. The 'nirvāna of the visible order' and the 'perfect nirvāna' are distinguished, according to the Buddha's teaching, only by the fact that in the latter the substrata of bodiliness, the residues of earlier *karma*, have fallen away. The question whether those who have entered into perfect Nirvāna continue to exist or not, the Buddha left unanswered.

Differing from this impersonal concept of the beyond is the idea of the eternal, personal communion with God in theistic mysticism and prophetic religion. Souls attain to blessedness in paradise in the presence of the personal saviour god. According to the *Bhagavadgītā* the soul who has escaped the cycle of rebirth enters into Krishna the saviour god, 'into his being', 'into his space', to 'dwell with him eternally'. In the theistic *bhakti* of India this idea, it is true, is mixed with the theopanic idea of merging into the endless Divine. In a more unmixed form there appears in Mahāyāna Buddhism this personal theistic idea of immortality. The *Buddha Amitābha* dwells in the land of happiness, the 'paradise of the west', in which the believers are happy in his love. The certainty of salvation in this world passes over into undisturbed blessedness in the beyond. Glorious descriptions of heavenly joys are found in the writings of Mahāyāna Buddhism (*SBE* vol. 49). According to the view of the Japanese Shin sect, in the paradise of the Buddha Amida the blessed wear gorgeous clothes, they see glorious visions, hear wonderful sermons, smell the incense of divine grace, taste divine joy with the tongue, bathe with their spirits in bliss, are delighted by the rustling of the winds which waft over the jewelled trees, listen to the notes which re-echo from their branches, leaves and fruits as in the song of the storks and the wild geese.

Israelite religion shows how faith in eternal life proceeds out of personal communion with God and certainty of God. In the spring-time of monotheism it knows of belief in the beyond only in the form of the idea of *she'ōl*. Not the individual, but only the elect people of Israel has eternal continuity. But out of the prophetic intercourse with God there sprang up out of itself the belief in eternal life. The psalmist prays: 'Whom have I in heaven but thee? And there is nothing upon earth that I desire besides thee. My flesh and my heart may fail, but God is the strength of my heart and my portion forever' (Ps. 73.25f.). This faith prepared the way for the belief in the resurrection of later Judaism.

Besides the mystic, pantheist view of eternal life and the personal theistic one there stands the universal, eschatological concept. Not only is eternal life a matter of the salvation and perfection of the individual soul, it also concerns the fulfilment of the whole of humanity and the cosmos. This universal view is first found on the grand scale in Zoroastrian Mazdaism. Zarathustra already announced the coming end of the world and its renewal, the setting up of the restored rule of Ahura Mazda on earth. Later Mazdayasnians developed his prophetic proclamation further and outlined a great scenario of the final cosmic events. The power of evil increases. Immense catastrophes, earthquakes, war, devastation overwhelm mankind. A fearful battle develops between the lord of the demons and the archangels of Ahura Mazda. The dragon *Azi Dahāka* is set free and destroys a third of mankind, but is conquered by the hero Kereshāspa. The saviour Saoshyant arises and effects the *frashokereti* (transfiguration, renewal). The dead, godless and good alike, arise; their souls are united with their bodies in heaven or in hell. The resurrected forgather and relatives recognize each other again. All people see their good and evil deeds; bad people appear as white sheep among black ones. There follows the separation of the righteous and the unrighteous; the first enter heaven in the 'House of Song', the latter go into hell where they are tormented. Now an immense ordeal by fire takes place: a torrent of molten metal which removes entire mountains, pours over the world. The righteous experience it as warm milk, the wicked as white-hot, molten metal. All who have passed the fire ordeal become of one mind and praise Ahura Mazda and the holy immortals. Saoshyant's assistants perform a sacrifice of the ox and the *haoma*. From the fat of the ox they prepare the elixir of life and give it to all men who thereupon become immortal. In the final battle between Ahura Mazda and Angra Mainyu, Ahura Mazda destroys the dragon, the holy immortals overwhelm the other powers. Then the world is completely pure, even hell is purified of all evil beings. The universe is now filled with divine, cosmic harmony (*asha*). All that live enter into a state of heavenly perfection.

No such cosmic eschatology was known by Israelite religion up to the time of the exile, only a prophetic hope of the restoration of the nation's glory. It was under Persian influence that Israelite cosmic eschatology was formed (*LThK* 3, 1084ff.; Mowinckel, 1956). It found expression in the apocalyptic literature of 'late' Judaism. The destruction of the world, the resurrection of the dead, the last judgement, the final salvation of the good and the eternal torment of the wicked – these are the main acts of the drama. India knows of a cosmic eschatology also, but in a cyclical sense of a periodic destruction and renewal of the world (see above, Chapter 4).

(5) Concepts of the beyond in Christianity

In many of the concepts considered so far Christianity has participated. For

Christianity is a religion of the beyond to an overwhelming degree (Althaus, 1933; Nigg, 1954; von Hügel, 1921; Quistorp, 1955; McNeile, 1925; Baillie, 1941; Hick, J., 1976). The Jewish concepts of the beyond, those of Zoroastrianism and of Greece flow together into it. The individual ideas in themselves were by no means new. What is new is twofold: first, the belief in the immediate nearness of the consummation. The gospel is an eschatological message, prepared through the preaching of John the Baptist concerning the nearness of the Kingdom of God (Matt. 3.2). Added to this comes the belief that Jesus revealed himself as the risen and living one to his disciples and thereby re-emphasized also the resurrection of those who believe in him (1 Cor. 15.12ff.). In the risen Christ the new aeon irrupts already into the present one. This world and the beyond are radically separate no longer. This world ruled by mortality is permeated by the powers of the new heavenly world.

The beginning of the disciples' belief in the resurrection of Jesus cannot be explained satisfactorily either by historical criticism or by modern psychology (see above, Chapter 15). The New Testament reports show a series of contradictions; two quite different views are at loggerheads: a strongly realistic, *materialistic* one ('handle . . . and see', Luke 24.39). The view of the sensorily-perceived resurrection body confronts the theory of the '*spiritual* body' or 'heavenly body' which despite an organic continuity with the 'natural' and 'earthly' body is completely different from it (1 Cor. 15.35ff.). A similar conception to this second view is that of being 'further clothed' with a new body which is prepared in heaven (2 Cor. 5.1ff.). Besides this there stands the purely spiritualistic view of the resurrection in the *gnōsis* of the Epistle to the Hebrews and the Gospel of John. But beyond all the divergences stands the certainty that Jesus has borne testimony to himself as the living one and that they who believe in him may share in the glory of the risen one who 'will change our lowly body to be like his glorious body' (Phil. 3.21). The different views and outlook of Christian circles rest on the basis of this resurrection faith. This manifoldness is already found within the New Testament writings.

(a) The original form of the Christian doctrine of the beyond is the *universal eschatological one* (Kennedy, 1904; Vos, 1954; see also section four above). It was taken over by Muhammad who appears to have received it for his part from Syrian Nestorian Christians. Jesus and Muhammad proclaimed the immediate nearness of the end of the world, the last judgement and the consummation of the world through the setting up of the perfect kingdom of glory and blessedness. In the New Testament apocalypse this hope is bound up with the idea of a thousand year interim kingdom (*RGG* 1, 1651ff.; *LThK* 2, 1058ff.; *RAC* 2, 1073; Bietenhard, 1944). The latter begins with the resurrection of the saints and martyrs. These become the kingdom's rulers (Rev. 20.4). Only after this does the final battle come and the general resurrection of the dead. The hope that the new Jerusalem would descend to the earth in the near future (Rev. 21.10) flared up again in the Montanist movement. When it was not fulfilled Christian theologians were forced into a renewed spiritualization of their expectations for the future. According to Origen the resurrection body does not resemble man's but has the most perfect form of body, that of a sphere (the form of the ancient Iranian primal man, Gayomart). This idea, however, was later condemned by the Church (Denzinger, no. 207).

Christian eschatology's view of the fate of the wicked and demons continued to be diverse in character. Jesus speaks of a 'destruction' of body and soul in hell fire (Matt. 10.28). The destruction of all demonic powers is also expected by the author of 1 Corinthians 15, apparently an early Christian Gnostic. This first makes possible that finally 'God may be everything to everyone' (1 Cor. 15.28). This view was further developed by Origen into the doctrine of the *apokatastasis hapantōn* (*RE* 1, 616ff.; *RAC* 1, 510ff.; *LThK* 1, 709ff.; *ER* 1, 344ff.). Christ himself is not able to attain complete beatitude as long as one single member of this body is missing, that is, as long as one created spirit is still entangled in evil or suffering. Therefore all spirits created by God, both men and even demons, finally attain to salvation in God after a period, no matter how long, of purification. When in this way the present aeon has reached its fulfilment a new aeon will begin, with a new fall of angels and men, a new salvation and finally its consummation. The influence of the Indian doctrine of the rhythm of the aeons (*kalpa*: see above, Chapter 4) may here be seen, even as the influence of the Buddhist idea of the Bodhisattva (see above, Chapter 12) is seen in the view of the yet unperfected salvation of Christ. Gregory of Nyssa followed in Origen's footsteps. But whereas the latter had taught only a temporary apokatastasis, the former held to its finality. Despite the Church's condemnation of the Origenist teaching (Denzinger, no. 223), the idea of apokatastasis has had its supporters in the Eastern Orthodox Church down to the present day. There have been even more supporters for this doctrine among the free Protestant spirits of all centuries, including Hans Denk and the radical Reformers, J. W. Peterson, Jane Lead and the mystic William Law in England, Jung Stilling, Oetinger and Bengel, for a time also Zinzendorf, in the modern period, Schleiermacher, Gustav Theodor Fechner, both Blumhardts, the Indian evangelist Sadhu Sundar Singh and, among recent theologians, John Hick (1976, 242ff.).

In opposition to this apokatastasis teaching, Catholic as well as Protestant orthodoxy has held fast to the eternity of hell's punishments and this by invoking the alleged sayings of Jesus (Matt. 18.8; 25.41; Mark 9.43, 48). Dante gave powerful expression in his *Inferno* to this teaching of the irrevocability of hell's torments with his words: 'Abandon hope all ye who enter here' (*Inf.* 3). But many faithful Christians are unable to live at peace with this teaching which stands in irreconcilable contradiction to the eternal love of God. The mystic Julian of Norwich received a divine revelation that God will make everything good in ways which people may not know of. Catherine of Genoa believed that the rays of divine love reach down even into hell and bring the damned mildness and refreshment in the midst of their torments. The Catholic systematic theologian Hermann Schell restricted the eternal punishments of hell to the 'sin with raised hand', the sin against the Holy Spirit, the radical hatred of God (Schell, 1893, 879ff.). Other theologians regard the harmonizing of the divine mercy, which wills the salvation of all people (1 Tim. 2.4), with the righteousness which demands the eternal rejection of flagrant sinners as one of the insoluble *a prioris* of the human spirit.

The universal, eschatological conception has been intersected since early Christian times by (b) the *Orphic, Platonic doctrine* of the beyond. The soul is freed at death from the chains of the body and goes bodiless into the eternal world. It is judged by God as an individual, at the moment of death or immediately after, as the Christian Gnostic already teaches in the Epistle to the Hebrews (9.27). In the parable of poor Lazarus and the rich glutton (Luke 16.19), a double state of the soul after death – the delights of the righteous in the bosom of Abraham and the tormenting of the wicked in hell-fire – is already assumed. On the basis of an individual judgement the sinless go straight to heaven, the wicked into hell. The first vivid description of the fate of souls in paradise and hell is contained in the Apocalypse of Peter which is influenced by Orphic ideas (MacCulloch, 1912). Paradise is depicted as an immeasurably large space outside our world, flooded with radiant light, covered with flowers that never fade, filled with fragrant odours, full of evergreen plants bearing luscious fruits. The inhabitants of paradise wear garments of light which are not less beautiful than their wonderful land and they praise God with joyful voice. Over against these paradisal delights of the righteous are the hellish torments of the wicked which, differentiated according to particular sins, are portrayed with Dantesque vividness. Murderers are gnawed away in a ravine full of worms. Women who have aborted, sit up to the neck in blood, whereby flames of fire are emitted by the children untimely born and strike the former in the face. The slanderers bite off their lips and receive red-hot molten iron poured into their eyes. The unmerciful, wrapped in rags, must dance on glowing flints. The homosexuals are repeatedly thrown down from a cliff and then have to climb up again. Those who fall away from the faith are roasted in frying-pans. (The Qur'ān contains similar portrayals of hellish torments, but these relate to souls who are reunited with their bodies at the resurrection.)

(c) The *linking* of early Christian eschatology with the Orphic, Platonic doctrine of the beyond engendered various *mixed forms*. To the degree that the return of the Lord – which the earliest congregations awaited in the immediate future – was postponed, the question became ever more burning as to the fate of the departed in the time between the individual's death and the general resurrection. There arose accordingly the doctrine of the 'intermediate state', which has in turn been conceived of in different ways:

1. The oldest view is the doctrine of soul sleep (*psychopannychia*; *LThK* 9, 114) which is already assumed to be the case in 1 Thessalonians (4.15f.). The sleeping ones are awakened at the last day by the sound of the trumpet, meanwhile those still living are caught up into the clouds to meet the Lord. This conception obtained especially in the Eastern Syrian and later Nestorian Church. As Semites the Syrian Christians shared the realistic view of the Jews who knew of no full continuation of the soul's life which had been separated from the body at death. Muhammad took over the doctrine of soul sleep, once

again from the Nestorian Christians (Qur'ān, *sura* 50, 19). Martin Luther shared the view that 'the souls of the righteous sleep and up to the judgement day know not where they are', they rest in the soul's little bedroom. John Calvin for his part produced a youthful work on psychopannychia. The same view may be found today in evangelical circles especially among Adventists and Apostolics and also among individual theologians. Especially characteristic in the Catholic Apostolic (Irvingite) liturgy is the intercessory prayer for the dead: 'Let them rest in thy peace and awaken to a joyous resurrection.'

2. Another direction is taken by the view predominant in the early Church and also in the present-day Churches of the East. According to it the departed find themselves in a conscious state of waiting for the last day, resurrection, judgement, reward and punishment. In this state of expectation the departed already participate in their eternal destiny: the righteous experience a foretaste of eternal blessedness, the wicked a premonition of hell's torments. The place of this waiting is variously depicted. Some look for it in the underworld which is thought of as being divided into paradise or the 'bosom of Abraham', and the place of darkness, the abyss or prison of hell. Others see the place of the righteous as an earthly paradise, that is, in that place where our first parents lived until their expulsion following the fall, and which now is to be found in an inaccessible spot on earth. It is described as a 'place of refreshment' (Cumont, 1956), of light and of peace. This view underlies the prayers in the liturgy for the dead of most Eastern Churches as well as of the old Latin Churches of the West. As long as the soul finds itself in this 'intermediate state' the final decision as to its fate has not yet taken place. This decision can therefore be influenced all the more by the intercessory prayers and alms of the faithful, above all by the offering of the eucharistic sacrifice. Indeed, this influence extends into the future as well as the present: thus, the dead achieve refreshment and relief in the intermediate state and protection from the wrath of God at the last judgement.

3. The third form in which the intermediate state is conceived is the 'refining fire'. The fathers of this Christian doctrine are Clement of Alexandria and Origen. It was shaped by the Stoic doctrine going back to Heraclitus, of the general conflagration at the end of a cosmic era, as well as by the Pauline idea of Persian origin, of a refining of people by fire at the last judgement (1 Cor. 3.13ff.). Both Alexandrians shared the view that the progressive refining in the beyond to which the individual person is subjected, is to be conceived of as a purifying through fire. This purifying fire is characterized as something intellectual and 'rational'. Every sinner lights the flame of his own fire and is not thrown into a fire which has already been lit by another beforehand. According to this Alexandrine view which attained its complete form in the Origenist teaching concerning the apokatastasis (see above), all spirits stained with sin, even the demons, are refined in this mental fire over long periods of time if necessary and so finally fitted for the vision of God. This view of the temporary nature of the punishment of hell coincides with the Hindu and Buddhist view of it as well.

The doctrine of the purifying fire was discredited in the Eastern Church through the condemnation of Origen's apokatastasis teaching. Yet it found acceptance in the West in a different and cruder form, above all through Gregory the Great (*LThK* 4, 9ff.; *HWDA* 2, 1294ff.; Le Goff, 1984). According to the medieval view, all those who depart hence burdened with venial sins or without having done sufficient penance for the serious sins they have left behind, are purified in the place of purgation until all the slack of their sinfulness is refined away and they are in a position to reach the vision of God. Those who depart in a state of mortal sin without repentance go straight to hell, while souls freed from sins and the consequences of sin come immediately to the vision of God in heaven. The purifying punishments are transferred to a special place which is mostly located in the earth's interior. The purgatorial fire is envisioned by popular piety and for the most part also by scholastic theology as a physical fire. The mystics, it is true, put forward mostly a sublimely spiritual view. Catherine of Genoa (Hügel, 1923), for instance, stressed that God himself is the fire of purification for those who are still not yet perfect just as he is the light of blessedness for the perfect; and that the soul conscious of its sinfulness plunges voluntarily into this spiritual fire in an act of love and penitence towards God. According to Roman doctrine the punishments of purgatory bear the character of expiation and satisfaction. They can be made milder and shorter in duration through the prayers and alms of the faithful by means of the application of 'indulgences', that is, ecclesiastical remission of temporal punishments for sins can be made available to 'poor souls in purgatory' by a process of substitution. The offering of the sacrifice of the Mass counts as one of the most important means of shortening the torments of purgatory. If this is celebrated on an altar specially 'licensed' by the pope the soul is freed from purgatory straight away. When the world comes to an end the intermediate state of purgatory ceases. The souls, reunited with their bodies at the resurrection, appear for the 'general judgement' before the throne of Christ. They then either enjoy God's glory with body and soul, or else suffer eternal torment in the fires of hell. In Dante's *Divina Commedia* with its three divisions of *Inferno*, *Purgatorio* and *Paradiso* this Western view of the beyond achieved its imperishable poetic form. At the Council of Trent (Sess. 25) the Roman Church raised the doctrine of purgatory to the status of an obligatory and binding dogma.

Although Protestantism is at one in its rejection of the Roman doctrine of purgatory, its view of the future life is extraordinarily diverse. Besides the doctrine of soul sleep there stands the acceptance of an immediate double decision (heaven or hell); and besides both runs the doctrine of an intermediate state as one of progressive development. In recent Protestant theology there is widespread rejection of the 'Platonic and Hellenistic' belief in immortality in favour of the view that at death body and soul are completely 'destroyed' and that at the last judgement God may create a new person with body and soul (*RGG* 1, 696ff.; Künneth, 1951).

(d) Besides the early Christian eschatological view and the Orphic-Platonic one stands yet another view of eternal life which moves both other approaches to one side as unimportant. Communion with God, for unshakeable faith, already includes eternal life. This is already expressed in Psalm 73 (see (4) above). This thought was most powerfully formulated by the author of the Fourth Gospel which stands in conscious opposition to the panorama of the future in early Christian eschatology. Christ says to John: 'He who hears my word and believes him who sent me, *has* eternal life; he does not come into judgement, but has passed from death to life. Truly, truly I say to you, the hour is coming, and now is, when the dead will hear the voice of the Son of God, and those who hear will live' (John 5.24f.). For this early Christian Gnostic, the resurrection is not an event that happens at the end of the world. It is rather the *present* benefits of salvation: '*I* am the resurrection and the life' (John 11.25). The judgement is not a future happening but a present one, it takes place immanently. Heaven and hell are in the heart of everyone. It was above all the German mystics of the sixteenth and seventeenth centuries who stressed with special emphasis the presence of heaven and hell in the human soul. Angelus Silesius gave this thought expression: 'Stop, where are you going? Heaven is within;/you seek it elsewhere, you will miss it forever.' Friedrich Schleiermacher in *Speeches on Religion*, this document of modern mysticism, expressed the view of eternal life's presence in the world in these oft-cited words (*Speeches* 2, 62): 'In the midst of the finite to be at one with the infinite and to experience eternity in a passing moment, that is immortality for religion.'

PART THREE

The World of
Christian Experience

19

Basic Forms

(1) Awe

Manifold is the world of ideas concerning God, God's activity in the world, and the human soul and its destiny after this earthly life. These conceptions can differ widely and yet be linked with the same basic *religious experience* (James, W., 1975; Pratt, 1930; Otto, 1972; Thouless, 1971; Grensted, 1952; Grühn, 1960; Argyle, 1961; Vergote, 1969; Sunden, 1982; *ER* 12, 323ff.). The most striking – and far-reaching – example of this is mysticism. In the most diverse religions, confessions and churches, races and peoples, cultures and epochs, *mystical experiences* (within certain types) are the same or similar (Underhill, 1911; Jones, 1919; Inge, 1947; Suzuki, 1957; Walther, 1955; Zaehner, 1971; Stace, 1961; Ellwood, 1980; Wainwright, 1981). The ecstatic state can be linked with traditional and shamanic deities, with Tao, Ātman-Brāhman, Vishnu-Krishna, Shiva, Kālī-Durgā, with Isis and Attis, and also, significantly, with Christ. Similarly, the saving history which gives the certainty of divine grace, can be just as much the ancient vow of Buddha Amitābha (see above, Chapter 17) or Israel's exodus from Egypt, as the cross of Christ, without changing the basic experience of faith, confidence, hope and security. Such an experience could be based on purely profane circumstances. It could be engendered by powerful political personalities just as a mystical experience of the 'highest good' can be found in association with beloved persons. There are erotic and artistic ecstasies as well as religious ones. The difference between the religious experiences and the profane one lies exclusively in the relationship to the supernatural, the transcendent, the beyond.

The basic religious experience, the substratum of it all, is reverence or awe or holy dread. This experience includes bowing to show honour and self-effacement, fear, admiration, longing and self-giving. It comes over a person especially when coming into or being in sacred space.

> God reveals his presence:
> Let us now adore him,
> And with awe appear before him.
> God is in his temple:
> All within keep silence,
> Prostrate lie with deepest reverence.
> Him alone
> God we own,
> Him our God and Saviour
> Praise his name for ever.

So runs a hymn (*CH* 234) of Gerhard Tersteegen which is often sung at the beginning of Protestant services of worship. The spontaneous expression of this reverence is the prayer gesture, especially prostration and kneeling (see above, Chapters 5 and 9).

(2) Fear

As admiration and longing fade, *awe* passes into *fear* (Scruton, 1985). So great is the significance attaching to fear that Lucretius saw in it the source of belief in the gods: 'As the first thing, fear created the gods in the world.' This saying contains a germ of truth. A large part of the religious practice of archaic and traditional peoples involves the fear of tabu objects, witches and sorcerers, and spirits, especially the spirits of the dead. The gods of antiquity are mostly feared, individual ones have a particularly frightful character, and, indeed, not just the war deities but even mother goddesses like Ishtar and present-day Kālī-Durgā have a fearful as well as a mild aspect. Yahweh who was originally a mountain, storm and volcano deity, also possesses a terrifying aspect. Even prophetic belief in God lays stress on fear: 'The fear of the Lord, that is wisdom' (Job 28.28), 'It is the beginning of wisdom' (Ps. 111.10), true worship (Ecclus. 2.17). 'Serve the Lord with fear, with trembling kiss his feet (Ps. 2.11f.). Fear reaches even into New Testament piety: 'Work out your own salvation with fear and trembling' (Phil. 2.12); 'It is a fearful thing to fall into the hands of the living God' (Heb. 10.31). Luther writes in the *Smaller Catechism*: 'God threatens to punish all who transgress this commandment; therefore we ought to be afraid of his wrath.'

There is nevertheless a tendency in religions towards an overcoming of fear by confidence and love. This holds above all for the New Testament in which the exhortation resounds again and again: 'Be not afraid' (e.g. Luke 2.10). The apostle says: 'You did not receive the spirit of slavery to fall back into fear, but you have received the spirit of sonship' (Rom. 8.15). In Johannine mysticism fear is completely removed at the highest level. 'There is no fear in love, but perfect love drives out fear. For fear has to do with punishment, and he who fears is not perfected in love' (1 John 4.18).

The heights of Pauline and Johannine mysticism were not held on to in subsequent Christianity. Motives of fear are found in large measure in Catholic piety, above all the fear of eternal punishment in hell. Gregoria, the lady-in-waiting, explained to Gregory the Great that she could not find peace, she felt compelled rather to be continually mistrustful and full of fear. The motive of fear is one of the strongest motives in the Church's education of the masses. It is built in to the Church's teaching on penance. The latter distinguishes a twofold repentance out of fear of eternal punishment and repentance out of love for God. Only in connection with confession and priestly absolution may the first form of repentance lead to the restoration of sanctifying grace and open the way to heaven. Medieval piety concentrated upon Christ as the fearful judge of the world. The *Dies Irae* of Thomas of Celano sings of the greatness of the fear when the judge shall come. Mary on the other hand embodies intercessory love; she stills her Son's wrath in showing him her maternal breast.

Besides the fear of the mighty, vengeful and judging God there is another kind of fear: the fear or anxiety (Pfister, 1948) concerning God's remoteness and being abandoned by him. The higher reaches of piety include not only happy confidence and blessedness, but also shuddering, dreadful states of loneliness, emptiness, barrenness, dryness, depression and anxiety; the mystics describe these as the 'dark night of the soul', the 'exile of the heart', the 'temporary hell'. The 'dryness' (*siccitās*) is especially to be found in the life of the passionate mystic as a reaction to experiences of bliss which have satiated the feelings. Luther also knows these dreadful states which he overcame through experiencing the certainty of justification. Anxiety drives the pious to ardent prayer in which there follows a swing back towards confidence and trust.

(3) Faith, trust, confidence

The opposite experience to fear is *faith, trust, confidence* as hope and present certainty, the sense of security and safety (*ER* 5, 250ff.). Without trust there can be no devotion to prayer. Trust is one of prayer's motifs as well; it grows and is increased by prayer (*ERE* 3, 325ff.). It is related to the power and goodness of the Deity, and the latter's helpfulness and joy in giving. It attains a pure form in prophetic piety. The most powerful expression of prophetic trust in the mighty and gracious God is the prayer of the Psalmist: 'Thou art my rock and my fortress, for thy name's sake lead me and guide me' (Ps. 31.3). 'In thee do I take refuge; let me never be put to shame' (Ps. 71.1).

The sense of being protected is maintained right in the midst of danger. 'Even though I walk through the valley of the shadow of death, I fear no evil; for thou art with me; thy rod and thy staff, they comfort me' (Ps. 23.4). The song of songs of safety and protection is Psalm 91 which Benedict selected as the chief Psalm of the night prayer: 'He will cover you with his pinions, and under his wings you will find refuge; his faithfulness is a shield and buckler' (Ps. 91.4). The certainty of God, described as virtually 'having God' is so great that it remains unshakeable in the face of complete external collapse: 'Whom have I in heaven but thee? And there is nothing upon earth that I desire besides thee. My flesh and my heart may fail, but God is the strength of my heart and my portion forever' (Ps. 73.25). Luther says: 'Whoever believes he has a gracious God and Father, that Christ the Son of God has destroyed death, sin, hell and the devil, ought he not to be happy and rejoice? Indeed he ought to make his way through mountains of iron and through all kinds of adversity with undaunted and unconquerable spirit.'

Faith is raised to defiant faith with the martyrs (see above, Chapter 12), beginning with the Maccabaean brothers, the apostles and early Christian witnesses unto blood. No agony of torture, no form of death however cruel could dissuade them from holding fast to their faith and making a good confession. Such martyrs, however, are also found in great numbers among Christian dissidents ('heretics'), as well as in Buddhism, Islam and Bahā'ism.

(4) Hope

Related to faith is *hope* (*ERE* 6, 779ff; *LThK* 5, 416ff.; Moltmann, 1967; *ER* 6, 459ff.). Religious hope is faith directed towards the future, be it for liberation from material need, for attaining eternal life and blessedness after death, or for the coming of the Kingdom of God (see above, Chapters 9 and 18). Hope defies even the appearance of the destruction of one's own life, it is the leap into uncertainty, it is believing in 'hope against hope' (Rom. 4.18).

(5) Love

Of the basic religious experiences 'the greatest is *love*' (*ERE* 8, 151–83; *RGG* 4, 361ff.; *ER* 9, 31ff.). The love of God is expressed in terms of human social relationships and that of friendship towards God (see above, Chapter 13). Mystical love is passionate turning towards the pure spiritual divine goods: divine truth, love, goodness (see above, ibid.). The Platonic *erōs* takes its starting point in the visible world, then ascends to the invisible one. Erōs is the son of *Ploutos* and *Penia*, of human need and divine fulness. Mystical love seeks absorption in the beloved object. The symbol of this spiritual love is the sexual eros in its absolute character and its tendency to be absorbed in the beloved and be merged into it (see above, Chapter 7). Very often heavenly and earthly eros are intermingled. Repressed sexual drives flow into the religious as in the loving intercourse of nuns with the heavenly bridegroom, for instance with the medieval Dominican Margareta Ebner (see above, Chapter 7). Besides the bridal love of God there is the child love as it unfolds in the cult of the *Bambino Gesu* and of the Krishna child.

A distinction should be drawn between mystical love and prophetic evangelical love, *agapē* (*ERE* 1, 166ff.; 3, 373ff.; *ThWNT* 5, 20–55; Nygren, 1953). Yet the latter like mystical love is also a love 'above all things' (Luther), a love 'with all your heart, and with all your soul, and with all your might' (Deut. 6.4; Mark 12.30). It rests on the personal relationship of trust in God who appears under the symbol of fatherhood and motherhood (see above, Chapter 14). This personal *agapē* is a response to the prevenient love of God: 'We love because he first loved us' (1 John 4.19). Love is the radiating outwards of the divine love into the human one: 'He who loves is born of God and knows God' (1 John 4.7). God's love is inseparably bound up with the love of one's neighbour: 'He who does not love his brother whom he has seen, cannot love God whom he has not seen' (1 John 4.20). In the suffering fellow-human the devotee loves the God who is present in him (see above, Chapter 12). This form of religious love is more sober and measured than mystical love which tends for its part towards excess.

(6) Peace

Faith, hope and love establish a religious state which is described as *peace* (Bammel, 1957). In a world without peace (*ER* 15, 339ff.) the religious person seeks peace and rest in God. The longing for 'peace in the heart' is found in many religions. It bears a different character, however, according to the two main types. Mystical peace (*shānti*), as it is praised in the Upanishads and in early Buddhism, is without passion, the extinguishing of desires (*apatheia, virāga*). The deepest peace of the soul is the 'nirvāna in the visible order' (see above, Chapter 17). The peace of the prophetic, evangelical religion of conscience (*ThWNT* 2, 398–418) takes a different form. Peace in the heart is attained on the basis of forgiveness of sins and the God-given experience of mercy. The Psalmist prays: 'Blessed is he whose transgression is forgiven, whose sin is covered. Blessed is the man to whom the Lord imputes no iniquity' (Ps. 32.1f.). Those to whom Jesus has assured forgiveness of sins he dismisses with the comforting words; 'Go in peace' (Mark 5.34; Luke 7.50). For Paul the peace of the heart is the state of those who are saved: 'Since we are justified by faith, we have peace with God through our Lord Jesus Christ' (Rom. 5.1). 'The fruit of the spirit is . . . peace' (Gal. 5.22). 'The kingdom of God is . . . peace and joy' (Rom. 14.17).

(7) Joy

Joy is closely associated with peace. The religious festivals are festivals of joy; sacrifices are often linked with joyful meals and banquets. Cultic joy often takes on an orgiastic and ecstatic character; there are sexual festivals of joy in which the 'bliss of creation' expresses itself in mass copulation (Schubart, 1941). Joy is a clear goal of the major religions, of the mystery cults, mysticism and the prophetic and evangelical religion of faith. In the festival rites of the mysteries, eternal blessedness is anticipated. Examples are the *Hilaria* of the Attis cult and the *Inventio* of the cult of Isis and Osiris (see above, Chapter 7). Despite all their renunciation of the world mystics are advocates of joy. The Taittirīya *Upanishad* (3, 6) says: 'All beings are born out of joy, through joy they are sustained, into joy they enter when they depart this life.' Joy is the natural feeling of the saved. Joy is the fruit of deep meditation (*ERE* 6, 510ff.). The second stage of meditation (*jnāna*) is described in Theravāda Buddhism as joy and delight free from all reflection. In the parallel scale of four feelings of endlessness, the 'states of Brāhma', the second stage is rejoicing with all fellow-beings. The final goal of the Buddhist way of salvation is happiness, but a happiness without excitement, without emotion and intoxication (see Chapter 17 above). This still, meditative joy stands in contrast to an extravagant emotional joy in love mysticism; examples include the Tamil mystic Mānikka Vāshagar, the Muslim poet Jelāl-ud-dīn Rūmī and the Franciscan poet Jacopone da Todi. This emotional joy alternates of course with the states of joylessness and 'dryness' (see under (2) above), as Mānikka Vāshagar, Vidyāpati Thākur, Bernard of Clairvaux and Mechthild of Magdeburg demonstrate.

Joy takes up equal space in prophetic, biblical religion (*LThK* 4, 361ff.; *ThWNT* 4, 365ff.; 9, 350ff.). The Hebrew language possesses a whole series of synonyms for joy. Joy animates the participants in the temple at Jerusalem at the presence of Yahweh, and indeed already during their pilgrimage there (Ps. 122). Many psalms have a joyful character: 'Let the righteous be joyful; let them exult before God; let them be jubilant with joy' (Ps. 68.3). 'My heart and flesh sing for joy to the living God' (Ps. 84.2). Religious joy widens out to cosmic joy: 'Let the heavens be glad and let the earth rejoice' (Ps. 96.11). Borne aloft by joy also is the sermon of the prophet of salvation looking out upon the coming time of deliverance: 'The ransomed of the Lord shall return, and come to Zion with singing, with everlasting joy upon their heads; they shall obtain joy and gladness, and sorrow and sighing shall flee away' (Isa. 35.10).

The call to joy sounds through the whole of the New Testament. Jesus proclaims a Kingdom of joy: 'Rejoice in that day and leap for joy, for behold, your reward is great in heaven' (Luke 6.23). Joy is also the basic tone of the first congregation's gathering for worship: 'They partook of food with glad and generous hearts' (Acts 2.46). Christians are described in the Epistle of Barnabas (7, 1) as 'children of joy'. Paul is a herald of eschatological joy: 'Rejoice in the Lord always; again I will say, Rejoice . . . the Lord is at hand' (Phil. 4.4f.). Joy is the goal of apostolic service: 'Not that we lord it over your faith; we work with you for your joy' (2 Cor. 1.24). Christian joy transfigures the suffering and the cross: 'With all our affliction, I am overjoyed' (2 Cor. 7.4). The breakthrough to joy out of suffering is depicted in the Fourth Gospel as the birth pangs of a woman (John 16.21). The Christian worship service is a constant source of joy; it has its high point in the liturgy of Easter night. Both the *Exsultet* of the Roman Easter liturgy and also the hymnic singing of the Greek Easter night show the cosmic scope of the joy. The Christian saints were heralds of joy to a remarkable degree. Understandably, therefore, Benedict XIV added a fourth requirement to the three hitherto valid in canon law for the canonization of a saint: a constant joy, even for someone with a melancholy temperament (see Chapter 12 above). Among the saints Francis of Assisi is especially outstanding as the embodiment of joy. He described as 'perfect joy' the willing endurance of deprivations, calumnies and wrongs. Luther was also a tireless preacher of joy, above all in his Christmas sermons. 'The stronger faith is, the happier the person becomes out of this boundless grace.' The narrow heart of man becomes 'drunk with joy'. Similarly Shinran says: 'We should have every occasion to rejoice heaven-high and to dance with joy like madmen' (see also above, Chapter 17).

(8) Eagerness to communicate, zeal

Religious experience has an *urge to communicate*. This impulse breaks through to a greater degree where the religious experience goes beyond the existing limits of tradition and creates new forms of the vision of God and salvation as also of the outward veneration of God. After his enlightenment, the Buddha was tempted to keep his saving knowledge for himself and to remain in the undisturbed freedom of Nirvāna; but compassion for all living beings who without his message cannot come to this saving knowledge, forced him to the decision to proclaim his teaching to the whole world (*Mahāvagga* I, 5, 2f.). He himself went out to preach and sent his disciples out for the same purpose, as the early formula of the Pāli canon puts it: 'For the salvation of many beings, for the happiness of many beings, out of compassion for gods and men' (*Mahāvagga* I, 11). The urge to communicate is not less pronounced in prophetic religion, though it is differently motivated. The prophet stands under the compulsion of the divine command which he must carry out. He cannot do otherwise than hand on the message of God which has been entrusted to him, especially before the mighty of this world, even when his preaching earns him dishonour and persecution (see Chapter 12 above). Paul considers himself 'set apart for the gospel of God' (Rom. 1.1). He must obey the divine command: 'Woe is me if I do not preach the gospel' (1 Cor. 9.16). The urge to proclaim impels towards missionary work. It is a question of bringing the liberating message to all who have not yet heard it and of incorporating them into the community of the redeemed. In this missionary impulse members of the three great world religions – Buddhism, Christianity and Islam – vie with one another. In recent years a fourth religion, Hinduism, has joined them (*ERE* 8, 700–51; *RGG* 4, 969–99; Neill, 1964; *ER* 9, 563ff.). Besides foreign missions, which seek to win members of other religions to one's own community, stand the home missions to those of one's own religion who have become alienated from it or have become indifferent in their religious life.

The urge to communicate becomes a matter of consuming zeal especially for members of prophetic religions but also for new religious movements (Mensching, 1966). 'The zeal for thy house has consumed me' – this saying (Ps. 69.9) the Fourth Evangelist applies to Jesus. This zeal for God's honour has again and again produced *fanaticism* (*RGG* 2, 873; *ER* 15, 268ff.) which even the followers of ethnic and state religions may manifest towards the advocates of 'new gods'. The prototype of prophetic fanaticism is Elijah who not only derided the priests of Ba'al but also massacred them (1 Kings 18.17–40). These signs of fanaticism are to be found in the writer of Deuteronomy and in the Deuteronomists who rewrote the early historical works. Fanaticism animated Saul who was 'breathing threats and murder against the disciples of the Lord' (Acts 9.1). It also spurred on the Jews who wanted to kill Paul as an alleged enemy of the law and the temple (Acts 21–23). In the history of Christianity dogmatic fanaticism has again and again led to the use of force against traditional religionists, Jews and Christian dissidents (Nigg, 1962). The history of Islam also shows sufficient examples of this. Thus Muslims have not only destroyed Buddhist and Hindu shrines but also killed Buddhist monks and in the nineteenth and twentieth centuries have bloodily persecuted the Bahā'i. Buddhism from its founder onwards is a religion of tolerance and yet its later followers have shown a fanaticism foreign to its nature towards the members of other religions, indeed those following other tendencies in its own religion, for example Nichiren the Japanese Buddhist (see above, Chapter 12) who called upon the regents to suppress other Buddhist sects by force, or the Sinhalese Theravāda monks who incited the populace against Hindus and Christians. This fanaticism proceeds from the consciousness of the absolute truth of one's own religion and possesses a contagious effect. Out of an individual experience it grows into a collective experience which joins together intellectual blindness with passion and a willingness to resort to force. It also, of course, may be based on fear and the genuine threat to the continuance of the religious cosmology concerned (McKenzie, P. R., 1977).

20
Supernormal Forms

(1) Inspiration

The basic religious experiences are exceeded by extraordinary ones which fall to the lot of especially gifted persons, above all creative religious personalities. These experiences touch in part the boundary of the pathological (*RGG* 5, 1025ff.; see further references above in Chapter 19). The first of these is the experience of *inspiration*, in which a devout person is given suddenly and with great distinctness an insight which relates to God, salvation and the future. The 'perfect illumination' which happened to the Buddha under the fig tree is such an experience. It consists of an insight into the 'causal connection' between suffering, the thirst for life and ignorance. It bore intuitive character such as comes to expression in the term 'visionary knowledge'. Such an insight is experienced by the one inspired as a gift of grace and a miracle (see above, Chapter 16). The experience of inspiration expresses itself insistently in inspired speech and inspired writing. The inspired person does not need to cast about for words. Words come by themselves (see above, Chapter 10). These words are in part incomprehensible and newly formed, in part poetic forms, for example, the 'solemn sayings of the Buddha', numerous sayings of the Hebrew prophets and portions of the New Testament, likewise a series of Quranic *suras*. Such portions of the text are sometimes not spoken orally but are written down as automatic writing and indeed at supernormal speed. To the one writing it is as if a compelling force were guiding one's pen (see above, ibid.).

(2) Visions and auditions

While the experience of inspiration is purely in the mind, *visions and auditions* (*LThK* 10, 646ff.; *ER* 15, 282ff.) take the form of sensory perception without a perceptible object being present. They must therefore be classified under hallucinatory or pseudo-hallucinatory experiences. Visions and auditions can be experienced in the form of a veritable dialogue between the person concerned and the higher power allegedly present. Visions and auditions are especially frequent in the area of mysticism. According to Buddhist psychology they are assigned to the fourth level of meditation, in the state of holy calm (*upekkhā*). The organs of this higher perception are described as the 'heavenly eye' and 'heavenly hearing'. Visions and auditions are no less frequent in prophetic religious experience (see above, Chapter 12). The experiences of the call of the Hebrew prophets are especially associated with auditions or visions (e.g. Isa. 6), likewise many Christian conversion experiences, beginning with the apostle Paul's conversion experience on the Damascus road (Acts 9.1ff.; 22.3ff.; 26.9ff.) down to this century, in the case of the Indian, Sadhu Sundar Singh. While Paul saw only a bright light and heard Jesus' voice, Sundar Singh saw the crucified with the marks of his wounds, in a bright cloud and heard his words: 'Why do you persecute me? Remember that I gave my life for you on the cross' (Heiler, 1926). Both visions and auditions are always dependent upon the conceptual and linguistic forms operating in the visionary's environment. Hindus have visions of their deities, as formerly the Greeks had of theirs. Israelites see angelic forms, Muslims the prophet, Christians the Trinity, Christ, Mary, the angels and saints. It does occur, however, that devout persons, e.g. the Hindu saint Ramakrishna, have had visions both of Hindu deities and also of Christ. Besides the heavenly beings, Satan and his followers also feature in the visions of the saints. The subjective character of all visions becomes clear precisely in the environmental conditioning of the whole world of visionary ideas. And yet, this does not exclude the fact that transcendent reality is disclosed to the devout within the framework of these subjective limits. The soul is touched with the image-less transcendent reality, but this contact is represented to the human spirit in images which are taken from the sensory world and indeed from the immediately accessible environment.

(3) Conversion

An important place in religions, including the traditional religions, is occupied by *conversion* (*RGG* 1, 976ff.; *LThK* 1, 163ff.; Nock, 1952; De Sanctis, 1927; Dollah, 1980; *ER* 4, 73ff.). It occurs partly in the form of an experience of inspiration, partly in that of vision and audition. Most conversions are sudden, as the examples given above (2) make clear. Conversion is commonly preceded by a period of inner uncertainty which sometimes seeks compensation through feverish activity but also can lead to despair. With conversion a state of inner peace and certainty supervenes and frequently evangelistic activity begins. Conversion follows either from an unspiritual and immoral life, or else from one religion to another or one religious tendency to another, or from a religious outlook to a more secular one. Besides conversion to Christianity (and Islam) from traditional religions should be placed conversion from Christianity to the Eastern religious movements. A series of Christian evangelical churches sees in the experience of conversion the criterion of Christian faith and seeks to bring this about in a more or less deliberate way, above all through the forceful revival sermon (*RGG* 2, 621ff.; *LThK* 2, 1063ff.). The latter's most important element is the appeal to repentance. Christianity is familiar with revival movements from Montanism in the second Christian century through the medieval Franciscan movement down to the revival movements of the eighteenth, nineteenth and twentieth centuries in the areas of the younger churches, as in more obviously 'Christian' countries.

(4) Ecstasy

The culmination of mystical experience is provided by *ecstasis* (Eliade, 1970; Sargant, 1973; Holm, N. G., 1982; *RGG* 2, 410ff.; *ER* 5, 11ff.). Ecstasy may be distinguished, as 'high ecstasy', from the states of trance and possession which are frequently met with in traditional religions. Nevertheless both kinds rest on the same 'shamanic' substratum. Ecstasy signifies the transcending of the normal psychic life to a more marked degree still than in the inspiration experience as met with in visions and auditions. Its preparatory stage is the 'intellectual vision', an experience of divine presence which is characterized by the absence of images, as are employed in meditation, and from ecstasy in that full consciousness is retained. Ecstasy is a 'supra-conscious' psychical state which is distinguished by the complete emptying of the soul of all normal experiences whether they be perceptions and ideas, or passions and desires, or of acts of knowing, valuing and desiring. Ecstasy is the experience of the complete oneness of the soul.

In the remoteness of this unitive experience from all normal experiences, ecstatics experience the 'wholly other' both in its alienness and weirdness and also in its fascinating power. They apprehend their own being as identical with the universal cosmic being. As soon as they have come out of the ecstasy, which can extend to hours and days, and have returned to normal psychic life, they feel impelled to interpret this inexplicable unifying experience in words and images. Such formulae include: 'I am God' in the Upanishads, 'I am Reality' (*anā'lhaqq*) in Islamic Sufism (Nicholson, 1978), and 'I in Thee and Thou in me' (Mechthild and Tersteegen). As images for the ecstatic experience of unity, the following are put forward: dreamless, deep sleep, the love union of the sexes, the dissolving of a lump of salt in water, and the burning of the butterfly in the flame into which it plunges. While Plotinus the prince of pre-Christian mystics was said to have experienced ecstasy only four times in his life, other devout persons have experienced ecstasy frequently, many for hours and days on end.

(5) Outward action

The extraordinary religious experience does not confine itself to the individual soul but also draws in other persons, indeed, even nature as well. (a) A special faculty of saints is *cardiognosia* ('knowing the heart'), in Pāli Buddhism 'knowledge of the other hearts' or 'miraculous knowing', a higher form of 'reading of thoughts'. The one at home in the world of inwardness is able to know and to judge the religious and moral state of other people, indeed is even able to see into their past life. When enumerating the extraordinary gifts of grace, Paul speaks of a 'distinguishing between spirits' (1 Cor. 12.10). With cardiognosia is linked telepathy, the perceiving of occurrences afar off and psychological states of distant persons, the prophetic vision of the future, as also the communication of one's own experience to others afar off, for instance, the communication of one's death ('Announcement').

(b) Whereas with the vision of the heart and the future it is mainly a matter of psychological phenomena, in a series of other extraordinary occurrences the psyche operates in the region of the corporeal and material, first and foremost in one's own bodily life (Thurston, 1952). The mystic's ecstatic ascent to God brings with it *a shining of the face*. At the transfiguration on Mt Tabor Jesus' face 'shone like the sun, and his garments became white as light' (Matt. 17.2). An observer tells of a dark-skinned South Indian yogi that at his entry into deep meditation the black of his body gradually changed into white; his white body became brighter and brighter, as if illumined from within, and began to shine. Another consequence of mystical ecstasy is *levitation*, the feeling of overcoming the weight of the body and floating above the ground. Disappearance of a person out of a circle of persons is based on the power of suggestion effecting the switching off of their powers of perception. *Bilocation* consists of a telekinetic generation of the hallucinatory perception of one's own body in a different place. In *self-healing* the devout person calls forth changes in his or her own body. In *anaesthesia*, the martyr switches off the sensation of pain and is able thus to bear the greatest affliction and torture to the amazement of tormentors and spectators alike.

(c) The effect of the psyche also extends further to the bodies of others. Saints possess the gift of *healing the sick* (*ThWNT* 3, 194–215; *RGG* 3, 194ff.; Weatherhead, 1951) and even the raising up of the apparently dead, be it through the laying on of hands or through words of command or even through operating at a distance. Psychic power is able to influence the animal world as well. The saints' love especially exercises a beneficent influence on wild animals (see above, Chapter 1). Thus the Buddha tamed an elephant incited against him, by means of the meditation of love. Buddhist, Islamic and Christian saints live in solitude with wild animals. Indeed, even an influence on wind and weather appears to lie in the realm of possibility. It is difficult to accept that the numerous magical influences on the atmospheric regions on the part of traditional religions, for instance the West African cult of Shango, as well as the nature miracles of great people of God, for example the stilling of the storm at sea by Jesus (Mark 4.35ff.), are all based simply on fiction and legendary accounts.

All these extraordinary phenomena are not miracles in the sense of apologetics of the various religions; they rest upon a conformity with natural law such as has been more and more brought to light by parapsychological research (*RGG* 5, 106f.; Beloff, 1974; McGeery, 1973; LeShan, 1980; Alcock, 1981). These capabilities presuppose a particular psychical, mainly psychosomatic, constitution; but they become more developed and numerous through the systematic practice of meditation, contemplation and prayer. In India a pronounced psycho-technical yoga was built up which followed on from still earlier shamanic traditions. This was further developed, then, in Indian, Tibetan, Chinese and Japanese Buddhism. These Indian techniques had their parallel in the Neoplatonic technique of spiritual exercises (Völker, 1958) and also the prayer technique of Eastern Christian monasticism (Ammann, 1938). The latter drew from Neoplatonic sources as well as Indian ones.

All religious experiences, especially the extraordinary ones, have a strongly contagious effect. There are mass ecstasies, just as there are mass visions and mass healings. Examples of mass visions in our time are the sun miracles of Fatima (*RGG* 4, 761ff.; De Marchi, 1956; see also above, Chapters 2 and 3) in which thousands saw the sun dancing, and the appearance of the Madonna of Heroldsbach. Mass healings occur at the place of pilgrimage at Lourdes (*RGG* 4, 458f.; Leuret, 1950; Schleyer, 1959; Marnham, 1980). In the field of the history of religions, especially in mysticism, psychological observation and description follow religious experience. The finest analysis and classification of mystical experience is found on the one hand in the Buddhist meditation technique which has grown out of yoga, and on the other, in Western mysticism. Among devout Christians the strongest psychological capacity was developed by Augustine (*Confessions*), Teresa of Jesus and Mme de Guyon. In modern theology the first to have described religious experience was Schleiermacher (*On Religion*); Rudolf Otto broadened and deepened his description; while from the viewpoint of religious experience Van der Leeuw (*Religion in Essence and Manifestation*) presented the totality of the world of religious manifestations. Others have been more cautious, whether by confining themselves to experimental psychology (Girgensohn, 1930) or by moving towards more detailed anthropology (Platvoet, 1982). Although religious experience appears always to be subjectively coloured and restricted, and the concept of God born of the imagination but a projection of this experience, nevertheless for the one undergoing the experience what is decisive is not the experience but the Divine towards which the experience is directed and by whom in the final analysis it was called forth.

Conclusion

Up to this point Christianity has been viewed in terms of a wide series of phenomenological categories, and in the context of other religious traditions. A further step has now to be taken. The manifold forms of religious manifestations, religious concepts and religious experiences point beyond themselves towards a final objective that lies beyond and above all sensory and spiritual phenomena. This objective, the holy, the Divine, embraces the three motifs of *mystērium* or *nūmen*, the *tremendum* and the *fascinans* (Otto, 1972; *ER* 6, 431ff.; 11, 139ff.). Towards this objective is directed not only the cult of personal deity but also that of the traditional *nūmen* and ways of salvation which do not recognize personal Deity, including Jainism and Theravāda Buddhism. This reality discloses itself at the same time as revealed and hidden (*deus revelātus, deus absconditus*; Schrade, 1949; Ikenga-Metuh, 1985). As revealed Deity (see above, Chapter 14), the Divine takes on personal form for devotees and appears to them with human countenance, perhaps in the image or icon (see above, Chapter 2). This 'humanness' of the Deity shows itself most strongly in the fact that the Deity confronts the person praying as 'Thou'. This Thou, however, is not confined to the countenance of Deity which is turned towards mankind. Both traditional religions as well as Christian trinitarian faith see this Thou also in the life within the godhead. For Christianity, Father, Son and Spirit coexist as 'persons' in an intimate I-Thou relationship. Otto agrees: 'Surely God is for us Thou and person', yet he goes on to add: 'The Thou in him is that in him which is turned towards us, (but) is at the same time . . . the foothills of a massif which . . . is lost to view in the eternal obscurity.' The one-sided stress on personalism robs the divine of its richness. Above the personal God, indeed above the trinitarian God, Meister Eckhart significantly placed the *Gottheit*, the Deity in its absolute *mystērium*, unfathomable, unknowable and ineffable (see above, Chapter 14). The person who dares to penetrate into this secret is shattered by it. Yahweh speaks to Moses: 'You cannot see my face; for man shall not see me and live' (Exod. 33.20). To Arjuna in the *Bhagavadgītā*, who asks Krishna to show him his countenance, Krishna reveals himself as a grisly and frightening figure (*BG* 11).

Although it may be argued that salvation requires the final, hidden part of God to be no different from the *Deus revelātus*, even the Reformers were cautious at this point. According to Luther, he who would climb up to the knowledge of the *Deus absconditus, Deus nūdus* or *Deus ipse* is consumed in the sea of flames of the divine wrath. This secret may be grasped only in imperfect similitudes and pictures (Brandt, 1958) be they objects or theological concepts.

Ignoring the character of all forms of revelation as similitude has led again and again to the misunderstanding of religion and its repression and desiccation through theological doctrine. Not only the manifestations of nature, but also the metaphors of the Bible and the concepts of theological doctrines constantly call to the seeker, in Augustine's words (*Conf.* 10, 6): 'We are not God, seek beyond us.'

Religion (Bousset, 1903; Brunner, 1948; Hessen, 1955; Holm, 1960; Hick, 1983; *LThK* 8, 783ff.; *ER* 12, 282ff.) has often been too narrowly interpreted on the basis of partial manifestations of religion, be they single ideas or experiences, be they individual religious systems. It does not consist of a particular, static concept of the divine to be grasped rationally but rather of a dynamic intercourse with the Divine (*ERE* 3, 736–76). It is not simply thinking about a transcendent object but an activity be that cultic action or the following of a mystical way of salvation or the life of faith in God's guidance and obedience to his will. Action is present even where prayer and meditation serve no other purpose than preparation for an illumination which arises spontaneously or a reception of grace in a passive state. It is not a theoretical affair but a highly practical one. It is also no merely marginal manifestation in human life (even in the West), but where it is taken seriously it permeates the whole life of a person.

Summed up in a brief formula, religion is worship of the *mystērium* and surrender to this. Such devotion need not be directed simply to the personal in Deity. It includes awe before impersonal, sacred power and the *nūmen*. It vibrates through the words of a teacher of salvation such as Gautama Buddha who is constantly – like the early Christians – accused of atheism. The surrender shows itself in the readiness to sacrifice (see above, Chapter 6), whether this takes the form of an ascetic action or the offering of an external gift or of one's self or an act of charity towards one's neighbour. This selfgiving has a tendency towards the heroic: the great religious personalities of all times are martyrs (see above, Chapter 12), whereby under martyrs should be understood not only those who have given their life once for their faith, but the daily martyrs who show their fellows in a life of renunciation and of service that there is a divine reality.

The pre-eminent activity of religion including Christianity is proclaimed in sacrifice. It consists not only in the preparation for an experience of grace, but also in the consequence of that experience. The mystic who has found salvation in the union with the infinite does not remain in permanent isolation from the world but takes an active part therein. As the disciples of Jesus descend again from the mount of transfiguration, to return to daily life (Mark 9.9), so worshippers and mystics return from the *vīta contemplatīva* to the *vīta actīva* though this may consist only in the hermit or solitary's constant intercessions for people living in the world. More than ever prophets are embued with the tireless activity which consists not only in proclaiming the divine message conveyed to them, but also in selfless service to their fellows and to all mankind. All religious activity in the world, it is true, takes place in the light of eternity.

The final goal of all sacrifice is the state of bliss; suffering is the 'breakthrough' to endless joy.

Religion, including Christianity, is not philosophy, not world-view, not theology, but intercourse with the sacred. This intercourse is a twofold one. It comes to expression very clearly in the dialogues between the soul and Christ as they are found in the most beautiful and popular writings of the German mystics: *The Booklet of Eternal Wisdom* of Henry Suso and the *Imitation of Christ* of Thomas à Kempis. This intercourse, however, is not a human invention of the religious person be it an inspired understanding of experience; it rests not in the realm of human initiative but in that of the Divine. It is not the person who comes to God, but the other way round: God comes to the person. 'It was you that first moved me and made me look for you' (*Imitation of Christ* 3, 21). The traditional devotee derives the cultus from instructions given by higher beings, the cult place from a divine revelation (Gen. 28.10ff.). It is not the person who seeks God but God who seeks the person. This central religious experience is depicted by Sadhu Sundar Singh in a similitude: A child loses its mother in the forest. As it discovers that the mother is away, it begins to seek her and finally finds her. Thereby it notices that the mother had gone to search for the child long before the latter had missed the mother.

Although religion (with Christianity) is *acting*, it is in the final analysis not human achievement, but grace. At all the high points of religion there follows a breakthrough of the experience of grace: in Upanishadic mysticism, in Buddhism in its original form as also in its Mahāyānic one, in Hindu Bhakti mysticism, in Platonic mysticism, in the mysticism of the Islamic Sūfī, in Deutero-Isaianic prophecy, in the piety of the Psalms, with Jesus, Paul, John, Augustine, Luther and Schleiermacher, as also, indeed in the festivals, sacrifices and divination of traditional religions.

Thus the nature of religion, including Christianity, is fellowship of men and women with transcendent reality, a fellowship which flows out of divine grace, which is accomplished in worship and sacrifice and leads to the blessedness of men and women and of humanity.

The act of surrender to the reality of the beyond distinguishes religion, and with it Christianity, from its secularist parallels and surrogates. These resemble religion in their forms of experience and form of expression, and the boundaries between both are fluid. Such parallels to religion are the modern ideologies, racist nationalism and communism, in which a value from the transcendent has been stripped away, or else the intended value is recognized as the highest good and one strives after a wordly goal in the future with eschatological fervour (*RGG* 4, 895ff.; *NDLW* 481ff.).

In contradistinction to these secular eschatologies authentic religion aims at the eternal and imperishable in the sense of Buddha's words: 'What is not eternal, that has no value that one should rejoice in it, no value that one should welcome it, no value that one should turn to it.' Authentic religion ever contains an element of world renunciation, for 'the form of this world is passing away (1 Cor. 7.31). Nothing transitory suffices for the soul, for 'our heart is restless until it rest in thee', as Augustine prays in the introduction to his *Confession*. 'Let grace come and let the world pass away', runs the early Christian communion prayer (*Did.* 10, 6).

Religion is a 'flight of the alone to the alone': so the concluding words of Plotinus' *Enneads*. Buddha appears as completely alone when, meditating under the fig-tree, he has a vision in a state of dispassionate equanimity of the truths of salvation. But the same Buddha took a decision out of compassion for the world to move out of solitude and to become active in the world with his disciples 'for the salvation and the benefit and the happiness' of all living beings. Jesus also stands in great solitariness when he sojourned in the desert for forty days and nights (Mark 1.13), and spent nights alone on a mountain in conversation with his Father (Luke 6.12). But the same Jesus proclaims the coming of God's Kingdom in which those who fulfil God's will find eternal blessedness. Above the individualism of the search for salvation there arises the belief that the final goal of mankind and the cosmos is God's Kingdom, 'the kingdom of truth and of life, the kingdom of holiness and of grace, the kingdom of righteousness, love and peace' (Preface to the Roman liturgy for the feast of Christ the King).

No lesser historian of religion than Nathan Söderblom saw in the Kingdom of God the 'end of all religions': 'Jesus who fulfilled Moses and the prophets did not come to found a new religion but to do away with religions and to found God's kingdom.' Georg Sebastian Huber, a Roman Catholic pricst filled with the prophetic spirit, published a book with the title *From Christianity to the Kingdom of God* (Regensburg, 1934). This rallying cry is correct in that God's Kingdom which forms the content of Jesus' gospel, is greater than all the religions, including Christianity, in that it signifies their final fulfilment. Nevertheless religion only ceases in God's Kingdom in part. In the state of fulfilment the painful sacrifice that forms an essential part of religion comes to an end; but the other essential element, fellowship with God in worship, praise and thanksgiving, spiritual sacrifice, continues for all eternity as Revelation, the last book of the Bible, shows so incisively. God's Kingdom is religion's fulfilment, not one religion's, not simply that of Christianity, but all religions'; for in it, according to the triumphant word of the apostle, God will be 'everything to everyone' (1 Cor. 15.28).

References

Abrahamsson, H., *The Origin of Death* (Stud. Ethnogr. Upsal. 3). Uppsala, 1951.

Adam, A., 'Das Fortwirken des Manichäismus bei Augustinus', *Zeitschrift für Kirchengeschichte*, 69 (1958), 1–25.

Aland, K., *Lutherlexikon*. Göttingen, Vandenhoeck & Ruprecht, 1983.

Alcock, J., *Parapsychology: Science or Magic – A psychological perspective*. Oxford – New York, Pergamon Press, 1981.

Altaner, B., *Patrologie: Leben, Schriften und Lehrer der Kirchenväter*. Freiburg, Herder, 1966.

Althaus, P., *Die letzten Dinge*. Gütersloh, Bertelsmann, 1933.

Ameer Ali, S., *The Legal Position of Women in Islam*. London, 1912.

Ammann, A. M., *Die Gottesschau im palamitischen Hesychasm: ein Handbuch der spätbyzantinischen Mystik*. Würzburg, Augustinus Verlag, 1948.

Andrae, T., *Die letzten Dinge*. Leipzig, J. C. Hinrichs Verlag, 1940.

——, *Mohammed: The Man and his Faith*. New York, Harper Torchbooks, 1960.

Angus, S., *The Mystery Religions and Christianity*. New York, C. Scribner's Sons; London, John Murray, 1928.

Antes, P., *Christentum: eine Einführung*. Stuttgart, Kohlhammer Verlag, 1985.

Appasamy, A. J., *Sundar Singh*. London, Lutterworth, 1958.

Arberry, A. J., *Revelation and Reason in Islam*. London, Geo. Allen & Unwin, 1957.

Arens, W., *The Man-Eating Myth: Anthropology and Anthropophagy*. New York, Oxford University Press, 1979.

Argyle, M., *Religious Behaviour*. London, Routledge & Kegan Paul, 1961.

Armstrong, E. A., *Saint Francis: Nature Mystic*. Berkeley *et al.*, University of California Press, 1973.

Arndt, W. F. and Gingrich, F. W., *A Greek Lexikon of the New Testament*. Chicago, University of Chicago Press; Cambridge, Cambridge University Press, 1957.

Arntz, H., *Handbuch der Runenkunde*. Halle, Niehmeyer, 1944.

Assaad, M. B., *Female Circumcision in Egypt*. Studies in Family Planning (Cairo, 1980), 1, 3–16.

Atchley, E. G. C. F., *History of the Use of Incense in Divine Worship*. London and New York, Longmans Green, 1909.

Aulen, G., *Christus Victor: An historical study of the three main types of the idea of the Atonement*. London, SPCK, 1950.

Bachofen, J. J., *Myth, Religion and Mother Right: Selected Writings*. London, Routledge & Kegan Paul, 1967.

Bächtold-Stäubli, H., ed., *Handwörterbuch des deutschen Aberglaubens*. Berlin, Walter de Gruyter, 10 vols. 1927–42.

Backman, E. L., *Religious Dances in the Christian Church and in Popular Medicine*. London, Allen & Unwin; Greenwood Press, 1952/1977.

Baillie, J., *Our Knowledge of God*. New York, Charles Scribner's Sons, 1939.

——, *And the Life Everlasting*. London, Oxford University Press, 1941.

Bainton, R. H. *Christendom: A short history of Christianity and its impact on Western Civilization*. New York ... London, Harper Colophon Books, 2 vols. 1966.

Baker, D., ed., *Medieval Women*. Oxford, Blackwell, 1978.

Bamberger, B. J., *Fallen Angels*. Philadelphia, Jewish Publication Society, 1952.

Bammel, F., *Das heilige Mahl im Glauben der Völker: Eine religionsgeschichtliche Untersuchung*. Gütersloh, Bertelsmann, 1950.

——, *Die Religionen der Welt und der Friede auf Erden: Eine religionsphänomenologische Studie*. Munich, Federmann Verlag, 1957.

Bandt, H., *Luthers Lehre vom verborgenen Gott*. Berlin, Evang. Verlags-Anstalt, 1958.

Barbour, I. G., ed., *Science and Religion: New Perspectives on the Dialogue*. London, SCM, 1968.

Barr, J., *The Bible in the Modern World*. London, SCM, 1973.

—— *Fundamentalism*. London, SCM, 1977.

——, *Holy Scripture: Canon, Authority, Criticism*. Oxford University Press, 1983.

Barrett, D. B., *Schism and Renewal in Africa: An analysis of six thousand contemporary religious movements*. Nairobi *et al.*, Oxford University Press, 1968.

——, *World Christian Encyclopedia*: A comparative study of churches and religions in the modern world A.D. 1900–2000. Nairobi – Oxford, Oxford University Press, 1982.

Barrows, J. H., ed., *The World's Parliament of Religions*. Chicago, Parliament Publishing, 1893.

Barth, K., *The Word of God and the Word of Man*. New York, Harper & Row, 1957.

——, *Church Dogmatics* I/1: The Doctrine of the Word of God. Edinburgh, Oliver & Boyd, 1963.

Bascom, W. R., *The Sociological Role of the Yoruba Cult-group*. New York, Kraus Reprint, 1944/1969.

Battenhouse, R. W., ed., *A Companion to the Study of St Augustine*. New York, Oxford University, Press, 1956.

Bauer, W., *Orthodoxy and Heresy in Earliest Christianity*. Philadelphia, Fortress Press, 1971.

Bauman, R., *Let Your Words be Few: Symbolism of speaking and silence among seventeenth-century Quakers*. Cambridge University Press, 1984.

Baumgartner, W., *Israelitische und altorientalische Weisheit*. Tübingen, Mohr, 1933.

Baus, K., *Der Kranz in Antike und Christentum*. Bonn, Hanstein, 1965.

Bavink, B., *Weltschöpfung in Mythos und Religionen, Philosophie und Naturwissenschaft*. Munich, Reinhardt, 1950.

Beloff, J., ed., *New Directions in Parapsychology*. London, Elek Science, 1974.

Bentzen, A., *King and Messiah*. London, Lutterworth Press, 1955.

Benz, E., *Ecclesia Spiritualis: Kirchenidee und Geschichtstheologie der franziskanischen Reformation*. Stuttgart, Kohlhammer Verlag, 1934.

——, *Russische Heiligenlegenden*. Zürich, Verlag die Waage, 1953.

——, *Evolution and Christian Hope: Man's concept of the future from the early Fathers to Teilhard de Chardin*. London, Gollancz, 1967.

Bergmann, E., *Die deutsche Nationalkirche*. Breslau, Hirt, 1934.

Bernhart, J., *Chaos und Dämonie*. Bonn, Borromäus-Vereins, 1950.

Bertell, R., *No Immediate Danger: Prognosis for a radioactive earth*. London, The Women's Press, 1985.

Bertholet, A., *Götterspaltung und Göttervereinigung*. Tübingen, Mohr, 1932.

——, *Die Geschlecht der Gottheit*. Tübingen, Mohr, 1934.

Bethge, E., *Dietrich Bonhoeffer: Theologian, Christian, Contemporary*. London, Collins, 1970.

Bettenson, H., *Documents of the Christian Church*. London, Oxford University Press, 1975.

Bevan, E. R., *Holy Images: An inquiry into idolatry and image-worship in ancient paganism and in Christianity*. London, Allen & Unwin, 1940.

Bianchi, U., ed., *Mysteria Mithrae*. Leiden, Brill, 1979.

Bietenhard, H., *Das tausendjährige Reich: Eine biblisch-theologische Studie*. Bern, BEG-Verlag in Komm, 1944.

Black, M. and Rowley, H. H., ed., *Peake's Commentary on the Bible*. London, Nelson, 1962.

Blackwood, A. W., *The Protestant Pulpit: An anthology of master sermons from the Reformation to our own day*. New York and Nashville, Abingdon-Cokesbury Press, 1947.

Bliss, K., *The Service and Status of Women in the Churches*. London, SCM, 1952.

Boff, L., *Church: Charism and Power – Liberation theology and the institutional Church*. New York, Crossroad; London, SCM, 1985.

Böklen, E., *Die Glückszahl Dreizehn und ihre mythische Bedeutung*. Leipzig, J. C. Hinrichs, 1913.

Bonino, J. M. *Revolutionary Theology comes of Age* (Orig. US title: *Doing Theology in a Revolutionary Situation*). London, SPCK, 1975.

Bonnet, H., ed., *Reallexikon der ägyptischen Religionsgeschichte*. Berlin, Walter de Gruyter, 1971.

Bornkamm, G., *Das Ende des Gesetzes: Paulusstudien* (Gesammelte Aufsätze I). Munich, Chr. Kaiser Verlag, 1961.

Borsinger, H., *Rechtstellung der Frau in der katholischen Kirche*. Dissertation Zürich, 1930.

Bottermann, M.-R., *Die Bedeutung des Kindes an der Liturgie von den Anfängen bie heute: eine liturgische Untersuchung*. Frankfurt, Lang, 1982.

Bouquet, A. C., *Sacred Books of the World: A source-book*. Harmondsworth, Penguin Books, 1967.

Bousset, W., *Das Wesen der Religion dargestellt in ihrer Geschichte*. Tübingen, Mohr, 1903.

Brandon, S. G. F., *Man and his Destiny in the Great Religions*. Manchester University Press, 1963a.

——, ed., *The Saviour God: Comparative studies in the concept of Salvation*. Manchester University Press, 1963b.

——, *The Judgment of the Dead: An historical and comparative study of the idea of a post-mortem judgment in the major religions*. London, Weidenfeld & Nicolson, 1967.

Braun, H., *Spätjudisch-häretischer und frühchristlicher Radikalismus: Jesus von Nazareth und die essenische Qumransekte*. Tübingen, J. C. B. Mohr (Paul Siebeck), 2 vols. 1957.

Braun, J., *Die liturgische Gewandung im Okzident und Orient*. Darmstadt, Wissenschaftliche Buchgesellschaft, 1907/1964.

——, *Handbuch der Paramentik*. Freiburg, Herder, 1912.

——, *Der christliche Altar in seiner geschichtlichen Entwicklung*. Munich, Alte Meister Guenther Koch, 2 vols. 1924.

——, *Die Reliquiare des christlichen Kults und ihre Entwicklung*. Freiburg, Herder, 1940.

Brennemann, W. L., et al., *The Seeing Eye: Hermeneutical phenomonology in the study of religion.* University Park and London, Pennsylvania State University Press, 1982.

Briffault, R., *The Mothers.* London, Geo Allen & Unwin, 1927/1959.

Brightman, F. E., ed., *Liturgies Eastern and Western* – I. Oxford, Clarendon Press, 1896.

Bring, R., *Das Verhältnis von Glauben und Werken in der lutherischen Theologie.* Munich, Kaiser, 1956.

Browe, P., *Die Verehrung der Eucharistie im Mittelalter.* Munich, Hueber Verlag, 1933.

——, *Die eucharistischen Wunder des Mittelalters.* Breslau, Müller & Seiffert, 1938.

Brown, D., *The Divine Trinity.* London, Duckworth, 1985.

Browne, L., *The World's Great Scriptures.* New York, Macmillan, 1961.

Browne, P., *The Dragon and its Relationship to the Landscape in English Folklore: A phenomenological study.* M.Phil. University of Leicester, 1985.

Bruce, F. F. and Rupp, E. G., ed., *Holy Book and Holy Tradition.* Manchester, Manchester University Press, 1968.

Brun, L., *Segen und Fluch im Urchristentum.* Oslo, Dybwad in Komm, 1932.

Brunner, E., *Revelation and Reason: The Christian Doctrine of Faith and Knowledge.* Philadelphia, Westminster Press, 1946.

——, *Religionsphilosophie evangelischer Theologie.* Munich, Leibniz (Oldenbourg), 1948.

Brunotte, W., *Das geistliche Amt bei Luther.* Berlin, Luther. Verlagshaus, 1959.

Buber, M., *The Prophetic Faith.* New York, Harper & Row, 1949/1960.

——, *Tales of the Hasidim.* New York, Harper Torchbooks, 2 vols. 1972.

Budde, K., *Die biblische Paradiesgeschichte.* Giessen, Töpelmann, 1932.

Bulgakov, S. N. *The Wisdom of God: A brief summary of Sophiology.* London, Williams & Norgate, 1937.

Bultmann, R., *Der Stil der paulinischen Predigt und die kynisch-stoische Diatribe.* Göttingen, FRLANT Heft 13, 1910.

——, *Jesus and the Word.* New York and London, Charles Scribner's Sons, 1934.

—— *Der Begriff der Offenbarung im Neuen Testament, Glauben und Verstehen* – III. Tübingen, J. C. B. Mohr (Paul Siebeck), 1–34. 1962.

——, *The Gospel of John: A commentary.* Oxford, Blackwell, 1971.

——, *The History of the Synoptic Tradition.* Oxford, Basil Blackwell, 1972.

Burkert, W., *Homo Necans.* Berlin, De Gruyter, 1972.

Burn, A. E., *The Hymn Te Deum and its Author.* London, Faith Press, 1926.

Butler, E. C., *Western Mysticism.* London, Constable, 1922.

Büttner, T., *Circumcellionen und Adamiten: Zwei Formen mittelalterlicher Haeresie.* Berlin, Akademie Verlag, 1959.

Cabrol, F., and Leclercq, H., ed., *Dictionnaire d'archéologie chrétienne et de liturgie.* Paris, Librairie Letouzey et Ane, 30 vols. 1924–53.

Caesarius of Heisterbach, *The Dialogue on Miracles.* London, George Routledge & Sons, 2 vols. 1929.

Caillet, E., *Pascal.* Philadelphia, Westminster Press, 1945.

Caird, G. B., *Principalities and Powers: A study in Pauline Theology.* Oxford, Clarendon Press, 1956.

Campenhausen, H. von, *Die Idee des Martyriums in der alten Kirche.* Göttingen, Vandenhoeck & Ruprecht, 1964.

——, *Ecclesiastical Authority and Spiritual Power in the Church of the First Three Centuries.* London, A. & C. Black, 1969.

Capps, W. H., and Wright, W. M., ed., *Silent Fire: An invitation to Western Mysticism.* New York ... and London, Harper Forum Books, 1978.

Carmody, D. L., *Women and World Religions.* Nashville, Abingdon, 1979.

——, *Feminism and Christianity.* Nashville, Abingdon, 1982.

Carrier, H., and Pin, E., *Sociologie du Christianisme: Bibliographie internationale.* Rome, 1964.

Cavendish, R., ed., *Man, Myth and Magic: An illustrated Encyclopedia of the Supernatural.* London, Purnell for BPC Publishing, 7 vols. 1970–2.

Chadwick, H., *Priscillian of Avila: The occult and the charismatic in the early Church.* London, Oxford University Press, 1976.

Chadwick, O., ed., *Western Mysticism.* Philadelphia, Westminster Press; London, SCM, Library of Christian Classics 12, 1958.

Chantepie de la Saussaye, P. D., *Lehrbuch der Religionsgeschichte.* Tübingen, J. C. B. Mohr (Paul Siebeck), 2 vols. 1925.

Charles, R. H., *Eschatology: Doctrine of a future life in Israel, Judaism and Christianity: A critical history.* New York, Schocken Books, 1970.

Charlesworth, J. H., ed., *The Old Testament Pseudepigrapha.* New York, Doubleday; London, Darton Longman & Todd, 2 vols. 1983–4.

Chauduri, N. C., *Scholar Extraordinary: The Life of Friedrich Max Müller.* London, Chatto & Windus, 1974.

Cheetham, E. *The Prophecies of Nostradamus.* Sudbury, Neville Spearman, 1979.

Chernus, I., 'Mythologies of Nuclear War', *Jnl. of the Amer. Acad. of Rel.* 50 (1982), 255–73.

The Church in a Changing Society (Proceedings of the CIHEC Congress 1977). Uppsala 1978.

The Church Missionary Society (CMS) Archives, Birmingham University.

Clark, E., and Richardson, H., ed., *Women and Religion: A feminist sourcebook of Christian thought.* New York – London, Harper & Row, 1977.

Clark, J. M., *The Dance of Death in the Middle Ages and the Renaissance.* Glasgow, 1950.

Clements, R. E., *God and Temple.* Oxford, Blackwell, 1965.

The Code of the Canon Law in English Translation (Codex Iuris Canonici), Canon Law Society of G. B. & I., London, Collins, 1983.

Cohen, A. D., *The Small Grey Bird.* B.Litt. Oxford, 1974.

Cohn, N. *The Pursuit of the Millennium.* London, Paladin Books, 1971.

Collins, R. F., *Introduction to the New Testament.* London, SCM, 1983.

Conolly, Ann, University of Leicester. Personal communication.

Cox, O. C., *Class, Caste and Race: A study in social dynamics.* New York, Doubleday, 1948.

Craig, H., *The English Religious Drama of the Middle Ages.* Oxford, Clarendon Press, 1955.

Cross, F. L., and Livingstone, E. A., ed., *The Oxford Dictionary of the Christian Church.* London – New York – Toronto, Oxford University, Press, 1974.

Cullmann, O., *Baptism in the New Testament.* London, SCM, 1950.

——, *Christ and Time: The primitive Christian conception of Time and History.* London, SCM, 1951.

Cumont, F., *Oriental Religions in Roman Paganism.* New York, Dover Publications, 1956.

——, *After Life in Roman Paganism.* New York, Dover Publications, 1959.

Curley, M. J. (tr.), *Physiologus.* London, University of Texas Press, 1979.

Cyril of Jerusalem., *The Works of St Cyril of Jerusalem.* Washington, Cath. Univ. of America Press, 2 vols. 1969/1970.

Dallapiccolo, A. L., *The Stupa: Its religious, historical and architectural significance.* Wiesbaden, F. Steiner, 1980.

Daly, M., *Beyond God the Father: Towards a philosophy of women's liberation.* Boston, Beacon Press, 1977.

——, *Gyn/ecology: The metaethics of radical feminism.* Boston, Beacon Press; London, Women's Press, 1978/1979.

——, *Pure Lust: Elemental feminist philosophy.* London, Women's Press, 1984.

Dargan, E. C., *A History of Preaching.* New York, Hodder & Stoughton, 2 vols. 1905/1912.

Dassmann, E., *Der Stachel im Fleisch: Paulus in der frühchristlichen Literatur bis Irenäus.* Münster, Aschendorff, 1979.

Davidson, R., and Leaney, A. R. C., *Biblical Criticism.* Harmondsworth, Penguin Books, 1970.

Davies, D. J., 'The Notion of Salvation in the Comparative Study of Religions', *Religion* 8(1978), 85–100.

Davies H. and M. H., *Holy Days and Holidays: The medieval pilgrimage to Compostela.* London & Toronto, Associated University Presses, 1982.

Davies, J. G., *The Early Christian Church.* London, Weidenfeld & Nicolson, 1965.

——, ed., *A (New) Dictionary of Liturgy and Worship.* London, SCM Press, 1972/1986.

——, *Temples, Churches, Mosques.* Oxford, Basil Blackwell, 1982.

Davis, E. G., *The First Sex.* Harmondsworth, Penguin, 1971.

D'avray, D. L., *The Preaching of the Friars: Sermons diffused from Paris before 1300.* Oxford, Clarendon Press, 1985.

Day, J., *God's Conflict with the Dragon and the Sea: Echoes of a Canaanite myth in the Old Testament.* Cambridge, Cambridge University Press, 1985.

De Bary, T., ed., *Sources of Japanese Tradition.* New York, Columbia University Press, 1958.

De Beauvoir, S., *The Second Sex.* Harmondsworth, Penguin, 1976.

De Marchi, J. *The True Story of Fatima.* St Paul, Minn., Catechetical Guild Educational Soc., 1956.

De Sanctis, S., *Religious Conversion: A bio-psychological study.* London, Kegan Paul, 1927.

Deanesley, M., *The Lollard Bible and other Medieval Versions.* Cambridge, Cambridge University Press, 1920.

Deissmann, A., *Light from the Ancient East: The New Testament illustrated by recently discovered texts of the Graeco-Roman world.* London, Hodder & Stoughton, 1911.

Delehaye, H., *The Legends of the Saints.* London, Geoffrey Chapman, 1962.

Denffer, A. von, *Fulani Evangelism Project in West Africa.* Leicester, Islamic Foundation, 1980.

——, *Christian Presence in the Gulf Region.* Leicester, Islamic Foundation, 1981.

Denzinger, H. J. D., *The Sources of Catholic Dogma* (Enchiridion Symbolorum). St Louis, Herder, 1957.

Deursen, A. van, *Der Heilbringer.* Groningen, Wolters, 1936.

Dix, G., *The Shape of the Liturgy.* London, Dacre Press, A. & C. Black, 1945/1975.

Dodd, C. H., *et al.*, *Man in God's Design according to the New Testament.* Newcastle upon Tyne, Studiorum Novi Testamenti Societas, 1952.

——, *The Bible Today*. Cambridge, Cambridge University Press, 1956.

——, *The Parables of the Kingdom*. Glasgow, Collins Fount Paperbacks, 1978.

Dollah, M. A., *The Social Psychology of Religious Conversion*. M.Litt. Glasgow, 1980.

Douglas, M., *Purity and Danger: an analysis of concepts of pollution and taboo*. Harmondsworth, Penguin Books, 1966.

Dowell, S., and Hurcombe, L., *Dispossessed Daughters of Eve: Faith and Feminism*. London, SCM, 1981.

Drinker, S. L., *Music and Women: The story of women in relation to music*. New York, Coward-McCann, 1948.

Dube, S. W. D., *The African Concept of Life as reflected in the Zionist Church Movement*. M.Litt. Aberdeen, 1985.

Duchesne-Guillemin, J., *The Hymns of Zarathustra*. Boston, Beacon Press, 1963.

Duckett, E. S., *The Wandering Saints*. London, Collins, 1959.

Dudden, F. H., *The Life and Times of Saint Ambrose*. Oxford, Clarendon Press, 2 vols. 1935.

Dunham, B. *The Heretics*. London, Eyre & Spottiswoode, 1965.

Dunkerley, R., ed., *Sacrament and Ministry in the Undivided and the Medieval Church*, London, 1937.

Dupont-Sommer, A., *The Essene Writings from Qumran*. Oxford, Blackwell, 1961.

Durkheim, E., *The Elementary Forms of the Religious Life*. London, Allen & Unwin, 1976.

Dye, T. W., 'Towards a Theology of Power for Melanesia', *Catalyst*, 14, Nos. 1 & 2 (1984), 57–75, 158–80.

Eckenstein, L., *Women under Monasticism*. Cambridge, Cambridge University Press, 1896.

Edsman, C. M., *The Body and Eternal Life: A comparative and exegetical study*. Stockholm, Sv. Kyrk. Diak. Bokförlag, 1946.

Edwards, D., *The Virgin Birth in History and Faith*. London, Faber & Faber, 1943.

Ehrenreich, P., 'Götter und Heilbringer', *Zeitschrift für Ethnologie* 38 (1906), 536–610.

Eichmann, E., *Vom Kaisergewandung im Mittelalter*, Historiches Jahrbuch 58 (1958), 268–304.

Eisenhöfer, L., *Handbuch der katholischen Liturgik*. Freiburg, Herder, vol. 1, 1932.

Eissfeldt, O., *Geschichtsschreibung im alten Testament*. Berlin, Evang. Verlagsanstalt, 1948.

——, *The Old Testament: An introduction* . . . Oxford, Blackwell, 1965/1974.

Eliade, M., *The Sacred and the Profane: The nature of religion*. New York, Harper Torchbooks, 1957.

——, *Rites and Symbols of Initiation: The mysteries of birth and rebirth*. New York, Harper, 1985a.

——, *Yoga: Immortality and Freedom*. London, Routledge & Kegan Paul, 1958b.

——, *Cosmos and History: The myth of the eternal return*. New York, Harper Torchbooks, 1959.

——, *Patterns in Comparative Religion*. Cleveland and New York, Meridian Books, 1963.

——, *Shamanism: Archaic techniques of ecstasy*. London, Routledge & Kegan Paul, 1970.

——, *From Primitives to Zen: A thematic sourcebook of the history of religions*. London, Collins, 1979.

——, ed., *The Encyclopedia of Religion*. New York, Macmillan; London, Collier Macmillan, 16 vols. 1987. (Intended to replace the *ERE*)

Eliot, T. S., *The Cocktail Party*. London, Faber, 1974.

Ellwood, R. S., *Mysticism and Religion*. Englewood Cliffs, N.J. and London, Prentice Hall, 1980.

Emmel, T. C., *Global Perspectives on Ecology*. Palo Alto, Cal., Mayfield Publishing, 1977.

Enang, K., *Salvation in a Nigerian Background: Its concepts and articulation in the Annang independent churches*. Berlin, Riemer, 1979.

Esslemont, J. E., *Baha'ullah and the New Era*. London, Baha'i Publishing Trust, 1974.

Evans-Wentz, W. L., ed., *The Tibetan Book of the Dead*. New York, Oxford University, Press, 1960.

Farnell, L. R., *Greek Hero Cults and Ideas of Immortality*. Oxford, Clarendon Press, 1970.

Fascher, E., 'Jesus der Lehrer', *Theol. Lit. Zeitung* 79 (1954), 325–42.

Fehrle, E., *Feste und Volksbräuche im Jahreslauf europäischer Völker*. Kassel, Hinnental, 1955.

Ferotin, M., *La liber ordinum en usage dans l'église wisigothique*. Paris, 1904.

Finegan, J., *Encountering New Testament Manuscripts: A working introduction to textual criticism*. London, SPCK, 1975.

Fischer, U., *Zur Liturgie des Umbandakultes: Eine Untersuchung zu den Riten und Amtshandlungen der synkretistischen Neureligion der Umbanda in Brasilien*. Leiden, Brill, 1970.

Fohrer, G., *Der heilige Weg*. Diss. Bonn, 1939.

——, *Die symbolischen Handlungen der Propheten*. Zürich, Zwingli Verlag, 1953.

Foster, H. E., *Jewish and Graeco-Roman Influences upon Paul's Attitude towards Women*. Ph.D. Chicago, 1936.

Franks, R. S., *The Work of Christ: A historical study of Christian doctrine*. London, Nelson. 1962.

Frazer, J. G., *The Golden Bough*. London, Macmillan, vol. 1, 1922.

Frend, W. H. C., *The Donatist Church*. Oxford, Clarendon Press, 1952.

——, *Martyrdom and Persecution in the Early Church*.Oxford, Blackwell, 1965.

Freud, S., *The Interpretation of Dreams*. Harmondsworth, Penguin Books, 1978.

Gager, J. G., *Kingdom and Community*. Englewood Cliffs, N.J., Prentice-Hall, 1975.

Galling, K., ed., *Die Religion in Geschichte und Gegenwart: Handwörterbuch für Theologie und Religionswissenschaft*. Tübingen, J. C. B. Mohr (Paul Siebeck), 7 vols. 1957–65.

Gandhi, M. K., *The Ethics of Fasting*. Lahore, Indian Printing Works, 1944.

Garcia, J., and Maitland, S., *Walking on the Water: Women talking about spirituality*. London, Virago Press, 1983.

Geering, L., *Resurrection: A symbol of hope*. London, Auckland, etc., Hodder & Stoughton, 1971.

Geiringer, K., *Haydn: A creative life in music*. London, Allen & Unwin, 1947.

Gelin, A., *The Key Concepts of the Old Testament*, London and New York, Sheed & Ward, 1955.

Gennep, A. van, *Rites of Passage*. London, Routledge & Kegan Paul, 1960.

George, C. T. T., 'Baptist Work in the Niger Delta', *Orita: Ibadan Journal of Religious Studies* 5 (1971), 77–9.

Georgi, D., *Die Kollekte des Paulus für Jerusalem.* Heidelberg, Habil.-Schrift, 1962.

Gerlitz, P., *Ausserchristliche Einflüsse auf die Entwicklung des christlichen Trinitätsdogmas.* Diss. Marburg, 1960.

Gervers, M., 'The Iconography of the Cave in Christian and Mithraic Tradition', *Mysteria Mithrae,* ed. U. Bianchi (Leiden, Brill, 1979), 579–99.

Giles, M. E. ed., *The Feminist Mystic, and other Essays on Women and Spirituality.* New York, Crossroad; London, SPCK, 1982.

Gill, J., *The Council of Florence.* Cambridge, Cambridge University Press, 1959.

Gilson, E., *The Spirit of Medieval Philosophy.* New York, Charles Scribner's Sons, 1940.

Gimbutas, M., *The Gods and Goddesses of Old Europe 7000 to 3500 B.C.: Myths, legends and cult images.* London, Thames & Hudson, 1974.

Girgensohn, K., *Der seelische Aufbau des religiösen Erlebens.* Gütersloh, C. Bertelsmann, 1930.

Glasenapp, H. von, *Buddhismus und Gottesidee.* Mainz, Akad. der Wiss. und der Lit., 1954.

Godwin, J., *Mystery Religions in the Ancient World.* London, Thames & Hudson, 1981.

Goldammer, K., *Die eucharistische Epiklese in der mittelalterlichen abendländischen Frömmigkeit.* Diss. Marburg, 1941.

——, 'Die Fahne: Zur Geschichte und Phänomenologie eines religiösen Urobjektes', *Zeitschrift für Ethnologie* 4/5 (1954/55), 13–55.

——, *Die Formenwelt des Religiösen: Grundriss der systematischen Religionswissenschaft.* Stuttgart, Alfred Kröner Verlag, 1960.

——, *Kirchliche Kunst im Mittelalter.* KüG G2. Göttingen, Vandenhoeck & Ruprecht, 1969.

Goodman, F. D., *Speaking in Tongues: A cross-cultural study of glossolalia.* Chicago, University of Chicago Press, 1974.

Grabmann, M., *Geschichte der scholastischen Methode.* Freiburg, Herder, 2 vols. 1909/1911.

Grant, R. M., *Miracle and Natural Law in Graeco-Roman and early Christian Thought.* Amsterdam, N. Holland Publishing, 1952.

——, and Tracy, D., *A Short History of the Interpretation of the Bible.* London, SCM, 1984.

Grass, H., *Ostergeschehen und Osterberichte.* Göttingen, Vandenhoeck & Ruprecht, 1962.

Grensted, L. W., *The Psychology of Religion.* London, Oxford University Press, 1952.

Greenoak, F., 'Symbols in the Churchyard', *Natural World* 13, (1985) 14–15.

Greschat, H.-J., *Westafrikanische Propheten: Morphologie eines religiösen Spezialisierung.* Marburg, Marburger Studien z. Asien u. Afrikakunde; E. T. Birmingham, CENERM, 1974/1984.

Grollenberg, L., *The Bible for our Time: Reading the Bible in the light of today's questions.* London, SCM, 1979.

Groupe de la Boussière, *Pratiques de la confession: des pères du désert à Vatican II.* Paris, Editions du Cerf, 1983.

Grühn, W., *Die Frömmigkeit der Gegenwart: Grundtatsachen der empirischen Psychologie.* Konstanz, Friedrich Bahn Verlag, 1960.

Guerber, H. A., *Myths and Legends of the Middle Ages.* London, Harrap, 1909.

Guillaume, A., *Prophecy and Divination among the Hebrews and Semites.* London, Hodder & Stoughton, 1938.

Gunkel, H., *Die Genesis.* Göttingen, Vandenhoeck & Ruprecht, 1964.

Günter, H., *Die christliche Legende des Abendlandes*. Heidelberg, Winter, 1910.

Gutierrez, G., *A Theology of Liberation*. London, SCM, 1974.

Haggeney, K., sj *Im Heerbann des Priesterkönigs*. Freiburg, Herder, 1921/22.

Hahn, F., *Christologische Hoheitstitel: Ihre Geschichte im frühen Christentum*. Göttingen, Vandenhoeck & Ruprecht, 1963.

Halifax, Lord (ed. Wood, C. L.,), *The Conversations at Malines 1921–25: Original documents*. London, P. Allen, 1930.

Hamilton, M., *Incubation or the Cure of Disease in Pagan Temples and Christian Churches*. St Andrews, Henderson & Son, 1906.

Hammond, P., *Liturgy and Architecture*. London, Barrie & Rockcliff, 1960.

Hanson, R. P. C., *Allegory and Event: Origen's Interpretation of Scripture*. London, SCM, 1959.

Harnack, A., *Marcion: Das Evangelium vom fremden Gott*. Leipzig; Darmstadt, Wiss. Buchgesellschaft, 1921/1960.

——, *History of Dogma*. New York, Dover Publications, 7 vols. in 4,1961.

——, *The Mission and Expansion of Christianity in the First Three Centuries*. New York, Harper Torchbooks, 1962.

Hartmann, M., *Die Frau im Islam*. Halle, Gebauer-Schwetschke, 1909.

Hasenfratz, H.-P., *Die toten Lebenden: Eine religionsphänomenologishe Studie zum sozialen Tod in archäischer Gesellschaft*. Leiden, Brill, 1982.

Hastings, J., *Encyclopaedia of Religion and Ethics*. Edinburgh, T. & T. Clark, 13 vols. 1908–26.

Hauck, A., ed., *Realencyklopädie für protestantische Theologie und Kirche*. Leipzig, J. C. Hinrichs, 1896–1909.

Haupt, G., *Die Farbensymbolik in der sakralen Kunst des abendländischen Mittelalters*. Dresden, Dittert, 1941.

Heidel, A., *The Gilgamesh Epic and Old Testament Parallels*. Chicago, Phoenix Books, 1949.

Heighton, M., *Paradox in Mysticism: A study and interpretation of the paradoxes found in the mystics' thought, language and action*. M.Phil. Leicester, 1980.

Heiler, A.-M., ed., *Interconfessiones: Beiträge zur Förderung des interkonfessionellen und interreligiösen Gesprächs*. Marburg, N. G. Elwert Verlag, 1972.

Heiler, F., *Das Gebet: Eine religionsgeschichtliche und religionspsychologische Untersuchung*. Munich, Ernst Reinhart, 1923a.

——, *Der Katholizismus: Seine Idee und seine Erscheinung*. Munich, Ernst Reinhardt, 1923b/1970.

——, *Sadhu Sundar Singh: Ein Apostel des Ostens und des Westens*. Munich, Ernst Reinhardt, 1924/1926.

——, 'Die Madonna als religiöses Symbol', *Eranos Jahrbuch* (1934), 277–317.

——, 'Der Dienst der Frau in den Religionen der Menschheit', *Einheit der Kirche* 21 (1939), 1–48.

——, *Altkirchliche Autonomie und päpstlicher Zentralismus*. Munich, Reinhardt, 1941.

——, 'Die Bedeutung der Religionen für die Entwicklung des Menschheits- und Friedensgedankens', *Ökumenische Einheit* 2 (1951), 1–29.

——, *Erscheinungsformen und Wesen der Religion*. Stuttgart Berlin Cologne Mainz, Kohlhammer Verlag, Die Religionen der Menschheit I, 1961/1979.

——, *Die Ostkirchen* (previously published as *Urkirche und Ostkirche*). Munich, Ernst Reinhardt, 1971.

Heller, A., *Biblische Zahlensymbolik*. Reutlingen-Betzingen, Zeitbild Verlag F. Braun, 1936.

Hellmann, M. *et al.*, ed., *Cyrillo-Methodiana: Zur Frühgeschichte des Christentums bei den Slaven*. Cologne – Graz, Böhlau Verlag, 1964.

Hepher, C., *The Fruits of Silence* . . . London, Macmillan, 1924.

Hessen, J., *Religionsphilosophie*. Munich, Ernst Reinhardt, 2 vols. 1955.

Hick, J. *Death and Eternal Life*. London, Collins, 1976/1985.

——, ed., *The Myth of God Incarnate*. London, SCM, 1977.

——, *Philosophy of Religion*. Englewood Cliffs, N.J., London, Prentice Hall, 1983.

Hick, L., *Die Stellung des heiligen Paulus zur Frau im Rahmen seiner Zeit*. Cologne, Amerikan.-Ungar. Verlag, 1957.

Hilgen, U., *The Attitude towards Death in the Becket Circle*, CIHEC Colloquium, Durham, 1981.

Hines, V., 'Pentecostal Glossolalia', *Jnl. for the Scientific Study of Rel.* 8 (1962), 211–62.

Hinnells, J. R. and Sharpe, E. J., *Hinduism*. Newcastle, Oriel Press, 1972.

——, ed., *A Handbook of Living Religions*. Harmondsworth, Viking, 1984.

Hocart, A. M., *Caste: A comparative study*. London, Methuen, 1950.

Hodgkin, L. V., *Silent Worship: The way of wonder*. London and Birmingham, Swarthmore Lecture, 1919.

Hodgson, L.,*The Doctrine of the Trinity*. London, Nisbet, 1946.

Höfer, J. and Rahner, K., *Lexikon für Theologie und Kirche*. Freiburg, Herder, 11 vols. 1957–67.

Hollenweger, W. J., *The Pentecostals*. London, SCM, 1969.

——, *Christen ohne Schriften: Fünf Fallstudien zur Socialethik mündlicher Religion*. Erlangen, Verlag der ev.-luth. Mission, 1977.

Hollis, C., *A History of the Jesuits*. London, Weidenfeld & Nicolson, 1968.

Holm, N. G., 'Glossolalia Experiences among Swedish-speaking Pentecostals in Finland', *History of Religions: IAHR proceedings 1975*, ed. M. Pye *et al.* Leicester, Dept. of Rel., (1980) 129f.

——, *Religious Ecstasy*. Uppsala, Almqvist & Wiksell, 1982.

Holm, S., *Religionsphilosophie*. Stuttgart, W. Kohlhammer Verlag, 1960.

Holzach, M. *Das Vergessene Volk: Ein Jahr bei den deutschen Hutteriten in Kanada*. Hamburg, Hoffmann & Campe, 1980.

Hooke, S. H., *Myth and Ritual*. London, Oxford University Press, 1934.

Hopper, V. F., *Medieval Number Symbolism: Its sources, meaning, and influence on thought and expression*. New York, Cooper Square Publishers, 1969.

Howes, M., *Amulets*. London, Robert Hale, 1975.

Howes, R.,*James Jones and the People's Temple*. Diss. Leicester, 1982.

Hubert, H. P. E. and Mauss, M., *Sacrifice: Its nature and function*. London, Cohen & West, 1964.

Hübscher, A., *Die grosse Weissagung: Texte, Geschichte und Deutung der Prophezeiung von den biblischen Propheten bis auf unsere Zeit*. Munich, Heimeran, 1952.

Hunter, A. M., *Interpreting the New Testament 1900–1950*. London, SCM, 1951.

Hussain, F., ed., *Muslim Women*. Beckenham, Kent, Croom Helm, 1984.

Idowu, E. B., *Towards an Indigenous Church*. Oxford University, Press, 1965.

——, *Olodumare: God in Yoruba Belief*. London, Longmans, 1966.

Inayat Khan, V., *The Unity of Religious Ideals*. Southampton, Sufi Movement, 1949.

——, *The Message of our Time: The life and teaching of the Sufi master Pir-O-Murshid*

Inayat Khan. New York – London, Harper & Row, 1978.

Inge, W. R., *Mysticism in Religion*. London, Hutchinson, 1947.

Inikori, J. E., ed., *Forced Migration: The impact of the export slave trade on African societies*. London, Hutchinson University Library, 1982.

Innes, W. C., *Social Concern in Calvin's Geneva*. Allison Park, Penn., Pickwick Publications, 1983.

Iremonger, F. A., *William Temple: Archbishop of Canterbury: Life and Letters*. London – New York – Toronto, Oxford University Press, 1948.

James, E. O., *The Origins of Sacrifice: A study in comparative religion*. London, John Murray, 1933.

——, *The Concept of Deity: A comparative and historical study*. London, Hutchinson's University Library, 1950.

——, *Myth and Ritual in the Ancient Near East*. London, Thames & Hudson, 1958.

——, *The Cult of the Mother Goddess: An archaeological and documentary study*. London, Thames & Hudson, 1959.

——, *Seasonal Feasts and Festivals*. London, Thames & Hudson, 1961.

——, *Sacrifice and Sacrament*. London, Thames & Hudson, 1962.

——, *From Cave to Cathedral: Temples and shrines of prehistoric, classical, and early Christian times*. London, Thames & Hudson, 1965.

——, *The Tree of Life: An archaeological study*. Leiden, Brill, 1966.

James, M. R., *The Apocryphal New Testament*. Oxford, Clarendon Press, 1983.

James, W., *The Varieties of Religious Experience: A study of human nature*. New York, Random House; London, Collins, 1902/1975.

Jeremias, J., *The Eucharistic Words of Jesus*. Oxford, Blackwell, 1955.

——, *The Parables of Jesus*. New York, Charles Scribner's Sons, 1962.

——, *Rediscovering the Parables*. London, SCM, 1966.

Jones, R. M., *Spiritual Reformers in the Sixteenth and Seventeenth Century*. London, Macmillan, 1914.

——, *Studies in Mystical Religion*. London, Macmillan, 1919.

——, *The Flowering of Mysticism: The Friends of God in the fourteenth century*. New York, Macmillan, 1939.

Jungman, J., *Liturgical Renewal in Retrospect and Prospect*. London, Burns Oates, 1965.

Kähler, E., *Die Stellung der Frau in den paulinischen und deuteropaulinischen Briefen*. Diss. Kiel, 1957.

Kalsbach, A., *Die altkirchliche Einrichtung der Diakonissen bis zu ihrem Erloschen*. Freiburg, Herder, 1926.

Katz, S., ed., *Mysticism and Philosophical Analysis*. London, Sheldon Press, 1978.

Kaupel, H., *Die Dämonen im Alten Testament*. Augsburg, Filser, 1930.

Kee, A. A., *Constantine versus Christ: The triumph of ideology*. London, SCM, 1982.

Kee, H. C., *Understanding the New Testament*. Englewood Cliffs, N.J., Prentice Hall Inc., 1983.

Kelly, H. A., *The Devil at Baptism: Ritual, theology and drama*. Ithaca & London, Cornell University Press, 1985.

Kennedy, H. A. A., *St. Paul's Conceptions of the Last Things*. London, Hodder & Stoughton, 1904.

Kent, R. G., *Old Persian: Grammar, texts, lexicon*. New Haven, American Oriental Society, 1953.

Kierkegaard, S., *Fear and Trembling: A dialectical lyric.* Princeton University Press and Oxford University Press, 1946.

Kilduff, M. and Javers, R., *The Suicide Cult.* New York, Bantam Books, 1978.

Kircher, K., *Die sakrale Bedeutung des Weines im Alterum.* Berlin, Walter de Gruyter, 1970.

Kirfel, W. *Der Rosenkrantz.* Walldorf-Hessen, Verlag für Orientkunde, 1949.

Kittel, G and Friedrich, G., ed., *Theologisches Wörterbuch zum Neuen Testament.* Stuttgart, W. Kohlhammer Verlag, 11 vols. 1949–1979.

Klauser, T., ed., *Reallexikon für Antike und Christentum: Sachwörterbuch zur Auseinandersetzung des Christentums mit der antiken Welt.* Stuttgart, Hiersemann, 1950–.

Knowles, D., *Christian Monasticism.* London, Weidenfeld & Nicolson, 1969.

Knox, J., *Marcion and the New Testament.* Chicago, Chicago University Press, 1942.

Koenker, E. B., *The Liturgical Renaissance in the Roman Catholic Church.* Chicago, Chicago University Press, 1954.

Koep, L., *Das himmlische Buch in Antike und Christentum: Eine religionsgeschichtliche Untersuchung zur altchristlichen Bildersprache,* Bonn, Hanstein, 1952.

Köhler, M., *Maria Ward: Ein Frauenschicksal des 17. Jahrhunderts.* Munich, Kössel Verlag, 1984.

Kornfeld, W., *Studien zum Heiligkeitsgesetz.* Vienna, Herder, 1952.

Korvin-Krasinski, C., 'The Turnus Sacralis', *History of Religions, IAHR proceedings* 1975, Leicester, Dept. of Religion (1980), 120f.

Koso-Thomas, O., *The Circumcision of Women: a strategy for eradication.* London and New Jersey, Zed Books, 1987.

Kötting, B., *Peregrina Religiosa: Wallfahrten in der Antike und das Pilgerwesen in der alten Kirche.* Münster, Regenberg, 1950.

Kraft, H., 'Die altchristliche Prophetie und die Entstehung des Montanismus', *Theologische Zeitschrift* 11 (1955), 249–71.

Kraus, H.-J., *Geschichte des historisch-kritischen Forschung des Alten Testaments von der Reformation bis zur Gegenwart.* Neukirchen, Verlag der Buchhandlung des Erziehungsvereins, 1956.

——, *Worship in Israel: A cultic history of the Old Testament.* Oxford, Basil Blackwell, 1966.

Krautheimer, R., *Early Christian and Byzantine Architecture.* Harmondsworth, Penguin Books, 1965.

Kretschmar, G., *Studien zur frühchristlichen Trinitätstheologie.* Tübingen, Mohr (Siebeck), 1956.

Kristensen, W. B., *The Meaning of Religion: Lectures in the Phenomenology of Religion.* The Hague, Martinus Nijhoff, 1960.

Krüger, G., *Abendländische Humanität.* Stuttgart, Kohlhammer, 1953.

Künneth, W., *Theologie der Auferstehung.* Munich, Claudius Verlag, 1951.

Lambert, M. D., *Medieval Heresy.* London, Edward Arnold, 1977.

Lampe, G. W. H., *The Seal of the Spirit: A study in the doctrine of baptism and confirmation in the New Testament and the Fathers.* London – New York – Toronto, Longmans Green, 1951.

Lanczkowski, G., *Sacred Writings.* London, Fontana Books, 1961.

——, 'Gotteshüter und verborgene Heilbringer', *IAHR Proceedings* XIIth Congress 1970 (Leiden, Brill, 1974), 290–7.

Lane, C., *Christian Religion in the Soviet Union: A sociological study.* London, Allen & Unwin, 1978.

Langton, E., *The Angel Teaching of the New Testament*. London, J. Clarke, 1937.

——, *Essentials of Demonology: A study of Jewish and Christian doctrine* . . . London, Epworth Press, 1949.

Latourette, K. S., *A History of Christianity*. New York . . . London, Harper & Row, 2 vols. 1975.

Laufer, O., *Der Weihnachtsbaum im Glauben und Brauch*. Berlin and Leipzig, de Gruyter, 1934.

Laun, B., *Heiliges Geld*. Tübingen, 1924.

Laurentin, R., *Catholic Pentecostalism*. London, Darton Longman & Todd, 1977.

Le Goff, J., *The Birth of Purgatory*. London, Scolar Press, 1984.

Lea, H. C., *A History of Sacerdotal Celibacy in the Christian Church*. London, Williams & Norgate, 1907.

——, *Materials towards a History of Witchcraft*, ed. A. E. Howland, Philadelphia, University of Pennsylvania Press, 3 vols. 1939.

——, *The Inquisition of the Middle Ages: Its organization and operation*. London, Eyre & Spottiswood, 1963.

Leenhardt, F. J. and Blanke, F., *Die Stellung der Frau im Neuen Testament und in der alten Kirche*. Zürich, Zwingli Verlag, 1949.

Leeuw, G. van der, *In dem Himmel ist ein Tanz: Über die Bedeutung des Tanzes und Fest-züges*. Munich, Dornverlag, 1930.

——, 'Unsterblichkeit', *Eranos Jahrbuch* 18 (1950), 183–208.

——, *Sacred and Profane Beauty: The holy in art*. London, Weidenfeld & Nicolson, 1963.

——, *Religion in Essence and Manifestation*. London, Geo Allen & Unwin, 1964.

Lehmann, E., *Stellet och Vagen* (Place and Way), Stockholm, 1917.

Leitmann, C., *Die Kirche und die Gottesurteile*. Vienna, 1953.

Leshan, L., *Clairvoyant Reality: Towards a general theory of the paranormal*. Wellingborough, Turnstone Press, 1980.

Leuret, F. and Bon, H., *Les guérisons miraculeuses modernes*. Paris, Presses universitaires de France, 1950.

Liebmann, H., *Ein Planet wird unbewohnbar: Ein Sündenregister der Menschheit von der Antike bis zur Gegenwart*. Munich, Piper Verlag, 1973.

Lietzmann, H., *Mass and Lord's Supper: A study in the history of Liturgy*. Leiden, Brill, 1979.

Lindblom, J., *Prophecy in Ancient Israel*. Oxford, Blackwell, 1967.

Linnemann, E., *The Parables of Jesus: Introduction and exposition*. London, SPCK, 1966.

Loewenich, W. von, *Luthers Theologia Crucis*. Munich, Kaiser, 1954.

Lohmeyer, E., *Das Vaterunser*. Göttingen, Vandenhoeck & Ruprecht, 1962.

Long, C. H., *Alpha: The myths of creation*. New York, Braziller, 1963.

Lonsdale, S., *Animals and the Origins of Dance*. London, Thames & Hudson, 1981.

Lotz, W., *Das hochzeitliche Kleid*. Kassel, Stauda, 1949.

Lyttleton, C. S., *The New Comparative Mythology: An anthropological assessment of the theories of Georges Dumezil*. Berkeley Los Angeles London, University of California Press, 1982.

McArthur, A. A., *The Evolution of the Christian Year*. London, SCM, 1953.

McCann, J., *Saint Benedict*. London, Sheed & Ward, 1928.

Maccoby, H., *The Sacred Executioner: Human sacrifice and the legacy of guilt*. London, Thames & Hudson, 1982.

McCreery, C., 'Psychic Phenomena and the Psychical World', *Proceedings of the Institute of Psychophysical Research*. London, Hamish Hamilton, 1973.

MacCulloch, J. A., *Early Christian Versions of the Other World*. Edinburgh, T. & T. Clark, 1912.

Machen, J. G., *The Virgin Birth of Christ*. New York and London, Harper & Brothers, 1932.

McIntyre, J., *Saint Anselm and his Critics: A re-interpretation of the* Cur Deus Homo. Edinburgh and London, Oliver & Boyd, 1954.

McKenzie, J. L., *The Roman Catholic Church*. London, Weidenfeld & Nicolson, 1969.

McKenzie, P. R., *The Invisibility of the Church for Luther and Calvin*, Ph.D. Edinburgh, 1953.

——, *Inter-religious Encounters in West Africa: Samuel Ajayi Crowther's attitude to African traditional religion and Islam*. Leicester University, Dept of Religion. 1976a.

——, 'Sango: A traditional Yoruba cult group', *Africana Marburgensia* 9 (1976b), 3–33.

——, 'The Persecution of Early Nigerian Converts', *Orita: Ibadan Journal of Religious Studies* 11 (1977), 3–14.

Maclagan, D., *Creation Myths*. London, Thames & Hudson, 1977.

McNeile, A. H., *The Problem of the Future Life*. Cambridge, W. Heffer, 1925.

McNeill, J. T., *Unitive Protestantism: A study of our religious resources*. New York, Abingdon, 1930.

MacQueen, J., *Allegory*. London, Methuen, 1970.

Mannhardt, W., *Wald- und Feldkulte*, Darmstadt, Wissenschaftliche Buchgesellschaft, 1905/1963.

Manson, W. *et al.*, 1952. *Eschatology*, Scottish Jnl. of Theol. Occ. Papers 2, 1952.

Marnham, P., *Lourdes: A modern pilgrimage*. London, Heinemann, 1980.

Martin, E. J., *A History of the Iconoclastic Controversy*. London, SPCK, 1930.

Marvell, J., *The English Place of Worship: A phenomenological study*. Ph.D. Leicester, 1985.

Massey, R., *British Pentecostalism: A historical and phenomenological study*. M.A. Leicester, 1976.

Mathiez, A., *Les origines des cultes revolutionnaires*. Paris, 1964.

Matson, K., *The Encyclopaedia of Reality: A guide to the new age*. London . . . New York, Paladin Granada Publishing, 1979.

Mauss, M., *The Gift: Forms and functions of exchange in archaic societies*. London, Cohen & West, 1954.

Mayer-Thurman, C. C., *Raiment for the Lord's Service: A thousand years of Western vestments*. Chicago, Art Institute of Chicago, 1975.

Mayo, J., *A History of Ecclesiastical Dress*. London, Batsford, 1984.

Mbiti, J. S., *The Prayers of African Religion*. London, SPCK, 1975.

Meer, F. van der, *Augustine the Bishop: The life and work of a Father of the church*, London and New York, Sheed & Ward, 1961.

Mensching, G., *Das heilige Schweigen: Eine religionsgeschichtliche Untersuchung*. Giessen, Töpelmann, 1926.

——, *Das heilige Wort: Eine religionsgeschichtliche Untersuchung*. Bonn, Röhrscheid, 1937.

——, *Gut und Böse im Glauben der Völker*. Leipzig, Hinrichs Verlag, 1941.

——, *Der Schicksalsgedanke in der Religionsgeschichte*. Bonn, Bonner Univ. Buchdr., 1942.

——, *Das Wunder im Glauben und Aberglauben der Völker*. Leiden, Brill, 1957.

——, *Toleranz und Wahrheit in den Religionen.* Munich and Hamburg, Siebenstern Taschenbuch Verlag, 1966.

Mersch, E., *The Whole Christ: The historical development of the doctrine of the mystical body in scripture and tradition.* London, Dennis Dobson, 1949.

Metz, R., *La consécration des vierges dans l'église romaine.* Paris, Presses Universitaires de France, 1954.

Michael, W. F., *Die geistlichen Prozessionsspiele in Deutschland.* Baltimore, Johns Hopkins Press, 1954.

Michaelis, W., *Paulus und die Frauen.* Bern, Buchhandlung der Evang. Gesellschaft, 1931.

Miguez-Bonino, J., see Bonino, J. M.

Mirbt, C., *Quellen Zur Geschichte des Papstums und des römischen Katholizismus.* Tübingen, Mohr, 1924.

Mirsky, J., *Houses of God.* Chicago and London, University of Chicago Press, 1976.

Misner, P., ed., *Friedrich von Hügel, Nathan Söderblom, Friedrich Heiler: Briefwechsel 1909–1931.* Paderborn, Bonifacius Druckerei, 1981.

Mitchell, D., *The Jesuits: A history.* London, Macdonald, 1980.

Mitchell, L. L., *Baptismal Anointing.* London, University of Notre Dame Press, 1978.

Mitterweiser, A., *Geschichte der Fronleichnamsprozession in Bayern.* Munich, Weinmayer, 1949.

Mol, H., *Identity and the Sacred: A sketch for a new socio-scientific theory of religion.* Oxford, Basil Blackwell, 1976.

Molland, E., *Christendom: The Christian churches, their doctrines, constitutional forms and ways of worship.* London, A. R. Mowbray, 1959.

Moltmann, J., *Theology of Hope.* London, SCM, 1967.

——, *God in Creation: An ecological doctrine of creation.* London, SCM, 1985.

Moltmann-Wendel, E., *The Women around Jesus.* London, SCM, 1982.

Moore, A. C., *Iconography of Religions.* London, SCM, 1977.

Moore, G. F., *Metempsychosis.* Cambridge, Mass., Harvard University Press, 1914.

Moore, P. C., *Tomorrow is too Late: Taizé, an experiment in Christian community.* London, A. R. Mowbray, 1970.

Morison, F., *Who moved the Stone?* London, 1930.

Mowinckel, S., *He that cometh.* Oxford, Basil Blackwell, 1956.

——, *Psalmen-Studien* I–VI. Amsterdam, Schippers, 1961.

Müller, F. M., *Lectures on the Origin and Growth of Religion.* London, Longmans Green, 1878.

——, *Natural Religion.* London, Longmans Green, 1889.

Muncey, R. W., *A History of the Consecration of Churches and Churchyards.* Cambridge, W. Heffer & Sons, 1930.

Münster, L., *Hochzeit des Lammes: Die Christusmystik der Jungfrauenweihe.* Düsseldorf, Patmos Verlag, 1955.

Murray, J. E., 'The Church Missionary Society and the "Female Circumcision" Issue in Kenya 1929–1932', *Jnl. of Rel. in Africa* 8 (1976), 92–104.

The Mysteries. Eranos Jahrbuch, English tr., New York, Pantheon Books, 1955.

Neill, S. C., *Christian Missions,* Pelican History of the Church 6. Harmondsworth, Penguin Books, 1964.

——, *Anglicanism.* Harmondsworth, Penguin Books, 1965.

Nelson, K., *The Art of Reciting the Qur'an,* Ph.D. California (Berkeley), 1980.

Nemecek, O., *Die Wertschätzung der Jungfräulichkeit*, Vienna, 1953.

Neumann, E., *The Great Mother: An analysis of an archetype*. Princeton, Princeton University Press, 1972.

Neve, J. L., *Churches and Sects of Christendom*. Blair Nebraska, Lutheran Publishing House, 1952.

Nicholson, R. A., *Studies in Islamic Mysticism*. Cambridge, Cambridge University Press, 1921/1978.

Nickalls, J. L., ed., *The Journal of George Fox*. Cambridge, Cambridge University Press, 1952.

Nida, E. A., ed., *The Book of a Thousand Tongues*. London, United Bible Societies, 1972.

Niebuhr, R., *The Nature and Destiny of Man: A Christian interpretation*. London, Nisbet, 2 vols. 1947.

Nielson, E., *Oral Tradition: A modern problem in Old Testament introduction*. London, SCM, 1954.

Nielson, K., *Incense in Ancient Israel*. Leiden, Brill, 1986.

Nigg, W., *Das ewige Reich*. Zürich, Artemis Verlag, 1954.

——, *Das Buch der Ketzer*. Zürich, Artemis Verlag, 1962a.

——, *Grosse Heiligen*. Zürich, Artemis Verlag, 1962b.

Nineham, D., *The Use and Abuse of the Bible in an Age of Rapid Change*. London, Macmillan, 1976.

Nock, A. D., *Conversion: The old and new in religion from Alexander the Great to Augustine of Hippo*. Oxford, Clarendon Press, 1952.

Nygren, A. *Eros and Agape: A study of the Christian idea of love*. London, SPCK, 1953.

O'Dea, T., *The Sociology of Religion*. Englewood Cliffs N.J., Prentice-Hall Inc., 1966.

Oden, T. C., *The Parables of Kierkegaard*. Princeton and Guildford, Princeton University Press, 1978.

Oesterley, W. O. E., *The Sacred Dance: A study in comparative folklore*. Cambridge, Cambridge University Press, 1923.

Ohm, T., *Die Gebetsgebärden der Völker und das Christentum*. Leiden, Brill, 1948.

Okafor, S. O., 'Inter-religious Encounters in the Context of the Theory of Commensality . . .', Africana Marburgensia 14 (1981), 26–37.

——, *Concepts of Salvation: African and European*. Ph.D. Leicester, 1984.

Omoyajowo, J. A., *The Cherubim and Seraphim, the Christ Apostolic Church and the Montanists*. Diss. Ibadan, 1966.

Oppenheim, P., *Symbolik und religiöse Wertung des Mönchskleides im christlichen Altertum*. Münster, Aschendorff, 1932.

(Orimolade, M.), *The Life of Moses Orimolade*. Lagos, Cherubim and Seraphim, n.d.

Otto, R., *Das Gefühl des Überweltlichen*. Munich, C. H. Beck, 1932a.

——, *Sünde und Urschuld*. Munich, C. H. Beck, 1932b.

——, *Religious Essays: A supplement to 'The Idea of the Holy'*. London, Oxford University, Press, 1937.

——, *The Kingdom of God and the Son of Man: A study in the history of religion*. London, United Society for Christian Literature, 1938.

——, *The Idea of the Holy*. Oxford, Oxford University, Press, 1972.

Pagels, E., *The Gnostic Gospels*. Harmondsworth, Penguin Books, 1982.

Pannenberg, W., *Die Prädestinationslehre bei Duns Scotus Eriugena*. Göttingen, Vandenhoeck & Ruprecht, 1954.

——, 'Die Aufnahme des philosophischen Gottesbegriff als dogmatisches Problem der frühchristlichen Theologie', *Zeitschrift für Kirchengeschichte* (1959), 1–45.

——, *et al.*, *Offenbarung als Geschichte*. Göttingen, Vandenhoeck & Ruprecht, 1963. (E.tr.: *Theology as History*, 1967).

Parker, T. H. L., *The Doctrine of God: A study in the theology of John Calvin*. Edinburgh, Oliver & Boyd, 1952.

Parrinder, E. G., *Jesus in the Qur'an*. London, Faber & Faber, 1965.

——, *Witchcraft: African and European*. London, Faber & Faber, 1968.

——, *Sex in the World's Religions*. London, Sheldon Press, 1980.

Peacock, A., *World Fellowship through Religion: The story of the World Congress of Faiths*. London, World Congress of Faiths, c.1938.

Peacocke, A. R., *Creation and the World of Science*. Oxford, Clarendon Press, 1979.

Perrin, N., *The Kingdom of God in the Teaching of Jesus*. London–Philadelphia, SCM – Westminster Press, 1963.

——, and Duling, D. C., *The New Testament: An introduction – proclamation and paranesis, myth and history*. New York – London, Harcourt Brace Jovanovich Inc., 1982.

Peters, N., *Die Frau im Alten Testament*. Düsseldorf, L. Schwann, 1927.

Pfister, O., *Christianity and Fear: A study in history and in the psychology and hygiene of religion*. London, Geo Allen & Unwin, 1948.

Platvoet, J. G., *Comparing Religions: A limitative approach . . .* The Hague – Paris – New York, Mouton Publishers, 1982.

Plummer, C., ed., *Irish Litanies*. London, Henry Bradshaw Society, vol. 62, 1925.

Pratt, J. B., *The Religious Consciousness: A psychological study*. New York, Macmillan, 1930.

Prestige, G. L., *God in Patristic Thought*. London, SPCK, 1952.

Quistorp, H., *Calvin's Doctrine of the Last Things*. London, Lutterworth Press, 1955.

Rahner, H., *Greek Myths and Christian Mystery*. London, Burns & Oates, 1963.

Rall, H. F., *Religion as Salvation*. Nashville, Abingdon–Cokesbury, 1953.

Raphael, F., *et al.*, *Les pèlerinages de l'antiquité biblique et classique à l'occident médiéval*. Paris, Paul Geuthener, 1973.

Ratschow, C. H., *et al.*, *Theologische Realenzyklopädie*. Berlin – New York, Walter de Gruyter, 1977–.

Reeves, M., *Joachim of Fiore and the Prophetic Future*. London, SPCK, 1976.

Reitzenstein, R., *Das iranische Erlösungsmysterium: Religionsgeschichtliche Untersuchungen*. Bonn, Weber, 1921.

——, *Hellenistic Mystery-Religions: Their basic ideas and experience*. Pittsburgh, Pickwick Press, 1927/1978.

Reno, S. J., *The Sacred Tree as an Early Christian Literary Symbol*. Saarbrücken, Homo et Religio, 1978.

Reynolds, S., *The Christian Religious Tradition*. Encino and Belmont, California, Dickinson Publishing, 1977.

Richards, G. A., *The Compulsive Prayer*. New York, Monographs of the Ethnological Soc. 7, 1944.

Richardson, A., *The Miracle Stories of the Gospels*. London, SCM, 1952.

Richardson, C. C., *et al.*, ed., The Library of Christian Classics. London, SCM, 26 vols. 1953–66.

Richter, P. J., 'Recent Sociological Approaches to the Study of the New Testament', *Religion* XIV (1984), 77–90.

Riesner, R., *Jesus als Lehrer: Eine Untersuchung zum Ursprung der Evangeliumüberlieferung*. Tübingen, J.C.B. Mohr (Paul Siebeck), 1984.

Riley, A., *Athos: Or the mountain of the monks*. London, Longmans Green; Ann Arbor – London, Univ. Microfilms Internat., 1887/1982.

Robertson, R., ed., *Sociology of Religion: Selected readings*. Harmondsworth, Penguin Books, 1969.

Rodd, C. S., ed., *Foundation Documents of the Faith*. Edinburgh, T. & T. Clark, 1987.

Roeder, H., *Saints and their Attributes*. London, Longmans, 1955.

Rogier, L. J., *et al.*, ed., *The Christian Centuries: A new history of the Catholic Church*. London, Darton Longman & Todd, 5 vols., 1964–78.

Rouse, R., and Neill, S. C., ed., *A History of the Ecumenical Movement*. London, SPCK, 1954.

Royster, J. E., *The Meaning of Muhammad for Muslims: A phenomenological study of recurrent images of the Prophet*. Ph.D. Hartford Seminary, Ann Arbor – London, Univ. Microfilms Internat., 1970/1981.

Rubinstein, R. L., *After Auschwitz: Radical theology and contemporary Judaism*. Indianapolis – New York, Bobs-Merrill, 1966.

Rüdiger, R. B., *Einhorn: Fabelwelt und Wirklichkeit*. Munich, Verlag Georg D. Callwey, 1977.

Rudloff, L. von, *Taufe und Firmung im byzantinischen Ritus*. Paderborn, Schöningh, 1938.

Rudolph, K., *Historical Fundamentals and the Study of Religions*. New York, Macmillan; London, Collier Macmillan, 1985.

Ruether, R. R., *Religion and Sexism: Images of woman in the Jewish and Christian traditions*. New York, Simon & Shuster, 1979.

——, *Sexism and God-Talk: Towards a feminist philosophy*. Boston, Beacon Press, 1983.

Russell, E., *History of Quakerism*. New York, 1942.

Russell, J. B., *The Devil: Perceptions of evil from antiquity to primitive Christianity*. New York – London . . . , Meridian Books, 1977.

Ryrie, C. C., *The Place of Woman in the Church*. New York, Macmillan, 1958.

'Sacral Kingship', *IAHR* VIIIth Congress, Rome 1955. Leiden, Brill, 1959.

Samarin, W. J., *Tongues of Men and of Angels: The religious language of Pentecostalism*. London, Collier Macmillan, 1972.

Sanday, W., *Inspiration*, Bampton lectures 1893. London, 1908.

Sankey, I. A., comp., *The Evangelistic Hymn Book No. 1*. London, n.d.

Sargant, W., *The Mind Possessed: A physiology of possession, mysticism and faith healing*. London, Heinemann, 1973.

Schaefer, P., *Die katholische Wiedergeburt der anglikanischen Kirche*. Munich, Reinhardt, 1933.

Schäfer, T., *Die Fusswaschung im monastischen Brauchtum und in der lateinischen Liturgie*. Beuron, Kunstverlag, 1956.

Schaff, P., *A History of the Creeds of Christendom*. London, Hodder & Stoughton, 1877.

Schell, H., *Katholische Dogmatik*. Paderborn, F. Schöningh, 1893.

Schilling, J., *Der Jenseitsgedanke im Alten Testament: Seine Entfaltung und deren Triebkräfte*. Mainz, 1951.

Schimmelpfennig, R., *Die Geschichte der Marienverehrung im deutschen Protestantismus*. Paderborn, Schöningh, 1955.

Schleiermacher, F., *Predigten*. 5 vols. Berlin, Eugen Grosser, 1876.

Schleyer, F. L., *Die Heilungen von Lourdes: Eine kritische Untersuchung*. Bonn, Bouvier, 1949.

Schlink, E., *Theologie der lutherischen Bekenntnisschriften*. Munich, Chr. Kaiser Verlag, 1949.

——, *Ökumenische Dogmatik: Grundzüge*. Göttingen, Vandenhoeck & Ruprecht, 1983.

Schmidt, K. D., *et al.*, ed., *Die Kirche in ihrer Geschichte: Ein Handbuch*. Göttingen, Vandenhoeck & Ruprecht, 1961–.

Schmidt, W., *Der Ursprung der Gottesidee: Eine historisch-kritische und positive Studie*. Münster, Aschendorff, vol. 2, 1926.

Schnackenberg, R., *Der Glaube im vierten Evangelium*. Diss. Breslau, 1937.

Schoeps, H. J., *Paul: The theology of the apostle in the light of Jewish religious history*. London, Lutterworth Press, 1961.

Schöne, W., *et al.*, *Das Gottesbild im Abendland*. Witten & Berlin, Eckhart Verlag, 1959.

Schopp, L., *et al.*, ed., *The Fathers of the Church: A new translation*. Washington D.C., Cath. Univ. of America Press, 72 vols. 1962ff.

Schrade, H., *Der verborgene Gott: Gottesbild und Gottesvorstellung in Israel und im alten Orient*. Stuttgart, Kohlhammer, 1949.

Schubart, W., *Religion und Eros*. Munich, Beck, 1952.

Schulte, R., *Die Messe als Opfer der Kirche*. Münster, Aschendorff, 1959.

Schütz, R., *Die Offenbarung des Johannes und Kaiser Domitian*. Göttingen, Vandenhoeck & Ruprecht, 1933.

Schutz, W. C., *Joy: Expanding Human Awareness*. Harmondsworth, Penguin Books, 1973.

Schweitzer, A., *The Quest of the Historical Jesus*. New York, Macmillan, 1948.

Scruton, D. L., ed., *Sociophobics: The anthropology of fear*. Godstone, Surrey, Westview Press, 1985.

Seeberg, R., *Lehrbuch der Dogmengeschichte*. Leipzig, Deichert, vol. 1. 1920.

Seters, J. van, *Abraham in History and Tradition*. Yale University Press, 1975.

Sharp, E. J., *Understanding Religion*. London, Duckworth, 1983.

Sholem, G., 'Kabbalah und Mythos', *Eranos Jahrbuch* (1949), 287–334.

Sierksma, F., *The Gods as we shape Them*. London, Routledge & Kegan Paul, 1960.

Simson, O. G. von, *The Gothic Cathedral: Origins of Gothic architecture and the medieval concept of order*. London – New York, Bollingen Foundation – Pantheon Books, 1962.

Smalley, B., *The Study of the Bible in the Middle Ages*, Oxford, Basil Blackwell, 1983.

Smart, N., *Secular Education and the Logic of Religion*. London, Faber & Faber, 1968.

——, *The Phenomenon of Christianity*. London, Collins, 1979.

——, 'Identity and a Dynamic Phenomenology of Religion', *Jnl. of the Inst. for the Study of Rel.* 11 (1985), 23–34.

——, and Hecht, R. D., *Sacred Texts of the World: A universal anthology*. London, Macmillan Reference Books, 1982.

Smith, M., *Rabi'a the Mystic and her fellow Saints in Islam*. Cambridge, 1928.

Smolitsch, I., *Russisches Mönchtum*, Würzburg, Augustinus Verlag, 1953.

Söderberg, H., *La religion des Cathares: Étude sur le Gnosticisme de la basse antiquité et du moyen age*, Uppsala, Almqvist & Wiksell, 1949.

Söderblom, N., *Das Werden des Gottesglaubens: Untersuchungen über die Anfänge der Religion*. Leipzig, Hinrichs'sche Buchhandlung, 1916/1926.

——, *The Living God: Basic forms of personal religion*. Boston, Beacon Press, 1962.

Soulen, R. N., *Handbook of Biblical Criticism*. London, Lutterworth Press, 1977.

Spamer, A., *Das kleine Andachtsbild vom 14. zum 20. Jahrhundert*. Munich, F. Bruckmann, 1930.

Spinka, M., *A History of Christianity in the Balkans*. Hamden, Conn., Archon Books, 1968.

Sproul, B. C., *Primal Myths: Creating the world*, London, Ryder, 1979.

Stace, W. T., *Mysticism and Philosophy*. London, Macmillan, 1961.

Stamm, J. J. and Andrew, M. E., *The Ten Commandments in Recent Research*. London, SCM, 1967.

Stange, A., *Das frühchristliche Gebäude als Bild des Himmels*, Cologne, Camel, 1950.

Stark, W., *Sociology of Religion*. London, Routledge & Kegan Paul, 5 vols. 1966–72.

Stendahl, K., *The Scrolls and the New Testament*, New York, Harper; Greenwood Reprints, 1957/1975.

——, *Paul among Jews and Gentiles*. London, SCM, 1977.

Sterne, L., *The Life and Opinions of Tristram Shandy*. Harmondsworth, Penguin Books, 1967.

Stevenson, L., *Seven Theories of Human Nature*. New York and Oxford, Oxford University, Press, 1979.

Stökl, G., *Geschichte der Sklavenmission, Die Kirche in ihrer Geschichte*. Göttingen, Vandenhoeck & Ruprecht, Part E, 1961.

Strack, H. L., and Billerbeck, P., *Kommentar zum Neuen Testament aus Talmud und Midrash*. Munich, C. H. Beck, 6 vols. 1928.

Stricker, K., *Die Frau in der Reformation*. Berlin, F. M. Herbig, 1927.

Strobel, A., *Das heilige Land der Montanisten*. Berlin, de Gruyter, 1980.

Summers, M., *The Physical Phenomena of Mysticism: With especial reference to the stigmata* ... London, Rider, 1950.

Sumption, J., *Pilgrimage: An image of medieval religion*. London, Faber & Faber, 1975.

Sunden, H., *Religionspsychologie: Probleme und Methoden*. Stuttgart, Calwer Verlag, 1982.

Sundkler, B., *Nathan Söderblom: His life and work*. Lund, Gleerups, 1968.

Sutcliffe, E. F., *The Monks of Qumran as depicted in the Dead Sea Scrolls*. London, Burns & Oates, 1960.

Suzuki, D. T., *Mysticism: Christian and Buddhist*. London, Allen & Unwin, 1957.

Swete, H. B., ed., *Essays on the Early History of the Church and Ministry*. London, Macmillan, 1921.

Sykes, S., *The Identity of Christianity*. London, SPCK; Philadelphia, Fortress Press, 1984.

Te Selle, S. M., *Speaking in Parables: A study in metaphor and theology*. Philadelphia, Fortress Press, 1975.

Temple, W., *Nature Man and God*. London, Macmillan, 1949.

Theissen, G., *The First Followers of Jesus*. London, SCM, 1978.

Thomas, D. W., ed., *Documents from Old Testament Times*. London ... and New York, Thomas Nelson & Sons, 1958.

Thomas, E. E., *The Problem of Sin in the New Testament*. London, 1927.

Thomas, E. J., *The Life of Buddha as Legend and History*. London, Routledge & Kegan Paul, 1949.

Thomas à Kempis, *The Imitation of Christ*. Glasgow, Collins Fount Paperbacks, 1977.

Thompson, T. L., *The Historicity of the Patriarchal Narratives*. Berlin, de Gruyter, 1974.

Thouless, R. T., *An Introduction to the Psychology of Religion*. London, Cambridge University Press, 1971.

Tierhilfswerk Karlsruhe e.V. (Animal Protection Society, Karlsruhe) *Statement* issued in 1981.

Thurston, H. H. C., *The Physical Phenomena of Mysticism*. London, Burns Oates, 1952.

Tillich, P., *Das Dämonische: Ein Beitrag zur Sinndeutung der Geschichte*. Tübingen, J. C. B. Mohr, 1926.

Tourn, G., *The Waldensians: The first eight hundred years 1174–1974*. Turin, Claudiana, 1980.

True, U., *Physiologus: Naturkunde im frühchristlicher Deutung*. Hanau, Werner Dausien, 1981.

Trimingham, J. S., *The Sufi Orders in Islam*. London, Oxford University Press, 1973.

Troeltsch, E., *The Social Teaching of the Christian Church*. London, Allen & Unwin, 1931.

Turner, B., *Religious Sects: A sociological study*. London, World University Library, Weidenfeld & Nicolson, 1970.

Turner, H. W., *African Independent Church*. Oxford, Clarendon Press, 2 vols. 1967.

——, *Bibliography of New Religious Movements in Primal Societies*. Boston, G. K. Hall; London, Prior, 2 vols. 1977/1978.

——, *From Temple to Meeting House: The phenomenology and theology of places of worship*. The Hague – Paris – New York, Mouton, 1979.

Turner, V., 'The Center out There: The pilgrim's goal', *History of Religions* 12 (1973), 191–230.

Underhill, E., *Mysticism: A study in the nature and development of man's spiritual consciousness*. London; New York, Dutton, 1911/1961.

Usener, H., *Götternamen: Versuch einer Lehre von der religiösen Begriffsbildung*. Frankfurt, Verlag Schulte-Bulmke, 1948.

Van der Leeuw, see Leeuw, G. van der.

Vansina, J., *Oral Tradition: A study in historical methodology*. London, Routledge & Kegan Paul, 1965.

——, *Oral Tradition as History*. London, James Currey; Nairobi, Heinemann, 1985.

Vaux, R. de, *Ancient Israel: Its life and institutions*. London, Darton Longman & Todd, 1965.

Vergote, A., *The Religious Man: A psychological study of religious attitudes*, Dublin, Gill & Macmillan, 1969.

Vermaseren, M. J., *Corpus Inscriptionum et Monumentorum Religionis Mithriacae*. The Hague, M. Nijhoff, 2 vols. 1956/1960.

——, *Mithras: The secret God*, tr. Therese and Vincent Megaw. London, Chatto & Windus, 1963.

——, *Cybele and Attis: The myth and the cult*. London, Thames & Hudson, 1977.

Versnel, H. S., 'Some Remarks on the Roman devotio', *History of Religions: IAHR proceedings* 1975. Leicester, Dept. of Religion, 1980.

Völker, W., *Kontemplation und Ekstase bei Pseudo-Dionysius Areopagite*. Wiesbaden, Steiner, 1958.

Von Hügel, F. *Eternal Life: A study of its implications and applications*. Edinburgh, T. & T. Clarke, 1912.

——, *The Mystical Element of Religion: As studied in St Catherine of Genoa and her friends*. London, Dent, 2 vols. 1923.

Vos, G., *Pauline Eschatology*. Grand Rapids, Mich., Erdmans, 1954.

Vrijhof, H. and Waardenburg, J., *Official and Popular Religion: Analysis of a theme for religious studies*. The Hague, Mouton, Religion & Society 19, 1979.

Wach, J., *Der Erlösungsgedanke und seine Deutung*. Leipzig, J. C. Hinrichs, 1922.

——, *Meister und Jünger*. Tübingen, J. C. B. Mohr, 1925.

——, *Typen religiöser Anthropologie: Vergleich der Lehre vom Menschen im religionsphilosophischen Denken vom Orient und Okzident*. Tübingen, J. C. B. Mohr, 1932.

——, *Sociology of Religion*. Chicago, Phoenix Books, 1964.

Wainwright, W. J., *Mysticism: A study of its nature, cognitive value and moral implications*. Brighton, Harvester Press, 1981.

Walther, G., *Phänomenologie der Mystik*. Freiburg, Walter, 1955.

Wakefield, W. L., and Evans, A. P., *Heresies of the High Middle Ages*, New York – London, Columbia University Press, 1969.

Wallace, R. S., *Calvin's Doctrine of the Word and Sacrament*, Edinburgh, Oliver & Boyd, 1953.

Wand, J. W. C., *Anglicanism in History and Today*. London, Weidenfeld & Nicolson, 1961.

Watson, P. S., *Let God be God: An interpretation of the Theology of Martin Luther*. London, Epworth Press, 1948.

Watt, W. M., *Muhammad: Prophet and statesman*. London – Oxford – New York, Oxford University Press, 1969.

Watts, A., *Myth and Ritual in Christianity*. Boston, Beacon Press, 1968.

Weatherhead, L., *Psychology, Religion and Healing*. London, Hodder & Stoughton, 1951.

Weber, M., *Sociology of Religion*. London, Methuen, 1966.

Weidkuhn, P., *Agressivität, Ritus, Säkularisierung: Biologische Grundformen religiöser Prozesse*, Basel, Pharos Verlag, 1965.

Weidmann, J. L., ed., *Christian Feminism: Visions of a new humanity*. San Francisco ... Cambridge ... London, Harper & Row, 1984.

Weman, H., *African Music and the Church in Africa*. Uppsala, Svenska Institutet för Missionsfosknig, 1960.

Wenschkewitz, H., 'Die Spiritualisierung der Kultusbegriffe Tempel, Priester und Opfer im Neuen Testament', *Angelos* 4 (1932), 71–230.

Westermarck, E., *The History of Human Marriage*. New York and London, Macmillan & Co, 1922.

——, *Origin and Development of Moral Ideas*, London, Macmillan, 2 vols. 1926.

Weymann, U., *Die seusesche Mystik und ihre Wirkung auf die bildende Kunst*. Berlin, Pfau, 1938.

Whaling, F., ed., *Contemporary Approaches to the Study of Religion I – The Humanities* (Berlin – New York – Amsterdam, Mouton, 1984), esp. 29–164.

Widengren, G., *The King and the Tree of Life in Ancient Near Eastern Religion*. Uppsala, Lundequist, 1951.

——, *Mani and Manichaeism*. London, Weidenfeld & Nicolson, 1965.

Wieschhoff, H., *Die afrikanischen Trommeln und ihre ausserafrikanischen Beziehungen*. Stuttgart, Strecker & Schröder, 1933.

Wikander, S., *Der arische Männerbund: Studien zur Sprach- und Religionsgeschichte*. Lund, H. Olsson, 1938.

Williams, C. G. *Tongues of the Spirit*. Cardiff, University of Wales Press, 1981.

Williams, N. P., *The Ideas of the Fall and of Original Sin*. London, Longmans, 1927.

Wilson, I., *The Turin Shroud*. London, Gollancz; Harmondsworth, Penguin Books, 1978/1979.

Winslow, J. C., *Narayan Vaman Tilak: The Christian poet of Maharashtra*. Calcutta, Association Press, 1923.

Workman, H. B., *The Evolution of the Monastic Ideal*. London, Epworth Press, 1927.

——, *John Wiclif: A study in the English medieval church*. Oxford, Clarendon Press, 2 vols. 1926.

Wyatt, N., 'Some Observations on the Idea of History among the West Semitic Peoples', *Ugarit-Forschungen* 11 (1979), 825–32.

Yates, N., *The Oxford Movement and Anglican Ritualism*. London, Historical Association Pamphlets Gen. Series 105, 1983.

Yinger, J. M., *Religion, Society and the Individual: An introduction to the sociology of religion*. New York, Macmillan, 1957.

——, *The Scientific Study of Religion*. New York, Macmillan, 1970.

Young, K., *The Drama of the Medieval Church*. Oxford, Clarendon Press, vol. 2. 1951.

Zaehner, R. C., *Mysticism Sacred and Profane: An inquiry into some varieties of praeternatural experience*. London, Oxford University, Press, 1971.

Zellinger, J., *Augustin und Volksfrömmigkeit: Blicke in dem frühchristlichen Alltag*. Munich, Hueber, 1933.

Index